41a *BENEDICTUS (THE SONG OF ZECHARIAH)*

1   ✠ Blessèd be the Lord the God of Israel, *
who has come to his people and set them free.

2   He has raised up for us a mighty Saviour, *
born of the house of his servant David.

3   Through his holy prophets God promised of old *
to save us from our enemies,
    from the hands of all that hate us,

4   To show mercy to our ancestors, *
and to remember his holy covenant.

5   This was the oath God swore to our father Abraham: *
to set us free from the hands of our enemies,

6   Free to worship him without fear, *
holy and righteous in his sight
    all the days of our life.

7   And you, child, shall be called the prophet of the Most High, *
for you will go before the Lord to prepare his way,

8   To give his people knowledge of salvation *
by the forgiveness of all their sins.

9   In the tender compassion of our God *
the dawn from on high shall break upon us,

10 To shine on those who dwell in darkness
    and the shadow of death, *
and to guide our feet into the way of peace.

Luke 1.68-79

Either:

**Glory to the Father and to the Son
    and to the Holy Spirit; ***
**as it was in the beginning, is now,
    and shall be for ever. Amen.**

or:

**Glory to God, Source of all being,
    Eternal Word and Holy Spirit; ***
**as it was in the beginning, is now,
    and shall be for ever. Amen.**

40a *MAGNIFICAT (THE SONG OF MARY)*

1   ✠ My soul proclaims the greatness of the Lord,
    my spirit rejoices in God my Saviour; *
    he has looked with favour on his lowly servant.

2   From this day all generations will call me blessèd; *
    the Almighty has done great things for me
    and holy is his name.

3   He has mercy on those who fear him, *
    from generation to generation.

4   He has shown strength with his arm *
    and has scattered the proud in their conceit,

5   Casting down the mighty from their thrones *
    and lifting up the lowly.

6   He has filled the hungry with good things *
    and sent the rich away empty.

7   He has come to the aid of his servant Israel, *
    to remember his promise of mercy,

8   The promise made to our ancestors, *
    to Abraham and his children for ever.

Luke 1.46-55

Either:

**Glory to the Father and to the Son
   and to the Holy Spirit; *
as it was in the beginning, is now,
   and shall be for ever. Amen.**

or:

**Glory to God, Source of all being,
   Eternal Word and Holy Spirit; *
as it was in the beginning, is now,
   and shall be for ever. Amen.**

The Daily Office SSF

BLOOMSBURY CONTINUUM
LONDON • OXFORD • NEW YORK • NEW DELHI • SYDNEY

Published for the Society of Saint Francis by
BLOOMSBURY CONTINUUM
Bloomsbury Publishing Plc
50 Bedford Square, London, WC1B 3DP, UK

BLOOMSBURY, BLOOMSBURY CONTINUUM and
the Diana logo are trademarks of
Bloomsbury Publishing Plc

Text and typography: © The European Province of
the Society of Saint Francis 2010 liturgysec@franciscans.org.uk
Revised edition 2010
Reprinted 2012, 2016, 2019

The Society of Saint Francis is indebted to churches, publishers
and individuals whose copyright texts have been included
with permission, in either original or adapted form.
For further information, see Acknowledgements, page 820.

A catalogue record for this book is available from the British Library

Library of Congress Cataloguing-in-Publication data has been applied for

ISBN: HB: 978-1-4729-7054-1

2 4 6 8 10 9 7 5 3 1

Typeset in Gill Sans MT 9 point by the Society of Saint Francis
Printed and bound in Great Britain by CPI Group (UK) Ltd, Croydon
CR0 4YY

To find out more about our authors and books
visit www.bloomsbury.com and sign up for our newsletters

TABLE OF CONTENTS

Common of Saints and the Departed

Special Occasions

Additional Liturgies

Prayers for Various Occasions

Foreword

To share in the daily prayer of the Church is to be drawn into something that shapes and forms us. It strengthens our hold on eternal life. It deepens our communion with Christian brothers and sisters and our experience of the mystery of God.

It has been a joy in the life of the Church of England to see a common form of daily liturgical prayer emerging, after a period when people went their separate ways in terms of the Daily Office or, in the case of too many, simply stopped saying the Office, seeing it as somehow irrelevant to contemporary life and ministry. If one can pinpoint a moment when the tide began to turn, it was the publication in 1992 of *Celebrating Common Prayer. Celebrating Common Prayer* was, of course, a Franciscan-inspired compilation, in which members of the then Church of England Liturgical Commission collaborated with members of religious communities, the Society of St Francis and others, to create an Office book that would be rich enough to meet the needs of religious communities and yet simple and flexible enough to be used in parish communities, by small groups and by individuals, from right across the traditions of the Church. With its two almost identical versions, the blue *Celebrating Common Prayer* and the brown *The Daily Office SSF*, it marked a return to common prayer and helped the offering of liturgical daily prayer to be reclaimed by the laity, for whom it had often seemed to be simply a clerical obligation.

When *Common Worship: Daily Prayer* was published, in a preliminary edition in 2002 and in a definitive form in 2005, it was immediately clear that *Celebrating Common Prayer* and *The Daily Office SSF* had judged rightly what the Church needed. They had provided a model that the Church could welcome, use and make its own. *Common Worship: Daily Prayer* is essentially *Celebrating Common Prayer* revised, enriched and recognised by the Church as part of its official provision for the 21st century. The Church has a Franciscan-led Office book and all that remains is to provide a version that, derived from it, meets the specific needs of the religious life and includes the liturgical material that celebrates Francis, Clare and the Franciscan saints. This volume, building on *Common Worship: Daily Prayer,* does just that.

The benefit is, of course, two-way. For Franciscans, whether gathered together in community or dispersed and praying alone, there is the encouragement of knowing they pray as part of a great company, much larger than those who particularly look to Francis and to Clare as their inspiration. For the wider Church, and for individuals sometimes praying in isolation, there is the joy of knowing that their praying is alongside, and supported by, the dependable disciplined prayer of religious houses, where it is always a priority and always at the heart of community life. For me and for many that is a huge blessing, for which to give thanks and praise to God.

+Michael Gloucester
Bishop Protector of the European Province of SSF *October 2009*

Daily Prayer in the Life of the Church

From the beginning of the life of the Church, the baptised 'devoted themselves to the apostles' teaching and fellowship, to the breaking of bread and the prayers' *(Acts 2.42)*. Individuals, continuing the Jewish custom, prayed at fixed times through the day and, in various parts of the Church, there developed the custom of devoting certain times of each day to pray together.

Daily prayer, offered by the whole Christian community, was an important feature of the developing life of the Church. Such prayer consisted of only a relatively small number of psalms and canticles. Certain psalms and canticles were chosen for their appropriateness to the time of day and repeated regularly. Praise, and the offering of intercession, formed the core of these daily prayers, together with the use of bodily gestures, and symbols such as light and incense. Such a 'city' (sometimes known as 'cathedral') style of prayer had an outward focus on the needs of the world, the whole creation and the company of heaven. A complementary development was that of a 'desert' (or 'monastic') style of praying together in solitude. Here the emphasis was much more on inward nourishing of the heart through the meditative use of the whole Psalter and extensive scripture readings. At different times and places in Christian history these two styles of praying daily have been combined in various ways. At the English Reformation, for example, the *Book of Common Prayer* used a simplified 'desert' style of Office in order to produce a 'city' result in every parish. The Anglican Communion is one of the few churches in the Christian world that has preserved the tradition of the Daily Office as the prayer of the whole people of God rather than it being restricted in practice to clerical and monastic use only.

1 The Ceaseless Praise of all Creation

Christian prayer and worship is offered to God the Father, the Creator; through God the Son, the Redeemer; and in God the Holy Spirit, the Sanctifier.

(a) *To the Father*

The prayer of the Daily Office is part of that praise that the whole creation, consciously or unconsciously, offers to its Creator. Through baptism, each Christian becomes part of that royal priesthood of believers able both to proclaim the word of God and, in faith and action, to respond to it, thereby giving voice to all creation in its ceaseless praise and glory of the eternal Creator, the source of all its being and life.

(b) *Through the Son*

Again and again, the gospels show us Jesus at prayer: 'Abba', he cries. His commands to his disciples are 'pray', 'ask', 'seek' ... 'in my name'. Above all, in his suffering and death, he showed us that it was prayer that enabled him to offer himself as a paschal sacrifice. Now, through his self-offering on the cross, and his being raised from the dead, 'he ever lives to intercede for us' *(Romans 8.34)*. In the communion of saints, all Christians pray with Christ and in Christ. Until the end of the world, we are joined to the heavenly worship of saints and angels; our liturgy is part of that heavenly liturgy of praise and intercession in which the whole Christ offers the whole Christ, before the throne of God.

(c) *In the Spirit*

We are only able to pray because we are in the Spirit: the Spirit of Christ, the Spirit of the whole Church, the Spirit present in each baptised person. 'We do not know how to pray as we ought, but the Spirit intercedes for us' *(Romans 8.26)*; 'the Spirit intercedes for the saints according to the will of God' *(Romans 8.27)*. In the Spirit, we can offer true prayer to God, for 'when we cry Abba! Father! it is that very Spirit bearing witness with our spirit' *(Romans 8.15)*. It is the Spirit who unites the whole Church and brings us through the Redeemer to the Creator.

2 Praise and Prayer in all our Days
The Sanctification of Time

In accordance with Jewish tradition, and sanctified by the practice of Christ, the Christian Church has, from the earliest times, consecrated moments of time so that, through praise and prayer, they become the vehicles of God's time, the time of the sovereignty of God. Principally this has been done through the use of two liturgical cycles: firstly of the day, the week and the year, and secondly of the memorial of the saints.

(a) *The Year*

The Church's Year has two major focal points, each proclaiming and illuminating the great acts of God in the saving events of history: the incarnation and the redemption. Each of these is centred on a double festival: the former on Christmas and Epiphany, the latter on Easter and Pentecost. Each has a time of preparation, a time of celebration and a time of fulfilment. For the festival of the incarnation, we prepare in the Advent season for the coming of Christ; we celebrate the birth and manifestation of Christ in Christmas and Epiphany; and find its fulfilment in the Epiphany season, as we explore the revelation of the glory of Christ through to the celebration of his presentation in the temple.

For the festival of our redemption, we begin to understand the obedience of Christ in the pre-Lent season and the season of Lent; we pass through the celebration of the passion in Holy Week and the celebration of the Lord's resurrection in the Easter season, finding its completion in the Ascension, when we acknowledge Christ as sovereign Lord of all. The season finds its fulfilment in the nine days leading up to Pentecost, when we, as the Church, make ready to receive the Holy Spirit of God. In the Ordinary Time after Pentecost, we explore the meaning of God the Holy Trinity's saving work in Christ through the life of the pilgrim Church on earth, in the power of the Holy Spirit, and in all of the Creator's creation, for God saw that 'it was good'. The year ends with a time, from All Saints to Advent, when we acknowledge that 'here we have no abiding city' but confess God's reign in our heart, our life and our death as we rejoice in the promise of sharing in God's glory, and look for the coming of his Kingdom in our midst.

(b) *The Week*

The week offers its praise to God through the sequence of the Daily Offices at morning, midday, evening and night, interspersing prayer In the regular pattern of work, study and rest, and continually recalling the presence of the love of Christ among us: 'Praise and prayer constitute the atmosphere in which we will strive to live' *(The Principles of the First Order SSF, Day 14)*. The revelation and redemption of God is made clear to us and provides the material for our personal reflection, through the proclamation of his word in psalmody and readings. Communal and personal prayer support one another and both find their source in holy scripture and in the fullness of the Christian mystery.

Each week begins with the eve of Sunday, the weekly feast of the Lord's resurrection. Evening Prayer may begin with the Blessing of the Light, to remind us of the light of the risen Christ coming into a darkened world. At the end of the Office, the gospel of Sunday may be solemnly proclaimed for the first time: the day of the Lord beginning with the word of the Lord. Sunday, the day of the Lord Jesus, celebrates both the completing of God's creation and the beginning of re-creation through the resurrection of Christ. It is the day of the Messiah, the eighth day, and, as both an end and a beginning, it gives meaning to all the other days of the week.

The Offices on Monday celebrate the gift of the Holy Spirit; on Tuesday they look forward to the advent of Christ; on Wednesday they celebrate the incarnation; on Thursday they focus on prayer for the unity and mission of the Church; on Friday they recall the suffering of Christ; and on Saturday they rejoice in the communion of saints. In these ways, echoing the celebrations of the seasons of the Church's Year, the Friday to Monday of each week recall the paschal mystery of the Lord's passion, resurrection and the presence of the Holy Spirit, and the Tuesday to Thursday his incarnation.

(c) *The Day*

Morning Prayer comes at the time of day when we 'pass over' from darkness to light. At the time of our greatest weakness, we welcome with joy Christ our light. Through the darkness of death he has brought us redemption, in the light and power of his resurrection. This theme is powerfully recalled in the gospel canticle, the Song of Zechariah (*Benedictus*): 'You have raised up for us a mighty saviour; the dawn from on high shall break upon us, to shine on those who dwell in darkness and the shadow of death; ... you have come to your people and set them free.' During the course of each day, we celebrate the light of Christ as we pray at sunrise and sunset, the 'pass over' moments of each day. At midday, we recall the glory of the ascended Christ at the time when the sun is at its height; and, coming as it does in the middle of the day's work, we are reminded to offer the whole of our life to God our Creator through the hands of the eternal high priest.

At the end of the day's work, when we have been concerned with our stewardship of creation, we are called to turn again to God, that we might be renewed by the light of God's word. Each day, the candles may be lit ceremonially, using the Blessing of the Light. This custom is the direct successor of the Jewish and early Christian practice of blessing God at 'the lighting of the lamps'. At the heart of the Office is the gospel canticle, the Song of Mary (*Magnificat*), we celebrate the incarnation of the Second Adam, the Word made flesh by a new act of the Spirit in the womb of Mary. As the world was at its evening, so the true light of Christ has been revealed in our midst. According to the biblical tradition, the day begins in the evening at sunset: witness the account of creation in Genesis: 'so evening came and morning came, the first day.' This tradition is preserved by observing the first Evening Prayer of Sunday and of major feasts.

At the end of the day at Night Prayer, we invoke 'the Master's blessing of protection and peace' *(The Principles of the First Order SSF, Day 15)*. In the Song of Simeon *(Nunc Dimittis)* are united both the expectation and longing of humanity and the fulfilment of this waiting; that the life of the world has been placed in our hands and here is not only the end but also the beginning, for we have 'seen the salvation' which is revealed for all people.

Each liturgical day, beginning with Evening Prayer, we celebrate God's redeeming love in creation and incarnation. Night Prayer takes us into the mystery of God's light, present even in suffering, darkness and death. Morning Prayer brings us into the gift of new life in resurrection 'each returning day'. Midday Prayer enables us to bring together our common life in Christ with Mary, Francis and Clare as we travel with the whole people of God towards that Day that has no ending.

(d) *The Memorials of the Saints*

The celebration of the Holy Spirit at work in many different ways in the lives of Christian men and women down the ages, whose examples excite us to holiness, is a sign of the great cloud of witnesses with which we are surrounded. They remind us, who are the Church on earth, of our unity in prayer and fellowship with the Church in heaven and that the liturgy of any particular Christian community, however small, is part of the heavenly liturgy of the angels and saints, as we await the glorious manifestation of Christ at the end of time.

3 The Word of God and our Response
The Structure and Contents of the Office

The local community prayer of each day has been divided into two major Offices, those for the morning and the evening, and two lesser Offices for midday and at night. Each Office has three sections:

The Preparation   the call to praise: versicles and responses, an opening canticle, a hymn and a prayer;

The Word of God   the proclamation and praise of the work of God: psalmody, scripture readings, the gospel and other canticles, a response to the word;

The Prayers	our response in intercession and thanksgiving for the Church and the world, combined with the Kyries, the collect and concluding with the Lord's Prayer and the blessing.

(a) *The Preparation*

This section prepares our hearts and minds that we may more readily respond to God's word. At Morning Prayer, after the opening versicles and responses, there may be an acclamation, which is followed by the opening canticle. At Evening Prayer, there is either the Blessing of the Light or versicles and responses, followed by the opening canticle. At Night Prayer, this section may be preceded by an opportunity to reflect upon the past day and an act of penitence. To conclude this section in every Office a hymn may be sung; at Morning and Evening Prayer, this section is concluded with a short prayer.

(b) *The Word of God*

This is the heart of the Office. At Morning and Evening Prayer, the gospel canticle with its refrain is the climax, bringing together the promises of the Old and New Covenant. The reading of scripture is both the proclamation of the word and works of God and also the means of building up God's people through a deeper understanding of God's ways with humanity and their response to God.

In each Office, the reading of scripture is preceded by psalmody. Through the words of the psalms, we come before God and enter into the joys and sorrows, hopes and failures of the people of God representing all humanity. This finds its fulfilment in the prayer and praise of the life, death and resurrection of Christ. At Midday Prayer, Psalm 119 is used to meditate upon the law of God, while the Psalms of Ascent enhance our awareness of God's presence on our pilgrim journey. At Night Prayer, the psalms express a trust in God's love and care in both life and death.

To the proclamation of the word of God, we respond in various ways: in silence for reflection; in canticles of praise drawn from the Old and New Testaments and the tradition of the Church; and through the use of a responsory.

(c) *The Prayers*

The pattern of all Christian prayer was given to us by Jesus in the Lord's Prayer. This may be preceded by the Kyries and, at Morning and Evening, its petitions may be extended; these prayers of the Church are 'collected' up in the collect of the day, the time or the feast and concluded with the Lord's Prayer. Any additional prayers and thanksgivings which the community or individuals may wish to offer should be included in this section within the structure of the Office. Thus the realities and concerns of the present moment are gathered up into the prayer of the praying Christ. Finally a blessing is said and at Morning and Evening Prayer we proclaim 'Let us bless the Lord – Thanks be to God!' as we are commanded to love, serve and praise God in one another and in the world.

4 The Eucharist and the Office

While prayer is essentially a whole, the distinction between sacrament and Office – sacraments with their sense of direction and power to transform, Offices with their cyclic, reflective form – mirrors to some extent our differing experiences of God.

Our prayer as a local community unites us with the whole Body of Christ as we seek to express not only our own prayer but the prayer of the whole Church, conscious always of the promise and presence of Christ in us and among us, 'for where two or three are gathered in my name, I am there among them' *(Matthew 18.20)*. Through prayer, we share in that worship which the Church and all creation are offering to the glory of God the Creator, through the intercession of Jesus the Redeemer, and in the power of the sanctifying Spirit.

5 The Celebration of the Office

The offering of prayer and praise to God in the form of a Daily Office is not primarily a duty to be performed but a liturgy to be celebrated in thanksgiving for the saving acts of God. We celebrate our common prayer as individuals of body, mind and spirit and as members of a community, whether large or small. Both these facts have certain consequences. The celebration of the Office is not just a mental exercise but something which involves the whole person, through, for example, movement and gesture; the use of visible signs of prayer, light and incense; the use of silence, of music and of song. Each group needs to find a form of prayer which is related both to its life together and to each individual, not forgetting to look forward to what that life in Christ might fully be. Nor must the needs of guests be forgotten – whether baptised members of the Body of Christ or not, all have a right to be able to participate in worship.

The book provides a considerable degree of flexibility, of choice and of optional extra texts. However, the effectiveness of the local community prayer in any particular group is to be measured by its quality rather than its quantity.

This book of prayer and praise represents a long period of exploration and experimentation in community prayer. It is for us all, as part of the Body of Christ and in union with his eternal offering, to bring our times of prayer to life through our commitment to it; our careful preparation for it; our use of all the means available and suitable to those participating in it; to make it a true sacrifice of praise which will bear fruit in the whole of our lives.

'For here we have no lasting city, but we are looking for the city that is to come. Through Jesus, then, let us continually offer a sacrifice of praise to God, that is, the fruit of lips that confess his name' *(Hebrews 13.14,15).*

Notes

A GENERAL

1 **Saying and Singing** In the rubrics, 'said' and 'sung' are interchangeable.

2 **Rubrics** In the rubrics, 'until' means 'up to and including'; whereas 'to' means 'as far as, but not including'.

3 **Brackets** Items in square brackets [ ] are optional. Items in round brackets, mostly (Alleluia), are for use in the Easter season.

4 **Before the Office** The material provided for use before the Office, pages 36-8, is optional.

5 **Hymns** The hymns suggested are optional and hymns may be sung at other points.

6 **Silence** Periods of silence may be kept before or after each Office, after each psalm or group of psalms, after each reading, before the collect, before the confession at Night Prayer and at other suitable points.

7 **Other Versions** Psalms, canticles, readings and prayers may be used from any authorised version.

8 **Office and Eucharist**
(a) When the Eucharist closely follows an Office, 'The Prayers' section may consist of the collect, preferably one different from that to be used at the Eucharist, and the blessing only.

(b) If Morning, Midday or Evening Prayer and the Eucharist are combined, the following order may be used:

The Office	• the Preparation
	• the Word of God, to the end of the psalmody
The Eucharist	• the Kyries *and/or* Gloria
	• the Collect
	• Old Testament *and/or* New Testament reading
	• the Second Canticle
	• the Gospel
	• the Intercessions
	• the Peace
	• Preparation of the Table

- Eucharistic Prayer, Communion
- the Gospel Canticle
- Post Communion Prayer
- Blessing
- Dismissal

9 **Scripture** Readings are announced in the order: book, chapter and verse and may be slightly adjusted if it is necessary to make sense in a particular translation. The readings are to be taken from the *Common Worship* Lectionary of the Church of England or another authorised lectionary. Readings are provided for those occasions in the SSF Calendar with no provision in the *Common Worship* Lectionary. At the conclusion, of either or both readings, silence for reflection may be kept. It may be preceded or followed by the reader saying '[This is] the word of the Lord' and the reply is 'Thanks be to God'.

10 **Intercessions** Petitions of intercession, thanksgivings and other forms of free prayer may be used before the confession at Night Prayer or in all Offices either at the beginning of 'The Prayers' section, or before the collect provided that they occur before 'The Blessing', which forms the conclusion of the Office. The Kyries may be used as responses to such petitions.

11 **The Collect** Only one collect should be used to collect up the petitions (silent or aloud) of the community. It may be preceded by 'Let us pray' and a brief bidding followed by a short silence. The collect 'of the day' is the prayer proper to the Sunday of the current week; the collect for a Holy Day takes precedence over the Sunday collect and becomes the collect of the day; the collect of a commemoration being observed locally, may take precedence over the Sunday collect and become the collect of the day. On any occasion, when more than one collect is provided, only one is to be used. In the case of any collect ending with the words 'Christ our Lord/Saviour/Redeemer . . .' etc., the officiant may add the Trinitarian ending, 'who is alive and reigns with you and the Holy Spirit, one God, now and for ever. Amen.'

12 **The Lord's Prayer** This prayer given by Jesus to his disciples forms the climax of the Office when used. From the early Church (*the Didache, c. 2nd century*) the tradition is that it should be prayed three times a day.

13 **A Sermon** A sermon or homily may be given after the reading(s) or after the gospel canticle (at Morning and Evening Prayer), before The Prayers section.

14 **The Gospel** The gospel reading for Sunday or for a Holy Day may follow the order for 'The Gospel Proclamation', page 738, on the Saturday evening or the Eve of a Holy Day.

15 **The Peace** The exchange of the Peace may replace the blessing on appropriate occasions, introduced by one of the following:
> The Peace of the Lord be always with you.
> Let us offer one another a sign of peace,
> God's seal on our prayers.

B THE CHURCH'S YEAR

1 **Sundays** Each Sunday is a celebration of the resurrection of the Lord and begins with Evening Prayer on the eve. The Blessing of the Light may precede either Evening Prayer or Night Prayer.

2 **Advent** Advent begins at Evening Prayer on the eve of the First Sunday of Advent and ends before Evening Prayer on Christmas Eve. The first collect for Advent 1 may be used each day at Midday Prayer except on Holy Days. A prayer to bless the Advent Wreath may replace the prayer in the Blessing of the Light on the eve or the first prayer in the Preparation at Morning Prayer for each Sunday in Advent. Form 3 is used daily, except for Midday Prayer when the appropriate day of Form 1-7 is used with seasonal propers.

3 **Christmas** Christmas begins at Evening Prayer on Christmas Eve and ends before Evening Prayer on the eve of the Epiphany. Form 4 is used daily, except for Midday Prayer when the appropriate day of Form 1-7 is used with seasonal propers.

4 **Epiphany** Epiphany begins at Evening Prayer on the eve of the Epiphany (5 January) and ends at Night Prayer on the feast of the Presentation (2 February) or, if that feast is being celebrated on the Sunday between 28 January and 3 February, at Night Prayer on that day. Form 5 is used daily, except for Midday Prayer when the appropriate day of Form 1-7 is used with seasonal propers.

5 **Lent** Lent begins at Morning Prayer on Ash Wednesday and ends after Evening Prayer or Night Prayer and before the Easter Vigil on Easter Eve. 'Alleluia' is not said in Lent. The first Collect for Ash Wednesday may be used each day at Midday Prayer, except on Holy Days. Although Passiontide is a part of Lent, the propers change to Passiontide from Evening Prayer on the eve of Lent 5. Form 6 is used daily, except for

Midday Prayer when the appropriate day of Form 1-7 is used with seasonal propers.

6   **Triduum Sacrum** or **the Great Three Days**   From the evening celebration of the Lord's Supper on Maundy Thursday to the Easter Vigil, the Office may be said in the following way:
    'The Preparation' section is omitted and the Office begins with the psalms;
    all Glorias and Doxologies are omitted;
    'The Responsory' at Morning, Evening and Night Prayer is omitted;
    'The Prayers' section consists of the collect alone;
    'The Conclusion' is omitted.

7   **Easter**   Easter begins with the Great Vigil of Easter and ends after Night Prayer on the feast of Pentecost. The Paschal Candle is lit at all Offices until Night Prayer on the Day of Pentecost. 'Alleluias' in brackets are added where indicated. The propers of Easter are used from the Vigil of Easter until Night Prayer on Ascension Day. Form 1 is used daily, except for Midday Prayer when the appropriate day of Form 1-7 is used with seasonal propers.

8   **Pentecost**   Although Pentecost is part of Easter, the propers change from the day after Ascension Day until the Day of Pentecost, traditionally nine days of prayer for the gifts of the Holy Spirit. Form 2 is used daily, except for Midday Prayer when the appropriate day of Form 1-7 is used with seasonal propers.

9   **From All Saints' Day to Advent**   Although this period is part of Ordinary Time the propers change from the eve of All Saints' Day to the eve of the First Sunday of Advent, reflecting a time of celebration of the reign of Christ in earth and in heaven. Form 7 is used daily, except for Midday Prayer when the appropriate day of Form 1-7 is used with seasonal propers.

10   **Ordinary Time**   Ordinary Time is the period from the day after the feast of the Presentation of Christ until Night Prayer on Shrove Tuesday; and then again the time from the day after the feast of Pentecost to Morning Prayer on the eve of All Saints' Day. During these times, the Office follows the regular Sunday to Saturday of Form 1 to Form 7 order, varying only on Holy Days.

C MORNING AND EVENING PRAYER

1 **Theme** Human beings have long responded in praise and prayer at the dawning and setting of the sun with its passage from darkness to light and light to darkness. Christians, following Jewish practice, have since earliest times gathered at regular times to respond to God's Word offering the sacrifice of praise and thanksgiving on behalf of all creation and with intercession for the salvation of the world. To take part in such prayer and praise is both a privilege and a duty for communities and individuals. The use of these common forms brings us together in a larger Franciscan and Christian community of prayer. This community extends through both time and space, heaven and earth, uniting those who seek to do what Jesus taught in praying together for the hallowing of God's name and for the coming of God's reign.

2 **Eve of a Holy Day** If a First Evening Prayer is needed because a Class II or Class III observance is celebrated as Class I locally, the propers may be taken from the appropriate Common of Saints.

3 **The Psalmody** The psalms appointed for the day are indicated in the Common Worship Lectionary of the Church of England or the scheme authorised in the local Province of the Anglican Communion. An alternative table, arranged thematically, is provided on page 817. At Morning Prayer, a psalm of praise (the *Laudate* psalm) may be said at the conclusion of the psalmody. The following cycle may be used.

Sunday	117
Monday	146
Tuesday	147.1-12
Wednesday	147.13-end
Thursday	148
Friday	149
Saturday	150

Alleluia is not said in Lent and these psalms are not appropriate in Passiontide. Further notes on the use of the Psalter will be found on page 254.

4 **Readings** One or two scriptural readings from an authorised lectionary may be used and a second or third non-scriptural reading may be added. When only one reading is used, the second canticle follows the psalmody. When three readings are used, the second and third readings follow the second canticle. Silence for reflection may follow each reading or one longer silence may follow the final reading.

5 **Canticles** On Holy Days observed locally, an appropriate second canticle may be chosen.

6 **Gospel Canticle** Whenever possible the Offices should include some singing, especially of the Gospel Canticle, which is the climax of the morning and evening praise for the work of God in Christ.

7 **The Prayers** The Prayers may include a litany, extempore prayer, biddings or a pattern of intercessions and thanksgivings. The Lord's Prayer may be introduced with other words than those provided. The longer form is for use in the appropriate season. The introduction may be omitted.

8 **Other Liturgies** These may replace The Prayers section but they should include petitions of thanksgiving or intercession, the Lord's Prayer, a collect and a blessing.

D MIDDAY PRAYER

1 **Theme** One or more pauses to pray during the working day, to 'sanctify the time', have been characteristics of Christian prayer since the earliest times. In *The Daily Office SSF* this time of prayer may also have a particular Franciscan emphasis. The Office follows the regular Sunday to Saturday order of Form 1 to Form 7 without variation.

2 **Psalmody** Two alternative patterns are provided. The first uses Psalm 119, the great psalm of contemplation of God's love made known through God's word. The second uses Psalms 121 to 133, the Psalms of Ascent, used by pilgrims on the way up to Jerusalem. It is desirable that in Ordinary Time these patterns are used consistently in alternate weeks. In the seasons the appropriate alternative is indicated in the Temporale.

3 **Reading** The appointed reading may be replaced by an appropriate non-scriptural one, for example, a Franciscan reading from *A Sense of the Divine,* edited by Austin SSF, Nicholas Alan SSF and Tristam SSF.

4 **The Prayers** This section may be replaced by other liturgical forms. On Sundays the Thanksgiving for Baptism, including the blessing of holy water, may be used. On Fridays, because the time is closely linked with the hour of the Lord's passion, Cross Prayers may be used either at this Office or at Evening Prayer.

E NIGHT PRAYER

1 **Theme** The Office of Night Prayer or Compline derives its name from the Latin word *completorium* for completion, the completing of the day's round of work and prayer of anticipating that final completion in death and rest in Christ. If an unchanging pattern is desired, Night Prayer Form 7 should be used.

2 **Blessing of the Light** On suitable occasions, Night Prayer may begin with 'The Blessing of the Light' (Lucernarium). After the Song of the Light, incense may be burnt during Psalm 141, which is of a penitential nature. Night Prayer then continues with the appropriate psalmody.

3 **Preparation** In the Preparation section, all that precedes 'O God, make speed to save us' may be omitted; this is appropriate if the Eucharist has been celebrated earlier in the evening.

4 **Reading** The reading may be replaced by a non-scriptural reading.

5 **Responsory** The Alleluias are used only from Easter Day until the Day of Pentecost.

6 **Anthems** An anthem of the BVM may be sung following Night Prayer and the community may gather around an appropriate icon to do so.

The Calendar SSF

This Calendar is essentially that of *Common Worship*. It has been augmented to include celebrations of Franciscan saints of the three Orders as well as significant lives in the history of the Religious Life.

CLASSIFICATION

Holy Days are either Principal Feasts (Class I) or Festivals (Class II), Lesser Festivals (Class III) or Commemorations where desired. Holy Days marked with an asterisk (*) are those additionally observed by SSF.

Holy Days are celebrated in the following way:

Principal Feasts (Class I) Morning and Evening Prayer are of the Feast, with proper psalms and readings. The celebration begins either with the First Evening Prayer or a Vigil and ends at Night Prayer the following day. Midday Prayer is of the day of the week (Form 1-7), with propers provided for use on Feasts and in the Seasons. Night Prayer is of the Feast, with a reading and the festal refrain on the gospel canticle.

Festivals (Class II) Morning and Evening Prayer are of the Festival, with proper psalms and readings. Midday Prayer is of the day of the week (Form 1-7), with propers provided for use on Festivals and in the Seasons. Night Prayer is of the Festival, with a reading and the festal refrain on the gospel canticle.

Lesser Festivals (Class III) Morning Prayer and Evening Prayer are of the ordinary day or Season, with the collect of the Lesser Festival. Common propers may be used, except during the Seasons, when the seasonal propers are used. Midday Prayer is of the day of the week (Form 1-7). Seasonal propers are used. Night Prayer is of the day of the week (Form 1-7) or the Season.

Commemorations When desired a Commemoration may be observed by use of a hagiography (from e.g. *Exciting Holiness)*, by mention in intercessions or by the use of texts from the appropriate Common of Saints. Commemorations from the Calendar of *Common Worship* are indicated by *(CW)*.

Local Observance Where desired a commemoration of a local saint or dedication may be celebrated by assigning it to an appropriate classification and the propers may be drawn from the Common of Saints.

DAYS OF SPECIAL OBSERVANCE

Christmas Eve and Easter Eve are days of preparation and vigil,
therefore the collects of Christmas Day and Easter Day are not said
on Christmas Eve and Easter Eve respectively.

Ash Wednesday, the days of Holy Week and the Commemoration of the
Faithful Departed (2 November) are days of special devotion. The days
after Christmas until 6 January, and the days of Easter Week, are days of
special thanksgiving. The nine days after Ascension Day until Pentecost are
days of prayer and preparation to celebrate the outpouring of the Spirit.

The Week of Prayer for Christian Unity, usually observed 18 to 25 January,
may be observed between the alternative dates of Ascension Day and the
feast of Pentecost (as it is in some parts of the world).

Ember Days, Rogation Days and Harvest Thanksgiving are observed at the
Eucharist. If there is no celebration of the Eucharist, a collect from
Common Worship may be used in the Office.

THE SEASONS (TEMPORALE)

ADVENT	*Use Form 3*	
The 1st Sunday of Advent		II
The 2nd Sunday of Advent		II
The 3rd Sunday of Advent		II
From 17 December (O Sapientia)		
begin the eight days of prayer before Christmas Day		
The 4th Sunday of Advent		II
Christmas Eve		

CHRISTMAS	*Use Form 4*	
Christmas Day – *25 December*		I
The 1st Sunday of Christmas		II
The 2nd Sunday of Christmas		II

*The days after Christmas Day until the Epiphany traditionally form
a unity of days of special thanksgiving for the Incarnation.*

EPIPHANY	*Use Form 5*	
The Epiphany – *6 January*		I
The Baptism of Christ – *The 1st Sunday of Epiphany*		I
(The 2nd Sunday of Epiphany when 6 January is a Sunday)		
The 2nd Sunday of Epiphany		II

The 3rd Sunday of Epiphany   II
The 4th Sunday of Epiphany   II
The Presentation of Christ in the Temple (Candlemas)
  – *2 February*   I

ORDINARY TIME
This begins on the day following the Presentation.
The 5th Sunday before Lent   II
The 4th Sunday before Lent   II
The 3rd Sunday before Lent   II
The 2nd Sunday before Lent   II
Sunday next before Lent   II

LENT   *Use Form 6*
Ash Wednesday   I
The 1st Sunday of Lent   II
The 2nd Sunday of Lent   II
The 3rd Sunday of Lent   II
The 4th Sunday of Lent – *Mothering Sunday*   II
PASSIONTIDE
The 5th Sunday of Lent   II
Palm Sunday   II
Monday of Holy Week
Tuesday of Holy Week
Wednesday of Holy Week
Maundy Thursday   I
Good Friday   I
Easter Eve and Vigil

EASTER   *Use Form 1*
Easter Day   I
Monday of Easter Week
Tuesday of Easter Week
Wednesday of Easter Week
Thursday of Easter Week
Friday of Easter Week
Saturday of Easter Week
The 2nd Sunday of Easter   II
The 3rd Sunday of Easter   II
The 4th Sunday of Easter   II
The 5th Sunday of Easter   II
The 6th Sunday of Easter   II
Ascension Day   I

PENTECOST   *Use Form 2*
From Friday after Ascension Day begin the nine days of prayer
before Pentecost.
The 7th Sunday of Easter – *Sunday after Ascension Day*   II
Pentecost (Whit Sunday)   I

ORDINARY TIME
This is resumed on the Monday following the Day of Pentecost.
Trinity Sunday   I
**Day of Thanksgiving for the Institution
 of Holy Communion** (Corpus Christi)
  – *Thursday after Trinity Sunday*   I
The 1st Sunday after Trinity   II
Divine Compassion of Christ
  – *Friday after The 1st Sunday after Trinity*   II *
The 2nd Sunday after Trinity   II
The 3rd Sunday after Trinity   II
The 4th Sunday after Trinity   II
The 5th Sunday after Trinity   II
The 6th Sunday after Trinity   II
The 7th Sunday after Trinity   II
The 8th Sunday after Trinity   II
The 9th Sunday after Trinity   II
The 10th Sunday after Trinity   II
The 11th Sunday after Trinity   II
The 12th Sunday after Trinity   II
The 13th Sunday after Trinity   II
The 14th Sunday after Trinity   II
The 15th Sunday after Trinity   II
The 16th Sunday after Trinity   II
The 17th Sunday after Trinity   II
The 18th Sunday after Trinity   II
The 19th Sunday after Trinity   II
The 20th Sunday after Trinity   II
The 21st Sunday after Trinity   II
The Last Sunday after Trinity   II

Dedication of All Franciscan Churches – *October 30*   I

ALL SAINTS' UNTIL ADVENT *Use Form 7*

All Saints' Day – *1 November*   I

The Sunday between 30 October and 5 November
may be kept as All Saints' Sunday or as:

The 4th Sunday before Advent   II

The 3rd Sunday before Advent   II

The 2nd Sunday before Advent   II

Christ the King – *The Sunday next before Advent*   I

HOLY DAYS (SANCTORALE)

JANUARY

1	*Eighth Day of Christmas*	
	Naming and Circumcision of Jesus the Christ	I
2	*Ninth Day of Christmas*	
	Basil the Great (379) & Gregory of Nazianzus (389),	
	Bishops, Teachers of the Faith	III
3	*Tenth Day of Christmas*	
4	*Eleventh Day of Christmas*	
5	*Twelfth Day of Christmas*	
6	The Epiphany	I
12	Aelred of Hexham, Abbot of Rievaulx, 1167	III
13	Hilary, Bishop of Poitiers, Teacher, 367	III
16	The First Franciscan Martyrs, 1220	III *
17	Antony of Egypt, Hermit, Abbot, 356	III
18-25	*Week of Prayer for Christian Unity*	
18	Confession of Peter	II *
19	Wulfstan, Bishop of Worcester, 1095	III
20	Founders of Anglican Franciscan Communities	II *
21	Agnes, Child Martyr at Rome, 304	III
24	Francis de Sales, Bishop of Geneva, Teacher, 1622	III
25	The Conversion of Paul	II
26	Timothy and Titus, Companions of Paul	III
28	Thomas Aquinas, Priest, Philosopher, Teacher, 1274	III
30	Charles, King, Martyr, 1649	III

Additional Commemorations where desired:

2 Seraphim, Monk of Sarov, Spiritual Guide, 1833 *(CW)*

2 Vedanayagam Samuel Azariah, Bishop in South India, Evangelist, 1945 *(CW)*

7 Angela of Foligno, Franciscan Tertiary, Contemplative, 1309

10 Paul of Thebes, first Christian Hermit, c. 342

10 William Laud, Archbishop of Canterbury, 1645 *(CW)*

11 Mary Slessor, Missionary in West Africa, 1915 *(CW)*

12 Benedict Biscop, Abbot of Wearmouth, Scholar, 689 *(CW)*

13 Kentigern (Mungo), Monk, Bishop in Strathclyde & Cumbria, 603 *(CW)*

13 George Fox, Founder of the Society of Friends (the Quakers), 1691 *(CW)*

14 Richard Meux Benson, Founder of the Society of St John the Evangelist, 1915

17 Charles Gore, Founder of the Community of the Resurrection, 1932 *(CW)*

18 Amy Carmichael, Spiritual Writer, 1951 *(CW)*

20 Richard Rolle of Hampole, Spiritual Writer, 1349 *(CW)*

22 Vincent of Saragossa, Deacon, first Martyr of Spain, 304 *(CW)*

30 Hyacinth of Mariscotti, Franciscan Tertiary, 1640

31 Louise degli Albertoni, Franciscan Tertiary, 1533

31 John Bosco, Priest Founder of the Salesian Teaching Order, 1888 *(CW)*

FEBRUARY

  2 The Presentation of Christ in the Temple (Candlemas)   I
  3 Anskar, Archbishop of Hamburg, Missionary in Denmark
     and Sweden, 865   III
  7 Colette, Poor Clare, Founder of the Colettine Reform,
     1447   III *
 14 Cyril, 869, and Methodius, 885, Missionaries to the Slavs III
 17 Janani Luwum, Archbishop of Uganda, Martyr, 1977   III
 23 Polycarp, Bishop of Smyrna, Martyr, c. 155   III
 24 Vocation of Francis, 1208/9   III *
 27 George Herbert, Priest, Pastor, Poet, 1633   III

Additional Commemorations where desired:

  1 Brigid (Bride), Abbess of Kildare, c. 525 *(CW)*

  1 Veridiana of Castelfiorentino, Franciscan Tertiary and Anchoress, 1242

  4 Gilbert of Sempringham, Founder of the Gilbertine Order, 1189 *(CW)*

  6 Peter Baptist, Paul Miki & Companions, Martyrs of Japan, 1597 *(CW)*

  6 Founding of the Community of St Clare, Freeland, 1950

 10 Scholastica, sister of Benedict, Abbess of Plombariola, c. 543 *(CW)*

 10 Clare Agolanti of Rimini, Franciscan Tertiary, 1346

 11 Our Lady of Lourdes

 14 Valentine, Martyr at Rome, c. 269 *(CW)*

 15 Sigfrid, Bishop, Apostle of Sweden, 1045 *(CW)*

 15 Thomas Bray, Priest, Founder of SPCK & SPG, 1730 *(CW)*

 15 George Potter, Friar, Founder of the Brotherhood of the Holy Cross, 1960

 16 Philippa Mareri, Poor Clare, Founding Abbess of Rieti, 1236

 20 Cecile Isherwood, Founder of the Community of the Resurrection,
     Grahamstown, South Africa, 1906

 25 Foundation of the Community of St Francis by Rosina Mary Rice, 1905

 26 Isabella of France, Poor Clare, 1270

 28 Antonia of Florence, Poor Clare, Founding Abbess of Aquila, 1472

Alternative Dates

Matthias may be celebrated on 24 February instead of 14 May.

MARCH

1	David, Bishop of Menevia, Patron of Wales, c. 601	II
2	Chad, Bishop of Lichfield, Missionary, 672	III
7	Perpetua, Felicity & their Companions, Martyrs at Carthage, 203	III
8	Edward King, Bishop of Lincoln, 1910	III
17	Patrick, Bishop of Armagh, Patron of Ireland, c. 460	II
19	Joseph of Nazareth	II
20	Cuthbert, Bishop of Lindisfarne, Missionary, 687	III
21	Thomas Cranmer, Archbishop of Canterbury, Martyr, 1556	III
25	Annunciation of our Lord to the Blessed Virgin Mary	I

Additional Commemorations where desired:

2 Agnes of Prague, Poor Clare, 1282

7 Helen Elizabeth Christmas, a Founder of the Community of St Francis, 1950

7 Joseph Crookston, Founder of the Order of St Francis, 1979

8 Felix, Bishop, Apostle to the East Angles, 647 *(CW)*

8 Geoffrey Studdert Kennedy, Priest, Poet, 1929 *(CW)*

11 Passing of Benedict of Nursia, Abbot, c. 550

18 Cyril, Bishop of Jerusalem, Teacher, 386 *(CW)*

20 John of Parma, Franciscan Friar, Spiritual, Solitary, 1289

24 Walter Hilton of Thurgarton, Augustinian Canon, Mystic, 1396 *(CW)*

24 Paul Couturier, Priest, Ecumenist, 1953 *(CW)*

24 Oscar Romero, Archbishop of San Salvador, Martyr, 1980 *(CW)*

26 June Ellacombe & Mary Bruce, Founders first Sisterhood in the C of E, 1845

26 Harriet Monsell, Founder of the Community of St John the Baptist, 1883 *(CW)*

28 William Sirr SDC, Franciscan Friar, Monk, Solitary, 1937

29 Jack Winslow, Scholar, Missionary, Evangelist, 1974

31 John Donne, Priest, Poet, 1631 *(CW)*

31 Andrew Ernest Hardy SDC, Franciscan Friar, 1946

Alternative Dates

Chad may be celebrated with Cedd on 26 October instead of 2 March.

Cuthbert may be celebrated on 4 September instead of 20 March.

APRIL

10	William Law, Priest, Spiritual Writer, 1761	III
16	Commemoration of the taking of Vows by Francis, 1209	III *
	Renewal of Commitment to Vows, First Order SSF	
19	Alphege, Archbishop of Canterbury, Martyr, 1012	III
21	Anselm, Abbot of Le Bec, Archbishop of Canterbury, Teacher, 1109	III
23	George, Martyr, Patron of England, c. 304	II
25	Mark the Evangelist	II
29	Catherine of Siena, Mystic, Dominican Tertiary, Teacher, 1380	III

Additional Commemorations where desired:

1 Frederick Denison Maurice, Priest, Teacher, 1872 *(CW)*

2 Francis of Paola, Franciscan Hermit, 1507

3 Benedict the Black, Franciscan Friar, 1589

4 Martin Luther King, Civil Rights Leader, 1968

5 Maria Crescentia Hoss, Franciscan Third Order Regular, 1744

9 Dietrich Bonhoeffer, Lutheran Pastor, Martyr, 1945 *(CW)*

10 William of Ockham, Franciscan Friar, Philosopher, Teacher, 1347 *(CW)*

10 Pierre Teilhard de Chardin, Visionary, 1955

11 George Augustus Selwyn, first Bishop of New Zealand, 1878 *(CW)*

16 Isabella Gilmore, Deaconess, 1923 *(CW)*

16 Foundation of the Poor Clares of Reparation & Adoration, USA, 1924

21 Conrad of Parzham, Franciscan Friar, 1894

23 Giles of Assisi, Franciscan Friar, 1252

23 Michael Ramsey, Archbishop of Canterbury, Teacher, 1988

24 Mellitus, Bishop of London, first Bishop at St Paul's, 624 *(CW)*

24 Fidelis Roy of Sigmaringen, Franciscan Friar, Martyr, 1622

24 The Seven Martyrs of the Melanesian Brotherhood, SI, 2003 *(CW)*

27 Christina Rosetti, Poet, 1894 *(CW)*

28 Luchesio & Buonadonna, Franciscan Tertiaries, 1260

28 Peter Chanel, Missionary in the South Pacific, Martyr, 1841 *(CW)*

30 Pandita Mary Ramabai, Translator of the Scriptures, 1922 *(CW)*

MAY

1	Philip and James, Apostles	II
2	Athanasius, Bishop of Alexandria, Teacher, 373	III
4	English Saints & Martyrs of the Reformation Era	III
8	Julian of Norwich, Mystic, c. 1417	III
14	Matthias the Apostle	II
15	Pachomius, Abbot, Founder of Monasticism, 346	III *
16	Margaret of Cortona, Penitent, Franciscan Tertiary, 1297	III *
19	Dunstan, Archbishop of Canterbury, Restorer of Monastic Life, 988	III
20	Bernardine of Siena, Franciscan Friar, 1444	III *
24	John, 1791, and Charles, 1788, Wesley, Evangelists, Hymn Writers	III
25	The Venerable Bede, Priest, Monk at Jarrow, Scholar, Historian, 735	III
26	Augustine, first Archbishop of Canterbury, 605	II
30	Josephine Butler, Social Reformer, 1906	III
31	Visit of the Blessed Virgin Mary to Elizabeth	II

Additional Commemorations where desired:

9 Catherine of Bologna, Poor Clare, Artist, 1463

12 Edward Willis, Co-Founder of the Oxford Mission to Calcutta, 1879

12 Leopold Mandich of Herceg Novi, Franciscan Friar, 1942

12 Gregory Dix, Benedictine, Liturgist, 1952 *(CW)*

16 Caroline Chisholm, Social Reformer, 1877 *(CW)*

17 Paschal Baylon, Franciscan Friar, 1592

18 Felix Porri of Cantallce, Franciscan Friar, 1587

19 Humiliana de' Cerchi, first cloistered Franciscan Tertiary, 1246

20 Alcuin of York, Deacon, Abbot of Tours, 804 *(CW)*

21 Helena, Protector of the Holy Places, 330 *(CW)*

25 Aldhelm, Bishop of Sherborne, 709 *(CW)*

26 John Calvin, Reformer, 1564 *(CW)*

28 Lanfranc, Prior of Le Bec, Archbishop of Canterbury, Scholar, 1089 *(CW)*

28 Mary Anne of Jesus of Paredes, Franciscan Tertiary, 1645

30 Joan of Arc, Visionary, 1431 *(CW)*

30 Baptista Varani, Poor Clare, 1527

30 Apolo Kivebulaya, Priest, Evangelist in Central Africa, 1933 *(CW)*

Alternative Dates

Matthias may be celebrated on 24 February instead of 14 May.
The Visit of the Blessed Virgin Mary to Elizabeth may be celebrated
on 2 July instead of 31 May.

JUNE

1	Justin, Martyr at Rome, c. 165	III
5	Boniface (Wynfrith) of Crediton, Bishop, Apostle of Germany, Martyr, 754	III
8	Thomas Ken, Bishop of Bath and Wells, Non-Juror, Hymn Writer, 1711	III
9	Columba (Columcille), Abbot of Iona, Missionary, 597	III
11	Barnabas the Apostle	II
13	Antony of Padua, Franciscan Friar, 1231	III *
16	Richard, Bishop of Chichester, 1253	III
22	Alban, first Martyr of Britain, c. 250	II
23	Etheldreda, Abbess of Ely, c. 678	III
24	The Birth of John the Baptist	I
28	Irenaeus, Bishop of Lyons, Teacher, c. 200	III
29	Peter and Paul, Apostles	II

Additional Commemorations where desired:

1 James Adderley, Founder of Anglican Franciscan Religious Life, 1942

3 Martyrs of Uganda, 1886 & 1978 *(CW)*

4 Petroc, Abbot of Padstow, 6th century *(CW)*

4 John XXIII, Bishop of Rome, Reformer, 1963

6 Marian Hughes, First to make Religious Vows in the C of E, 1841

6 Ini Kopuria, Founder of the Melanesian Brotherhood, 1945 *(CW)*

9 Ephrem of Syria, Deacon, Hymn Writer, Teacher, 373 *(CW)*

14 Richard Baxter, Puritan Divine, 1691 *(CW)*

15 Evelyn Underhill, Spiritual Writer, 1941 *(CW)*

16 Joseph Butler, Bishop of Durham, Philosopher, 1752 *(CW)*

17 Samuel and Henrietta Barnett, Social Reformers, 1913 & 1936 *(CW)*

18 Bernard Mizeki, Apostle to the Mashona, Martyr, 1896 *(CW)*

19 Sundar Singh of India, Sadhu (holy man), Evangelist, Teacher, 1929 *(CW)*

20 Michelina of Pesaro, Franciscan Tertiary, 1356

27 Cyril, Bishop of Alexandria, Teacher, 444 *(CW)*

30 Ramon Lull, Franciscan Tertiary, Martyr, 1315

Alternative Dates

Peter the Apostle may be celebrated alone, without Paul, on 29 June.

JULY

3	Thomas the Apostle	II
11	Benedict of Nursia, Abbot of Monte Casino, Father of Western Monasticism, c. 550	II
14	John Keble, Priest, Tractarian Poet, 1866	III
15	Bonaventure, Franciscan Friar, Bishop, Teacher, 1274	III *
19	Gregory, Bishop of Nyssa, & his sister Macrina, Deacon, Teachers, 394 & 379	III
22	Mary Magdalene, Apostle to the Apostles	II
25	James the Apostle	II
26	Anne and Joachim, Parents of the Blessed Virgin Mary	III
29	Mary, Martha & Lazarus, Companions of our Lord	III
30	Thomas Clarkson, Olaudah Equiano and William Wilberforce, Anti-Slavery Campaigners, 1846, 1797 and 1833	III

Additional Commemorations where desired:

1 Junipero Serra, Franciscan Friar, Missionary, 1784

4 Elizabeth of Portugal, Franciscan Tertiary, 1336

9 Nicholas Pieck & Companions, Martyrs of Gorkum, 1572

10 Veronica Giuliani, Poor Clare, 1727

13 Angelina of Foligno, Founder of Third Order Congregation, 1435

14 Francis Solano, Franciscan Friar, 1610

15 Swithun, Bishop of Winchester, c. 862 *(CW)*

16 Osmund, Bishop of Salisbury, 1099 *(CW)*

18 Elizabeth Ferard, first Deaconess of the Church of England, Founder of the Community of St Andrew, 1883 *(CW)*

20 Margaret of Antioch, Martyr, 4th century *(CW)*

20 Bartolomé de las Casas, Apostle to the Indies, 1566 *(CW)*

21 Lawrence of Brindisi, Franciscan Friar, Teacher, 1619

23 John Cassian, Monk, Author, 435

23 Bridget of Sweden, Abbess of Vadstena, 1373 *(CW)*

24 Cunegunde, Franciscan Third Order Regular, 1292

27 Mary Magdalene of Martinengo, Poor Clare (Capucine), 1737

27 Brooke Foss Westcott, Bishop of Durham, Teacher, 1901 *(CW)*

31 Ignatius of Loyola, Founder of the Society of Jesus, 1556 *(CW)*

Alternative Dates

The Visit of the Blessed Virgin Mary to Elizabeth may be celebrated on 2 July instead of 31 May

Thomas the Apostle may be celebrated on 21 December instead of 3 July.

Thomas Becket may be celebrated on 7 July instead of 29 December.

AUGUST

2	Mary of the Angels	III *
4	John Vianney, Curé d'Ars, Patron of the Parish Clergy, Franciscan Tertiary, 1859	III *
5	Oswald, King of Northumbria, Martyr, 642	III
6	Transfiguration of Christ	I
8	Dominic, Priest, Founder of the Order of Preachers, 1221	III
9	Mary Sumner, Founder of the Mothers Union, 1921	III
10	Laurence, Deacon at Rome, Martyr, 258	III
11	Clare, Founder of the Minoresses (Poor Clares), 1253	I *
13	Jeremy Taylor, Bishop of Down and Connor, Pastor, Teacher, 1667	III
14	Maximilian Kolbe, Franciscan Friar, Martyr, 1941	III *
15	The Blessed Virgin Mary	I *
20	Bernard, Founding Abbot of Clairvaux, Teacher, 1153	III
24	Bartholomew the Apostle	II
25	Louis Capet, Christian Monarch, Crusader for Christ, Patron of the Third Order, 1270	II *
27	Monica, mother of Augustine of Hippo, 387	III
28	Augustine, Bishop of Hippo, Teacher, 430	III
29	Beheading of John the Baptist	III *
30	John Bunyan, Spiritual Writer, 1688	III
31	Aidan, Bishop of Lindisfarne, Missionary, 651	III

Additional Commemorations where desired:

7 John Mason Neale, Priest, Hymn Writer, 1866 *(CW)*

11 John Henry Newman, Priest, Tractarian, 1890 *(CW)*

13 Florence Nightingale, Social Reformer, 1910 *(CW)*

13 Octavia Hill, Social Reformer, 1912 *(CW)*

20 William & Catherine Booth, Founders of the Salvation Army, 1912 & 1890 *(CW)*

SEPTEMBER

3	Gregory the Great, Bishop of Rome, Teacher, 604	III
8	The Birth of the Blessed Virgin Mary	II
10	Agnellus of Pisa, and the Coming of the Friars Minor to England, 1224	III *
13	John Chrysostom, Bishop of Constantinople, Teacher, 407	III
14	Holy Cross Day	II
15	Mary at the Cross	III *
16	Ninian, Bishop of Galloway, Apostle of the Picts, c. 432	III
17	Stigmata of Francis, 1224	II *
20	John Coleridge Patteson, First Bishop of Melanesia, & his Companions, Martyrs, 1871	III
21	Matthew the Apostle	II
25	Lancelot Andrewes, Bishop of Winchester, Spiritual Writer, 1626	III
27	Vincent de Paul, Founder of the Congregation of the Mission (Lazarists), 1660	III
29	Michael and All Angels	II

Additional Commemorations where desired:

1 Giles of Provence, Hermit, c. 710 *(CW)*

1 Beatrix da Silva, Founder of Conceptionist Poor Clares, 1490

2 Martyrs of Papua New Guinea, 1901 & 1942 *(CW)*

4 Birinus, Bishop of Dorchester (Oxon), Apostle of Wessex, 650 *(CW)*

4 Rose of Viterbo, Franciscan Tertiary, 1251

7 Douglas Downes, Franciscan Friar, Founder of the Brotherhood of St Francis of Assisi, 1957

9 Charles Fuge Lowder, Priest, 1880 *(CW)*

15 Cyprian, Bishop of Carthage, Martyr, 258 *(CW)*

16 Edward Bouverie Pusey, Priest, Tractarian, 1882 *(CW)*

17 Hildegard, Abbess of Bingen, Visionary, 1179 *(CW)*

18 Joseph of Cupertino, Franciscan Friar, 1663

19 Theodore of Tarsus, Archbishop of Canterbury, 690 *(CW)*

23 Finding of the Body of Clare, 1850

23 Padre Pio, Franciscan Friar, Mystic, 1968

24 Our Lady of Walsingham

25 Sergei of Radonezh, Russian Monastic Reformer, Teacher, 1392 *(CW)*

26 Delphina & Elzear of Sabran, Franciscan Tertiaries, 1358

26 Wilson Carlisle, Founder of the Church Army, 1942 *(CW)*

30 Jerome, Translator of the Scriptures, 420 *(CW)*

Alternative Dates

Cuthbert may be celebrated on 4 September instead of 20 March.

OCTOBER

3	*The Transitus of Francis*	*
4	Francis of Assisi, Friar, Deacon, Founder of the Friars Minor, 1226	I
6	William Tyndale, Translator of the Scriptures, Martyr, 1536	III
10	Paulinus, Monk, Bishop of York, Missionary, 644	III
12	Wilfrid of Ripon, Bishop, Missionary, 709	III
13	Edward the Confessor, King of England, 1066	III
15	Teresa of Avila, Mystic, Teacher, 1582	III
17	Ignatius, Bishop of Antioch, Martyr, c. 107	III
18	Luke the Evangelist	II
19	Henry Martyn, Translator of the Scriptures Missionary in India & Persia, 1812	III
22	Peter of Alcantara, Franciscan Friar, Reformer, 1562	III *
26	Alfred the Great, King of the West Saxons, Scholar, 899	III
28	Simon and Jude, Apostles	II
29	James Hannington, Bishop of Eastern Equatorial Africa, Martyr in Uganda, 1885	III
30	Dedication of all Franciscan Churches	I *

Additional Commemorations where desired:

1 Remigius, Bishop of Rheims, Apostle of the Franks, 533 *(CW)*

1 Anthony Ashley Cooper, Earl of Shaftesbury, Social Reformer, 1885 *(CW)*

3 George Bell, Bishop, Ecumenist, Peacemaker, 1958 *(CW)*

9 Denys, Bishop of Paris, and his Companions, Martyrs, c. 250 *(CW)*

9 Robert Grosseteste, Bishop of Lincoln, Philosopher, Scientist, 1253 *(CW)*

10 Thomas Traherne, Poet, Spiritual Writer, 1674 *(CW)*

11 Ethelburga, Abbess of Barking, 675 *(CW)*

11 James the Deacon, companion of Paulinus, 7th century *(CW)*

12 Elizabeth Fry, Prison Reformer, 1845 *(CW)*

12 Edith Cavell, Nurse, 1915 *(CW)*

16 Nicholas Ridley and Hugh Latimer, Bishops, Reformation Martyrs, 1555 *(CW)*

23 John of Capistrano, Franciscan Friar, 1456

25 Crispin and Crispinian, Martyrs at Rome, c. 287 *(CW)*

26 Cedd, Bishop of the East Saxons, Founding Abbot of Lastingham, 664 *(CW)*

29 Paula of Montaldo, Poor Clare, Mystic, 1514

31 Martin Luther, Ecclesiastical Reformer, 1546 *(CW)*

Alternative Dates

Chad may be celebrated with Cedd on 26 October instead of 2 March.

NOVEMBER

1	All Saints' Day	I
2	Commemoration of the Faithful Departed	
	(All Souls' Day)	II
3	Richard Hooker, Priest, Anglican Apologist, Teacher,	
	1600	III
7	Willibrord of York, Bishop, Apostle of Frisia, 739	III
8	The Saints and Martyrs of England	III
10	Leo the Great, Bishop of Rome, Teacher, 461	III
11	Martin, Bishop of Tours, c. 397	III
13	Charles Simeon, Priest, Evangelical Divine, 1836	III
16	Margaret, Queen of Scotland, Philanthropist,	
	Reformer of the Church, 1093	III
17	Hugh, Bishop of Lincoln, 1200	III
18	Elizabeth of Hungary, Philanthropist,	
	Franciscan Tertiary, Patron of the Third Order, 1231	II *
19	Hilda, Abbess of Whitby, 680	III
20	Edmund, King of the East Angles, Martyr, 870	III
23	Clement, Bishop of Rome, Martyr, c. 100	III
24	All Departed Franciscans	III *
29	All Franciscan Saints	III *
30	Andrew the Apostle, Patron of Scotland	II

Additional Commemorations where desired:

3 Martin de Porres, Dominican Friar, 1639 *(CW)*

4 Helen Enselmini of Padua, Poor Clare, 1242

6 Leonard, Hermit, 6th century *(CW)*

6 William Temple, Archbishop of Canterbury, Teacher, 1944 *(CW)*

7 Didacus (Diego) of Alcalá, Franciscan Friar, 1463

8 John Duns Scotus, Franciscan Friar, Theologian, Teacher 1308

9 Margery Kempe, Mystic, c. 1440 *(CW)*

14 Samuel Seabury, first Anglican Bishop in North America, 1796 *(CW)*

15 Mary of the Passion, Founder of the Franciscan Missionaries of Mary, 1904

16 Edmund Rich of Abingdon, Archbishop of Canterbury, 1240 *(CW)*

19 Agnes of Assisi, Poor Clare, 1253

19 Mechtild, Béguine of Magdeburg, Mystic, 1280 *(CW)*

20 Priscilla Lydia Sellon, a Restorer of the Religious Life
   in the Church of England, 1876 *(CW)*

22 Cecilia, Martyr at Rome, c. 230 *(CW)*

23 Algy Robertson, co-Founder of the Society of St Francis, 1955

25 Catherine of Alexandria, Martyr, 4th century *(CW)*

25 Isaac Watts, Hymn Writer, 1748 *(CW)*

26 Leonard of Port Maurice, Franciscan Friar, 1751

28 James of the March, Franciscan Friar, 1476

29 *Day of Intercession and Thanksgiving for the Missionary Work of the Church*

DECEMBER

6	Nicholas, Bishop of Myra, c. 326	III
7	Ambrose, Bishop of Milan, Teacher, 397	III
8	Conception of the Blessed Virgin Mary	II
13	Lucy, Martyr at Syracuse, 304	III
14	John of the Cross, Poet, Teacher, 1591	III
17	*O Sapientia*	
18	*O Adonai*	
19	*O Radix Jesse*	
20	*O Clavis David*	
21	*O Oriens*	
22	*O Rex Gentium*	
23	*O Emmanuel*	
24	Eve and Vigil of Christmas	
25	Christmas Day	I
26	*Second Day of Christmas*	
	Stephen, Deacon, First Martyr	II
27	*Third Day of Christmas*	
	John, Apostle & Evangelist	II
28	*Fourth Day of Christmas*	
	The Holy Innocents	II
29	*Fifth Day of Christmas*	
	Thomas Becket, Archbishop of Canterbury, Martyr, 1170	III
30	*Sixth Day of Christmas*	
31	*Seventh Day of Christmas*	

Additional Commemorations where desired:

1 Charles de Foucauld, Hermit in the Sahara, 1916 *(CW)*
3 Francis Xavier, Missionary, Apostle of the Indies, 1552 *(CW)*
4 John of Damascus, Monk, Teacher, c. 749 *(CW)*
4 Nicholas Ferrar, Founder of the Little Gidding Community, 1637 *(CW)*
8 John Pecham, Archbishop of Canterbury, Franciscan friar, 1292
10 Thomas Merton, Monk, Spiritual Writer, 1968
12 Our Lady of Guadalupe, 1531
12 Finding of the Body of Francis, 1818
13 Samuel Johnson, Moralist, 1784 *(CW)*
15 Mary Frances Schervier, Franciscan Tertiary, 1876
17 Eglantyne Jebb, Founder of 'Save the Children', 1928 *(CW)*
24 Jacopone da Todi, Franciscan Friar, Poet, 1306
30 Margaret Colonna, Poor Clare, 1284
31 John Wyclif, Reformer, 1384 *(CW)*

Alternative Dates

Thomas the Apostle may be celebrated on 21 December instead of 3 July.
Thomas Becket may be celebrated on 7 July instead of 29 December.

The Date of Easter
and Other Variable Dates

Year		Ash Wed	Easter Day	Asc Day	Pente-cost	Advent Sunday
2010	C	17 Feb	4 Apr	13 May	23 May	28 Nov
2011	A	9 Mar	24 Apr	2 Jun	12 Jun	27 Nov
2012	B	22 Feb	8 Apr	17 May	27 May	2 Dec
2013	C	13 Feb	31 Mar	9 May	19 May	1 Dec
2014	A	5 Mar	20 Apr	29 May	8 Jun	30 Nov
2015	B	18 Feb	5 Apr	14 May	24 May	29 Nov
2016	C	10 Feb	27 Mar	5 May	15 May	27 Nov
2017	A	1 Mar	16 Apr	25 May	4 Jun	3 Dec
2018	B	14 Feb	1 Apr	10 May	20 May	2 Dec
2019	C	6 Mar	21 Apr	30 May	9 Jun	1 Dec
2020	A	26 Feb	12 Apr	21 May	31 May	29 Nov
2021	B	17 Feb	4 Apr	13 May	23 May	28 Nov
2022	C	2 Mar	17 Apr	26 May	5 Jun	27 Nov
2023	A	22 Feb	9 Apr	18 May	28 May	3 Dec
2024	B	14 Feb	31 Mar	9 May	19 May	1 Dec
2025	C	5 Mar	20 Apr	29 May	8 Jun	30 Nov
2026	A	18 Feb	5 Apr	14 May	24 May	29 Nov
2027	B	10 Feb	28 Mar	6 May	16 May	28 Nov
2028	C	1 Mar	16 Apr	25 May	4 Jun	3 Dec
2029	A	14 Feb	1 Apr	10 May	20 May	2 Dec
2030	B	6 Mar	21 Apr	30 May	9 Jun	1 Dec
2031	C	26 Feb	13 Apr	22 May	1 Jun	30 Nov
2032	A	11 Feb	28 Mar	6 May	16 May	28 Nov
2033	B	2 Mar	17 Apr	26 May	5 Jun	27 Nov
2034	C	22 Feb	9 Apr	18 May	28 May	3 Dec
2035	A	7 Feb	25 Mar	3 May	13 May	2 Dec

Before the Office

– *MEMORIAL OF THE INCARNATION*

The Angelus is traditionally observed at dawn, midday and sunset from the Monday after Pentecost to Maundy Thursday.

*Either **A**:*

The angel of the Lord brought tidings to Mary
and she conceived by the Holy Spirit.

Hail Mary, full of grace, the Lord is with you.
Blessèd are you among women,
and blessèd is the fruit of your womb, Jesus.
**Holy Mary, Mother of God, pray for us sinners,
now, and at the hour of our death.**

'Behold the handmaid of the Lord;
let it be to me according to your word.'

Hail Mary, . . .
Holy Mary, . . .

The Word was made flesh
and dwelt among us.

Hail Mary, . . .
Holy Mary, . . .

Pray for us, holy Mother of God,
that we may be made worthy of the promises of Christ.

Let us pray.

We beseech you, O Lord,
pour your grace into our hearts;
that as we have known the incarnation of your Son Jesus Christ
    by the message of an angel,
so by his cross and passion
we may be brought to the glory of his resurrection;
through Jesus Christ our Lord. **Amen.**

*or **B**:*

The angel brought good news to Mary:
The Holy Spirit will come upon you.

Hail Mary, full of grace, the Lord is with you.
Blessèd are you among women,
and blessèd is the fruit of your womb, Jesus.
Son of Mary, Son of God, have mercy on us,
now, and at the hour of our death.

'Here am I, the servant of the Lord;
let it be with me according to your word.'

Hail Mary, . . .
Son of Mary, . . .

The Word became flesh
and lived among us.

Hail Mary, . . .
Son of Mary, . . .

Blessèd is she who believed,
blessèd are those who hear the word of God
and keep it.

Let us pray.

We beseech you, O Lord,
pour your grace into our hearts;
that as we have known the incarnation of your Son Jesus Christ
   by the message of an angel,
so by his cross and passion
we may be brought to the glory of his resurrection;
through Jesus Christ our Lord. **Amen.**

REGINA COELI – *MEMORIAL OF THE RESURRECTION*

The Regina Coeli is traditionally observed at dawn, midday and sunset from Easter Day until Pentecost.

Queen of Heaven, rejoice this day.
Alleluia.

He whom you were called to bear.
Alleluia.

As he promised has arisen.
Alleluia.

Pour for us, to God, your prayer.
Alleluia.

Rejoice and be glad, O Virgin Mary. Alleluia.
For the Lord has risen indeed. Alleluia.

Let us pray.

O God, who by the resurrection of your Son,
our Lord Jesus Christ,
you have brought joy to the whole world;
grant that, aided by the prayers
    of his Mother, the Virgin Mary,
we may know the joys of eternal life;
through Jesus Christ our Lord. **Amen.**

A PRAYER ON ENTERING A CHURCH

*Either **A**:*

We adore you, most holy Lord Jesus Christ,
here, and in all your churches
    throughout all the world;
and we bless you
because, by your holy cross,
you have redeemed the world.

from The Testament, Francis of Assisi
after the European Province SSF

*or **B**:*

Both here, and in all your churches
    throughout the whole world;
we adore you, O Christ,
and we bless you
because by your holy cross,
you have redeemed the world.

from The Testament, Francis of Assisi
after the Province of the Americas SSF

Form 1 – Morning Prayer

Sundays in Ordinary Time
and daily in Easter Season

THE PREPARATION

A *is used on Sundays in Ordinary Time.*
B *is used daily in Easter season, on specified Class I & II Holy Days and may also be used on Sundays in Ordinary Time. For Ascension Day, see page 586.*

A:

O Lord, open our lips
and our mouth shall proclaim your praise.

Lead your people to freedom, O God,
and banish all darkness from our hearts and minds.

Glory . . .   Alleluia.

THE OPENING CANTICLE

BENEDICITE – A SONG OF CREATION (37b) or Number 37a, page 499

1   Bless the Lord all you works of the Lord: *
    sing his praise and exalt him for ever.

2   Bless the Lord you heavens: *
    sing his praise and exalt him for ever.

3   Bless the Lord you angels of the Lord: *
    sing his praise and exalt him for ever.

4   Bless the Lord all people on earth: *
    sing his praise and exalt him for ever.

5   O people of God bless the Lord: *
    sing his praise and exalt him for ever.

6   Bless the Lord you priests of the Lord: *
    sing his praise and exalt him for ever.

7   Bless the Lord you servants of the Lord: *
    sing his praise and exalt him for ever.

8   Bless the Lord all you of upright spirit: *
     bless the Lord you that are holy and humble in heart.

Bless the Father, the Son and the Holy Spirit: *
sing his praise and exalt him for ever.

The Song of the Three 35-37,60-65

Morning Prayer continues with the HYMN and/or THE OPENING PRAYER.

B:

O Lord, open our lips
and our mouth shall proclaim your praise.

Blessèd are you, Lord God of our salvation,
to you be praise and glory for ever.
As once you ransomed your people from Egypt
and led them to freedom in the promised land,
so now you have delivered us from the dominion of darkness
and brought us into the kingdom of your risen Son.
May we, the first fruits of your new creation,
rejoice in this new day you have made,
and praise you for your mighty acts,
Father, Son and Holy Spirit:
Blessèd be God for ever.

The following is said:

In Ordinary Time:

God is the creator and redeemer of all.
O come, let us worship.

or, in Easter:

Alleluia. Christ is risen indeed.
O come, let us worship. Alleluia.

THE OPENING CANTICLE

THE EASTER ANTHEMS (62a), number 62b, page 523, or Psalm 100, page 392

1   Christ our passover has been sacrificed for us, *
     so let us celebrate the feast,

2   Not with the old leaven of corruption and wickedness *
     but with the unleavened bread of sincerity and truth.

3   Christ once raised from the dead dies no more; *
     death has no more dominion over him.

4   In dying, he died to sin once for all; *
     in living, he lives to God.

5   See yourselves, therefore, as dead to sin *
     and alive to God in Jesus Christ our Lord.

6   Christ has been raised from the dead; *
     the first fruits of those who sleep.

7   For since by one man came death, *
     by another has come also the resurrection of the dead,

8   For as in Adam all die, *
     even so in Christ shall all be made alive.

   Glory . . .

                        I Corinthians 5.7b-8; Romans 6.9-11; I Corinthians 15.20-22

A HYMN may be sung.

THE OPENING PRAYER may be said.

The night has passed and the day lies open before us;
let us pray with one heart and mind.
(Silence may be kept.)

As we rejoice in the gift of this new day,
so may the light of your presence, O God,
set our hearts on fire with love for you;
now and for ever. Amen.

THE WORD OF GOD

THE PSALMODY, as appointed

Each psalm, or group of psalms, may end with:
Glory . . .

If there are two SCRIPTURE READINGS, the first may be read here, or both may be read after the Second Canticle.

THE SECOND CANTICLE

In Ordinary Time:

Either A SONG OF THE NEW CREATION (14) or number 36, page 498

Refrain: **I will make a way in the wilderness,
and rivers in the desert.**

1   'I am the Lord, your Holy One, *
    the Creator of Israel, your King.'

2   Thus says the Lord, who makes a way in the sea, *
    a path in the mighty waters,

3   'Remember not the former things, *
    nor consider the things of old.

4   'Behold, I am doing a new thing; *
    now it springs forth, do you not perceive it?

5   'I will make a way in the wilderness
       and rivers in the desert, *
    to give drink to my chosen people,

6   'The people whom I formed for myself, *
    that they might declare my praise.'

   Glory . . .   *Isaiah 43.15,16,18,19,20c,21*

   **I will make a way in the wilderness,
   and rivers in the desert.**

In Easter:

Either THE SONG OF MOSES & MIRIAM (1) or numbers 5, page 474, or 14, page 481

Refrain: **In your unfailing love, O Lord,**
you lead the people whom you have redeemed.

1   I will sing to the Lord, who has triumphed gloriously; *
     the horse and his rider have been thrown into the sea.

2   The Lord is my strength and my song *
     and has become my salvation.

3   This is my God whom I will praise *
     the God of my ancestors whom I will exalt.

4   The Lord is a warrior; *
     the Lord is his name.

5   Your right hand, O Lord, is glorious in power: *
     your right hand, O Lord, shatters the enemy.

6   At the blast of your nostrils, the sea covered them; *
     they sank as lead in the mighty waters.

7   In your unfailing love, O Lord, *
     you lead the people whom you have redeemed,

8   And by your invincible strength *
     you will guide them to your holy dwelling.

9   You will bring them in and plant them, O Lord, *
     in the sanctuary which your hands have established.

   Glory ...   *Exodus 15.1b-3,6,10,13,17*

   In your unfailing love, O Lord,
   you lead the people whom you have redeemed.

THE SCRIPTURE READING(S)

A RESPONSORY may be said.

Awake, O sleeper, and arise from the dead.
And Christ shall give you light.

You have died,
and your life is hid with Christ in God.
Awake, O sleeper, and arise from the dead.

Set your minds on things that are above,
not on things that are on the earth.
And Christ shall give you light.

When Christ our life appears
you will appear with him in glory.
Awake, O sleeper, and arise from the dead,
and Christ shall give you light.

from Colossians 3

THE GOSPEL CANTICLE: BENEDICTUS – THE SONG OF ZECHARIAH (41)

See either inside front cover, inside back cover or page 506 for another version.

In Ordinary Time:

Refrain: **You have raised up for us a mighty Saviour,**
   born of the house of your servant David.

or, in Easter:

   Alleluia. Christ is risen from the dead;
   by his death he has trampled down death
   and through the grave
   all life has been set free. Alleluia.

The refrain is repeated after the canticle.

THE PRAYERS

INTERCESSIONS may be offered.

THE KYRIES may be used as responses to intercession.

Lord, have mercy.
Lord, have mercy.

Christ, have mercy.
Christ, have mercy.

Lord, have mercy.
Lord, have mercy.

God of glory,
by the raising of your Son
you have broken the chains of death and hell:
fill your Church with faith and hope;
for a new day has dawned
and the way to life stands open
in our Saviour Jesus Christ. **Amen.**

or, in Easter:

God of life,
who for our redemption gave your only-begotten Son
    to the death of the cross,
and by his glorious resurrection
have delivered us from the power of our enemy:
grant us so to die daily to sin,
that we may evermore live with him in the joy of his risen life;
through Jesus Christ our Lord. **Amen.**

THE LORD'S PRAYER may be said.

[Rejoicing in God's new creation,]
as our Saviour taught us, so we pray
Our Father in heaven, . . .

THE CONCLUSION

In Ordinary Time:

**The Lord bless us, and preserve us from all evil,
and keep us in eternal life. Amen.**

Let us bless the Lord.
Thanks be to God.

or, in Easter:

May the risen Christ grant us the joys of eternal life. Amen.

Let us bless the Lord. Alleluia, alleluia.
Thanks be to God. Alleluia, alleluia.

or, on Class I & II Holy Days:

May our blessèd Lady pray for us.
May Saint Francis and Saint Clare pray for us.
[May Saint N pray for us.]
May all the saints of God pray for us.
May the angels of God befriend us
    and watch around us to protect us.
May the Lord Jesus give us his blessing of peace. Amen.

Let us bless the Lord. (Alleluia, alleluia.)
Thanks be to God. (Alleluia, alleluia.)

Form 1 – Midday Prayer

Sundays through the Year

Seasonal Propers are found beginning page 539.

THE PREPARATION

O God, make speed to save us.
O Lord, make haste to help us.

Glory . . .   **Alleluia.** *(Omitted in Lent)*

A HYMN may be sung, the following or some other.

To God our Father, thanks and praise
For this, the first and dawn of days:
The day when through your word of might
From chaos was created light.

The day on which your well-loved Son
O'er death and hell the triumph won;
The day on which the Spirit came,
Your gift to us, in wind and flame.

Ordinary Time Doxology
To you, our Father, through your Son,
And in the Spirit, Three in One:
We, new-created on this day,
New songs of love and glory pay. Amen.

tr. Order of Preachers, Oxford *

THE WORD OF GOD

THE PSALMODY

Either A: PSALM 119.1-32

1 Aleph

1   Blessèd are those whose way is pure, *
     who walk in the law of the Lord.

2   Blessèd are those who keep his testimonies *
     and seek him with their whole heart,

3   Those who do no wickedness, *
     but walk in his ways.

4   You, O Lord, have charged *
     that we should diligently keep your commandments.

5   O that my ways were made so direct *
     that I might keep your statutes.

6   Then should I not be put to shame, *
     because I have regard for all your commandments.

7   I will thank you with an unfeigned heart, *
     when I have learned your righteous judgements.

8   I will keep your statutes; *
     O forsake me not utterly.

2 Beth

9   How shall young people cleanse their way *
     to keep themselves according to your word?

10   With my whole heart have I sought you; *
     O let me not go astray from your commandments.

11   Your words have I hidden within my heart, *
     that I should not sin against you.

12   Blessèd are you, O Lord; *
     O teach me your statutes.

13   With my lips have I been telling *
     of all the judgements of your mouth.

14   I have taken greater delight in the way of your testimonies *
     than in all manner of riches.

15   I will meditate on your commandments *
     and contemplate your ways.

16   My delight shall be in your statutes *
     and I will not forget your word.

3   Gimel

17   O do good to your servant that I may live, *
     and so shall I keep your word.

18 Open my eyes, that I may see *
    the wonders of your law.

19 I am a stranger upon earth; *
    hide not your commandments from me.

20 My soul is consumed at all times *
    with fervent longing for your judgements.

21 You have rebuked the arrogant; *
    cursed are those who stray from your commandments.

22 Turn from me shame and rebuke, *
    for I have kept your testimonies.

23 Rulers also sit and speak against me, *
    but your servant meditates on your statutes.

24 For your testimonies are my delight; *
    they are my faithful counsellors.

4 Daleth

25 My soul cleaves to the dust; *
    O give me life according to your word.

26 I have acknowledged my ways and you have answered me; *
    O teach me your statutes.

27 Make me understand the way of your commandments, *
    and so shall I meditate on your wondrous works.

28 My soul melts away in tears of sorrow; *
    raise me up according to your word.

29 Take from me the way of falsehood; *
    be gracious to me through your law.

30 I have chosen the way of truth *
    and your judgements have I laid before me.

31 I hold fast to your testimonies; *
    O Lord, let me not be put to shame.

32 I will run the way of your commandments, *
    when you have set my heart at liberty.

PSALM 121

1   I lift up my eyes to the hills; *
    from where is my help to come?

2   My help comes from the Lord, *
    the maker of heaven and earth.

3   He will not suffer your foot to stumble; *
    he who watches over you will not sleep.

4   Behold, he who keeps watch over Israel *
    shall neither slumber nor sleep.

5   The Lord himself watches over you; *
    the Lord is your shade at your right hand,

6   So that the sun shall not strike you by day, *
    neither the moon by night.

7   The Lord shall keep you from all evil; *
    it is he who shall keep your soul.

8   The Lord shall keep watch over your going out
        and your coming in, *
    from this time forth for evermore.

PSALM 122

1   I was glad when they said to me, *
    'Let us go to the house of the Lord.'

2   And now our feet are standing *
    within your gates, O Jerusalem;

3   Jerusalem, built as a city *
    that is at unity in itself.

4   Thither the tribes go up, the tribes of the Lord, *
    as is decreed for Israel,
        to give thanks to the name of the Lord.

5   For there are set the thrones of judgement, *
    the thrones of the house of David.

6   O pray for the peace of Jerusalem: *
    'May they prosper who love you.

7   'Peace be within your walls *
    and tranquillity within your palaces.'

8   For my kindred and companions' sake, *
    I will pray that peace be with you.

9   For the sake of the house of the Lord our God, *
    I will seek to do you good.

Each psalm, or group of psalms, may end with:

   Glory . . .

THE READING

In Ordinary Time, week 1 begins on the first Sunday of the month and so on.

Either:

Week 1: Genesis 1.1-5
    2: 2 Corinthians 5.17-19a
    3: John 5.15-18
    4: Revelation 21.1-4
    5: Proverbs 8.30-31

or one of the following readings:

Jesus said, I am the living bread that came down from heaven. Whoever
eats of this bread will live for ever.   *John 6.51a*

Blessèd are the poor in spirit, for theirs is the kingdom of heaven.

                                                        Matthew 5.3

or some other suitable reading.

THE RESPONSE.

In Ordinary Time:

*Either **A**:*

The wolf shall live with the lamb,
the leopard lie down with the kid;

The calf and the lion together,
and a little child shall lead them.

They will not hurt or destroy
on all my holy mountain.

For the earth will be full of the knowledge of God
as the waters cover the sea.

or B:

Blessèd are you, O God: Father, Son and Holy Spirit;
we give you praise and honour for ever.

For you have loved us from all eternity,
and remembered us when we were in trouble.

Blessèd are you, Lord Jesus Christ,
who, for our salvation, came down from heaven.

By the power of the Holy Spirit,
you became incarnate of the Virgin Mary.

You loosed us from our sins by your own blood:
and on the third day rose from the dead.

You ascended up on high,
and opened wide for us the everlasting doors.

You are seated at the right hand of the Father
and ever live to intercede for us.

Blessèd are you, O God: Source of all being,
eternal Word and Spirit of life;
we give you praise and honour for ever.

THE PRAYERS

INTERCESSIONS may be offered.

THE KYRIES may be used as responses to intercession.

Lord, have mercy.
Lord, have mercy.

Christ, have mercy.
Christ, have mercy.

Lord, have mercy.
Lord, have mercy.

THE COLLECT of the day or one of the following:

Maker of all,
you have created the heavens and the earth
and made us in your own image:
may we discern your hand in all your works
and serve you with reverence and thanksgiving;
through Jesus Christ our Lord,
who with you and the Holy Spirit
reigns supreme over all things
now and for ever. **Amen.**

David Silk

Almighty, eternal, just and merciful God,
give to us poor creatures the grace to do for you alone
    that which we know to be your will,
and always desire that which pleases you,
so that, inwardly purified, enlightened
and inflamed by the fire of your Holy Spirit,
we may be enabled to follow in the footprints
    of your belovèd Son, our Lord Jesus Christ,
and, by your grace alone, make our way to you,
    the Most High;
who in perfect Trinity and simple Unity,
live and reign, God all-powerful,
for ever and ever. **Amen.**

A Letter to the Entire Order, Francis of Assisi

THE LORD'S PRAYER may be said.

[Lord Jesus remember us in your kingdom
and teach us to pray.]
Our Father in heaven, . . .

THE CONCLUSION

Let us bless the Lord God living and true!
Let us always give him
praise, glory, honour, blessing and every good.
Amen. Amen. (Alleluia, alleluia.)

Prayer said by Francis of Assisi at the end of the office

Form 1 – Evening Prayer

Sundays in Ordinary Time and daily in Easter Season

THE BLESSING OF THE LIGHT *may replace THE PREPARATION.*

A light, which may be the Paschal Candle, is brought in, or a candle may simply be lit. From Easter to Pentecost, the Paschal Candle may be burning in its customary place.
For Ascension Day, see page 586.

You, O Lord, are my lamp; you turn our darkness into light.

The light and peace of Jesus Christ be with you
and also with you.

Blessèd are you, Sovereign Lord,
the God and Father of our Lord Jesus Christ;
to you be glory and praise for ever.
From the deep waters of death
you brought your people to new birth
by raising your Son to life in triumph.
Through him dark death has been destroyed
and radiant life is everywhere restored.
As you call us out of darkness into his marvellous light
may our lives reflect his glory
and our lips repeat the endless song,
Father, Son and Holy Spirit:
Blessèd be God for ever.

While the other candles are lit the following, or another version of number 63, page 524, or another suitable hymn may be sung A SONG OF THE LIGHT (63c)

1   **Hail, gladdening Light, of his pure glory poured,**
     Who is the immortal Father, heavenly, blest,
     Holiest of holies, Jesus Christ our Lord.

2   **Now we are come to the sun's hour of rest,**
     The lights of evening round us shine,
     We hymn the Father, Son and Holy Spirit divine.

3   **Worthy are you at all times to be sung**
    With undefilèd tongue,
    Son of our God, giver of life, alone:
    Therefore in all the world your glories,
        Lord, they own.

Verses from PSALM 141 may be said and incense may be burned.

Let my prayer rise before you as incense,
the lifting up of my hands as the evening sacrifice.

O Lord, I call to you; come to me quickly;
hear my voice when I cry to you.
Set a watch before my mouth, O Lord,
and guard the door of my lips.

Let my prayer rise before you as incense,
the lifting up of my hands as the evening sacrifice.

Let not my heart incline to any evil thing;
let me not be occupied in wickedness with evildoers.
But my eyes are turned to you, Lord God,
in you I take refuge;
do not leave me defenceless.

Let my prayer rise before you as incense,
the lifting up of my hands as the evening sacrifice.

Psalm 141.1-4b,8

This prayer may be said:

That this evening may be holy, good and peaceful,
let us pray with one heart and mind.
(Silence may be kept.)

As our evening prayer rises before you, O God,
so may your mercy come down upon us
    to cleanse our hearts
and set us free to sing your praise,
now and forever. Amen.

Evening Prayer continues with the appointed Psalmody.

THE PREPARATION

O God, make speed to save us.
O Lord, make haste to help us.

Lead your people to freedom, O God,
and banish all darkness from our hearts and minds.

Glory . . .   Alleluia.

THE OPENING CANTICLE

A SONG OF DAVID (4)

1   Blessèd are you, God of Israel, for ever and ever, *
     for yours is the greatness, the power,
          the glory, the splendour and the majesty.

2   Everything in heaven and on earth is yours; *
     yours is the kingdom, O Lord,
          and you are exalted as head over all.

3   Riches and honour come from you *
     and you rule over all.

4   In your hand are power and might; *
     yours it is to give power and strength to all.

5   And now we give you thanks, our God, *
     and praise your glorious name.

6   For all things come from you, *
     and of your own have we given you.

     Glory . . .   *1 Chronicles 29.10b-13,14b*

A HYMN may be sung.

THE OPENING PRAYER may be said.

That this evening may be holy, good and peaceful,
let us pray with one heart and mind.
(Silence may be kept.)

**May we, Lord,
who walk in the light of your presence
acclaim your Christ, rising victorious,
as he banishes all darkness
from our hearts and minds,
now and for ever. Amen.**

THE WORD OF GOD

THE PSALMODY, as appointed

Each psalm, or group of psalms, may end with:
Glory . . .

*If there are two SCRIPTURE READINGS, the first may be read here, or both may
be read after the Second Canticle.*

THE SECOND CANTICLE

In Ordinary Time:

Either A SONG OF THE HEAVENLY CITY (60) or number 48, page 512

Refrain: **By the river stood the tree of life,
with healing for all the nations.**

1   I saw no temple in the city, *
    for its temple is the Lord God the Almighty
       and the Lamb.

2   And the city has no need of sun or moon
       to shine upon it, *
    for the glory of God is its light,
       and its lamp is the Lamb.

3   By its light the nations shall walk, *
    and the rulers of the earth
       shall bring their glory into it.

4   Its gates shall never be shut by day,
       nor shall there be any night; *
    they shall bring into it
       the glory and honour of the nations.

5   I saw the river of the water of life,
        bright as crystal, *
    flowing from the throne of God and of the Lamb.

6   And either side of the river stood the tree of life,
        yielding its fruit each month, *
    and the leaves of the tree
        were for the healing of the nations.

7   The throne of God and of the Lamb shall be there,
        and his servants shall worship him; *
    and they shall see his face
        and his name shall be on their foreheads.

To the One who sits on the throne and to the Lamb *
be blessing and honour and glory and might,
for ever and ever. Amen.

Revelation 21.22-26; 22.1,2b,d,3b,4

By the river stood the tree of life,
with healing for all the nations.

In Easter:

Either A SONG OF FAITH (51) or numbers 46, page 511, or 68, page 530

Refrain: **God raised Christ from the dead,**
                the Lamb without spot or stain.

I   Blessèd be the God and Father *
    of our Lord Jesus Christ!

2   By his great mercy we have been born anew to a living hope *
    through the resurrection of Jesus Christ from the dead,

3   Into an inheritance that is imperishable, undefiled and unfading, *
    kept in heaven for you,

4   Who are being protected by the power of God through faith, *
    for a salvation ready to be revealed in the last time.

5   You were ransomed from the futile ways of your ancestors *
    not with perishable things like silver or gold

6   But with the precious blood of Christ *
    like that of a lamb without spot or stain.

7   Through him you have confidence in God,
      who raised him from the dead and gave him glory, *
    so that your faith and hope are set on God.

    Glory ...

1 Peter 1.3-5,18,19,21

God raised Christ from the dead,
the Lamb without spot or stain.

THE SCRIPTURE READING(S)

A RESPONSORY may be said.

The Lord is my light and my salvation;
the Lord is the strength of my life.
The Lord is my light and my salvation;
the Lord is the strength of my life.

The light shines in the darkness
and the darkness has not overcome it.
The Lord is the strength of my life.

Glory to the Father and to the Son
and to the Holy Spirit.
The Lord is my light and my salvation;
the Lord is the strength of my life.   *from Psalm 27 and John 1*

THE GOSPEL CANTICLE: MAGNIFICAT – THE SONG OF MARY (40)

See either inside front cover, inside back cover or page 504 for another version.

In Ordinary Time:

Refrain: **You have done great things, O God,**
          and holy is your name.

or, in Easter:

     Alleluia. Mary of Magdala said to the disciples,
     I have seen the Lord!
     The Lord is risen indeed! Alleluia.

The refrain is repeated after the canticle.

THE PRAYERS

INTERCESSIONS may be offered.

THE KYRIES may be used as responses to intercession.

Lord, have mercy.
Lord, have mercy.

Christ, have mercy.
Christ, have mercy.

Lord, have mercy.
Lord, have mercy.

THE COLLECT of the day or one of the following:

Grant to us, Lord, we pray,
the spirit to think and do always
such things as be rightful;
that we, who cannot do anything that is good without you
may by you be enabled to live
   according to your will;
through Jesus Christ our Lord. **Amen.**

or, in Easter:

God of life,
who for our redemption gave your only-begotten Son
   to the death of the cross,
and by his glorious resurrection
have delivered us from the power of our enemy:
grant us so to die daily to sin,
that we may evermore live with him in the joy of his risen life;
through Jesus Christ our Lord. **Amen.**

THE LORD'S PRAYER may be said.

[Rejoicing in God's new creation,]
as our Saviour taught us, so we pray
Our Father in heaven, . . .

THE CONCLUSION

In Ordinary Time:

**The grace of our Lord Jesus Christ,
and the love of God,
and the fellowship of the Holy Spirit,
be with us all evermore. Amen.**

Let us bless the Lord.
Thanks be to God.

or, in Easter:

May the risen Christ grant us the joys of eternal life. Amen.

Let us bless the Lord. Alleluia, alleluia.
Thanks be to God. Alleluia, alleluia.

or, on Class I & II Holy Days:

May our blessèd Lady pray for us.
May Saint Francis and Saint Clare pray for us.
[May Saint N pray for us.]
May all the saints of God pray for us.
May the angels of God befriend us
    and watch around us to protect us.
May the Lord Jesus give us his blessing of peace. Amen.

Let us bless the Lord. (Alleluia, alleluia.)
Thanks be to God. (Alleluia, alleluia.)

Form 1 – Night Prayer

Sundays in Ordinary Time and daily in Easter Season

THE PREPARATION

The Lord almighty grant us a quiet night and a perfect end.
Amen.

Our help is in the name of the Lord
who made heaven and earth.

A period of silence for reflection on the past day may follow.
The following or other suitable words of penitence may be used.

Holy God,
we confess to you before the company
**   of the faithful in heaven and on earth,**
that we have sinned against you,
against one another
and against your creation.
Forgive us in your mercy,
help us to forgive each other
and to hold in reverence
**   all that you have made. Amen.**

OSB West Malling

or:

Holy God,
holy and strong,
holy and immortal:
have mercy on us.

O God, make speed to save us.
O Lord, make haste to help us.

Glory . . .   Alleluia.

The following or another suitable HYMN may be sung.

Before the ending of the day,
Creator of the world, we pray
That you, with steadfast love, would keep
Your watch around us while we sleep.

From evil dreams defend our sight,
From fears and terrors of the night;
Tread under foot our deadly foe
That we no sinful thought may know.

Ordinary Time Doxology
O Father, that we ask be done
Through Jesus Christ, your only Son;
And Holy Spirit, by whose breath
Our souls are raised to life from death. Amen.

Easter Doxology
All praise be yours, O risen Lord,
From death to endless life restored;
Whom, with the Father, we adore
And Holy Spirit evermore. Amen.

THE WORD OF GOD

THE PSALMODY

Psalm 104.1,21-33

1   Bless the Lord, O my soul. *
    O Lord my God, how excellent is your greatness!

2   You appointed the moon to mark the seasons, *
    and the sun knows the time for its setting.

3   You make darkness that it may be night, *
    in which all the beasts of the forest creep forth.

4   The lions roar for their prey *
    and seek their food from God.

5   The sun rises and they are gone *
    to lay themselves down in their dens.

6   People go forth to their work *
    and to their labour until the evening.

7   O Lord, how manifold are your works! *
    In wisdom you have made them all;
        the earth is full of your creatures.

8   There is the sea, spread far and wide, *
    and there move creatures beyond number, both small and great.

9   There go the ships, and there is that Leviathan *
    which you have made to play in the deep.

10 All of these look to you *
    to give them their food in due season.

11 When you give it them, they gather it; *
    you open your hand and they are filled with good.

12 When you hide your face they are troubled; *
    when you take away their breath,
        they die and return again to the dust.

13 When you send forth your spirit, they are created, *
    and you renew the face of the earth.

14 May the glory of the Lord endure for ever; *
    may the Lord rejoice in his works.

    Glory . . .

THE READING: one of the following or some other.

Either, in Ordinary Time:

You, O Lord, are in the midst of us and we are called by your name; leave us not, O Lord our God.

Jeremiah. 14.9

or, in Easter:

The servants of the Lamb shall see the face of God, whose name will be on their foreheads. There will be no more night: they will not need the light of a lamp or the light of the sun, for God will be their light; and they will reign for ever and ever.

Revelation 22.4,5

THE RESPONSORY may be said.

Either in Ordinary Time:

Into your hands, O Lord, I commend my spirit.
Into your hands, O Lord, I commend my spirit.

For you have redeemed me, Lord God of truth.
I commend my spirit.

Glory to the Father and to the Son
and to the Holy Spirit.
Into your hands, O Lord, I commend my spirit.

Keep me as the apple of your eye.
Hide me under the shadow of your wings.

or, in Easter:

Into your hands, O Lord, I commend my spirit.
Alleluia, alleluia.
Into your hands, O Lord, I commend my spirit.
Alleluia, alleluia.

For you have redeemed me, Lord God of truth.
Alleluia, alleluia.

Glory to the Father and to the Son
and to the Holy Spirit.
Into your hands, O Lord, I commend my spirit.
Alleluia, alleluia.

Keep me as the apple of your eye.
Hide me under the shadow of your wings.

THE GOSPEL CANTICLE: NUNC DIMITTIS — THE SONG OF SIMEON (42) or
another version on page 508

Refrain: **Save us, O Lord, while waking,**
and guard us while sleeping,
that awake we may watch with Christ,
and asleep may rest in peace.

or, in Easter:

Alleluia. The Lord is risen, alleluia,
as he promised to you. Alleluia, alleluia.

or, on Class I & II Holy Days:

> **Grant us your light, O Lord,**
> **that the darkness of our hearts being overcome,**
> **we may receive the true light,**
> **even Christ our Saviour. (Alleluia.)**

1 ✠ Now, Lord, you let your servant go in peace: *
   your word has been fulfilled.

2 My own eyes have seen the salvation *
   which you have prepared in the sight of every people:

3 A light to reveal you to the nations *
   and the glory of your people Israel.

Luke 2.29-32

Glory . . .

The refrain is repeated after the canticle.

THE PRAYERS

Intercessions and thanksgivings may be offered here.

THE COLLECT: one of the following or some other.

Either, in Ordinary Time:

Lighten our darkness,
Lord, we pray;
and in your mercy defend us
from all perils and dangers of this night;
for the love of your only Son,
our Saviour Jesus Christ. **Amen.**

or, in Easter:

Almighty God,
by triumphing over the powers of darkness
Christ has prepared a place for us
   in the new Jerusalem:
may we, who have this day given thanks
   for his resurrection,
praise him in the eternal city
of which he is the light;
through Jesus Christ our Lord. **Amen.**

David Silk

THE LORD'S PRAYER may be said.

[As we come to the ending of the day,]
as our Saviour taught us, so we pray
Our Father in heaven, . . .

THE CONCLUSION

In peace, we will lie down and sleep;
for you alone, Lord, make us dwell in safety.

Abide with us, Lord Jesus,
for the night is at hand and the day is now past.

As the night-watch looks for the morning,
so do we look for you, O Christ.

[Come with the dawning of the day
and make yourself known
in the breaking of the bread.]

May the risen Lord Jesus bless us.
May he watch over us and renew us
   as he renews the whole of creation.
May our hearts and lives echo his love. Amen.

A MARIAN ANTHEM may be sung.

SALVE REGINA

Traditionally, this anthem is sung at the end of Night Prayer from after Pentecost to Advent; or it may be the unchanging final anthem. The other Marian anthems may be found on page 775.

Salve, Regina, mater misericordiae;
vita, dulcedo, et spes nostra, salve.
Ad te clamamus, exsules, filii Evae,
ad te suspiramus,
gementes et flentes in hac lacrimarum valle;
eia ergo, advocata nostra,
illos tuos misericordes oculos ad nos converte,
Et Iesum, benedictum fructum ventris tui,
nobis post hoc exsilium ostende.
O clemens, O pia, O dulcis Virgo Maria.

Form 2 – Morning Prayer

Mondays in Ordinary Time
and daily from the day after Ascension
until the Day of Pentecost

THE PREPARATION

A *is used on Mondays in Ordinary Time.*
B *is used daily from the day after Ascension until Pentecost and on specified Class I & II Holy Days.*

A:

O Lord, open our lips
and our mouth shall proclaim your praise.

Pour your love into our hearts, O God,
through the Holy Spirit you have given to us.

Glory . . .   Alleluia.

THE OPENING CANTICLE

A SONG OF GOD'S COMPASSION

1   The Lord is full of compassion and mercy, *
    slow to anger and of great kindness.

2   He will not always accuse us, *
    neither will he keep his anger for ever.

3   He has not dealt with us according to our sins, *
    nor rewarded us according to our wickedness.

4   For as the heavens are high above the earth, *
    so great is his mercy upon those who fear him.

5   As far as the east is from the west, *
    so far has he set our sins from us.

6   As a father has compassion on his children, *
    so is the Lord merciful towards those who fear him.

7   For he knows of what we are made; *
    he remembers that we are but dust.

8   Our days are but as grass; *
    we flourish as a flower of the field;

9   For as soon as the wind goes over it, it is gone, *
    and its place shall know it no more.

10 But the merciful goodness of the Lord is from of old
        and endures for ever on those who fear him, *
    and his righteousness on children's children;

11 On those who keep his covenant *
    and remember his commandments to do them.

    Glory . . .   *Psalm 103.8-18*

Morning Prayer continues with the HYMN and/or THE OPENING PRAYER.

B:

O Lord, open our lips
and our mouth shall proclaim your praise.

Blessèd are you, creator God;
to you be glory and praise for ever.
As your Spirit moved over the face of the waters
bringing light and life to your creation,
pour out your Spirit on us today,
that we may walk as children of light
and by your grace reveal your presence,
Father, Son and Holy Spirit:
Blessèd be God for ever.

The following is said:

From the day after Ascension until Pentecost:

Alleluia. The Spirit of God fills the whole world:
O come, let us worship. Alleluia.

or, on feasts of Missionaries and of Evangelists:

(Alleluia.) Christ has proclaimed his gospel in all lands:
O come, let us worship. (Alleluia.)

THE OPENING CANTICLE

A SONG OF GOD'S RIGHTEOUSNESS

1   Bless the Lord, O my soul, *
    and all that is within me bless his holy name.

2   Bless the Lord, O my soul, *
    and forget not all his benefits;

3   Who forgives all your sins *
    and heals all your infirmities;

4   Who redeems your life from the Pit *
    and crowns you with faithful love and compassion;

5   Who satisfies you with good things, *
    so that your youth is renewed like an eagle's.

6   The Lord executes righteousness *
    and judgement for all who are oppressed.

7   He made his ways known to Moses *
    and his works to the children of Israel.

8   The Lord has established his throne in heaven, *
    and his kingdom has dominion over all.

9   Bless the Lord, you angels of his, *
    you mighty ones who do his bidding
       and hearken to the voice of his word.

10 Bless the Lord, all you his hosts, *
    you ministers of his who do his will.

11 Bless the Lord, all you works of his,
       in all places of his dominion; *
    bless the Lord, O my soul.

   Glory . . .   *Psalm 103.1-7,19-22*

A HYMN may be sung.

THE OPENING PRAYER may be said.

The night has passed and the day lies open before us;
let us pray with one heart and mind.
(Silence may be kept.)

As we rejoice in the gift of this new day,
so may the light of your presence, O God,
set our hearts on fire with love for you;
now and for ever. Amen.

THE WORD OF GOD

THE PSALMODY, as appointed

Each psalm, or group of psalms, may end with:
Glory . . .

*If there are two SCRIPTURE READINGS, the first may be read here, or both may
be read after the Second Canticle.*

THE SECOND CANTICLE

In Ordinary Time:

Either A SONG OF DELIVERANCE (9) or number 29, page 493

Refrain: **All the earth, shout and sing for joy,**
for great in your midst is the Holy One.

1   'Behold, God is my salvation; *
    I will trust and will not be afraid;

2   'For the Lord God is my strength and my song, *
    and has become my salvation.'

3   With joy you will draw water *
    from the wells of salvation.

4   On that day you will say, *
    'Give thanks to the Lord, call upon his name;

5   'Make known his deeds among the nations, *
    proclaim that his name is exalted.

6   'Sing God's praises, who has triumphed gloriously; *
    let this be known in all the world.

7   'Shout and sing for joy, you that dwell in Zion, *
    for great in your midst is the Holy One of Israel.'

Glory . . .   *Isaiah 12.2-6*

**All the earth, shout and sing for joy,
for great in your midst is the Holy One.**

From the day after Ascension until Pentecost:

Either A SONG OF EZEKIEL (22) or numbers 27, page 491, or 30, page 494

Refrain: **I will put a new spirit within you,
and you shall be my people.**

1   I will take you from the nations, *
    and gather you from all the countries.

2   I will sprinkle clean water upon you, *
    and you shall be clean from all
        your uncleannesses.

3   A new heart I will give you, *
    and put a new spirit within you,

4   And I will remove from your body the heart of stone *
    and give you a heart of flesh.

5   You shall be my people, *
    and I will be your God.

Glory . . .   *Ezekiel 36.24-26,28b*

**I will put a new spirit within you,
and you shall be my people**

On feasts of Missionaries, numbers 9 or 22, above, are alternative canticles.

*On feasts of Evangelists, numbers 9 above or 17, page 483, are alternative
canticles*

THE SCRIPTURE READING(S)

A RESPONSORY may be said.

Come, Holy Spirit, fill the hearts of your people,
and kindle in us the fire of your love.

All who are led by the Spirit of God
are children of God and fellow-heirs with Christ.
Come, Holy Spirit, fill the hearts of your people.

Renew the face of your creation, Lord,
pouring on us the gifts of your Spirit,
and kindle in us the fire of your love.

For the creation waits with eager longing
for the glorious liberty of the children of God.
**Come, Holy Spirit, fill the hearts of your people
and kindle in us the fire of your love.**

cf Romans 8

THE GOSPEL CANTICLE: BENEDICTUS – THE SONG OF ZECHARIAH (41)

See either inside front cover, inside back cover or page 506 for another version.

In Ordinary Time:

Refrain: **You have set us free to worship you without fear,
holy and righteous in your sight.**

or, from the day after Ascension until Pentecost:

> **Christ has gone up on high
> and has led captivity captive. Alleluia.**

or, on feasts of Missionaries:

> **Christ gave them as a light to the nations,
> that his salvation might reach to the ends
> of the earth. (Alleluia.)**

or, on feasts of Evangelists:

> **We bring you the good news that what God promised
> to our ancestors he has fulfilled for us their children
> by raising Jesus. (Alleluia.)**

The refrain is repeated after the canticle.

THE PRAYERS

INTERCESSIONS may be offered.

THE KYRIES may be used as responses to intercession.

Lord, have mercy.
Lord, have mercy.

Christ, have mercy.
Christ, have mercy.

Lord, have mercy.
Lord, have mercy.

THE COLLECT of the day or one of the following:

Lord our God,
as with all creation
we offer you the life of this new day,
give us grace to love and serve you
to the praise of Jesus Christ our Lord. **Amen.**

or, from the day after Ascension until Pentecost:

Almighty God,
who sent your Holy Spirit
to be the life and light of your Church:
open our hearts to the riches of your grace,
that we may bring forth the fruit of the Spirit
in love and joy and peace;
through Jesus Christ our Lord. **Amen.**

THE LORD'S PRAYER may be said.

[Being made one by the power of the Spirit,]
as our Saviour taught us, so we pray
Our Father in heaven, . . .

THE CONCLUSION

In Ordinary Time:

**The Lord bless us, and preserve us from all evil,
and keep us in eternal life. Amen.**

Let us bless the Lord.
Thanks be to God.

or, from the day after Ascension until Pentecost:

May the Spirit kindle in us the fire of God's love. Amen.

Let us bless the Lord. Alleluia, alleluia.
Thanks be to God. Alleluia, alleluia.

or, on Class I & II Holy Days:

May our blessèd Lady pray for us.
May Saint Francis and Saint Clare pray for us.
[May Saint N pray for us.]
May all the saints of God pray for us.
May the angels of God befriend us
    and watch around us to protect us.
May the Lord Jesus give us his blessing of peace. Amen.

Let us bless the Lord. (Alleluia, alleluia.)
Thanks be to God. (Alleluia, alleluia.)

Form 2 – Midday Prayer

Mondays through the Year

Seasonal Propers are found beginning page 539.

THE PREPARATION

O God, make speed to save us.
O Lord, make haste to help us.

Glory . . .   Alleluia. *(Omitted in Lent)*

A HYMN may be sung, the following or some other.

Come, Holy Spirit, ever One
With God the Father and the Son:
Come swiftly, Fount of grace, and pour
Into our hearts your boundless store.

With all our strength, with heart and tongue,
By word and deed your praise be sung:
And love light up our mortal frame
Till others catch the living flame.

Ordinary Time Doxology
O Father, that we ask be done
Through Jesus Christ, your only Son,
Who, with the Spirit, reigns above;
Three Persons in one God of love. Amen.

tr. J.H. Newman *

THE WORD OF GOD

THE PSALMODY

*Either **A**: PSALM 119.33-56*

5 He

33   Teach me, O Lord, the way of your statutes *
     and I shall keep it to the end.

34   Give me understanding and I shall keep your law; *
     I shall keep it with my whole heart.

35 Lead me in the path of your commandments, *
for therein is my delight.

36 Incline my heart to your testimonies *
and not to unjust gain.

37 Turn away my eyes lest they gaze on vanities; *
O give me life in your ways.

38 Confirm to your servant your promise, *
which stands for all who fear you.

39 Turn away the reproach which I dread, *
because your judgements are good.

40 Behold, I long for your commandments; *
in your righteousness give me life.

6 Waw

41 Let your faithful love come unto me, O Lord, *
even your salvation, according to your promise.

42 Then shall I answer those who taunt me, *
for my trust is in your word.

43 O take not the word of truth utterly out of my mouth, *
for my hope is in your judgements.

44 So shall I always keep your law; *
I shall keep it for ever and ever.

45 I will walk at liberty, *
because I study your commandments.

46 I will tell of your testimonies, even before kings, *
and will not be ashamed.

47 My delight shall be in your commandments, *
which I have greatly loved.

48 My hands will I lift up to your commandments, which I love, *
and I will meditate on your statutes.

7 Zayin

49 Remember your word to your servant, *
on which you have built my hope.

50   This is my comfort in my trouble, *
      that your promise gives me life.

51   The proud have derided me cruelly, *
      but I have not turned aside from your law.

52   I have remembered your everlasting judgements, O Lord, *
      and have been comforted.

53   I am seized with indignation at the wicked, *
      for they have forsaken your law.

54   Your statutes have been like songs to me *
      in the house of my pilgrimage.

55   I have thought on your name in the night, O Lord, *
      and so have I kept your law.

56   These blessings have been mine, *
      for I have kept your commandments.

*or **B:**   Psalms of Ascent*

PSALM 123

1   To you I lift up my eyes, *
      to you that are enthroned in the heavens.

2   As the eyes of servants look to the hand of their master, *
      or the eyes of a maid to the hand of her mistress,

3   So our eyes wait upon the Lord our God, *
      until he have mercy upon us.

4   Have mercy upon us, O Lord, have mercy upon us, *
      for we have had more than enough of contempt.

5   Our soul has had more than enough of the scorn of the arrogant, *
      and of the contempt of the proud.

PSALM 124

1   If the Lord himself had not been on our side, *
      now may Israel say;

2   If the Lord had not been on our side, *
      when enemies rose up against us;

3 Then would they have swallowed us alive *
   when their anger burned against us;

4 Then would the waters have overwhelmed us
     and the torrent gone over our soul; *
   over our soul would have swept the raging waters.

5 But blessèd be the Lord *
   who has not given us over to be a prey for their teeth.

6 Our soul has escaped
     as a bird from the snare of the fowler; *
   the snare is broken and we are delivered.

7 Our help is in the name of the Lord, *
   who has made heaven and earth.

Each psalm, or group of psalms, may end with:

   Glory . . .

THE READING

In Ordinary Time, week 1 begins on the first Sunday of the month and so on.

Either:

Week 1: Isaiah 49.1b-4
     2: Proverbs 3.7-12
     3: Mark 4.26-29
     4. Matthew 25.19-21
     5: Matthew 11.28

or one of the following readings:

Jesus said, I am the true vine. My Father is glorified by this, that you bear
much fruit and become my disciples.

John 15.1a,8

Blessèd are the meek, for they will inherit the earth.

Matthew 5.5

or some other suitable reading.

In Ordinary Time:

*Either **A:***

He shall be called the Prince of Peace,
and his throne shall be established for ever.

His kingdom is an everlasting kingdom,
and all nations shall serve and obey him.

He shall be great to the ends of the earth,
and he shall be their peace.

The Lord has given him the dominion and glory and a kingdom:
that all peoples, nations and languages shall serve him.

*or **B**:*

You are not in the flesh but in the Spirit
since the Spirit of God dwells in you.

If Christ lives in you, though the body is dead because of sin,
the Spirit is alive because of righteousness.

If the Spirit of God who raised up Jesus from the dead lives in you,
God will give life to your mortal bodies also,
through the Spirit which lives in you.

For you are not in the flesh,
but in the Spirit.

THE PRAYERS

INTERCESSIONS may be offered.

THE KYRIES may be used as responses to intercession.

Lord, have mercy.
Lord, have mercy.

Christ, have mercy.
Christ, have mercy.

Lord, have mercy.
Lord, have mercy.

Eternal light, shine into our hearts,
eternal goodness, deliver us from evil,
eternal power, be our support,
eternal wisdom, scatter the darkness of our ignorance,
eternal pity, have mercy upon us;
that with all our heart and mind and soul and strength
we may seek your face and be brought by your infinite mercy
    to your holy presence;
through Jesus Christ our Lord. **Amen.**

Alcuin of York (804)

Lord, make us to walk in your Way:
'Where there is love and wisdom,
there is neither fear nor ignorance;
where there is patience and humility,
there is neither anger nor disturbance;
where there is poverty with joy,
there is neither greed nor avarice;
where there is peace and contemplation,
there is neither anxiety nor restlessness;
where there is the fear of God to guard the dwelling,
there no enemy can enter;
where there is mercy and discernment,
there is neither excess nor hardness of heart';
this we know through your Son,
Jesus Christ our Lord. **Amen.**

The Admonitions XXVII, Francis of Assisi

THE LORD'S PRAYER may be said.

[Lord Jesus remember us in your kingdom
and teach us to pray.]
Our Father in heaven, . . .

THE CONCLUSION

Let us bless the Lord God living and true!
Let us always give him
praise, glory, honour, blessing and every good.
Amen. Amen. (Alleluia, alleluia.)

Prayer said by Francis of Assisi at the end of the office

Form 2 – Evening Prayer

Mondays in Ordinary Time
and daily from the day after Ascension
until the Day of Pentecost

THE BLESSING OF THE LIGHT *may replace THE PREPARATION.*

A light, which may be the Paschal Candle, is brought in, or a candle may simply be lit. From Easter to Pentecost, the Paschal Candle may be burning in its customary place.

With you, O God, is the well of life
and in your light shall we see light.

The light and peace of Jesus Christ be with you
and also with you.

Blessèd are you, Sovereign God, our light and our life;
to you be glory and praise for ever!
When we turned away to darkness and chaos,
like a mother you would not forsake us.
You cried out like a woman in labour
and rejoiced to bring forth a new people.
Your living Word brings light out of darkness
and daily your Spirit renews the face of the earth,
bending our wills to the gentle rule of your love,
Father, Son and Holy Spirit:
Blessèd be God for ever.

While the other candles are lit the following, or another version of number 63, page 524, or another suitable hymn may be sung.

A SONG OF THE LIGHT (63c)

1   **Hail, gladdening Light, of his pure glory poured,
    Who is the immortal Father, heavenly, blest,
    Holiest of holies, Jesus Christ our Lord.**

2   **Now we are come to the sun's hour of rest,
    The lights of evening round us shine,
    We hymn the Father, Son and Holy Spirit divine.**

3   **Worthy are you at all times to be sung**
    With undefilèd tongue,
    Son of our God, giver of life, alone:
    Therefore in all the world your glories,
        Lord, they own.

Verses from PSALM 141 may be said and incense may be burned.

Let my prayer rise before you as incense,
the lifting up of my hands as the evening sacrifice.

O Lord, I call to you; come to me quickly;
hear my voice when I cry to you.
Set a watch before my mouth, O Lord,
and guard the door of my lips.

Let my prayer rise before you as incense,
the lifting up of my hands as the evening sacrifice.

Let not my heart incline to any evil thing;
let me not be occupied in wickedness with evildoers.
But my eyes are turned to you, Lord God,
in you I take refuge;
do not leave me defenceless.

Let my prayer rise before you as incense,
the lifting up of my hands as the evening sacrifice.

Psalm 141.1-4b,8

This prayer may be said:

That this evening may be holy, good and peaceful,
let us pray with one heart and mind.
(Silence may be kept.)

As our evening prayer rises before you, O God,
so may your mercy come down upon us
    to cleanse our hearts
and set us free to sing your praise,
now and for ever. Amen.

Evening Prayer continues with the appointed Psalmody.

THE PREPARATION

O God, make speed to save us.
O Lord, make haste to help us.

Pour your love into our hearts, O God,
through the Holy Spirit you have given to us.

Glory . . .   **Alleluia.**

THE OPENING CANTICLE

A SONG OF GOD'S GREATNESS

1   Bless the Lord, O my soul. *
     O Lord my God, how excellent is your greatness!

2   You are clothed with majesty and honour, *
     wrapped in light as in a garment.

3   The sun knows the time for its setting. *
     You make darkness that it may be night.

4   O Lord, how manifold are your works! *
     In wisdom you have made them all;
        the earth is full of your creatures.

5   When you send forth your spirit, they are created, *
     and you renew the face of the earth.

6   May the glory of the Lord endure for ever; *
     may the Lord rejoice in his works;

7   I will sing to the Lord as long as I live; *
     I will make music to my God while I have my being.

     Glory . . .   *Psalm 104.1,2,21b,22a,26,32,33,35*

A HYMN may be sung.

THE OPENING PRAYER may be said.

That this evening may be holy, good and peaceful,
let us pray with one heart and mind.
(Silence may be kept.)

As your living Word
   brings light out of darkness, O Lord,
so may your Spirit renew the face of the earth,
bending our wills to the gentle rule of your love,
now and for ever. Amen.

THE WORD OF GOD

THE PSALMODY, as appointed.

Each psalm, or group of psalms, may end with:

Glory . . .

If there are two SCRIPTURE READINGS, the first may be read here, or both may be read after the Second Canticle.

THE SECOND CANTICLE

In Ordinary Time:

Either A SONG OF GOD'S GRACE (46) or number 44, page 86

Refrain: **The glorious grace of God**
            is freely bestowed on us in the Beloved.

1   Blessèd are you,
       the God and Father of our Lord Jesus Christ, *
    for you have blest us in Christ Jesus
       with every spiritual blessing in the heavenly places.

2   You chose us to be yours in Christ
    before the foundation of the world, *
    that we should be holy and blameless before you.

3   In love you destined us for adoption as your children,
    through Jesus Christ, *
    according to the purpose of your will,

4   To the praise of your glorious grace, *
    which you freely bestowed on us in the Beloved.

5   In you, we have redemption
    through the blood of Christ, *
    the forgiveness of our sins,

6 According to the riches of your grace, *
   which you have lavished upon us.

7 You have made known to us, in all wisdom and insight, *
   the mystery of your will,

8 According to your purpose
   which you set forth in Christ, *
   as a plan for the fullness of time,

9 To unite all things in Christ, *
   things in heaven and things on earth.

   Glory ...   *Ephesians 1.3-10*

   **The glorious grace of God
   is freely bestowed on us in the Beloved.**

From Ascension until Pentecost:

*Either A SONG OF GOD'S CHILDREN (44) or numbers 49, page 513, or 71,
page 534*

Refrain: **The Spirit of the Father,
         who raised Christ Jesus from the dead,
         gives life to the people of God.**

1 The law of the Spirit of life in Christ Jesus *
   has set us free from the law of sin and death.

2 All who are led by the Spirit of God are children of God; *
   for we have received the Spirit that enables us to cry, 'Abba, Father'.

3 The Spirit himself bears witness that we are children of God *
   and if God's children, then heirs of God;

4 If heirs of God, then fellow-heirs with Christ; *
   since we suffer with him now, that we may be glorified with him.

5 These sufferings that we now endure *
   are not worth comparing to the glory that shall be revealed.

6 For the creation waits with eager longing *
   for the revealing of the children of God.

   Glory ...   *Romans 8.2,14,15b-19*

**The Spirit of the Father,
who raised Christ Jesus from the dead,
gives life to the people of God.**

*On feasts of Missionaries, numbers 49, page 513, or 53, page 515, are
alternative canticles.*

*On feasts of Evangelists, numbers 49, page 513, or 57, page 518, are
alternative canticles.*

THE SCRIPTURE READING(S)

A RESPONSORY may be said.

When you send forth your Spirit, we are created:
you renew the face of the earth.
**When you send forth your Spirit, we are created:
you renew the face of the earth.**

O Lord, how manifold are your works:
in wisdom you have made them all.
You renew the face of the earth.

Glory to the Father and to the Son
and to the Holy Spirit.
**When you send forth your Spirit, we are created;
you renew the face of the earth.**

from Psalm 104

THE GOSPEL CANTICLE: MAGNIFICAT – THE SONG OF MARY (40)

See either inside front cover, inside back cover or page 504 for another version.

In Ordinary Time:

Refrain: **My spirit rejoices in you, O God,
my soul proclaims your greatness.**

or, from the day after Ascension until Pentecost:

**How excellent is your name in all the world,
you have set your glory above the heavens. Alleluia.**

or, on feasts of Missionaries:

> **How beautiful on the mountains**
> **are the feet of those who bring good news**
> **and proclaim the gospel of peace. (Alleluia.)**

or, on feasts of Evangelists:

> **The one who saw what Jesus did has borne witness,**
> **that you also may believe. (Alleluia.)**

The refrain is repeated after the canticle.

THE PRAYERS

INTERCESSIONS may be offered.

THE KYRIES may be used as responses to intercession.

Lord, have mercy.
Lord, have mercy.

Christ, have mercy.
Christ, have mercy.

Lord, have mercy.
Lord, have mercy.

THE COLLECT of the day, or one of the following:

Guide us, Lord, in all our doings,
with your most gracious favour
and further us with your continual help;
that in all our works begun, continued
    and ended in you,
we may glorify your holy name,
and by your mercy attain everlasting life;
through Jesus Christ our Lord. **Amen.**

or, from the day after Ascension until Pentecost:

Lord, you have taught us
that all our doings without love are nothing worth:
send your Holy Spirit
and pour into our hearts
that most excellent gift of love,
the true bond of peace and of all virtues,

without which whoever lives
is counted dead before you.
Grant this for the sake of your only Son,
Jesus Christ our Lord. **Amen.**

THE LORD'S PRAYER may be said.

[Being made one by the power of the Spirit,]
as our Saviour taught us, so we pray
Our Father in heaven, . . .

THE CONCLUSION

In Ordinary Time:

**The grace of our Lord Jesus Christ,
and the love of God,
and the fellowship of the Holy Spirit,
be with us all evermore. Amen.**

Let us bless the Lord.
Thanks be to God.

or, from the day after Ascension until Pentecost:

May the Spirit kindle in us the fire of God's love. Amen.

Let us bless the Lord. Alleluia, alleluia.
Thanks be to God. Alleluia, alleluia.

or, on Class I & II Holy Days:

May our blessèd Lady pray for us.
May Saint Francis and Saint Clare pray for us.
[May Saint N pray for us.]
May all the saints of God pray for us.
May the angels of God befriend us
    and watch around us to protect us.
May the Lord Jesus give us his blessing of peace. Amen.

Let us bless the Lord. (Alleluia, alleluia.)
Thanks be to God. (Alleluia, alleluia.)

Form 2 – Night Prayer

Mondays in Ordinary Time
and daily from the day after Ascension
until the Day of Pentecost

THE PREPARATION

The Lord almighty grant us a quiet night and a perfect end.
Amen.

Our help is in the name of the Lord
who made heaven and earth.

A period of silence for reflection on the past day may follow.
The following or other suitable words of penitence may be used.

Holy God,
we confess to you before the company
of the faithful in heaven and on earth,
that we have sinned against you,
against one another
and against your creation.
Forgive us in your mercy,
help us to forgive each other
and to hold in reverence
all that you have made. Amen.

OSB West Malling

or:

Holy God,
holy and strong,
holy and immortal:
have mercy on us.

O God, make speed to save us.
O Lord, make haste to help us.

Glory . . .   Alleluia.

The following or another suitable HYMN may be sung.

Before the ending of the day,
Creator of the world, we pray
That you, with steadfast love, would keep
Your watch around us while we sleep.

From evil dreams defend our sight,
From fears and terrors of the night;
Tread under foot our deadly foe
That we no sinful thought may know.

Ordinary Time Doxology
O Father, that we ask be done
Through Jesus Christ, your only Son;
And Holy Spirit, by whose breath
Our souls are raised to life from death. Amen.

Ascension until Pentecost Doxology
To God the Father, God the Son,
And God the Spirit praise be done:
May Christ the Lord upon us pour
The Spirit's gift for evermore. Amen.

THE WORD OF GOD

THE PSALMODY

Psalm 86

1   Incline your ear, O Lord, and answer me, *
for I am poor and in misery.

2   Preserve my soul, for I am faithful; *
save your servant, for I put my trust in you.

3   Be merciful to me, O Lord, for you are my God; *
I call upon you all the day long.

4   Gladden the soul of your servant, *
for to you, O Lord, I lift up my soul.

5   For you, Lord, are good and forgiving, *
abounding in steadfast love to all who call upon you.

6   Give ear, O Lord, to my prayer *
and listen to the voice of my supplication.

7   In the day of my distress I will call upon you, *
    for you will answer me.

8   Among the gods there is none like you, O Lord, *
    nor any works like yours.

9   All nations you have made shall come and worship you, O Lord, *
    and shall glorify your name.

10 For you are great and do wonderful things; *
    you alone are God.

11 Teach me your way, O Lord, and I will walk in your truth; *
    knit my heart to you, that I may fear your name.

12 I will thank you, O Lord my God, with all my heart, *
    and glorify your name for evermore;

13 For great is your steadfast love towards me, *
    for you have delivered my soul from the depths of the grave.

14 O God, the proud rise up against me
        and a ruthless horde seek after my life; *
    they have not set you before their eyes.

15 But you, Lord, are gracious and full of compassion, *
    slow to anger and full of kindness and truth.

16 Turn to me and have mercy upon me; *
    give your strength to your servant
        and save the child of your handmaid.

17 Show me a token of your favour,
        that those who hate me may see it and be ashamed; *
    because you, O Lord, have helped and comforted me.

Glory . . .

THE READING: one of the following or some other.

Either, in Ordinary Time:

Thus says the Lord God, the Holy One of Israel: in returning and rest you
shall be saved; in quietness and in trust shall be your strength.

Isaiah 30.15

or, in Ascension until Pentecost:

I will pour out my spirit on all flesh; your sons and your daughters shall prophesy. The old shall dream dreams and the young see visions.

Joel 2.28

or, on feasts of Missionaries or Evangelists:

You are no longer strangers and aliens but citizens with the saints and also members of the household of God, built upon the foundation of the apostles and the prophets, with Christ Jesus himself as the cornerstone. In him the whole structure is joined together and grows into a holy temple in the Lord.

Ephesians 2.19-21

THE RESPONSORY may be said.

Either, in Ordinary Time:

Into your hands, O Lord, I commend my spirit.
Into your hands, O Lord, I commend my spirit.

For you have redeemed me, Lord God of truth.
I commend my spirit.

Glory to the Father and to the Son
and to the Holy Spirit.
Into your hands, O Lord, I commend my spirit.

Keep me as the apple of your eye.
Hide me under the shadow of your wings.

or, in Easter and Ascension until Pentecost:

Into your hands, O Lord, I commend my spirit.
Alleluia, alleluia.
Into your hands, O Lord, I commend my spirit.
Alleluia, alleluia.

For you have redeemed me, Lord God of truth.
Alleluia, alleluia.

Glory to the Father and to the Son
and to the Holy Spirit;
Into your hands, O Lord, I commend my spirit.
Alleluia, alleluia.

Keep me as the apple of your eye.
Hide me under the shadow of your wings.

THE GOSPEL CANTICLE: NUNC DIMITTIS – THE SONG OF SIMEON (42) or another version on page 508

Refrain: **Save us, O Lord, while waking,**
and guard us while sleeping,
that awake we may watch with Christ,
and asleep may rest in peace.

or, in Ascension until Pentecost:

Alleluia. The Holy Spirit, the Advocate, alleluia,
shall teach you all things. Alleluia, alleluia.

or, on Class I & II Holy Days:

Grant us your light, O Lord,
that the darkness of our hearts being overcome,
we may receive the true light,
even Christ our Saviour. (Alleluia.)

1 ✠ Now, Lord, you let your servant go in peace: *
your word has been fulfilled.

2 My own eyes have seen the salvation *
which you have prepared in the sight of every people:

3 A light to reveal you to the nations *
and the glory of your people Israel.

Luke 2.29-32

Glory . . .

The refrain is repeated after the canticle.

THE PRAYERS

Intercessions and thanksgivings may be offered here.

Either, in Ordinary Time:

Be present, O merciful God,
and protect us through the silent hours of this night,
so that we who are wearied by the changes
   and chances of this fleeting world,
may rest upon your eternal changelessness;
through Jesus Christ our Lord. **Amen.**

or:

Lighten our darkness,
Lord, we pray;
and in your mercy defend us
from all perils and dangers of this night;
for the love of your only Son,
our Saviour Jesus Christ. **Amen.**

or, in Ascension until Pentecost:

Come, O Spirit of God,
and make within us your dwelling place and home.
May our darkness be dispelled by your light,
and our troubles calmed by your peace;
may all evil be redeemed by your love,
all pain transformed through the suffering of Christ,
and all dying glorified in his risen life. **Amen.**

THE LORD'S PRAYER may be said.

[As we come to the ending of the day,]
as our Saviour taught us, so we pray
Our Father in heaven, . . .

THE CONCLUSION

In peace, we will lie down and sleep;
for you alone, Lord, make us dwell in safety.

Abide with us, Lord Jesus,
for the night is at hand and the day is now past.

As the night-watch looks for the morning,
so do we look for you, O Christ.

[Come with the dawning of the day
**and make yourself known
in the breaking of the bread.**]

Either, in Ordinary Time:

**The Lord bless us and watch over us,
the Lord make his face shine upon us
   and be gracious to us,
the Lord look kindly on us and give us peace. Amen.**

or, in Ascension until Pentecost:

**May the Holy Spirit of God bless and sanctify us
so that we may be consecrated in the truth. Amen.**

A MARIAN ANTHEM may be sung.

SALVE REGINA

*Traditionally, this anthem is sung at the end of Night Prayer from after Pentecost
to Advent; or it may be the unchanging final anthem. The other Marian anthems
may be found on page 775.*

Salve, Regina, mater misericordiae;
vita, dulcedo, et spes nostra, salve.
Ad te clamamus, exsules, filii Evae,
ad te suspiramus,
gementes et flentes in hac lacrimarum valle;
eia ergo, advocata nostra,
illos tuos misericordes oculos ad nos converte,
Et Iesum, benedictum fructum ventris tui,
nobis post hoc exsilium ostende.
O clemens, O pia, O dulcis Virgo Maria.

Form 3 – Morning Prayer

Tuesdays in Ordinary Time and daily in Advent

THE PREPARATION

A *is used on Tuesdays in Ordinary Time.*
B *is used daily in Advent and on specified Class I & II Holy Days.*

A:

O Lord, open our lips;
and our mouth shall proclaim your praise.

Reveal among us the light of your presence,
that we may behold your power and glory.

Glory . . .   Alleluia.

Morning Prayer continues with THE OPENING CANTICLE.

B:

O Lord, open our lips
and our mouth shall proclaim your praise.

On Sundays in Advent, the following prayer may be replaced by Prayer I from Common Worship, 'Times and Seasons', page 51ff, for the lighting of a new candle of the Advent Wreath.

Blessèd are you, Sovereign God of all,
to you be glory and praise for ever!
In your tender compassion,
the dawn from on high is breaking upon us
to dispel the lingering shadows of night.
As we look for your coming among us this day,
open our eyes to behold your presence
and strengthen our hands to do your will,
that the world may rejoice and give you praise,
Father, Son and Holy Spirit.
Blessèd be God for ever.

The following is said:

In Advent:

Our Sovereign and Saviour draws near.
O come, let us worship.

or, on feasts of Members of Religious Communities:

(Alleluia.) Christ, the pure and lowly in heart.
O come, let us worship. (Alleluia.)

THE OPENING CANTICLE

A SONG OF THE KING'S GLORY

1   The earth is the Lord's and all that fills it, *
     the compass of the world and all who dwell therein.

2   For he has founded it upon the seas *
     and set it firm upon the rivers of the deep.

3   'Who shall ascend the hill of the Lord, *
     or who can rise up in his holy place?'

4   'Those who have clean hands and a pure heart, *
     who have not lifted up their soul to an idol,
         nor sworn an oath to a lie;

5   'They shall receive a blessing from the Lord, *
     a just reward from the God of their salvation.'

6   Such is the company of those who seek him, *
     of those who seek your face, O God of Jacob.

7   Lift up your heads, O gates;
     be lifted up, you everlasting doors; *
         and the King of glory shall come in.

8   'Who is the King of glory?' *
     'The Lord, strong and mighty,
         the Lord who is mighty in battle.'

9   Lift up your heads, O gates;
         be lifted up, you everlasting doors; *
     and the King of glory shall come in.

10 'Who is this King of glory?' *
    'The Lord of hosts,
       he is the King of glory.'

Glory . . .   *Psalm 24*

A HYMN may be sung.

THE OPENING PRAYER may be said.

The night has passed and the day lies open before us;
let us pray with one heart and mind.
(Silence may be kept.)

**As we rejoice in the gift of this new day,
so may the light of your presence, O God,
set our hearts on fire with love for you;
now and for ever. Amen.**

THE WORD OF GOD

THE PSALMODY, as appointed

Each psalm, or group of psalms, may end with:

Glory . . .

*If there are two SCRIPTURE READINGS, the first may be read here, or both may
be read after the Second Canticle.*

THE SECOND CANTICLE

In Ordinary Time:

Either A SONG OF PEACE (6) or number 11, page 479

Refrain: **Spirit of God, teach us your ways
           that we may walk in the paths of peace.**

1   Come, let us go up to the mountain of God, *
    to the house of the God of Jacob;

2   That God may teach us his ways, *
    and that we may walk in his paths.

3   For the law shall go out from Zion, *
    and the word of the Lord from Jerusalem.

4   God shall judge between the nations, *
    and shall mediate for many peoples.

5   They shall beat their swords into ploughshares, *
    and their spears into pruning hooks.

6   Nation shall not lift up sword against nation, *
    neither shall they learn war any more.

7   O people of Jacob, come: *
    let us walk in the light of the Lord.

    Glory . . .   *Isaiah 2.3-5*

    **Spirit of God, teach us your ways,
    that we may walk in the paths of peace.**

In Advent:

*Either A SONG OF GOD'S HERALD (12) or numbers 32, page 495, or
35, page 497*

Refrain: **God will feed his flock like a shepherd,
          and gather the lambs in his arms.**

I   Go up to a high mountain,
        herald of good tidings to Zion; *
    lift up your voice with strength,
        herald of good tidings to Jerusalem.

2   Lift up your voice, fear not; *
    say to the cities of Judah, 'Behold your God!'

3   See, the Lord God comes with might, *
    and his arm rules for him.

4   Behold, his reward is with him, *
    and his recompense before him.

5   God will feed his flock like a shepherd, *
    and gather the lambs in his arms;

6   He will carry them in his breast, *
    and gently lead those that are with young.

Glory . . .

Isaiah 40.9-11

**God will feed his flock like a shepherd,
and gather the lambs in his arms.**

On feasts of Members of Religious Communities, number 34, page 497, is an alternative canticle.

THE SCRIPTURE READING(S)

A RESPONSORY may be said.

Now it is time to awake out of sleep,
for the night is far spent and the day is at hand.

Now is our salvation nearer than when we first believed,
for the night is far spent.

Let us therefore cast off the works of darkness
and put on the armour of light,
for the day is at hand.

Put on the Lord Jesus Christ
and make no provision for the flesh,
for the night is far spent and the day is at hand.

from Romans 13

THE GOSPEL CANTICLE: BENEDICTUS – TI IE SONG OF ZECHARIAH (11)

See either inside front cover, inside back cover or page 506 for another version.

In Ordinary Time:

Refrain: **In your tender compassion, O God,
the dawn from on high shall break upon us.**

or, from Advent Sunday until 16 December:

**Look towards the east, O Jerusalem,
and see the glory that is coming from God.**

or, from 17 December until Christmas Eve:

> **Like the sun in the morning sky,**
> **the Saviour of the world will dawn;**
> **like rain upon the meadows,**
> **the Christ will come down upon us.**

or, on feasts of Members of Religious Communities:

> **They who wait upon the Lord**
> **shall renew their strength;**
> **they shall mount up with wings as an eagle. (Alleluia.)**

The refrain is repeated after the canticle.

THE PRAYERS

INTERCESSIONS may be offered.

THE KYRIES may be used as responses to intercession.

Lord, have mercy.
Lord, have mercy.

Christ, have mercy.
Christ, have mercy.

Lord, have mercy.
Lord, have mercy.

THE COLLECT of the day or one of the following:

Eternal God and Father,
you create and redeem us by the power of your love:
guide and strengthen us by your Spirit,
that we may give ourselves in love and service
to one another and to you;
through Jesus Christ our Lord. **Amen.**

or, in Advent:

O God,
who set before us the great hope
that your Kingdom shall come on earth
and taught us to pray for its coming:
give us grace to discern the signs of its dawning
and to work for the perfect day
when the whole world shall reflect your glory;
through Jesus Christ our Lord. **Amen.** *Percy Dearmer*

THE LORD'S PRAYER may be said.

[Awaiting his coming in glory,]
as our Saviour taught us, so we pray
Our Father in heaven, . . .

THE CONCLUSION

In Ordinary Time:

**The Lord bless us, and preserve us from all evil,
and keep us in eternal life. Amen.**

Let us bless the Lord.
Thanks be to God.

or, in Advent:

**May the Lord, when he comes,
find us watching and waiting. Amen.**

Let us bless the Lord.
Thanks be to God.

or, on Class I & II Holy Days:

May our blessèd Lady pray for us.
May Saint Francis and Saint Clare pray for us.
[May Saint N pray for us.]
May all the saints of God pray for us.
May the angels of God befriend us
    and watch around us to protect us.
May the Lord Jesus give us his blessing of peace. Amen.

Let us bless the Lord. (Alleluia, alleluia.)
Thanks be to God. (Alleluia, alleluia.)

Form 3 – Midday Prayer
Tuesdays through the Year

Seasonal Propers are found beginning page 539.

THE PREPARATION

O God, make speed to save us.
O Lord, make haste to help us.

Glory . . .   **Alleluia.** *(Omitted in Lent)*

A HYMN may be sung, the following or some other.

O God of truth, O Lord of might,
You order time and change aright,
And send the early morning ray
And light the glow of perfect day.

Extinguish every sinful fire
And banish all our ill desire;
And, while you keep the body whole,
Shed forth your peace upon the soul.

Ordinary Time Doxology
O Father, that we ask be done
Through Jesus Christ, your only Son,
Who, with the Spirit, reigns above,
Three Persons in one God of love. Amen.

tr. J.M. Neale *

THE WORD OF GOD

THE PSALMODY

Either A: PSALM 119.57-80

8 Heth

57   You only are my portion, O Lord; *
      I have promised to keep your words.

58   I entreat you with all my heart, *
      be merciful to me according to your promise.

59   I have considered my ways *
       and turned my feet back to your testimonies.

60   I made haste and did not delay *
       to keep your commandments.

61   Though the cords of the wicked entangle me, *
       I do not forget your law.

62   At midnight I will rise to give you thanks, *
       because of your righteous judgements.

63   I am a companion of all those who fear you, *
       those who keep your commandments.

64   The earth, O Lord, is full of your faithful love; *
       instruct me in your statutes.

9 Teth

65   You have dealt graciously with your servant, *
       according to your word, O Lord.

66   O teach me true understanding and knowledge, *
       for I have trusted in your commandments.

67   Before I was afflicted I went astray, *
       but now I keep your word.

68   You are gracious and do good; *
       O Lord, teach me your statutes.

69   The proud have smeared me with lies, *
       but I will keep your commandments with my whole heart.

70   Their heart has become gross with fat, *
       but my delight is in your law.

71   It is good for me that I have been afflicted, *
       that I may learn your statutes.

72   The law of your mouth is dearer to me *
       than a hoard of gold and silver.

10 Yodh

73   Your hands have made me and fashioned me; *
       give me understanding, that I may learn your commandments.

74   Those who fear you will be glad when they see me, *
       because I have hoped in your word.

75   I know, O Lord, that your judgements are right, *
       and that in very faithfulness you caused me to be troubled.

76   Let your faithful love be my comfort, *
       according to your promise to your servant.

77   Let your tender mercies come to me, that I may live, *
       for your law is my delight.

78   Let the proud be put to shame, for they wrong me with lies; *
       but I will meditate on your commandments.

79   Let those who fear you turn to me, *
       even those who know your testimonies.

80   Let my heart be sound in your statutes, *
       that I may not be put to shame.

*or **B:** Psalms of Ascent*

PSALM 125

1   Those who trust in the Lord are like Mount Zion, *
       which cannot be moved, but stands fast for ever.

2   As the hills stand about Jerusalem, *
       so the Lord stands round about his people,
         from this time forth for evermore.

3   The sceptre of wickedness shall not hold sway
        over the land allotted to the righteous, *
       lest the righteous turn their hands to evil.

4   Do good, O Lord, to those who are good, *
       and to those who are true of heart.

5   Those who turn aside to crooked ways
        the Lord shall take away with the evildoers; *
       but let there be peace upon Israel.

PSALM 126

1   When the Lord restored the fortunes of Zion, *
       then were we like those who dream.

2   Then was our mouth filled with laughter *
    and our tongue with songs of joy.

3   Then said they among the nations, *
    'The Lord has done great things for them.'

4   The Lord has indeed done great things for us, *
    and therefore we rejoiced.

5   Restore again our fortunes, O Lord, *
    as the river beds of the desert.

6   Those who sow in tears *
    shall reap with songs of joy.

7   Those who go out weeping, bearing the seed, *
    will come back with shouts of joy,
       bearing their sheaves with them.

The psalm, or group of psalms, may end with:

Glory . . .

THE READING

In Ordinary Time, week 1 begins on the first Sunday of the month and so on.

Either:
Week 1: Deuteronomy 28.1-6
     2: Isaiah 35.2c-6
     3: John 9.1-5
     4: Revelation 22.1,2
     5: Matthew 15.30

or one of the following readings:
Jesus said to them, I am the light of the world. Whoever follows me will
never walk in darkness but will have the light of life.

John 8.12

Blessèd are those who hunger and thirst for righteousness, for they shall be
filled.

Matthew 5.6

or some other suitable reading.

THE RESPONSE

In Ordinary Time:

*Either **A**:*

Blessèd are you who are poor,
for yours is the kingdom of heaven.

Blessèd are you who hunger now,
for you will be fed.

Blessèd are you who weep now,
for you will laugh.

Blessèd are you when people hate you,
  and when they exclude you,
when they revile and defame you,

Rejoice in that day and leap for joy,
for surely your reward is great in heaven.

*or **B**:*

Awake, O sleeper, and arise from the dead,
and Christ shall give you light.

If you have been raised with Christ, seek the things that are above,
where Christ is, who is seated at the right hand of God.

Set your minds on things that are above,
not on things that are on the earth.

You have died,
and your life is hid with Christ in God.

When Christ who is our life shall appear,
then you will appear with him in glory.

Awake, O sleeper, and arise from the dead,
and Christ shall give you light.

THE PRAYERS

INTERCESSIONS may be offered.

THE KYRIES may be used as responses to intercession.

Lord, have mercy.
Lord, have mercy.

Christ, have mercy.
Christ, have mercy.

Lord, have mercy.
Lord, have mercy.

THE COLLECT of the day or one of the following:

Eternal God,
the light of the minds that know you,
the joy of the hearts that love you,
and the strength of the wills that serve you:
grant us so to know you
that we may truly love you,
so to love you that we may truly serve you,
whose service is perfect freedom;
through Jesus Christ our Lord. **Amen.**

after Augustine of Hippo (430)

Holy, holy, holy Lord God almighty,
who is, who was, and who is to come:
We praise and glorify you for ever.

O Lord our God, you are worthy
to receive praise, glory and honour and blessing.
We praise and glorify you for ever.

Worthy is the Lamb who was slain
to receive power and divinity, wisdom and strength,
honour and glory and blessing.
We praise and glorify you for ever.

Let us bless the Father and the Son with the Holy Spirit.
We praise and glorify you for ever.

Bless the Lord, all you works of the Lord.
We praise and glorify you for ever.

Sing praise to our God, all you his servants,
and you who fear God, the small and the great.
We praise and glorify you for ever.

Let heaven and earth praise him who is glorious.
We praise and glorify you for ever.

Every creature in heaven, on earth and under the earth;
and in the sea, and those which are in it.
We praise and glorify you for ever.

Glory to the Father and to the Son and to the Holy Spirit.
We praise and glorify you for ever.

As it was in the beginning, is now,
and shall be for ever.
We praise and glorify you for ever.

after The Praises to be Said at all the Hours, Francis of Assisi

THE LORD'S PRAYER may be said.

[Lord Jesus remember us in your kingdom
and teach us to pray.]
Our Father in heaven, . . .

THE CONCLUSION

Let us bless the Lord God living and true!
Let us always give him
praise, glory, honour, blessing and every good.
Amen. Amen. (Alleluia, alleluia.)

Prayer said by Francis of Assisi at the end of the office

Form 3 – Evening Prayer

Tuesdays in Ordinary Time
and daily in Advent

THE BLESSING OF THE LIGHT *may replace THE PREPARATION.*

A light, which may be the Paschal Candle, is brought in, or a candle may simply be lit.

Your word, O God, is a lantern to our feet
 and a light upon our path.

The light and peace of Jesus Christ be with you
and also with you.

On Sundays in Advent, the following prayer may be replaced by Prayer 1 from 'Common Worship: Times and Seasons', page 51ff, for the lighting of a new candle of the Advent Wreath.

Blessèd are you, Sovereign God,
creator of light and darkness,
to you be glory and praise for ever.
As evening falls, you renew your promise
to reveal among us the light of your presence.
May your word be a lantern to our feet
and a light upon our path
that we may behold your coming among us.
Strengthen us in our stumbling weakness
and free our tongues to sing your praise,
Father, Son and Holy Spirit:
Blessèd be God for ever.

While the other candles are lit the following, or another version of number 63, page 524, or another suitable hymn may be sung.

A SONG OF THE LIGHT (63c)

1   **Hail, gladdening Light, of his pure glory poured,**
    Who is the immortal Father, heavenly, blest,
    Holiest of holies, Jesus Christ our Lord.

2 **Now we are come to the sun's hour of rest,**
The lights of evening round us shine,
We hymn the Father, Son and Holy Spirit divine.

3 **Worthy are you at all times to be sung**
With undefilèd tongue,
Son of our God, giver of life, alone:
Therefore in all the world your glories,
   Lord, they own.

Verses from PSALM 141 may be said and incense may be burned.

Let my prayer rise before you as incense,
the lifting up of my hands as the evening sacrifice.

O Lord, I call to you; come to me quickly;
hear my voice when I cry to you.
Set a watch before my mouth, O Lord,
and guard the door of my lips.

Let my prayer rise before you as incense,
the lifting up of my hands as the evening sacrifice.

Let not my heart incline to any evil thing;
let me not be occupied in wickedness with evildoers.
But my eyes are turned to you, Lord God,
in you I take refuge;
do not leave me defenceless.

Let my prayer rise before you as incense,
the lifting up of my hands as the evening sacrifice.

Psalm 141.1-4b,8

This prayer may be said:

That this evening may be holy, good and peaceful,
let us pray with one heart and mind.
(Silence may be kept.)

As our evening prayer rises before you, O God,
so may your mercy come down upon us
   to cleanse our hearts
and set us free to sing your praise,
now and for ever. Amen.

Evening Prayer continues with the appointed Psalmody.

THE PREPARATION

O God, make speed to save us.
O Lord, make haste to help us.

Reveal among us the light of your presence,
that we may behold your power and glory.

Glory . . .   Alleluia.

THE OPENING CANTICLE

A SONG OF MERCY AND TRUTH

1   O God, will you not give us life again, *
    that your people may rejoice in you?

2   Show us your mercy, O Lord, *
    and grant us your salvation.

3   Truly, his salvation is near to those who fear him, *
    that his glory may dwell in our land.

4   Mercy and truth are met together, *
    righteousness and peace have kissed each other;

5   Truth shall spring up from the earth *
    and righteousness look down from heaven.

6   Righteousness shall go before him *
    and direct his steps in the way.

    Glory . . .   *Psalm 85.6,7,9-11,13*

A HYMN may be sung.

THE OPENING PRAYER may be said.

That this evening may be holy, good and peaceful,
let us pray with one heart and mind.
(Silence may be kept.)

As your word, O Lord,
  gives light to our path,
may we behold the glory of your presence
and so rejoice to sing your praise,
now and for ever. Amen.

THE WORD OF GOD

THE PSALMODY, as appointed

Each psalm, or group of psalms, may end with:

Glory . . .

*If there are two SCRIPTURE READINGS, the first may be read here, or both may
be read after the Second Canticle.*

THE SECOND CANTICLE

In Ordinary Time:

Either A SONG OF THE LAMB (58) or number 43, page 508

Refrain: **Let us rejoice and exult
      and give glory and homage to our God.**

1   Salvation and glory and power belong to our God, *
    whose judgements are true and just.

2   Praise our God, all you his servants, *
    all who fear him, both small and great.

3   The Lord our God, the Almighty, reigns: *
    let us rejoice and exult and give him the glory.

4   For the marriage of the Lamb has come *
    and his bride has made herself ready.

5   Blessèd are those who are invited *
    to the wedding banquet of the Lamb.

    **To the One who sits on the throne and to the Lamb *
    be blessing and honour and glory and might,
    for ever and ever. Amen.**

Revelation 19.1b,2a,5b,6b,7,9b

**Let us rejoice and exult
and give glory and homage to our God.**

In Advent:

Either A SONG OF THE SPIRIT (61) or numbers 59, page 520, or 66, page 528

Refrain: **Surely I am coming soon.
Amen. Come, Lord Jesus!**

1   'Behold, I am coming soon', says the Lord,
        and bringing my reward with me, *
    to give to everyone according to their deeds.

2   'I am the Alpha and the Omega, the first and the last, *
    the beginning and the end.'

3   Blessèd are those who do God's commandments,
        that they may have the right to the tree of life, *
    and may enter into the city through the gates.

4   'I, Jesus, have sent my angel to you, *
    with this testimony for all the churches.

5   'I am the root and the offspring of David, *
    I am the bright morning star.'

6   'Come!' say the Spirit and the Bride; *
    'Come!' let each hearer reply.

7   Come forward, you who are thirsty, *
    let those who desire
        take the water of life as a gift.

**To the One who sits on the throne and to the Lamb *
be blessing and honour and glory and might,
for ever and ever. Amen.**

Revelation 22.12-14,16,17

**Surely I am coming soon.
Amen. Come, Lord Jesus!**

*On feasts of Members of Religious Communities, number 39, page 502, is an
alternative canticle.*

THE SCRIPTURE READING(S)

A RESPONSORY may be said.

My soul is waiting for you, O Lord:
in your word is my hope.
**My soul is waiting for you, O Lord:
in your word is my hope.**

There is forgiveness with you,
so that you shall be feared.
In your word is my hope.

Glory to the Father and to the Son
and to the Holy Spirit.
**My soul is waiting for you, O Lord:
in your word is my hope.**

from Psalm 130

THE GOSPEL CANTICLE: MAGNIFICAT – THE SONG OF MARY (40)

See either inside front cover, inside back cover or page 504 for another version.

In Ordinary Time:

Refrain: **You have mercy on those who fear you,
from generation to generation.**

or, from Advent Sunday until 16 December:

**Lord Jesus, you are the one who is to come,
the one whom we await with longing hearts.**

or, from 17 to 23 December, see page 543

or, on feasts of Members of Religious Communities:

**You have left all things and followed me:
you will be rewarded a hundred times over
and gain eternal life. (Alleluia.)**

The refrain is repeated after the canticle.

THE PRAYERS

INTERCESSIONS may be offered.

THE KYRIES may be used as responses to intercession.

Lord, have mercy.
Lord, have mercy.

Christ, have mercy.
Christ, have mercy.

Lord, have mercy.
Lord, have mercy.

THE COLLECT of the day, or one of the following:

O God, by whose command
   the order of time runs its course:
forgive our restlessness, perfect our faith
and, while we await the fulfilment of your promise,
grant us to have a good hope
through the Word made flesh,
even Jesus Christ our Lord. **Amen.**

Gregory Nazianzus

or, in Advent:

O Lord our God,
make us watchful and keep us faithful
as we await the coming of your Son our Lord;
that, when he shall appear,
he may not find us sleeping in sin
but active in his service
and joyful in his praise;
through Jesus Christ our Lord. **Amen.**

David Silk

THE LORD'S PRAYER may be said.

[Awaiting his coming in glory,]
as our Saviour taught us, so we pray
Our Father in heaven, . . .

In Ordinary Time:

**The grace of our Lord Jesus Christ,
and the love of God,
and the fellowship of the Holy Spirit,
be with us all evermore. Amen.**

Let us bless the Lord.
Thanks be to God.

or, in Advent:

**May the Lord, when he comes,
find us watching and waiting. Amen.**

Let us bless the Lord.
Thanks be to God.

or, on Class I & II Holy Days:

May our blessèd Lady pray for us.
May Saint Francis and Saint Clare pray for us.
[May Saint N pray for us.]
May all the saints of God pray for us.
May the angels of God befriend us
   and watch around us to protect us.
May the Lord Jesus give us his blessing of peace. Amen.

Let us bless the Lord. (Alleluia, alleluia.)
Thanks be to God. (Alleluia, alleluia.)

Form 3 – Night Prayer

Tuesdays in Ordinary Time
and daily in Advent

THE PREPARATION

The Lord almighty grant us a quiet night and a perfect end.
Amen.

Our help is in the name of the Lord
who made heaven and earth.

A period of silence for reflection on the past day may follow.
The following or other suitable words of penitence may be used.

Holy God,
we confess to you before the company
**   of the faithful in heaven and on earth,**
that we have sinned against you,
against one another
and against your creation.
Forgive us in your mercy,
help us to forgive each other
and to hold in reverence
**   all that you have made. Amen.**

OSB West Malling

or:

Holy God,
holy and strong,
holy and immortal:
have mercy on us.

O God, make speed to save us.
O Lord, make haste to help us.

Glory . . .   Alleluia.

The following or another suitable HYMN may be sung.

Before the ending of the day,
Creator of the world, we pray
That you, with steadfast love, would keep
Your watch around us while we sleep.

From evil dreams defend our sight,
From fears and terrors of the night;
Tread under foot our deadly foe
That we no sinful thought may know.

Ordinary Time Doxology
O Father, that we ask be done
Through Jesus Christ, your only Son;
And Holy Spirit, by whose breath
Our souls are raised to life from death. Amen.

Advent Doxology
To you, O Christ, all glory be,
Whose advent sets your people free;
Whom, with the Father, we adore,
And Holy Spirit, evermore. Amen.

THE WORD OF GOD

THE PSALMODY

Psalm 143.1-11

1   Hear my prayer, O Lord,
      and in your faithfulness give ear to my supplications; *
      answer me in your righteousness.

2   Enter not into judgement with your servant, *
      for in your sight shall no one living be justified.

3   For the enemy has pursued me,
      crushing my life to the ground, *
      making me sit in darkness like those long dead.

4   My spirit faints within me; *
      my heart within me is desolate.

5   I remember the time past; I muse upon all your deeds; *
      I consider the works of your hands.

6   I stretch out my hands to you; *
     my soul gasps for you like a thirsty land.

7   O Lord, make haste to answer me; my spirit fails me; *
     hide not your face from me
       lest I be like those who go down to the Pit.

8   Let me hear of your loving-kindness in the morning,
       for in you I put my trust; *
     show me the way I should walk in,
       for I lift up my soul to you.

9   Deliver me, O Lord, from my enemies, *
     for I flee to you for refuge.

10   Teach me to do what pleases you, for you are my God; *
     let your kindly spirit lead me on a level path.

11   Revive me, O Lord, for your name's sake; *
     for your righteousness' sake, bring me out of trouble.

Glory . . .

THE READING: one of the following or some other.

Either, in Ordinary Time:

Jesus said, 'Come to me, all you that are weary and are carrying heavy
burdens, and I will give you rest. Take my yoke upon you, and learn from
me; for I am gentle and humble in heart, and you will find rest for your
souls. For my yoke is easy, and my burden is light.'

Matthew 11.28-30

or, in Advent:

Keep awake – for you do not know when the master of the house will
come, in the evening, or at midnight, or at cockcrow, or at dawn – or else
he may find you asleep. And what I say to you I say to all: Keep awake.

Mark 13.35-end

or, on feasts of Members of Religious Communities:

Jesus said, 'Blessèd are the poor in spirit, for theirs is the kingdom of
heaven. Blessèd are the pure in heart, for they will see God.

Matthew 5.3,8

THE RESPONSORY may be said.

Into your hands, O Lord,
I commend my spirit. (Alleluia, alleluia)
Into your hands, O Lord,
I commend my spirit. (Alleluia, alleluia.)

For you have redeemed me, Lord God of truth.
I commend my spirit. (*or:* **Alleluia, alleluia.)**

Glory to the Father and to the Son
and to the Holy Spirit.
Into your hands, O Lord,
I commend my spirit. (Alleluia, alleluia.)

Keep me as the apple of your eye.
Hide me under the shadow of your wings.

THE GOSPEL CANTICLE: NUNC DIMITTIS – THE SONG OF SIMEON (42) or
another version on page 508

Refrain: **Save us, O Lord, while waking,**
and guard us while sleeping,
that awake we may watch with Christ,
and asleep may rest in peace.

or, in Advent:

Come, O Lord, and visit us in peace;
let us rejoice before you with a perfect heart.

or, on Class I & II Holy Days:

Grant us your light, O Lord,
that the darkness of our hearts being overcome,
we may receive the true light,
even Christ our Saviour. (Alleluia.)

1   ✠ Now, Lord, you let your servant go in peace: *
    your word has been fulfilled.

2   My own eyes have seen the salvation *
    which you have prepared in the sight of every people:

3   A light to reveal you to the nations *
    and the glory of your people Israel.

Luke 2.29-32

Glory . . .

The refrain is repeated after the canticle.

THE PRAYERS

Intercessions and thanksgivings may be offered here.

THE COLLECT: one of the following or some other.

Either, in Ordinary Time:

Look down, O God,
from your heavenly throne,
illuminate the darkness of this night
with your celestial brightness,
and from the children of light
banish the deeds of darkness;
through Jesus Christ our Saviour. **Amen.**

or:

Lighten our darkness,
Lord, we pray;
and in your mercy defend us
from all perils and dangers of this night;
for the love of your only Son,
our Saviour Jesus Christ. **Amen.**

or, in Advent:

Stir up your power, O God,
and come among us.
Heal our wounds,
calm our fears
and give us peace;
through Jesus our Redeemer. **Amen.**

THE LORD'S PRAYER may be said.

[As we come to the ending of the day,]
as our Saviour taught us, so we pray
Our Father in heaven, . . .

THE CONCLUSION

In peace, we will lie down and sleep;
for you alone, Lord, make us dwell in safety.

Abide with us, Lord Jesus,
for the night is at hand and the day is now past.

As the night-watch looks for the morning,
so do we look for you, O Christ.

[Come with the dawning of the day
**and make yourself known
in the breaking of the bread.**]

Either, in Ordinary Time:

**The Lord bless us and watch over us,
the Lord make his face shine upon us
    and be gracious to us,
the Lord look kindly on us and give us peace. Amen.**

or, in Advent:

**Restore us again, O God of hosts,
Show us the light of your countenance
and we shall be saved.
Bless and keep us, this night and always. Amen.**

A MARIAN ANTHEM may be sung.

SALVE REGINA

Traditionally, this anthem is sung at the end of Night Prayer from after Pentecost to Advent; or it may be the unchanging final anthem. The other Marian anthems may be found on page 775.

Salve, Regina, mater misericordiae;
vita, dulcedo, et spes nostra, salve.
Ad te clamamus, exsules, filii Evae,
ad te suspiramus,
gementes et flentes in hac lacrimarum valle;
eia ergo, advocata nostra,
illos tuos misericordes oculos ad nos converte,
Et Iesum, benedictum fructum ventris tui,
nobis post hoc exsilium ostende.
O clemens, O pia, O dulcis Virgo Maria.

Form 4 – Morning Prayer

Wednesdays in Ordinary Time and daily in Christmas Season

THE PREPARATION

A *is used on Wednesdays in Ordinary Time.*
B *is used daily in Christmas season and on specified Class I & II Holy Days.*

A:

O Lord, open our lips
and our mouth shall proclaim your praise.

You laid the foundation of the earth
and the heavens are the work of your hands.

Glory . . .   Alleluia.

Morning Prayer continues with THE OPENING CANTICLE.

B:

O Lord, open our lips
and our mouth shall proclaim your praise.

Blessèd are you, sovereign God,
creator of heaven and earth,
to you be praise and glory for ever.
As your living Word, eternal in heaven,
assumed the frailty of our mortal flesh,
may the light of your love be born in us
to fill our hearts with joy as we sing to you:
Father, Son and Holy Spirit:
Blessèd be God for ever.

The following is said:

In Christmas:

Alleluia. The Word was made flesh and dwelt among us.
O come, let us worship. Alleluia.

Alleluia. Christ is the Son of Mary.
O come, let us worship. Alleluia.

THE OPENING CANTICLE

A SONG OF GOD'S GLORIOUS NAME

1   O Lord our governor, *
     how glorious is your name in all the world!

2   Your majesty above the heavens is praised *
     out of the mouths of babes at the breast.

3   You have founded a stronghold against your foes, *
     that you might still the enemy and the avenger.

4   When I consider your heavens, the work of your fingers, *
     the moon and the stars that you have ordained,

5   What are mortals, that you should be mindful of them; *
     mere human beings, that you should seek them out?

6   You have made them little lower than the angels *
     and crown them with glory and honour.

7   You have given them dominion over the works of your hands *
     and put all things under their feet,

8   All sheep and oxen, *
     even the wild beasts of the field,

9   The birds of the air, the fish of the sea *
     and whatsoever moves in the paths of the sea.

10   O Lord our governor, *
     how glorious is your name in all the world!

     Glory ...

Psalm 8

A HYMN may be sung.

THE OPENING PRAYER may be said.

The night has passed and the day lies open before us;
let us pray with one heart and mind.
(Silence may be kept.)

**As we rejoice in the gift of this new day,
so may the light of your presence, O God,
set our hearts on fire with love for you;
now and for ever. Amen.**

THE WORD OF GOD

THE PSALMODY, as appointed

Each psalm, or group of psalms, may end with:

Glory . . .

If there are two SCRIPTURE READINGS, the first may be read here, or both may be read after the Second Canticle.

THE SECOND CANTICLE

In Ordinary Time:

Either A SONG OF THE WORD (15) or number 17, page 483

Refrain: **Return to the Lord, who will have mercy,
to our God, who will richly pardon.**

1   Seek the Lord while he may be found, *
    call upon him while he is near;

2   Let the wicked abandon their ways, *
    and the unrighteous their thoughts;

3   Return to the Lord, who will have mercy; *
    to our God, who will richly pardon.

4   'For my thoughts are not your thoughts, *
    neither are your ways my ways,' says the Lord.

5   'For as the heavens are higher than the earth, *
    so are my ways higher than your ways
        and my thoughts than your thoughts.

6 'As the rain and the snow come down from above, *
and return not again but water the earth,

7 'Bringing forth life and giving growth, *
seed for sowing and bread to eat,

8 'So is my word that goes forth from my mouth; *
it will not return to me fruitless,

9 'But it will accomplish that which I purpose, *
and succeed in the task I gave it.'

Glory . . . *Isaiah 55.6-11*

**Return to the Lord, who will have mercy,
to our God, who will richly pardon.**

In Christmas:

Either A SONG OF THE MESSIAH (7) or numbers 3, page 473, or 8, page 476

Refrain: **To us a child is born,
to us a son is given.**

1 The people who walked in darkness
have seen a great light; *
those who dwelt in a land of deep darkness,
upon them the light has dawned.

2 You have increased their joy
and given them great gladness; *
they rejoiced before you as with joy at the harvest.

3 For you have shattered the yoke that burdened them; *
the collar that lay heavy on their shoulders.

4 For to us a child is born and to us a son is given, *
and the government will be upon his shoulder.

5 And his name will be called: Wonderful Counsellor;
the Mighty God; *
the Everlasting Father; the Prince of Peace.

6 Of the increase of his government and of peace *
there will be no end,

7   Upon the throne of David and over his kingdom, *
    to establish and uphold it
        with justice and righteousness.

8   From this time forth and for evermore; *
    the zeal of the Lord of hosts will do this.

    Glory . . .   *Isaiah 9.2, 3b, 4a, 6, 7*

    **To us a child is born,
    to us a son is given.**

*On feasts of the BVM, numbers 3, page 473, 20, page 485, or 30, page 494, are
alternative canticles.*

THE SCRIPTURE READING(S)

A RESPONSORY may be said.

The Word of Life which was from the beginning,
we proclaim to you.

The darkness is passing away
and the true light is already shining:
the Word of Life which was from the beginning.

That which we heard, which we saw with our eyes
and touched with our hands,
we proclaim to you.

For our fellowship is with the Father
and with his Son, Jesus Christ our Lord.
**The Word of Life which was from the beginning,
we proclaim to you.**

                                                    from 1 John 1

THE GOSPEL CANTICLE: BENEDICTUS – THE SONG OF ZECHARIAH (41)

See either inside front cover, inside back cover or page 506 for another version.

In Ordinary Time:

Refrain: **You show mercy to our ancestors,
and remember your holy covenant.**

or, in Christmas:

> **To us is born a Saviour, who is Christ the Lord,**
> **and all the heavenly hosts now sing,**
> **Glory to God in the highest.**

or, on feasts of the BVM:

> **In the womb of Mary,**
> **you found a dwelling place on earth, O Christ;**
> **remain for ever in our hearts. (Alleluia.)**

The refrain is repeated after the canticle.

THE PRAYERS

INTERCESSIONS may be offered.

THE KYRIES may be used as responses to intercession.

Lord, have mercy.
Lord, have mercy.

Christ, have mercy.
Christ, have mercy.

Lord, have mercy.
Lord, have mercy.

THE COLLECT of the day or one of the following:

Almighty and everlasting God,
we thank you that you have brought us safely
to the beginning of this day.
Keep us from falling into sin
or running into danger,
order us in all our doings
and guide us to do always
what is righteous in your sight;
through Jesus Christ our Lord. **Amen.**

or, in Christmas:

Almighty God,
who wonderfully created us in your own image
and yet more wonderfully restored us
through your Son Jesus Christ:
grant that, as he came to share our humanity,
so we may share the life of his divinity;
who is alive and reigns with you,
in the unity of the Holy Spirit,
one God, now and for ever. **Amen.**

THE LORD'S PRAYER may be said.

[Rejoicing in the presence of God here among us,]
as our Saviour taught us, so we pray
Our Father in heaven, . . .

THE CONCLUSION

In Ordinary Time:

**The Lord bless us, and preserve us from all evil,
and keep us in eternal life. Amen.**

Let us bless the Lord.
Thanks be to God.

or, in Christmas:

**May God, who has called us out of darkness
into his marvellous light,
bless us and fill us with peace. Amen.**

Let us bless the Lord.
Thanks be to God.

or, on Class I & II Holy Days:

May our blessèd Lady pray for us.
May Saint Francis and Saint Clare pray for us.
[May Saint N pray for us.]
May all the saints of God pray for us.
May the angels of God befriend us
  and watch around us to protect us.
May the Lord Jesus give us his blessing of peace. Amen.

Let us bless the Lord. (Alleluia. Alleluia.)
Thanks be to God. (Alleluia. Alleluia.)

Form 4 – Midday Prayer
Wednesdays through the Year

Seasonal Propers are found beginning page 539.

THE PREPARATION

O God, make speed to save us.
O Lord, make haste to help us.

Glory . . .   **Alleluia.** *(Omitted in Lent)*

A HYMN may be sung, the following or some other.

Lord Christ, you came on us to shine
True light from the eternal Light!
And now the Father's brightness rests
On those who long have dwelt in night.

O see how all that lives and breathes
True homage gives in deed and word:
The glory of almighty God,
The Father's image, Christ our Lord.

Ordinary Time Doxology
We bless the Father, Fount of light,
And you, O Christ, belovèd Son,
Who, with the Spirit, dwell in us;
The only God; the Three in One. Amen.

*Panel of Monastic Musicians**

THE WORD OF GOD

THE PSALMODY

*Either **A:** PSALM 119.81-104*

11 Kaph

81 My soul is pining for your salvation; *
    I have hoped in your word.

82 My eyes fail with watching for your word, *
    while I say, 'O when will you comfort me?'

83   I have become like a wineskin in the smoke, *
       yet I do not forget your statutes.

84   How many are the days of your servant? *
       When will you bring judgement on those who persecute me?

85   The proud have dug pits for me *
       in defiance of your law.

86   All your commandments are true; *
       help me, for they persecute me with falsehood.

87   They had almost made an end of me on earth, *
       but I have not forsaken your commandments.

88   Give me life according to your loving-kindness; *
       so shall I keep the testimonies of your mouth.

12 Lamedh

89   O Lord, your word is everlasting; *
       it ever stands firm in the heavens.

90   Your faithfulness also remains from one generation to another; *
       you have established the earth and it abides.

91   So also your judgements stand firm this day, *
       for all things are your servants.

92   If your law had not been my delight, *
       I should have perished in my trouble.

93   I will never forget your commandments, *
       for by them you have given me life.

94   I am yours, O save me! *
       For I have sought your commandments.

95   The wicked have waited for me to destroy me, *
       but I will meditate on your testimonies.

96   I have seen an end of all perfection, *
       but your commandment knows no bounds.

13 Mem

97   Lord, how I love your law! *
       All the day long it is my study.

98   Your commandments have made me wiser than my enemies, *
      for they are ever with me.

99   I have more understanding than all my teachers, *
      for your testimonies are my meditation.

100 I am wiser than the aged, *
      because I keep your commandments.

101 I restrain my feet from every evil way, *
      that I may keep your word.

102 I have not turned aside from your judgements, *
      for you have been my teacher.

103 How sweet are your words on my tongue! *
      They are sweeter than honey to my mouth.

104 Through your commandments I get understanding; *
      therefore I hate all lying ways.

*or **B:** Psalms of Ascent*

PSALM 127

1   Unless the Lord builds the house, *
    those who build it labour in vain.

2   Unless the Lord keeps the city, *
    the guard keeps watch in vain.

3   It is in vain that you hasten to rise up early
      and go so late to rest, eating the bread of toil, *
    for he gives his beloved sleep.

4   Children are a heritage from the Lord *
    and the fruit of the womb is his gift.

5   Like arrows in the hand of a warrior, *
    so are the children of one's youth.

6   Happy are those who have their quiver full of them: *
    they shall not be put to shame
      when they dispute with their enemies in the gate.

1   Blessèd are all those who fear the Lord, *
    and walk in his ways.

2   You shall eat the fruit of the toil of your hands; *
    it shall go well with you, and happy shall you be.

3   Your wife within your house
        shall be like a fruitful vine; *
    your children round your table,
        like fresh olive branches.

4   Thus shall the one be blest *
    who fears the Lord.

5   The Lord from out of Zion bless you, *
    that you may see Jerusalem in prosperity
        all the days of your life.

6   May you see your children's children, *
    and may there be peace upon Israel.

The psalm, or group of psalms, may end with:

Glory . . .

THE READING

In Ordinary Time, week 1 begins on the first Sunday of the month and so on.

Either:
Week 1: Isaiah 61.1-3a
      2: Micah 4.1-4a
      3: Matthew 9.35-end
      4: John 18.33,36-38
      5: Habakkuk 2.14

or one of the following readings:

Jesus said to him, I am the way and the truth and the life. No one comes to
the Father except through me.   John 14.6

Blessèd are the merciful, for they will receive mercy.   *Matthew 5.7*

or some other suitable reading.

THE RESPONSE

In Ordinary Time:

*Either **A**:*

Come, you that are blessèd of my Father,
inherit the kingdom prepared for you.

I was hungry and you gave me food,
I was thirsty and you gave me drink,

I was a stranger and you welcomed me,
I was naked and you clothed me,

I was sick and you took care of me,
I was in prison and you visited me.

As you did it to one of the least,
you did it to me.

*or **B**:*

There are diversities of gifts but the same Spirit;
there are differences of service but the same Lord.

To one is given, by the Spirit, the word of wisdom:
to another the word of knowledge by the same Spirit.

To another faith, by the same Spirit:
to another gifts of healing, by the same Spirit.

The grace of our Lord Jesus Christ, and the love of God,
and the fellowship of the Holy Spirit,
be with us all evermore.

THE PRAYERS

INTERCESSIONS may be offered.

THE KYRIES may be used as responses to intercession.

Lord, have mercy.
Lord, have mercy.

Christ, have mercy.
Christ, have mercy.

Lord, have mercy.
Lord, have mercy.

THE COLLECT of the day or one of the following:

O Lord our God,
grant us grace to desire you with our whole heart;
that so desiring, we may seek and find you;
and so finding, may love you;
and so loving, may hate those sins from which
    you have delivered us;
through Jesus Christ our Lord. **Amen.**

Anselm (1109)

You are the holy Lord God
who does wonderful things.
You are strong, you are great.
You are the Most High, you are the almighty King.
You, holy Father, are King of heaven and earth.
You are three and one, the Lord God of gods.
You are the good, all good, the highest good,
Lord God living and true.
You are love, you are wisdom,
You are humility, you are patience,
You are security, you are rest,
You are gladness and joy, you are our hope,
You are justice, you are moderation,
You are all our riches and you suffice for us.
You are beauty, you are meekness,
You are the protector,
You are our guardian and defender.
You are strength, you are refreshment,
You are our faith, you are all our sweetness,
You are our eternal life:
great and wonderful Lord,
Almighty God, merciful Saviour. **Amen.**

The Praises of God, Francis of Assisi

THE LORD'S PRAYER may be said.

[Lord Jesus remember us in your kingdom
and teach us to pray.]
Our Father in heaven, . . .

Let us bless the Lord God living and true!
Let us always give him
praise, glory, honour, blessing and every good.
Amen. Amen. (Alleluia, alleluia.)

Prayer said by Francis of Assisi at the end of the office

Form 4 – Evening Prayer

Wednesday in Ordinary Time
and daily in Christmas Season

THE BLESSING OF THE LIGHT *may replace THE PREPARATION.*

A light, which may be the Paschal Candle, is brought in, or a candle may simply be lit.

In the beginning was the Word,
and the Word was with God and the Word was God.
In him was life, and the life was the light of all.

The light and peace of Jesus Christ be with you
and also with you.

Blessèd are you, Sovereign God,
our light and our salvation,
to you be glory and praise for ever.
To dispel the darkness of our night
you sent forth your Son, the firstborn of all creation,
to be the Christ, the light of the world.
Rejoicing in the mystery of the Word made flesh,
we acclaim him Emmanuel, as all creation sings to you:
Father, Son and Holy Spirit:
Blessèd be God for ever.

While the other candles are lit the following, or another version of number 63, page 524, or another suitable hymn may be sung.

A SONG OF THE LIGHT (63c)

1 **Hail, gladdening Light, of his pure glory poured,**
   Who is the immortal Father, heavenly, blest,
   Holiest of holies, Jesus Christ our Lord.

2 **Now we are come to the sun's hour of rest,**
   The lights of evening round us shine,
   We hymn the Father, Son and Holy Spirit divine.

3   **Worthy are you at all times to be sung**
       With undefilèd tongue,
       Son of our God, giver of life, alone:
       Therefore in all the world your glories,
          Lord, they own.

Verses from PSALM 141 may be said and incense may be burned.

Let my prayer rise before you as incense,
the lifting up of my hands as the evening sacrifice.

O Lord, I call to you; come to me quickly;
hear my voice when I cry to you.
Set a watch before my mouth, O Lord,
and guard the door of my lips.

Let my prayer rise before you as incense,
the lifting up of my hands as the evening sacrifice.

Let not my heart incline to any evil thing;
let me not be occupied in wickedness with evildoers.
But my eyes are turned to you, Lord God,
in you I take refuge;
do not leave me defenceless.

Let my prayer rise before you as incense,
the lifting up of my hands as the evening sacrifice.

Psalm 141.1-4b,8

This prayer may be said.

That this evening may be holy, good and peaceful,
let us pray with one heart and mind.
(Silence may be kept.)

As our evening prayer rises before you, O God,
so may your mercy come down upon us
   to cleanse our hearts
and set us free to sing your praise,
now and for ever. Amen.

Evening Prayer continues with the appointed Psalmody.

THE PREPARATION

O God, make speed to save us.
O Lord, make haste to help us.

You laid the foundation of the earth
and the heavens are the work of your hands.

Glory . . .   Alleluia.

THE OPENING CANTICLE

A SONG OF GOD'S DESCENDING

1   I love you, O Lord my strength. *
     The Lord is my crag, my fortress and my deliverer.

2   In my distress I called upon the Lord *
     and cried out to my God for help.

3   He heard my voice in his temple *
     and my cry came to his ears.

4   He parted the heavens and came down *
     and thick darkness was under his feet.

5   He rode upon the cherubim and flew; *
     he came flying on the wings of the wind.

6   He made darkness his covering round about him, *
     dark waters and thick clouds his pavilion.

7   From the brightness of his presence, through the clouds *
     burst hailstones and coals of fire.

8   The Lord also thundered out of heaven; *
     the Most High uttered his voice
         with hailstones and coals of fire.

9   For you will save a lowly people *
     and bring down the high looks of the proud.

10   You also shall light my candle; *
     the Lord my God shall make my darkness to be bright.

11   As for God, his way is perfect;
         the word of the Lord is tried in the fire; *
     he is a shield to all who trust in him.

A HYMN may be sung.

THE OPENING PRAYER may be said.

That this evening may be holy, good and peaceful,
let us pray with one heart and mind.
(Silence may be kept.)

As your word, O Lord,
  gives light to our path,
may we behold the glory of your presence
and so rejoice to sing your praise,
now and for ever. Amen.

THE WORD OF GOD

THE PSALMODY, as appointed

Each psalm, or group of psalms, may end with:

Glory . . .

*If there are two SCRIPTURE READINGS, the first may be read here, or both may
be read after the Second Canticle.*

THE SECOND CANTICLE

In Ordinary Time:

Either A SONG OF GOD'S LOVE (54) or number 55, page 517

Refrain: **God's love was revealed among us**
       so that we might live through Jesus.

1   Beloved, let us love one another,
     for love is of God; *
    everyone who loves is born of God and knows God.

2   Whoever does not love does not know God, *
    for God is love.

3   In this the love of God was revealed among us, *
    that God sent his only Son into the world,
        so that we might live through him.

4   In this is love,
        not that we loved God but that he loved us, *
    and sent his Son to be the expiation for our sins.

5   Beloved, since God loved us so much, *
    we ought also to love one another.

6   For if we love one another, God abides in us, *
    and God's love will be perfected in us.

   Glory . . .   *1 John 4.7-11,12b*

   **God's love was revealed among us
   so that we might live through Jesus.**

In Christmas:

*Either A SONG OF REDEMPTION (48) or numbers 59, page 520, or 73,
page 536*

Refrain: **Christ is the image of the invisible God,
        the firstborn of all creation.**

1   The Father has delivered us from the dominion of darkness, *
    and transferred us to the kingdom of his beloved Son;

2   In whom we have redemption, *
    the forgiveness of our sins.

3   He is the image of the invisible God, *
    the firstborn of all creation.

4   For in him all things were created, *
    in heaven and on earth, visible and invisible.

5   All things were created through him and for him, *
    he is before all things and in him all things hold together.

6   He is the head of the body, the Church, *
    he is the beginning, the firstborn from the dead.

7   In him all the fullness of God was pleased to dwell; *
    and through him God was pleased to reconcile all things.

Glory . . .   *Colossians 1.13-18a,19,20a*

**Christ is the image of the invisible God,
the firstborn of all creation.**

*On feasts of the BVM, numbers 59, page 520, and 72, page 535, are alternative
canticles.*

THE SCRIPTURE READING(S)

A RESPONSORY may be said.

Your salvation is near to those who fear you,
that glory may dwell in our land.
**Your salvation is near to those who fear you,
that glory may dwell in our land.**

Mercy and truth have met together;
righteousness and peace have kissed each other.
That glory may dwell in our land.

Glory to the Father and to the Son
and to the Holy Spirit.
**Your salvation is near to those who fear you;
that glory may dwell in our land.**

from Psalm 85

THE GOSPEL CANTICLE: MAGNIFICAT – THE SONG OF MARY (40)

See either inside front cover, inside back cover or page 504 for another version.

In Ordinary Time:

Refrain: **Remember your promise of mercy,
to Abraham and his children for ever.**

or, in Christmas:

**When peaceful silence lay over all,
and night was in the midst of her swift course:
from your royal throne O God, down from the heavens,
leapt your almighty Word.**

Form 4, Evening   145

**Mary gave birth to the Word of God;
truly she is the ever-blessèd Mother
of Christ our Lord. (Alleluia.)**

The refrain is repeated after the canticle.

THE PRAYERS

INTERCESSIONS may be offered.

THE KYRIES may be used as responses to intercession.

Lord, have mercy.
Lord, have mercy.

Christ, have mercy.
Christ, have mercy.

Lord, have mercy.
Lord, have mercy.

THE COLLECT of the day or one of the following:

Eternal Lord,
our beginning and our end:
bring us with the whole creation
to your glory, hidden through past ages
and made known
in Jesus Christ our Lord. **Amen.**

or, in Christmas:

Almighty God,
who wonderfully created us in your own image
and yet more wonderfully restored us
through your Son Jesus Christ:
grant that, as he came to share our humanity,
so we may share the life of his divinity;
who is alive and reigns with you,
in the unity of the Holy Spirit,
one God, now and for ever. **Amen.**

THE LORD'S PRAYER may be said.

[Rejoicing in the presence of God here among us,]
as our Saviour taught us, so we pray
Our Father in heaven, . . .

THE CONCLUSION

In Ordinary Time:

**The grace of our Lord Jesus Christ,
and the love of God,
and the fellowship of the Holy Spirit,
be with us all evermore. Amen.**

Let us bless the Lord.
Thanks be to God.

or, in Christmas:

**May God, who has called us out of darkness
into his marvellous light,
bless us and fill us with peace. Amen.**

Let us bless the Lord.
Thanks be to God.

or, on Class I & II Holy Days:

May our blessèd Lady pray for us.
May Saint Francis and Saint Clare pray for us.
[May Saint N pray for us.]
May all the saints of God pray for us.
May the angels of God befriend us
    and watch around us to protect us.
May the Lord Jesus give us his blessing of peace. Amen.

Let us bless the Lord. (Alleluia. Alleluia.)
Thanks be to God. (Alleluia. Alleluia.)

Form 4 – Night Prayer

Wednesdays in Ordinary Time and daily in Christmas Season

THE PREPARATION

The Lord almighty grant us a quiet night and a perfect end.
Amen.

Our help is in the name of the Lord
who made heaven and earth.

A period of silence for reflection on the past day may follow.
The following or other suitable words of penitence may be used.

Most merciful God,
we confess to you,
before the whole company of heaven
  and one another,
that we have sinned in thought, word and deed,
and in what we have failed to do.
Forgive us our sins,
heal us by your Spirit
and raise us to new life in Christ. Amen.

or:

Holy God,
holy and strong,
holy and immortal:
have mercy on us.

O God, make speed to save us.
O Lord, make haste to help us.

Glory . . .   Alleluia.

The following or another suitable HYMN may be sung.

Before the ending of the day,
Creator of the world, we pray
That you, with steadfast love, would keep
Your watch around us while we sleep.

From evil dreams defend our sight,
From fears and terrors of the night;
Tread under foot our deadly foe
That we no sinful thought may know.

Ordinary Time Doxology
O Father, that we ask be done
Through Jesus Christ, your only Son;
And Holy Spirit, by whose breath
Our souls are raised to life from death. Amen.

Christmas and feasts of the BVM Doxology
Lord Jesus, King of heaven and earth:
We praise you for your virgin birth;
You are the Father's only Son,
With God the Spirit, ever one. Amen.

THE WORD OF GOD

THE PSALMODY

Psalm 31.1-5,19-24

1   In you, O Lord, have I taken refuge;
        let me never be put to shame; *
     deliver me in your righteousness.

2   Incline your ear to me; *
     make haste to deliver me.

3   Be my strong rock, a fortress to save me,
        for you are my rock and my stronghold; *
     guide me, and lead me for your name's sake.

4   Take me out of the net
        that they have laid secretly for me, *
     for you are my strength.

5   Into your hands I commend my spirit, *
    for you have redeemed me, O Lord God of truth.

6   How abundant is your goodness, O Lord,
        which you have laid up for those who fear you; *
    which you have prepared in the sight of all
        for those who put their trust in you.

7   You hide them in the shelter of your presence
        from those who slander them; *
    you keep them safe in your refuge from the strife of tongues.

8   Blessèd be the Lord! *
    For he has shown me his steadfast love
        when I was as a city besieged.

9   I had said in my alarm,
        'I have been cut off from the sight of your eyes.' *
    Nevertheless, you heard the voice of my prayer
        when I cried out to you.

10 Love the Lord, all you his servants; *
    for the Lord protects the faithful,
        but repays to the full the proud.

11 Be strong and let your heart take courage, *
    all you who wait in hope for the Lord.

    Glory . . .

THE READING: one of the following or some other.

Either, in Ordinary Time:

Humble yourselves under the mighty hand of God, so that he may exalt you
in due time. Cast all your anxiety on him, because he cares for you.

1 Peter.5.6,7

or, in Christmas:

In him was life and the life was the light of all people. The light shines in the
darkness and the darkness did not overcome it.

John 1.4-5

or, on feasts of the BVM:

Mary said, 'Here am I, the servant of the Lord; let it be with me according to your word'.

Luke 1.38a

THE RESPONSORY may be said.

Into your hands, O Lord,
I commend my spirit. (Alleluia, alleluia)
Into your hands, O Lord,
I commend my spirit. (Alleluia, alleluia.)

For you have redeemed me, Lord God of truth.
I commend my spirit. (*or:* Alleluia, alleluia.)

Glory to the Father and to the Son
and to the Holy Spirit:
Into your hands, O Lord,
I commend my spirit. (Alleluia, alleluia.)

Keep me as the apple of your eye.
Hide me under the shadow of your wings.

THE GOSPEL CANTICLE: NUNC DIMITTIS – THE SONG OF SIMEON (42) or another version on page 508

Refrain: **Save us, O Lord, while waking,**
and guard us while sleeping,
that awake we may watch with Christ,
and asleep may rest in peace.

or, in Christmas:

Alleluia. The Word was made flesh, alleluia,
and dwelt among us. Alleluia, alleluia.

or, on feasts of the BVM:

Blessèd is she whose soul was pierced
by the sword of the cross.

> **Grant us your light, O Lord,**
> **that the darkness of our hearts being overcome,**
> **we may receive the true light,**
> **even Christ our Saviour. (Alleluia.)**

1   ✠ Now, Lord, you let your servant go in peace: *
     your word has been fulfilled.

2   My own eyes have seen the salvation *
     which you have prepared in the sight of every people:

3   A light to reveal you to the nations *
     and the glory of your people Israel.

Luke 2.29-32

Glory . . .

The refrain is repeated after the canticle.

THE PRAYERS

Intercessions and thanksgivings may be offered here.

THE COLLECT: one of the following or some other.

Either, in Ordinary Time:

Visit this house, O Lord, we pray,
drive far from it all the snares of the enemy;
may your holy angels dwell with us
    and guard us in peace
and may your blessing be always upon us;
through Jesus Christ our Lord. **Amen.**

or:

Lighten our darkness,
Lord, we pray;
and in your mercy defend us from all perils
    and dangers of this night;
for the love of your only Son,
our Saviour Jesus Christ. **Amen.**

or, in Christmas and on feasts of the BVM:

We give you thanks, O God,
for the gift to the world of our Redeemer;
as we sing your glory at the close of this day,
so may we know his presence in our hearts,
who is our Saviour and our Lord,
now and for ever. **Amen.**

THE LORD'S PRAYER may be said.

[As we come to the ending of the day,]
as our Saviour taught us, so we pray
Our Father in heaven, . . .

THE CONCLUSION

In peace, we will lie down and sleep;
for you alone, Lord, make us dwell in safety.

Abide with us, Lord Jesus,
for the night is at hand and the day is now past.

As the night-watch looks for the morning,
so do we look for you, O Christ.

[Come with the dawning of the day
**and make yourself known
in the breaking of the bread.**]

Either, in Ordinary Time:

**The Lord bless us and watch over us,
the Lord make his face shine upon us
    and be gracious to us,
the Lord look kindly on us and give us peace. Amen.**

or, in Christmas and on feasts of the BVM:

**May the love of the Word made flesh enfold us,
his joy fill our lives,
his peace be in our hearts;
and the blessing of God be with us
this night and always. Amen.**

A MARIAN ANTHEM may be sung.

SALVE REGINA

Traditionally, this anthem is sung at the end of Night Prayer from after Pentecost to Advent; or it may be the unchanging final anthem. The other Marian anthems may be found on page 775.

Salve, Regina, mater misericordiae;
vita, dulcedo, et spes nostra, salve.
Ad te clamamus, exsules, filii Evae,
ad te suspiramus,
gementes et flentes in hac lacrimarum valle;
eia ergo, advocata nostra,
illos tuos misericordes oculos ad nos converte,
Et Iesum, benedictum fructum ventris tui,
nobis post hoc exsilium ostende.
O clemens, O pia, O dulcis Virgo Maria.

Form 5 – Morning Prayer

Thursdays in Ordinary Time and daily in Epiphany Season

THE PREPARATION

A *is used on Thursdays in Ordinary Time.*
B *is used daily in Epiphany season and on specified Class I & II Holy Days.*

A:

O Lord, open our lips
and our mouth shall proclaim your praise.

From the rising of the sun to its setting
your glory is proclaimed in all the world.

Glory . . .   Alleluia.

Morning Prayer continues with THE OPENING CANTICLE.

B:

O Lord, open our lips
and our mouth shall proclaim your praise.

Blessèd are you, Sovereign God,
king of the nations,
to you be praise and glory for ever!
From the rising of the sun to its setting
your name is proclaimed in all the world.
As the Sun of Righteousness dawns in our hearts,
anoint our lips with the seal of your Spirit
that we may witness to your gospel
and sing your praise in all the earth,
Father, Son and Holy Spirit:
Blessèd be God for ever.

The following is said:

In Epiphany:

God in Christ has revealed his glory.
O come, let us worship.

or, on feasts of Teachers of the Faith:

(Alleluia.) Christ speaks the truth in every age.
O come, let us worship. (Alleluia.)

or, on feasts of Bishops and other Pastors:

(Alleluia.) Christ feeds his flock in every age.
O come, let us worship. (Alleluia.)

THE OPENING CANTICLE

JUBILATE – A SONG OF JOY

1   O be joyful in the Lord, all the earth; *
      serve the Lord with gladness
          and come before his presence with a song.

2   Know that the Lord is God; *
      it is he that has made us and we are his;
          we are his people and the sheep of his pasture.

3   Enter his gates with thanksgiving
          and his courts with praise; *
      give thanks to him and bless his name.

4   For the Lord is gracious; his steadfast love is everlasting, *
      and his faithfulness endures from generation to generation.

      Glory . . .   *Psalm 100*

A HYMN may be sung.

THE OPENING PRAYER may be said.

The night has passed and the day lies open before us;
let us pray with one heart and mind:
(Silence may be kept.)

As we rejoice in the gift of this new day,
so may the light of your presence, O God,
set our hearts on fire with love for you;
now and for ever. Amen.

THE WORD OF GOD

THE PSALMODY, as appointed

Each psalm, or group of psalms, may end with:

Glory . . .

*If there are two SCRIPTURE READINGS, the first may be read here, or both may
be read after the Second Canticle.*

THE SECOND CANTICLE

In Ordinary Time:

Either A SONG OF THE COVENANT (13) or number 26, page 491

Refrain: **I have given you as a light to the nations,
and I have called you in righteousness.**

1   Thus says God, who created the heavens, *
who fashioned the earth and all that dwells in it;

2   Who gives breath to the people upon It †
and spirit to those who walk in it,

3   'I am the Lord and I have called you in righteousness, *
I have taken you by the hand and kept you;

4   'I have given you as a covenant to the people, *
a light to the nations, to open the eyes that are blind,

5   'To bring out the captives from the dungeon, *
from the prison, those who sit in darkness.

6   'I am the Lord, that is my name; *
my glory I give to no other.'

     Glory . . .   *Isaiah 42.5-8a*

     **I have given you as a light to the nations,
and I have called you in righteousness.**

In Epiphany:

Either A SONG OF THE NEW JERUSALEM (16) or numbers 13 above or 18, page 484

Refrain: **Above you the Holy One arises,
and above you God's glory appears.**

1   Arise, shine out, for your light has come, *
the glory of the Lord is rising upon you.

2   Though night still covers the earth, *
and darkness the peoples;

3   Above you the Holy One arises, *
and above you God's glory appears.

4   The nations will come to your light, *
and kings to your dawning brightness.

5   Your gates will lie open continually, *
shut neither by day nor by night.

6   The sound of violence
shall be heard no longer in your land, *
or ruin and devastation within your borders.

7   You will call your walls, Salvation, *
and your gates, Praise.

8   No more will the sun give you daylight, *
nor moonlight shine upon you;

9   But the Lord will be your everlasting light, *
your God will be your splendour.

10 For you shall be called the city of God, *
the dwelling of the Holy One of Israel.

Glory . . .   *Isaiah 60.1-3,11a,18,19,14b*

**Above you the Holy One arises,
and above you God's glory appears.**

On feasts of Teachers of the Faith, numbers 29, page 493, and 30, page 494, are alternative canticles.

On feasts of Bishops and other Pastors, number 31, page 495, is an alternative canticle.

THE SCRIPTURE READING(S)

A RESPONSORY may be said.

O worship the Lord in the beauty of holiness;
let the whole earth tremble before him.

Tell it out among the nations that the Lord is King.
O worship the Lord in the beauty of holiness.

Tell out his salvation from day to day.
Let the whole earth tremble before him.

Declare his glory among the nations
and his wonders among all peoples.
**O worship the Lord in the beauty of holiness;
let the whole earth tremble before him.**

from Psalm 96

THE GOSPEL CANTICLE: BENEDICTUS – THE SONG OF ZECHARIAH (41)

See either inside front cover, inside back cover or page 506 for another version.

In Ordinary Time.

Refrain: **You promised, O God, to save us from our enemies,
from the hands of all that hate us.**

or, in Epiphany:

> **This is the Christ, the Chosen of God,
> the one who will bring healing to the nations.**

or, on feasts of Teachers of the Faith:

> **Those who are wise will shine as brightly as the heavens,
> and those who have instructed many in virtue
> will shine like stars for all eternity. (Alleluia.)**

or, on feasts of Bishops and other Pastors:

> **I will give you shepherds after my own heart
> who will feed you with knowledge
> and understanding. (Alleluia.)**

The refrain is repeated after the canticle.

THE PRAYERS

INTERCESSIONS may be offered.

THE KYRIES may be used as responses to intercession.

Lord, have mercy.
Lord, have mercy.

Christ, have mercy.
Christ, have mercy.

Lord, have mercy.
Lord, have mercy.

THE COLLECT of the day or one of the following:.

O God, the author of peace
and lover of concord,
whom to know is eternal life,
whose service is perfect freedom:
defend us your servants
from all assaults of our enemies,
that we, surely trusting in your defence,
may not fear the power of any adversaries;
through Jesus Christ our Lord. **Amen.**

or, in Epiphany:

Almighty God,
in Christ you make all things new:
transform the poverty of our nature by the riches of your grace,
and in the renewal of our lives
make known your heavenly glory;
through Jesus Christ our Lord. **Amen.**

THE LORD'S PRAYER may be said.

[Praying for the unity of all peoples on earth,]
as our Saviour taught us, so we pray
Our Father in heaven, . . .

In Ordinary Time:

**The Lord bless us, and preserve us from all evil,
and keep us in eternal life. Amen.**

Let us bless the Lord.
Thanks be to God.

or, in Epiphany:

**May Christ, who sends us to the nations,
give us the power of his Spirit. Amen.**

Let us bless the Lord.
Thanks be to God.

or, on Class I & II Holy Days:

May our blessèd Lady pray for us.
May Saint Francis and Saint Clare pray for us.
[May Saint N pray for us.]
May all the saints of God pray for us.
May the angels of God befriend us
    and watch around us to protect us.
May the Lord Jesus give us his blessing of peace. Amen.

Let us bless the Lord. (Alleluia. Alleluia)
Thanks be to God. (Alleluia. Alleluia.)

Form 5 – Midday Prayer
Thursdays through the Year

Seasonal Propers are found beginning page 539.

THE PREPARATION

O God, make speed to save us.
O Lord, make haste to help us.

Glory . . .   **Alleluia.** *(Omitted in Lent)*

A HYMN may be sung, the following or some other.

O God, creation's secret force,
Yourself unmoved, all motion's source,
Who from the morn till evening's ray
Through all its changes guide the day.

Grant us, when this short life is past
The glorious evening that shall last,
That, by a holy death attained,
Eternal glory may be gained.

Ordinary Time Doxology
O Father, that we ask be done
Through Jesus Christ, your only Son,
Who, with the Spirit, reigns above,
Three Persons in one God of love. Amen.

tr. Order of the Holy Cross, New York

THE WORD OF GOD

THE PSALMODY

Either A: PSALM 119.105-128

14 Nun

105   Your word is a lantern to my feet *
         and a light upon my path.

106   I have sworn and will fulfil it, *
         to keep your righteous judgements.

107 I am troubled above measure; *
give me life, O Lord, according to your word.

108 Accept the freewill offering of my mouth, O Lord, *
and teach me your judgements.

109 My soul is ever in my hand, *
yet I do not forget your law.

110 The wicked have laid a snare for me, *
but I have not strayed from your commandments.

111 Your testimonies have I claimed as my heritage for ever; *
for they are the very joy of my heart.

112 I have applied my heart to fulfil your statutes: *
always, even to the end.

15 Samekh

113 I hate those who are double-minded, *
but your law do I love.

114 You are my hiding place and my shield *
and my hope is in your word.

115 Away from me, you wicked! *
I will keep the commandments of my God.

116 Sustain me according to your promise, that I may live, *
and let me not be disappointed in my hope.

117 Hold me up and I shall be saved, *
and my delight shall be ever in your statutes.

118 You set at nought those who depart from your statutes, *
for their deceiving is in vain.

119 You consider all the wicked as dross; *
therefore I love your testimonies.

120 My flesh trembles for fear of you *
and I am afraid of your judgements.

16 Ayin

121 I have done what is just and right; *
O give me not over to my oppressors.

122 Stand surety for your servant's good; *
let not the proud oppress me.

123 My eyes fail with watching for your salvation *
and for your righteous promise.

124 O deal with your servant according to your faithful love *
and teach me your statutes.

125 I am your servant; O grant me understanding, *
that I may know your testimonies.

126 It is time for you to act, O Lord, *
for they frustrate your law.

127 Therefore I love your commandments *
above gold, even much fine gold.

128 Therefore I direct my steps by all your precepts, *
and all false ways I utterly abhor.

or B: Psalm of Ascent

PSALM 132

1 Lord, remember for David *
all the hardships he endured;

2 How he swore an oath to the Lord *
and vowed a vow to the Mighty One of Jacob:

3 'I will not come within the shelter of my house, *
nor climb up into my bed;

4 'I will not allow my eyes to sleep, *
nor let my eyelids slumber,

5 'Until I find a place for the Lord, *
a dwelling for the Mighty One of Jacob.'

6 Now, we heard of the ark in Ephrathah *
and found it in the fields of Ja-ar.

7   Let us enter his dwelling place *
    and fall low before his footstool.

8   Arise, O Lord, into your resting place, *
    you and the ark of your strength.

9   Let your priests be clothed with righteousness *
    and your faithful ones sing with joy.

10 For your servant David's sake, *
    turn not away the face of your anointed.

11 The Lord has sworn an oath to David, *
    a promise from which he will not shrink:

12 'Of the fruit of your body *
    shall I set upon your throne.

13 'If your children keep my covenant
        and my testimonies that I shall teach them, *
    their children also shall sit upon your throne for evermore.'

14 For the Lord has chosen Zion for himself; *
    he has desired her for his habitation:

15 'This shall be my resting place for ever; *
    here will I dwell, for I have longed for her.

16 'I will abundantly bless her provision; *
    her poor will I satisfy with bread.

17 'I will clothe her priests with salvation, *
    and her faithful ones shall rejoice and sing.

18 'There will I make a horn to spring up for David; *
    I will keep a lantern burning for my anointed.

19 'As for his enemies, I will clothe them with shame; *
    but on him shall his crown be bright.'

Each psalm, or group of psalms, may end with:

Glory . . .

THE READING

In Ordinary Time, week 1 begins on the first Sunday of the month and so on.

Either:

Week 1: Deuteronomy 15.7,8,10,11
     2: Isaiah 43.5-7
     3: 1Peter 2.9,10
     4: John 17.18-23
     5: 1Corinthians 12.12,13a

or one of the following readings:

Jesus said to them, I am the gate for the sheep. I came that they may have life, and have it abundantly.

John 10.7,10b

Blessed are the peacemakers, for they will be called children of God.

Matthew 5.9

or some other suitable reading.

THE RESPONSE

In Ordinary Time:

*Either **A**:*

Let us keep the unity of the Spirit in the bond of peace,
for there is one body and one Spirit,
   one hope of our calling.

There is one Lord, one faith, one baptism,
one God and Father of us all.

Grace was given to each of us
according to the measure of the gift of Christ.

He gave some to be apostles, some prophets,
   evangelists, pastors and teachers,
for building up the body of Christ.

Until we all attain to the unity of the faith,
to the knowledge of the Son of God.

No longer shall we be children, but fully mature,
measured by the stature of the fullness of Christ.

*or **B**:*

The Lord will bring us to his holy mountain
and make us joyful in his house of prayer.

Enter the gates of the Lord with thanksgiving.
Walk into his courts with praise.

All our offerings and sacrifices
will be accepted on your altar.

For your house shall be called
a house of prayer for all peoples.

THE PRAYERS

INTERCESSIONS may be offered.

THE KYRIES may be used as responses to intercession.

Lord, have mercy.
Lord, have mercy.

Christ, have mercy.
Christ, have mercy.

Lord, have mercy.
Lord, have mercy.

THE COLLECT of the day or one of the following:

O gracious and holy Father,
give us wisdom to perceive you,
diligence to seek you,
patience to wait for you,
eyes to behold you,
a heart to meditate upon you,
and a life to proclaim you,
through the power of the Spirit
of Jesus Christ our Lord. **Amen.**

Benedict of Nursia (c. 550)

Most High and glorious God,
enlighten the darkness of our hearts
and give us a true faith, a certain hope
and a perfect love.
Give us a sense of the divine
and knowledge of yourself,
so that we may do everything
in fulfilment of your holy will;
through Jesus Christ our Lord. **Amen.**

The Prayer before the Crucifix, Francis of Assisi

THE LORD'S PRAYER may be said.

[Lord Jesus remember us in your kingdom
and teach us to pray.]
Our Father in heaven, . . .

THE CONCLUSION

Let us bless the Lord God living and true!
Let us always give him
praise, glory, honour, blessing and every good.
Amen. Amen. (Alleluia, alleluia.)

Prayer said by Francis of Assisi at the end of the office

Form 5 – Evening Prayer

Thursdays in Ordinary Time and daily in Epiphany Season

THE BLESSING OF THE LIGHT *may replace THE PREPARATION.*

A light, which may be the Paschal Candle, is brought in, or a candle may simply be lit.

Jesus Christ is the light of the world,
a light no darkness can quench.

The light and peace of Jesus Christ be with you
and also with you.

Blessèd are you, Sovereign God,
our light and our salvation,
to you be glory and praise for ever.
You gave your Christ as a light to the nations,
and through the anointing of the Spirit
you established us as a royal priesthood.
As you call us into your marvellous light,
may our lives bear witness to your truth
and our lips never cease to proclaim your praise,
Father, Son and Holy Spirit:
Blessèd be God for ever.

While the other candles are lit the following, or another version of number 63, page 524, or another suitable hymn may be sung.

A SONG OF THE LIGHT (63c)

1   **Hail, gladdening Light, of his pure glory poured,**
    Who is the immortal Father, heavenly, blest,
    Holiest of holies, Jesus Christ our Lord.

2   **Now we are come to the sun's hour of rest,**
    The lights of evening round us shine,
    We hymn the Father, Son and Holy Spirit divine.

3   **Worthy are you at all times to be sung**
    With undefilèd tongue,
    Son of our God, giver of life, alone:
    Therefore in all the world your glories,
      Lord, they own.

Verses from PSALM 141 may be said and incense may be burned.

Let my prayer rise before you as incense,
the lifting up of my hands as the evening sacrifice.

O Lord, I call to you; come to me quickly;
hear my voice when I cry to you.
Set a watch before my mouth, O Lord,
and guard the door of my lips.

Let my prayer rise before you as incense,
the lifting up of my hands as the evening sacrifice.

Let not my heart incline to any evil thing;
let me not be occupied in wickedness with evildoers.
But my eyes are turned to you, Lord God,
in you I take refuge;
do not leave me defenceless.

Let my prayer rise before you as incense,
the lifting up of my hands as the evening sacrifice.

Psalm 141.1-4b,8

This prayer may be said:

That this evening may be holy, good and peaceful,
let us pray with one heart and mind.
(Silence may be kept.)

As our evening prayer rises before you, O God,
so may your mercy come down upon us
   to cleanse our hearts
and set us free to sing your praise,
now and for ever. Amen.

Evening Prayer continues with the appointed Psalmody.

THE PREPARATION

O God, make speed to save us.
O Lord, make haste to help us.

From the rising of the sun to its setting
your glory is proclaimed in all the world.

Glory . . .   Alleluia.

THE OPENING CANTICLE

A SONG OF GOD'S SPLENDOUR

1   Sing to the Lord a new song; *
    sing to the Lord, all the earth.

2   Sing to the Lord and bless his name; *
    tell out his salvation from day to day.

3   Declare his glory among the nations *
    and his wonders among all peoples.

4   Honour and majesty are before him; *
    power and splendour are in his sanctuary.

5   Ascribe to the Lord, you families of the peoples; *
    ascribe to the Lord honour and strength.

6   Ascribe to the Lord the honour due to his name; *
    bring offerings and come into his courts.

7   O worship the Lord in the beauty of holiness; *
    let the whole earth tremble before him.

8   Tell it out among the nations that the Lord is king. *
    with righteousness he will judge the world
        and the peoples with his truth.

    Glory . . .

Psalm 96.1-3,6-10a,13b

A HYMN may be sung.

THE OPENING PRAYER may be said.

That this evening may be holy, good and peaceful,
let us pray with one heart and mind.
(Silence may be kept.)

**As you call us into your marvellous light, O God,
may our lives bear witness to your truth
and our lips never cease to proclaim your praise,
now and for ever. Amen.**

THE WORD OF GOD

THE PSALMODY, as appointed

Each psalm, or group of psalms, may end with:

Glory . . .

*If there are two SCRIPTURE READINGS, the first may be read here, or both may
be read after the Second Canticle.*

THE SECOND CANTICLE

In Ordinary Time:

Either A SONG OF PRAISE (55) or number 49, page 513

Refrain: **You created all things, O God,
and are worthy of our praise for ever.**

1   You are worthy, our Lord and God, *
    to receive glory and honour and power.

2   For you have created all things, *
    and by your will they have their being.

3   You are worthy, O Lamb, for you were slain, *
    and by your blood you ransomed for God
    saints from every tribe and language and nation.

4   You have made them to be a kingdom and priests
       serving our God, *
    and they will reign with you on earth.

To the One who sits on the throne and to the Lamb *
be blessing and honour and glory and might,
for ever and ever. Amen.

Revelation 4.11; 5.9b,10

You created all things, O God,
and are worthy of our praise for ever.

In Epiphany:

Either GREAT AND WONDERFUL (57) or numbers 49, page 513, or 65,
page 528

Refrain: **All nations shall come and worship you, O Christ,**
and share in the feast of your kingdom.

1   Great and wonderful are your deeds, *
    Lord God the Almighty.

2   Just and true are your ways, *
    O ruler of the nations.

3   Who shall not revere and praise your name, O Lord? *
    for you alone are holy.

4   All nations shall come and worship in your presence: *
    for your just dealings have been revealed.

To the One who sits on the throne and to the Lamb *
be blessing and honour and glory and might,
for ever and ever. Amen.

Revelation 15.3,4

All nations shall come and worship you, O Christ,
and share in the feast of your kingdom.

On feasts of Teachers of the Faith, numbers 39, page 502, and 53, page 515,
are alternative canticles.

On feasts of Bishops and other Pastors, numbers 47, page 512, and 54,
page 516, are alternative canticles.

THE SCRIPTURE READING(S)

A RESPONSORY may be said.

Arise, shine, for your light has come;
the glory of the Lord is rising upon you.
Arise, shine, for your light has come;
the glory of the Lord is rising upon you.

God's salvation has been openly shown to all people.
The glory of the Lord is rising upon you.

Glory to the Father and to the Son
and to the Holy Spirit.
Arise, shine, for your light has come;
the glory of the Lord is rising upon you.

from Isaiah 60

THE GOSPEL CANTICLE: MAGNIFICAT – THE SONG OF MARY (40)

See either inside front cover, inside back cover or page 504 for another version.

In Ordinary Time:

Refrain: **You have filled the hungry with good things,**
and sent the rich away empty.

or, in Epiphany:

Behold, my servant, whom I uphold,
my chosen, in whom my soul delights;
the anointed one on whom my Spirit rests.

or, on feasts of Teachers of the Faith:

Those who keep and teach the commandments
will be considered great in heaven. (Alleluia.)

or, on feasts of Bishops and other Pastors:

Well done, good and faithful servant:
you have been faithful over a little:
I will make you ruler over much. (Alleluia.)

The refrain is repeated after the canticle.

THE PRAYERS

INTERCESSIONS may be offered.

THE KYRIES may be used as responses to intercession.

Lord, have mercy.
Lord, have mercy.

Christ, have mercy.
Christ, have mercy.

Lord, have mercy.
Lord, have mercy.

THE COLLECT of the day or one of the following:

O God,
the source of all good desires,
all right judgements and all just works:
give to your servants that peace
    which the world cannot give;
that our hearts may be set to obey
    your commandments
and that, freed from the fear of our enemies,
we may pass our time in rest and quietness;
through Jesus Christ our Lord. **Amen.**

or, in Epiphany:

Almighty God,
in Christ you make all things new:
transform the poverty of our nature
by the riches of your grace,
and in the renewal of our lives
make known your heavenly glory;
through Jesus Christ our Lord. **Amen.**

THE LORD'S PRAYER may be said.

[Praying for the unity of all peoples on earth,]
as our Saviour taught us, so we pray
Our Father in heaven, . . .

THE CONCLUSION

In Ordinary Time:

**The grace of our Lord Jesus Christ,
and the love of God,
and the fellowship of the Holy Spirit,
be with us all evermore. Amen.**

Let us bless the Lord.
Thanks be to God.

or, in Epiphany:

**May Christ, who sends us to the nations,
give us the power of his Spirit. Amen.**

Let us bless the Lord.
Thanks be to God.

or, on Class I & II Holy Days:

May our blessèd Lady pray for us.
May Saint Francis and Saint Clare pray for us.
[May Saint N pray for us.]
May all the saints of God pray for us.
May the angels of God befriend us
     and watch around us to protect us.
May the Lord Jesus give us his blessing of peace. Amen.

Let us bless the Lord. (Alleluia, Alleluia.)
Thanks be to God. (Alleluia, Alleluia.)

Form 5 – Night Prayer

Thursdays in Ordinary Time
and daily in Epiphany Season

THE PREPARATION

The Lord almighty grant us a quiet night and a perfect end.
Amen.

Our help is in the name of the Lord
who made heaven and earth.

A period of silence for reflection on the past day may follow.
The following or other suitable words of penitence may be used.

Holy God,
we confess to you before the company
**   of the faithful in heaven and on earth,**
that we have sinned against you,
against one another
and against your creation.
Forgive us in your mercy,
help us to forgive each other
and to hold in reverence
**   all that you have made. Amen.**

OSB West Malling

or:

Holy God,
holy and strong,
holy and immortal:
have mercy on us.

O God, make speed to save us.
O Lord, make haste to help us.

Glory . . .   Alleluia.

The following or another suitable HYMN may be sung.

Before the ending of the day,
Creator of the world, we pray
That you, with steadfast love, would keep
Your watch around us while we sleep.

From evil dreams defend our sight,
From fears and terrors of the night;
Tread under foot our deadly foe
That we no sinful thought may know.

Ordinary Time Doxology
O Father, that we ask be done
Through Jesus Christ, your only Son;
And Holy Spirit, by whose breath
Our souls are raised to life from death. Amen.

Epiphany Doxology
Your glory, Christ, is manifest:
All peoples, Lord, by you are blest;
Whom, with the Father, we adore,
And Holy Spirit evermore. Amen.

THE WORD OF GOD

THE PSALMODY

Psalm 16

1   Preserve me, O God, for in you have I taken refuge; *
    I have said to the Lord, 'You are my lord,
       all my good depends on you.'

2   All my delight is upon the godly that are in the land, *
    upon those who are noble in heart.

3   Though the idols are legion that many run after, *
    their drink offerings of blood I will not offer,
       neither make mention of their names upon my lips.

4   The Lord himself is my portion and my cup; *
    in your hands alone is my fortune.

5   My share has fallen in a fair land; *
    indeed, I have a goodly heritage.

6   I will bless the Lord who has given me counsel, *
     and in the night watches he instructs my heart.

7   I have set the Lord always before me; *
     he is at my right hand; I shall not fall.

8   Wherefore my heart is glad and my spirit rejoices; *
     my flesh also shall rest secure.

9   For you will not abandon my soul to Death, *
     nor suffer your faithful one to see the Pit.

10   You will show me the path of life;
        in your presence is the fullness of joy *
     and in your right hand are pleasures for evermore.

   Glory . . .

THE READING: one of the following or some other.

Either, in Ordinary Time:

Be sober, be vigilant, because your adversary the devil is prowling round
like a roaring lion, seeking for someone to devour. Resist him, strong in the
faith.

1 Peter 5.8,9

or, in Epiphany:

The grace of God has appeared, bringing salvation to all.

Titus 2.11

or, on feasts of Teachers of the Faith, Bishops and other Pastors:

Wisdom guided the righteous on straight paths; she showed them the
kingdom of God and gave them knowledge of holy things.

Wisdom 10.10

THE RESPONSORY may be said.

Into your hands, O Lord,
I commend my spirit. (Alleluia, alleluia.)
Into your hands, O Lord,
I commend my spirit. (Alleluia, alleluia.)

For you have redeemed me, Lord God of truth.
I commend my spirit. (*or:* **Alleluia, alleluia.)**

Glory to the Father and to the Son
and to the Holy Spirit.
**Into your hands, O Lord,
I commend my spirit. (Alleluia, alleluia.)**

Keep me as the apple of your eye.
Hide me under the shadow of your wings.

*THE GOSPEL CANTICLE: NUNC DIMITTIS – THE SONG OF SIMEON (42) or
another version on page 508*

Refrain: **Save us, O Lord, while waking,
and guard us while sleeping,
that awake we may watch with Christ,
and asleep may rest in peace.**

or, in Epiphany:

> **Alleluia. Christ the light of the world, alleluia,
> has manifested his glory. Alleluia, alleluia.**

or, on Class I & II Holy Days:

> **Grant us your light, O Lord,
> that the darkness of our hearts being overcome,
> we may receive the true light,
> even Christ our Saviour. (Alleluia.)**

1   ✠ Now, Lord, you let your servant go in peace: *
     your word has been fulfilled.

2   My own eyes have seen the salvation *
     which you have prepared in the sight of every people:

3   A light to reveal you to the nations *
     and the glory of your people Israel.

Luke 2.29-32

Glory . . .

The refrain is repeated after the canticle.

THE PRAYERS

Intercessions and thanksgivings may be offered here.

Either, in Ordinary Time:

Keep watch, dear Lord,
with those who wake, or watch, or weep this night,
and give your angels charge over those who sleep.
Tend the sick, give rest to the weary,
sustain the dying, calm the suffering,
and pity the distressed;
all for your love's sake,
O Christ our Redeemer. **Amen.**

or:

Lighten our darkness,
Lord, we pray;
and in your mercy defend us from all perils
    and dangers of this night;
for the love of your only Son,
our Saviour Jesus Christ. **Amen.**

or, in Epiphany:

King of kings and Lord of lords,
making the true light to shine:
lighten our darkness now and evermore
that with our lips and in our lives
we may praise you;
for you are our God, now and for ever. **Amen.**

THE LORD'S PRAYER may be said.

[As we come to the ending of the day,]
as our Saviour taught us, so we pray
Our Father in heaven, . . .

THE CONCLUSION

In peace, we will lie down and sleep;
for you alone, Lord, make us dwell in safety.

Abide with us, Lord Jesus,
for the night is at hand and the day is now past.

As the night-watch looks for the morning,
so do we look for you, O Christ.

[Come with the dawning of the day
**and make yourself known
in the breaking of the bread.]**

Either, in Ordinary Time:

**May God's love surround us,
God's joy fill our lives,
God's peace be in our hearts,
and God's blessing be with us
this night and always. Amen.**

or, in Epiphany:

**May the living waters of Christ cleanse us,
may the Spirit descend upon us,
and the blessing of God be with us
this night and always. Amen.**

A MARIAN ANTHEM may be sung.

SALVE REGINA

Traditionally, this anthem is sung at the end of Night Prayer from after Pentecost to Advent; or it may be the unchanging final anthem. The other Marian anthems may be found on page 775.

Salve, Regina, mater misericordiae;
vita, dulcedo, et spes nostra, salve.
Ad te clamamus, exsules, filii Evae,
ad te suspiramus,
gementes et flentes in hac lacrimarum valle;
eia ergo, advocata nostra,
illos tuos misericordes oculos ad nos converte,
Et Iesum, benedictum fructum ventris tui,
nobis post hoc exsilium ostende.
O clemens, O pia, O dulcis Virgo Maria.

Form 6 – Morning Prayer

Fridays in Ordinary Time
and daily in Lent & Passiontide

THE PREPARATION

A *is used on Fridays in Ordinary Time.*
B *is used in Lent and Passiontide and on specified Class I & II Holy Days.*

A:

O Lord, open our lips
and our mouth shall proclaim your praise.

Let your ways be known upon earth,
your saving power among the nations.

Glory . . .   Alleluia.

THE OPENING CANTICLE

VENITE – A SONG OF TRIUMPH

1   O come, let us sing to the Lord; *
     let us heartily rejoice in the rock of our salvation.

2   Let us come into his presence with thanksgiving *
     and be glad in him with psalms.

3   For the Lord is a great God *
     and a great king above all gods.

4   In his hand are the depths of the earth *
     and the heights of the mountains are his also.

5   The sea is his, for he made it, *
     and his hands have moulded the dry land.

6   Come, let us worship and bow down *
     and kneel before the Lord our Maker.

7   For he is our God; *
     we are the people of his pasture
        and the sheep of his hand.

The canticle may end here.

8   O that today you would listen to his voice: *
      'Harden not your hearts as at Meribah,
          on that day at Massah in the wilderness,

9   'When your forebears tested me,
          and put me to the proof, *
      though they had seen my works.

10   'Forty years long I detested that generation and said, *
      "This people are wayward in their hearts;
          they do not know my ways."

11   'So I swore in my wrath, *
      "They shall not enter into my rest." '

Glory . . .   *Psalm 95*

Morning Prayer continues with the Hymn and/or THE OPENING PRAYER.

B:

O Lord, open our lips
and our mouth shall proclaim your praise.

Either, in Lent:

Blessèd are you, God of compassion and mercy,
to you be praise and glory for ever.
In the darkness of our sin,
your light breaks forth like the dawn
and your healing springs up for deliverance.
As we rejoice in the gift of your saving help,
sustain us with your bountiful Spirit
and open our lips to sing your praise,
Father, Son and Holy Spirit:
Blessèd be God for ever.

or, in Passiontide or on specified Class I & II Holy Days:

Blessèd are you, Lord God of our salvation,
to you be praise and glory for ever.
As a man of sorrows and acquainted with grief
your only Son was lifted up
that he might draw the whole world to himself.
May we walk this day in the way of the cross
and always be ready to share its weight,
declaring your love for all the world,
Father, Son and Holy Spirit:
Blessèd be God for ever.

The following is said:

In Lent:

Christ, though tempted like us, was without sin.
O come, let us worship.

or, in Passiontide:

Christ suffered and died for us.
O come, let us worship.

or, on feasts of Martyrs:

(Alleluia.) Christ is the strength of the martyrs.
O come, let us worship. (Alleluia.)

THE OPENING CANTICLE

In Lent:

A SONG OF PENITENCE

1   Have mercy on me, O God, in your great goodness; *
    according to the abundance of your compassion
        blot out my offences.

2   Wash me thoroughly from my wickedness *
    and cleanse me from my sin.

3   For I acknowledge my faults *
    and my sin is ever before me.

4   Against you only have I sinned *
     and done what is evil in your sight,

5   So that you are justified in your sentence *
     and righteous in your judgement.

6   Cast me not away from your presence *
     and take not your holy spirit from me.

7   Give me again the joy of your salvation *
     and sustain me with your gracious spirit;

8   Then shall I teach your ways to the wicked *
     and sinners shall return to you.

9   Deliver me from my guilt, O God,
        the God of my salvation, *
     and my tongue shall sing of your righteousness.

Glory . . .   *Psalm 51.1-5,12-15*

or, in Passiontide:

A SONG OF LAMENTATION (21)

1   Is it nothing to you, all you who pass by? *
     Look and see if there is any sorrow like my sorrow,

2   Which was brought upon me, *
     which the Lord inflicted
        on the day of his fierce anger.

3   For these things I weep;
        my eyes flow with tears; *
     for a comforter is far from me,
        one to revive my courage.

4   Remember my affliction and my bitterness, *
     the wormwood and the gall!

5   But this I call to mind, *
     and therefore I have hope:

6   The steadfast love of the Lord never ceases, *
     his mercies never come to an end;

7   They are new every morning; *
     great is your faithfulness.

8   'The Lord is my portion,' says my soul, *
     'therefore I will hope in him.'

9   The Lord is good to those who wait for him, *
     to the soul that seeks him.

10   It is good that we should wait quietly *
     for the salvation of the Lord.

11   For the Lord will not reject for ever; *
     though he causes grief, he will have compassion,

12   According to the abundance of his steadfast love; *
     for he does not willingly afflict or grieve anyone.

     Glory . . .   *Lamentations 1.12,16a,b; 3.19,21-26,31-33*

A HYMN may be sung.

THE OPENING PRAYER may be said.

The night has passed and the day lies open before us;
let us pray with one heart and mind.
(Silence may be kept.)

**As we rejoice in the gift of this new day,
so may the light of your presence, O God,
set our hearts on fire with love for you;
now and for ever. Amen.**

THE WORD OF GOD

THE PSALMODY, as appointed

Each psalm, or group of psalms, may end with:

Glory . . .

*If there are two SCRIPTURE READINGS, the first may be read here, or both may
be read after the Second Canticle.*

THE SECOND CANTICLE

In Ordinary Time:

Either A SONG OF HUMILITY (23) or number 15, page 481

Refrain: **Raise us up, O God,
that we may live in your presence.**

1 Come, let us return to the Lord *
   who has torn us and will heal us.

2 God has stricken us *
   and will bind up our wounds.

3 After two days, he will revive us, *
   and on the third day will raise us up,
      that we may live in his presence.

4 Let us strive to know the Lord; *
   his appearing is as sure as the sunrise.

5 He will come to us like the showers, *
   like the spring rains that water the earth.

6 'O Ephraim, how shall I deal with you? *
   How shall I deal with you, O Judah?

7 'Your love for me is like the morning mist, *
   like the dew that goes early away.

8 'Therefore, I have hewn them by the prophets, *
   and my judgement goes forth as the light.

9 'For loyalty is my desire and not sacrifice, *
   and the knowledge of God rather than burnt offerings.'

   Glory . . .   *Hosea 6.1-6*

   **Raise us up, O God,
   that we may live in your presence.**

or, in Lent:

Either THE SONG OF MANASSEH (38) or numbers 2, page 472, or 24, page 489

Refrain: **Full of compassion and mercy and love is God, the Most High, the Almighty.**

1   Lord almighty and God of our ancestors, *
    you who made heaven and earth in all their glory:

2   All things tremble with awe at your presence, *
    before your great and mighty power.

3   Immeasurable and unsearchable is your promised mercy, *
    for you are God, Most High.

4   You are full of compassion, long-suffering
        and very merciful, *
    and you relent at human suffering.

5   O God, according to your great goodness, *
    you have promised forgiveness for repentance
        to those who have sinned against you.

6   The sins I have committed against you *
    are more in number than the sands of the sea.

7   I am not worthy to look up to the height of heaven, *
    because of the multitude of my iniquities.

8   And now I bend the knee of my heart before you, *
    imploring your kindness upon me.

9   I have sinned, O God, I have sinned, *
    and I acknowledge my transgressions.

10 Unworthy as I am, you will save me, *
    according to your great mercy.

11 For all the host of heaven sings your praise, *
    and your glory is for ever and ever.

Glory . . .   *Manasseh 1a,2,4,6,7a,b,9a,c,11,12,14b,15b*

**Full of compassion and mercy and love
is God, the Most High, the Almighty.**

or, in Passiontide:

Either A SONG OF SOLOMON (5) or numbers 19, page 485, or 25, page 489

Refrain: **Many waters cannot quench love;**
neither can the floods drown it.

1   Set me as a seal upon your heart, *
       as a seal upon your arm;

2   For love is strong as death,
           passion fierce as the grave; *
       its flashes are flashes of fire,
           a raging flame.

3   Many waters cannot quench love, *
       neither can the floods drown it.

4   If all the wealth of our house
           were offered for love, *
       it would be utterly scorned.

     Glory . . .   *cf Song of Solomon 8.6,7*

     Many waters cannot quench love;
     neither can the floods drown it.

On feasts of Martyrs, numbers 5 above, 19, page 485, and 24, page 489, are
alternative canticles.

THE SCRIPTURE READING(S)

A RESPONSORY may be said.

To you, O Lord, I lift up my soul;
O my God, in you I trust.

You are the God of my salvation.
To you, O Lord, I lift up my soul.

In you I hope all the day long.
O my God, in you I trust.

Remember, Lord, your compassion and love,
for they are from everlasting.
To you, O Lord, I lift up my soul;
O my God, in you I trust.

from Psalm 25

THE GOSPEL CANTICLE: BENEDICTUS – THE SONG OF ZECHARIAH (41)

See either inside front cover, inside back cover or page 506 for another version.

In Ordinary Time:

Refrain: **Give your people knowledge of salvation, O God,**
by the forgiveness of all their sins.

or, in Lent:

> **Blessèd are those who hunger and thirst**
> **for righteousness,**
> **for they shall be satisfied.**

or, in Passiontide:

> **The word of the cross is folly**
> **to those who are perishing,**
> **but to those who are being saved,**
> **it is the power of God.**

or, on feasts of Martyrs:

> **Blessèd are those who are persecuted**
> **for the cause of right,**
> **for theirs is the kingdom of heaven. (Alleluia.)**

The refrain is repeated after the canticle.

THE PRAYERS

INTERCESSIONS may be offered.

THE KYRIES may be used as responses to intercession.

Lord, have mercy.
Lord, have mercy.

Christ, have mercy.
Christ, have mercy.

Lord, have mercy.
Lord, have mercy.

THE COLLECT of the day, or one of the following:

Gracious Father,
you gave up your Son
out of love for the world:
lead us to ponder the mysteries of his passion,
that we may know eternal peace
through the shedding of our Saviour's blood,
Jesus Christ our Lord. **Amen.**

or, in Lent and Passiontide:

Almighty and everlasting God,
you hate nothing that you have made
and forgive the sins of all those who are penitent:
create and make in us new and contrite hearts
that we, worthily lamenting our sins

   and acknowledging our wretchedness,
may receive from you, the God of all mercy,
perfect remission and forgiveness;
through Jesus Christ our Lord. **Amen.**

THE LORD'S PRAYER may be said.

[Trusting in the compassion of God,]
as our Saviour taught us, so we pray
Our Father in heaven, . . .

THE CONCLUSION

In Ordinary Time:

**The Lord bless us, and preserve us from all evil,
and keep us in eternal life. Amen.**

Let us bless the Lord.
Thanks be to God.

or, in Lent:

May God our Redeemer show us compassion and love. Amen.

Let us bless the Lord.
Thanks be to God.

or, in Passiontide:

**May Christ, who bore our sins on the cross,
set us free to serve him with joy. Amen.**

Let us bless the Lord.
Thanks be to God.

or, on Class I & II Holy Days:

May our blessèd Lady pray for us.
May Saint Francis and Saint Clare pray for us.
[May Saint N pray for us.]
May all the saints of God pray for us.
May the angels of God befriend us
    and watch around us to protect us.
May the Lord Jesus give us his blessing of peace.   Amen.

Let us bless the Lord. (Alleluia. Alleluia.)
Thanks be to God. (Alleluia. Alleluia.)

Form 6 – Midday Prayer
Fridays through the Year

Seasonal Propers are found beginning page 539.

THE PREPARATION

O God, make speed to save us.
O Lord, make haste to help us.

Glory . . .　　　**Alleluia.** *(Omitted in Lent)*

A HYMN may be sung, the following or some other.

We bless you, Father, Lord of life,
To whom all living beings tend,
The source of holiness and grace,
Our first beginning and our end.

We give you thanks, redeeming Christ,
Who bore the weight of sin and shame;
In dark defeat you conquered sin,
And death, by dying, overcame.

Come, Holy Spirit, searching fire,
Whose flame all evil burns away.
With light and love come down to us
In silence and in peace to stay.

Ordinary Time Doxology
We praise you, God, the Three in One,
Sublime in majesty and might:
You reign for ever, Lord of all,
In splendour and unending light.　Amen.

*OSB Stanbrook Abbey *

THE WORD OF GOD

THE PSALMODY

Either **A:** *PSALM 119.129-152*

17 Pe

129 Your testimonies are wonderful; *
    therefore my soul keeps them.

130 The opening of your word gives light; *
    it gives understanding to the simple.

131 I open my mouth and draw in my breath, *
    as I long for your commandments.

132 Turn to me and be gracious to me, *
    as is your way with those who love your name.

133 Order my steps by your word, *
    and let no wickedness have dominion over me.

134 Redeem me from earthly oppressors *
    so that I may keep your commandments.

135 Show the light of your countenance upon your servant *
    and teach me your statutes.

136 My eyes run down with streams of water, *
    because the wicked do not keep your law.

18 Tsadhe

137 Righteous are you, O Lord, *
    and true are your judgements.

138 You have ordered your decrees in righteousness *
    and in great faithfulness.

139 My indignation destroys me, *
    because my adversaries forget your word.

140 Your word has been tried to the uttermost *
    and so your servant loves it.

141 I am small and of no reputation, *
    yet do I not forget your commandments.

142 Your righteousness is an everlasting righteousness *
and your law is the truth.

143 Trouble and heaviness have taken hold upon me, *
yet my delight is in your commandments.

144 The righteousness of your testimonies is everlasting; *
O grant me understanding and I shall live.

19 Qoph

145 I call with my whole heart; *
answer me, O Lord, that I may keep your statutes.

146 To you I call, O save me! *
And I shall keep your testimonies.

147 Early in the morning I cry to you, *
for in your word is my trust.

148 My eyes are open before the night watches, *
that I may meditate on your word.

149 Hear my voice, O Lord, according to your faithful love; *
according to your judgement, give me life.

150 They draw near that in malice persecute me, *
who are far from your law.

151 You, O Lord, are near at hand, *
and all your commandments are true.

152 Long have I known of your testimonies, *
that you have founded them for ever.

or B: Psalms of Ascent

PSALM 129

1 'Many a time have they fought against me from my youth,' *
may Israel now say;

2 'Many a time have they fought against me from my youth, *
but they have not prevailed against me.'

3 The ploughers ploughed upon my back *
and made their furrows long.

4   But the righteous Lord *
     has cut the cords of the wicked in pieces.

5   Let them be put to shame and turned backwards, *
     as many as are enemies of Zion.

6   Let them be like grass upon the housetops, *
     which withers before it can grow,

7   So that no reaper can fill his hand, *
     nor a binder of sheaves his bosom;

8   And none who go by may say,
       'The blessing of the Lord be upon you. *
     We bless you in the name of the Lord.'

PSALM 130

1   Out of the depths have I cried to you, O Lord;
       Lord, hear my voice; *
     let your ears consider well the voice of my supplication.

2   If you, Lord, were to mark what is done amiss, *
     O Lord, who could stand?

3   But there is forgiveness with you, *
     so that you shall be feared.

4   I wait for the Lord; my soul waits for him; *
     in his word is my hope.

5   My soul waits for the Lord,
       more than the night watch for the morning, *
     more than the night watch for the morning.

6   O Israel, wait for the Lord, *
     for with the Lord there is mercy;

7   With him is plenteous redemption *
     and he shall redeem Israel from all their sins.

Each psalm, or group of psalms, may end with:

Glory . . .

THE READING

In Ordinary Time, week 1 begins on the first Sunday of the month and so on.

Either:

Week 1: 2 Chronicles 7.13,14
     2: Isaiah 57.15-19
     3: Ephesians 2.13-18
     4: Luke 9.22-25
     5: Luke 6.27b,28

or one of the following readings:

Jesus said to them, I am the good shepherd. The good shepherd lays down his life for the sheep.   John 10.11

Blessèd are those who are persecuted for righteousness' sake, for theirs is the kingdom of heaven.   *Matthew 5.10*

or some other suitable reading.

THE RESPONSE

In Ordinary Time:

Either **A**:

Do not fear for I have redeemed you,
I have called you by name; you are mine.

When you pass through the waters, I will be with you;
and when you pass through rivers, they shall not overwhelm you.

When you walk through fire, you shall not be burned:
and the flame shall not consume you.

Do not fear, for I am with you,
I am the Holy One, your Saviour.

or **B**:

The preaching of the cross is folly to those who are perishing,
but to those who are being saved, it is the power of God.

To those who are called,
Christ is the power of God and the wisdom of God.

For the folly of God is wiser than human wisdom,
and the weakness of God is stronger than human strength.

We adore you, O Christ, and we bless you;
because by your holy cross, you have redeemed the world.

THE PRAYERS

On Fridays, the 'Cross Prayers', page 737, may conclude the Office by replacing all that follows.

INTERCESSIONS may be offered.

THE KYRIES may be used as responses to intercession.

Lord, have mercy.
Lord, have mercy.

Christ, have mercy.
Christ, have mercy.

Lord, have mercy.
Lord, have mercy.

THE COLLECT of the day, or one of the following:

Lord Jesus Christ, we thank you
for all the benefits that you have won for us,
for all the pains and insults that you have borne for us.
Most merciful redeemer,
friend and brother,
may we know you more clearly,
love you more dearly,
and follow you more nearly,
day by day. **Amen.**

after Richard of Chichester (1253)

May the power of your love, Lord Christ,
fiery and sweet,
so absorb our hearts
as to withdraw them from all that is under heaven;
grant that we may be ready
to die for love of your love,
as you died for love of our love. **Amen.**

Absorbeat, after Francis of Assisi

THE LORD'S PRAYER may be said.

[Lord Jesus remember us in your kingdom
and teach us to pray.]
Our Father in heaven, . . .

THE CONCLUSION

**Let us bless the Lord God living and true!
Let us always give him
praise, glory, honour, blessing and every good.
Amen. Amen. (Alleluia, alleluia.)**

Prayer said by Francis of Assisi at the end of the office

Form 6 – Evening Prayer

Fridays in Ordinary Time
and daily in Lent and Passiontide

THE BLESSING OF THE LIGHT *may replace THE PREPARATION.*

A light, which may be the Paschal Candle, is brought in, or a candle may simply be lit.

Christ your light shall rise in the darkness
and your healing shall spring up like the dawn.

The light and peace of Jesus Christ be with you
and also with you.

Blessèd are you, Lord God of our salvation,
to you be glory and praise for ever.
As we behold your Son, enthroned on the cross,
stir up in us the fire of your love,
that we may be cleansed from all our sins,
and walk with you in newness of life
singing the praise of him who died
for us and for our salvation,
Father, Son and Holy Spirit:
Blessèd be God for ever.

While the other candles are lit the following, or another version of number 63, page 524, or another suitable hymn may be sung.

A SONG OF THE LIGHT (63c)

1   **Hail, gladdening Light, of his pure glory poured,
    Who is the immortal Father, heavenly, blest,
    Holiest of holies, Jesus Christ our Lord.**

2   **Now we are come to the sun's hour of rest,
    The lights of evening round us shine,
    We hymn the Father, Son and Holy Spirit divine.**

3   **Worthy are you at all times to be sung**
    With undefilèd tongue,
    Son of our God, giver of life, alone:
    Therefore in all the world your glories,
        Lord, they own.

Verses from PSALM 141 may be said and incense may be burned.

Let my prayer rise before you as incense,
the lifting up of my hands as the evening sacrifice.

O Lord, I call to you; come to me quickly;
hear my voice when I cry to you.
Set a watch before my mouth, O Lord,
and guard the door of my lips.

Let my prayer rise before you as incense,
the lifting up of my hands as the evening sacrifice.

Let not my heart incline to any evil thing;
let me not be occupied in wickedness with evildoers.
But my eyes are turned to you, Lord God,
in you I take refuge;
do not leave me defenceless.

Let my prayer rise before you as incense,
the lifting up of my hands as the evening sacrifice.

Psalm 141.1-4b,8

This prayer may be said:

That this evening may be holy good and peaceful,
let us pray with one heart and mind.
(Silence may be kept.)

As our evening prayer rises before you, O God,
so may your mercy come down upon us
    to cleanse our hearts
and set us free to sing your praise,
now and for ever. Amen.

Evening Prayer continues with the appointed Psalmody.

THE PREPARATION

O God, make speed to save us.
O Lord, make haste to help us.

Let your ways be known upon earth,
your saving power among the nations.

Glory . . .   **Alleluia.** *(Omitted in Lent)*

THE OPENING CANTICLE

A SONG OF ENTREATY

1   Hear my prayer, O Lord,
        and in your faithfulness give ear to my supplications; *
     answer me in your righteousness.

2   Enter not into judgement with your servant, *
     for in your sight shall no one living be justified.

3   My spirit faints within me; *
     my heart within me is desolate.

4   I stretch out my hands to you; *
     my soul gasps for you like a thirsty land.

5   O Lord, make haste to answer me; my spirit fails me; *
     hide not your face from me
        lest I be like those who go down to the Pit.

6   Let me hear of your loving-kindness in the morning,
        for in you I put my trust; *
     show me the way I should walk in,
        for I lift up my soul to you.

7   Teach me to do what pleases you, for you are my God; *
     let your kindly spirit lead me on a level path.

8   Revive me, O Lord, for your name's sake; *
     for your righteousness' sake, bring me out of trouble.

     Glory . . .   *Psalm 143.1,2,4,6-8,10,11*

A HYMN may be sung.

THE OPENING PRAYER may be said.

That this evening may be holy good and peaceful,
let us pray with one heart and mind.
(Silence may be kept.)

**Stir up in us, O God, the fire of your love,
that we may be cleansed of all our sins
and so be made ready to come into your presence,
singing your praises now and for ever. Amen.**

THE WORD OF GOD

THE PSALMODY, as appointed

Each psalm, or group of psalms, may end with:

Glory . . .

*If there are two SCRIPTURE READINGS, the first may be read here, or both may
be read after the Second Canticle.*

THE SECOND CANTICLE

In Ordinary Time:

Either A SONG OF CHRIST'S GLORY (47) or number 67, page 529

Refrain: **At the name of Jesus
every knee shall bow.**

1   Christ Jesus was in the form of God, *
     but he did not cling to equality with God.

2   He emptied himself, taking the form of a servant, *
     and was born in our human likeness.

3   Being found in human form he humbled himself, *
     and became obedient unto death, even death on a cross.

4   Therefore God has highly exalted him, *
     and bestowed on him the name above every name,

5   That at the name of Jesus every knee should bow, *
     in heaven and on earth and under the earth;

6   And every tongue confess that Jesus Christ is Lord, *
     to the glory of God the Father.

     Glory . . .   *Philippians 2.5-11*

     At the name of Jesus
     every knee shall bow.

or, in Lent:

Either A SONG OF THE JUSTIFIED (43) or numbers 47 above or 53,
page 515

Refrain: **Our hope is not in vain,**
          because God's love
          has been poured into our hearts.

1   God reckons as righteous those who believe, *
     who believe in him who raised Jesus from the dead;

2   For Christ was handed over to death for our sins, *
     and raised to life for our justification.

3   Since we are justified by faith, *
     we have peace with God through our Lord Jesus Christ.

4   Through Christ we have gained access
        to the grace in which we stand, *
     and rejoice in our hope of the glory of God.

5   We even exult in our sufferings, *
     for suffering produces endurance,

6   And endurance brings hope, *
     and our hope is not in vain,

7   Because God's love has been poured into our hearts, *
     through the Holy Spirit, given to us.

8   God proves his love for us: *
     while we were yet sinners Christ died for us.

9   Since we have been justified by his death, *
     how much more shall we be saved from God's wrath.

10   Therefore, we exult in God through our Lord Jesus Christ, *
     in whom we have now received our reconciliation.

Glory . . . *Romans 4.24,25; 5.1-5,8,9,11*

**Our hope is not in vain,
because God's love
has been poured into our hearts.**

or, in Passiontide:

*Either A SONG OF CHRIST THE SERVANT (52) or numbers 74, page 537, or
75, page 538*

Refrain: **Christ committed no sin,
no guile was found on his lips.**

1   Christ suffered for you, leaving you an example, *
    that you should follow in his steps.

2   He committed no sin, no guile was found on his lips, *
    when he was reviled, he did not revile in turn.

3   When he suffered, he did not threaten, *
    but he trusted himself to God who judges justly.

4   Christ himself bore our sins in his body on the tree, *
    that we might die to sin and live to righteousness.

5   By his wounds, you have been healed,
       for you were straying like sheep, *
    but have now returned
       to the shepherd and guardian of your souls.

Glory . . . *I Peter 2.21b-25*

**Christ committed no sin,
no guile was found on his lips.**

*On feasts of Martyrs, numbers 43 above and 56, page 517, are alternative
canticles.*

THE SCRIPTURE READING(S)

A RESPONSORY may be said.

O Lord, do not forsake me;
be not far from me, O my God.
O Lord, do not forsake me;
be not far from me, O my God.

Make haste to help me,
O Lord of my salvation.
Be not far from me, O my God.

Glory to the Father and to the Son
and to the Holy Spirit.
O Lord, do not forsake me;
be not far from me, O my God.

from Psalm 38

THE GOSPEL CANTICLE: MAGNIFICAT – THE SONG OF MARY (40)

See either inside front cover, inside back cover or page 504 for another version.

In Ordinary Time:

Refrain: **You have scattered the proud in their conceit,**
and lifted up the lowly.

or, in Lent:

Come, let us return to the Lord,
for our God will richly pardon.

or, in Passiontide:

God's love for us is revealed
in that, while we were yet sinners,
Christ died for us.

or, on feasts of Martyrs:

Those who gave up their lives for Christ,
and followed in the Way,
rejoice with God now and for ever. (Alleluia.)

The refrain is repeated after the canticle.

THE PRAYERS

On Fridays, if not said at Midday Prayer, the 'Cross Prayers', page 737, may conclude the Office by replacing all that follows.

INTERCESSIONS may be offered.

THE KYRIES may be used as responses to intercession.

Lord, have mercy.
Lord, have mercy.

Christ, have mercy.
Christ, have mercy.

Lord, have mercy.
Lord, have mercy.

THE COLLECT of the day, or one of the following:

Heal us, O God, from all our afflictions
and keep us steadfast in your love;
bind up our wounds,
raise us from death,
and lead us to fullness of life;
through Jesus Christ our Saviour. **Amen.**

or, in Lent and Passiontide:

Most merciful God,
who by the death and resurrection
of your Son Jesus Christ
delivered and saved the world:
grant that by faith in him who suffered on the cross
we may triumph in the power of his victory;
through Jesus Christ our Lord. **Amen.**

THE LORD'S PRAYER may be said.

[Trusting in the compassion of God,]
as our Saviour taught us, so we pray
Our Father in heaven, . . .

THE CONCLUSION

In Ordinary Time:

**The grace of our Lord Jesus Christ,
and the love of God,
and the fellowship of the Holy Spirit,
be with us all evermore. Amen.**

Let us bless the Lord.
Thanks be to God.

or, in Lent:

May God our Redeemer show us compassion and love. Amen.

Let us bless the Lord.
Thanks be to God.

or, in Passiontide:

**May Christ, who bore our sins on the cross,
set us free to serve him with joy. Amen.**

Let us bless the Lord.
Thanks be to God.

or, on Class I & II Holy Days:

May our blessèd Lady pray for us.
May Saint Francis and Saint Clare pray for us.
[May Saint N pray for us.]
May all the saints of God pray for us.
May the angels of God befriend us
    and watch around us to protect us.
May the Lord Jesus give us his blessing of peace. Amen.

Let us bless the Lord. (Alleluia. Alleluia.)
Thanks be to God. (Alleluia. Alleluia.)

Form 6 – Night Prayer

Fridays in Ordinary Time
and daily in Lent and Passiontide

THE PREPARATION

The Lord almighty grant us a quiet night and a perfect end.
Amen.

Our help is in the name of the Lord
who made heaven and earth.

A period of silence for reflection on the past day may follow.
The following or other suitable words of penitence may be used.

Most merciful God,
we confess to you,
before the whole company of heaven
  and one another,
that we have sinned in thought, word and deed,
and in what we have failed to do.
Forgive us our sins,
heal us by your Spirit
and raise us to new life in Christ. Amen.

or:

Holy God,
holy and strong,
holy and immortal:
have mercy on us.

O God, make speed to save us.
O Lord, make haste to help us.

Glory . . .　　　**Alleluia.** *(Omitted in Lent)*

The following or another suitable HYMN may be sung.

Before the ending of the day,
Creator of the world, we pray
That you, with steadfast love, would keep
Your watch around us while we sleep.

From evil dreams defend our sight,
From fears and terrors of the night;
Tread under foot our deadly foe
That we no sinful thought may know.

Ordinary Time Doxology
O Father, that we ask be done
Through Jesus Christ, your only Son;
And Holy Spirit, by whose breath
Our souls are raised to life from death. Amen.

Lent Doxology
Grant, ever blessèd Trinity,
And ever perfect Unity,
That this, our fast of forty days,
May work our profit and your praise. Amen.

Passiontide Doxology
To you, O saving Three in One,
Let homage due by all be done;
And grant us, by the cross restored,
To share the Victor's great reward. Amen.

THE WORD OF GOD

THE PSALMODY

Psalm 139.1-18

1   O Lord, you have searched me out and known me; *
    you know my sitting down and my rising up;
    you discern my thoughts from afar.

2   You mark out my journeys and my resting place *
    and are acquainted with all my ways.

3   For there is not a word on my tongue, *
    but you, O Lord, know it altogether.

4   You encompass me behind and before *
    and lay your hand upon me.

5   Such knowledge is too wonderful for me, *
    so high that I cannot attain it.

6   Where can I go then from your spirit? *
    Or where can I flee from your presence?

7   If I climb up to heaven, you are there; *
    if I make the grave my bed, you are there also.

8   If I take the wings of the morning *
    and dwell in the uttermost parts of the sea,

9   Even there your hand shall lead me, *
    your right hand hold me fast.

10 If I say, 'Surely the darkness will cover me *
    and the light around me turn to night,'

11 Even darkness is no darkness with you;
     the night is as clear as the day; *
    darkness and light to you are both alike.

12 For you yourself created my inmost parts; *
    you knit me together in my mother's womb.

13 I thank you, for I am fearfully and wonderfully made; *
    marvellous are your works, my soul knows well.

14 My frame was not hidden from you, *
    when I was made in secret
     and woven in the depths of the earth.

15 Your eyes beheld my form, as yet unfinished; *
    already in your book were all my members written,

16 As day by day they were fashioned *
    when as yet there was none of them.

17 How deep are your counsels to me, O God! *
    How great is the sum of them!

18 If I count them, they are more in number than the sand, *
    and at the end, I am still in your presence.

    Glory . . .

THE READING: one of the following or some other.

Either, in Ordinary Time:

God has destined us not for wrath but for obtaining salvation through our Lord Jesus Christ, who died for us, so that whether we are awake or asleep we may live with him.

1 Thessalonians 5.9,10

or, in Lent:

Is not this the fast that I choose: to loose the bonds of injustice, to undo the thongs of the yoke, to let the oppressed go free and to break every yoke? Is it not to share your bread with the hungry and bring the homeless poor into your house; when you see the naked, to cover them and not to hide yourself from your own kin?

Isaiah 58.6,7

or, in Passiontide:

I will pour out a spirit of compassion and supplication on the house of David and the inhabitants of Jerusalem so that, when they look on the one whom they have pierced, they shall mourn for him, as one mourns for an only child, and weep bitterly over him, as one weeps over a first-born.

Zechariah 12.10

or, on feasts of Martyrs:

Set me as a seal upon your heart, as a seal upon your arm; for love is strong as death, passion fierce as the grave. Its flashes are flashes of fire, a raging flame. Many waters cannot quench love, neither can floods drown it.

Song of Solomon 8.6,7a

THE RESPONSORY may be said.

Into your hands, O Lord,
I commend my spirit. (Alleluia, alleluia.)
Into your hands, O Lord,
I commend my spirit. (Alleluia, alleluia.)

For you have redeemed me, Lord God of truth.
I commend my spirit. (*or:* Alleluia, alleluia.)

Glory to the Father and to the Son
and to the Holy Spirit.
Into your hands, O Lord,
I commend my spirit. (Alleluia, alleluia.)

Keep me as the apple of your eye.
Hide me under the shadow of your wings.

THE GOSPEL CANTICLE: NUNC DIMITTIS – THE SONG OF SIMEON (42) or
another version on page 508

Refrain: **Save us, O Lord, while waking,**
and guard us while sleeping,
that awake we may watch with Christ,
and asleep may rest in peace.

or, in Lent:

Christ died for us,
so that, whether we wake or sleep,
we might live with him.

or, in Passiontide:

Christ himself bore our sins
in his body on the tree,
that we might die to sin
and live to righteousness.

or, on Class I & II Holy Days:

Grant us your light, O Lord,
that the darkness of our hearts being overcome,
we may receive the true light,
even Christ our Saviour. (Alleluia.)

1   ✠ Now, Lord, you let your servant go in peace: *
     your word has been fulfilled.

2   My own eyes have seen the salvation *
     which you have prepared in the sight of every people:

3   A light to reveal you to the nations *
     and the glory of your people Israel.

Luke 2.29-32

Glory . . .

The refrain is repeated after the canticle.

THE PRAYERS

Intercessions and thanksgivings may be offered here.

THE COLLECT: one of the following or some other.

Either, in Ordinary Time:

Lord Jesus Christ, Son of the living God,
who at this evening hour lay in the tomb
and so hallowed the grave
to be a bed of hope
for all who put their trust in you:
give us such sorrow for our sins,
which were the cause of your passion,
that, when our bodies lie in the dust,
our souls may live with you for ever. **Amen.**

or:

Lighten our darkness,
Lord, we pray;
and in your mercy defend us from all perils
    and dangers of this night;
for the love of your only Son,
our Saviour Jesus Christ. **Amen.**

or, in Lent:

Almighty God,
may we, by the prayer and discipline of Lent,
enter into the mystery of Christ's sufferings;
that by following in the Way,
we may come to share in the glory;
through Jesus Christ our Lord. **Amen.**

Almighty God,
as we stand at the foot of the cross of your Son,
help us to see and know your love for us,
so that in humility, love and joy
we may place at his feet
all that we have and all that we are;
through Jesus Christ our Saviour. **Amen.**

THE LORD'S PRAYER may be said.

[As we come to the ending of the day,]
as our Saviour taught us, so we pray
Our Father in heaven, . . .

THE CONCLUSION

In peace, we will lie down and sleep;
for you alone, Lord, make us dwell in safety.

Abide with us, Lord Jesus,
for the night is at hand and the day is now past.

As the night-watch looks for the morning,
so do we look for you, O Christ.

[Come with the dawning of the day
**and make yourself known
in the breaking of the bread.]**

Either, in Ordinary Time:

**May God's love surround us,
God's joy fill our lives,
God's peace be in our hearts,
and God's blessing be with us
this night and always. Amen.**

or, in Lent and Passiontide:

**May God bless us,
that in us may be found love and humility,
obedience and thanksgiving,
discipline, gentleness and peace. Amen.**

A MARIAN ANTHEM may be sung.

SALVE REGINA

Traditionally, this anthem is sung at the end of Night Prayer from after Pentecost to Advent; or it may be the unchanging final anthem. The other Marian anthems may be found on page 775.

Salve, Regina, mater misericordiae;
vita, dulcedo, et spes nostra, salve.
Ad te clamamus, exsules, filii Evae,
ad te suspiramus,
gementes et flentes in hac lacrimarum valle;
eia ergo, advocata nostra,
illos tuos misericordes oculos ad nos converte,
Et Iesum, benedictum fructum ventris tui,
nobis post hoc exsilium ostende.
O clemens, O pia, O dulcis Virgo Maria.

Form 7 – Morning Prayer

Saturdays in Ordinary Time
and daily from All Saints' Day to Advent

THE PREPARATION

A *is used on Saturdays in Ordinary Time.*
B *is used daily from All Saints' Day to the day before the First Sunday of Advent and on specified Class I & II Holy Days.*

A:

O Lord, open our lips
and our mouth shall proclaim your praise.

Your faithful servants bless you.
They make known the glory of your kingdom.

Glory . . .   Alleluia.

Morning Prayer continues with THE OPENING CANTICLE.

B:

O Lord, open our lips
and our mouth shall proclaim your praise.

Blessèd are you, Sovereign God,
ruler and judge of all,
to you be praise and glory for ever.
In the darkness of this age that is passing away
may the light of your presence which the saints enjoy
surround our steps as we journey on.
May we reflect your glory this day
and so be made ready to see your face
in the heavenly city where night shall be no more,
Father, Son and Holy Spirit:
Blessèd be God for ever.

The following is said:

From All Saints to Advent:

God ever reigns on high.
O come, let us worship.

or, on feasts of Apostles:

(Alleluia.) Christ the corner-stone has built
his church upon the apostles and prophets.
O come let us worship. (Alleluia.)

or, on feasts of any Saint:

(Alleluia.) Our God is the God of Peace,
whom to serve is perfect freedom.
O come, let us worship. (Alleluia.)

or, for the Departed:

God is our Redeemer, for whom all are alive.
O come, let us worship.

THE OPENING CANTICLE

A SONG OF GOD'S PRAISE

1   O God, you are my God; eagerly I seek you; *
     my soul is athirst for you

2   My flesh also faints for you, *
     as in a dry and thirsty land where there is no water.

3   So would I gaze upon you in your holy place, *
     that I might behold your power and your glory.

4   Your loving-kindness is better than life itself *
     and so my lips shall praise you.

5   I will bless you as long as I live *
     and lift up my hands in your name.

6   My soul shall be satisfied, as with marrow and fatness, *
     and my mouth shall praise you with joyful lips,

7   When I remember you upon my bed *
     and meditate on you in the watches of the night.

8   For you have been my helper *
     and under the shadow of your wings will I rejoice.

9   My soul clings to you; *
     your right hand shall hold me fast.

Glory ...   *Psalm 63.1-9*

A HYMN may be sung.

THE OPENING PRAYER may be said.

The night has passed and the day lies open before us;
let us pray with one heart and mind.
(Silence may be kept.)

As we rejoice in the gift of this new day,
so may the light of your presence, O God,
set our hearts on fire with love for you;
now and for ever. Amen.

THE WORD OF GOD

THE PSALMODY, as appointed

Each psalm, or group of psalms, may end with:

Glory ...

*If there are two SCRIPTURE READINGS, the first may be read here, or both may
be read after the Second Canticle.*

THE SECOND CANTICLE

In Ordinary Time:

Either A SONG OF JERUSALEM OUR MOTHER (20) or number 34, page 497

Refrain: **Thus says our God, I will comfort you,**
       you shall see and your heart shall rejoice.

1   'Rejoice with Jerusalem and be glad for her, *
     all you who love her,' says the Lord.

2   'Rejoice with her in joy, *
     all you who mourn over her,

3 'That you may drink deeply with delight *
   from her consoling breast.'

4 For thus says our God, *
   'You shall be nursed and carried on her arm.

5 'As a mother comforts her children, *
   so I will comfort you;

6 'You shall see and your heart shall rejoice; *
   you shall flourish like the grass of the fields.'

   Glory . . .   *Isaiah 66.10,11a,12a,12c,13a,14a,b*

   Thus says our God, I will comfort you,
   you shall see and your heart shall rejoice.

From All Saints to Advent:

Either A SONG OF THE BRIDE (18) or numbers 10, page 478, or 29, page 493

Refrain: **God makes righteousness and praise**
          blossom before all the nations.

1 I will greatly rejoice in the Lord, *
   my soul shall exult in my God;

2 Who has clothed me with the garments of salvation, *
   and has covered me with the cloak of integrity,

3 As a bridegroom decks himself with a garland, *
   and as a bride adorns herself with her jewels.

4 For as the earth puts forth her blossom, *
   and as seeds in the garden spring up,

5 So shall God make righteousness and praise *
   blossom before all the nations.

6 For Zion's sake I will not keep silent, *
   and for Jerusalem's sake I will not rest,

7 Until her deliverance shines out like the dawn, *
   and her salvation as a burning torch.

8 The nations shall see your deliverance, *
   and all rulers shall see your glory;

9   Then you shall be called by a new name *
    which the mouth of God will give.

10 You shall be a crown of glory in the hand of the Lord, *
    a royal diadem in the hand of your God.

Glory . . .   *Isaiah 61.10,11; 62.1-3*

**God makes righteousness and praise
blossom before all the nations.**

On feasts of Apostles, number 17, page 483, is an alternative canticle.

*On feasts of any Saint, numbers 10, page 478, and 26, page 491, are alternative
canticles.*

For the Departed, number 24, page 489, is an alternative canticle.

THE SCRIPTURE READING(S)

A RESPONSORY may be said.

I will sing for ever of your love, O Lord.
My lips shall proclaim your faithfulness.

The heavens bear witness to your wonders.
I will sing for ever of your love, O Lord.

The assembly of your saints proclaims your truth.
My lips shall proclaim your faithfulness.

Righteousness and justice are the foundation of your throne;
steadfast love and faithfulness go before you.
**I will sing for ever of your love, O Lord,
my lips shall proclaim your faithfulness.**

                                                        from Psalm 89

THE GOSPEL CANTICLE: BENEDICTUS – THE SONG OF ZECHARIAH (41)

See either inside front cover, inside back cover or page 506 for another version.

In Ordinary Time:

Refrain: **Shine on us, O God, who dwell in darkness,
        and guide us into the way of peace.**

or, from All Saints to Advent:

**You will guide us with your counsel, O God,
and afterwards receive us with glory.**

or, on feasts of Apostles:

**You did not choose me but I chose you
and I appointed you to go out and bear fruit,
the fruit that shall last. (Alleluia.)**

or, on feasts of any Saint:

**They were faithful until death
and God has given them the crown of life. (Alleluia.)**

or, for the Departed:

**I am the resurrection and the life;
whoever believes in me,
even though they die, will live.**

The refrain is repeated after the canticle.

THE PRAYERS

INTERCESSIONS may be offered.

THE KYRIES may be used as responses to intercession.

Lord, have mercy.
Lord, have mercy.

Christ, have mercy.
Christ, have mercy.

Lord, have mercy.
Lord, have mercy.

THE COLLECT of the day, or one of the following:

Merciful God, you have prepared for those who love you
such good things as pass our understanding:
pour into our hearts such love towards you
that we, loving you above all things,
may obtain your promises, which exceed all that we can desire;
through Jesus Christ our Lord. **Amen.**

or, from All Saints to Advent:

Almighty God, you have knit together your elect
into one communion and fellowship
in the mystical body of your Son Christ our Lord:
give us grace so to follow your blessèd saints
in all virtuous and godly living
that we may come to those inexpressible joys
which you have prepared for those who truly love you;
through Jesus Christ our Lord. **Amen.**

THE LORD'S PRAYER may be said.

[Uniting our prayers with the whole company of heaven,]
as our Saviour taught us, so we pray
Our Father in heaven, . . .

THE CONCLUSION

In Ordinary Time:

**The Lord bless us, and preserve us from all evil,
and keep us in eternal life. Amen.**

Let us bless the Lord.
Thanks be to God.

or, from All Saints to Advent:

**May Christ, who has opened the kingdom of heaven,
bring us to reign with him in glory. Amen.**

Let us bless the Lord.
Thanks be to God.

or, on Class I & II Holy Days:

May our blessèd Lady pray for us.
May Saint Francis and Saint Clare pray for us.
[May Saint N pray for us.]
May all the saints of God pray for us.
May the angels of God befriend us
   and watch around us to protect us.
May the Lord Jesus give us his blessing of peace.   Amen.

Let us bless the Lord. (Alleluia. Alleluia.)
Thanks be to God. (Alleluia. Alleluia.)

Form 7 – Midday Prayer

Saturdays through the Year

Seasonal Propers are found beginning page 539.

THE PREPARATION

O God, make speed to save us.
O Lord, make haste to help us.

Glory . . .   **Alleluia.** *(Omitted in Lent)*

A HYMN may be sung, the following or some other.

**Christ yesterday and Christ today,
For all eternity the same,
The image of our hidden God:
Eternal Wisdom is his name.**

**Christ keeps his word from age to age,
Is with us to the end of days;
A cloud by day, a flame by night,
To go before us on our ways.**

Ordinary Time Doxology
**We bless the Father, Fount of light,
And you, O Christ, belovèd Son,
Who, with the Spirit, dwell in us;
The only God; the Three in One. Amen.**

OSB Stanbrook Abbey*

THE WORD OF GOD

THE PSALMODY

*Either **A:** PSALM 119.153-176*

20 Resh

153   O consider my affliction and deliver me, *
         for I do not forget your law.

154   Plead my cause and redeem me; *
         according to your promise, give me life.

155 Salvation is far from the wicked, *
    for they do not seek your statutes.

156 Great is your compassion, O Lord; *
    give me life, according to your judgements.

157 Many there are that persecute and oppress me, *
    yet do I not swerve from your testimonies.

158 It grieves me when I see the treacherous, *
    for they do not keep your word.

159 Consider, O Lord, how I love your commandments; *
    give me life according to your loving-kindness.

160 The sum of your word is truth, *
    and all your righteous judgements endure for evermore.

21 Shin

161 Princes have persecuted me without a cause, *
    but my heart stands in awe of your word.

162 I am as glad of your word *
    as one who finds great spoils.

163 As for lies, I hate and abhor them, *
    but your law do I love.

164 Seven times a day do I praise you, *
    because of your righteous judgements.

165 Great peace have they who love your law; *
    nothing shall make them stumble.

166 Lord, I have looked for your salvation *
    and I have fulfilled your commandments.

167 My soul has kept your testimonies *
    and greatly have I loved them.

168 I have kept your commandments and testimonies, *
    for all my ways are before you.

22 Taw

169 Let my cry come before you, O Lord; *
    give me understanding, according to your word.

170 Let my supplication come before you; *
　　deliver me, according to your promise.

171 My lips shall pour forth your praise, *
　　when you have taught me your statutes.

172 My tongue shall sing of your word, *
　　for all your commandments are righteous.

173 Let your hand reach out to help me, *
　　for I have chosen your commandments.

174 I have longed for your salvation, O Lord, *
　　and your law is my delight.

175 Let my soul live and it shall praise you, *
　　and let your judgements be my help.

176 I have gone astray like a sheep that is lost; *
　　O seek your servant, for I do not forget your commandments.

or B: Psalms of Ascent

PSALM 131

1　O Lord, my heart is not proud; *
　　my eyes are not raised in haughty looks.

2　I do not occupy myself with great matters, *
　　with things that are too high for me.

3　But I have quieted and stilled my soul,
　　　like a weaned child on its mother's breast; *
　　so my soul is quieted within me.

4　O Israel, trust in the Lord, *
　　from this time forth for evermore.

PSALM 133

1　Behold how good and pleasant it is *
　　to dwell together in unity.

2　It is like the precious oil upon the head, *
　　running down upon the beard,

3 Even on Aaron's beard, *
 running down upon the collar of his clothing.

4 It is like the dew of Hermon *
 running down upon the hills of Zion.

5 For there the Lord has promised his blessing: *
 even life for evermore.

Each psalm, or group of psalms, may end with:

Glory . . .

THE READING

In Ordinary Time, week 1 begins on the first Sunday of the month and so on.

Either:
Week 1: Isaiah 11.6-9
 2: Ephesians 3.14-19
 3: John 11.17-26a
 4: Revelation 5.8-10
 5: 2 Corinthians 4.18

or one of the following readings:

Jesus said to Martha, I am the resurrection and the life. Those who believe in
me, even though they die, will live. John 11.25

Blessèd are the pure in heart, for they will see God. *Matthew 5.8*

or some other suitable reading.

THE RESPONSE

In Ordinary Time:

Either A:

I know that my Redeemer lives,
and that at the last he shall stand upon the earth.

Then without my flesh,
I shall see God.

I want to know Christ,
and the power of his resurrection.

Come all you who have heard my word and do it,
inherit the kingdom prepared for you.

or **B**:

To him who loves us and has freed us from our sins by his blood:
to him be glory and dominion for ever.

You are a chosen race, a royal priesthood, a holy nation,
   God's own people,
**that you may declare the wonderful deeds of him who has
   called you out of darkness into his marvellous light.**

Once you were no people, but now you are God's people;
**once you had not received mercy, but now
   you have received mercy.**

To him who loves us and has freed us from our sins by his blood:
to him be glory and dominion for ever.

THE PRAYERS

INTERCESSIONS may be offered.

THE KYRIES may be used as responses to intercession.

Lord, have mercy.
Lord, have mercy.

Christ, have mercy.
Christ, have mercy.

Lord, have mercy.
Lord, have mercy.

THE COLLECT of the day or one of the following:

Lord, make us instruments of your peace.
Where there is hatred, let us sow love;
where there is injury, pardon;
where there is doubt, faith;
where there is despair, hope;
where there is darkness, light;
where there is sadness, joy.

O Divine Master, grant that we may not so much
seek to be consoled as to console,
to be understood as to understand,
to be loved as to love.
For it is in giving that we receive,
it is in pardoning that we are pardoned,
and it is in dying that we are born to
eternal life. **Amen.**

19th century French Prayer, after Francis of Assisi

Hail, O Lady, holy Queen,
Mary, holy Mother of God,
who are the Virgin made Church,
chosen by the most holy Father in heaven
whom he consecrated, with his most holy belovèd Son
and with the Holy Spirit, the Paraclete,
in whom there was and is
all fullness of grace and every good.
Hail his Palace! Hail his Tabernacle!
Hail his Dwelling! Hail his Robe!
Hail his Servant! Hail his Mother!
and hail all you holy virtues,
which are poured into the hearts of the faithful
through the grace and inspiration of the Holy Spirit,
that from being unbelievers,
you may make them faithful to God. **Amen.**

A Salutation of the Blessed Virgin Mary, Francis of Assisi

THE LORD'S PRAYER may be said.

[Lord Jesus remember us in your kingdom
and teach us to pray.]
Our Father in heaven, . . .

THE CONCLUSION

Let us bless the Lord God living and true!
Let us always give him
praise, glory, honour, blessing and every good.
Amen. Amen. (Alleluia, alleluia.)

Prayer said by Francis of Assisi at the end of the office

Form 7 – Evening Prayer

Saturdays in Ordinary Time
and daily from All Saints' Day to Advent

THE BLESSING OF THE LIGHT *may replace THE PREPARATION*

A light, which may be the Paschal Candle, is brought in, or a candle may simply be lit.

Let us give thanks to our God,
who has delivered us from the dominion of darkness
and made us partakers in the inheritance
of the saints in light.

The light and peace of Jesus Christ be with you
and also with you.

Either, in Ordinary Time:

Blessèd are you, Lord God, creator of day and night:
to you be praise and glory for ever.
As darkness falls you renew your promise
to reveal among us the light of your presence.
By the light of Christ, your living Word,
dispel the darkness of our hearts
that we may walk as children of light
and sing your praise throughout the world,
Father, Son and Holy Spirit:
Blessèd be God for ever.

or, from All Saints to Advent:

Blessèd are you, Sovereign God,
our light and our salvation,
to you be glory and praise for ever.
Now, as darkness is falling,
wash away our transgressions,
cleanse us by your refining fire
and make us temples of your Holy Spirit.
By the light of Christ,
dispel the darkness of our hearts

and make us ready to enter your kingdom,
where songs of praise for ever sound,
Father, Son and Holy Spirit:
Blessèd be God for ever.

*While the other candles are lit the following, another version of number 63,
page 524, or another suitable hymn may be sung.*

A SONG OF THE LIGHT (63c)

1   **Hail, gladdening Light, of his pure glory poured,
    Who is the immortal Father, heavenly, blest,
    Holiest of holies, Jesus Christ our Lord.**

2   **Now we are come to the sun's hour of rest,
    The lights of evening round us shine,
    We hymn the Father, Son and Holy Spirit divine.**

3   **Worthy are you at all times to be sung
    With undefilèd tongue,
    Son of our God, giver of life, alone:
    Therefore in all the world your glories,
        Lord, they own.**

Verses from PSALM 141 may be said and incense may be burned.

**Let my prayer rise before you as incense,
the lifting up of my hands as the evening sacrifice.**

O Lord, I call to you; come to me quickly;
hear my voice when I cry to you.
Set a watch before my mouth, O Lord,
and guard the door of my lips.

**Let my prayer rise before you as incense,
the lifting up of my hands as the evening sacrifice.**

Let not my heart incline to any evil thing;
let me not be occupied in wickedness with evildoers.
But my eyes are turned to you, Lord God,
in you I take refuge;
do not leave me defenceless.

Let my prayer rise before you as incense,
the lifting up of my hands as the evening sacrifice.

Psalm 141.1-4b,8

This prayer may be said:

That this evening may be holy good and peaceful,
let us pray with one heart and mind.
(Silence may be kept.)

As our evening prayer rises before you, O God,
so may your mercy come down upon us
    to cleanse our hearts
and set us free to sing your praise,
now and for ever. Amen.

Evening Prayer continues with the appointed Psalmody.

THE PREPARATION

O God, make speed to save us.
O Lord, make haste to help us.

Your faithful servants bless you.
They make known the glory of your kingdom.

Glory . . .   Alleluia.

THE OPENING CANTICLE

A SONG OF GOD'S LIGHT

1   The Lord is my light and my salvation;
        whom then shall I fear? *
     The Lord is the strength of my life;
        of whom then shall I be afraid?

2   Though a host encamp against me,
        my heart shall not be afraid, *
     and though there rise up war against me,
        yet will I put my trust in him.

3   One thing have I asked of the Lord
        and that alone I seek: *
    that I may dwell in the house of the Lord
        all the days of my life,

4   To behold the fair beauty of the Lord *
    and to seek his will in his temple.

5   For in the day of trouble
        he shall hide me in his shelter; *
    in the secret place of his dwelling shall he hide me
        and set me high upon a rock.

6   Therefore will I offer in his dwelling an oblation
        with great gladness; *
    I will sing and make music to the Lord.

Glory . . .   *Psalm 27.1,3-6,8*

A HYMN may be sung.

The following prayer may be said.

That this evening may be holy good and peaceful,
let us pray with one heart and mind.
(Silence may be kept.)

As our evening prayer rises before you, O God,
so may your mercy come down upon us
**   to cleanse our hearts**
and set us free to sing your praise,
now and for ever. Amen.

THE WORD OF GOD

THE PSALMODY, as appointed

Each psalm, or group of psalms, may end with:

Glory . . .

*If there are two SCRIPTURE READINGS, the first may be read here, or both may
be read after the Second Canticle.*

THE SECOND CANTICLE

In Ordinary Time:

Either A SONG OF THE BLESSÈD (39) or number 54, page 516

Refrain: **Rejoice and be glad**
for you are the light of the world,
and great is your reward in heaven.

1   Blessèd are the poor in spirit, *
    for theirs is the kingdom of heaven.

2   Blessèd are those who mourn, *
    for they shall be comforted.

3   Blessèd are the meek, *
    for they shall inherit the earth.

4   Blessèd are those who hunger
        and thirst after righteousness, *
    for they shall be satisfied.

5   Blessèd are the merciful, *
    for they shall obtain mercy.

6   Blessèd are the pure in heart, *
    for they shall see God.

7   Blessèd are the peacemakers, *
    for they shall be called children of God.

8   Blessèd are those who suffer persecution
        for righteousness' sake, *
    for theirs is the kingdom of heaven.

   Glory . . .   *Matthew 5.3-10*

   Rejoice and be glad
   for you are the light of the world,
   and great is your reward in heaven.

From All Saints to Advent:

Either A SONG OF THE REDEEMED (56) or numbers 50, page 513, or 59, page 520

Refrain: **Salvation belongs to our God,
who will guide us to springs of living water.**

1   Behold, a great multitude *
     which no one could number,

2   From every nation,
        from all tribes and peoples and tongues, *
     standing before the throne and the Lamb.

3   They were clothed in white robes
        and had palms in their hands, *
     and they cried with a loud voice, saying,

4   'Salvation belongs to our God
        who sits on the throne, *
     and to the Lamb.'

5   These are they
        who have come out of the great tribulation, *
     they have washed their robes
        and made them white in the blood of the Lamb;

6   Therefore they stand before the throne of God, *
     whom they serve day and night within the temple.

7   And the One who sits upon the throne *
     will shelter them with his presence.

8   They shall never again feel hunger or thirst, *
     the sun shall not strike them,
        nor any scorching heat.

9   For the Lamb at the heart of the throne *
     will be their Shepherd,

10 He will guide them to springs of living water, *
     and God will wipe away every tear from their eyes.

To the One who sits on the throne and to the Lamb *
be blessing and honour and glory and might,
for ever and ever. Amen.   *Revelation 7.9, 10, 14b-17*

**Salvation belongs to our God,
who will guide us to springs of living water.**

On feasts of Apostles, numbers 49, page 513, and 56, page 517, are alternative canticles.

On feasts of any Saint, numbers 50, page 513, and 52, page 515, are alternative canticles.

For the Departed, number 43, page 508, is an alternative canticle.

THE SCRIPTURE READING(S)

A RESPONSORY may be said.

Lord, you will guide me with your counsel
and afterwards receive me with glory.
**Lord, you will guide me with your counsel
and afterwards receive me with glory.**

For I am always with you;
you hold me by my right hand.
And afterwards receive me with glory.

Glory to the Father and to the Son
and to the Holy Spirit.
**Lord, you will guide me with your counsel
and afterwards receive me with glory.**

from Psalm 73

THE GOSPEL CANTICLE: MAGNIFICAT – THE SONG OF MARY (40)

See either inside front cover, inside back cover or page 504 for another version.

In Ordinary Time:

Refrain: **You have looked with favour on your lowly servant,
from this day all generations will call her blessèd.**

or, from All Saints to Advent:

**The righteous will shine like the sun
in the kingdom of their Father.**

or, on feasts of Apostles:

> **On the foundation stones of the heavenly city
> are written the names of the apostles of the Lamb.
> (Alleluia.)**

or, on feasts of any Saint:

> **In the heavenly kingdom,
> the blessèd have their dwelling place
> and their rest for ever and ever. (Alleluia.)**

or, for the Departed:

> **All that the Father gives to me will come to me;
> and the one who comes to me I will not cast out.**

The refrain is repeated after the canticle.

THE PRAYERS

INTERCESSIONS may be offered.

THE KYRIES may be used as responses to intercession.

Lord, have mercy.
Lord, have mercy.

Christ, have mercy.
Christ, have mercy.

Lord, have mercy.
Lord, have mercy.

THE COLLECT of the day, or one of the following:

O God, our protector,
by whose mercy the world turns safely into darkness
and returns again to light:
we give into your hands our unfinished tasks,
our unsolved problems,
and our unfulfilled hopes;
for you alone are our sure defence
and bring us lasting peace
in Jesus Christ our Lord. **Amen.**

or, from All Saints to Advent:

Almighty God,
from whom all thoughts of truth and peace proceed:
kindle, we pray, in the hearts of all, the true love of peace
and guide with your pure and peaceable wisdom
those who take counsel for the nations of the earth
that in tranquillity your kingdom may go forward,
till the earth is filled with the knowledge of your love;
through Jesus Christ our Lord. **Amen.**

THE LORD'S PRAYER may be said.

[Uniting our prayers with the whole company of heaven,]
as our Saviour taught us, so we pray
Our Father in heaven, . . .

THE CONCLUSION

In Ordinary Time:

**The grace of our Lord Jesus Christ,
and the love of God,
and the fellowship of the Holy Spirit,
be with us all evermore. Amen.**

Let us bless the Lord.
Thanks be to God.

or, from All Saints to Advent:

**May Christ, who has opened the kingdom of heaven,
bring us to reign with him in glory. Amen.**

Let us bless the Lord.
Thanks be to God.

or, on Class I & II Holy Days:

May our blessèd Lady pray for us.
May Saint Francis and Saint Clare pray for us.
[May Saint N pray for us.]
May all the saints of God pray for us.
May the angels of God befriend us
   and watch around us to protect us.
May the Lord Jesus give us his blessing of peace.   Amen.

Let us bless the Lord. (Alleluia. Alleluia.)
Thanks be to God. (Alleluia. Alleluia.)

Form 7 – Night Prayer

Saturdays in Ordinary Time
and daily from All Saints' Day to Advent

THE PREPARATION

The Lord almighty grant us a quiet night and a perfect end.
Amen.

Our help is in the name of the Lord
who made heaven and earth.

A period of silence for reflection on the past day may follow.
The following or other suitable words of penitence may be used.

Holy God,
we confess to you before the company
**   of the faithful in heaven and on earth,**
that we have sinned against you,
against one another
and against your creation.
Forgive us in your mercy,
help us to forgive each other
and to hold in reverence
**   all that you have made. Amen.**

OSB West Malling

or:

Holy God,
holy and strong,
holy and immortal:
have mercy on us.

O God, make speed to save us.
O Lord, make haste to help us.

Glory . . .   Alleluia.

The following or another suitable HYMN may be sung.

Before the ending of the day,
Creator of the world, we pray
That you, with steadfast love, would keep
Your watch around us while we sleep.

From evil dreams defend our sight,
From fears and terrors of the night;
Tread under foot our deadly foe
That we no sinful thought may know.

Ordinary Time Doxology
O Father, that we ask be done
Through Jesus Christ, your only Son;
And Holy Spirit, by whose breath
Our souls are raised to life from death. Amen.

All Saints to Advent Doxology
Most loving Father, hear our plea!
You rule the world with equity,
Together with your only Son,
And with your Spirit, three in one. Amen.

THE WORD OF GOD

THE PSALMODY
One or more of the following psalms may be used.

Psalm 4

1   Answer me when I call, O God of my righteousness; *
     you set me at liberty when I was in trouble;
      have mercy on me and hear my prayer.

2   How long will you nobles dishonour my glory; *
     how long will you love vain things and seek after falsehood?

3   But know that the Lord has shown me his marvellous kindness; *
     when I call upon the Lord, he will hear me.

4   Stand in awe, and sin not; *
     commune with your own heart upon your bed, and be still.

5   Offer the sacrifices of righteousness *
     and put your trust in the Lord.

6   There are many that say, 'Who will show us any good?' *
     Lord, lift up the light of your countenance upon us.

7   You have put gladness in my heart, *
     more than when their corn and wine and oil increase.

8   In peace I will lie down and sleep, *
     for it is you Lord, only, who make me dwell in safety.

Psalm 91

I   Whoever dwells in the shelter of the Most High *
     and abides under the shadow of the Almighty,

2   Shall say to the Lord, 'My refuge and my stronghold, *
     my God, in whom I put my trust.'

3   For he shall deliver you from the snare of the fowler *
     and from the deadly pestilence.

4   He shall cover you with his wings
      and you shall be safe under his feathers; *
     his faithfulness shall be your shield and buckler.

5   You shall not be afraid of any terror by night, *
     nor of the arrow that flies by day;

6   Of the pestilence that stalks in darkness, *
     nor of the sickness that destroys at noonday.

7   Though a thousand fall at your side
      and ten thousand at your right hand, *
     yet it shall not come near you.

8   Your eyes have only to behold *
     to see the reward of the wicked.

9   Because you have made the Lord your refuge *
     and the Most High your stronghold,

10   There shall no evil happen to you, *
     neither shall any plague come near your tent.

11   For he shall give his angels charge over you, *
     to keep you in all your ways.

12   They shall bear you in their hands, *
     lest you dash your foot against a stone.

13   You shall tread upon the lion and adder; *
     the young lion and the serpent you shall trample underfoot.

14   Because they have set their love upon me,
       therefore will I deliver them; *
     I will lift them up, because they know my name.

15   They will call upon me and I will answer them; *
     I am with them in trouble,
       I will deliver them and bring them to honour.

16   With long life will I satisfy them *
     and show them my salvation.

Psalm 134

1   Come, bless the Lord, all you servants of the Lord, *
     you that by night stand in the house of the Lord.

2   Lift up your hands towards the sanctuary *
     and bless the Lord.

3   The Lord who made heaven and earth *
     give you blessing out of Zion.

     Glory . . .

THE READING: one of the following or some other.

Either, in Ordinary Time:

A sabbath rest still remains for the people of God; for those who enter
God's rest also cease from their labours, as God did from his. Let us,
therefore, make every effort to enter that rest.

Hebrews 4. 9-11

or, in All Saints to Advent:

The one who endures to the end will be saved. And this good news of the
kingdom will be proclaimed throughout the world as a testimony to all the
nations.

Matthew 24.13,14a

or, on feasts of Apostles:

You are no longer strangers and aliens but citizens with the saints and also members of the household of God, built upon the foundation of the apostles and the prophets, with Christ Jesus himself as the cornerstone. In him the whole structure is joined together and grows into a holy temple in the Lord.

Ephesians 2.19-21

or, on feasts of any Saint:

Finally, belovèd, whatever is true, whatever is honourable, whatever is just, whatever is pure, whatever is pleasing, whatever is commendable, if there is any excellence and if there is anything worthy of praise, think about these things. Keep on doing the things that you have learned and received and heard and seen in me, and the God of peace will be with you.

Philippians 4..8,9

or, for the Departed:

For if we have been united with Christ in a death like his, we will certainly be united with him in a resurrection like his.

Romans 6.5

THE RESPONSORY may be said.

Into your hands, O Lord,
I commend my spirit. (Alleluia, alleluia.)
Into your hands, O Lord,
I commend my spirit. (Alleluia, alleluia.)

For you have redeemed me, Lord God of truth.
I commend my spirit. (*or:* Alleluia, alleluia.)

Glory to the Father and to the Son
and to the Holy Spirit.
Into your hands, O Lord,
I commend my spirit. (Alleluia, alleluia.)

Keep me as the apple of your eye.
Hide me under the shadow of your wings.

THE GOSPEL CANTICLE: NUNC DIMITTIS – THE SONG OF SIMEON (42) or another version on page 508

When Night Prayer for Saturday is being used as standard, the appropriate seasonal refrain should be used.

Refrain: **Save us, O Lord, while waking,**
and guard us while sleeping,
that awake we may watch with Christ,
and asleep may rest in peace.

or, in All Saints to Advent:

O King most blessèd,
on the day of judgement
number us among your chosen.

or, on Class I & II Holy Days:

Grant us your light, O Lord,
that the darkness of our hearts being overcome,
we may receive the true light,
even Christ our Saviour. (Alleluia.)

1 ✠ Now, Lord, you let your servant go in peace: *
your word has been fulfilled.

2 My own eyes have seen the salvation *
which you have prepared in the sight of every people:

3 A light to reveal you to the nations *
and the glory of your people Israel.

Glory . . . *Luke 2. 29-32*

The refrain is repeated after the canticle.

THE PRAYERS

Intercessions and thanksgivings may be offered here.

THE COLLECT: one of the following or some other.

Either, in Ordinary Time:

Stay with us, O God, this night,
so that by your strength
we may rise with the new day
to rejoice in the resurrection of your Son,
Jesus Christ our Saviour. **Amen.**

or:

Lighten our darkness,
Lord, we pray;
and in your mercy defend us from all perils
    and dangers of this night;
for the love of your only Son,
our Saviour Jesus Christ. **Amen.**

or, in All Saints to Advent:

God and Father of our Lord Jesus Christ,
bring us to the dwelling which your Son is preparing
    for all who love you;
give us the will each day to live in life eternal;
let our citizenship be in heaven with the blessèd,
with the whole company of the redeemed
and with countless angels,
praising, worshipping and adoring your Son,
our Lord Jesus Christ,
who sits upon the throne for ever and ever. **Amen.**

THE LORD'S PRAYER may be said.

[As we come to the ending of the day,]
as our Saviour taught us, so we pray
Our Father in heaven, . . .

THE CONCLUSION

In peace, we will lie down and sleep;
for you alone, Lord, make us dwell in safety.

Abide with us, Lord Jesus,
for the night is at hand and the day is now past.

As the night-watch looks for the morning,
so do we look for you, O Christ.

[Come with the dawning of the day
**and make yourself known
in the breaking of the bread.**]

Either, in Ordinary Time:

**The Lord bless us and watch over us;
the Lord make his face shine upon us
    and be gracious to us;
the Lord look kindly on us
    and give us peace. Amen.**

or, in All Saints to Advent:

**May the light of Christ, the King of all,
shine ever brighter in our hearts,
that with all the saints in light
we may shine forth as lights in the world. Amen.**

A MARIAN ANTHEM may be sung.

SALVE REGINA

Traditionally, this anthem is sung at the end of Night Prayer from after Pentecost to Advent; or it may be the unchanging final anthem. The other Marian anthems may be found on page 775.

Salve, Regina, mater misericordiae;
vita, dulcedo, et spes nostra, salve.
Ad te clamamus, exsules, filii Evae,
ad te suspiramus,
gementes et flentes in hac lacrimarum valle;
eia ergo, advocata nostra,
illos tuos misericordes oculos ad nos converte,
Et Iesum, benedictum fructum ventris tui,
nobis post hoc exsilium ostende.
O clemens, O pia, O dulcis Virgo Maria.

The Vigil Office

*This Office, which replaces both Evening Prayer and Night Prayer, may be used on
the evening before a Sunday or Principal Feast in the following order: it begins
with the Blessing of Light and then continues with a repeating pattern of reading,
psalm or canticle, silence and prayer; it concludes with the Gospel proclamation,
the Gospel Canticle, the prayers and the blessing.*

*Alternatively, a Vigil may be kept less formally; those present participate
by contributing readings and poetry, music and song, testimony and prayer.*

PREPARATION

The Blessing of Light

In the evening, Jesus came and stood among the disciples and said to them:
'Peace be with you.' (Alleluia.)   *John 20.19*

The light and peace of Jesus Christ be with you all
and also with you.

Blessèd are you, Sovereign God,
our light and our salvation,
eternal creator of day and night,
to you be glory and praise for ever.
Now, as darkness is falling,
hear the prayer of your faithful people.
As we look for your coming in glory,
wash away our transgressions,
cleanse us by your refining fire
and make us temples of your Holy Spirit.
By the light of Christ,
dispel the darkness of our hearts
and make us ready to enter your kingdom,
where songs of praise for ever sound,
Father, Son and Holy Spirit.
Blessèd be God for ever.

*Other candles may be lit as Phos Hilaron, A SONG OF THE LIGHT (63),
page 524, the following, or another suitable hymn or canticle, is sung.*

**Hail, gladdening Light, of his pure glory poured
Who is the immortal Father, heavenly, blest,
Holiest of holies, Jesus Christ our Lord.**

Now we are come to the sun's hour of rest,
The lights of evening round us shine,
We hymn the Father, Son, and Holy Spirit divine.

Worthy are you at all times to be sung
With undefilèd tongue,
Son of our God, giver of life, alone:
Therefore in all the world your glories,
   Lord, they own.

Verses from PSALM 141 may be said and incense may be burned.

Let my prayer rise before you as incense,
the lifting up of my hands as the evening sacrifice.

O Lord, I call to you; come to me quickly;
hear my voice when I cry to you.
Set a watch before my mouth, O Lord, *
and guard the door of my lips;

Let my prayer rise before you as incense,
the lifting up of my hands as the evening sacrifice.

Let not my heart incline to any evil thing;
let me not be occupied in wickedness with evildoers.
But my eyes are turned to you, Lord God;
in you I take refuge;
do not leave me defenceless.

Let my prayer rise before you as incense,
the lifting up of my hands as the evening sacrifice.

Psalm 141.1-4b, 8

This prayer may be said:

That this evening may be holy, good and peaceful,
let us pray with one heart and mind.
(Silence may be kept.)

As our evening prayer rises before you, O God,
so may your mercy come down upon us
   to cleanse our hearts
and set us free to sing your praise
now and for ever. Amen.

THE WORD OF GOD

An Old Testament reading, a psalm, silence and this or another suitable Collect follow.

God of glory,
you nourish us with your word
which is the bread of life.
Fill us with your Holy Spirit,
that through us the light of your glory
   may shine in all the world;
we ask this in the name of Jesus Christ, our Saviour. **Amen.**

A NEW TESTAMENT READING

THE SONG OF CHRIST'S GLORY or another suitable canticle

Refrain: **At the name of Jesus
     every knee shall bow.**

1   Christ Jesus was in the form of God, *
    but he did not cling to equality with God.

2   He emptied himself, taking the form of a servant, *
    and was born in our human likeness.

3   Being found in human form he humbled himself, *
    and became obedient unto death, even death on a cross.

4   Therefore God has highly exalted him, *
    and bestowed on him the name above every name,

5   That at the name of Jesus every knee should bow, *
    in heaven and on earth and under the earth;

6   And every tongue confess that Jesus Christ is Lord, *
    to the glory of God the Father.

Glory . . .   *Philippians 2.5-11*

**At the name of Jesus
every knee shall bow.**

Silence

THE COLLECT

Kindle in our hearts, O God,
the flame of love which never ceases,
that it may burn in us, giving light to others.
May we shine for ever in your temple,
set on fire with your eternal light,
even your Son Jesus Christ,
our Saviour and our Redeemer. **Amen.**

Columba (597)

THE GOSPEL READING for the Sunday or Principal Feast is read.
The reading may be introduced by this acclamation.

We proclaim not ourselves, but Christ Jesus as Lord
and ourselves as your servants for Jesus' sake.

For the God who said, Let light shine out of darkness,
has caused the light to shine within us:

to give the light of the knowledge of the glory of God
in the face of Jesus Christ.

Hear the Gospel of our Lord Jesus Christ according to N.
Glory to you, O Lord.

After the Gospel reading:

This is the Gospel of the Lord.
Praise to you, O Christ.

Lord, you will guide me with your counsel
and afterwards receive me with glory.
**Lord, you will guide me with your counsel
and afterwards receive me with glory.**

For I am always with you;
you hold me by my right hand.
And afterwards receive me with glory.

Glory to the Father and to the Son
and to the Holy Spirit.
**Lord, you will guide me with your counsel
and afterwards receive me with glory.**

from Psalm 73

THE GOSPEL CANTICLE: MAGNIFICAT – THE SONG OF MARY (40)
follows with the appropriate Refrain.

See either inside front cover, inside back cover or page 504 for another version.

THE PRAYERS

A litany or a suitable chant may be said or sung.

THE COLLECT of the morrow

THE LORD'S PRAYER

[Awaiting the fulfilment of all God's promises,]
as our Saviour taught us, so we pray
Our Father in heaven, . . .

THE CONCLUSION

**The Lord bless us with every spiritual gift
as we wait for our Lord Jesus Christ to be revealed.
Amen.**

Let us bless the Lord. (Alleluia, alleluia.)
Thanks be to God. (Alleluia, alleluia.)

The Psalter

Introduction

The psalms have had a staple place in the daily prayer of Christians from earliest times. They constitute the nearest thing to a Jewish 'hymn book' that exists and phrases of the psalms were on the lips of Jesus. Down the centuries Christians have found nothing better to express the different moods and experiences of human beings before God. Extreme feelings, both good and bad, are included and can be expressed by individuals or groups as a way of sharing in the need for redemption through the mercy and love of God. If a group or individual considers such verses are not suitable for public worship they can omit the verses in brackets.

In Christian history there have been two main methods of organising the Psalter for public worship. In one the psalms are recited 'in course', basically in numerical order, morning and evening, over a period of weeks. *Common Worship: Daily Prayer* uses this arrangement for the psalms on weekdays in Ordinary Time, with some allowance either to suitability for the time of day or the day of the week. The other is to use psalms in a 'thematic' way reflecting the nature of a season or Sunday or Holy Day.

How to Recite

Even when praying alone individuals may find it helpful to pray the psalms aloud. When two or more gather together in worship, psalms may be sung or said in a number of different ways. The two commonest methods are:

(a) with the verses alternated between one half of the group and the other with the 'boundary' between the two groups clearly defined beforehand;

(b) with the verses alternated between the leader and the others.

Less common methods are:

(c) by a solo voice, while everyone listens in silence – particularly suitable for more personal or penitential psalms;

(d) by everyone together – particularly suitable for praise psalms;

(e) responsorially, with a solo voice reciting the psalm and the rest of the people responding with the refrain after groups of verses; certain psalms have refrains printed in italics which can also be used in this way.

Helps in Praying the Psalter

1 **The Refrain** Optional Refrains, also known as Antiphons, are provided at the beginning of each psalm, and may also be used at the end (see below). These are drawn either from the same psalm or elsewhere in the Psalter. They express one of the themes of a psalm to help focus its use in prayer and praise. The refrain before the psalm may be said or sung by the Officiant or Cantor and then repeated by the community. If it is used after the psalm, the Refrain is said or sung by all.

2 **The Psalm Prayer** Each psalm is provided with an optional short prayer, which develops a theme from the text and places it in the context of Jesus Christ, the fulfiller of the Old Covenant and the giver of the New Covenant. The Psalm Prayer may be said either by an individual or the whole group.

3 **The Mid-Point** An asterisk (*) marks the mid-point of each psalm, where a pause is observed as an aid to recollection. Recitation with a gentle and regular pace will help to unite the group and focus the worship on God.

4 **Silence** A pause for reflection and individual prayer may follow each psalm. This is particularly suitable if the Psalm Prayer is being used.

5 **Doxology** Each psalm or group of psalms may end with

either:

**Glory to the Father and to the Son
 and to the Holy Spirit; ***
**as it was in the beginning, is now,
 and shall be for ever. Amen.**

or:

**Glory to God, Source of all being,
 Eternal Word and Holy Spirit; ***
**as it was in the beginning, is now,
 and shall be for ever. Amen.**

In this way the prayer of the psalm is drawn into the never-ending prayer and praise of the Triune God.

6 **Examples** Three possible ways of using the material provided with the Psalter are as follows:

A	B	C
Refrain	Refrain	Refrain
Psalm	Psalm	Psalm
Gloria	Silence	Silence
Refrain	Gloria, at end of each psalm or group of psalms	Psalm Prayer

Psalm 1

[Refrain: The Lord knows the way of the righteous.]

1   Blessèd are they who have not walked
        in the counsel of the wicked, *
    nor lingered in the way of sinners,
        nor sat in the assembly of the scornful.

2   Their delight is in the law of the Lord *
    and they meditate on his law day and night.

3   Like a tree planted by streams of water
    bearing fruit in due season, with leaves that do not wither, *
        whatever they do, it shall prosper.

4   As for the wicked, it is not so with them; *
    they are like chaff which the wind blows away.

5   Therefore the wicked shall not be able to stand
        in the judgement, *
    nor the sinner in the congregation of the righteous.

6   For the Lord knows the way of the righteous, *
    but the way of the wicked shall perish.

    [Christ our wisdom,
    give us delight in your law,
    that we may bear fruits of patience and peace
    in the kingdom of the righteous;
    for your mercy's sake. Amen.]

Psalm 2

[Refrain: The Lord is the strength of his people,
            a sure refuge for his anointed.]

1   Why are the nations in tumult, *
    and why do the peoples devise a vain plot?

2   The kings of the earth rise up,
        and the rulers take counsel together, *
    against the Lord and against his anointed:

3   'Let us break their bonds asunder *
    and cast away their cords from us.'

4   He who dwells in heaven shall laugh them to scorn; *
    the Lord shall have them in derision.

5   Then shall he speak to them in his wrath *
    and terrify them in his fury:

6   'Yet have I set my king *
    upon my holy hill of Zion.'

7   I will proclaim the decree of the Lord; *
    he said to me: 'You are my Son;
       this day have I begotten you.

8   'Ask of me and I will give you the nations
       for your inheritance *
    and the ends of the earth for your possession.

9   'You shall break them with a rod of iron *
    and dash them in pieces like a potter's vessel.'

10 Now therefore be wise, O kings; *
    be prudent, you judges of the earth.

11 Serve the Lord with fear, and with trembling kiss his feet, *
    lest he be angry and you perish from the way,
       for his wrath is quickly kindled.

12 Happy are all they *
    who take refuge in him.

    *[Most high and holy God,
    lift our eyes to your Son
    enthroned on Calvary;
    and as we behold his meekness,
    shatter our earthly pride;
    for he is Lord for ever and ever. Amen.]*

Psalm 3

[Refrain: You, Lord, are a shield about me.]

1   Lord, how many are my adversaries; *
    many are they who rise up against me.

2   Many are they who say to my soul, *
    'There is no help for you in your God.'

3   But you, Lord, are a shield about me; *
     you are my glory, and the lifter up of my head.

4   When I cry aloud to the Lord, *
     he will answer me from his holy hill;

5   I lie down and sleep and rise again, *
     because the Lord sustains me.

6   I will not be afraid of hordes of the peoples *
     that have set themselves against me all around.

7   Rise up, O Lord, and deliver me, O my God, *
     for you strike all my enemies on the cheek
        and break the teeth of the wicked.

8   Salvation belongs to the Lord: *
     may your blessing be upon your people.

     *[Shield us, Lord, from all evil,
     and lift us from apathy and despair,
     that even when we are terrified,
     we may trust your power to save;
     through Jesus Christ our Lord. Amen.]*

Psalm 4

[Refrain: In peace I will lie down and sleep.]

1   Answer me when I call, O God of my righteousness; *
     you set me at liberty when I was in trouble;
        have mercy on me and hear my prayer.

2   How long will you nobles dishonour my glory; *
     how long will you love vain things and seek after falsehood?

3   But know that the Lord has shown me his marvellous kindness; *
     when I call upon the Lord, he will hear me.

4   Stand in awe, and sin not; *
     commune with your own heart upon your bed, and be still.

5   Offer the sacrifices of righteousness *
     and put your trust in the Lord.

6   There are many that say, 'Who will show us any good?' *
     Lord, lift up the light of your countenance upon us.

7   You have put gladness in my heart, *
    more than when their corn and wine and oil increase.

8   In peace I will lie down and sleep, *
    for it is you Lord, only, who make me dwell in safety.

    *[Give us today, O God,
    a glad heart and a clear conscience,
    that when we come to this day's end
    we may rest in peace with Christ our Lord. Amen.]*

Psalm 5

[Refrain: You, O Lord, will bless the righteous.]

1   Give ear to my words, O Lord; *
    consider my lamentation.

2   Hearken to the voice of my crying, my King and my God, *
    for to you I make my prayer.

3   In the morning, Lord, you will hear my voice; *
    early in the morning I make my appeal to you, and look up.

4   For you are the God who takes no pleasure in wickedness; *
    no evil can dwell with you.

5   The boastful cannot stand in your sight; *
    you hate all those that work wickedness.

6   You destroy those who speak lies; *
    the bloodthirsty and deceitful the Lord will abhor.

7   But as for me, through the greatness of your mercy,
        I will come into your house; *
    I will bow down towards your holy temple in awe of you.

8   Lead me, Lord, in your righteousness,
        because of my enemies; *
    make your way straight before my face.

9   For there is no truth in their mouth,
        in their heart is destruction, *
    their throat is an open sepulchre,
        and they flatter with their tongue.

10 Punish them, O God; *
    let them fall through their own devices.

11 Because of their many transgressions cast them out, *
    for they have rebelled against you.

12 But let all who take refuge in you be glad; *
    let them sing out their joy for ever.

13 You will shelter them, *
    so that those who love your name may exult in you.

14 For you, O Lord, will bless the righteous; *
    and with your favour you will defend them as with a shield.

*[Lord, protect us from the deceit
of flattering tongues and lying lips;
give us words of life which speak your truth
and bless your name;
through Jesus Christ our Lord. Amen.]*

Psalm 6

[Refrain: Turn again, O Lord, and deliver my soul.]

1 O Lord, rebuke me not in your wrath; *
    neither chasten me in your fierce anger.

2 Have mercy on me, Lord, for I am weak; *
    Lord, heal me, for my bones are racked.

3 My soul also shakes with terror; *
    how long, O Lord, how long?

4 Turn again, O Lord, and deliver my soul; *
    save me for your loving mercy's sake.

5 For in death no one remembers you; *
    and who can give you thanks in the grave?

6 I am weary with my groaning; *
    every night I drench my pillow
      and flood my bed with my tears.

7 My eyes are wasted with grief *
    and worn away because of all my enemies.

8   Depart from me, all you that do evil, *
       for the Lord has heard the voice of my weeping.

9   The Lord has heard my supplication; *
       the Lord will receive my prayer.

10   All my enemies shall be put to shame and confusion; *
       they shall suddenly turn back in their shame.

       [Lord Jesus Christ,
       may the tears shed in your earthly life
       be balm for all who weep,
       and may the prayers of your pilgrimage
       give strength to all who suffer;
       for your mercy's sake. Amen.]

Psalm 7

       [Refrain: Give judgement for me
       *   according to my righteousness, O Lord.]*

1   O Lord my God, in you I take refuge; *
       save me from all who pursue me, and deliver me,

2   Lest they rend me like a lion and tear me in pieces *
       while there is no one to help me.

3   O Lord my God, if I have done these things: *
       if there is any wickedness in my hands,

4   If I have repaid my friend with evil, *
       or plundered my enemy without a cause,

5   Then let my enemy pursue me and overtake me, *
       trample my life to the ground,
          and lay my honour in the dust.

6   Rise up, O Lord, in your wrath;
          lift yourself up against the fury of my enemies. *
       Awaken, my God, the judgement that you have commanded.

7   Let the assembly of the peoples gather round you; *
       be seated high above them: O Lord, judge the nations.

8   Give judgement for me
          according to my righteousness, O Lord, *
       and according to the innocence that is in me.

9   Let the malice of the wicked come to an end,
        but establish the righteous; *
    for you test the mind and heart, O righteous God.

10   God is my shield that is over me; *
    he saves the true of heart.

11   God is a righteous judge; *
    he is provoked all day long.

12   If they will not repent, God will whet his sword; *
    he has bent his bow and made it ready.

13   He has prepared the weapons of death; *
    he makes his arrows shafts of fire.

14   Behold those who are in labour with wickedness, *
    who conceive evil and give birth to lies.

15   They dig a pit and make it deep *
    and fall into the hole that they have made for others.

16   Their mischief rebounds on their own head; *
    their violence falls on their own scalp.

17   I will give thanks to the Lord for his righteousness, *
    and I will make music to the name of the Lord Most High.

[Lord, your justice turns evil on itself:
move us to examine our hearts
and repent of all duplicity;
for the sake of Jesus Christ,
our Judge and righteous Saviour. Amen.]

Psalm 8

1   *O Lord our governor, ***
    how glorious is your name in all the world!

2   Your majesty above the heavens is praised *
    out of the mouths of babes at the breast.

3   You have founded a stronghold against your foes, *
    that you might still the enemy and the avenger.

4   When I consider your heavens, the work of your fingers, *
    the moon and the stars that you have ordained,

5   What is man, that you should be mindful of him; *
     the son of man, that you should seek him out?

6   You have made him little lower than the angels *
     and crown him with glory and honour.

7   You have given him dominion over the works of your hands *
     and put all things under his feet,

8   All sheep and oxen, *
     even the wild beasts of the field,

9   The birds of the air, the fish of the sea *
     and whatsoever moves in the paths of the sea.

10   *O Lord our governor, *
     how glorious is your name in all the world!*

     *[We bless you, master of the heavens,
     for the wonderful order which enfolds this world;
     grant that your whole creation
     may find fulfilment in the Son of Man,
     Jesus Christ our Saviour. Amen.]*

Psalm 9

     [Refrain: You, Lord, have never failed those who seek you.]

1   I will give thanks to you, Lord, with my whole heart; *
     I will tell of all your marvellous works.

2   I will be glad and rejoice in you; *
     I will make music to your name, O Most High.

3   When my enemies are driven back, *
     they stumble and perish at your presence.

4   For you have maintained my right and my cause; *
     you sat on your throne giving righteous judgement.

5   You have rebuked the nations and destroyed the wicked; *
     you have blotted out their name for ever and ever.

6   The enemy was utterly laid waste. *
     You uprooted their cities;
        their very memory has perished.

7   But the Lord shall endure for ever; *
      he has made fast his throne for judgement.

8   For he shall rule the world with righteousness *
      and govern the peoples with equity.

9   Then will the Lord be a refuge for the oppressed, *
      a refuge in the time of trouble.

10   And those who know your name will put their trust in you, *
      for you, Lord, have never failed those who seek you.

11   Sing praises to the Lord who dwells in Zion; *
      declare among the peoples the things he has done.

12   The avenger of blood has remembered them; *
      he did not forget the cry of the oppressed.

13   Have mercy upon me, O Lord; *
      consider the trouble I suffer from those who hate me,
        you that lift me up from the gates of death;

14   That I may tell all your praises in the gates of the city of Zion *
      and rejoice in your salvation.

15   The nations shall sink into the pit of their making *
      and in the snare which they set will their own foot be taken.

16   The Lord makes himself known by his acts of justice; *
      the wicked are snared in the works of their own hands.

17   They shall return to the land of darkness, *
      all the nations that forget God.

18   For the needy shall not always be forgotten *
      and the hope of the poor shall not perish for ever.

19   Arise, O Lord, and let not mortals have the upper hand; *
      let the nations be judged before your face.

20   Put them in fear, O Lord, *
      that the nations may know themselves to be but mortal.

[Remember, Lord, all who cry to you
from death's dark gates;
do not forget those whom the world forgets,
but raise your faithful ones to Zion's gate,

with your all-conquering Son,
Jesus Christ our Lord. Amen.]

Psalm 10

[Refrain: You, Lord, have never failed those who seek you.]

1   Why stand so far off, O Lord? *
     Why hide yourself in time of trouble?

2   The wicked in their pride persecute the poor; *
     let them be caught in the schemes they have devised.

3   The wicked boast of their heart's desire; *
     the covetous curse and revile the Lord.

4   The wicked in their arrogance say, 'God will not avenge it'; *
     in all their scheming God counts for nothing.

5   They are stubborn in all their ways,
        for your judgements are far above out of their sight; *
     they scoff at all their adversaries.

6   They say in their heart, 'I shall not be shaken; *
     no harm shall ever happen to me.'

7   Their mouth is full of cursing, deceit and fraud; *
     under their tongue lie mischief and wrong.

8   They lurk in the outskirts
        and in dark alleys they murder the innocent; *
     their eyes are ever watching for the helpless.

9   They lie in wait, like a lion in his den;
        they lie in wait to seize the poor; *
     they seize the poor when they get them into their net.

10   The innocent are broken and humbled before them; *
     the helpless fall before their power.

11   They say in their heart, 'God has forgotten; *
     he hides his face away; he will never see it.'

12   Arise, O Lord God, and lift up your hand; *
     forget not the poor.

13   Why should the wicked be scornful of God? *
       Why should they say in their hearts, 'You will not avenge it'?

14   Surely, you behold trouble and misery; *
       you see it and take it into your own hand.

15   The helpless commit themselves to you, *
       for you are the helper of the orphan.

16   Break the power of the wicked and malicious; *
       search out their wickedness until you find none.

17   The Lord shall reign for ever and ever; *
       the nations shall perish from his land.

18   Lord, you will hear the desire of the poor; *
       you will incline your ear to the fullness of their heart,

19   To give justice to the orphan and oppressed, *
       so that people are no longer driven in terror from the land.

*[When wickedness triumphs
and the poor are betrayed,
come to your kingdom, strong and holy God,
destroy the masks of evil
and reign in our broken hearts;
through Jesus Christ our Lord. Amen.]*

Psalm 11

[Refrain: The Lord's throne is in heaven.]

1   In the Lord have I taken refuge; *
      how then can you say to me,
        'Flee like a bird to the hills,

2   'For see how the wicked bend the bow
      and fit their arrows to the string, *
      to shoot from the shadows at the true of heart.

3   'When the foundations are destroyed, *
      what can the righteous do?'

4   The Lord is in his holy temple; *
      the Lord's throne is in heaven.

5　His eyes behold, *
　　his eyelids try every mortal being.

6　The Lord tries the righteous as well as the wicked, *
　　but those who delight in violence his soul abhors.

7　Upon the wicked he shall rain coals of fire
　　　and burning sulphur; *
　　scorching wind shall be their portion to drink.

8　For the Lord is righteous;
　　　he loves righteous deeds, *
　　and those who are upright shall behold his face.

[God of heaven,
when the foundations are shaken
and there is no escape,
test us, but not to destruction,
look on the face of your anointed
and heal us in Jesus Christ your Son. Amen.]

Psalm 12

[Refrain:　You, O Lord, will watch over us.]

1　Help me, Lord, for no one godly is left; *
　　the faithful have vanished from the whole human race.

2　They all speak falsely with their neighbour; *
　　they flatter with their lips, but speak from a double heart.

3　O that the Lord would cut off all flattering lips *
　　and the tongue that speaks proud boasts!

4　Those who say, 'With our tongue will we prevail; *
　　our lips we will use; who is lord over us?'

5　'Because of the oppression of the needy,
　　　and the groaning of the poor, *
　　I will rise up now,' says the Lord,
　　　'and set them in the safety that they long for.'

6　The words of the Lord are pure words, *
　　like silver refined in the furnace
　　　and purified seven times in the fire.

7   You, O Lord, will watch over us *
    and guard us from this generation for ever.

8   The wicked strut on every side, *
    when what is vile is exalted by the whole human race.

    *[Lord, when faith is faint
    and speech veils our intentions,
    restore us by your word of power and purity,
    both now and for ever. Amen.]*

Psalm 13

[Refrain: I love the Lord, for he has heard the voice of my supplication.]

1   How long will you forget me, O Lord; for ever? *
    How long will you hide your face from me?

2   How long shall I have anguish in my soul
        and grief in my heart, day after day? *
    How long shall my enemy triumph over me?

3   Look upon me and answer, O Lord my God; *
    lighten my eyes, lest I sleep in death;

4   Lest my enemy say, 'I have prevailed against him,' *
    and my foes rejoice that I have fallen.

5   But I put my trust in your steadfast love; *
    my heart will rejoice in your salvation.

6   I will sing to the Lord, *
    for he has dealt so bountifully with me.

    *[Jesus Christ, Son of God,
    who passed through the dark sleep of death,
    remember those who cry to you
    in shame and silence and defeat
    and raise them to your risen life,
    for you are alive and reign for ever. Amen.]*

Psalm 14

[Refrain: The fear of the Lord is the beginning of wisdom.]

1   The fool has said in his heart, 'There is no God.' *
    Corrupt are they, and abominable in their wickedness;
        there is no one that does good.

2   The Lord has looked down from heaven
        upon the children of earth, *
    to see if there is anyone who is wise
        and seeks after God.

3   But every one has turned back;
        all alike have become corrupt: *
    there is none that does good; no, not one.

4   Have they no knowledge, those evildoers, *
    who eat up my people as if they ate bread
        and do not call upon the Lord?

5   There shall they be in great fear; *
    for God is in the company of the righteous.

6   Though they would confound the counsel of the poor, *
    yet the Lord shall be their refuge.

7   O that Israel's salvation would come out of Zion! *
    When the Lord restores the fortunes of his people,
        then will Jacob rejoice and Israel be glad.

*[God of heaven,
look with mercy on all who are consumed
by ignorance and greed,
and let the children of earth know
that you are God for ever. Amen.]*

Psalm 15

*[Refrain: Through the greatness of your mercy,
            I will come into your house.]*

1   Lord, who may dwell in your tabernacle? *
    Who may rest upon your holy hill?

2   Whoever leads an uncorrupt life *
      and does the thing that is right;

3   Who speaks the truth from the heart *
      and bears no deceit on the tongue;

4   Who does no evil to a friend *
      and pours no scorn on a neighbour;

5   In whose sight the wicked are not esteemed, *
      but who honours those who fear the Lord.

6   Whoever has sworn to a neighbour *
      and never goes back on that word;

7   Who does not lend money in hope of gain, *
      nor takes a bribe against the innocent;

8   Whoever does these things *
      shall never fall.

[Lord, lead us to our heavenly home
by single steps of self-restraint
and deeds of righteousness;
through the grace of Jesus Christ our Lord. Amen.]

Psalm 16

[Refrain: The Lord is at my right hand; I shall not fall.]

1   Preserve me, O God, for in you have I taken refuge; *
      I have said to the Lord, 'You are my lord,
        all my good depends on you.'

2   All my delight is upon the godly that are in the land, *
      upon those who are noble in heart.

3   Though the idols are legion that many run after, *
      their drink offerings of blood I will not offer,
        neither make mention of their names upon my lips.

4   The Lord himself is my portion and my cup; *
      in your hands alone is my fortune.

5   My share has fallen in a fair land; *
      indeed, I have a goodly heritage.

6   I will bless the Lord who has given me counsel, *
     and in the night watches he instructs my heart.

7   I have set the Lord always before me; *
     he is at my right hand; I shall not fall.

8   Wherefore my heart is glad and my spirit rejoices; *
     my flesh also shall rest secure.

9   For you will not abandon my soul to Death, *
     nor suffer your faithful one to see the Pit.

10   You will show me the path of life;
        in your presence is the fullness of joy *
     and in your right hand are pleasures for evermore.

     [Give to us, Lord Christ,
     the fullness of grace,
     your presence and your very self,
     for you are our portion and our delight,
     now and for ever. Amen.]

Psalm 17

[Refrain: Deliver me, O Lord, by your hand.]

1   Hear my just cause, O Lord; consider my complaint; *
     listen to my prayer, which comes not from lying lips.

2   Let my vindication come forth from your presence; *
     let your eyes behold what is right.

3   Weigh my heart, examine me by night, *
     refine me, and you will find no impurity in me.

4   My mouth does not trespass for earthly rewards; *
     I have heeded the words of your lips.

5   My footsteps hold fast in the ways of your commandments; *
     my feet have not stumbled in your paths.

6   I call upon you, O God, for you will answer me; *
     incline your ear to me, and listen to my words.

7   Show me your marvellous loving-kindness, *
     O Saviour of those who take refuge at your right hand
        from those who rise up against them.

8   Keep me as the apple of your eye; *
    hide me under the shadow of your wings,

9   From the wicked who assault me, *
    from my enemies who surround me to take away my life.

10 They have closed their heart to pity *
    and their mouth speaks proud things.

11 They press me hard, they surround me on every side, *
    watching how they may cast me to the ground,

12 Like a lion that is greedy for its prey, *
    like a young lion lurking in secret places.

13 Arise, Lord; confront them and cast them down; *
    deliver me from the wicked by your sword.

14 Deliver me, O Lord, by your hand *
    from those whose portion in life is unending,

15 Whose bellies you fill with your treasure, *
    who are well supplied with children
        and leave their wealth to their little ones.

16 As for me, I shall see your face in righteousness; *
    when I awake and behold your likeness, I shall be satisfied.

    *[Generous Lord,
    deliver us from all envious thoughts,
    and when we are tempted by the desire for wealth,
    let us see your face;
    for your abundance is enough to clothe our lack;
    through Jesus Christ our Lord. Amen.]*

Psalm 18

[Refrain: The Lord my God shall make my darkness to be bright.]

Part 1

1   I love you, O Lord my strength. *
    The Lord is my crag, my fortress and my deliverer,

2   My God, my rock in whom I take refuge, *
    my shield, the horn of my salvation and my stronghold.

3   I cried to the Lord in my anguish *
     and I was saved from my enemies.

4   The cords of death entwined me *
     and the torrents of destruction overwhelmed me.

5   The cords of the Pit fastened about me *
     and the snares of death entangled me.

6   In my distress I called upon the Lord *
     and cried out to my God for help.

7   He heard my voice in his temple *
     and my cry came to his ears.

8   The earth trembled and quaked; *
     the foundations of the mountains shook;
      they reeled because he was angry.

9   Smoke rose from his nostrils
     and a consuming fire went out of his mouth; *
     burning coals blazed forth from him.

10   He parted the heavens and came down *
     and thick darkness was under his feet.

11   He rode upon the cherubim and flew; *
     he came flying on the wings of the wind.

12   He made darkness his covering round about him, *
     dark waters and thick clouds his pavilion.

13   From the brightness of his presence, through the clouds *
     burst hailstones and coals of fire.

14   The Lord also thundered out of heaven; *
     the Most High uttered his voice
      with hailstones and coals of fire.

15   He sent out his arrows and scattered them; *
     he hurled down lightnings and put them to flight.

16   The springs of the ocean were seen,
     and the foundations of the world uncovered *
     at your rebuke, O Lord,
      at the blast of the breath of your displeasure.

17 He reached down from on high and took me; *
    he drew me out of the mighty waters.

18 He delivered me from my strong enemy, *
    from foes that were too mighty for me.

19 They came upon me in the day of my trouble; *
    but the Lord was my upholder.

20 He brought me out into a place of liberty; *
    he rescued me because he delighted in me.

Part 2

21 The Lord rewarded me after my righteous dealing; *
    according to the cleanness of my hands he recompensed me,

22 Because I had kept the ways of the Lord *
    and had not gone wickedly away from my God,

23 For I had an eye to all his laws, *
    and did not cast out his commandments from me.

24 I was also wholehearted before him *
    and kept myself from iniquity;

25 Therefore the Lord rewarded me
      after my righteous dealing, *
    and according to the cleanness of my hands in his sight.

26 With the faithful you show yourself faithful; *
    with the true you show yourself true;

27 With the pure you show yourself pure, *
    but with the crooked you show yourself perverse.

28 For you will save a lowly people *
    and bring down the high looks of the proud.

29 You also shall light my candle; *
    the Lord my God shall make my darkness to be bright.

30 By your help I shall run at an enemy host; *
    with the help of my God I can leap over a wall.

31 As for God, his way is perfect;
      the word of the Lord is tried in the fire; *
    he is a shield to all who trust in him.

32 For who is God but the Lord, *
and who is the rock except our God?

33 It is God who girds me about with strength *
and makes my way perfect.

34 He makes my feet like hinds' feet *
so that I tread surely on the heights.

35 He teaches my hands to fight *
and my arms to bend a bow of bronze.

36 You have given me the shield of your salvation; *
your right hand upholds me
and your grace has made me great.

37 You enlarge my strides beneath me, *
yet my feet do not slide.

38 I will pursue my enemies and overtake them, *
nor turn again until I have destroyed them.

39 I will smite them down so they cannot rise; *
they shall fall beneath my feet.

40 You have girded me with strength for the battle; *
you will cast down my enemies under me;

41 You will make my foes turn their backs upon me *
and I shall destroy them that hate me.

42 They will cry out, but there shall be none to help them; *
they will cry to the Lord, but he will not answer.

43 I shall beat them as small as the dust on the wind; *
I will cast them out as the mire in the streets.

44 You will deliver me from the strife of the peoples; *
you will make me the head of the nations.

45 A people I have not known shall serve me;
as soon as they hear me, they shall obey me; *
strangers will humble themselves before me.

46 The foreign peoples will lose heart *
and come trembling out of their strongholds.

47   The Lord lives, and blessèd be my rock! *
       Praised be the God of my salvation,

48   Even the God who vindicates me *
       and subdues the peoples under me!

49   You that deliver me from my enemies,
         you will set me up above my foes; *
       from the violent you will deliver me;

50   Therefore will I give you thanks, O Lord, among the nations *
       and sing praises to your name,

51   To the one who gives great victory to his king *
       and shows faithful love to his anointed,
         to David and his seed for ever.

[From your royal throne, O God, you sent your living Word
to pierce the gloom of oppression;
so, in our souls' night,
come with your saving help
and penetrate our darkness with the
   rays of your glory
in Jesus Christ our Lord. Amen.]

Psalm 19

[Refrain: The commandment of the Lord is pure
             and gives light to the eyes.]

1   The heavens are telling the glory of God *
       and the firmament proclaims his handiwork.

2   One day pours out its song to another *
       and one night unfolds knowledge to another.

3   They have neither speech nor language *
       and their voices are not heard,

4   Yet their sound has gone out into all lands *
       and their words to the ends of the world.

5   In them has he set a tabernacle for the sun, *
       that comes forth as a bridegroom out of his chamber
         and rejoices as a champion to run his course.

6   It goes forth from the end of the heavens
       and runs to the very end again, *
    and there is nothing hidden from its heat.

7   The law of the Lord is perfect, reviving the soul; *
    the testimony of the Lord is sure
       and gives wisdom to the simple.

8   The statutes of the Lord are right and rejoice the heart; *
    the commandment of the Lord is pure
       and gives light to the eyes.

9   The fear of the Lord is clean and endures for ever; *
    the judgements of the Lord are true
       and righteous altogether.

10 More to be desired are they than gold,
       more than much fine gold, *
    sweeter also than honey,
       dripping from the honeycomb.

11 By them also is your servant taught *
    and in keeping them there is great reward.

12 Who can tell how often they offend? *
    O cleanse me from my secret faults!

13 Keep your servant also from presumptuous sins
       lest they get dominion over me; *
    so shall I be undefiled,
       and innocent of great offence.

14 Let the words of my mouth and the meditation of my heart
       be acceptable in your sight, *
    O Lord, my strength and my redeemer.

    *[Christ, the sun of righteousness,
    rise in our hearts this day,
    enfold us in the brightness of your love
    and bear us at the last to heaven's horizon;
    for your love's sake. Amen.]*

Psalm 20

[Refrain: We will call on the name of the Lord our God.]

1   May the Lord hear you in the day of trouble, *
      the name of the God of Jacob defend you;

2   Send you help from his sanctuary *
      and strengthen you out of Zion;

3   Remember all your offerings *
      and accept your burnt sacrifice;

4   Grant you your heart's desire *
      and fulfil all your mind.

5   May we rejoice in your salvation
      and triumph in the name of our God; *
      may the Lord perform all your petitions.

6   Now I know that the Lord will save his anointed; *
      he will answer him from his holy heaven,
      with the mighty strength of his right hand.

7   Some put their trust in chariots and some in horses, *
      but we will call only on the name of the Lord our God.

8   They are brought down and fallen, *
      but we are risen and stand upright.

9   O Lord, save the king *
      and answer us when we call upon you.

[Merciful God,
purify our hearts in the flame of your Spirit
and transform our toil into an offering of praise,
that we may reject the proud rule of might
and trust in Christ alone,
for he is our Lord for ever and ever. Amen.]

Psalm 21

[Refrain: The king puts his trust in the Lord.]

1   The king shall rejoice in your strength, O Lord; *
      how greatly shall he rejoice in your salvation!

2   You have given him his heart's desire *
      and have not denied the request of his lips.

3   For you come to meet him with blessings of goodness *
      and set a crown of pure gold upon his head.

4   He asked of you life and you gave it him, *
      length of days, for ever and ever.

5   His honour is great because of your salvation; *
      glory and majesty have you laid upon him.

6   You have granted him everlasting felicity *
      and will make him glad with joy in your presence.

7   For the king puts his trust in the Lord; *
      because of the loving-kindness of the Most High,
         he shall not be overthrown.

[8   Your hand shall mark down all your enemies; *
      your right hand will find out those who hate you.

9   You will make them like a fiery oven
         in the time of your wrath; *
      the Lord will swallow them up in his anger
         and the fire will consume them.

10   Their fruit you will root out of the land *
      and their seed from among its inhabitants.

11   Because they intend evil against you *
      and devise wicked schemes
         which they cannot perform,

12   You will put them to flight *
      when you aim your bow at their faces.]

13   Be exalted, O Lord, in your own might; *
      we will make music and sing of your power.

      *[Crown us, O God, but with humility,
      and robe us with compassion,
      that, as you call us into the kingdom of your Son,
      we may strive to overcome all evil
         by the power of good
      and so walk gently on the earth
      with you, our God, for ever. Amen.]*

Psalm 22

[Refrain: Be not far from me, O Lord.]

1   My God, my God, why have you forsaken me, *
    and are so far from my salvation,
       from the words of my distress?

2   O my God, I cry in the daytime,
       but you do not answer; *
    and by night also, but I find no rest.

3   Yet you are the Holy One, *
    enthroned upon the praises of Israel.

4   Our forebears trusted in you; *
    they trusted, and you delivered them.

5   They cried out to you and were delivered; *
    they put their trust in you and were not confounded.

6   But as for me, I am a worm and no man, *
    scorned by all and despised by the people.

7   All who see me laugh me to scorn; *
    they curl their lips and wag their heads, saying,

8   'He trusted in the Lord; let him deliver him; *
    let him deliver him, if he delights in him.'

9   But it is you that took me out of the womb *
    and laid me safe upon my mother's breast.

10   On you was I cast ever since I was born; *
    you are my God even from my mother's womb.

11   Be not far from me, for trouble is near at hand *
    and there is none to help.

12   Mighty oxen come around me; *
    fat bulls of Bashan close me in on every side.

13   They gape upon me with their mouths, *
    as it were a ramping and a roaring lion.

14   I am poured out like water;
      all my bones are out of joint; *
    my heart has become like wax
      melting in the depths of my body.

15   My mouth is dried up like a potsherd;
      my tongue cleaves to my gums; *
    you have laid me in the dust of death.

16   For the hounds are all about me,
      the pack of evildoers close in on me; *
    they pierce my hands and my feet.

17   I can count all my bones; *
    they stand staring and looking upon me.

18   They divide my garments among them; *
    they cast lots for my clothing.

19   Be not far from me, O Lord; *
    you are my strength; hasten to help me.

20   Deliver my soul from the sword, *
    my poor life from the power of the dog.

21   Save me from the lion's mouth,
      from the horns of wild oxen. *
    You have answered me!

22   I will tell of your name to my people; *
    in the midst of the congregation will I praise you.

23   Praise the Lord, you that fear him; *
    O seed of Jacob, glorify him;
      stand in awe of him, O seed of Israel.

24   For he has not despised nor abhorred the suffering of the poor;
      neither has he hidden his face from them; *
    but when they cried to him he heard them.

25   From you comes my praise in the great congregation; *
    I will perform my vows
      in the presence of those that fear you.

26   The poor shall eat and be satisfied; *
    those who seek the Lord shall praise him;
      their hearts shall live for ever.

27   All the ends of the earth
        shall remember and turn to the Lord, *
     and all the families of the nations shall bow before him.

28   For the kingdom is the Lord's *
     and he rules over the nations.

29   How can those who sleep in the earth
        bow down in worship, *
     or those who go down to the dust kneel before him?

30   He has saved my life for himself;
        my descendants shall serve him; *
     this shall be told of the Lord for generations to come.

31   They shall come and make known his salvation,
        to a people yet unborn, *
     declaring that he, the Lord, has done it.

     *[Restless with grief and fear,
     the abandoned turn to you:
     in every hour of trial,
     good Lord, deliver us,
     O God most holy, God most strong,
     whose wisdom is the cross of Christ. Amen.]*

Psalm 23

     [Refrain: I will dwell in the house of the Lord for ever.]

I   The Lord is my shepherd; *
     therefore can I lack nothing.

2   He makes me lie down in green pastures *
     and leads me beside still waters.

3   He shall refresh my soul *
     and guide me in the paths of righteousness for his name's sake.

4   Though I walk through the valley of the shadow of death,
        I will fear no evil; *
     for you are with me;
        your rod and your staff, they comfort me.

5   You spread a table before me
        in the presence of those who trouble me; *
    you have anointed my head with oil
        and my cup shall be full.

6   Surely goodness and loving mercy shall follow me
        all the days of my life, *
    and I will dwell in the house of the Lord for ever.

    [O God, our sovereign and shepherd,
    who brought again your Son Jesus Christ
        from the valley of death,
    comfort us with your protecting presence
    and your angels of goodness and love,
    that we also may come home
    and dwell with him in your house for ever. Amen.]

Psalm 24

[Refrain: The Lord of hosts: he is the King of glory.]

1   The earth is the Lord's and all that fills it, *
    the compass of the world and all who dwell therein.

2   For he has founded it upon the seas *
    and set it firm upon the rivers of the deep.

3   'Who shall ascend the hill of the Lord, *
    or who can rise up in his holy place?'

4   'Those who have clean hands and a pure heart, *
    who have not lifted up their soul to an idol,
        nor sworn an oath to a lie;

5   'They shall receive a blessing from the Lord, *
    a just reward from the God of their salvation.'

6   Such is the company of those who seek him, *
    of those who seek your face, O God of Jacob.

7   Lift up your heads, O gates;
        be lifted up, you everlasting doors; *
    and the King of glory shall come in.

8   'Who is the King of glory?' *
    'The Lord, strong and mighty,
      the Lord who is mighty in battle.'

9   Lift up your heads, O gates;
      be lifted up, you everlasting doors; *
    and the King of glory shall come in.

10 'Who is this King of glory?' *
    'The Lord of hosts,
      he is the King of glory.'

*[O Lord of hosts,
purify our hearts
that the King of glory may come in,
your Son, Jesus our redeemer. Amen.]*

Psalm 25

[Refrain: Remember, Lord, your compassion and love.]

1   To you, O Lord, I lift up my soul;
      O my God, in you I trust; *
    let me not be put to shame;
      let not my enemies triumph over me.

2   Let none who look to you be put to shame, *
    but let the treacherous be shamed and frustrated.

3   Make me to know your ways, O Lord, *
    and teach me your paths.

4   Lead me in your truth and teach me, *
    for you are the God of my salvation;
      for you have I hoped all the day long.

5   Remember, Lord, your compassion and love, *
    for they are from everlasting.

6   Remember not the sins of my youth
      or my transgressions, *
    but think on me in your goodness, O Lord,
      according to your steadfast love.

7   Gracious and upright is the Lord; *
    therefore shall he teach sinners in the way.

8   He will guide the humble in doing right *
       and teach his way to the lowly.

9   All the paths of the Lord are mercy and truth *
       to those who keep his covenant and his testimonies.

10   For your name's sake, O Lord, *
       be merciful to my sin, for it is great.

11   Who are those who fear the Lord? *
       Them will he teach in the way that they should choose.

12   Their soul shall dwell at ease *
       and their offspring shall inherit the land.

13   The hidden purpose of the Lord is for those who fear him *
       and he will show them his covenant.

14   My eyes are ever looking to the Lord, *
       for he shall pluck my feet out of the net.

15   Turn to me and be gracious to me, *
       for I am alone and brought very low.

16   The sorrows of my heart have increased; *
       O bring me out of my distress.

17   Look upon my adversity and misery *
       and forgive me all my sin.

18   Look upon my enemies, for they are many *
       and they bear a violent hatred against me.

19   O keep my soul and deliver me; *
       let me not be put to shame, for I have put my trust in you.

20   Let integrity and uprightness preserve me, *
       for my hope has been in you.

21   Deliver Israel, O God, *
       out of all his troubles.

       [Free us, God of mercy,
       from all that keeps us from you;
       relieve the misery of the anxious and the ashamed
       and fill us with the hope of peace;
       through Jesus Christ our Lord. Amen.]

Psalm 26

[Refrain: Lord, I love the place where your glory abides.]

1   Give judgement for me, O Lord,
    for I have walked with integrity; *
    I have trusted in the Lord and have not faltered.

2   Test me, O Lord, and try me; *
    examine my heart and my mind.

3   For your love is before my eyes; *
    I have walked in your truth.

4   I have not joined the company of the false, *
    nor consorted with the deceitful.

5   I hate the gathering of evildoers *
    and I will not sit down with the wicked.

6   I will wash my hands in innocence, O Lord, *
    that I may go about your altar,

7   To make heard the voice of thanksgiving *
    and tell of all your wonderful deeds.

8   Lord, I love the house of your habitation *
    and the place where your glory abides.

9   Sweep me not away with sinners, *
    nor my life with the bloodthirsty,

10   Whose hands are full of wicked schemes *
    and their right hand full of bribes.

11   As for me, I will walk with integrity; *
    redeem me, Lord, and be merciful to me.

12   My foot stands firm; *
    in the great congregation I will bless the Lord.

[Have mercy on us and redeem us, O Lord,
for our merits are your mercies
and in your judgement is our salvation;
through Jesus Christ our Lord. Amen.]

Psalm 27

[Refrain: The Lord is my light and my salvation.]

1   The Lord is my light and my salvation;
        whom then shall I fear? *
    The Lord is the strength of my life;
        of whom then shall I be afraid?

2   When the wicked, even my enemies and my foes,
        came upon me to eat up my flesh, *
    they stumbled and fell.

3   Though a host encamp against me,
        my heart shall not be afraid, *
    and though there rise up war against me,
        yet will I put my trust in him.

4   One thing have I asked of the Lord
        and that alone I seek: *
    that I may dwell in the house of the Lord
        all the days of my life,

5   To behold the fair beauty of the Lord *
    and to seek his will in his temple.

6   For in the day of trouble
        he shall hide me in his shelter; *
    in the secret place of his dwelling shall he hide me
        and set me high upon a rock.

7   And now shall he lift up my head *
    above my enemies round about me;

8   Therefore will I offer in his dwelling an oblation
        with great gladness; *
    I will sing and make music to the Lord.

9   Hear my voice, O Lord, when I call; *
    have mercy upon me and answer me.

10   My heart tells of your word, 'Seek my face.' *
    Your face, Lord, will I seek.

11   Hide not your face from me, *
    nor cast your servant away in displeasure.

12   You have been my helper; *
      leave me not, neither forsake me, O God of my salvation.

13   Though my father and my mother forsake me, *
      the Lord will take me up.

14   Teach me your way, O Lord; *
      lead me on a level path,
         because of those who lie in wait for me.

15   Deliver me not into the will of my adversaries, *
      for false witnesses have risen up against me,
         and those who breathe out violence.

16   I believe that I shall see the goodness of the Lord *
      in the land of the living.

17   Wait for the Lord;
         be strong and he shall comfort your heart; *
      wait patiently for the Lord.

      *[God, our light and our salvation,
      illuminate our lives,
      that we may see your goodness in the land of the living,
      and, looking on your beauty,
      may be changed into the likeness of Jesus Christ our Lord. Amen.]*

Psalm 28

      [Refrain: The Lord is my strength and my shield.]

1   To you I call, O Lord my rock;
         be not deaf to my cry, *
      lest, if you do not hear me,
         I become like those who go down to the Pit.

2   Hear the voice of my prayer when I cry out to you, *
      when I lift up my hands to your holy of holies.

3   Do not snatch me away with the wicked,
         with the evildoers, *
      who speak peaceably with their neighbours,
         while malice is in their hearts.

[4   Repay them according to their deeds *
      and according to the wickedness of their devices.

5   Reward them according to the work of their hands *
      and pay them their just deserts.]

6   They take no heed of the Lord's doings,
         nor of the works of his hands; *
      therefore shall he break them down
         and not build them up.

7   Blessèd be the Lord, *
      for he has heard the voice of my prayer.

8   The Lord is my strength and my shield; *
      my heart has trusted in him and I am helped;

9   Therefore my heart dances for joy *
      and in my song will I praise him.

10   The Lord is the strength of his people, *
      a safe refuge for his anointed.

11   Save your people and bless your inheritance; *
      shepherd them and carry them for ever.

      [Hear us, Shepherd of your people,
      forgive us our sins
      and, in a world of pretences,
      make us true in heart and mind;
      through Jesus Christ our Lord. Amen.]

Psalm 29

      [Refrain: The Lord shall give his people the blessing of peace.]

1   Ascribe to the Lord, you powers of heaven, *
      ascribe to the Lord glory and strength.

2   Ascribe to the Lord the honour due to his name; *
      worship the Lord in the beauty of holiness.

3   The voice of the Lord is upon the waters;
         the God of glory thunders; *
      the Lord is upon the mighty waters.

4   The voice of the Lord is mighty in operation; *
      the voice of the Lord is a glorious voice.

5   The voice of the Lord breaks the cedar trees; *
       the Lord breaks the cedars of Lebanon;

6   He makes Lebanon skip like a calf *
       and Sirion like a young wild ox.

7   The voice of the Lord splits the flash of lightning;
       the voice of the Lord shakes the wilderness; *
       the Lord shakes the wilderness of Kadesh.

8   The voice of the Lord makes the oak trees writhe
       and strips the forests bare; *
       in his temple all cry, 'Glory!'

9   The Lord sits enthroned above the water flood; *
       the Lord sits enthroned as king for evermore.

10   The Lord shall give strength to his people; *
       the Lord shall give his people the blessing of peace.

> *[Open our ears, glorious Lord Christ,*
> *to hear the music of your voice*
> *above the chaos of this world;*
> *open our eyes to see the vision of your glory,*
> *for you are our King, now and for ever. Amen.]*

Psalm 30

[Refrain: You brought me up, O Lord, from the dead.]

1   I will exalt you, O Lord,
       because you have raised me up *
       and have not let my foes triumph over me.

2   O Lord my God, I cried out to you *
       and you have healed me.

3   You brought me up, O Lord, from the dead; *
       you restored me to life from among those that go down to the Pit.

4   Sing to the Lord, you servants of his; *
       give thanks to his holy name.

5   For his wrath endures but the twinkling of an eye,
       his favour for a lifetime. *
     Heaviness may endure for a night,
       but joy comes in the morning.

6   In my prosperity I said,
      'I shall never be moved. *
    You, Lord, of your goodness,
      have made my hill so strong.'

7   Then you hid your face from me *
    and I was utterly dismayed.

8   To you, O Lord, I cried; *
    to the Lord I made my supplication:

9   'What profit is there in my blood,
      if I go down to the Pit? *
    Will the dust praise you or declare your faithfulness?

10   'Hear, O Lord, and have mercy upon me; *
    O Lord, be my helper.'

11   You have turned my mourning into dancing; *
    you have put off my sackcloth and girded me with gladness;

12   Therefore my heart sings to you without ceasing; *
    O Lord my God, I will give you thanks for ever.

*[Lord, you hide your face
when we trust in ourselves;
strip us of false security
and re-clothe us in your praise,
that we may know you
as the one who raises us from death,
as you raised your Son, our Saviour Jesus Christ. Amen.]*

Psalm 31

[Refrain: Into your hands I commend my spirit.]

1   In you, O Lord, have I taken refuge;
      let me never be put to shame; *
    deliver me in your righteousness.

2   Incline your ear to me; *
    make haste to deliver me.

3   Be my strong rock, a fortress to save me,
      for you are my rock and my stronghold; *
    guide me, and lead me for your name's sake.

4 Take me out of the net
   that they have laid secretly for me, *
  for you are my strength.

5 Into your hands I commend my spirit, *
  for you have redeemed me, O Lord God of truth.

6 I hate those who cling to worthless idols; *
  I put my trust in the Lord.

7 I will be glad and rejoice in your mercy, *
  for you have seen my affliction
   and known my soul in adversity.

8 You have not shut me up in the hand of the enemy; *
  you have set my feet in an open place.

9 Have mercy on me, Lord, for I am in trouble; *
  my eye is consumed with sorrow,
   my soul and my body also.

10 For my life is wasted with grief,
   and my years with sighing; *
  my strength fails me because of my affliction,
   and my bones are consumed.

11 I have become a reproach to all my enemies
   and even to my neighbours,
   an object of dread to my acquaintances; *
  when they see me in the street they flee from me.

12 I am forgotten like one that is dead, out of mind; *
  I have become like a broken vessel.

13 For I have heard the whispering of the crowd;
   fear is on every side; *
  they scheme together against me,
   and plot to take my life.

14 But my trust is in you, O Lord. *
  I have said, 'You are my God.

15 'My times are in your hand; *
  deliver me from the hand of my enemies,
   and from those who persecute me.

16   'Make your face to shine upon your servant, *
     and save me for your mercy's sake.'

17   Lord, let me not be confounded
      for I have called upon you; *
     but let the wicked be put to shame;
      let them be silent in the grave.

18   Let the lying lips be put to silence *
     that speak against the righteous
      with arrogance, disdain and contempt.

19   How abundant is your goodness, O Lord,
     which you have laid up for those who fear you; *
     which you have prepared in the sight of all
      for those who put their trust in you.

20   You hide them in the shelter of your presence
      from those who slander them; *
     you keep them safe in your refuge from the strife of tongues.

21   Blessèd be the Lord! *
     For he has shown me his steadfast love
      when I was as a city besieged.

22   I had said in my alarm,
     'I have been cut off from the sight of your eyes.' *
     Nevertheless, you heard the voice of my prayer
      when I cried out to you.

23   Love the Lord, all you his servants; *
     for the Lord protects the faithful,
      but repays to the full the proud.

24   Be strong and let your heart take courage, *
     all you who wait in hope for the Lord.

     [Lord Jesus Christ,
     when scorn and shame besiege us
     and hope is veiled in grief,
     hold us in your wounded hands
     and make your face shine on us again,
     for you are our Lord and God. Amen.]

Psalm 32

[Refrain: Be glad, you righteous, and rejoice in the Lord.]

1   Happy the one whose transgression is forgiven, *
and whose sin is covered.

2   Happy the one to whom the Lord imputes no guilt, *
and in whose spirit there is no guile.

3   For I held my tongue; *
my bones wasted away
   through my groaning all the day long.

4   Your hand was heavy upon me day and night; *
my moisture was dried up like the drought in summer.

5   Then I acknowledged my sin to you *
and my iniquity I did not hide.

6   I said, 'I will confess my transgressions to the Lord,' *
and you forgave the guilt of my sin.

7   Therefore let all the faithful make their prayers to you
   in time of trouble; *
in the great water flood, it shall not reach them.

8   You are a place for me to hide in;
   you preserve me from trouble; *
you surround me with songs of deliverance

9   'I will instruct you and teach you
   in the way that you should go; *
I will guide you with my eye.

10   'Be not like horse and mule which have no understanding; *
whose mouths must be held with bit and bridle,
   or else they will not stay near you.'

11   Great tribulations remain for the wicked, *
but mercy embraces those who trust in the Lord.

12   Be glad, you righteous, and rejoice in the Lord; *
shout for joy, all who are true of heart.

[Give us honest hearts, O God,
and send your kindly Spirit
to help us confess our sins
and bring us the peace of your forgiveness;
in Jesus Christ our Lord. Amen.]

Psalm 33

[Refrain: The earth is full of the loving-kindness of the Lord.]

1   Rejoice in the Lord, O you righteous, *
    for it is good for the just to sing praises.

2   Praise the Lord with the lyre; *
    on the ten-stringed harp sing his praise.

3   Sing for him a new song; *
    play skilfully, with shouts of praise.

4   For the word of the Lord is true *
    and all his works are sure.

5   He loves righteousness and justice; *
    the earth is full of the loving-kindness of the Lord.

6   By the word of the Lord were the heavens made *
    and all their host by the breath of his mouth.

7   He gathers up the waters of the sea as in a waterskin *
    and lays up the deep in his treasury.

8   Let all the earth fear the Lord; *
    stand in awe of him, all who dwell in the world.

9   For he spoke, and it was done; *
    he commanded, and it stood fast.

10 The Lord brings the counsel of the nations to naught; *
    he frustrates the designs of the peoples.

11 But the counsel of the Lord shall endure for ever *
    and the designs of his heart from generation to generation.

12 Happy the nation whose God is the Lord *
    and the people he has chosen for his own.

13 The Lord looks down from heaven *
    and beholds all the children of earth.

14 From where he sits enthroned he turns his gaze *
    on all who dwell on the earth.

15 He fashions all the hearts of them *
    and understands all their works.

16 No king is saved by the might of his host; *
    no warrior delivered by his great strength.

17 A horse is a vain hope for deliverance; *
    for all its strength it cannot save.

18 Behold, the eye of the Lord
      is upon those who fear him, *
    on those who wait in hope for his steadfast love,

19 To deliver their soul from death *
    and to feed them in time of famine.

20 Our soul waits longingly for the Lord; *
    he is our help and our shield.

21 Indeed, our heart rejoices in him; *
    in his holy name have we put our trust.

22 Let your loving-kindness, O Lord, be upon us, *
    as we have set our hope on you.

    *[Feed your people, Lord,
    with your holy word
    and free us from the emptiness of our
       wrongful desires,
    that we may sing the new song of salvation;
    through Jesus Christ our Lord. Amen.]*

Psalm 34

[Refrain: O taste and see that the Lord is gracious.]

1   I will bless the Lord at all times; *
    his praise shall ever be in my mouth.

2   My soul shall glory in the Lord; *
    let the humble hear and be glad.

3   O magnify the Lord with me; *
     let us exalt his name together.

4   I sought the Lord and he answered me *
     and delivered me from all my fears.

5   Look upon him and be radiant *
     and your faces shall not be ashamed.

6   This poor soul cried, and the Lord heard me *
     and saved me from all my troubles.

7   The angel of the Lord encamps around those who fear him *
     and delivers them.

8   O taste and see that the Lord is gracious; *
     blessèd is the one who trusts in him.

9   Fear the Lord, all you his holy ones, *
     for those who fear him lack nothing.

10   Lions may lack and suffer hunger, *
     but those who seek the Lord
       lack nothing that is good.

11   Come, my children, and listen to me; *
     I will teach you the fear of the Lord.

12   Who is there who delights in life *
     and longs for days to enjoy good things?

13   Keep your tongue from evil *
     and your lips from lying words.

14   Turn from evil and do good; *
     seek peace and pursue it.

15   The eyes of the Lord are upon the righteous *
     and his ears are open to their cry.

16   The face of the Lord is against those who do evil, *
     to root out the remembrance of them from the earth.

17   The righteous cry and the Lord hears them *
     and delivers them out of all their troubles.

18   The Lord is near to the brokenhearted *
     and will save those who are crushed in spirit.

19 Many are the troubles of the righteous; *
    from them all will the Lord deliver them.

20 He keeps all their bones, *
    so that not one of them is broken.

21 But evil shall slay the wicked *
    and those who hate the righteous will be condemned.

22 The Lord ransoms the life of his servants *
    and will condemn none who seek refuge in him.

    *[Send your holy angels
    to watch over us, O God,
    that on our lips will be found your truth
    and in our hearts your love;
    so we may ever taste your goodness
    in the land of the living;
    through Jesus Christ our Lord. Amen.]*

Psalm 35

*[Refrain: Give me justice, O Lord my God,
            according to your righteousness.]*

1   Contend, O Lord, with those that contend with me; *
    fight against those that fight against me.

2   Take up shield and buckler *
    and rise up to help me.

3   Draw the spear and bar the way
        against those who pursue me; *
    say to my soul, 'I am your salvation.'

4   Let those who seek after my life be shamed and disgraced; *
    let those who plot my ruin fall back and be put to confusion.

[5 Let them be as chaff before the wind, *
    with the angel of the Lord thrusting them down.

6   Let their way be dark and slippery, *
    with the angel of the Lord pursuing them.

7   For they have secretly spread a net for me without a cause; *
    without any cause they have dug a pit for my soul.

8   Let ruin come upon them unawares; *
      let them be caught in the net they laid;
         let them fall in it to their destruction.]

9   Then will my soul be joyful in the Lord *
      and glory in his salvation.

10   My very bones will say, 'Lord, who is like you? *
      You deliver the poor from those that are too strong for them,
       the poor and needy from those who would despoil them.'

11   False witnesses rose up against me; *
      they charged me with things I knew not.

12   They rewarded me evil for good, *
      to the desolation of my soul.

13   But as for me, when they were sick I put on sackcloth *
      and humbled myself with fasting;

14   When my prayer returned empty to my bosom, *
      it was as though I grieved for my friend or brother;

15   I behaved as one who mourns for his mother, *
      bowed down and brought very low.

16   But when I stumbled, they gathered in delight;
      they gathered together against me; *
     as if they were strangers I did not know
      they tore at me without ceasing.

17   When I fell they mocked me; *
      they gnashed at me with their teeth.

18   O Lord, how long will you look on? *
      Rescue my soul from their ravages,
      and my poor life from the young lions.

19   I will give you thanks in the great congregation; *
      I will praise you in the mighty throng.

20   Do not let my treacherous foes rejoice over me, *
      or those who hate me without a cause
      mock me with their glances.

21 For they do not speak of peace, *
    but invent deceitful schemes against those
        that are quiet in the land.

22 They opened wide their mouths and derided me, saying *
    'We have seen it with our very eyes.'

23 This you have seen, O Lord; do not keep silent; *
    go not far from me, O Lord.

24 Awake, arise, to my cause, *
    to my defence, my God and my Lord!

25 Give me justice, O Lord my God,
        according to your righteousness; *
    let them not triumph over me.

26 Let them not say to themselves,
        'Our heart's desire!' *
    Let them not say, 'We have swallowed him up.'

27 Let all who rejoice at my trouble be put to shame and confusion; *
    let those who boast against me
        be clothed with shame and dishonour.

28 Let those who favour my cause rejoice and be glad; *
    let them say always,
        'Great is the Lord, who delights in his servant's well-being.'

29 So shall my tongue be talking of your righteousness *
    and of your praise all the day long.

    *[Free us, righteous God, from all oppression,
    and bring justice to the nations,
    that all the world may know you
    as King of kings and Lord of lords,
    now and for ever. Amen.]*

Psalm 36

    [Refrain: With you, O God, is the well of life.]

1   Sin whispers to the wicked, in the depths of their heart; *
    there is no fear of God before their eyes.

2   They flatter themselves in their own eyes *
    that their abominable sin will not be found out.

3   The words of their mouth are unrighteous and full of deceit; *
     they have ceased to act wisely and to do good.

4   They think out mischief upon their beds
        and have set themselves in no good way; *
     nor do they abhor that which is evil.

5   Your love, O Lord, reaches to the heavens *
     and your faithfulness to the clouds.

6   Your righteousness stands like the strong mountains,
        your justice like the great deep; *
     you, Lord, shall save both man and beast.

7   How precious is your loving mercy, O God! *
     All mortal flesh shall take refuge
        under the shadow of your wings.

8   They shall be satisfied with the abundance of your house; *
     they shall drink from the river of your delights.

9   For with you is the well of life *
     and in your light shall we see light.

10   O continue your loving-kindness to those who know you *
     and your righteousness to those who are true of heart.

11   Let not the foot of pride come against me, *
     nor the hand of the ungodly thrust me away.

12   There are they fallen, all who work wickedness. *
     They are cast down and shall not be able to stand.

     *[O God, the well of life,
     make us bright with wisdom,
     that we may be lightened with the knowledge of your glory
     in the face of Jesus Christ our Lord. Amen.]*

Psalm 37

[Refrain: The salvation of the righteous comes from the Lord.]

Part I

1   Fret not because of evildoers; *
     be not jealous of those who do wrong.

2   For they shall soon wither like grass *
    and like the green herb fade away.

3   Trust in the Lord and be doing good; *
    dwell in the land and be nourished with truth.

4   Let your delight be in the Lord *
    and he will give you your heart's desire.

5   Commit your way to the Lord and put your trust in him, *
    and he will bring it to pass.

6   He will make your righteousness as clear as the light *
    and your just dealing as the noonday.

7   Be still before the Lord and wait for him; *
    do not fret over those that prosper
      as they follow their evil schemes.

8   Refrain from anger and abandon wrath; *
    do not fret, lest you be moved to do evil.

9   For evildoers shall be cut off, *
    but those who wait upon the Lord shall possess the land.

10   Yet a little while and the wicked shall be no more; *
    you will search for their place and find them gone.

11   But the lowly shall possess the land *
    and shall delight in abundance of peace.

12   The wicked plot against the righteous *
    and gnash at them with their teeth.

13   The Lord shall laugh at the wicked, *
    for he sees that their day is coming.

14   The wicked draw their sword and bend their bow
      to strike down the poor and needy, *
    to slaughter those who walk in truth.

15   Their sword shall go through their own heart *
    and their bows shall be broken.

16   The little that the righteous have *
    is better than great riches of the wicked.

17   For the arms of the wicked shall be broken, *
      but the Lord upholds the righteous.

Part 2

18   The Lord knows the days of the godly, *
      and their inheritance shall stand for ever.

19   They shall not be put to shame in the perilous time, *
      and in days of famine they shall have enough.

20   But the wicked shall perish;
      like the glory of the meadows
      the enemies of the Lord shall vanish; *
    they shall vanish like smoke.

21   The wicked borrow and do not repay, *
      but the righteous are generous in giving.

22   For those who are blest by God shall possess the land, *
      but those who are cursed by him shall be rooted out.

23   When your steps are guided by the Lord *
      and you delight in his way,

24   Though you stumble, you shall not fall headlong, *
      for the Lord holds you fast by the hand.

25   I have been young and now am old, *
      yet never have I seen the righteous forsaken,
      or their children begging their bread.

26   All the day long they are generous in lending, *
      and their children also shall be blest.

27   Depart from evil and do good *
      and you shall abide for ever.

28   For the Lord loves the thing that is right *
      and will not forsake his faithful ones.

29   The unjust shall be destroyed for ever, *
      and the offspring of the wicked shall be rooted out.

30   The righteous shall possess the land *
      and dwell in it for ever.

31   The mouth of the righteous utters wisdom, *
      and their tongue speaks the thing that is right.

32   The law of their God is in their heart *
      and their footsteps shall not slide.

33   The wicked spy on the righteous *
      and seek occasion to slay them.

34   The Lord will not leave them in their hand, *
      nor let them be condemned when they are judged.

35   Wait upon the Lord and keep his way; *
      he will raise you up to possess the land,
        and when the wicked are uprooted, you shall see it.

36   I myself have seen the wicked in great power *
      and flourishing like a tree in full leaf.

37   I went by and lo, they were gone; *
      I sought them, but they could nowhere be found.

38   Keep innocence and heed the thing that is right, *
      for that will bring you peace at the last.

39   But the sinners shall perish together, *
      and the posterity of the wicked shall be rooted out.

40   The salvation of the righteous comes from the Lord; *
      he is their stronghold in the time of trouble.

41   The Lord shall stand by them and deliver them; *
      he shall deliver them from the wicked and shall save them,
        because they have put their trust in him.

*[Blessèd and holy God,
ever merciful and forgiving,
may we turn from what is evil
and do what is good in your sight,
for you have saved us by the cross of your Son,
our Saviour Jesus Christ. Amen.]*

Psalm 38

[Refrain: Make haste to help me,
O Lord of my salvation.]

1   Rebuke me not, O Lord, in your anger, *
    neither chasten me in your heavy displeasure.

2   For your arrows have stuck fast in me *
    and your hand presses hard upon me.

3   There is no health in my flesh
       because of your indignation; *
    there is no peace in my bones because of my sin.

4   For my iniquities have gone over my head; *
    their weight is a burden too heavy to bear.

5   My wounds stink and fester *
    because of my foolishness.

6   I am utterly bowed down and brought very low; *
    I go about mourning all the day long.

7   My loins are filled with searing pain; *
    there is no health in my flesh.

8   I am feeble and utterly crushed; *
    I roar aloud because of the disquiet of my heart.

9   O Lord, you know all my desires *
    and my sighing is not hidden from you.

10 My heart is pounding, my strength has failed me; *
    the light of my eyes is gone from me.

11 My friends and companions stand apart from my affliction; *
    my neighbours stand afar off.

12 Those who seek after my life lay snares for me; *
    and those who would harm me whisper evil
       and mutter slander all the day long.

13 But I am like one who is deaf and hears not, *
    like one that is dumb, who does not open his mouth.

14 I have become like one who does not hear *
    and from whose mouth comes no retort.

15　For in you, Lord, have I put my trust; *
　　you will answer me, O Lord my God.

16　For I said, 'Let them not triumph over me, *
　　those who exult over me when my foot slips.'

17　Truly, I am on the verge of falling *
　　and my pain is ever with me.

18　I will confess my iniquity *
　　and be sorry for my sin.

19　Those that are my enemies without any cause are mighty, *
　　and those who hate me wrongfully are many in number.

20　Those who repay evil for good are against me, *
　　because the good is what I seek.

21　Forsake me not, O Lord; *
　　be not far from me, O my God.

22　Make haste to help me, *
　　O Lord of my salvation.

　　[Almighty Lord and Saviour,
　　behold with pity the wounds of your people;
　　do not forsake us, sinful as we are,
　　but for the sake of the passion of your
　　　Beloved One, Jesus,
　　come quickly to our aid,
　　for his mercy's sake. Amen.]

Psalm 39

　　[Refrain: Lord, let me know my end and the number of my days.]

1　I said, 'I will keep watch over my ways, *
　　so that I offend not with my tongue.

2　'I will guard my mouth with a muzzle, *
　　while the wicked are in my sight.'

3　So I held my tongue and said nothing; *
　　I kept silent but to no avail.

4   My distress increased, my heart grew hot within me; *
     while I mused, the fire was kindled
       and I spoke out with my tongue:

5   'Lord, let me know my end and the number of my days, *
     that I may know how short my time is.

6   'You have made my days but a handsbreadth,
       and my lifetime is as nothing in your sight; *
     truly, even those who stand upright are but a breath.

7   'We walk about like a shadow
       and in vain we are in turmoil; *
     we heap up riches and cannot tell who will gather them.

8   'And now, what is my hope? *
     Truly my hope is even in you.

9   'Deliver me from all my transgressions *
     and do not make me the taunt of the fool.'

10   I fell silent and did not open my mouth, *
     for surely it was your doing.

11   Take away your plague from me; *
     I am consumed by the blows of your hand.

12   With rebukes for sin you punish us;
       like a moth you consume our beauty; *
     truly, everyone is but a breath.

13   Hear my prayer, O Lord, and give ear to my cry; *
     hold not your peace at my tears.

14   For I am but a stranger with you, *
     a wayfarer, as all my forebears were.

15   Turn your gaze from me, that I may be glad again, *
     before I go my way and am no more.

     *[O Christ, Son of the living God,
     help us when we are too cast down to pray,
     and grant that we may trust you all our days,
     for you are with us in our living and our dying,
     Jesus, Lord and God. Amen.]*

Psalm 40

[Refrain: Great are the wonders you have done, O Lord my God.]

1 I waited patiently for the Lord; *
   he inclined to me and heard my cry.

2 He brought me out of the roaring pit,
      out of the mire and clay; *
   he set my feet upon a rock and made my footing sure.

3 He has put a new song in my mouth,
      a song of praise to our God; *
   many shall see and fear
      and put their trust in the Lord.

4 Blessèd is the one who trusts in the Lord, *
   who does not turn to the proud that follow a lie.

5 Great are the wonders you have done, O Lord my God.
      How great your designs for us! *
   There is none that can be compared with you.

6 If I were to proclaim them and tell of them *
   they would be more than I am able to express.

7 Sacrifice and offering you do not desire *
   but my ears you have opened;

8 Burnt offering and sacrifice for sin you have not required; *
   then said I. 'Lo, I come.

9 'In the scroll of the book it is written of me
      that I should do your will, O my God; *
   I delight to do it: your law is within my heart.'

10 I have declared your righteousness in the great congregation; *
    behold, I did not restrain my lips,
       and that, O Lord, you know.

11 Your righteousness I have not hidden in my heart;
       I have spoken of your faithfulness and your salvation; *
    I have not concealed your loving-kindness and truth
       from the great congregation.

12 Do not withhold your compassion from me, O Lord; *
    let your love and your faithfulness always preserve me,

13 For innumerable troubles have come about me;
    my sins have overtaken me so that I cannot look up; *
  they are more in number than the hairs of my head,
    and my heart fails me.

14 Be pleased, O Lord, to deliver me; *
  O Lord, make haste to help me.

15 Let them be ashamed and altogether dismayed
    who seek after my life to destroy it; *
  let them be driven back and put to shame
    who wish me evil.

16 Let those who heap insults upon me *
  be desolate because of their shame.

17 Let all who seek you rejoice in you and be glad; *
  let those who love your salvation say always,
    'The Lord is great.'

18 Though I am poor and needy, *
  the Lord cares for me.

19 You are my helper and my deliverer; *
  O my God, make no delay.

*[Free us from our sins, O God,
and may our sacrifices be of praise
to the glory of your Son,
our Redeemer, Jesus Christ. Amen.]*

Psalm 41

[Refrain: O Lord, be merciful to me.]

1 Blessèd are those who consider the poor and needy; *
  the Lord will deliver them in the time of trouble.

2 The Lord preserves them and restores their life,
    that they may be happy in the land; *
  he will not hand them over to the will of their enemies.

3 The Lord sustains them on their sickbed; *
  their sickness, Lord, you will remove.

4 And so I said, 'Lord, be merciful to me; *
  heal me, for I have sinned against you.'

5   My enemies speak evil about me, *
      asking when I shall die and my name perish.

6   If they come to see me, they utter empty words; *
      their heart gathers mischief;
        when they go out, they tell it abroad.

7   All my enemies whisper together against me, *
      against me they devise evil,

8   Saying that a deadly thing has laid hold on me, *
      and that I will not rise again from where I lie.

9   Even my bosom friend, whom I trusted,
      who ate of my bread, *
      has lifted up his heel against me.

10   But you, O Lord, be merciful to me *
      and raise me up, that I may reward them.

11   By this I know that you favour me, *
      that my enemy does not triumph over me.

12   Because of my integrity you uphold me *
      and will set me before your face for ever.

13   Blessèd be the Lord God of Israel, *
      from everlasting to everlasting. Amen and Amen.

*[God our deliverer,
raise up the poor and comfort the betrayed,
through the one who for our sakes became poor
and whose betrayal brought our salvation,
Jesus Christ our Lord. Amen.]*

Psalm 42

1   As the deer longs for the water brooks, *
      so longs my soul for you, O God.

2   My soul is athirst for God, even for the living God; *
      when shall I come before the presence of God?

3   My tears have been my bread day and night, *
      while all day long they say to me, 'Where is now your God?'

4   Now when I think on these things, I pour out my soul: *
     how I went with the multitude
       and led the procession to the house of God,

5   With the voice of praise and thanksgiving, *
     among those who kept holy day.

6   *Why are you so full of heaviness, O my soul,* *
     and why are you so disquieted within me?

7   *O put your trust in God;* *
     for I will yet give him thanks,
       who is the help of my countenance, and my God.

8   My soul is heavy within me; *
     therefore I will remember you from the land of Jordan,
       and from Hermon and the hill of Mizar.

9   Deep calls to deep in the thunder of your waterfalls; *
     all your breakers and waves have gone over me.

10   The Lord will grant his loving-kindness in the daytime; *
     through the night his song will be with me,
       a prayer to the God of my life.

11   I say to God my rock,
       'Why have you forgotten me, *
     and why go I so heavily, while the enemy oppresses me?'

12   As they crush my bones, my enemies mock me; *
     while all day long they say to me, 'Where is now your God?'

13   *Why are you so full of heaviness, O my soul,* *
     and why are you so disquieted within me?

14   *O put your trust in God;* *
     for I will yet give him thanks,
       who is the help of my countenance, and my God.

     [Come, creator Spirit, source of life;
     sustain us when our hearts are heavy
     and our wells have run dry,
     for you are the Father's gift,
     with him who is our living water, Jesus Christ our Lord. Amen.]

If desired, Psalms 42 and 43 may be said as one psalm.

Psalm 43

1   Give judgement for me, O God,
         and defend my cause against an ungodly people; *
     deliver me from the deceitful and the wicked.

2   For you are the God of my refuge;
         why have you cast me from you, *
     and why go I so heavily, while the enemy oppresses me?

3   O send out your light and your truth, that they may lead me, *
     and bring me to your holy hill and to your dwelling,

4   That I may go to the altar of God,
         to the God of my joy and gladness; *
     and on the lyre I will give thanks to you, O God my God.

5   *Why are you so full of heaviness, O my soul, *
     and why are you so disquieted within me?*

6   *O put your trust in God; *
     for I will yet give him thanks,
         who is the help of my countenance, and my God.*

     *[Come, creator Spirit, light and truth;
     bring us to the altar of life
     and renew our joy and gladness
     in Jesus Christ our Lord. Amen.]*

Psalm 44

     [Refrain: Rise up, O Lord, to help us.]

1   We have heard with our ears, O God, our forebears have told us, *
     all that you did in their days, in time of old;

2   How with your hand you drove out nations and planted us in, *
     and broke the power of peoples and set us free.

3   For not by their own sword did our ancestors take the land *
     nor did their own arm save them,

4   But your right hand, your arm, and the light of your countenance, *
     because you were gracious to them.

5   You are my King and my God, *
     who commanded salvation for Jacob.

6   Through you we drove back our adversaries; *
    through your name we trod down our foes.

7   For I did not trust in my bow; *
    it was not my own sword that saved me;

8   It was you that saved us from our enemies *
    and put our adversaries to shame.

9   We gloried in God all the day long, *
    and were ever praising your name.

10 But now you have rejected us and brought us to shame, *
    and go not out with our armies.

11 You have made us turn our backs on our enemies, *
    and our enemies have despoiled us.

12 You have made us like sheep to be slaughtered, *
    and have scattered us among the nations.

13 You have sold your people for a pittance *
    and made no profit on their sale.

14 You have made us the taunt of our neighbours, *
    the scorn and derision of those that are round about us.

15 You have made us a byword among the nations; *
    among the peoples they wag their heads.

16 My confusion is daily before me, *
    and shame has covered my face,

17 At the taunts of the slanderer and reviler, *
    at the sight of the enemy and avenger.

18 All this has come upon us,
      though we have not forgotten you *
    and have not played false to your covenant.

19 Our hearts have not turned back, *
    nor our steps gone out of your way,

20 Yet you have crushed us in the haunt of jackals, *
    and covered us with the shadow of death.

21 If we have forgotten the name of our God, *
    or stretched out our hands to any strange god,

22   Will not God search it out? *
       For he knows the secrets of the heart.

23   But for your sake are we killed all the day long, *
       and are counted as sheep for the slaughter.

24   Rise up! Why sleep, O Lord? *
       Awake, and do not reject us for ever.

25   Why do you hide your face *
       and forget our grief and oppression?

26   Our soul is bowed down to the dust; *
       our belly cleaves to the earth.

27   Rise up, O Lord, to help us *
       and redeem us for the sake of your steadfast love.

[In the darkness of unknowing,
when your love seems absent,
draw near to us, O God,
in Christ forsaken,
in Christ risen,
our Redeemer and our Lord. Amen.]

Psalm 45

[Refrain: Behold our defender, O God,
*   and look upon the face of your anointed.]*

1   My heart is astir with gracious words; *
       as I make my song for the king,
         my tongue is the pen of a ready writer.

2   You are the fairest of men; *
       full of grace are your lips,
         for God has blest you for ever.

3   Gird your sword upon your thigh, O mighty one; *
       gird on your majesty and glory.

4   Ride on and prosper in the cause of truth *
       and for the sake of humility and righteousness.

5   Your right hand will teach you terrible things; *
       your arrows will be sharp in the heart of the king's enemies,
         so that peoples fall beneath you.

6   Your throne is God's throne, for ever; *
       the sceptre of your kingdom is the sceptre of righteousness.

7   You love righteousness and hate iniquity; *
       therefore God, your God, has anointed you
         with the oil of gladness above your fellows.

8   All your garments are fragrant with myrrh, aloes and cassia; *
       from ivory palaces the music of strings makes you glad.

9   Kings' daughters are among your honourable women; *
       at your right hand stands the queen in gold of Ophir.

10   Hear, O daughter; consider and incline your ear; *
       forget your own people and your father's house.

11   So shall the king have pleasure in your beauty; *
       he is your lord, so do him honour.

12   The people of Tyre shall bring you gifts; *
       the richest of the people shall seek your favour.

13   The king's daughter is all glorious within; *
       her clothing is embroidered cloth of gold.

14   She shall be brought to the king in raiment of needlework; *
       after her the virgins that are her companions.

15   With joy and gladness shall they be brought *
       and enter into the palace of the king.

16   'Instead of your fathers you shall have sons, *
       whom you shall make princes over all the land.

17   'I will make your name to be remembered
         through all generations; *
       therefore shall the peoples praise you for ever and ever.'

[Lord our God,
bring your bride, your holy Church,
with joy to the marriage feast of heaven,
and unite us with your anointed Son,
Jesus Christ our Lord. Amen.]

Psalm 46

1   God is our refuge and strength, *
    a very present help in trouble;

2   Therefore we will not fear, though the earth be moved, *
    and though the mountains tremble in the heart of the sea;

3   Though the waters rage and swell, *
    and though the mountains quake at the towering seas.

4   There is a river whose streams make glad the city of God, *
    the holy place of the dwelling of the Most High.

5   God is in the midst of her;
        therefore shall she not be removed; *
    God shall help her at the break of day.

6   The nations are in uproar and the kingdoms are shaken, *
    but God utters his voice and the earth shall melt away.

7   *The Lord of hosts is with us; *
    the God of Jacob is our stronghold.*

8   Come and behold the works of the Lord, *
    what destruction he has wrought upon the earth.

9   He makes wars to cease in all the world; *
    he shatters the bow and snaps the spear
        and burns the chariots in the fire.

10 'Be still, and know that I am God; *
    I will be exalted among the nations;
        I will be exalted in the earth.'

11 *The Lord of hosts is with us; *
    the God of Jacob is our stronghold.*

    *[God of Jacob,
    when the earth shakes
    and the nations are in uproar,
    speak, and let the storm be still;
    through Jesus Christ our Lord. Amen.]*

Psalm 47

[Refrain: O sing praises to God, sing praises.]

1 Clap your hands together, all you peoples; *
   O sing to God with shouts of joy.

2 For the Lord Most High is to be feared; *
   he is the great King over all the earth.

3 He subdued the peoples under us *
   and the nations under our feet.

4 He has chosen our heritage for us, *
   the pride of Jacob, whom he loves.

5 God has gone up with a merry noise, *
   the Lord with the sound of the trumpet.

6 O sing praises to God, sing praises; *
   sing praises to our King, sing praises.

7 For God is the King of all the earth; *
   sing praises with all your skill.

8 God reigns over the nations; *
   God has taken his seat upon his holy throne.

9 The nobles of the peoples are gathered together *
   with the people of the God of Abraham.

10 For the powers of the earth belong to God *
   and he is very highly exalted.

[As Christ was raised by your glory, O Father,
so may we be raised to new life
and rejoice to be called your children,
both now and for ever. Amen.]

Psalm 48

[Refrain: We have waited on your loving-kindness, O God.]

1 Great is the Lord and highly to be praised, *
   in the city of our God.

2 His holy mountain is fair and lifted high, *
   the joy of all the earth.

3 On Mount Zion, the divine dwelling place, *
  stands the city of the great king.

4 In her palaces God has shown himself *
  to be a sure refuge.

5 For behold, the kings of the earth assembled *
  and swept forward together.

6 They saw, and were dumbfounded; *
  dismayed, they fled in terror.

7 Trembling seized them there;
  they writhed like a woman in labour, *
  as when the east wind shatters the ships of Tarshish.

8 As we had heard, so have we seen
  in the city of the Lord of hosts, the city of our God: *
  God has established her for ever.

9 We have waited on your loving-kindness, O God, *
  in the midst of your temple.

10 As with your name, O God,
  so your praise reaches to the ends of the earth; *
  your right hand is full of justice.

11 Let Mount Zion rejoice and the daughters of Judah be glad, *
  because of your judgements, O Lord.

12 Walk about Zion and go round about her;
  count all her towers; *
  consider well her bulwarks; pass through her citadels,

13 That you may tell those who come after
  that such is our God for ever and ever. *
  It is he that shall be our guide for evermore.

*[Father of lights,
raise us with Christ to your eternal city,
that, with kings and nations,
we may wait in the midst of your temple
and see your glory for ever and ever. Amen.]*

Psalm 49

[Refrain: Blessèd is the one who trusts in the Lord.]

1   Hear this, all you peoples; *
    listen, all you that dwell in the world,

2   You of low or high degree, *
    both rich and poor together.

3   My mouth shall speak of wisdom *
    and my heart shall meditate on understanding.

4   I will incline my ear to a parable; *
    I will unfold my riddle with the lyre.

5   Why should I fear in evil days, *
    when the malice of my foes surrounds me,

6   Such as trust in their goods *
    and glory in the abundance of their riches?

7   For no one can indeed ransom another *
    or pay to God the price of deliverance.

8   To ransom a soul is too costly; *
    there is no price one could pay for it,

9   So that they might live for ever, *
    and never see the grave.

10 For we see that the wise die also;
      with the foolish and ignorant they perish *
    and leave their riches to others.

11 Their tomb is their home for ever,
      their dwelling through all generations, *
    though they call their lands after their own names.

12 Those who have honour, but lack understanding, *
    are like the beasts that perish.

13 Such is the way of those who boast in themselves, *
    the end of those who delight in their own words.

14 Like a flock of sheep they are destined to die;
      death is their shepherd; *
    they go down straight to the Pit.

15 Their beauty shall waste away, *
    and the land of the dead shall be their dwelling.

16 But God shall ransom my soul; *
    from the grasp of death will he take me.

17 Be not afraid if some grow rich *
    and the glory of their house increases,

18 For they will carry nothing away when they die, *
    nor will their glory follow after them.

19 Though they count themselves happy while they live *
    and praise you for your success,

20 They shall enter the company of their ancestors *
    who will nevermore see the light.

21 Those who have honour, but lack understanding, *
    are like the beasts that perish.

    *[Save us from envy, God our Redeemer,
    and deliver us from the chains of wealth,
    that, ransomed through your Son,
    we may inherit the crown of everlasting life;
    through Jesus Christ our Lord. Amen.]*

Psalm 50

[Refrain: Offer to God a sacrifice of thanksgiving.]

1   The Lord, the most mighty God, has spoken *
    and called the world from the rising of the sun to its setting.

2   Out of Zion, perfect in beauty, God shines forth; *
    our God comes and will not keep silence.

3   Consuming fire goes out before him *
    and a mighty tempest stirs about him.

4   He calls the heaven above, *
    and the earth, that he may judge his people:

5   'Gather to me my faithful, *
    who have sealed my covenant with sacrifice.'

6   Let the heavens declare his righteousness, *
         for God himself is judge.

7   Hear, O my people, and I will speak: *
         'I will testify against you, O Israel;
            for I am God, your God.

8   'I will not reprove you for your sacrifices, *
         for your burnt offerings are always before me.

9   'I will take no bull out of your house, *
         nor he-goat out of your folds,

10   'For all the beasts of the forest are mine, *
         the cattle upon a thousand hills.

11   'I know every bird of the mountains *
         and the insect of the field is mine.

12   'If I were hungry, I would not tell you, *
         for the whole world is mine and all that fills it.

13   'Do you think I eat the flesh of bulls, *
         or drink the blood of goats?

14   'Offer to God a sacrifice of thanksgiving *
         and fulfil your vows to God Most High.

15   'Call upon me in the day of trouble; *
         I will deliver you and you shall honour me.'

16   But to the wicked, says God: *
         'Why do you recite my statutes
            and take my covenant upon your lips,

17   'Since you refuse to be disciplined *
         and have cast my words behind you?

18   'When you saw a thief, you made friends with him *
         and you threw in your lot with adulterers.

19   'You have loosed your lips for evil *
         and harnessed your tongue to deceit.

20   'You sit and speak evil of your brother; *
         you slander your own mother's son.

21 'These things have you done, and should I keep silence? *
Did you think that I am even such a one as yourself?

22 'But no, I must reprove you, *
and set before your eyes the things that you have done.

23 'You that forget God, consider this well, *
lest I tear you apart and there is none to deliver you.

24 'Whoever offers me the sacrifice of thanksgiving honours me *
and to those who keep my way
will I show the salvation of God.'

*[Mighty God,
dwelling in unapproachable light,
forgive our vain attempts to appease you,
and show us your full salvation
in Jesus Christ your Son our Lord. Amen.]*

Psalm 51

[Refrain: The sacrifice of God is a broken spirit.]

1 Have mercy on me, O God, in your great goodness; *
according to the abundance of your compassion
blot out my offences.

2 Wash me thoroughly from my wickedness *
and cleanse me from my sin.

3 For I acknowledge my faults *
and my sin is ever before me.

4 Against you only have I sinned *
and done what is evil in your sight,

5 So that you are justified in your sentence *
and righteous in your judgement.

6 I have been wicked even from my birth, *
a sinner when my mother conceived me.

7 Behold, you desire truth deep within me *
and shall make me understand wisdom
in the depths of my heart.

8   Purge me with hyssop and I shall be clean; *
     wash me and I shall be whiter than snow.

9   Make me hear of joy and gladness, *
     that the bones you have broken may rejoice.

10   Turn your face from my sins *
     and blot out all my misdeeds.

11   Make me a clean heart, O God, *
     and renew a right spirit within me.

12   Cast me not away from your presence *
     and take not your holy spirit from me.

13   Give me again the joy of your salvation *
     and sustain me with your gracious spirit;

14   Then shall I teach your ways to the wicked *
     and sinners shall return to you.

15   Deliver me from my guilt, O God,
       the God of my salvation, *
     and my tongue shall sing of your righteousness.

16   O Lord, open my lips *
     and my mouth shall proclaim your praise.

17   For you desire no sacrifice, else I would give it; *
     you take no delight in burnt offerings.

18   The sacrifice of God is a broken spirit; *
     a broken and contrite heart, O God, you will not despise.

19   O be favourable and gracious to Zion; *
     build up the walls of Jerusalem.

20   Then you will accept sacrifices offered in righteousness,
       the burnt offerings and oblations; *
     then shall they offer up bulls on your altar.

     *[Take away, good Lord, the sin that corrupts us;
     give us the sorrow that heals
     and the joy that praises
     and restore by grace your own image within us,
     that we may take our place among your people;
     in Jesus Christ our Lord. Amen.]*

Psalm 52

[Refrain: I trust in the goodness of God for ever and ever.]

1   Why do you glory in evil, you tyrant, *
    while the goodness of God endures continually?

2   You plot destruction, you deceiver; *
    your tongue is like a sharpened razor.

3   You love evil rather than good, *
    falsehood rather than the word of truth.

4   You love all words that hurt, *
    O you deceitful tongue.

5   Therefore God shall utterly bring you down; *
    he shall take you and pluck you out of your tent
        and root you out of the land of the living.

6   The righteous shall see this and tremble; *
    they shall laugh you to scorn, and say:

7   'This is the one who did not take God for a refuge, *
    but trusted in great riches and relied upon wickedness.'

8   But I am like a spreading olive tree in the house of God; *
    I trust in the goodness of God for ever and ever.

9   I will always give thanks to you for what you have done; *
    I will hope in your name,
        for your faithful ones delight in it.

    [Faithful and steadfast God,
    nourish your people in this wicked world,
    and, through prayer and the Scriptures,
    give us our daily bread;
    through Jesus Christ our Lord. Amen.]

Psalm 53

[Refrain: The fear of the Lord is the beginning of wisdom.]

1   The fool has said in his heart, 'There is no God.' *
    Corrupt are they, and abominable in their wickedness;
        there is no one that does good.

2   God has looked down from heaven upon the children of earth, *
    to see if there is anyone who is wise and seeks after God.

3   They are all gone out of the way;
        all alike have become corrupt; *
    there is no one that does good, no not one.

4   Have they no knowledge, those evildoers, *
    who eat up my people as if they ate bread,
        and do not call upon God?

5   There shall they be in great fear,
        such fear as never was; *
    for God will scatter the bones of the ungodly.

6   They will be put to shame, *
    because God has rejected them.

7   O that Israel's salvation would come out of Zion! *
    When God restores the fortunes of his people
        then will Jacob rejoice and Israel be glad.

    *[Without you, O God, nothing is real,
    all things are open to corruption
    and we are deadened by deceit;
    do not abandon us to our folly,
    but give us hearts that seek you
    and, at the last, joy in your heavenly city;
    through Jesus Christ our Lord. Amen.]*

Psalm 54

[Refrain: Behold, God is my helper.]

1   Save me, O God, by your name *
    and vindicate me by your power.

2   Hear my prayer, O God; *
    give heed to the words of my mouth.

3   For strangers have risen up against me,
        and the ruthless seek after my life; *
    they have not set God before them.

4   Behold, God is my helper; *
    it is the Lord who upholds my life.

[5   May evil rebound on those who lie in wait for me; *
       destroy them in your faithfulness.]

6   An offering of a free heart will I give you *
       and praise your name, O Lord, for it is gracious.

7   For he has delivered me out of all my trouble, *
       and my eye has seen the downfall of my enemies.

     [O living God,
     reach through the violence of the proud
     and the despair of the weak
     to create in Jesus Christ
     a people free to praise your holy name,
     now and for ever. Amen.]

Psalm 55

     [Refrain: Cast your burden upon the Lord and he will sustain you.]

1   Hear my prayer, O God; *
       hide not yourself from my petition.

2   Give heed to me and answer me; *
       I am restless in my complaining.

3   I am alarmed at the voice of the enemy *
       and at the clamour of the wicked;

4   For they would bring down evil upon me *
       and are set against me in fury.

5   My heart is disquieted within me, *
       and the terrors of death have fallen upon me.

6   Fearfulness and trembling are come upon me, *
       and a horrible dread has overwhelmed me.

7   And I said: 'O that I had wings like a dove, *
       for then would I fly away and be at rest.

8   'Then would I flee far away *
       and make my lodging in the wilderness.

9   'I would make haste to escape *
       from the stormy wind and tempest.'

10   Confuse their tongues, O Lord, and divide them, *
      for I have seen violence and strife in the city.

11   Day and night they go about on her walls; *
      mischief and trouble are in her midst.

12   Wickedness walks in her streets; *
      oppression and guile never leave her squares.

13   For it was not an open enemy that reviled me, *
      for then I could have borne it;

14   Nor was it my adversary that puffed himself up against me, *
      for then I would have hid myself from him.

15   But it was even you, one like myself, *
      my companion and my own familiar friend.

16   We took sweet counsel together *
      and walked with the multitude in the house of God.

[17   Let death come suddenly upon them;
         let them go down alive to the Pit; *
      for wickedness inhabits their dwellings, their very hearts.]

18   As for me, I will call upon God *
      and the Lord will deliver me.

19   In the evening and morning and at noonday
         I will pray and make my supplication, *
      and he shall hear my voice.

20   He shall redeem my soul in peace
         from the battle waged against me, *
      for many have come upon me.

21   God, who is enthroned of old,
         will hear and bring them down; *
      they will not repent, for they have no fear of God.

22   My companion stretched out his hands against his friend *
      and has broken his covenant;

23   His speech was softer than butter, though war was in his heart; *
      his words were smoother than oil, yet are they naked swords.

24   Cast your burden upon the Lord and he will sustain you, *
      and will not let the righteous fall for ever.

25   But those that are bloodthirsty and deceitful, O God, *
     you will bring down to the pit of destruction.

26   They shall not live out half their days, *
     but my trust shall be in you, O Lord.

     *[Lord, in all times of fear and dread,
     grant that we may so cast our burdens upon you,
     that you may bear us on the holy wings of the Spirit
     to the stronghold of your peace;
     through Jesus Christ our Lord. Amen.]*

Psalm 56

[Refrain: In God I trust, and will not fear.]

1   Have mercy on me, O God, for they trample over me; *
     all day long they assault and oppress me.

2   My adversaries trample over me all the day long; *
     many are they that make proud war against me.

3   In the day of my fear I put my trust in you, *
     in God whose word I praise.

4   In God I trust, and will not fear, *
     for what can flesh do to me?

5   All day long they wound me with words; *
     their every thought is to do me evil.

6   They stir up trouble; they lie in wait; *
     marking my steps, they seek my life.

7   Shall they escape for all their wickedness? *
     In anger, O God, cast the peoples down.

8   You have counted up my groaning;
        put my tears into your bottle; *
     are they not written in your book?

9   Then shall my enemies turn back
        on the day when I call upon you; *
     this I know, for God is on my side.

10   In God whose word I praise,
      in the Lord whose word I praise, *
    in God I trust and will not fear:
      what can flesh do to me?

11   To you, O God, will I fulfil my vows; *
    to you will I present my offerings of thanks,

12   For you will deliver my soul from death
      and my feet from falling, *
    that I may walk before God in the light of the living.

[Faithful God,
your deliverance is nearer than we know;
free us from fear
and help us to find courage in your Word,
Jesus Christ our Lord. Amen.]

Psalm 57

1   Be merciful to me, O God, be merciful to me, *
    for my soul takes refuge in you;

2   In the shadow of your wings will I take refuge *
    until the storm of destruction has passed by.

3   I will call upon the Most High God, *
    the God who fulfils his purpose for me.

4   He will send from heaven and save me
      and rebuke those that would trample upon me; *
    God will send forth his love and his faithfulness.

5   I lie in the midst of lions, *
    people whose teeth are spears and arrows,
      and their tongue a sharp sword.

6   *Be exalted, O God, above the heavens, **
    and your glory over all the earth.

7   They have laid a net for my feet;
      my soul is pressed down; *
    they have dug a pit before me
      and will fall into it themselves.

8   My heart is ready, O God, my heart is ready; *
      I will sing and give you praise.

9   Awake, my soul; awake, harp and lyre, *
      that I may awaken the dawn.

10   I will give you thanks, O Lord, among the peoples; *
      I will sing praise to you among the nations.

11   For your loving-kindness is as high as the heavens, *
      and your faithfulness reaches to the clouds.

12   *Be exalted, O God, above the heavens, *
      and your glory over all the earth.*

      [Tender God,
      gentle protector in time of trouble,
      pierce the gloom of despair
      and give us, with all your people,
      the song of freedom and the shout of praise;
      in Jesus Christ our Lord. Amen.]

Psalm 58

[Refrain: The Lord makes himself known by his acts of justice.]

[1   Do you indeed speak justly, you mighty? *
      Do you rule the peoples with equity?

2   With unjust heart you act throughout the land; *
      your hands mete out violence.

3   The wicked are estranged, even from the womb; *
      those who speak falsehood go astray from their birth.

4   They are as venomous as a serpent; *
      they are like the deaf adder which stops its ears,

5   Which does not heed the voice of the charmers, *
      and is deaf to the skilful weaver of spells.

6   Break, O God, their teeth in their mouths; *
      smash the fangs of these lions, O Lord.

7   Let them vanish like water that runs away; *
      let them wither like trodden grass.

8   Let them be as the slimy track of the snail, *
      like the untimely birth that never sees the sun.

9   Before ever their pots feel the heat of the thorns, *
      green or blazing, let them be swept away.

10   The righteous will be glad when they see God's vengeance; *
      they will bathe their feet in the blood of the wicked.

11   So that people will say,
      'Truly, there is a harvest for the righteous; *
      truly, there is a God who judges in the earth.']

[Living God,
deliver us from a world without justice
and a future without mercy;
in your mercy, establish justice,
and in your justice, remember the mercy
revealed to us in Jesus Christ our Lord. Amen.]

Psalm 59

[Refrain: You, O God, are my strong tower.]

1   Rescue me from my enemies, O my God; *
      set me high above those that rise up against me.

2   Save me from the evildoers *
      and from murderous foes deliver me.

3   For see how they lie in wait for my soul *
      and the mighty stir up trouble against me.

4   Not for any fault or sin of mine, O Lord; *
      for no offence, they run and prepare themselves for war.

5   Rouse yourself, come to my aid and see; *
      for you are the Lord of hosts, the God of Israel.

[6   Awake, and judge all the nations; *
      show no mercy to the evil traitors.]

7   They return at nightfall and snarl like dogs *
      and prowl about the city.

8   They pour out evil words with their mouths;
        swords are on their lips; *
    'For who', they say, 'can hear us?'

[9 But you laugh at them, O Lord; *
    you hold all the nations in derision.

10 For you, O my strength, will I watch; *
    you, O God, are my strong tower.

11 My God in his steadfast love will come to me; *
    he will let me behold the downfall of my enemies.

12 Slay them not, lest my people forget; *
    send them reeling by your might
        and bring them down, O Lord our shield.

13 For the sins of their mouth, for the words of their lips, *
    let them be taken in their pride.

14 For the cursing and falsehood they have uttered, *
    consume them in wrath, consume them till they are no more.]

15 And they shall know that God rules in Jacob, *
    and to the ends of the earth.

16 And still they return at nightfall and snarl like dogs *
    and prowl about the city.

17 Though they forage for something to devour, *
    and howl if they are not filled,

18 Yet will I sing of your strength *
    and every morning praise your steadfast love;

19 For you have been my stronghold, *
    my refuge in the day of my trouble.

20 To you, O my strength, will I sing; *
    for you, O God, are my refuge,
        my God of steadfast love.

    *[Strong and merciful God,
    stand with the oppressed
    against the triumph of evil
    and the complacency of your people,
    and establish in Jesus Christ*

your new order of generosity and joy,
for he is alive and reigns now and for ever. Amen.]

Psalm 60

[Refrain: Restore us again, O God our Saviour.]

1 O God, you have cast us off and broken us; *
you have been angry; restore us to yourself again.

2 You have shaken the earth and torn it apart; *
heal its wounds, for it trembles.

3 You have made your people drink bitter things; *
we reel from the deadly wine you have given us.

4 You have made those who fear you to flee, *
to escape from the range of the bow.

5 That your beloved may be delivered, *
save us by your right hand and answer us.

6 God has spoken in his holiness: *
'I will triumph and divide Shechem,
  and share out the valley of Succoth.

7 'Gilead is mine and Manasseh is mine; *
Ephraim is my helmet and Judah my sceptre.

8 'Moab shall be my washpot;
  over Edom will I cast my sandal; *
across Philistia will I shout in triumph.'

9 Who will lead me into the strong city? *
Who will bring me into Edom?

10 Have you not cast us off, O God? *
Will you no longer go forth with our troops?

11 Grant us your help against the enemy, *
for earthly help is in vain.

12 Through God will we do great acts, *
for it is he that shall tread down our enemies.

[Risen Christ,
you claim your own among the nations;
mend what is broken in us, loving Saviour;
do not forsake us when we fail,
but in your service grant us daring and love;
for your name's sake. Amen.]

Psalm 61

[Refrain: You are my refuge, O God,
a strong tower against the enemy.]

1   Hear my crying, O God, *
and listen to my prayer.

2   From the end of the earth I call to you with fainting heart; *
O set me on the rock that is higher than I.

3   For you are my refuge, *
a strong tower against the enemy.

4   Let me dwell in your tent for ever *
and take refuge under the cover of your wings.

5   For you, O God, will hear my vows; *
you will grant the request of those who fear your name.

6   You will add length of days to the life of the king, *
that his years may endure throughout all generations.

7   May he sit enthroned before God for ever; *
may steadfast love and truth watch over him.

8   So will I always sing praise to your name, *
and day by day fulfil my vows.

[Risen Christ,
as you knew the discipline of suffering
and the victory that brings us salvation,
so grant us your presence in our weakness
and a place in your unending kingdom
now and for evermore. Amen.]

Psalm 62

[Refrain: Wait on God alone in stillness, O my soul.]

1 On God alone my soul in stillness waits; *
   from him comes my salvation.

2 He alone is my rock and my salvation, *
   my stronghold, so that I shall never be shaken.

3 How long will all of you assail me to destroy me, *
   as you would a tottering wall or a leaning fence?

4 They plot only to thrust me down from my place of honour;
     lies are their chief delight; *
   they bless with their mouth, but in their heart they curse.

5 Wait on God alone in stillness, O my soul; *
   for in him is my hope.

6 He alone is my rock and my salvation, *
   my stronghold, so that I shall not be shaken.

7 In God is my strength and my glory; *
   God is my strong rock; in him is my refuge.

8 Put your trust in him always, my people; *
   pour out your hearts before him, for God is our refuge.

9 The peoples are but a breath,
     the whole human race a deceit; *
   on the scales they are altogether lighter than air.

10 Put no trust in oppression; in robbery take no empty pride; *
   though wealth increase, set not your heart upon it.

11 God spoke once, and twice have I heard the same, *
   that power belongs to God.

12 Steadfast love belongs to you, O Lord, *
   for you repay everyone according to their deeds.

[O God, teach us to seek security,
not in money or theft,
not in human ambition or malice,
not in our own ability or power,
but in you, the only God,
our rock and our salvation. Amen.]

Psalm 63

[Refrain: My soul is athirst for God, even for the living God.]

1   O God, you are my God; eagerly I seek you; *
    my soul is athirst for you.

2   My flesh also faints for you, *
    as in a dry and thirsty land where there is no water.

3   So would I gaze upon you in your holy place, *
    that I might behold your power and your glory.

4   Your loving-kindness is better than life itself *
    and so my lips shall praise you.

5   I will bless you as long as I live *
    and lift up my hands in your name.

6   My soul shall be satisfied, as with marrow and fatness, *
    and my mouth shall praise you with joyful lips,

7   When I remember you upon my bed *
    and meditate on you in the watches of the night.

8   For you have been my helper *
    and under the shadow of your wings will I rejoice.

9   My soul clings to you; *
    your right hand shall hold me fast.

10 But those who seek my soul to destroy it *
    shall go down to the depths of the earth;

11 Let them fall by the edge of the sword *
    and become a portion for jackals.

12 But the king shall rejoice in God;
      all those who swear by him shall be glad, *
    for the mouth of those who speak lies shall be stopped.

*[To you we come, radiant Lord,
the goal of all our desiring,
beyond all earthly beauty;
gentle protector, strong deliverer,
in the night you are our confidence;
from first light be our joy;
through Jesus Christ our Lord. Amen.]*

Psalm 64

[Refrain: The righteous shall rejoice in the Lord.]

1   Hear my voice, O God, in my complaint; *
    preserve my life from fear of the enemy.

2   Hide me from the conspiracy of the wicked, *
    from the gathering of evildoers.

3   They sharpen their tongue like a sword *
    and aim their bitter words like arrows,

4   That they may shoot at the blameless from hiding places; *
    suddenly they shoot, and are not seen.

5   They hold fast to their evil course; *
    they talk of laying snares, saying, 'Who will see us?'

6   They search out wickedness and lay a cunning trap, *
    for deep are the inward thoughts of the heart.

7   But God will shoot at them with his swift arrow, *
    and suddenly they shall be wounded.

8   Their own tongues shall make them fall, *
    and all who see them shall wag their heads in scorn.

9   All peoples shall fear and tell what God has done, *
    and they will ponder all his works.

10 The righteous shall rejoice in the Lord
      and put their trust in him, *
    and all that are true of heart shall exult.

*[Cut through the malice of our hearts, redeeming God,
with the Spirit's sword,
wound the pride of our rebellion
with the grace that makes righteous
and bring near the day of Christ,
when love shall reign in joy;
for he is alive and reigns, now and for ever. Amen.]*

Psalm 65

[Refrain: Be joyful in God, all the earth.]

1   Praise is due to you, O God, in Zion; *
    to you that answer prayer shall vows be paid.

2   To you shall all flesh come to confess their sins; *
    when our misdeeds prevail against us,
        you will purge them away.

3   Happy are they whom you choose
        and draw to your courts to dwell there. *
    We shall be satisfied with the blessings of your house,
        even of your holy temple.

4   With wonders you will answer us in your righteousness,
        O God of our salvation, *
    O hope of all the ends of the earth
        and of the farthest seas.

5   In your strength you set fast the mountains *
    and are girded about with might.

6   You still the raging of the seas, *
    the roaring of their waves
        and the clamour of the peoples.

7   Those who dwell at the ends of the earth
        tremble at your marvels; *
    the gates of the morning and evening sing your praise.

8   You visit the earth and water it; *
    you make it very plenteous.

9   The river of God is full of water; *
    you prepare grain for your people,
        for so you provide for the earth.

10   You drench the furrows and smooth out the ridges; *
    you soften the ground with showers and bless its increase.

11   You crown the year with your goodness, *
    and your paths overflow with plenty.

12   May the pastures of the wilderness flow with goodness *
    and the hills be girded with joy.

13 May the meadows be clothed with flocks of sheep *
and the valleys stand so thick with corn
that they shall laugh and sing.

*[May the richness of your creation, Lord,
and the mystery of your providence
lead us to that heavenly city
where all peoples will bring their wealth,
forsake their sins and find their true joy,
Jesus Christ our Lord. Amen.]*

Psalm 66

[Refrain: All the earth shall worship you, O Lord.]

1 Be joyful in God, all the earth; *
sing the glory of his name;
sing the glory of his praise.

2 Say to God, 'How awesome are your deeds! *
Because of your great strength
your enemies shall bow before you.

3 'All the earth shall worship you, *
sing to you, sing praise to your name.'

4 Come now and behold the works of God, *
how wonderful he is in his dealings with humankind.

5 He turned the sea into dry land;
the river they passed through on foot; *
there we rejoiced in him.

6 In his might he rules for ever;
his eyes keep watch over the nations; *
let no rebel rise up against him.

7 Bless our God, O you peoples; *
make the voice of his praise to be heard,

8 Who holds our souls in life *
and suffers not our feet to slip.

9 For you, O God, have proved us; *
you have tried us as silver is tried.

10   You brought us into the snare; *
      you laid heavy burdens upon our backs.

11   You let enemies ride over our heads;
      we went through fire and water; *
      but you brought us out into a place of liberty.

12   I will come into your house with burnt offerings
      and will pay you my vows, *
      which my lips uttered
      and my mouth promised when I was in trouble.

13   I will offer you fat burnt sacrifices
      with the smoke of rams; *
      I will sacrifice oxen and goats.

14   Come and listen, all you who fear God, *
      and I will tell you what he has done for my soul.

15   I called out to him with my mouth *
      and his praise was on my tongue.

16   If I had nursed evil in my heart, *
      the Lord would not have heard me,

17   But in truth God has heard me; *
      he has heeded the voice of my prayer.

18   Blessèd be God, who has not rejected my prayer, *
      nor withheld his loving mercy from me.

> *[How generous is your goodness, O God,*
> *how great is your salvation,*
> *how faithful is your love;*
> *help us to trust you in trial*
> *and praise you in deliverance;*
> *through Jesus Christ our Lord. Amen.]*

Psalm 67

1   God be gracious to us and bless us *
      and make his face to shine upon us,

2   That your way may be known upon earth, *
      your saving power among all nations.

3   *Let the peoples praise you, O God;* *
    let all the peoples praise you.

4   O let the nations rejoice and be glad, *
    for you will judge the peoples righteously
       and govern the nations upon earth.

5   *Let the peoples praise you, O God;* *
    let all the peoples praise you.

6   Then shall the earth bring forth her increase, *
    and God, our own God, will bless us.

7   God will bless us, *
    and all the ends of the earth shall fear him.

    [In the face of Jesus Christ
    your light and glory have blazed forth,
    O God of all the nations;
    with all your people,
    may we make known your grace
    and walk in the ways of peace;
    for your name's sake. Amen.]

Psalm 68

   [Refrain: Sing to God, sing praises to his name.]

1   Let God arise and let his enemies be scattered; *
    let those that hate him flee before him.

2   As the smoke vanishes, so may they vanish away; *
    as wax melts at the fire,
       so let the wicked perish at the presence of God.

3   But let the righteous be glad and rejoice before God; *
    let them make merry with gladness.

4   Sing to God, sing praises to his name;
       exalt him who rides on the clouds. *
    The Lord is his name; rejoice before him.

5   Father of the fatherless, defender of widows, *
    God in his holy habitation!

6   God gives the solitary a home
        and brings forth prisoners to songs of welcome, *
    but the rebellious inhabit a burning desert.

7   O God, when you went forth before your people, *
    when you marched through the wilderness,

8   The earth shook and the heavens dropped down rain,
        at the presence of God, the Lord of Sinai, *
    at the presence of God, the God of Israel.

9   You sent down a gracious rain, O God; *
    you refreshed your inheritance when it was weary.

10 Your people came to dwell there; *
    in your goodness, O God, you provide for the poor.

11 The Lord gave the word;
        great was the company of women who bore the tidings: *
    'Kings and their armies they flee, they flee!'
        and women at home are dividing the spoil.

12 Though you stayed among the sheepfolds, *
    see now a dove's wings covered with silver
        and its feathers with green gold.

13 When the Almighty scattered the kings, *
    it was like snowflakes falling on Zalmon.

14 You mighty mountain, great mountain of Bashan! *
    You towering mountain, great mountain of Bashan!

15 Why look with envy, you towering mountains,
        at the mount which God has desired for his dwelling, *
    the place where the Lord will dwell for ever?

16 The chariots of God are twice ten thousand,
        even thousands upon thousands; *
    the Lord is among them, the Lord of Sinai in holy power.

17 You have gone up on high and led captivity captive; *
    you have received tribute,
        even from those who rebelled,
        that you may reign as Lord and God.

18 Blessèd be the Lord who bears our burdens day by day, *
    for God is our salvation.

19   God is for us the God of our salvation; *
      God is the Lord who can deliver from death.

[20   God will smite the head of his enemies, *
      the hairy scalp of those who walk in wickedness.

21   The Lord has said, 'From the heights of Bashan, *
      from the depths of the sea will I bring them back,

22   'Till you dip your foot in blood *
      and the tongue of your dogs has a taste of your enemies.']

23   We see your solemn processions, O God, *
      your processions into the sanctuary, my God and my King.

24   The singers go before, the musicians follow after, *
      in the midst of maidens playing on timbrels.

25   In your companies, bless your God; *
      bless the Lord, you that are of the fount of Israel.

26   At the head there is Benjamin, least of the tribes,
       the princes of Judah in joyful company, *
      the princes of Zebulun and Naphtali.

27   Send forth your strength, O God; *
      establish, O God, what you have wrought in us.

28   For your temple's sake in Jerusalem *
      kings shall bring their gifts to you.

29   Drive back with your word the wild beast of the reeds, *
      the herd of the bull-like, the brutish hordes.

30   Trample down those who lust after silver; *
      scatter the peoples that delight in war.

31   Vessels of bronze shall be brought from Egypt; *
      Ethiopia will stretch out her hands to God.

32   Sing to God, you kingdoms of the earth; *
      make music in praise of the Lord;

33   He rides on the ancient heaven of heavens *
      and sends forth his voice, a mighty voice.

34   Ascribe power to God, whose splendour is over Israel, *
      whose power is above the clouds.

35   How terrible is God in his holy sanctuary, *
       the God of Israel, who gives power and strength to his people!
         Blessèd be God.

[Blessèd are you, gracious God;
you make your home among the weak,
you deliver us from death,
you bring us joy beyond our imagining
to the praise of Jesus Christ our Lord. Amen.]

Psalm 69

[Refrain: Hide not your face from your servant, O Lord.]

1   Save me, O God, *
      for the waters have come up, even to my neck.

2   I sink in deep mire where there is no foothold; *
      I have come into deep waters and the flood sweeps over me.

3   I have grown weary with crying; my throat is raw; *
      my eyes have failed from looking so long for my God.

4   Those who hate me without any cause *
      are more than the hairs of my head;

5   Those who would destroy me are mighty; *
      my enemies accuse me falsely:
        must I now give back what I never stole?

6   O God, you know my foolishness, *
      and my faults are not hidden from you.

7   Let not those who hope in you
        be put to shame through me, Lord God of hosts; *
      let not those who seek you be disgraced because of me,
        O God of Israel.

8   For your sake have I suffered reproach; *
      shame has covered my face.

9   I have become a stranger to my kindred, *
      an alien to my mother's children.

10   Zeal for your house has eaten me up; *
      the scorn of those who scorn you has fallen upon me.

11 I humbled myself with fasting, *
  but that was turned to my reproach.

12 I put on sackcloth also *
  and became a byword among them.

13 Those who sit at the gate murmur against me, *
  and the drunkards make songs about me.

14 But as for me, I make my prayer to you, O Lord; *
  at an acceptable time, O God.

15 Answer me, O God, in the abundance of your mercy *
  and with your sure salvation.

16 Draw me out of the mire, that I sink not; *
  let me be rescued from those who hate me
   and out of the deep waters.

17 Let not the water flood drown me,
   neither the deep swallow me up; *
  let not the Pit shut its mouth upon me.

18 Answer me, Lord, for your loving-kindness is good; *
  turn to me in the multitude of your mercies.

19 Hide not your face from your servant; *
  be swift to answer me, for I am in trouble.

20 Draw near to my soul and redeem me; *
  deliver me because of my enemies.

21 You know my reproach, my shame and my dishonour; *
  my adversaries are all in your sight.

22 Reproach has broken my heart; I am full of heaviness. *
  I looked for some to have pity, but there was no one,
   neither found I any to comfort me.

23 They gave me gall to eat, *
  and when I was thirsty, they gave me vinegar to drink.

[24 Let the table before them be a trap *
  and their sacred feasts a snare.

25 Let their eyes be darkened, that they cannot see, *
  and give them continual trembling in their loins.

26   Pour out your indignation upon them, *
      and let the heat of your anger overtake them.

27   Let their camp be desolate, *
      and let there be no one to dwell in their tents.

28   For they persecute the one whom you have stricken, *
      and increase the sorrows of him whom you have pierced.

29   Lay to their charge guilt upon guilt, *
      and let them not receive your vindication.

30   Let them be wiped out of the book of the living *
      and not be written among the righteous.]

31   As for me, I am poor and in misery; *
      your saving help, O God, will lift me up.

32   I will praise the name of God with a song; *
      I will proclaim his greatness with thanksgiving.

33   This will please the Lord more than an offering of oxen, *
      more than bulls with horns and hooves.

34   The humble shall see and be glad; *
      you who seek God, your heart shall live.

35   For the Lord listens to the needy, *
      and his own who are imprisoned he does not despise.

36   Let the heavens and the earth praise him, *
      the seas and all that moves in them;

37   For God will save Zion and rebuild the cities of Judah; *
      they shall live there and have it in possession.

38   The children of his servants shall inherit it, *
      and they that love his name shall dwell therein.

*[Thirsting on the cross,
your Son shared the reproach of the oppressed
and carried the sins of all;
in him, O God, may the despairing find you,
the afflicted gain life
and the whole creation know its true king,
Jesus Christ our Lord. Amen.]*

Psalm 70

[Refrain: Come to me quickly, O God.]

1   O God, make speed to save me; *
    O Lord, make haste to help me.

2   Let those who seek my life
        be put to shame and confusion; *
    let them be turned back and disgraced
        who wish me evil.

3   Let those who mock and deride me *
    turn back because of their shame.

4   But let all who seek you rejoice and be glad in you; *
    let those who love your salvation say always, 'Great is the Lord!'

5   As for me, I am poor and needy; *
    come to me quickly, O God.

6   You are my help and my deliverer; *
    O Lord, do not delay.

[O God, our helper and defender,
deliver us in our weakness,
answer our longings
and vindicate our faith,
that we may see your glory
in Jesus Christ our Lord. Amen.]

Psalm 71

[Refrain: O God, be not far from me.]

1   In you, O Lord, do I seek refuge; *
    let me never be put to shame.

2   In your righteousness, deliver me and set me free; *
    incline your ear to me and save me.

3   Be for me a stronghold to which I may ever resort; *
    send out to save me, for you are my rock and my fortress.

4   Deliver me, my God, from the hand of the wicked, *
    from the grasp of the evildoer and the oppressor.

5   For you are my hope, O Lord God, *
       my confidence, even from my youth.

6   Upon you have I leaned from my birth,
        when you drew me from my mother's womb; *
       my praise shall be always of you.

7   I have become a portent to many, *
       but you are my refuge and my strength.

8   Let my mouth be full of your praise *
       and your glory all the day long.

9   Do not cast me away in the time of old age; *
       forsake me not when my strength fails.

10   For my enemies are talking against me, *
       and those who lie in wait for my life take counsel together.

11   They say, 'God has forsaken him;
        pursue him and take him, *
       because there is none to deliver him.'

12   O God, be not far from me; *
       come quickly to help me, O my God.

13   Let those who are against me
        be put to shame and disgrace; *
       let those who seek to do me evil
        be covered with scorn and reproach.

14   But as for me I will hope continually *
       and will praise you more and more.

15   My mouth shall tell of your righteousness
        and salvation all the day long, *
       for I know no end of the telling.

16   I will begin with the mighty works of the Lord God; *
       I will recall your righteousness, yours alone.

17   O God, you have taught me since I was young, *
       and to this day I tell of your wonderful works.

18   Forsake me not, O God,
       when I am old and grey-headed, *
      till I make known your deeds to the next generation
       and your power to all that are to come.

19   Your righteousness, O God, reaches to the heavens; *
      in the great things you have done, who is like you, O God?

20   What troubles and adversities you have shown me, *
      and yet you will turn and refresh me
       and bring me from the deep of the earth again.

21   Increase my honour; *
      turn again and comfort me.

22   Therefore will I praise you upon the harp
       for your faithfulness, O my God; *
      I will sing to you with the lyre, O Holy One of Israel.

23   My lips will sing out as I play to you, *
      and so will my soul, which you have redeemed.

24   My tongue also will tell of your righteousness all the day long, *
      for they shall be shamed and disgraced
       who sought to do me evil.

[Faithful Lord, living Saviour,
in youth and old age,
from the womb to the grave,
may we know your protection
and proclaim your great salvation
to the glory of God the Father. Amen.]

Psalm 72

[Refrain: The Lord is king; let the earth rejoice.]

1   Give the king your judgements, O God, *
    and your righteousness to the son of a king.

2   Then shall he judge your people righteously *
    and your poor with justice.

3   May the mountains bring forth peace, *
    and the little hills righteousness for the people.

4 May he defend the poor among the people, *
   deliver the children of the needy and crush the oppressor.

5 May he live as long as the sun and moon endure, *
   from one generation to another.

6 May he come down like rain upon the mown grass, *
   like the showers that water the earth.

7 In his time shall righteousness flourish, *
   and abundance of peace
     till the moon shall be no more.

8 May his dominion extend from sea to sea *
   and from the River to the ends of the earth.

9 May his foes kneel before him *
   and his enemies lick the dust.

10 The kings of Tarshish and of the isles shall pay tribute; *
    the kings of Sheba and Seba shall bring gifts.

11 All kings shall fall down before him; *
    all nations shall do him service.

12 For he shall deliver the poor that cry out, *
    the needy and those who have no helper.

13 He shall have pity on the weak and poor; *
    he shall preserve the lives of the needy.

14 He shall redeem their lives from oppression and violence, *
    and dear shall their blood be in his sight.

15 Long may he live;
      unto him may be given gold from Sheba; *
    may prayer be made for him continually
      and may they bless him all the day long.

16 May there be abundance of grain on the earth,
      standing thick upon the hilltops; *
    may its fruit flourish like Lebanon
      and its grain grow like the grass of the field.

17 May his name remain for ever
        and be established as long as the sun endures; *
    may all nations be blest in him
        and call him blessèd.

18 Blessèd be the Lord, the God of Israel, *
    who alone does wonderful things.

19 And blessèd be his glorious name for ever. *
    May all the earth be filled with his glory.
        Amen. Amen.

    *[May your kingdom come, O God,
    with deliverance for the needy,
    with peace for the righteous,
    with overflowing blessing for all nations,
    with glory, honour and praise
    for Christ, the only Saviour. Amen.]*

Psalm 73

    [Refrain: In the Lord God have I made my refuge.]

1   Truly, God is loving to Israel, *
    to those who are pure in heart.

2   Nevertheless, my feet were almost gone; *
    my steps had well-nigh slipped.

3   For I was envious of the proud; *
    I saw the wicked in such prosperity;

4   For they suffer no pains *
    and their bodies are sleek and sound;

5   They come to no misfortune like other folk; *
    nor are they plagued as others are;

6   Therefore pride is their necklace *
    and violence wraps them like a cloak.

7   Their iniquity comes from within; *
    the conceits of their hearts overflow.

8   They scoff, and speak only of evil; *
    they talk of oppression from on high.

9 They set their mouth against the heavens, *
   and their tongue ranges round the earth;

10 And so the people turn to them *
   and find in them no fault.

11 They say, 'How should God know? *
   Is there knowledge in the Most High?'

12 Behold, these are the wicked; *
   ever at ease, they increase their wealth.

13 Is it in vain that I cleansed my heart *
   and washed my hands in innocence?

14 All day long have I been stricken *
   and chastened every morning.

15 If I had said, 'I will speak as they do,' *
   I should have betrayed the generation of your children.

16 Then thought I to understand this, *
   but it was too hard for me,

17 Until I entered the sanctuary of God *
   and understood the end of the wicked:

18 How you set them in slippery places; *
   you cast them down to destruction.

19 How suddenly do they come to destruction, *
   perish and come to a fearful end!

20 As with a dream when one awakes, *
   so, Lord, when you arise you will despise their image.

21 When my heart became embittered *
   and I was pierced to the quick,

22 I was but foolish and ignorant; *
   I was like a brute beast in your presence.

23 Yet I am always with you; *
   you hold me by my right hand.

24 You will guide me with your counsel *
   and afterwards receive me with glory.

25 Whom have I in heaven but you? *
And there is nothing upon earth that I desire
  in comparison with you.

26 Though my flesh and my heart fail me, *
God is the strength of my heart and my portion for ever.

27 Truly, those who forsake you will perish; *
you will put to silence the faithless who betray you.

28 But it is good for me to draw near to God; *
in the Lord God have I made my refuge,
  that I may tell of all your works.

[Holy God,
may we find wisdom in your presence
and set our hope not on uncertain riches
but on the love that holds us to the end;
in Jesus Christ our Lord. Amen.]

Psalm 74

[Refrain: Arise, O God, maintain your own cause.]

1 O God, why have you utterly disowned us? *
Why does your anger burn
  against the sheep of your pasture?

2 Remember your congregation that you purchased of old, *
the tribe you redeemed for your own possession,
  and Mount Zion where you dwelt.

3 Hasten your steps towards the endless ruins, *
where the enemy has laid waste all your sanctuary.

4 Your adversaries roared in the place of your worship; *
they set up their banners as tokens of victory.

5 Like men brandishing axes on high in a thicket of trees, *
all her carved work they smashed down with hatchet and hammer.

6 They set fire to your holy place; *
they defiled the dwelling place of your name
  and razed it to the ground.

7 They said in their heart, 'Let us make havoc of them altogether,' *
and they burned down all the sanctuaries of God in the land.

8   There are no signs to see, not one prophet left, *
     not one among us who knows how long.

9   How long, O God, will the adversary scoff? *
     Shall the enemy blaspheme your name for ever?

10   Why have you withheld your hand *
     and hidden your right hand in your bosom?

11   Yet God is my king from of old, *
     who did deeds of salvation in the midst of the earth.

12   It was you that divided the sea by your might *
     and shattered the heads of the dragons on the waters;

13   You alone crushed the heads of Leviathan *
     and gave him to the beasts of the desert for food.

14   You cleft the rock for fountain and flood; *
     you dried up ever-flowing rivers.

15   Yours is the day, yours also the night; *
     you established the moon and the sun.

16   You set all the bounds of the earth; *
     you fashioned both summer and winter.

17   Remember now, Lord, how the enemy scoffed, *
     how a foolish people despised your name.

18   Do not give to wild beasts the soul of your turtle dove; *
     forget not the lives of your poor for ever.

19   Look upon your creation,
        for the earth is full of darkness, *
     full of the haunts of violence.

20   Let not the oppressed turn away ashamed, *
     but let the poor and needy praise your name.

21   Arise, O God, maintain your own cause; *
     remember how fools revile you all the day long.

22   Forget not the clamour of your adversaries, *
     the tumult of your enemies that ascends continually.

[Redeeming God,
renew your broken people
with your Holy Spirit,
that they may walk your narrow way,
and greet your coming dawn
in Jesus Christ our Lord. Amen.]

Psalm 75

[Refrain: God alone is judge.]

1   We give you thanks, O God, we give you thanks, *
    for your name is near, as your wonderful deeds declare.

2   'I will seize the appointed time; *
    I, the Lord, will judge with equity.

3   'Though the earth reels and all that dwell in her, *
    it is I that hold her pillars steady.

4   'To the boasters I say, "Boast no longer," *
    and to the wicked, "Do not lift up your horn.

5   ' "Do not lift up your horn on high; *
    do not speak with a stiff neck." '

6   For neither from the east nor from the west, *
    nor yet from the wilderness comes exaltation.

7   But God alone is judge; *
    he puts down one and raises up another.

8   For in the hand of the Lord there is a cup, *
    well mixed and full of foaming wine.

9   He pours it out for all the wicked of the earth; *
    they shall drink it, and drain the dregs.

10 But I will rejoice for ever *
    and make music to the God of Jacob.

11 All the horns of the wicked will I break, *
    but the horns of the righteous shall be exalted.

    [Judge of all the earth,
    restrain the ambition of the proud
    and establish among us the reign of the Messiah,

who drained for us the cup of judgement
and is alive with you and the Holy Spirit,
one God, for ever and ever. Amen.]

Psalm 76

[Refrain: The Lord has made fast his throne for judgement.]

1   In Judah God is known; *
     his name is great in Israel.

2   At Salem is his tabernacle, *
     and his dwelling place in Zion.

3   There broke he the flashing arrows of the bow, *
     the shield, the sword and the weapons of war.

4   In the light of splendour you appeared, *
     glorious from the eternal mountains.

5   The boastful were plundered; they have slept their sleep; *
     none of the warriors can lift their hand.

6   At your rebuke, O God of Jacob, *
     both horse and chariot fell stunned.

7   Terrible are you in majesty: *
     who can stand before your face when you are angry?

8   You caused your judgement to be heard from heaven; *
     the earth trembled and was still,

9   When God arose to judgement, *
     to save all the meek upon earth.

10   You crushed the wrath of the peoples *
     and bridled the wrathful remnant.

11   Make a vow to the Lord your God and keep it; *
     let all who are round about him bring gifts
      to him that is worthy to be feared.

12   He breaks down the spirit of princes *
     and strikes terror in the kings of the earth.

[Majestic and gracious God,
more awesome than the agents of war,
more powerful than the wrath of nations,
restrain the violence of the peoples
and draw the despised of the earth
into the joyful life of your kingdom,
where you live and reign for ever and ever. Amen.]

Psalm 77

[Refrain: In the day of my trouble I have sought the Lord.]

1   I cry aloud to God; *
     I cry aloud to God and he will hear me.

2   In the day of my trouble I have sought the Lord; *
     by night my hand is stretched out and does not tire;
         my soul refuses comfort.

3   I think upon God and I groan; *
     I ponder, and my spirit faints.

4   You will not let my eyelids close; *
     I am so troubled that I cannot speak.

5   I consider the days of old; *
     I remember the years long past;

6   I commune with my heart in the night; *
     my spirit searches for understanding.

7   Will the Lord cast us off for ever? *
     Will he no more show us his favour?

8   Has his loving mercy clean gone for ever? *
     Has his promise come to an end for evermore?

9   Has God forgotten to be gracious? *
     Has he shut up his compassion in displeasure?

10   And I said, 'My grief is this: *
     that the right hand of the Most High has lost its strength.'

11   I will remember the works of the Lord *
     and call to mind your wonders of old time.

12 I will meditate on all your works *
and ponder your mighty deeds.

13 Your way, O God, is holy; *
who is so great a god as our God?

14 You are the God who worked wonders *
and declared your power among the peoples.

15 With a mighty arm you redeemed your people, *
the children of Jacob and Joseph.

16 The waters saw you, O God;
the waters saw you and were afraid; *
the depths also were troubled.

17 The clouds poured out water; the skies thundered; *
your arrows flashed on every side;

18 The voice of your thunder was in the whirlwind;
your lightnings lit up the ground; *
the earth trembled and shook.

19 Your way was in the sea, and your paths in the great waters, *
but your footsteps were not known.

20 You led your people like sheep *
by the hand of Moses and Aaron.

[God our shepherd,
you led us and saved us in times of old;
do not forget your people in their troubles,
but raise up your power
to sustain the poor and helpless;
for the honour of Jesus Christ our Lord. Amen.]

Psalm 78

Part 1

[Refrain: O Lord, how glorious are your works.]

1 Hear my teaching, O my people; *
incline your ears to the words of my mouth.

2 I will open my mouth in a parable; *
I will pour forth mysteries from of old,

3 Such as we have heard and known, *
  which our forebears have told us.

4 We will not hide from their children,
    but will recount to generations to come, *
  the praises of the Lord and his power
    and the wonderful works he has done.

5 He laid a solemn charge on Jacob
    and made it a law in Israel, *
  which he commanded them to teach their children,

6 That the generations to come might know,
    and the children yet unborn, *
  that they in turn might tell it to their children;

7 So that they might put their trust in God *
  and not forget the deeds of God,
    but keep his commandments,

8 And not be like their forebears,
    a stubborn and rebellious generation, *
  a generation whose heart was not steadfast,
    and whose spirit was not faithful to God.

9 The people of Ephraim, armed with the bow, *
  turned back in the day of battle;

10 They did not keep the covenant of God *
  and refused to walk in his law;

11 They forgot what he had done *
  and the wonders he had shown them.

12 For he did marvellous things in the sight of their forebears, *
  in the land of Egypt, in the field of Zoan.

13 He divided the sea and let them pass through; *
  he made the waters stand still in a heap.

14 He led them with a cloud by day *
  and all the night through with a blaze of fire.

15 He split the hard rocks in the wilderness *
  and gave them drink as from the great deep.

16 He brought streams out of the rock *
    and made water gush out like rivers.

17 Yet for all this they sinned more against him *
    and defied the Most High in the wilderness.

18 They tested God in their hearts *
    and demanded food for their craving.

19 They spoke against God and said, *
    'Can God prepare a table in the wilderness?

20 'He struck the rock indeed, so that the waters gushed out
        and the streams overflowed, *
    but can he give bread or provide meat for his people?'

21 When the Lord heard this, he was full of wrath; *
    a fire was kindled against Jacob
        and his anger went out against Israel,

22 For they had no faith in God *
    and put no trust in his saving help.

23 So he commanded the clouds above *
    and opened the doors of heaven.

24 He rained down upon them manna to eat *
    and gave them the grain of heaven.

25 So mortals ate the bread of angels; *
    he sent them food in plenty.

26 He caused the east wind to blow in the heavens *
    and led out the south wind by his might.

27 He rained flesh upon them as thick as dust *
    and winged fowl like the sand of the sea.

28 He let it fall in the midst of their camp *
    and round about their tents.

29 So they ate and were well filled, *
    for he gave them what they desired.

30 But they did not stop their craving; *
    their food was still in their mouths,

31   When the anger of God rose against them, *
    and slew their strongest men
      and felled the flower of Israel.

32   But for all this, they sinned yet more *
    and put no faith in his wonderful works.

33   So he brought their days to an end like a breath *
    and their years in sudden terror.

34   Whenever he slew them, they would seek him; *
    they would repent and earnestly search for God.

35   They remembered that God was their rock *
    and the Most High God their redeemer.

36   Yet they did but flatter him with their mouth *
    and dissembled with their tongue.

37   Their heart was not steadfast towards him, *
    neither were they faithful to his covenant.

38   But he was so merciful that he forgave their misdeeds
    and did not destroy them; *
  many a time he turned back his wrath
    and did not suffer his whole displeasure to be roused.

39   For he remembered that they were but flesh, *
    a wind that passes by and does not return.

[God our deliverer,
as you led our ancestors through the wilderness,
so lead us through the wilderness of this world,
that we may be saved through Christ for ever. Amen.]

Part 2

[Refrain: Tremble, O earth, at the presence of the Lord.]

40   How often they rebelled against him in the wilderness *
    and grieved him in the desert!

41   Again and again they tempted God *
    and provoked the Holy One of Israel.

42   They did not remember his power *
    in the day when he redeemed them from the enemy;

43 How he had wrought his signs in Egypt *
    and his wonders in the field of Zoan.

44 He turned their rivers into blood, *
    so that they could not drink of their streams.

45 He sent swarms of flies among them, which devoured them, *
    and frogs which brought them ruin.

46 He gave their produce to the caterpillar, *
    the fruit of their toil to the locust.

47 He destroyed their vines with hailstones *
    and their sycamore trees with the frost.

48 He delivered their cattle to hailstones *
    and their flocks to thunderbolts.

49 He set loose on them his blazing anger: *
    fury, displeasure and trouble,
        a troop of destroying angels.

50 He made a way for his anger
        and spared not their souls from death, *
    but gave their life over to the pestilence.

51 He smote the firstborn of Egypt, *
    the first fruits of their strength in the tents of Ham.

52 But he led out his people like sheep *
    and guided them in the wilderness like a flock.

53 He led them to safety and they were not afraid, *
    but the sea overwhelmed their enemies.

54 He brought them to his holy place, *
    the mountain which his right hand took in possession.

55 He drove out the nations before them
        and shared out to them their inheritance; *
    he settled the tribes of Israel in their tents.

56 Yet still they tested God Most High
        and rebelled against him, *
    and would not keep his commandments.

57 They turned back and fell away like their forebears, *
    starting aside like an unstrung bow.

58   They grieved him with their hill altars *
       and provoked him to displeasure with their idols.

59   God heard and was greatly angered, *
       and utterly rejected Israel.

60   He forsook the tabernacle at Shiloh, *
       the tent of his presence on earth.

61   He gave the ark of his strength into captivity, *
       his splendour into the adversary's hand.

62   He delivered his people to the sword *
       and raged against his inheritance.

63   The fire consumed their young men; *
       there was no one to lament their maidens.

64   Their priests fell by the sword, *
       and their widows made no lamentation.

65   Then the Lord woke as out of sleep, *
       like a warrior who had been overcome with wine.

66   He struck his enemies from behind *
       and put them to perpetual shame.

67   He rejected the tent of Joseph *
       and chose not the tribe of Ephraim,

68   But he chose the tribe of Judah *
       and the hill of Zion, which he loved.

69   And there he built his sanctuary like the heights of heaven, *
       like the earth which he founded for ever.

70   He chose David also, his servant, *
       and took him away from the sheepfolds.

71   From following the ewes with their lambs he took him, *
       that he might shepherd Jacob his people
         and Israel his inheritance.

72   So he shepherded them with a devoted heart *
       and with skilful hands he guided them.

[God our shepherd,
in all our wanderings and temptations,

teach us to rest in your mercy
and trust in your defence;
through him who laid down his life for us,
Jesus Christ our Lord. Amen.]

Psalm 79

[Refrain: Help us, O God of our salvation, for the glory of your name.]

1   O God, the heathen have come into your heritage; *
      your holy temple have they defiled
         and made Jerusalem a heap of stones.

2   The dead bodies of your servants they have given
         to be food for the birds of the air, *
      and the flesh of your faithful to the beasts of the field.

3   Their blood have they shed like water
         on every side of Jerusalem, *
      and there was no one to bury them.

4   We have become the taunt of our neighbours, *
      the scorn and derision of those that are round about us.

5   Lord, how long will you be angry, for ever? *
      How long will your jealous fury blaze like fire?

6   Pour out your wrath upon the nations that have not known you, *
      and upon the kingdoms that have not called upon your name.

7   For they have devoured Jacob *
      and laid waste his dwelling place.

8   Remember not against us our former sins; *
      let your compassion make haste to meet us,
         for we are brought very low.

9   Help us, O God of our salvation, for the glory of your name; *
      deliver us, and wipe away our sins for your name's sake.

[10   Why should the heathen say, *
      'Where is now their God?'

11   Let vengeance for your servants' blood that is shed *
      be known among the nations in our sight.]

12   Let the sorrowful sighing of the prisoners come before you, *
and by your mighty arm
    preserve those who are condemned to die.

[13 May the taunts with which our neighbours taunted you, Lord, *
return sevenfold into their bosom.]

14   But we that are your people and the sheep of your pasture
    will give you thanks for ever, *
and tell of your praise from generation to generation.

*[When faith is scorned
and love grows cold,
then, God of hosts, rebuild your Church
on lives of thankfulness and patient prayer;
through Christ your eternal Son. Amen.]*

Psalm 80

1   Hear, O Shepherd of Israel, *
you that led Joseph like a flock;

2   Shine forth, you that are enthroned upon the cherubim, *
before Ephraim, Benjamin and Manasseh.

3   Stir up your mighty strength *
and come to our salvation.

4   *Turn us again, O God; *
show the light of your countenance, and we shall be saved.*

5   O Lord God of hosts, *
how long will you be angry at your people's prayer?

6   You feed them with the bread of tears; *
you give them abundance of tears to drink.

7   You have made us the derision of our neighbours, *
and our enemies laugh us to scorn.

8   *Turn us again, O God of hosts; *
show the light of your countenance, and we shall be saved.*

9   You brought a vine out of Egypt; *
you drove out the nations and planted it.

10   You made room around it, *
     and when it had taken root, it filled the land.

11   The hills were covered with its shadow *
     and the cedars of God by its boughs.

12   It stretched out its branches to the Sea *
     and its tendrils to the River.

13   Why then have you broken down its wall, *
     so that all who pass by pluck off its grapes?

14   The wild boar out of the wood tears it off, *
     and all the insects of the field devour it.

15   Turn again, O God of hosts, *
     look down from heaven and behold;

16   Cherish this vine which your right hand has planted, *
     and the branch that you made so strong for yourself.

17   Let those who burnt it with fire, who cut it down, *
     perish at the rebuke of your countenance.

18   Let your hand be upon the man at your right hand, *
     the son of man you made so strong for yourself.

19   And so will we not go back from you; *
     give us life, and we shall call upon your name.

20   *Turn us again, O Lord God of hosts; *
     show the light of your countenance, and we shall be saved.*

     *[Faithful shepherd of your people,
     as we look for the light of your countenance,
     restore in us the image of your glory
     and graft us into the risen life of your Son,
     Jesus Christ our Lord. Amen.]*

Psalm 81

     [Refrain: O come, let us sing to the Lord.]

1   Sing merrily to God our strength, *
     shout for joy to the God of Jacob.

2   Take up the song and sound the timbrel, *
        the tuneful lyre with the harp.

3   Blow the trumpet at the new moon, *
        as at the full moon, upon our solemn feast day.

4   For this is a statute for Israel, *
        a law of the God of Jacob,

5   The charge he laid on the people of Joseph, *
        when they came out of the land of Egypt.

6   I heard a voice I did not know, that said: *
        'I eased their shoulder from the burden;
          their hands were set free from bearing the load.

7   'You called upon me in trouble and I delivered you; *
        I answered you from the secret place of thunder
          and proved you at the waters of Meribah.

8   'Hear, O my people, and I will admonish you: *
        O Israel, if you would but listen to me!

9   'There shall be no strange god among you; *
        you shall not worship a foreign god.

10   'I am the Lord your God,
        who brought you up from the land of Egypt; *
        open your mouth wide and I shall fill it.'

11   But my people would not hear my voice *
        and Israel would not obey me.

12   So I sent them away in the stubbornness of their hearts, *
        and let them walk after their own counsels.

13   O that my people would listen to me, *
        that Israel would walk in my ways!

14   Then I should soon put down their enemies *
        and turn my hand against their adversaries.

15   Those who hate the Lord would be humbled before him, *
        and their punishment would last for ever.

16   But Israel would I feed with the finest wheat *
        and with honey from the rock would I satisfy them.

[Father of mercy,
keep us joyful in your salvation
and faithful to your covenant;
and, as we journey to your kingdom,
ever feed us with the bread of life,
your Son, our Saviour Jesus Christ. Amen.]

Psalm 82

[Refrain: Arise, O God and judge the earth.]

1   God has taken his stand in the council of heaven; *
    in the midst of the gods he gives judgement:

2   'How long will you judge unjustly *
    and show such favour to the wicked?

3   'You were to judge the weak and the orphan; *
    defend the right of the humble and needy;

4   'Rescue the weak and the poor; *
    deliver them from the hand of the wicked.

5   'They have no knowledge or wisdom;
       they walk on still in darkness: *
    all the foundations of the earth are shaken.

6   'Therefore I say that though you are gods *
    and all of you children of the Most High,

7   'Nevertheless, you shall die like mortals *
    and fall like one of their princes.'

8   Arise, O God, and judge the earth, *
    for it is you that shall take all nations for your possession.

    [God our deliverer,
    when the foundations are shaken
    and justice has departed,
    defend the poor and needy
    and give your people strength to fight all wrong
    in the name of your Son, Jesus Christ our Lord. Amen.]

Psalm 83

[Refrain: The wicked shall not be able to stand in the judgement.]

1   Hold not your peace, O God, do not keep silent; *
    be not unmoved, O God;

2   For your enemies are in tumult *
    and those who hate you lift up their heads.

3   They take secret counsel against your people *
    and plot against those whom you treasure.

4   They say, 'Come, let us destroy them as a nation, *
    that the name of Israel be remembered no more.'

5   They have conspired together with one mind; *
    they are in league against you:

6   The tents of Edom and the Ishmaelites, *
    Moab and the Hagarenes,

7   Gebal and Ammon and Amalek, *
    the Philistines and those who dwell in Tyre.

8   Ashur also has joined them *
    and has lent a strong arm to the children of Lot.

[9 Do to them as you did to Midian, *
    to Sisera and to Jabin at the river of Kishon,

10 Who perished at Endor *
    and became as dung for the earth.

11 Make their commanders like Oreb and Zeëb, *
    and all their princes like Zebah and Zalmunna,

12 Who said, 'Let us take for ourselves *
    the pastures of God as our possession.'

13 O my God, make them like thistledown, *
    like chaff before the wind.

14 Like fire that consumes a forest, *
    like the flame that sets mountains ablaze,

15 So drive them with your tempest *
    and dismay them with your storm.

16 Cover their faces with shame, O Lord, *
    that they may seek your name.

17 Let them be disgraced and dismayed for ever; *
    let them be put to confusion and perish;]

18 And they shall know that you, whose name is the Lord, *
    are alone the Most High over all the earth.

    [Lord God, most high over all the world,
    when the pride of nations obscures
    *   your glorious purpose,*
    draw us into that unity which is your will for all people
    in Jesus Christ our Lord. Amen.]

Psalm 84

[Refrain: Blessèd are they who dwell in your house.]

1   How lovely is your dwelling place, O Lord of hosts! *
    My soul has a desire and longing to enter the courts of the Lord;
       my heart and my flesh rejoice in the living God.

2   The sparrow has found her a house
       and the swallow a nest where she may lay her young: *
    at your altars, O Lord of hosts, my King and my God.

3   Blessèd are they who dwell in your house: *
    they will always be praising you.

4   Blessèd are those whose strength is in you, *
    in whose heart are the highways to Zion,

5   Who going through the barren valley find there a spring, *
    and the early rains will clothe it with blessing.

6   They will go from strength to strength *
    and appear before God in Zion.

7   O Lord God of hosts, hear my prayer; *
    listen, O God of Jacob.

8   Behold our defender, O God, *
    and look upon the face of your anointed.

9   For one day in your courts *
    is better than a thousand.

10   I would rather be a doorkeeper in the house of my God *
       than dwell in the tents of ungodliness.

11   For the Lord God is both sun and shield;
         he will give grace and glory; *
       no good thing shall the Lord withhold
          from those who walk with integrity.

12   O Lord God of hosts, *
       blessèd are those who put their trust in you.

[Lord God,
sustain us in this vale of tears
with the vision of your grace and glory,
that, strengthened by the bread of life,
we may come to your eternal dwelling place;
in the power of Jesus Christ our Lord. Amen.]

Psalm 85

[Refrain: Show us your mercy, O Lord.]

1   Lord, you were gracious to your land; *
       you restored the fortunes of Jacob.

2   You forgave the offence of your people *
       and covered all their sins.

3   You laid aside all your fury *
       and turned from your wrathful indignation.

4   Restore us again, O God our Saviour, *
       and let your anger cease from us.

5   Will you be displeased with us for ever? *
       Will you stretch out your wrath from one generation to another?

6   Will you not give us life again, *
       that your people may rejoice in you?

7   Show us your mercy, O Lord, *
       and grant us your salvation.

8   I will listen to what the Lord God will say, *
       for he shall speak peace to his people and to the faithful,
         that they turn not again to folly.

9   Truly, his salvation is near to those who fear him, *
     that his glory may dwell in our land.

10   Mercy and truth are met together, *
     righteousness and peace have kissed each other;

11   Truth shall spring up from the earth *
     and righteousness look down from heaven.

12   The Lord will indeed give all that is good, *
     and our land will yield its increase.

13   Righteousness shall go before him *
     and direct his steps in the way.

     [Most holy God,
     when we come to you fearing that
       truth condemns us,
     show us that truth is one with love
     in your Word made flesh,
     our Saviour Jesus Christ. Amen.]

Psalm 86

     [Refrain: All nations you have made will come and worship
                 you, O Lord.]

1   Incline your ear, O Lord, and answer me, *
     for I am poor and in misery.

2   Preserve my soul, for I am faithful; *
     save your servant, for I put my trust in you.

3   Be merciful to me, O Lord, for you are my God; *
     I call upon you all the day long.

4   Gladden the soul of your servant, *
     for to you, O Lord, I lift up my soul.

5   For you, Lord, are good and forgiving, *
     abounding in steadfast love to all who call upon you.

6   Give ear, O Lord, to my prayer *
     and listen to the voice of my supplication.

7   In the day of my distress I will call upon you, *
     for you will answer me.

8   Among the gods there is none like you, O Lord, *
      nor any works like yours.

9   All nations you have made shall come and worship you, O Lord, *
      and shall glorify your name.

10   For you are great and do wonderful things; *
      you alone are God.

11   Teach me your way, O Lord, and I will walk in your truth; *
      knit my heart to you, that I may fear your name.

12   I will thank you, O Lord my God, with all my heart, *
      and glorify your name for evermore;

13   For great is your steadfast love towards me, *
      for you have delivered my soul from the depths of the grave.

14   O God, the proud rise up against me
      and a ruthless horde seek after my life; *
      they have not set you before their eyes.

15   But you, Lord, are gracious and full of compassion, *
      slow to anger and full of kindness and truth.

16   Turn to me and have mercy upon me; *
      give your strength to your servant
      and save the child of your handmaid.

17   Show me a token of your favour,
      that those who hate me may see it and be ashamed; *
      because you, O Lord, have helped and comforted me.

*[God of mercy,
who in your great love
drew your Son from the depths of the Pit,
bring your people from death to life,
that we may rejoice in your compassion
and praise you now and for ever. Amen.]*

Psalm 87

[Refrain: The Lord has chosen Zion for himself.]

1   His foundation is on the holy mountains. *
      The Lord loves the gates of Zion
      more than all the dwellings of Jacob.

2   Glorious things are spoken of you, *
    Zion, city of our God.

3   I record Egypt and Babylon as those who know me; *
    behold Philistia, Tyre and Ethiopia:
        in Zion were they born.

4   And of Zion it shall be said, 'Each one was born in her, *
    and the Most High himself has established her.'

5   The Lord will record as he writes up the peoples, *
    'This one also was born there.'

6   And as they dance they shall sing, *
    'All my fresh springs are in you.'

        *[Lord, as you call us to your city
        founded on the rock of ages,
        let the springs of living water
        rise within us to eternal life;
        in Jesus Christ our Lord. Amen.]*

Psalm 88

[Refrain: You are my refuge, my portion in the land of the living.]

1   O Lord, God of my salvation, *
    I have cried day and night before you.

2   Let my prayer come into your presence; *
    incline your ear to my cry.

3   For my soul is full of troubles; *
    my life draws near to the land of death.

4   I am counted as one gone down to the Pit; *
    I am like one that has no strength,

5   Lost among the dead, *
    like the slain who lie in the grave,

6   Whom you remember no more, *
    for they are cut off from your hand.

7   You have laid me in the lowest pit, *
    in a place of darkness in the abyss.

8 Your anger lies heavy upon me, *
and you have afflicted me with all your waves.

9 You have put my friends far from me *
and made me to be abhorred by them.

10 I am so fast in prison that I cannot get free; *
my eyes fail from all my trouble.

11 Lord, I have called daily upon you; *
I have stretched out my hands to you.

12 Do you work wonders for the dead? *
Will the shades stand up and praise you?

13 Shall your loving-kindness be declared in the grave, *
your faithfulness in the land of destruction?

14 Shall your wonders be known in the dark *
or your righteous deeds in the land where all is forgotten?

15 But as for me, O Lord, I will cry to you; *
early in the morning my prayer shall come before you.

16 Lord, why have you rejected my soul? *
Why have you hidden your face from me?

17 I have been wretched and at the point of death from my youth; *
I suffer your terrors and am no more seen.

18 Your wrath sweeps over me; *
your horrors are come to destroy me;

19 All day long they come about me like water; *
they close me in on every side.

20 Lover and friend have you put far from me *
and hid my companions out of my sight.

*[In the depths of our isolation
we cry to you, Lord God;
give light in our darkness
and bring us out of the prison of our despair;
through Jesus Christ our Lord. Amen.]*

Psalm 89

Part 1

[Refrain: Truly the Lord is our shield.]

1   My song shall be always of the loving-kindness of the Lord: *
     with my mouth will I proclaim your faithfulness
        throughout all generations.

2   I will declare that your love is established for ever; *
     you have set your faithfulness as firm as the heavens.

3   For you said: 'I have made a covenant with my chosen one; *
     I have sworn an oath to David my servant:

4   ' "Your seed will I establish for ever *
     and build up your throne for all generations." '

5   The heavens praise your wonders, O Lord, *
     and your faithfulness in the assembly of the holy ones;

6   For who among the clouds can be compared to the Lord? *
     Who is like the Lord among the host of heaven?

7   A God feared in the council of the holy ones, *
     great and terrible above all those round about him.

8   Who is like you, Lord God of hosts? *
     Mighty Lord, your faithfulness is all around you.

9   You rule the raging of the sea; *
     you still its waves when they arise.

10   You crushed Rahab with a deadly wound *
     and scattered your enemies with your mighty arm.

11   Yours are the heavens; the earth also is yours; *
     you established the world and all that fills it.

12   You created the north and the south; *
     Tabor and Hermon rejoice in your name.

13   You have a mighty arm; *
     strong is your hand and high is your right hand.

14   Righteousness and justice are the foundation of your throne; *
     steadfast love and faithfulness go before your face.

15 Happy are the people who know the shout of triumph: *
   they walk, O Lord, in the light of your countenance.

16 In your name they rejoice all the day long *
   and are exalted in your righteousness.

17 For you are the glory of their strength, *
   and in your favour you lift up our heads.

18 Truly the Lord is our shield; *
   the Holy One of Israel is our king.

   [As we sing of your love, O Lord,
   anoint us with the Spirit's seal,
   that we may praise your faithfulness
   and proclaim your truth from age to age;
   through Jesus Christ our Lord. Amen.]

Part 2

   [Refrain: The Lord has sworn an oath to David,
   a promise from which he will not shrink.]

19 You spoke once in a vision and said to your faithful people: *
   'I have set a youth above the mighty;
     I have raised a young man over the people.

20 'I have found David my servant; *
   with my holy oil have I anointed him.

21 'My hand shall hold him fast *
   and my arm shall strengthen him.

22 'No enemy shall deceive him, *
   nor any wicked person afflict him.

23 'I will strike down his foes before his face *
   and beat down those that hate him.

24 'My truth also and my steadfast love shall be with him, *
   and in my name shall his head be exalted.

25 'I will set his dominion upon the sea *
   and his right hand upon the rivers.

26 'He shall call to me, "You are my Father, *
   my God, and the rock of my salvation;"

27 'And I will make him my firstborn, *
    the most high above the kings of the earth.

28 'The love I have pledged to him will I keep for ever, *
    and my covenant will stand fast with him.

29 'His seed also will I make to endure for ever *
    and his throne as the days of heaven.

30 'But if his children forsake my law *
    and cease to walk in my judgements,

31 'If they break my statutes *
    and do not keep my commandments,

32 'I will punish their offences with a rod *
    and their sin with scourges.

33 'But I will not take from him my steadfast love *
    nor suffer my truth to fail.

34 'My covenant will I not break *
    nor alter what has gone out of my lips.

35 'Once for all have I sworn by my holiness *
    that I will not prove false to David.

36 'His seed shall endure for ever *
    and his throne as the sun before me;

37 'It shall stand fast for ever as the moon, *
    the enduring witness in the heavens.'

> *[Faithful God,*
> *remember your promise*
> *fulfilled in your anointed Son Jesus Christ,*
> *in whose strength alone we stand,*
> *now and for ever. Amen.]*

Part 3

> *[Refrain: For your servant David's sake,*
> *turn not away the face of your anointed.]*

38 But you have cast off and rejected your anointed; *
    you have shown fierce anger against him.

39 You have broken the covenant with your servant, *
    and have cast his crown to the dust.

40 You have broken down all his walls *
    and laid his strongholds in ruins.

41 All who pass by despoil him, *
    and he has become the scorn of his neighbours.

42 You have exalted the right hand of his foes *
    and made all his enemies rejoice.

43 You have turned back the edge of his sword *
    and have not upheld him in battle.

44 You have made an end of his radiance *
    and cast his throne to the ground.

45 You have cut short the days of his youth *
    and have covered him with shame.

46 How long will you hide yourself so utterly, O Lord? *
    How long shall your anger burn like fire?

47 Remember how short my time is, *
    how frail you have made all mortal flesh.

48 Which of the living shall not see death, *
    and shall deliver their soul from the power of darkness?

49 Where, O Lord, is your steadfast love of old, *
    which you swore to David in your faithfulness?

50 Remember, O Lord, how your servant is scorned, *
    how I bear in my bosom the taunts of many peoples,

51 While your enemies mock, O Lord, *
    while they mock the footsteps of your anointed.

52 Blessèd be the Lord for evermore. *
    Amen and Amen.

    [Lord, when death appals us
    and you hide your face,
    may we know our life is hidden with Christ,
    our hope of glory and our risen Lord. Amen.]

Psalm 90

[Refrain: O Lord my God, in you I take refuge.]

1   Lord, you have been our refuge *
     from one generation to another.

2   Before the mountains were brought forth,
        or the earth and the world were formed, *
     from everlasting to everlasting you are God.

3   You turn us back to dust and say: *
     'Turn back, O children of earth.'

4   For a thousand years in your sight are but as yesterday, *
     which passes like a watch in the night.

5   You sweep them away like a dream; *
     they fade away suddenly like the grass.

6   In the morning it is green and flourishes; *
     in the evening it is dried up and withered.

7   For we consume away in your displeasure; *
     we are afraid at your wrathful indignation.

8   You have set our misdeeds before you *
     and our secret sins in the light of your countenance.

9   When you are angry, all our days are gone; *
     our years come to an end like a sigh.

10   The days of our life are three score years and ten,
        or if our strength endures, even four score; *
     yet the sum of them is but labour and sorrow,
        for they soon pass away and we are gone.

11   Who regards the power of your wrath *
     and your indignation like those who fear you?

12   So teach us to number our days *
     that we may apply our hearts to wisdom.

13   Turn again, O Lord; how long will you delay? *
     Have compassion on your servants.

14   Satisfy us with your loving-kindness in the morning, *
     that we may rejoice and be glad all our days.

15   Give us gladness for the days you have afflicted us, *
       and for the years in which we have seen adversity.

16   Show your servants your works, *
       and let your glory be over their children.

17   May the gracious favour of the Lord our God be upon us; *
       prosper our handiwork; O prosper the work of our hands.

[Almighty God,
our eternal refuge,
teach us to live with the knowledge of our death
and to rejoice in the promise of your glory,
revealed to us in Jesus Christ our Lord. Amen.]

Psalm 91

[Refrain: Keep me as the apple of your eye.]

1   Whoever dwells in the shelter of the Most High *
      and abides under the shadow of the Almighty,

2   Shall say to the Lord, 'My refuge and my stronghold, *
      my God, in whom I put my trust.'

3   For he shall deliver you from the snare of the fowler *
      and from the deadly pestilence.

4   He shall cover you with his wings
      and you shall be safe under his feathers; *
      his faithfulness shall be your shield and buckler.

5   You shall not be afraid of any terror by night, *
      nor of the arrow that flies by day;

6   Of the pestilence that stalks in darkness, *
      nor of the sickness that destroys at noonday.

7   Though a thousand fall at your side
      and ten thousand at your right hand, *
      yet it shall not come near you.

8   Your eyes have only to behold *
      to see the reward of the wicked.

9   Because you have made the Lord your refuge *
      and the Most High your stronghold,

10   There shall no evil happen to you, *
       neither shall any plague come near your tent.

11   For he shall give his angels charge over you, *
       to keep you in all your ways.

12   They shall bear you in their hands, *
       lest you dash your foot against a stone.

13   You shall tread upon the lion and adder; *
       the young lion and the serpent you shall trample underfoot.

14   Because they have set their love upon me,
       therefore will I deliver them; *
       I will lift them up, because they know my name.

15   They will call upon me and I will answer them; *
       I am with them in trouble,
        I will deliver them and bring them to honour.

16   With long life will I satisfy them *
       and show them my salvation.

*[Keep us, good Lord,
under the shadow of your mercy
and, as you have bound us to yourself in love,
leave us not who call upon your name,
but grant us your salvation,
made known in the cross of Jesus Christ our Lord. Amen.]*

Psalm 92

[Refrain: You, O Lord, shall be exalted for evermore.]

1   It is a good thing to give thanks to the Lord *
       and to sing praises to your name, O Most High;

2   To tell of your love early in the morning *
       and of your faithfulness in the night-time,

3   Upon the ten-stringed instrument, upon the harp, *
       and to the melody of the lyre.

4   For you, Lord, have made me glad by your acts, *
       and I sing aloud at the works of your hands.

5   O Lord, how glorious are your works! *
      Your thoughts are very deep.

6   The senseless do not know, *
      nor do fools understand,

7   That though the wicked sprout like grass *
      and all the workers of iniquity flourish,

8   It is only to be destroyed for ever; *
      but you, O Lord, shall be exalted for evermore.

9   For lo, your enemies, O Lord,
        lo, your enemies shall perish, *
      and all the workers of iniquity shall be scattered.

10   But my horn you have exalted
        like the horns of wild oxen; *
      I am anointed with fresh oil.

11   My eyes will look down on my foes; *
      my ears shall hear the ruin of the evildoers
        who rise up against me.

12   The righteous shall flourish like a palm tree, *
      and shall spread abroad like a cedar of Lebanon.

13   Such as are planted in the house of the Lord *
      shall flourish in the courts of our God.

14   They shall still bear fruit in old age; *
      they shall be vigorous and in full leaf;

15   That they may show that the Lord is true; *
      he is my rock,
        and there is no unrighteousness in him.

      *[Give us the music of your praise, Lord,
      morning, noon and night,
      that our lives may be fruitful
      and our lips confess you as the true and only God. Amen.]*

Psalm 93

[Refrain: The Lord shall reign for ever and ever.]

1 The Lord is king and has put on glorious apparel; *
   the Lord has put on his glory
      and girded himself with strength.

2 He has made the whole world so sure *
   that it cannot be moved.

3 Your throne has been established from of old; *
   you are from everlasting.

4 The floods have lifted up, O Lord,
      the floods have lifted up their voice; *
   the floods lift up their pounding waves.

5 Mightier than the thunder of many waters,
      mightier than the breakers of the sea, *
   the Lord on high is mightier.

6 Your testimonies are very sure; *
   holiness adorns your house, O Lord, for ever.

[Christ our King,
you put on the apparel of our nature
and raised us to your glory;
reign from your royal throne
above the chaos of this world,
that all may see the victory you have won
and trust in your salvation;
for your glory's sake. Amen.]

Psalm 94

[Refrain: Righteous are you, O Lord, and true are your judgements.]

1 Lord God to whom vengeance belongs, *
   O God to whom vengeance belongs, shine out in majesty.

2 Rise up, O Judge of the earth; *
   give the arrogant their just deserts.

3 Lord, how long shall the wicked, *
   how long shall the wicked triumph?

4   How long shall the evildoers boast *
     and pour out such impudent words?

5   They crush your people, O Lord, *
     and afflict your heritage.

6   They murder the widow and the stranger; *
     the orphans they put to death.

7   And yet they say, 'The Lord will not see, *
     neither shall the God of Jacob regard it.'

8   Consider, most stupid of people; *
     you fools, when will you understand?

9   He that planted the ear, shall he not hear? *
     He that formed the eye, shall he not see?

10   He who corrects the nations, shall he not punish? *
     He who teaches the peoples, does he lack knowledge?

11   The Lord knows every human thought, *
     that they are but a breath.

12   Blessèd are those whom you chasten, O Lord, *
     whom you instruct from your law;

13   That you may give them rest in days of adversity, *
     until a pit is dug for the wicked.

14   For the Lord will not fail his people, *
     neither will he forsake his inheritance.

15   For justice shall return to the righteous, *
     and all that are true of heart shall follow it.

16   Who will rise up for me against the wicked? *
     Who will take my part against the evildoers?

17   If the Lord had not helped me, *
     my soul would soon have been put to silence.

18   And when I said, 'My foot has slipped', *
     your loving mercy, O Lord, upheld me.

19   In the multitude of cares that troubled my heart, *
     your comforts have refreshed my soul.

20   Will you have anything to do with the throne of wickedness, *
     which fashions evil through its law?

21   They gather together against the life of the righteous *
     and condemn the innocent to death.

22   But the Lord has become my stronghold *
     and my God the rock of my trust.

23   He will turn against them their own wickedness
        and silence them through their own malice; *
     the Lord our God will put them to silence.

     [Lord God, judge of all,
     before whom no secrets are hidden,
     let your justice shine out
     and your righteousness sweep wickedness from its throne,
     that we may live free from fear and stumbling;
     through Jesus Christ our Lord. Amen.]

Psalm 95

     [Refrain: Come, let us worship and bow down.]

1   O come, let us sing to the Lord; *
     let us heartily rejoice in the rock of our salvation.

2   Let us come into his presence with thanksgiving *
     and be glad in him with psalms.

3   For the Lord is a great God *
     and a great king above all gods.

4   In his hand are the depths of the earth *
     and the heights of the mountains are his also.

5   The sea is his, for he made it, *
     and his hands have moulded the dry land.

6   Come, let us worship and bow down *
     and kneel before the Lord our Maker.

7   For he is our God; *
     we are the people of his pasture and the sheep of his hand.

8   O that today you would listen to his voice: *
      'Harden not your hearts as at Meribah,
         on that day at Massah in the wilderness,

9   'When your forebears tested me, and put me to the proof, *
      though they had seen my works.

10   'Forty years long I detested that generation and said, *
      "This people are wayward in their hearts;
         they do not know my ways."

11   'So I swore in my wrath, *
      "They shall not enter into my rest." '

[Lord God, the maker of all,
as we bow down in praise this day,
make us attentive to your voice
and do not test us beyond our enduring;
through Jesus Christ our Lord. Amen.]

Psalm 96

[Refrain: O worship the Lord in the beauty of holiness.]

1   Sing to the Lord a new song; *
    sing to the Lord, all the earth.

2   Sing to the Lord and bless his name; *
    tell out his salvation from day to day.

3   Declare his glory among the nations *
    and his wonders among all peoples.

4   For great is the Lord and greatly to be praised; *
    he is more to be feared than all gods.

5   For all the gods of the nations are but idols; *
    it is the Lord who made the heavens.

6   Honour and majesty are before him; *
    power and splendour are in his sanctuary.

7   Ascribe to the Lord, you families of the peoples; *
    ascribe to the Lord honour and strength.

8   Ascribe to the Lord the honour due to his name; *
      bring offerings and come into his courts.

9   O worship the Lord in the beauty of holiness; *
      let the whole earth tremble before him.

10   Tell it out among the nations that the Lord is king. *
      He has made the world so firm that it cannot be moved;
        he will judge the peoples with equity.

11   Let the heavens rejoice and let the earth be glad; *
      let the sea thunder and all that is in it;

12   Let the fields be joyful and all that is in them; *
      let all the trees of the wood shout for joy before the Lord.

13   For he comes, he comes to judge the earth; *
      with righteousness he will judge the world
        and the peoples with his truth.

      [Lord God, you draw us by your beauty
      and transform us by your holiness;
      let our worship echo all creation's praise
      and declare your glory to the nations;
      through Jesus Christ our Lord. Amen.]

Psalm 97

      [Refrain· You, Lord, are most high over all the earth.]

1   The Lord is king: let the earth rejoice; *
      let the multitude of the isles be glad.

2   Clouds and darkness are round about him; *
      righteousness and justice are the foundation of his throne.

3   Fire goes before him *
      and burns up his enemies on every side.

4   His lightnings lit up the world; *
      the earth saw it and trembled.

5   The mountains melted like wax at the presence of the Lord, *
      at the presence of the Lord of the whole earth.

6   The heavens declared his righteousness, *
      and all the peoples have seen his glory.

7   Confounded be all who worship carved images
        and delight in mere idols. *
    Bow down before him, all you gods.

8   Zion heard and was glad, and the daughters of Judah rejoiced, *
    because of your judgements, O Lord.

9   For you, Lord, are most high over all the earth; *
    you are exalted far above all gods.

10 The Lord loves those who hate evil; *
    he preserves the lives of his faithful
        and delivers them from the hand of the wicked.

11 Light has sprung up for the righteous *
    and joy for the true of heart.

12 Rejoice in the Lord, you righteous, *
    and give thanks to his holy name.

    *[Most high and holy God,
    enthroned in fire and light,
    burn away the dross of our lives
    and kindle in us the fire of your love,
    that our lives may reveal the light and life
    we find in your Son, our Lord Jesus Christ. Amen.]*

Psalm 98

[Refrain: The Lord has made known his salvation.]

1   Sing to the Lord a new song, *
    for he has done marvellous things.

2   His own right hand and his holy arm *
    have won for him the victory.

3   The Lord has made known his salvation; *
    his deliverance has he openly shown in the sight of the nations.

4   He has remembered his mercy and faithfulness
        towards the house of Israel, *
    and all the ends of the earth have seen the salvation of our God.

5   Sound praises to the Lord, all the earth; *
    break into singing and make music.

6   Make music to the Lord with the lyre, *
         with the lyre and the voice of melody.

7   With trumpets and the sound of the horn *
         sound praises before the Lord, the King.

8   Let the sea thunder and all that fills it, *
         the world and all that dwell upon it.

9   Let the rivers clap their hands *
         and let the hills ring out together before the Lord,
           for he comes to judge the earth.

10   In righteousness shall he judge the world *
         and the peoples with equity.

> *[Lord God, just and true,*
> *you make your salvation known in the sight of the nations;*
> *tune the song of our hearts to the music of creation*
> *as you come among us to judge the earth;*
> *through our Saviour Jesus Christ. Amen.]*

Psalm 99

1   The Lord is king: let the peoples tremble; *
         he is enthroned above the cherubim: let the earth shake.

2   The Lord is great in Zion *
         and high above all peoples.

3   Let them praise your name, which is great and awesome; *
         the Lord our God is holy.

4   Mighty king, who loves justice,
           you have established equity; *
         you have executed justice and righteousness in Jacob.

5   *Exalt the Lord our God; *
         bow down before his footstool, for he is holy.*

6   Moses and Aaron among his priests
           and Samuel among those who call upon his name; *
         they called upon the Lord and he answered them.

7   He spoke to them out of the pillar of cloud; *
         they kept his testimonies and the law that he gave them.

8   You answered them, O Lord our God; *
     you were a God who forgave them
        and pardoned them for their offences.

9   *Exalt the Lord our God*
        and worship him upon his holy hill, *
     for the Lord our God is holy.

     [Lord God, mighty king,
     you love justice and establish equity;
     may we love justice more than gain
     and mercy more than power;
     through Jesus Christ our Lord. Amen.]

Psalm 100

[Refrain: The Lord is gracious; his steadfast love is everlasting.]

1   O be joyful in the Lord, all the earth; *
     serve the Lord with gladness
        and come before his presence with a song.

2   Know that the Lord is God; *
     it is he that has made us and we are his;
        we are his people and the sheep of his pasture.

3   Enter his gates with thanksgiving
        and his courts with praise; *
     give thanks to him and bless his name.

4   For the Lord is gracious; his steadfast love is everlasting, *
     and his faithfulness endures from generation to generation.

     [O Christ, door of the sheepfold,
     may we enter your gates with praise
     and go from your courts to serve you
     in the poor, the lost and the wandering,
     this day and all our days. Amen.]

Psalm 101

[Refrain: Blessèd are those who fear the Lord.]

1   I will sing of faithfulness and justice; *
     to you, O Lord, will I sing.

2   Let me be wise in the way that is perfect: *
when will you come to me?

3   I will walk with purity of heart *
within the walls of my house.

4   I will not set before my eyes *
a counsel that is evil.

5   I abhor the deeds of unfaithfulness; *
they shall not cling to me.

6   A crooked heart shall depart from me; *
I will not know a wicked person.

7   One who slanders a neighbour in secret *
I will quickly put to silence.

8   Haughty eyes and an arrogant heart *
I will not endure.

9   My eyes are upon the faithful in the land, *
that they may dwell with me.

10   One who walks in the way that is pure *
shall be my servant.

11   There shall not dwell in my house *
one that practises deceit.

12   One who utters falsehood *
shall not continue in my sight.

13   Morning by morning will I put to silence *
all the wicked in the land,

14   To cut off from the city of the Lord *
all those who practise evil.

*[Keep us, O Lord,
in purity of heart and faithfulness to your commands,
that your servants may walk before you
in the way that is perfect;
through Jesus Christ our Lord. Amen.]*

Psalm 102

1   O Lord, hear my prayer *
    and let my crying come before you.

2   Hide not your face from me *
    in the day of my distress.

3   Incline your ear to me; *
    when I call, make haste to answer me,

4   For my days are consumed in smoke *
    and my bones burn away as in a furnace.

5   My heart is smitten down and withered like grass, *
    so that I forget to eat my bread.

6   From the sound of my groaning *
    my bones cleave fast to my skin.

7   I am become like a vulture in the wilderness, *
    like an owl that haunts the ruins.

8   I keep watch and am become like a sparrow *
    solitary upon the housetop.

9   My enemies revile me all the day long, *
    and those who rage at me have sworn together against me.

10 I have eaten ashes for bread *
    and mingled my drink with weeping,

11 Because of your indignation and wrath, *
    for you have taken me up and cast me down.

12 My days fade away like a shadow, *
    and I am withered like grass.

13 But you, O Lord, shall endure for ever *
    and your name through all generations.

14 You will arise and have pity on Zion; *
    it is time to have mercy upon her;
      surely the time has come.

15   For your servants love her very stones *
        and feel compassion for her dust.

16   Then shall the nations fear your name, O Lord, *
        and all the kings of the earth your glory,

17   When the Lord has built up Zion *
        and shown himself in glory;

18   When he has turned to the prayer of the destitute *
        and has not despised their plea.

19   This shall be written for those that come after, *
        and a people yet unborn shall praise the Lord.

20   For he has looked down from his holy height; *
        from the heavens he beheld the earth,

21   That he might hear the sighings of the prisoner *
        and set free those condemned to die;

22   That the name of the Lord may be proclaimed in Zion *
        and his praises in Jerusalem,

23   When peoples are gathered together *
        and kingdoms also, to serve the Lord.

24   He has brought down my strength in my journey *
        and has shortened my days.

25   I pray, 'O my God, do not take me in the midst of my days; *
        your years endure throughout all generations.

26   'In the beginning you laid the foundations of the earth, *
        and the heavens are the work of your hands;

27   'They shall perish, but you will endure; *
        they all shall wear out like a garment.

28   'You change them like clothing, and they shall be changed; *
        but you are the same, and your years will not fail.

29   'The children of your servants shall continue, *
        and their descendants shall be established in your sight.'

[Have pity on our frailty, O God,
and in the hour of our death
cast us not away as clothing that is worn,
for you are our eternal refuge;
through Jesus Christ our Lord. Amen.]

Psalm 103

[Refrain: The Lord is full of compassion and mercy.]

1   Bless the Lord, O my soul, *
    and all that is within me bless his holy name.

2   Bless the Lord, O my soul, *
    and forget not all his benefits;

3   Who forgives all your sins *
    and heals all your infirmities;

4   Who redeems your life from the Pit *
    and crowns you with faithful love and compassion;

5   Who satisfies you with good things, *
    so that your youth is renewed like an eagle's.

6   The Lord executes righteousness *
    and judgement for all who are oppressed.

7   He made his ways known to Moses *
    and his works to the children of Israel.

8   The Lord is full of compassion and mercy, *
    slow to anger and of great kindness.

9   He will not always accuse us, *
    neither will he keep his anger for ever.

10 He has not dealt with us according to our sins, *
    nor rewarded us according to our wickedness.

11 For as the heavens are high above the earth, *
    so great is his mercy upon those who fear him.

12 As far as the east is from the west, *
    so far has he set our sins from us.

13　As a father has compassion on his children, *
　　so is the Lord merciful towards those who fear him.

14　For he knows of what we are made; *
　　he remembers that we are but dust.

15　Our days are but as grass; *
　　we flourish as a flower of the field;

16　For as soon as the wind goes over it, it is gone, *
　　and its place shall know it no more.

17　But the merciful goodness of the Lord is from of old
　　　and endures for ever on those who fear him, *
　　and his righteousness on children's children;

18　On those who keep his covenant *
　　and remember his commandments to do them.

19　The Lord has established his throne in heaven, *
　　and his kingdom has dominion over all.

20　Bless the Lord, you angels of his, *
　　you mighty ones who do his bidding
　　　and hearken to the voice of his word.

21　Bless the Lord, all you his hosts, *
　　you ministers of his who do his will.

22　Bless the Lord, all you works of his,
　　　in all places of his dominion; *
　　bless the Lord, O my soul.

[Merciful Lord,
as we come from dust and return to dust,
show us the face of our Redeemer,
that in our frailty we may bless your name
and praise you all our days;
through Jesus Christ our Lord. Amen.]

Psalm 104

[Refrain: I will sing to the Lord as long as I live.]

1　Bless the Lord, O my soul. *
　　O Lord my God, how excellent is your greatness!

2   You are clothed with majesty and honour, *
       wrapped in light as in a garment.

3   You spread out the heavens like a curtain *
       and lay the beams of your dwelling place in the waters above.

4   You make the clouds your chariot *
       and ride on the wings of the wind.

5   You make the winds your messengers *
       and flames of fire your servants.

6   You laid the foundations of the earth, *
       that it never should move at any time.

7   You covered it with the deep like a garment; *
       the waters stood high above the hills.

8   At your rebuke they fled; *
       at the voice of your thunder they hastened away.

9   They rose up to the hills and flowed down to the valleys beneath, *
       to the place which you had appointed for them.

10   You have set them their bounds that they should not pass, *
       nor turn again to cover the earth.

11   You send the springs into the brooks, *
       which run among the hills.

12   They give drink to every beast of the field, *
       and the wild asses quench their thirst.

13   Beside them the birds of the air make their nests *
       and sing among the branches.

14   You water the hills from your dwelling on high; *
       the earth is filled with the fruit of your works.

15   You make grass to grow for the cattle *
       and plants to meet our needs,

16   Bringing forth food from the earth *
       and wine to gladden our hearts,

17   Oil to give us a cheerful countenance *
       and bread to strengthen our hearts.

18   The trees of the Lord are full of sap, *
       the cedars of Lebanon which he planted,

19   In which the birds build their nests, *
       while the fir trees are a dwelling for the stork.

20   The mountains are a refuge for the wild goats *
       and the stony cliffs for the conies.

21   You appointed the moon to mark the seasons, *
       and the sun knows the time for its setting.

22   You make darkness that it may be night, *
       in which all the beasts of the forest creep forth.

23   The lions roar for their prey *
       and seek their food from God.

24   The sun rises and they are gone *
       to lay themselves down in their dens.

25   People go forth to their work *
       and to their labour until the evening.

26   O Lord, how manifold are your works! *
       In wisdom you have made them all;
          the earth is full of your creatures.

27   There is the sea, spread far and wide, *
       and there move creatures beyond number, both small and great.

28   There go the ships, and there is that Leviathan *
       which you have made to play in the deep.

29   All of these look to you *
       to give them their food in due season.

30   When you give it them, they gather it; *
       you open your hand and they are filled with good.

31   When you hide your face they are troubled; *
       when you take away their breath,
          they die and return again to the dust.

32   When you send forth your spirit, they are created, *
       and you renew the face of the earth.

33 May the glory of the Lord endure for ever; *
   may the Lord rejoice in his works;

34 He looks on the earth and it trembles; *
   he touches the mountains and they smoke.

35 I will sing to the Lord as long as I live; *
   I will make music to my God while I have my being.

36 So shall my song please him *
   while I rejoice in the Lord.

37 Let sinners be consumed out of the earth
      and the wicked be no more. *
   Bless the Lord, O my soul.
      Alleluia.

   [Creator God,
   send your Holy Spirit to renew this living world,
   that the whole creation,
   in its groaning and striving,
   may know your loving purpose
   and come to reflect your glory;
   in Jesus Christ our Lord. Amen.]

Psalm 105

   [Refrain: Remember the marvels the Lord has done.]

1 O give thanks to the Lord and call upon his name; *
   make known his deeds among the peoples.

2 Sing to him, sing praises, *
   and tell of all his marvellous works.

3 Rejoice in the praise of his holy name; *
   let the hearts of them rejoice who seek the Lord.

4 Seek the Lord and his strength; *
   seek his face continually.

5 Remember the marvels he has done, *
   his wonders and the judgements of his mouth,

6 O seed of Abraham his servant, *
   O children of Jacob his chosen.

7   He is the Lord our God; *
    his judgements are in all the earth.

8   He has always been mindful of his covenant, *
    the promise that he made for a thousand generations:

9   The covenant he made with Abraham, *
    the oath that he swore to Isaac,

10 Which he established as a statute for Jacob, *
    an everlasting covenant for Israel,

11 Saying, 'To you will I give the land of Canaan *
    to be the portion of your inheritance.'

12 When they were but few in number, *
    of little account, and sojourners in the land,

13 Wandering from nation to nation, *
    from one kingdom to another people,

14 He suffered no one to do them wrong *
    and rebuked even kings for their sake,

15 Saying, 'Touch not my anointed *
    and do my prophets no harm.'

16 Then he called down famine over the land *
    and broke every staff of bread.

17 But he had sent a man before them, *
    Joseph, who was sold as a slave.

18 They shackled his feet with fetters; *
    his neck was ringed with iron.

19 Until all he foretold came to pass, *
    the word of the Lord tested him.

20 The king sent and released him; *
    the ruler of peoples set him free.

21 He appointed him lord of his household *
    and ruler of all he possessed,

22 To instruct his princes as he willed *
    and to teach his counsellors wisdom.

            *   *   *

23   Then Israel came into Egypt; *
        Jacob sojourned in the land of Ham.

24   And the Lord made his people exceedingly fruitful; *
        he made them too many for their adversaries,

25   Whose heart he turned, so that they hated his people *
        and dealt craftily with his servants.

26   Then sent he Moses his servant *
        and Aaron whom he had chosen.

27   He showed his signs through their word *
        and his wonders in the land of Ham.

28   He sent darkness and it grew dark; *
        yet they did not heed his words.

29   He turned their waters into blood *
        and slew all their fish.

30   Their land swarmed with frogs, *
        even in their kings' chambers.

31   He spoke the word, and there came clouds of flies, *
        swarms of gnats within all their borders.

32   He gave them hailstones for rain *
        and flames of lightning in their land.

33   He blasted their vines and their fig trees *
        and shattered trees across their country.

34   He spoke the word, and the grasshoppers came *
        and young locusts without number;

35   They ate every plant in their land *
        and devoured the fruit of their soil.

36   He smote all the firstborn in their land, *
        the first fruits of all their strength.

37   Then he brought them out with silver and gold; *
        there was not one among their tribes that stumbled.

38   Egypt was glad at their departing, *
        for a dread of them had fallen upon them.

39 He spread out a cloud for a covering *
and a fire to light up the night.

40 They asked and he brought them quails; *
he satisfied them with the bread of heaven.

41 He opened the rock, and the waters gushed out *
and ran in the dry places like a river.

42 For he remembered his holy word *
and Abraham, his servant.

43 So he brought forth his people with joy, *
his chosen ones with singing.

44 He gave them the lands of the nations *
and they took possession of the fruit of their toil,

45 That they might keep his statutes *
and faithfully observe his laws. Alleluia.

*[God of our earthly pilgrimage,
feed your Easter people with the bread of heaven,
that we may hunger and thirst for righteousness
until we reach our promised land;
through Jesus Christ our Lord. Amen.]*

Psalm 106

[Refrain: The Lord remembered his covenant.]

1 Alleluia.
Give thanks to the Lord, for he is gracious, *
for his faithfulness endures for ever.

2 Who can express the mighty acts of the Lord *
or show forth all his praise?

3 Blessèd are those who observe what is right *
and always do what is just.

4 Remember me, O Lord, in the favour you bear for your people; *
visit me in the day of your salvation;

5 That I may see the prosperity of your chosen
and rejoice in the gladness of your people, *
and exult with your inheritance.

6   We have sinned like our forebears; *
       we have done wrong and dealt wickedly.

7   In Egypt they did not consider your wonders,
       nor remember the abundance of your faithful love; *
       they rebelled against the Most High at the Red Sea.

8   But he saved them for his name's sake, *
       that he might make his power to be known.

9   He rebuked the Red Sea and it was dried up; *
       so he led them through the deep as through the wilderness.

10   He saved them from the adversary's hand *
       and redeemed them from the hand of the enemy.

11   As for those that troubled them, the waters overwhelmed them; *
       there was not one of them left.

12   Then they believed his words *
       and sang aloud his praise.

13   But soon they forgot his deeds *
       and would not wait for his counsel.

14   A craving seized them in the wilderness, *
       and they put God to the test in the desert.

15   He gave them their desire, *
       but sent a wasting sickness among them.

16   They grew jealous of Moses in the camp *
       and of Aaron, the holy one of the Lord.

17   So the earth opened and swallowed up Dathan *
       and covered the company of Abiram.

18   A fire was kindled in their company; *
       the flame burnt up the wicked.

19   They made a calf at Horeb *
       and worshipped the molten image;

20   Thus they exchanged their glory *
       for the image of an ox that feeds on hay.

21   They forgot God their saviour, *
       who had done such great things in Egypt,

22   Wonderful deeds in the land of Ham *
      and fearful things at the Red Sea.

23   So he would have destroyed them,
       had not Moses his chosen stood before him in the breach, *
      to turn away his wrath from consuming them.

         *   *   *

24   Then they scorned the Promised Land *
      and would not believe his word,

25   But murmured in their tents *
      and would not heed the voice of the Lord.

26   So he lifted his hand against them *
      and swore to overthrow them in the wilderness,

27   To disperse their descendants among the nations, *
      and to scatter them throughout the lands.

28   They joined themselves to the Baal of Peor *
      and ate sacrifices offered to the dead.

29   They provoked him to anger with their evil deeds *
      and a plague broke out among them.

30   Then Phinehas stood up and interceded *
      and so the plague was stayed.

31   This was counted to him for righteousness *
      throughout all generations for ever.

32   They angered him also at the waters of Meribah, *
      so that Moses suffered for their sake;

33   For they so embittered his spirit *
      that he spoke rash words with his lips.

34   They did not destroy the peoples *
      as the Lord had commanded them.

35   They mingled with the nations *
      and learned to follow their ways,

36   So that they worshipped their idols, *
      which became to them a snare.

37 Their own sons and daughters *
   they sacrificed to evil spirits.

38 They shed innocent blood, *
   the blood of their sons and daughters,

39 Which they offered to the idols of Canaan, *
   and the land was defiled with blood.

40 Thus were they polluted by their actions, *
   and in their wanton deeds went whoring after other gods.

41 Therefore was the wrath of the Lord
      kindled against his people, *
   and he abhorred his inheritance.

42 He gave them over to the hand of the nations, *
   and those who hated them ruled over them.

43 So their enemies oppressed them *
   and put them in subjection under their hand.

44 Many a time did he deliver them,
      but they rebelled through their own devices *
   and were brought down through their wickedness.

45 Nevertheless, he saw their adversity, *
   when he heard their lamentation.

46 He remembered his covenant with them *
   and relented according to the greatness of his faithful love.

47 He made them also to be pitied *
   by all who had taken them captive.

48 Save us, O Lord our God,
      and gather us from among the nations, *
   that we may give thanks to your holy name
      and glory in your praise.

49 Blessèd be the Lord, the God of Israel,
      from everlasting and to everlasting; *
   and let all the people say, Amen.
      Alleluia.

[Holy God,
when our memories blot out your kindness
and we ignore your patient love,
remember us, re-make us,
and give to us poor sinners
the rich inheritance of Jesus Christ our Lord. Amen.]

Psalm 107

1   O give thanks to the Lord, for he is gracious, *
for his steadfast love endures for ever.

2   Let the redeemed of the Lord say this, *
those he redeemed from the hand of the enemy,

3   And gathered out of the lands
   from the east and from the west, *
from the north and from the south.

4   Some went astray in desert wastes *
and found no path to a city to dwell in.

5   Hungry and thirsty, *
their soul was fainting within them.

6   So they cried to the Lord in their trouble *
and he delivered them from their distress.

7   He set their feet on the right way *
till they came to a city to dwell in.

8   *Let them give thanks to the Lord for his goodness *
and the wonders he does for his children.

9   *For he satisfies the longing soul *
and fills the hungry soul with good.

10   Some sat in darkness and in the shadow of death, *
bound fast in misery and iron,

11   For they had rebelled against the words of God *
and despised the counsel of the Most High.

12   So he bowed down their heart with heaviness; *
they stumbled and there was none to help them.

13   Then they cried to the Lord in their trouble, *
and he delivered them from their distress.

14   He brought them out of darkness and out of the shadow of death, *
and broke their bonds asunder.

15   *Let them give thanks to the Lord for his goodness* *
and the wonders he does for his children.

16   *For he has broken the doors of bronze* *
and breaks the bars of iron in pieces.

17   Some were foolish and took a rebellious way, *
and were plagued because of their wrongdoing.

18   Their soul abhorred all manner of food *
and drew near to the gates of death.

19   Then they cried to the Lord in their trouble, *
and he delivered them from their distress.

20   He sent forth his word and healed them, *
and saved them from destruction.

21   *Let them give thanks to the Lord for his goodness* *
and the wonders he does for his children.

22   *Let them offer him sacrifices of thanksgiving* *
and tell of his acts with shouts of joy.

23   Those who go down to the sea in ships *
and ply their trade in great waters,

24   These have seen the works of the Lord *
and his wonders in the deep.

25   For at his word the stormy wind arose *
and lifted up the waves of the sea.

26   They were carried up to the heavens
   and down again to the deep; *
their soul melted away in their peril.

27   They reeled and staggered like a drunkard *
and were at their wits' end.

28   Then they cried to the Lord in their trouble, *
and he brought them out of their distress.

29　He made the storm be still *
　　and the waves of the sea were calmed.

30　Then were they glad because they were at rest, *
　　and he brought them to the haven they desired.

31　*Let them give thanks to the Lord for his goodness* *
　　and the wonders he does for his children.

32　*Let them exalt him in the congregation of the people* *
　　and praise him in the council of the elders.

33　The Lord turns rivers into wilderness *
　　and water springs into thirsty ground;

34　A fruitful land he makes a salty waste, *
　　because of the wickedness of those who dwell there.

35　He makes the wilderness a pool of water *
　　and water springs out of a thirsty land.

36　There he settles the hungry *
　　and they build a city to dwell in.

37　They sow fields and plant vineyards *
　　and bring in a fruitful harvest.

38　He blesses them, so that they multiply greatly; *
　　he does not let their herds of cattle decrease.

39　He pours contempt on princes *
　　and makes them wander in trackless wastes.

40　They are diminished and brought low, *
　　through stress of misfortune and sorrow,

41　But he raises the poor from their misery *
　　and multiplies their families like flocks of sheep.

42　The upright will see this and rejoice, *
　　but all wickedness will shut its mouth.

43　Whoever is wise will ponder these things *
　　and consider the loving-kindness of the Lord.

[O living Christ,
rescue us from foolish passion
and the storms of our self-will;
and, as you are our anchor in this life,
so bring us to the haven you have prepared for us;
for your mercy's sake. Amen.]

Psalm 108

[Refrain: Be exalted, O God, above the heavens.]

1   My heart is ready, O God, my heart is ready; *
    I will sing and give you praise.

2   Awake, my soul; awake, harp and lyre, *
    that I may awaken the dawn.

3   I will give you thanks, O Lord, among the peoples; *
    I will sing praise to you among the nations.

4   For your loving-kindness is as high as the heavens *
    and your faithfulness reaches to the clouds.

5   Be exalted, O God, above the heavens *
    and your glory over all the earth.

6   That your beloved may be delivered, *
    save us by your right hand and answer me.

7   God has spoken in his holiness: *
    'I will triumph and divide Shechem
       and share out the valley of Succoth.

8   'Gilead is mine and Manasseh is mine; *
    Ephraim is my helmet and Judah my sceptre.

9   'Moab shall be my washpot,
    over Edom will I cast my sandal, *
       across Philistia will I shout in triumph.'

10 Who will lead me into the strong city? *
    Who will bring me into Edom?

11 Have you not cast us off, O God? *
    Will you no longer go forth with our troops?

12 O grant us your help against the enemy, *
    for earthly help is in vain.

13 Through God will we do great acts, *
    for it is he that shall tread down our enemies.

    *[In times of terror, O God,
    give us boldness
    to act with courage, yet with mercy,
    for you rule the nations with the
        sword of truth;
    in Jesus Christ our Lord. Amen.]*

Psalm 109

*[Refrain: O Lord my God
            save me for your loving mercy's sake.]*

1   Keep silent no longer, O God of my praise, *
    for the mouth of wickedness and treachery
        is opened against me.

2   They have spoken against me with a lying tongue; *
    they encompassed me with words of hatred
        and fought against me without a cause.

3   In return for my love, they set themselves against me, *
    even though I had prayed for them.

4   Thus have they repaid me with evil for good, *
    and hatred for my good will.

[5 They say, 'Appoint a wicked man over him, *
    and let an accuser stand at his right hand.

6   'When he is judged, let him be found guilty, *
    and let his prayer be counted as sin.

7   'Let his days be few *
    and let another take his office.

8   'Let his children be fatherless *
    and his wife become a widow.

9   'Let his children wander to beg their bread; *
    let them seek it in desolate places.

10　'Let the creditor seize all that he has; *
　　let strangers plunder the fruit of his toil.

11　'Let there be no one to keep faith with him, *
　　or have compassion on his fatherless children.

12　'Let his line soon come to an end *
　　and his name be blotted out in the next generation.

13　'Let the wickedness of his fathers
　　　be remembered before the Lord, *
　　and no sin of his mother be blotted out;

14　'Let their sin be always before the Lord, *
　　that he may root out their name from the earth;

15　'Because he was not minded to keep faith, *
　　but persecuted the poor and needy
　　　and sought to kill the brokenhearted.

16　'He loved cursing and it came to him; *
　　he took no delight in blessing and it was far from him.

17　'He clothed himself with cursing as with a garment: *
　　it seeped into his body like water
　　　and into his bones like oil;

18　'Let it be to him like the cloak which he wraps around him *
　　and like the belt that he wears continually.'

19　Thus may the Lord repay my accusers *
　　and those who speak evil against me.]

20　But deal with me, O Lord my God, according to your name; *
　　O deliver me, for sweet is your faithfulness.

21　For I am helpless and poor *
　　and my heart is disquieted within me.

22　I fade like a shadow that lengthens; *
　　I am shaken off like a locust.

23　My knees are weak through fasting *
　　and my flesh is dried up and wasted.

24　I have become a reproach to them; *
　　those who see me shake their heads in scorn.

25   Help me, O Lord my God; *
     save me for your loving mercy's sake,

26   And they shall know that this is your hand, *
     that you, O Lord, have done it.

27   Though they curse, may you bless; *
     let those who rise up against me be confounded,
         but let your servant rejoice.

28   Let my accusers be clothed with disgrace *
     and wrap themselves in their shame as in a cloak.

29   I will give great thanks to the Lord with my mouth; *
     in the midst of the multitude will I praise him;

30   Because he has stood at the right hand of the needy, *
     to save them from those who would condemn them.

     [Lord, when we are repaid with evil for good,
     help us not to return evil for evil,
     but to bear witness to your steadfast love,
     shown in the face of your dear Son,
     our Saviour Jesus Christ. Amen.]

Psalm 110

[Refrain: The Lord is king and has put on glorious apparel.]

1   The Lord said to my lord, 'Sit at my right hand, *
     until I make your enemies your footstool.'

2   May the Lord stretch forth the sceptre of your power; *
     rule from Zion in the midst of your enemies.

3   'Noble are you on this day of your birth; *
     on the holy mountain, from the womb of the dawn
         the dew of your new birth is upon you.'

4   The Lord has sworn and will not retract: *
     'You are a priest for ever after the order of Melchizedek.'

[5   The king at your right hand, O Lord, *
     shall smite down kings in the day of his wrath.

6   In all his majesty, he shall judge among the nations, *
     smiting heads over all the wide earth.

7   He shall drink from the brook beside the way; *
        therefore shall he lift high his head.**]**

[Lord Jesus, divine Son and eternal priest,
inspire us with the confidence of your final conquest of evil,
and grant that daily on our way
we may drink of the brook of your eternal life
and so find courage against all adversities;
for your mercy's sake. Amen.]

Psalm 111

[Refrain: The Lord is gracious and full of compassion.]

1   Alleluia.
     I will give thanks to the Lord with my whole heart, *
    in the company of the faithful and in the congregation.

2   The works of the Lord are great, *
    sought out by all who delight in them.

3   His work is full of majesty and honour *
    and his righteousness endures for ever.

4   He appointed a memorial for his marvellous deeds; *
    the Lord is gracious and full of compassion.

5   He gave food to those who feared him; *
    he is ever mindful of his covenant.

6   He showed his people the power of his works *
    in giving them the heritage of the nations.

7   The works of his hands are truth and justice; *
    all his commandments are sure.

8   They stand fast for ever and ever; *
    they are done in truth and equity.

9   He sent redemption to his people;
     he commanded his covenant for ever; *
    holy and awesome is his name.

10   The fear of the Lord is the beginning of wisdom;
     a good understanding have those who live by it; *
    his praise endures for ever.

[Gracious God, you are full of compassion;
may we who long for your kingdom to come
rejoice to do your will
and acknowledge your power alone to save;
through Jesus Christ our Lord. Amen.]

Psalm 112

[Refrain: The righteous will be held in everlasting remembrance.]

1   Alleluia.
      Blessèd are those who fear the Lord *
      and have great delight in his commandments.

2   Their descendants will be mighty in the land, *
      a generation of the faithful that will be blest.

3   Wealth and riches will be in their house, *
      and their righteousness endures for ever.

4   Light shines in the darkness for the upright; *
      gracious and full of compassion are the righteous.

5   It goes well with those who are generous in lending *
      and order their affairs with justice,

6   For they will never be shaken; *
      the righteous will be held in everlasting remembrance.

7   They will not be afraid of any evil tidings; *
      their heart is steadfast, trusting in the Lord.

8   Their heart is sustained and will not fear, *
      until they see the downfall of their foes.

9   They have given freely to the poor;
        their righteousness stands fast for ever; *
      their head will be exalted with honour.

10   The wicked shall see it and be angry;
        they shall gnash their teeth in despair; *
      the desire of the wicked shall perish.

[Generous God,
save us from the meanness
that calculates its interest and hoards its earthly gain;
as we have freely received,
so may we freely give;
in the grace of Jesus Christ our Lord. Amen.]

Psalm 113

[Refrain: From the rising of the sun to its setting
let the name of the Lord be praised.]

1   Alleluia.
      Give praise, you servants of the Lord, *
    O praise the name of the Lord.

2   Blessèd be the name of the Lord, *
    from this time forth and for evermore.

3   From the rising of the sun to its setting *
    let the name of the Lord be praised.

4   The Lord is high above all nations *
    and his glory above the heavens.

5   Who is like the Lord our God,
         that has his throne so high, *
    yet humbles himself to behold
         the things of heaven and earth?

6   He raises the poor from the dust *
    and lifts the needy from the ashes,

7   To set them with princes, *
    with the princes of his people.

8   He gives the barren woman a place in the house *
    and makes her a joyful mother of children.
         Alleluia.

[From the rising of the sun to its setting
we praise your name, O Lord;
may your promise to raise the poor from the dust
and turn the fortunes of the needy upside down
be fulfilled in our time also,
as it was in your Son, Jesus Christ our Lord. Amen.]

Psalm 114

[Refrain: Tremble, O earth, at the presence of the Lord.]

1   When Israel came out of Egypt, *
the house of Jacob from a people of a strange tongue,

2   Judah became his sanctuary, *
Israel his dominion.

3   The sea saw that, and fled; *
Jordan was driven back.

4   The mountains skipped like rams, *
the little hills like young sheep.

5   What ailed you, O sea, that you fled? *
O Jordan, that you were driven back?

6   You mountains, that you skipped like rams, *
you little hills like young sheep?

7   Tremble, O earth, at the presence of the Lord, *
at the presence of the God of Jacob,

8   Who turns the hard rock into a pool of water, *
the flint-stone into a springing well.

[Strike the rock of our hard hearts, O God,
and let our tears of joy and sorrow
mould us to bear the imprint of your love,
given in Christ our risen Lord. Amen.]

Psalm 115

[Refrain: The Lord has been mindful of us and he will bless us.]

1   Not to us, Lord, not to us,
        but to your name give the glory, *
    for the sake of your loving mercy and truth.

2   Why should the nations say, *
    'Where is now their God?'

3   As for our God, he is in heaven; *
    he does whatever he pleases.

4   Their idols are silver and gold, *
    the work of human hands.

5   They have mouths, but cannot speak; *
    eyes have they, but cannot see;

6   They have ears, but cannot hear; *
    noses have they, but cannot smell;

7   They have hands, but cannot feel;
        feet have they, but cannot walk; *
    not a whisper do they make from their throats.

8   Those who make them shall become like them *
    and so will all who put their trust in them.

9   But you, Israel, put your trust in the Lord; *
    he is their help and their shield.

10 House of Aaron, trust in the Lord; *
    he is their help and their shield.

11 You that fear the Lord, trust in the Lord; *
    he is their help and their shield.

12 The Lord has been mindful of us and he will bless us; *
    may he bless the house of Israel;
        may he bless the house of Aaron;

13 May he bless those who fear the Lord, *
    both small and great together.

14 May the Lord increase you more and more, *
    you and your children after you.

15 May you be blest by the Lord, *
   the maker of heaven and earth.

16 The heavens are the heavens of the Lord, *
   but the earth he has entrusted to his children.

17 The dead do not praise the Lord, *
   nor those gone down into silence;

18 But we will bless the Lord, *
   from this time forth for evermore.
      Alleluia.

   *[Living God,
   defend us from the idols which our hearts enthrone,
   that we may not go down into silence
   but be raised to our heaven of heavens
   in Jesus Christ our Lord. Amen.]*

Psalm 116

   [Refrain: Gracious is the Lord and righteous.]

1 I love the Lord,
      for he has heard the voice of my supplication; *
   because he inclined his ear to me
      on the day I called to him.

2 The snares of death encompassed me;
      the pains of hell took hold of me; *
   by grief and sorrow was I held.

3 Then I called upon the name of the Lord: *
   'O Lord, I beg you, deliver my soul.'

4 Gracious is the Lord and righteous; *
   our God is full of compassion.

5 The Lord watches over the simple; *
   I was brought very low and he saved me.

6 Turn again to your rest, O my soul, *
   for the Lord has been gracious to you.

7 For you have delivered my soul from death, *
   my eyes from tears and my feet from falling.

8 I will walk before the Lord *
   in the land of the living.

9 I believed that I should perish
      for I was sorely troubled; *
   and I said in my alarm, 'Everyone is a liar.'

10 How shall I repay the Lord *
   for all the benefits he has given to me?

11 I will lift up the cup of salvation *
   and call upon the name of the Lord.

12 I will fulfil my vows to the Lord *
   in the presence of all his people.

13 Precious in the sight of the Lord *
   is the death of his faithful servants.

14 O Lord, I am your servant, *
   your servant, the child of your handmaid;
      you have freed me from my bonds.

15 I will offer to you a sacrifice of thanksgiving *
   and call upon the name of the Lord.

16 I will fulfil my vows to the Lord *
   in the presence of all his people,

17 In the courts of the house of the Lord, *
   in the midst of you, O Jerusalem.
      Alleluia.

[As we walk through the valley of the shadow of death,
may we call upon your name,
raise the cup of salvation,
and so proclaim your death, O Lord,
until you come in glory. Amen.]

Psalm 117

[Refrain: Alleluia.]

1 O praise the Lord, all you nations; *
   praise him, all you peoples.

2   For great is his steadfast love towards us, *
    and the faithfulness of the Lord endures for ever.
        Alleluia.

    [Gracious God,
    we praise you for your faithfulness
    and pray that every nation may find your blessing
    in the face of Jesus Christ our Lord. Amen.]

Psalm 118

[Refrain: I will give thanks to you,
for you have become my salvation.]

1   O give thanks to the Lord, for he is good; *
    his mercy endures for ever.

2   Let Israel now proclaim, *
    'His mercy endures for ever.'

3   Let the house of Aaron now proclaim, *
    'His mercy endures for ever.'

4   Let those who fear the Lord proclaim, *
    'His mercy endures for ever.'

5   In my constraint I called to the Lord; *
    the Lord answered and set me free.

6   The Lord is at my side; I will not fear; *
    what can flesh do to me?

7   With the Lord at my side as my saviour, *
    I shall see the downfall of my enemies.

8   It is better to take refuge in the Lord *
    than to put any confidence in flesh.

9   It is better to take refuge in the Lord *
    than to put any confidence in princes.

10 All the nations encompassed me, *
    but by the name of the Lord I drove them back.

11 They hemmed me in, they hemmed me in on every side, *
    but by the name of the Lord I drove them back.

12 They swarmed about me like bees;
    they blazed like fire among thorns, *
    but by the name of the Lord I drove them back.

13 Surely, I was thrust to the brink, *
    but the Lord came to my help.

14 The Lord is my strength and my song, *
    and he has become my salvation.

15 Joyful shouts of salvation *
    sound from the tents of the righteous:

16 'The right hand of the Lord does mighty deeds;
    the right hand of the Lord raises up; *
    the right hand of the Lord does mighty deeds.'

17 I shall not die, but live *
    and declare the works of the Lord.

18 The Lord has punished me sorely, *
    but he has not given me over to death.

19 Open to me the gates of righteousness, *
    that I may enter and give thanks to the Lord.

20 This is the gate of the Lord; *
    the righteous shall enter through it.

21 I will give thanks to you, for you have answered me *
    and have become my salvation.

22 The stone which the builders rejected *
    has become the chief cornerstone.

23 This is the Lord's doing, *
    and it is marvellous in our eyes.

24 This is the day that the Lord has made; *
    we will rejoice and be glad in it.

25 Come, O Lord, and save us we pray. *
    Come, Lord, send us now prosperity.

26 Blessèd is he who comes in the name of the Lord; *
    we bless you from the house of the Lord.

27   The Lord is God; he has given us light; *
        link the pilgrims with cords
          right to the horns of the altar.

28   You are my God and I will thank you; *
        you are my God and I will exalt you.

29   O give thanks to the Lord, for he is good; *
        his mercy endures for ever.

[Saving God,
open the gates of righteousness,
that your pilgrim people may enter
and be built into a living temple
on the cornerstone of our salvation,
Jesus Christ our Lord. Amen.]

Psalm 119

1   Aleph

[Refrain: Teach me, O Lord, the way of your statutes.]

1   Blessèd are those whose way is pure, *
        who walk in the law of the Lord.

2   Blessèd are those who keep his testimonies *
        and seek him with their whole heart,

3   Those who do no wickedness, *
        but walk in his ways.

4   You, O Lord, have charged *
        that we should diligently keep your commandments.

5   O that my ways were made so direct *
        that I might keep your statutes.

6   Then should I not be put to shame, *
        because I have regard for all your commandments.

7   I will thank you with an unfeigned heart, *
        when I have learned your righteous judgements.

8   I will keep your statutes; *
        O forsake me not utterly.

2 Beth

9   How shall young people cleanse their way *
     to keep themselves according to your word?

10   With my whole heart have I sought you; *
     O let me not go astray from your commandments.

11   Your words have I hidden within my heart, *
     that I should not sin against you.

12   Blessèd are you, O Lord; *
     O teach me your statutes.

13   With my lips have I been telling *
     of all the judgements of your mouth.

14   I have taken greater delight in the way of your testimonies *
     than in all manner of riches.

15   I will meditate on your commandments *
     and contemplate your ways.

16   My delight shall be in your statutes *
     and I will not forget your word.

3 Gimel

17   O do good to your servant that I may live, *
     and so shall I keep your word.

18   Open my eyes, that I may see *
     the wonders of your law.

19   I am a stranger upon earth; *
     hide not your commandments from me.

20   My soul is consumed at all times *
     with fervent longing for your judgements.

21   You have rebuked the arrogant; *
     cursed are those who stray from your commandments.

22   Turn from me shame and rebuke, *
     for I have kept your testimonies.

23   Rulers also sit and speak against me, *
     but your servant meditates on your statutes.

24   For your testimonies are my delight; *
       they are my faithful counsellors.

4 Daleth

25   My soul cleaves to the dust; *
       O give me life according to your word.

26   I have acknowledged my ways and you have answered me; *
       O teach me your statutes.

27   Make me understand the way of your commandments, *
       and so shall I meditate on your wondrous works.

28   My soul melts away in tears of sorrow; *
       raise me up according to your word.

29   Take from me the way of falsehood; *
       be gracious to me through your law.

30   I have chosen the way of truth *
       and your judgements have I laid before me.

31   I hold fast to your testimonies; *
       O Lord, let me not be put to shame.

32   I will run the way of your commandments, *
       when you have set my heart at liberty.

> [Faithful God,
> let your word be the treasure of our hearts,
> that we may delight in your truth
> and walk in the glorious liberty of your
>   Son Jesus Christ. Amen.]

5 He

> [Refrain: My delight shall be in your commandments.]

33   Teach me, O Lord, the way of your statutes *
       and I shall keep it to the end.

34   Give me understanding and I shall keep your law; *
       I shall keep it with my whole heart.

35   Lead me in the path of your commandments, *
       for therein is my delight.

36 Incline my heart to your testimonies *
and not to unjust gain.

37 Turn away my eyes lest they gaze on vanities; *
O give me life in your ways.

38 Confirm to your servant your promise, *
which stands for all who fear you.

39 Turn away the reproach which I dread, *
because your judgements are good.

40 Behold, I long for your commandments; *
in your righteousness give me life.

6 Waw

41 Let your faithful love come unto me, O Lord, *
even your salvation, according to your promise.

42 Then shall I answer those who taunt me, *
for my trust is in your word.

43 O take not the word of truth utterly out of my mouth, *
for my hope is in your judgements.

44 So shall I always keep your law; *
I shall keep it for ever and ever.

45 I will walk at liberty, *
because I study your commandments.

46 I will tell of your testimonies, even before kings, *
and will not be ashamed.

47 My delight shall be in your commandments, *
which I have greatly loved.

48 My hands will I lift up to your commandments, which I love, *
and I will meditate on your statutes.

7 Zayin

49 Remember your word to your servant, *
on which you have built my hope.

50 This is my comfort in my trouble, *
that your promise gives me life.

51 The proud have derided me cruelly, *
   but I have not turned aside from your law.

52 I have remembered your everlasting judgements, O Lord, *
   and have been comforted.

53 I am seized with indignation at the wicked, *
   for they have forsaken your law.

54 Your statutes have been like songs to me *
   in the house of my pilgrimage.

55 I have thought on your name in the night, O Lord, *
   and so have I kept your law.

56 These blessings have been mine, *
   for I have kept your commandments.

   [God of loving mercy,
   in this place of our pilgrimage
   turn your laws into songs,
   that we may find your promises
   fulfilled in Jesus Christ our Lord. Amen.]

8   Heth

[Refrain: I know, O Lord, that your judgements are right.]

57 You only are my portion, O Lord; *
   I have promised to keep your words.

58 I entreat you with all my heart, *
   be merciful to me according to your promise.

59 I have considered my ways *
   and turned my feet back to your testimonies.

60 I made haste and did not delay *
   to keep your commandments.

61 Though the cords of the wicked entangle me, *
   I do not forget your law.

62 At midnight I will rise to give you thanks, *
   because of your righteous judgements.

63 I am a companion of all those who fear you, *
   those who keep your commandments.

64   The earth, O Lord, is full of your faithful love; *
      instruct me in your statutes.

9 Teth

65   You have dealt graciously with your servant, *
      according to your word, O Lord.

66   O teach me true understanding and knowledge, *
      for I have trusted in your commandments.

67   Before I was afflicted I went astray, *
      but now I keep your word.

68   You are gracious and do good; *
      O Lord, teach me your statutes.

69   The proud have smeared me with lies, *
      but I will keep your commandments with my whole heart.

70   Their heart has become gross with fat, *
      but my delight is in your law.

71   It is good for me that I have been afflicted, *
      that I may learn your statutes.

72   The law of your mouth is dearer to me *
      than a hoard of gold and silver.

10 Yodh

73   Your hands have made me and fashioned me; *
      give me understanding, that I may learn your commandments.

74   Those who fear you will be glad when they see me, *
      because I have hoped in your word.

75   I know, O Lord, that your judgements are right, *
      and that in very faithfulness you caused me to be troubled.

76   Let your faithful love be my comfort, *
      according to your promise to your servant.

77   Let your tender mercies come to me, that I may live, *
      for your law is my delight.

78   Let the proud be put to shame, for they wrong me with lies; *
      but I will meditate on your commandments.

79   Let those who fear you turn to me, *
       even those who know your testimonies.

80   Let my heart be sound in your statutes, *
       that I may not be put to shame.

[God our comforter,
send your Holy Spirit
to reveal your hidden mercy
even in our failures and troubles;
for the sake of Jesus Christ our Lord. Amen.]

11 Kaph

[Refrain: Give me life, O Lord, according to your word.]

81   My soul is pining for your salvation; *
       I have hoped in your word.

82   My eyes fail with watching for your word, *
       while I say, 'O when will you comfort me?'

83   I have become like a wineskin in the smoke, *
       yet I do not forget your statutes.

84   How many are the days of your servant? *
       When will you bring judgement on those who persecute me?

85   The proud have dug pits for me *
       in defiance of your law.

86   All your commandments are true; *
       help me, for they persecute me with falsehood.

87   They had almost made an end of me on earth, *
       but I have not forsaken your commandments.

88   Give me life according to your loving-kindness; *
       so shall I keep the testimonies of your mouth.

12 Lamedh

89   O Lord, your word is everlasting; *
       it ever stands firm in the heavens.

90   Your faithfulness also remains from one generation to another; *
       you have established the earth and it abides.

91   So also your judgements stand firm this day, *
      for all things are your servants.

92   If your law had not been my delight, *
      I should have perished in my trouble.

93   I will never forget your commandments, *
      for by them you have given me life.

94   I am yours, O save me! *
      For I have sought your commandments.

95   The wicked have waited for me to destroy me, *
      but I will meditate on your testimonies.

96   I have seen an end of all perfection, *
      but your commandment knows no bounds.

13 Mem

97   Lord, how I love your law! *
      All the day long it is my study.

98   Your commandments have made me wiser than my enemies, *
      for they are ever with me.

99   I have more understanding than all my teachers, *
      for your testimonies are my meditation.

100   I am wiser than the aged, *
      because I keep your commandments.

101   I restrain my feet from every evil way, *
      that I may keep your word.

102   I have not turned aside from your judgements, *
      for you have been my teacher.

103   How sweet are your words on my tongue! *
      They are sweeter than honey to my mouth.

104   Through your commandments I get understanding; *
      therefore I hate all lying ways.

[Lord Christ,
as we sit at your feet,
teach us your living way;
for you are our Word and Wisdom,
one God with the Father and the Holy Spirit,
now and for ever. Amen.]

14 Nun

[Refrain: O deal with your servant according to your faithful love.]

105 Your word is a lantern to my feet *
and a light upon my path.

106 I have sworn and will fulfil it, *
to keep your righteous judgements.

107 I am troubled above measure; *
give me life, O Lord, according to your word.

108 Accept the freewill offering of my mouth, O Lord, *
and teach me your judgements.

109 My soul is ever in my hand, *
yet I do not forget your law.

110 The wicked have laid a snare for me, *
but I have not strayed from your commandments.

111 Your testimonies have I claimed as my heritage for ever; *
for they are the very joy of my heart.

112 I have applied my heart to fulfil your statutes: *
always, even to the end.

15 Samekh

113 I hate those who are double-minded, *
but your law do I love.

114 You are my hiding place and my shield *
and my hope is in your word.

115 Away from me, you wicked! *
I will keep the commandments of my God.

116 Sustain me according to your promise, that I may live, *
and let me not be disappointed in my hope.

117 Hold me up and I shall be saved, *
and my delight shall be ever in your statutes.

118 You set at nought those who depart from your statutes, *
for their deceiving is in vain.

119 You consider all the wicked as dross; *
therefore I love your testimonies.

120 My flesh trembles for fear of you *
and I am afraid of your judgements.

16 Ayin

121 I have done what is just and right; *
O give me not over to my oppressors.

122 Stand surety for your servant's good; *
let not the proud oppress me.

123 My eyes fail with watching for your salvation *
and for your righteous promise.

124 O deal with your servant according to your faithful love *
and teach me your statutes.

125 I am your servant; O grant me understanding, *
that I may know your testimonies.

126 It is time for you to act, O Lord, *
for they frustrate your law.

127 Therefore I love your commandments *
above gold, even much fine gold.

128 Therefore I direct my steps by all your precepts, *
and all false ways I utterly abhor.

[O God, save us from ourselves,
from double standards
and divided hearts,
and give us light and life
in Jesus Christ our Lord. Amen.]

17 Pe

[Refrain: The opening of your word gives light.]

129 Your testimonies are wonderful; *
therefore my soul keeps them.

130 The opening of your word gives light; *
it gives understanding to the simple.

131 I open my mouth and draw in my breath, *
as I long for your commandments.

132 Turn to me and be gracious to me, *
as is your way with those who love your name.

133 Order my steps by your word, *
and let no wickedness have dominion over me.

134 Redeem me from earthly oppressors *
so that I may keep your commandments.

135 Show the light of your countenance upon your servant *
and teach me your statutes.

136 My eyes run down with streams of water, *
because the wicked do not keep your law.

18 Tsadhe

137 Righteous are you, O Lord, *
and true are your judgements.

138 You have ordered your decrees in righteousness *
and in great faithfulness.

139 My indignation destroys me, *
because my adversaries forget your word.

140 Your word has been tried to the uttermost *
and so your servant loves it.

141 I am small and of no reputation, *
yet do I not forget your commandments.

142 Your righteousness is an everlasting righteousness *
and your law is the truth.

143 Trouble and heaviness have taken hold upon me, *
     yet my delight is in your commandments.

144 The righteousness of your testimonies is everlasting; *
     O grant me understanding and I shall live.

19 Qoph

145 I call with my whole heart; *
     answer me, O Lord, that I may keep your statutes.

146 To you I call, O save me! *
     And I shall keep your testimonies.

147 Early in the morning I cry to you, *
     for in your word is my trust.

148 My eyes are open before the night watches, *
     that I may meditate on your word.

149 Hear my voice, O Lord, according to your faithful love; *
     according to your judgement, give me life.

150 They draw near that in malice persecute me, *
     who are far from your law.

151 You, O Lord, are near at hand, *
     and all your commandments are true.

152 Long have I known of your testimonies, *
     that you have founded them for ever.

*[Lord, you are just
and your commandments are eternal;
teach us to love you with all our heart
and our neighbour as ourselves,
for the sake of Jesus Christ our Lord. Amen.]*

20 Resh

[Refrain: I have longed for your salvation, O Lord.]

153 O consider my affliction and deliver me, *
     for I do not forget your law.

154 Plead my cause and redeem me; *
     according to your promise, give me life.

155　Salvation is far from the wicked, *
　　　for they do not seek your statutes.

156　Great is your compassion, O Lord; *
　　　give me life, according to your judgements.

157　Many there are that persecute and oppress me, *
　　　yet do I not swerve from your testimonies.

158　It grieves me when I see the treacherous, *
　　　for they do not keep your word.

159　Consider, O Lord, how I love your commandments; *
　　　give me life according to your loving-kindness.

160　The sum of your word is truth, *
　　　and all your righteous judgements endure for evermore.

21 Shin

161　Princes have persecuted me without a cause, *
　　　but my heart stands in awe of your word.

162　I am as glad of your word *
　　　as one who finds great spoils.

163　As for lies, I hate and abhor them, *
　　　but your law do I love.

164　Seven times a day do I praise you, *
　　　because of your righteous judgements.

165　Great peace have they who love your law; *
　　　nothing shall make them stumble.

166　Lord, I have looked for your salvation *
　　　and I have fulfilled your commandments.

167　My soul has kept your testimonies *
　　　and greatly have I loved them.

168　I have kept your commandments and testimonies, *
　　　for all my ways are before you.

22 Taw

169　Let my cry come before you, O Lord; *
　　　give me understanding, according to your word.

170   Let my supplication come before you; *
      deliver me, according to your promise.

171   My lips shall pour forth your praise, *
      when you have taught me your statutes.

172   My tongue shall sing of your word, *
      for all your commandments are righteous.

173   Let your hand reach out to help me, *
      for I have chosen your commandments.

174   I have longed for your salvation, O Lord, *
      and your law is my delight.

175   Let my soul live and it shall praise you, *
      and let your judgements be my help.

176   I have gone astray like a sheep that is lost; *
      O seek your servant, for I do not forget your commandments.

*[God of mercy, swift to help us,
as our lips pour forth your praise,
fill our hearts with the peace you give
to those who wait for your salvation
in Jesus Christ our Lord. Amen.]*

Psalm 120

[Refrain: Deliver me, O Lord from lying lips.]

1   When I was in trouble I called to the Lord; *
      I called to the Lord and he answered me.

2   Deliver me, O Lord, from lying lips *
      and from a deceitful tongue.

3   What shall be given to you? *
      What more shall be done to you, deceitful tongue?

4   The sharp arrows of a warrior, *
      tempered in burning coals!

5   Woe is me, that I must lodge in Meshech *
      and dwell among the tents of Kedar.

6   My soul has dwelt too long *
with enemies of peace.

7   I am for making peace, *
but when I speak of it, they make ready for war.

*[God of consolation,
look on us, pilgrims in a strange land;
preserve us from slander and deceit,
show us the truth
and give to our souls the peace of Christ. Amen.]*

Psalm 121

[Refrain: The Lord shall keep you from all evil.]

1   I lift up my eyes to the hills; *
from where is my help to come?

2   My help comes from the Lord, *
the maker of heaven and earth.

3   He will not suffer your foot to stumble; *
he who watches over you will not sleep.

4   Behold, he who keeps watch over Israel *
shall neither slumber nor sleep.

5   The Lord himself watches over you; *
the Lord is your shade at your right hand,

6   So that the sun shall not strike you by day, *
neither the moon by night.

7   The Lord shall keep you from all evil; *
it is he who shall keep your soul.

8   The Lord shall keep watch over your going out
and your coming in, *
from this time forth for evermore.

*[Lord, ever watchful and faithful,
we look to you to be our defence
and we lift our hearts to know your help;
through Jesus Christ our Lord. Amen.]*

Psalm 122

[Refrain: How lovely is your dwelling place, O Lord of hosts.]

1   I was glad when they said to me, *
    'Let us go to the house of the Lord.'

2   And now our feet are standing *
    within your gates, O Jerusalem;

3   Jerusalem, built as a city *
    that is at unity in itself.

4   Thither the tribes go up, the tribes of the Lord, *
    as is decreed for Israel,
      to give thanks to the name of the Lord.

5   For there are set the thrones of judgement, *
    the thrones of the house of David.

6   O pray for the peace of Jerusalem: *
    'May they prosper who love you.

7   'Peace be within your walls *
    and tranquillity within your palaces.'

8   For my kindred and companions' sake, *
    I will pray that peace be with you.

9   For the sake of the house of the Lord our God, *
    I will seek to do you good.

[God of our pilgrimage,
bring us with joy to the eternal city
founded on the rock,
and give to our earthly cities
the peace that comes from above;
through Jesus Christ our Lord. Amen.]

Psalm 123

[Refrain: Our eyes wait upon the Lord our God.]

1   To you I lift up my eyes, *
    to you that are enthroned in the heavens.

2   As the eyes of servants look to the hand of their master, *
    or the eyes of a maid to the hand of her mistress,

3   So our eyes wait upon the Lord our God, *
    until he have mercy upon us.

4   Have mercy upon us, O Lord, have mercy upon us, *
    for we have had more than enough of contempt.

5   Our soul has had more than enough of the scorn of the arrogant, *
    and of the contempt of the proud.

    *[Sovereign God, enthroned in the heavens,
    look upon us with your eyes of mercy,
    as we look on you with humility and love,
    and fill our souls with your peace;
    through Jesus Christ our Lord. Amen.]*

Psalm 124

    [Refrain: Our help is in the name of the Lord.]

1   If the Lord himself had not been on our side, *
    now may Israel say;

2   If the Lord had not been on our side, *
    when enemies rose up against us;

3   Then would they have swallowed us alive *
    when their anger burned against us;

4   Then would the waters have overwhelmed us
        and the torrent gone over our soul; *
    over our soul would have swept the raging waters.

5   But blessèd be the Lord *
    who has not given us over to be a prey for their teeth.

6   Our soul has escaped
        as a bird from the snare of the fowler; *
    the snare is broken and we are delivered.

7   Our help is in the name of the Lord, *
    who has made heaven and earth.

[O God, maker of heaven and earth,
you save us in the water of baptism
and by the suffering of your Son you set us free;
help us to put our trust in his victory
and to know the salvation won for us
by Jesus Christ our Lord. Amen.]

Psalm 125

[Refrain: Glorious things are spoken of you,
Zion, city of our God.]

1   Those who trust in the Lord are like Mount Zion, *
    which cannot be moved, but stands fast for ever.

2   As the hills stand about Jerusalem, *
    so the Lord stands round about his people,
        from this time forth for evermore.

3   The sceptre of wickedness shall not hold sway
        over the land allotted to the righteous, *
    lest the righteous turn their hands to evil.

4   Do good, O Lord, to those who are good, *
    and to those who are true of heart.

5   Those who turn aside to crooked ways
        the Lord shall take away with the evildoers; *
    but let there be peace upon Israel.

[God of power,
you are strong to save
and you never fail those who trust in you;
keep us under your protection
and spread abroad your reign of peace;
through Jesus Christ our Lord. Amen.]

Psalm 126

[Refrain: The Lord has indeed done great things for us.]

1   When the Lord restored the fortunes of Zion, *
    then were we like those who dream.

2   Then was our mouth filled with laughter *
     and our tongue with songs of joy.

3   Then said they among the nations, *
     'The Lord has done great things for them.'

4   The Lord has indeed done great things for us, *
     and therefore we rejoiced.

5   Restore again our fortunes, O Lord, *
     as the river beds of the desert.

6   Those who sow in tears *
     shall reap with songs of joy.

7   Those who go out weeping, bearing the seed, *
     will come back with shouts of joy,
        bearing their sheaves with them.

*[Lord, as you send rain and flowers
even to the wilderness,
renew us by your Holy Spirit,
help us to sow good seed in time of adversity
and to live to rejoice in your good harvest of all creation;
through Jesus Christ our Lord. Amen.]*

Psalm 127

*[Refrain: The Lord shall keep watch over your going out
            and your coming in.]*

1   Unless the Lord builds the house, *
     those who build it labour in vain.

2   Unless the Lord keeps the city, *
     the guard keeps watch in vain.

3   It is in vain that you hasten to rise up early
        and go so late to rest, eating the bread of toil, *
     for he gives his beloved sleep.

4   Children are a heritage from the Lord *
     and the fruit of the womb is his gift.

5   Like arrows in the hand of a warrior, *
     so are the children of one's youth.

6   Happy are those who have their quiver full of them: *
     they shall not be put to shame
        when they dispute with their enemies in the gate.

[Lord, you are ever watchful
and bless us with your gifts;
as you provide for all our needs,
so help us to build only what pleases you;
through Jesus Christ our Lord. Amen.]

Psalm 128

[Refrain: How abundant is your goodness, O Lord.]

1   Blessèd are all those who fear the Lord, *
     and walk in his ways.

2   You shall eat the fruit of the toil of your hands; *
     it shall go well with you, and happy shall you be.

3   Your wife within your house
        shall be like a fruitful vine; *
     your children round your table,
        like fresh olive branches.

4   Thus shall the one be blest *
     who fears the Lord.

5   The Lord from out of Zion bless you, *
     that you may see Jerusalem in prosperity
        all the days of your life.

6   May you see your children's children, *
     and may there be peace upon Israel.

[O Christ our true vine,
may we your branches
be ever fruitful in your service
and share your love and peace with all your children,
in the power of the Spirit and to the glory of the Father. Amen.]

Psalm 129

[Refrain: The Lord ransoms the life of his servants.]

1   'Many a time have they fought against me from my youth,' *
may Israel now say;

2   'Many a time have they fought against me from my youth, *
but they have not prevailed against me.'

3   The ploughers ploughed upon my back *
and made their furrows long.

4   But the righteous Lord *
has cut the cords of the wicked in pieces.

5   Let them be put to shame and turned backwards, *
as many as are enemies of Zion.

6   Let them be like grass upon the housetops, *
which withers before it can grow,

7   So that no reaper can fill his hand, *
nor a binder of sheaves his bosom;

8   And none who go by may say,
'The blessing of the Lord be upon you. *
We bless you in the name of the Lord.'

[Jesus our redeemer,
you bore the cut of the lash
for us and our salvation;
help us to bear our sufferings
and to share in the affliction
of all who suffer for your holy name.   Amen.]

Psalm 130

[Refrain: My soul waits for the Lord.]

1   Out of the depths have I cried to you, O Lord;
Lord, hear my voice; *
let your ears consider well the voice of my supplication.

2   If you, Lord, were to mark what is done amiss, *
O Lord, who could stand?

3　　But there is forgiveness with you, *
　　　so that you shall be feared.

4　　I wait for the Lord; my soul waits for him; *
　　　in his word is my hope.

5　　My soul waits for the Lord,
　　　　more than the night watch for the morning, *
　　　more than the night watch for the morning.

6　　O Israel, wait for the Lord, *
　　　for with the Lord there is mercy;

7　　With him is plenteous redemption *
　　　and he shall redeem Israel from all their sins.

*[Father, we commend to your faithful love
those who are crying from the depths;
help them to watch and pray
through their time of darkness,
in sure hope of the dawn of your
　　forgiveness and redemption;
through Jesus Christ our Lord. Amen.]*

Psalm 131

[Refrain:　O Israel, trust in the Lord.]

1　　O Lord, my heart is not proud; *
　　　my eyes are not raised in haughty looks.

2　　I do not occupy myself with great matters, *
　　　with things that are too high for me.

3　　But I have quieted and stilled my soul,
　　　　like a weaned child on its mother's breast; *
　　　so my soul is quieted within me.

4　　O Israel, trust in the Lord, *
　　　from this time forth for evermore.

*[Eternal God,
calm and quieten our souls;
keep us humble and full of wonder
and trusting as we live in your love;
through Jesus Christ our Lord. Amen.]*

Psalm 132

[Refrain: Arise, O Lord, into your resting place.]

1   Lord, remember for David *
    all the hardships he endured;

2   How he swore an oath to the Lord *
    and vowed a vow to the Mighty One of Jacob:

3   'I will not come within the shelter of my house, *
    nor climb up into my bed;

4   'I will not allow my eyes to sleep, *
    nor let my eyelids slumber,

5   'Until I find a place for the Lord, *
    a dwelling for the Mighty One of Jacob.'

6   Now, we heard of the ark in Ephrathah *
    and found it in the fields of Ja-ar.

7   Let us enter his dwelling place *
    and fall low before his footstool.

8   Arise, O Lord, into your resting place, *
    you and the ark of your strength.

9   Let your priests be clothed with righteousness *
    and your faithful ones sing with joy

10 For your servant David's sake, *
    turn not away the face of your anointed.

11 The Lord has sworn an oath to David, *
    a promise from which he will not shrink:

12 'Of the fruit of your body *
    shall I set upon your throne.

13 'If your children keep my covenant
      and my testimonies that I shall teach them, *
    their children also shall sit upon your throne for evermore.'

14 For the Lord has chosen Zion for himself; *
    he has desired her for his habitation:

15   'This shall be my resting place for ever; *
     here will I dwell, for I have longed for her.

16   'I will abundantly bless her provision; *
     her poor will I satisfy with bread.

17   'I will clothe her priests with salvation, *
     and her faithful ones shall rejoice and sing.

18   'There will I make a horn to spring up for David; *
     I will keep a lantern burning for my anointed.

19   'As for his enemies, I will clothe them with shame; *
     but on him shall his crown be bright.'

     [Jesus, Son of David,
     make us a priestly people;
     clothe us in righteousness,
     make us fruitful,
     and give us hearts to shout for joy in your salvation;
     we pray in the power of the Spirit. Amen.]

Psalm 133

[Refrain: Mercy and truth have met together,
righteousness and peace have kissed each other.]

1   Behold how good and pleasant it is *
     to dwell together in unity.

2   It is like the precious oil upon the head, *
     running down upon the beard,

3   Even on Aaron's beard, *
     running down upon the collar of his clothing.

4   It is like the dew of Hermon *
     running down upon the hills of Zion.

5   For there the Lord has promised his blessing: *
     even life for evermore.

*[Grant to your people, good Lord,
the spirit of unity,
that they may dwell together in your love,
and so bear to the world
the ointment of your healing and the
    dew of your blessing;
through Jesus Christ our Lord. Amen.]*

Psalm 134

[Refrain: Bless the Lord, O my soul.]

1   Come, bless the Lord, all you servants of the Lord, *
    you that by night stand in the house of the Lord.

2   Lift up your hands towards the sanctuary *
    and bless the Lord.

3   The Lord who made heaven and earth *
    give you blessing out of Zion.

    *[Guard all your household, Lord,
    through the dark night of faith,
    and purify the hearts of those who wait on you,
    until your kingdom dawns with the
        rising of your Son,
    Christ, the morning star. Amen.]*

Psalm 135

[Refrain: Praise the Lord, for the Lord is good.]

1   Alleluia.
    Praise the name of the Lord; *
    give praise, you servants of the Lord,

2   You that stand in the house of the Lord, *
    in the courts of the house of our God.

3   Praise the Lord, for the Lord is good; *
    make music to his name, for it is lovely.

4   For the Lord has chosen Jacob for himself *
    and Israel for his own possession.

5   For I know that the Lord is great *
    and that our Lord is above all gods.

6   The Lord does whatever he pleases
      in heaven and on earth, *
    in the seas and in all the deeps.

7   He brings up the clouds from the ends of the earth; *
    he makes lightning with the rain
      and brings the winds out of his treasuries.

8   He smote the firstborn of Egypt, *
    the firstborn of man and beast.

9   He sent signs and wonders into your midst, O Egypt, *
    upon Pharaoh and all his servants.

10 He smote many nations *
    and slew mighty kings:

11 Sihon, king of the Amorites,
      and Og, the king of Bashan, *
    and all the kingdoms of Canaan.

12 He gave their land as a heritage, *
    a heritage for Israel his people.

13 Your name, O Lord, endures for ever *
    and shall be remembered through all generations.

14 For the Lord will vindicate his people *
    and have compassion on his servants.

15 The idols of the nations are but silver and gold, *
    the work of human hands.

16 They have mouths, but cannot speak; *
    eyes have they, but cannot see;

17 They have ears, but cannot hear; *
    neither is there any breath in their mouths.

18 Those who make them shall become like them, *
    and so will all who put their trust in them.

19 Bless the Lord, O house of Israel; *
    O house of Aaron, bless the Lord.

20   Bless the Lord, O house of Levi; *
     you who fear the Lord, bless the Lord.

21   Blessèd be the Lord from Zion, *
     who dwells in Jerusalem.
       Alleluia.

*[Wise and gracious God,
save us from the idols of our hearts
and keep us in your living presence,
that we may become a people for your praise
in Jesus Christ our Lord. Amen.]*

Psalm 136

1   Give thanks to the Lord, for he is gracious, *
     for his mercy endures for ever.

2   Give thanks to the God of gods, *
     for his mercy endures for ever.

3   Give thanks to the Lord of lords, *
     for his mercy endures for ever;

4   Who alone does great wonders, *
     for his mercy endures for ever;

5   Who by wisdom made the heavens, *
     for his mercy endures for ever;

6   Who laid out the earth upon the waters, *
     for his mercy endures for ever;

7   Who made the great lights, *
     for his mercy endures for ever;

8   The sun to rule the day, *
     for his mercy endures for ever;

9   The moon and the stars to govern the night, *
     for his mercy endures for ever;

10   Who smote the firstborn of Egypt, *
     for his mercy endures for ever;

11   And brought out Israel from among them, *
     for his mercy endures for ever;

12 With a mighty hand and outstretched arm, *
   for his mercy endures for ever;

13 Who divided the Red Sea in two, *
   for his mercy endures for ever;

14 And made Israel to pass through the midst of it, *
   for his mercy endures for ever;

15 But Pharaoh and his host he overthrew in the Red Sea, *
   for his mercy endures for ever;

16 Who led his people through the wilderness, *
   for his mercy endures for ever;

17 Who smote great kings, *
   for his mercy endures for ever;

18 And slew mighty kings, *
   for his mercy endures for ever;

19 Sihon, king of the Amorites, *
   for his mercy endures for ever;

20 And Og, the king of Bashan, *
   for his mercy endures for ever;

21 And gave away their land for a heritage, *
   for his mercy endures for ever;

22 A heritage for Israel his servant, *
   for his mercy endures for ever;

23 Who remembered us when we were in trouble, *
   for his mercy endures for ever;

24 And delivered us from our enemies, *
   for his mercy endures for ever;

25 Who gives food to all creatures, *
   for his mercy endures for ever.

26 Give thanks to the God of heaven, *
   for his mercy endures for ever.

[Remember us, O God, and shape our history,
form our inward eyes
to see the shadow of the life-giving cross
in the turbulence of our time;
for his sake who died for all,
Christ our Lord. Amen.]

Psalm 137

[Refrain: O pray for the peace of Jerusalem.]

1   By the waters of Babylon we sat down and wept, *
    when we remembered Zion.

2   As for our lyres, we hung them up *
    on the willows that grow in that land.

3   For there our captors asked for a song,
       our tormentors called for mirth: *
    'Sing us one of the songs of Zion.'

4   How shall we sing the Lord's song *
    in a strange land?

5   If I forget you, O Jerusalem, *
    let my right hand forget its skill.

6   Let my tongue cleave to the roof of my mouth
       if I do not remember you, *
    if I set not Jerusalem above my highest joy.

[7   Remember, O Lord, against the people of Edom
       the day of Jerusalem, *
    how they said, 'Down with it, down with it,
       even to the ground.'

8   O daughter of Babylon, doomed to destruction, *
    happy the one who repays you
       for all you have done to us;

9   Who takes your little ones, *
    and dashes them against the rock.]

[God of our pilgrimage,
you sent your Son to our strange land
to bring us home to you;
give us your songs to sing,
that even in our exile
we may be filled with the breath of the Spirit
of Jesus Christ our Lord. Amen.]

Psalm 138

[Refrain: Your loving-kindness, O Lord, endures for ever.]

1   I will give thanks to you, O Lord, with my whole heart; *
     before the gods will I sing praise to you.

2   I will bow down towards your holy temple and praise your name,
        because of your love and faithfulness; *
     for you have glorified your name
        and your word above all things.

3   In the day that I called to you, you answered me; *
     you put new strength in my soul.

4   All the kings of the earth shall praise you, O Lord, *
     for they have heard the words of your mouth.

5   They shall sing of the ways of the Lord, *
     that great is the glory of the Lord.

6   Though the Lord be high, he watches over the lowly; *
     as for the proud, he regards them from afar.

7   Though I walk in the midst of trouble,
        you will preserve me; *
     you will stretch forth your hand against the fury of my enemies;
        your right hand will save me.

8   The Lord shall make good his purpose for me; *
     your loving-kindness, O Lord, endures for ever;
        forsake not the work of your hands.

Psalm 139

[Refrain: Search me out, O God, and know my heart.]

1   O Lord, you have searched me out and known me; *
    you know my sitting down and my rising up;
        you discern my thoughts from afar.

2   You mark out my journeys and my resting place *
    and are acquainted with all my ways.

3   For there is not a word on my tongue, *
    but you, O Lord, know it altogether.

4   You encompass me behind and before *
    and lay your hand upon me.

5   Such knowledge is too wonderful for me, *
    so high that I cannot attain it.

6   Where can I go then from your spirit? *
    Or where can I flee from your presence?

7   If I climb up to heaven, you are there; †
    if I make the grave my bed, you are there also.

8   If I take the wings of the morning *
    and dwell in the uttermost parts of the sea,

9   Even there your hand shall lead me, *
    your right hand hold me fast.

10 If I say, 'Surely the darkness will cover me *
    and the light around me turn to night,'

11 Even darkness is no darkness with you;
        the night is as clear as the day; *
    darkness and light to you are both alike.

12   For you yourself created my inmost parts; *
      you knit me together in my mother's womb.

13   I thank you, for I am fearfully and wonderfully made; *
      marvellous are your works, my soul knows well.

14   My frame was not hidden from you, *
      when I was made in secret
        and woven in the depths of the earth.

15   Your eyes beheld my form, as yet unfinished; *
      already in your book were all my members written,

16   As day by day they were fashioned *
      when as yet there was none of them.

17   How deep are your counsels to me, O God! *
      How great is the sum of them!

18   If I count them, they are more in number than the sand, *
      and at the end, I am still in your presence.

[19   O that you would slay the wicked, O God, *
      that the bloodthirsty might depart from me!

20   They speak against you with wicked intent; *
      your enemies take up your name for evil.

21   Do I not oppose those, O Lord, who oppose you? *
      Do I not abhor those who rise up against you?

22   I hate them with a perfect hatred; *
      they have become my own enemies also.]

23   Search me out, O God, and know my heart; *
      try me and examine my thoughts.

24   See if there is any way of wickedness in me *
      and lead me in the way everlasting.

      [Creator God,
      may every breath we take be for your glory,
      may every footstep show you as our way,
      that, trusting in your presence in this world,
      we may, beyond this life, still be with you
      where you are alive and reign
      for ever and ever. Amen.]

Psalm 140

[Refrain: Keep me, O Lord, from the hands of the wicked.]

1   Deliver me, O Lord, from evildoers *
    and protect me from the violent,

2   Who devise evil in their hearts *
    and stir up strife all the day long.

3   They have sharpened their tongues like a serpent; *
    adder's poison is under their lips.

4   Keep me, O Lord, from the hands of the wicked; *
    protect me from the violent
       who seek to make me stumble.

5   The proud have laid a snare for me
       and spread out a net of cords; *
    they have set traps along my path.

6   I have said to the Lord, 'You are my God; *
    listen, O Lord, to the voice of my supplication.

7   'O Lord God, the strength of my salvation, *
    you have covered my head in the day of battle.

8   'Do not grant the desires of the wicked, O Lord, *
    do not prosper their wicked plans.

[9 'Let not those who surround me lift up their heads; *
    let the evil of their own lips fall upon them.

10 'Let hot burning coals rain upon them; *
    let them be cast into the depths, that they rise not again.'

11 No slanderer shall prosper on the earth, *
    and evil shall hunt down the violent to overthrow them.]

12 I know that the Lord will bring justice for the oppressed *
    and maintain the cause of the needy.

13 Surely, the righteous will give thanks to your name, *
    and the upright shall dwell in your presence.

[Glorious Saviour,
rescue us from the subtle evils that are too strong for us,
from poisonous words and the spirit of war;
by your judgement overthrow the forces of violence,
that all the world may join to worship you
in thanksgiving and peace,
now and for ever. Amen.]

Psalm 141

[Refrain: Set a watch before my mouth, O Lord.]

1   O Lord, I call to you; come to me quickly; *
    hear my voice when I cry to you.

2   Let my prayer rise before you as incense, *
    the lifting up of my hands as the evening sacrifice.

3   Set a watch before my mouth, O Lord, *
    and guard the door of my lips;

4   Let not my heart incline to any evil thing; *
    let me not be occupied in wickedness with evildoers,
        nor taste the pleasures of their table.

5   Let the righteous smite me in friendly rebuke;
        but let not the oil of the unrighteous anoint my head; *
    for my prayer is continually against their wicked deeds.

[6   Let their rulers be overthrown in stony places; *
    then they may know that my words are sweet.

7   As when a plough turns over the earth in furrows, *
    let their bones be scattered at the mouth of the Pit.]

8   But my eyes are turned to you, Lord God; *
    in you I take refuge; do not leave me defenceless.

9   Protect me from the snare which they have laid for me *
    and from the traps of the evildoers.

10 Let the wicked fall into their own nets, *
    while I pass by in safety.

[Lord God, our protector and guide,
who made us knowing both good and evil,
help us to desire all that is good,
that the offering of our lives may be acceptable to you;
through Jesus Christ our Lord. Amen.]

Psalm 142

[Refrain: Bring my soul out of prison,
that I may give thanks to your name.]

1   I cry aloud to the Lord; *
    to the Lord I make my supplication.

2   I pour out my complaint before him *
    and tell him of my trouble.

3   When my spirit faints within me, you know my path; *
    in the way wherein I walk have they laid a snare for me.

4   I look to my right hand, and find no one who knows me; *
    I have no place to flee to, and no one cares for my soul.

5   I cry out to you, O Lord, and say: *
    'You are my refuge, my portion in the land of the living.

6   'Listen to my cry, for I am brought very low; *
    save me from my persecutors, for they are too strong for me.

7   'Bring my soul out of prison,
       that I may give thanks to your name; *
    when you have dealt bountifully with me,
       then shall the righteous gather around me.'

[God of compassion,
you regard the forsaken
and give hope to the crushed in spirit;
hear those who cry to you in distress
and bring your ransomed people to sing your glorious praise,
now and for ever. Amen.]

Psalm 143

[Refrain: Show me, O Lord, the way that I should walk in.]

1   Hear my prayer, O Lord,
        and in your faithfulness give ear to my supplications; *
    answer me in your righteousness.

2   Enter not into judgement with your servant, *
    for in your sight shall no one living be justified.

3   For the enemy has pursued me,
        crushing my life to the ground, *
    making me sit in darkness like those long dead.

4   My spirit faints within me; *
    my heart within me is desolate.

5   I remember the time past; I muse upon all your deeds; *
    I consider the works of your hands.

6   I stretch out my hands to you; *
    my soul gasps for you like a thirsty land.

7   O Lord, make haste to answer me; my spirit fails me; *
    hide not your face from me
        lest I be like those who go down to the Pit.

8   Let me hear of your loving-kindness in the morning,
        for in you I put my trust; *
    show me the way I should walk in,
        for I lift up my soul to you.

9   Deliver me, O Lord, from my enemies, *
    for I flee to you for refuge.

10 Teach me to do what pleases you, for you are my God; *
    let your kindly spirit lead me on a level path.

11 Revive me, O Lord, for your name's sake; *
    for your righteousness' sake, bring me out of trouble.

[12 In your faithfulness, slay my enemies,
        and destroy all the adversaries of my soul, *
    for truly I am your servant.]

[Jesus, our companion,
when we are driven to despair,
help us, through the friends and strangers
    we encounter on our path,
to know you as our refuge,
our way, our truth, our life. Amen.]

Psalm 144

[Refrain: Happy are the people who have the Lord for their God.]

1   Blessèd be the Lord my rock, *
    who teaches my hands for war and my fingers for battle;

2   My steadfast help and my fortress,
       my stronghold and my deliverer,
       my shield in whom I trust, *
    who subdues the peoples under me.

3   O Lord, what are mortals that you should consider them; *
    mere human beings, that you should take thought for them?

4   They are like a breath of wind; *
    their days pass away like a shadow.

5   Bow your heavens, O Lord, and come down; *
    touch the mountains and they shall smoke.

6   Cast down your lightnings and scatter them; *
    shoot out your arrows and let thunder roar.

7   Reach down your hand from on high; *
    deliver me and take me out of the great waters,
       from the hand of foreign enemies,

8   Whose mouth speaks wickedness *
    and their right hand is the hand of falsehood.

9   O God, I will sing to you a new song; *
    I will play to you on a ten-stringed harp,

10 You that give salvation to kings *
    and have delivered David your servant.

11 Save me from the peril of the sword *
    and deliver me from the hand of foreign enemies,

12   Whose mouth speaks wickedness *
      and whose right hand is the hand of falsehood;

13   So that our sons in their youth
         may be like well-nurtured plants, *
      and our daughters like pillars
         carved for the corners of the temple;

14   Our barns be filled with all manner of store; *
      our flocks bearing thousands,
         and ten thousands in our fields;

15   Our cattle be heavy with young: *
      may there be no miscarriage or untimely birth,
         no cry of distress in our streets.

16   Happy are the people whose blessing this is. *
      Happy are the people who have the Lord for their God.

      *[God our deliverer,
      stir our weak wills,
      revive our weary spirits,
      and give us the courage
      to strive for the freedom of all your children,
      to the praise of your glorious name. Amen.]*

Psalm 145

[Refrain: Great is the Lord and highly to be praised.]

1   I will exalt you, O God my King, *
      and bless your name for ever and ever.

2   Every day will I bless you *
      and praise your name for ever and ever.

3   Great is the Lord and highly to be praised; *
      his greatness is beyond all searching out.

4   One generation shall praise your works to another *
      and declare your mighty acts.

5   They shall speak of the majesty of your glory, *
      and I will tell of all your wonderful deeds.

6   They shall speak of the might of your marvellous acts, *
      and I will also tell of your greatness.

7   They shall pour forth the story of your abundant kindness *
    and joyfully sing of your righteousness.

8   The Lord is gracious and merciful, *
    long-suffering and of great goodness.

9   The Lord is loving to everyone *
    and his mercy is over all his creatures.

10 All your works praise you, O Lord, *
    and your faithful servants bless you.

11 They tell of the glory of your kingdom *
    and speak of your mighty power,

12 To make known to all peoples your mighty acts *
    and the glorious splendour of your kingdom.

13 Your kingdom is an everlasting kingdom; *
    your dominion endures throughout all ages.

14 The Lord is sure in all his words *
    and faithful in all his deeds.

15 The Lord upholds all those who fall *
    and lifts up all those who are bowed down.

16 The eyes of all wait upon you, O Lord, *
    and you give them their food in due season.

17 You open wide your hand *
    and fill all things living with plenty.

18 The Lord is righteous in all his ways *
    and loving in all his works.

19 The Lord is near to those who call upon him, *
    to all who call upon him faithfully.

20 He fulfils the desire of those who fear him; *
    he hears their cry and saves them.

21 The Lord watches over those who love him, *
    but all the wicked shall he destroy.

22 My mouth shall speak the praise of the Lord, *
    and let all flesh bless his holy name for ever and ever.

[King of the universe,
you show the bright glory of your reign
in acts of mercy and enduring love;
raise the spirits of the downcast
and restore those who have fallen away,
that we may sing for ever of your love;
through Jesus Christ our Lord. Amen.]

Psalm 146

[Refrain: The Lord shall reign for ever.]

1   Alleluia.
      Praise the Lord, O my soul:
      while I live will I praise the Lord; *
   as long as I have any being,
      I will sing praises to my God.

2   Put not your trust in princes,
         nor in any human power, *
      for there is no help in them.

3   When their breath goes forth, they return to the earth; *
      on that day all their thoughts perish.

4   Happy are those who have the God of Jacob for their help, *
      whose hope is in the Lord their God;

5   Who made heaven and earth,
         the sea and all that is in them; *
      who keeps his promise for ever;

6   Who gives justice to those that suffer wrong *
      and bread to those who hunger.

7   The Lord looses those that are bound; *
      the Lord opens the eyes of the blind;

8   The Lord lifts up those who are bowed down; *
      the Lord loves the righteous;

9   The Lord watches over the stranger in the land;
         he upholds the orphan and widow; *
      but the way of the wicked he turns upside down.

10   The Lord shall reign for ever, *
     your God, O Zion, throughout all generations.
       Alleluia.

[Lord of all,
our breath and being come from you,
yet our earthly end is dust;
as you loose the bound and feed the hungry,
so bring us in your mercy through the grave and gate of death
to the feast of eternal life,
where you reign for evermore. Amen.]

Psalm 147

[Refrain: Great is our Lord and mighty in power.]

Part I

1   Alleluia.
       How good it is to make music for our God, *
       how joyful to honour him with praise.

2   The Lord builds up Jerusalem *
     and gathers together the outcasts of Israel.

3   He heals the brokenhearted *
     and binds up all their wounds.

4   He counts the number of the stars *
     and calls them all by their names.

5   Great is our Lord and mighty in power; *
     his wisdom is beyond all telling.

6   The Lord lifts up the poor, *
     but casts down the wicked to the ground.

7   Sing to the Lord with thanksgiving; *
     make music to our God upon the lyre;

8   Who covers the heavens with clouds *
     and prepares rain for the earth;

9   Who makes grass to grow upon the mountains *
     and green plants to serve our needs.

10 He gives the beasts their food *
    and the young ravens when they cry.

11 He takes no pleasure in the power of a horse, *
    no delight in human strength;

12 But the Lord delights in those who fear him, *
    who put their trust in his steadfast love.

Part 2

13 Sing praise to the Lord, O Jerusalem; *
    praise your God, O Zion;

14 For he has strengthened the bars of your gates *
    and has blest your children within you.

15 He has established peace in your borders *
    and satisfies you with the finest wheat.

16 He sends forth his command to the earth *
    and his word runs very swiftly.

17 He gives snow like wool *
    and scatters the hoarfrost like ashes.

18 He casts down his hailstones like morsels of bread; *
    who can endure his frost?

19 He sends forth his word and melts them; *
    he blows with his wind and the waters flow.

20 He declares his word to Jacob, *
    his statutes and judgements to Israel.

21 He has not dealt so with any other nation; *
    they do not know his laws.
       Alleluia.

    *[Compassionate God,
    as you know each star you have created,
    so you know the secrets of every heart;
    in your loving mercy bring to your table
    all who are fearful and broken,
    all who are wounded and needy,*

*that our hungers may be satisfied
in the city of your peace;
through Christ who is our peace. Amen.]*

Psalm 148

[Refrain: O praise the name of the Lord.]

1 Alleluia.
   Praise the Lord from the heavens; *
   praise him in the heights.

2 Praise him, all you his angels; *
   praise him, all his host.

3 Praise him, sun and moon; *
   praise him, all you stars of light.

4 Praise him, heaven of heavens, *
   and you waters above the heavens.

5 Let them praise the name of the Lord, *
   for he commanded and they were created.

6 He made them fast for ever and ever; *
   he gave them a law which shall not pass away.

7 Praise the Lord from the earth, *
   you sea monsters and all deeps;

8 Fire and hail, snow and mist, *
   tempestuous wind, fulfilling his word;

9 Mountains and all hills, *
   fruit trees and all cedars;

10 Wild beasts and all cattle, *
   creeping things and birds on the wing;

11 Kings of the earth and all peoples, *
   princes and all rulers of the world;

12 Young men and women,
   old and young together; *
   let them praise the name of the Lord.

13 For his name only is exalted, *
    his splendour above earth and heaven.

14 He has raised up the horn of his people
        and praise for all his faithful servants, *
    the children of Israel, a people who are near him.
        Alleluia.

[O glorious God,
your whole creation sings your marvellous work;
may heaven's praise so echo in our hearts
that we may be good stewards of the earth;
through Jesus Christ our Lord. Amen.]

Psalm 149

[Refrain: Sound praises to the Lord, all the earth.]

1   Alleluia.
        O sing to the Lord a new song; *
    sing his praise in the congregation of the faithful.

2   Let Israel rejoice in their maker; *
    let the children of Zion be joyful in their king.

3   Let them praise his name in the dance; *
    let them sing praise to him with timbrel and lyre.

4   For the Lord has pleasure in his people *
    and adorns the poor with salvation.

5   Let the faithful be joyful in glory; *
    let them rejoice in their ranks,

6   With the praises of God in their mouths *
    and a two-edged sword in their hands;

[7 To execute vengeance on the nations *
    and punishment on the peoples;

8   To bind their kings in chains *
    and their nobles with fetters of iron;

9   To execute on them the judgement decreed: *
    such honour have all his faithful servants.]
        Alleluia.

[Glorious and redeeming God,
give us hearts to praise you all our days
and wills to reject the world's deceits,
that we may bind the evils of our age
and proclaim the good news of salvation
in Jesus Christ our Lord. Amen.]

Psalm 150

[Refrain: Let everything that has breath praise the Lord.]

1   Alleluia.
     O praise God in his holiness; *
     praise him in the firmament of his power.

2   Praise him for his mighty acts; *
     praise him according to his excellent greatness.

3   Praise him with the blast of the trumpet; *
     praise him upon the harp and lyre.

4   Praise him with timbrel and dances; *
     praise him upon the strings and pipe.

5   Praise him with ringing cymbals; *
     praise him upon the clashing cymbals.

6   Let everything that has breath *
     praise the Lord.
        Alleluia.

     [God of life and love,
     whose Son was victorious over sin and death,
     make us alive with his life,
     that the whole world may resound with your praise;
     through Jesus Christ our Lord. Amen.]

The Canticles

Index

Old Testament & Apocrypha Canticles

New Testament Canticles

Other Canticles

THE DOXOLOGY

Canticles which have **Glory . . .** *printed at the end may conclude with,
Either:*

**Glory to the Father and to the Son
    and to the Holy Spirit: ***
**as it was in the beginning, is now,
    and shall be for ever. Amen.**

or:

**Glory to God, Source of all being,
    Eternal Word and Holy Spirit: ***
**as it was in the beginning, is now,
    and shall be for ever. Amen.**

Old Testament and Apocrypha Canticles

1 *THE SONG OF MOSES AND MIRIAM*

Refrain: **In your unfailing love, O Lord,**
you lead the people whom you have redeemed.

1   I will sing to the Lord, who has triumphed gloriously, *
the horse and his rider have been thrown into the sea.

2   The Lord is my strength and my song *
and has become my salvation.

3   This is my God whom I will praise, *
the God of my ancestors whom I will exalt.

4   The Lord is a warrior, *
the Lord is his name.

5   Your right hand, O Lord, is glorious in power: *
your right hand, O Lord, shatters the enemy.

6   At the blast of your nostrils, the sea covered them; *
they sank as lead in the mighty waters.

7   In your unfailing love, O Lord, *
you lead the people whom you have redeemed.

8   And by your invincible strength *
you will guide them to your holy dwelling.

9   You will bring them in and plant them, O Lord, *
in the sanctuary which your hands have established.

Glory . . .   *Exodus 15.1b-3,6,10,13,17*

In your unfailing love, O Lord,
you lead the people whom you have redeemed.

2 *A SONG OF THE ROCK*

Refrain: **The word is very near to you;**
it is in your mouth and in your heart for you to observe.

1   Give ear, O heavens, and I will speak; *
and let the earth hear the words of my mouth.

2 May my teaching drop as the rain,
 my speech distil as the dew, *
as the gentle rain on the grass,
 and as the showers upon the meadow.

3 For I will proclaim the name of the Lord. *
Ascribe greatness to our God!

4 The Rock, his work is perfect; for all his ways are just: *
a faithful God without deceit, just and upright is he.

5 His degenerate children have dealt corruptly with him; *
a perverse and crooked generation.

6 Do you thus repay the Lord, you foolish and senseless people? *
Is not he your father, who created you,
 who made you and established you?

7 Remember the days of old, consider the years long past; *
ask your father, and he will show you;
 your elders, and they will tell you.

8 When the Most High gave the nations their inheritance,
 when he divided the children of earth, *
he fixed the bounds of the peoples
 according to the number of the children of God.

9 For the Lord's own portion is his people, *
Jacob his allotted heritage.

10 He sustained him in a desert land,
 in the howling waste of the wilderness; *
he shielded him and cared for him;
 he kept him as the apple of his eye.

11 As an eagle stirs up its nest, and hovers over its young, *
spreading out its wings, takes them,
 and bears them aloft on its pinions,

12 So the Lord alone did guide him, *
and no foreign god was with him.

Glory . . .   *Deuteronomy 32.1-12*

**The word is very near to you;
it is in your mouth and in your heart for you to observe.**

3 *A SONG OF HANNAH*

Refrain: **Blessèd are those who believe,
for what God has promised will be fulfilled.**

1   My heart exults in the Lord; *
    my strength is exalted in my God.

2   My mouth derides my enemies, *
    because I rejoice in your salvation.

3   There is no Holy One like you, O Lord, *
    nor any Rock like you, our God.

4   For you are a God of knowledge *
    and by you our actions are weighed.

5   The bows of the mighty are broken, *
    but the feeble gird on strength.

6   Those who were full now hire themselves out for bread, *
    but those who were hungry are well fed.

7   The barren woman has borne sevenfold, *
    but she who has many children is forlorn.

8   Both the poor and the rich are of your making; *
    you bring low and you also exalt.

9   You raise up the poor from the dust, *
    and lift the needy from the ash heap.

10 You make them sit with the rulers *
    and inherit a place of honour.

11 For the pillars of the earth are yours *
    and on them you have set the world.

Glory . . .   *1 Samuel 2.1,2,3b-5,7,8*

**Blessèd are those who believe,
for what God has promised will be fulfilled.**

4 *A SONG OF DAVID*

Refrain: **Splendour and majesty are yours, O God;**
you are exalted as head over all.

1   Blessèd are you, God of Israel, for ever and ever, *
    for yours is the greatness, the power,
        the glory, the splendour and the majesty.

2   Everything in heaven and on earth is yours; *
    yours is the kingdom, O Lord,
        and you are exalted as head over all.

3   Riches and honour come from you *
    and you rule over all.

4   In your hand are power and might; *
    yours it is to give power and strength to all.

5   And now we give you thanks, our God, *
    and praise your glorious name.

6   For all things come from you, *
    and of your own have we given you.

    Glory . . .   *1 Chronicles 29.10b-13,14b*

    Splendour and majesty are yours, O God;
    you are exalted as head over all.

5 *A SONG OF SOLOMON*

Refrain: **Many waters cannot quench love;**
neither can the floods drown it.

1   Set me as a seal upon your heart, *
    as a seal upon your arm;

2   For love is strong as death,
        passion fierce as the grave; *
    its flashes are flashes of fire,
        a raging flame.

3   Many waters cannot quench love, *
    neither can the floods drown it.

4 If all the wealth of our house
    were offered for love, *
    it would be utterly scorned.

Glory . . .   *cf Song of Solomon 8.6,7*

Many waters cannot quench love;
neither can the floods drown it.

6 *A SONG OF PEACE*

Refrain: **Spirit of God, teach us your ways**
          that we may walk in the paths of peace.

1 Come, let us go up to the mountain of God, *
    to the house of the God of Jacob;

2 That God may teach us his ways, *
    and that we may walk in his paths.

3 For the law shall go out from Zion, *
    and the word of the Lord from Jerusalem.

4 God shall judge between the nations, *
    and shall mediate for many peoples.

5 They shall beat their swords into ploughshares, *
    and their spears into pruning hooks.

6 Nation shall not lift up sword against nation, *
    neither shall they learn war any more.

7 O people of Jacob, come: *
    let us walk in the light of the Lord.

Glory . . .   *Isaiah 2.3-5*

Spirit of God, teach us your ways,
that we may walk in the paths of peace.

7 *A SONG OF THE MESSIAH*

Refrain: **To us a child is born,**
      to us a son is given.

1   The people who walked in darkness
      have seen a great light; *
    those who dwelt in a land of deep darkness,
      upon them the light has dawned.

2   You have increased their joy
      and given them great gladness; *
    they rejoiced before you as with joy at the harvest.

3   For you have shattered the yoke that burdened them; *
    the collar that lay heavy on their shoulders.

4   For to us a child is born and to us a son is given, *
    and the government will be upon his shoulder.

5   And his name will be called: Wonderful Counsellor;
      the Mighty God; *
    the Everlasting Father; the Prince of Peace.

6   Of the increase of his government and of peace *
    there will be no end,

7   Upon the throne of David and over his kingdom, *
    to establish and uphold it
      with justice and righteousness.

8   From this time forth and for evermore; *
    the zeal of the Lord of hosts will do this.

    Glory . . .   *Isaiah 9.2,3b,4a,6,7*

    To us a child is born,
    to us a son is given.

8 *A SONG OF GOD'S CHOSEN ONE*

Refrain: **The earth shall be full**
      of the knowledge of the Lord.

1   There shall come forth a shoot from the stock of Jesse, *
    and a branch shall grow out of his roots.

2   And the Spirit of the Lord shall rest upon him, *
    the spirit of wisdom and understanding,

3   The spirit of counsel and might, *
    the spirit of knowledge and the fear of the Lord.

4   He shall not judge by what his eyes see, *
    or decide by what his ears hear,

5   But with righteousness he shall judge the poor, *
    and decide with equity for the meek of the earth.

6   The wolf shall dwell with the lamb, *
    and the leopard shall lie down with the kid.

7   The calf, the lion and the fatling together, *
    with a little child to lead them.

8   They shall not hurt or destroy in all my holy mountain, *
    for the earth shall be full of the knowledge of the Lord
       as the waters cover the sea.

   Glory . . .   *Isaiah 11.1,2,3b-4a,6,9*

   **The earth shall be full
   of the knowledge of the Lord.**

9 *A SONG OF DELIVERANCE*

Refrain: **All the earth, shout and sing for joy,
            for great in your midst is the Holy One.**

1   'Behold, God is my salvation; *
    I will trust and will not be afraid;

2   'For the Lord God is my strength and my song, *
    and has become my salvation.'

3   With joy you will draw water *
    from the wells of salvation.

4   On that day you will say, *
    'Give thanks to the Lord, call upon his name;

5   'Make known his deeds among the nations, *
    proclaim that his name is exalted.

6   'Sing God's praises, who has triumphed gloriously; *
     let this be known in all the world.

7   'Shout and sing for joy, you that dwell in Zion, *
     for great in your midst is the Holy One of Israel.'

Glory . . .   *Isaiah 12.2-6*

**All the earth, shout and sing for joy,
for great in your midst is the Holy One.**

10 *A SONG OF TRUST*

Refrain: **Trust in the Lord for ever,
           for the Lord God is an everlasting rock.**

1   We have a strong city; he sets up salvation
        as walls and bulwarks. *
     Open the gates, that the righteous nation which keeps faith
        may enter in.

2   You will keep him in perfect peace,
        whose mind is stayed on you, *
     because he trusts in you.

3   Trust in the Lord for ever, *
     for the Lord God is an everlasting rock.

4   The way of the righteous is level; *
     you who are upright make smooth the path of the righteous.

5   In the path of your judgements, O Lord, we wait for you; *
     your name and renown is the desire of our soul.

6   My soul yearns for you in the night, *
     my spirit within me earnestly seeks you.

7   For when your judgements are in the earth, *
     the inhabitants of the world learn righteousness.

8   O Lord, you will ordain peace for us, *
     for indeed all that we have done you have done for us.

Glory . . .   *Isaiah 26.1-4,7-9,12*

**Trust in the Lord for ever,
for the Lord God is an everlasting rock.**

11 *A SONG OF THE WILDERNESS*

Refrain: **The ransomed of the Lord shall return,**
        and sorrow and sighing shall flee away.

1   The wilderness and the dry land shall rejoice, *
      the desert shall blossom and burst into song.

2   They shall see the glory of the Lord, *
      the majesty of our God.

3   Strengthen the weary hands, *
      and make firm the feeble knees.

4   Say to the anxious, 'Be strong, fear not,
      your God is coming with judgement, *
    coming with judgement to save you.'

5   Then shall the eyes of the blind be opened, *
      and the ears of the deaf unstopped;

6   Then shall the lame leap like a hart, *
      and the tongue of the dumb sing for joy.

7   For waters shall break forth in the wilderness, *
      and streams in the desert;

8   The ransomed of the Lord shall return with singing, *
      with everlasting joy upon their heads.

9   Joy and gladness shall be theirs, *
      and sorrow and sighing shall flee away.

    Glory . . .   *Isaiah 35.1,2b-4a,4c-6,10*

    The ransomed of the Lord shall return,
    and sorrow and sighing shall flee away.

12 *A SONG OF GOD'S HERALD*

Refrain: **God will feed his flock like a shepherd,**
        and gather the lambs in his arms.

1   Go up to a high mountain,
      herald of good tidings to Zion; *
    lift up your voice with strength,
      herald of good tidings to Jerusalem.

2   Lift up your voice, fear not; *
      say to the cities of Judah, 'Behold your God!'

3   See, the Lord God comes with might, *
      and his arm rules for him.

4   Behold, his reward is with him, *
      and his recompense before him.

5   God will feed his flock like a shepherd, *
      and gather the lambs in his arms;

6   He will carry them in his breast, *
      and gently lead those that are with young.

Glory . . .   *Isaiah 40.9-11*

**God will feed his flock like a shepherd,
and gather the lambs in his arms.**

13 *A SONG OF THE COVENANT*

Refrain: **I have given you as a light to the nations,
and I have called you in righteousness.**

1   Thus says God, who created the heavens, *
      who fashioned the earth and all that dwells in it;

2   Who gives breath to the people upon it *
      and spirit to those who walk in it,

3   'I am the Lord and I have called you in righteousness, *
      I have taken you by the hand and kept you;

4   'I have given you as a covenant to the people, *
      a light to the nations, to open the eyes that are blind,

5   'To bring out the captives from the dungeon, *
      from the prison, those who sit in darkness.

6   'I am the Lord, that is my name; *
      my glory I give to no other.'

Glory . . .   *Isaiah 42.5-8a*

**I have given you as a light to the nations,
and I have called you in righteousness.**

14 *A SONG OF THE NEW CREATION*

Refrain: **I will make a way in the wilderness,
and rivers in the desert.**

1 'I am the Lord, your Holy One, *
    the Creator of Israel, your King.'

2 Thus says the Lord, who makes a way in the sea, *
    a path in the mighty waters,

3 'Remember not the former things, *
    nor consider the things of old.

4 'Behold, I am doing a new thing; *
    now it springs forth, do you not perceive it?

5 'I will make a way in the wilderness
        and rivers in the desert, *
    to give drink to my chosen people,

6 'The people whom I formed for myself, *
    that they might declare my praise.'

   Glory . . .   *Isaiah 43.15,16,18,19,20c,21*

   **I will make a way in the wilderness,
   and rivers in the desert.**

15 *A SONG OF THE WORD OF THE LORD*

Refrain: **Return to the Lord, who will have mercy,
to our God, who will richly pardon.**

1 Seek the Lord while he may be found, *
    call upon him while he is near;

2 Let the wicked abandon their ways, *
    and the unrighteous their thoughts;

3 Return to the Lord, who will have mercy; *
    to our God, who will richly pardon.

4 'For my thoughts are not your thoughts, *
    neither are your ways my ways,' says the Lord.

5   'For as the heavens are higher than the earth, *
       so are my ways higher than your ways
          and my thoughts than your thoughts.

6   'As the rain and the snow come down from above, *
       and return not again but water the earth,

7   'Bringing forth life and giving growth, *
       seed for sowing and bread to eat,

8   'So is my word that goes forth from my mouth; *
       it will not return to me fruitless,

9   'But it will accomplish that which I purpose, *
       and succeed in the task I gave it.'

     Glory . . .   *Isaiah 55.6-11*

     **Return to the Lord, who will have mercy,
to our God, who will richly pardon.**

16   *A SONG OF THE NEW JERUSALEM*

Refrain: **Above you the Holy One arises,
              and above you God's glory appears.**

1   Arise, shine out, for your light has come, *
       the glory of the Lord is rising upon you.

2   Though night still covers the earth, *
       and darkness the peoples;

3   Above you the Holy One arises, *
       and above you God's glory appears.

4   The nations will come to your light, *
       and kings to your dawning brightness.

5   Your gates will lie open continually, *
       shut neither by day nor by night.

6   The sound of violence
       shall be heard no longer in your land, *
     or ruin and devastation within your borders.

7   You will call your walls, Salvation, *
       and your gates, Praise.

8   No more will the sun give you daylight, *
    nor moonlight shine upon you;

9   But the Lord will be your everlasting light, *
    your God will be your splendour.

10 For you shall be called the city of God, *
    the dwelling of the Holy One of Israel.

    Glory . . .   *Isaiah 60.1-3,11a,18,19,14b*

    Above you the Holy One arises,
    and above you God's glory appears.

17 *A SONG OF THE LORD'S ANOINTED*

Refrain: **The Lord has anointed me**
          and sent me to bring good news to the oppressed.

1   The Spirit of the Lord is upon me *
    because he has anointed me.

2   He has sent me to bring good news to the oppressed, *
    to bind up the broken-hearted,

3   To proclaim liberty to the captives, *
    and the opening of the prison to those who are bound;

4   To proclaim the year of the Lord's favour, *
    to comfort all who mourn,

5   To give them a garland instead of ashes, *
    the oil of gladness instead of mourning,
      the mantle of praise instead of a faint spirit,

6   That they may be called oaks of righteousness, *
    the planting of the Lord, that he may be glorified.

7   For as the earth puts forth her blossom, *
    and as seeds in the garden spring up,

8   So shall the Lord God make righteousness and praise *
    blossom before all the nations.

9   You shall be called priests of the Lord; *
    they shall speak of you as ministers of our God.

    Glory . . .   *Isaiah 61.1-3,11,6a*

**The Lord has anointed me
and sent me to bring good news to the oppressed.**

18 *A SONG OF THE BRIDE*

Refrain: **God makes righteousness and praise
blossom before all the nations.**

1   I will greatly rejoice in the Lord, *
     my soul shall exult in my God;

2   Who has clothed me with the garments of salvation, *
     and has covered me with the cloak of integrity,

3   As a bridegroom decks himself with a garland, *
     and as a bride adorns herself with her jewels.

4   For as the earth puts forth her blossom, *
     and as seeds in the garden spring up,

5   So shall God make righteousness and praise *
     blossom before all the nations.

6   For Zion's sake I will not keep silent, *
     and for Jerusalem's sake I will not rest,

7   Until her deliverance shines out like the dawn, *
     and her salvation as a burning torch.

8   The nations shall see your deliverance, *
     and all rulers shall see your glory;

9   Then you shall be called by a new name *
     which the mouth of God will give.

10   You shall be a crown of glory in the hand of the Lord, *
     a royal diadem in the hand of your God.

   Glory . . .   *Isaiah 61.10,11;62.1-3*

   **God makes righteousness and praise
   blossom before all the nations.**

19 *A SONG OF THE LORD'S GRACIOUS DEEDS*

Refrain: **I will recount the gracious deeds of the Lord,
the praises of the Most High.**

1   Who is this that comes from Edom, *
    coming from Bozrah, his garments stained crimson?

2   Who is this in glorious apparel, *
    marching in the greatness of his strength?

3   'It is I, who announce that right has won the day, *
    it is I,' says the Lord, 'for I am mighty to save.'

4   Why are your robes all red, O Lord, *
    and your garments like theirs who tread the winepress?

5   'I have trodden the winepress alone, *
    and from the peoples no one was with me.'

6   I will recount the gracious deeds of the Lord, *
    the praises of the Most High;

7   All that God has done for us in his mercy, *
    by his many acts of love.

8   For God said, 'Surely, they are my people,
       my children who will not deal falsely,' *
    and he became their Saviour in all their distress.

9   So God redeemed them by his love and pity; *
    he lifted them up and carried them
       through all the days of old.

    Glory . . .   *Isaiah 63.1-3a,7-9*

    **I will recount the gracious deeds of the Lord,
the praises of the Most High.**

20 *A SONG OF JERUSALEM OUR MOTHER*

Refrain: **Thus says our God, I will comfort you,
you shall see and your heart shall rejoice.**

1   'Rejoice with Jerusalem and be glad for her, *
    all you who love her,' says the Lord.

2 'Rejoice with her in joy, *
   all you who mourn over her,

3 'That you may drink deeply with delight *
   from her consoling breast.'

4 For thus says our God, *
   'You shall be nursed and carried on her arm.

5 'As a mother comforts her children, *
   so I will comfort you;

6 'You shall see and your heart shall rejoice; *
   you shall flourish like the grass of the fields.'

   Glory . . .   *Isaiah 66.10,11a,12a,12c,13a,14a,b*

   **Thus says our God, I will comfort you,
   you shall see and your heart shall rejoice.**

21 *A SONG OF LAMENTATION*

Refrain: **Great is your faithfulness, O Lord.
            Therefore I will hope in you.**

1 Is it nothing to you, all you who pass by? *
   Look and see if there is any sorrow like my sorrow,

2 Which was brought upon me, *
   which the Lord inflicted
      on the day of his fierce anger.

3 For these things I weep;
      my eyes flow with tears; *
   for a comforter is far from me,
      one to revive my courage.

4 Remember my affliction and my bitterness, *
   the wormwood and the gall!

5 But this I call to mind, *
   and therefore I have hope:

6 The steadfast love of the Lord never ceases, *
   his mercies never come to an end;

7 They are new every morning; *
  great is your faithfulness.

8 'The Lord is my portion,' says my soul, *
  'therefore I will hope in him.'

9 The Lord is good to those who wait for him, *
  to the soul that seeks him.

10 It is good that we should wait quietly *
  for the salvation of the Lord.

11 For the Lord will not reject for ever; *
  though he causes grief, he will have compassion,

12 According to the abundance of his steadfast love; *
  for he does not willingly afflict or grieve anyone.

 Glory . . .   *Lamentations 1.12,16a,b;3.19,21-26,31-33*

 Great is your faithfulness, O Lord.
 Therefore I will hope in you.

22 *A SONG OF EZEKIEL*

Refrain: **I will put a new spirit within you,**
   and you shall be my people.

1 I will take you from the nations, *
  and gather you from all the countries.

2 I will sprinkle clean water upon you, *
  and you shall be clean
    from all your uncleannesses.

3 A new heart I will give you, *
  and put a new spirit within you,

4 And I will remove from your body the heart of stone *
  and give you a heart of flesh.

5 You shall be my people, *
  and I will be your God.

 Glory . . .   *Ezekiel 36.24-26,28b*

 I will put a new spirit within you,
 and you shall be my people.

Refrain: **Raise us up, O God,**
        that we may live in your presence.

1   Come, let us return to the Lord *
    who has torn us and will heal us.

2   God has stricken us *
    and will bind up our wounds.

3   After two days, he will revive us, *
    and on the third day will raise us up,
        that we may live in his presence.

4   Let us strive to know the Lord; *
    his appearing is as sure as the sunrise.

5   He will come to us like the showers, *
    like the spring rains that water the earth.

6   'O Ephraim, how shall I deal with you? *
    How shall I deal with you, O Judah?

7   'Your love for me is like the morning mist, *
    like the dew that goes early away.

8   'Therefore, I have hewn them by the prophets, *
    and my judgement goes forth as the light.

9   'For loyalty is my desire and not sacrifice, *
    and the knowledge of God rather than burnt offerings.'

Glory . . .   *Hosea 6.1-6*

Raise us up, O God,
that we may live in your presence.

24 *A SONG OF JONAH*

Refrain: **My prayer came to you in your holy temple,
and you brought up my life from the depths.**

1   I called to you, O God, out of my distress
        and you answered me; *
     out of the belly of Sheol I cried,
        and you heard my voice.

2   You cast me into the deep,
        into the heart of the seas, *
     and the flood surrounded me,
        all your waves and billows passed over me.

3   Then I said, I am driven away from your sight; *
     how shall I ever look again upon your holy temple?

4   The waters closed in over me,
        the deep was round about me; *
     weeds were wrapped around my head
        at the roots of the mountains.

5   I went down to the land whose bars closed upon me for ever, *
     yet you brought up my life from the depths, O God.

6   As my life was ebbing away, I remembered you, O God, *
     and my prayer came to you, into your holy temple.

7   With the voice of thanksgiving, I will sacrifice to you; *
     what I have vowed I will pay;
        deliverance belongs to the Lord!

   Glory . . .   *Jonah 2.2-7,9*

   **My prayer came to you in your holy temple,
   and you brought up my life from the depths.**

25 *THE PRAYER OF HABAKKUK*

Refrain: **You came forth to save your people,
to save your anointed, O God.**

1   O Lord, I have heard of your renown, *
     and I stand in awe, O Lord, of your work.

2   In the midst of the years renew it;
        in the midst of the years make it known; *
    in wrath remember mercy.

3   God came from Teman, and the Holy One from Mount Paran. *
    His glory covered the heavens, and the earth was full of his praise.

4   His brightness was like the sun, *
    rays flashed from his hand; there he veiled his power.

5   You came forth to save your people, *
    to save your anointed.

6   You trampled the sea with your horses, *
    churning the mighty waters.

7   I hear, and my belly trembles, *
    my lips quiver at the sound;

8   Rottenness enters into my bones, *
    and my steps totter beneath me.

9   I will quietly wait for the day of trouble *
    to come upon the people that invade us.

10 Though the fig tree does not blossom,
        nor fruit appear on the vines, *
    the produce of the olive fail, and the fields yield no food,

11 Though the flock be cut off from the fold *
    and there be no herd in the stalls,

12 Yet will I rejoice in the Lord, *
    I will exult in the God of my salvation.

13 God, the Lord, is my strength; *
    he makes my feet like hinds' feet,
        and makes me tread upon the high places.

Glory . . .   *Habakkuk 3.2-4,13a,15-19*

**You came forth to save your people,
to save your anointed, O God.**

26 *A SONG OF TOBIT*

Refrain: **See what the Lord our God has done**
      and exalt him in the sight of the living.

1   Blessèd be God, who lives for ever, *
      whose reign endures throughout all ages.

2   Declare God's praise before the nations, *
      you who are the children of Israel.

3   For if our God has scattered you among them, *
      there too has he shown you his greatness.

4   Exalt him in the sight of the living, *
      because he is our Lord and God and our Father for ever.

5   Though God punishes you for your wickedness, *
      mercy will be shown to you all.

6   God will gather you from every nation, *
      from wherever you have been scattered.

7   When you turn to the Lord
         with all your heart and soul, *
      God will hide his face from you no more.

8   See what the Lord has done for you *
      and give thanks with a loud voice.

9   Praise the Lord of righteousness *
      and exalt the King of the ages.

   Glory . . .   *Tobit 13.1,3,4-6a*

   See what the Lord our God has done
   and exalt him in the sight of the living.

27 *A SONG OF JUDITH*

Refrain: **You sent forth your Spirit, O God,**
      and you continue to show mercy to all.

1   I will sing a new song to my God, *
      for you are great and glorious,
         truly strong and invincible.

2   May your whole creation serve you, *
    for you spoke and all things came to be.

3   You sent forth your Spirit and they were formed, *
    for no one can resist your voice.

4   Mountains and seas are stirred to their depths; *
    at your presence rocks shall melt like wax.

5   But to those who fear you, *
    you continue to show mercy.

6   No sacrifice, however fragrant, can please you, *
    but whoever fears the Lord
        shall stand in your sight for ever.

   Glory . . .   *Judith 16.13-16*

   **You sent forth your Spirit, O God,
   and you continue to show mercy to all.**

28 *A SONG OF THE RIGHTEOUS*

Refrain: **God has found the righteous worthy
           and their hope is full of immortality.**

1   The souls of the righteous are in the hand of God *
    and no torment will ever touch them.

2   In the eyes of the foolish, they seem to have died; *
    but they are at peace.

3   For though, in the sight of others, they were punished, *
    their hope is full of immortality.

4   Having been disciplined a little,
        they will receive great good, *
    because God tested them and found them worthy.

5   Like gold in the furnace, God tried them *
    and, like a sacrificial burnt offering, accepted them.

6   In the time of their visitation, they will shine forth *
    and will run like sparks through the stubble.

7   They will govern nations and rule over peoples *
    and God will reign over them for ever.

Glory . . . Wisdom 3.1,2a,3b-8

**God has found the righteous worthy
and their hope is full of immortality.**

29 *A SONG OF THE SPIRIT OF WISDOM*

Refrain: **All good things came to me along with Wisdom;
those who receive her obtain friendship with God.**

1 I prayed and understanding was given me; *
   I called on God
      and the Spirit of Wisdom came to me.

2 I preferred her to sceptres and thrones *
   and I accounted wealth as nothing
      in comparison with her.

3 I loved her more than health or beauty *
   and I chose to have her rather than light,
      because her radiance never ceases.

4 All good things came to me along with her, *
   and in her hands uncounted wealth.

5 I rejoiced in them all,
      because Wisdom leads them, *
   but I did not know that she was their mother.

6 I learned without guile
      and I impart without grudging, *
   I do not hide her wealth.

7 For Wisdom is an unfailing treasure for mortals: *
   those who receive her obtain friendship with God.

Glory . . . Wisdom 7.7-8,10-14a

**All good things came to me along with Wisdom;
those who receive her obtain friendship with God.**

30 *A SONG OF WISDOM*

Refrain: **Send Wisdom forth from your holy heavens;
from the throne of your glory
send what is pleasing to you.**

1   O God of our ancestors and Lord of mercy, *
    you have made all things by your word.

2   By your wisdom you have formed us *
    to have dominion over the creatures you have made;

3   To rule the world in holiness and righteousness *
    and to pronounce judgement in uprightness of soul.

4   Give us the Wisdom that sits by your throne; *
    do not reject us from among your servants,

5   For we are your servants, *
    with little understanding of judgement and laws.

6   Even one who is perfect among us *
    will be regarded as nothing
       without the wisdom that comes from you.

7   With you is Wisdom, she who knows your works, *
    and was present when you made the world.

8   She understands what is pleasing in your sight *
    and what is right according to your commandments.

9   Send her forth from the holy heavens, *
    from the throne of your glory send her.

10 That she may labour at our side *
    and that we may learn what is pleasing to you.

11 For she knows and understands all things, *
    she will guide us wisely in our actions
       and guard us with her glory.

Glory . . .   *Wisdom 9.1-5a,c,6,9-11*

**Send Wisdom forth from your holy heavens;
from the throne of your glory
send what is pleasing to you.**

31 A SONG OF THE REDEEMING SPIRIT

Refrain: **The righteous shall sing hymns
to your holy name, O God.**

1   A holy people and a blameless race *
    Wisdom delivered from a nation of oppressors.

2   She entered the soul of a servant of God *
    and withstood dread rulers with wonders and signs.

3   She gave to holy people the reward of their labours; *
    she guided them along a marvellous way.

4   She became a shelter to them by day *
    and a starry flame through the night.

5   She brought them over the Red Sea *
    and led them through deep waters.

6   The righteous sang hymns to your holy name, O God, *
    and praised with one accord your defending hand.

7   For Wisdom opened the mouths of those who were mute *
    and made the tongues of infants speak clearly.

   Glory . . .   *Wisdom 10.15-18,20b-21*

   **The righteous shall sing hymns
   to your holy name, O God.**

32 A SONG OF GOD'S SERVANTS

Refrain: **Hear the prayers of your servants,
those you have named as your own.**

1   Gather all the tribes of Jacob; *
    give them their inheritance,
       as at the beginning.

2   Have mercy on the people called by your name, O God, *
    on those you have named as your first-born.

3   Have pity on the city of your sanctuary, *
    Jerusalem, the place of your dwelling.

4   Fill it with your majesty, *
    and your people with your glory.

5   Bear witness to those you created in the beginning *
    and fulfil the prophecies spoken in your name.

6   Reward those who wait for you *
    and let your prophets be found worthy of trust.

7   Hear the prayers of your servants, *
    that all who are on the earth will know
        that you are the God of the ages.

Glory . . .   *Ecclesiasticus 36.13-22*

**Hear the prayers of your servants,
those you have named as your own.**

33 *A SONG IN PRAISE OF THE WORKS OF GOD*

Refrain: **Ascribe majesty to the name of the Most High;
        let all creation give thanks with praise.**

1   Listen to me, my faithful children, *
    and blossom like a rose
        growing by a stream of water.

2   Send out fragrance like incense
        and sing a hymn of praise, *
    bless our God for all creation.

3   Ascribe majesty to the name of the Most High, *
    give thanks with praise, with songs on your lips
        and with harps.

4   All your works are good, O God, *
    and whatever you command will be done.

Glory . . .   *Ecclesiasticus 39.13-15a,16*

**Ascribe majesty to the name of the Most High;
let all creation give thanks with praise.**

34 *A SONG OF PILGRIMAGE*

Refrain: **In prayer I inclined my ear**
and my heart was stirred to seek Wisdom.

1   While I was still young, *
     I sought Wisdom openly in my prayer.

2   Before the temple I asked for her, *
     and I will search for her until the end.

3   From the first blossom to the ripening grape, *
     my heart delighted in her.

4   My foot walked on the straight path, *
     from my youth I followed her steps.

5   I inclined my ear a little and received her, *
     I found for myself much instruction.

6   I made progress in Wisdom; *
     to the One who sent her, I will give glory.

7   I directed my soul to Wisdom, *
     and in purity have I found her.

8   With her, I gained understanding from the first, *
     therefore will I never be forsaken.

9   My heart was stirred to seek her, *
     with my tongue will I sing God's praise.

      Glory . . .   *Ecclesiasticus 51.13a,13c-17,20,21a,22b*

In prayer I inclined my ear
and my heart was stirred to seek Wisdom.

35 *A SONG OF BARUCH*

Refrain: **Lead us, O God, with joy**
to walk in the light of glory.

1   Arise, O Jerusalem, stand upon the height: *
     look to the east and see your children,

2   Gathered from the west and the east *
     at the word of the Holy One.

3   They rejoice that God has remembered them *
    and has brought them back to you.

4   For God has ordered that every high mountain *
    and the everlasting hills be made low,

5   And the valleys filled up to make level ground *
    so that they may walk safely in the glory of God.

6   The woods and every fragrant tree *
    have shaded them at God's command.

7   For God will lead his people with joy
      in the light of his glory *
    with the mercy and righteousness that comes from God.

Glory . . .   *Baruch 5.5,6c,7-9*

Lead us, O God, with joy
to walk in the light of glory.

36 *BLESS THE LORD*

1   Blessèd are you, the God of our ancestors, *
    worthy to be praised and exalted for ever.

2   Blessèd is your holy and glorious name, *
    worthy to be praised and exalted for ever.

3   Blessèd are you, in your holy and glorious temple, *
    worthy to be praised and exalted for ever.

4   Blessèd are you who look into the depths, *
    worthy to be praised and exalted for ever.

5   Blessèd are you, enthroned on the cherubim, *
    worthy to be praised and exalted for ever.

6   Blessèd are you on the throne of your kingdom, *
    worthy to be praised and exalted for ever.

7   Blessèd are you in the heights of heaven, *
    worthy to be praised and exalted for ever.

Bless the Father, the Son and the Holy Spirit, *
worthy to be praised and exalted for ever.

                                    The Song of the Three 29-34

37a *BENEDICITE – A SONG OF CREATION*

1   Bless the Lord all you works of the Lord:
     sing his praise and exalt him for ever.

2   Bless the Lord you heavens:
     sing his praise and exalt him for ever.

3   Bless the Lord you angels of the Lord:
     bless the Lord all you his hosts;
     bless the Lord you waters above the heavens:
     sing his praise and exalt him for ever.

4   Bless the Lord sun and moon:
     bless the Lord you stars of heaven;
     bless the Lord all rain and dew:
     sing his praise and exalt him for ever.

5   Bless the Lord all winds that blow:
     bless the Lord you fire and heat;
     bless the Lord scorching wind and bitter cold:
     sing his praise and exalt him for ever.

6   Bless the Lord dews and falling snows:
     bless the Lord you nights and days;
     bless the Lord light and darkness:
     sing his praise and exalt him for ever.

7   Bless the Lord frost and cold:
     bless the Lord you ice and snow;
     bless the Lord lightnings and clouds:
     sing his praise and exalt him for ever.

8   O let the earth bless the Lord:
     bless the Lord you mountains and hills;
     bless the Lord all that grows in the ground:
     sing his praise and exalt him for ever.

9   Bless the Lord you springs:
     bless the Lord you seas and rivers;
     bless the Lord you whales
       and all that swim in the waters:
     sing his praise and exalt him for ever.

10   Bless the Lord all birds of the air:
      bless the Lord you beasts and cattle;
      bless the Lord all people on earth:
      sing his praise and exalt him for ever.

11   O people of God bless the Lord:
      bless the Lord you priests of the Lord;
      bless the Lord you servants of the Lord:
      sing his praise and exalt him for ever.

12   **Bless the Lord all you of upright spirit:**
      bless the Lord you that are holy and humble in heart.
      Bless the Father, the Son and the Holy Spirit:
      sing his praise and exalt him for ever.

The Song of the Three 35-65

37b *BENEDICITE – A SONG OF CREATION (shorter version)*

1   Bless the Lord all you works of the Lord: *
      sing his praise and exalt him for ever.

2   Bless the Lord you heavens: *
      sing his praise and exalt him for ever.

3   Bless the Lord you angels of the Lord: *
      sing his praise and exalt him for ever.

4   Bless the Lord all people on earth: *
      sing his praise and exalt him for ever.

5   O people of God bless the Lord: *
      sing his praise and exalt him for ever.

6   Bless the Lord you priests of the Lord: *
      sing his praise and exalt him for ever.

7   Bless the Lord you servants of the Lord: *
      sing his praise and exalt him for ever.

8   Bless the Lord all you of upright spirit: *
      bless the Lord you that are holy and humble in heart.

      Bless the Father, the Son and the Holy Spirit: *
      sing his praise and exalt him for ever.

The Song of the Three 35-37,60-65

Refrain: **Full of compassion and mercy and love**
       is God, the Most High, the Almighty.

1   Lord almighty and God of our ancestors, *
      you who made heaven and earth in all their glory:

2   All things tremble with awe at your presence, *
      before your great and mighty power.

3   Immeasurable and unsearchable is your promised mercy, *
      for you are God, Most High.

4   You are full of compassion, long-suffering
       and very merciful, *
      and you relent at human suffering.

5   O God, according to your great goodness, *
      you have promised forgiveness for repentance
       to those who have sinned against you.

6   The sins I have committed against you *
      are more in number than the sands of the sea.

7   I am not worthy to look up to the height of heaven, *
      because of the multitude of my iniquities.

8   And now I bend the knee of my heart before you, *
      imploring your kindness upon me.

9   I have sinned, O God, I have sinned, *
      and I acknowledge my transgressions.

10   Unworthy as I am, you will save me, *
      according to your great mercy.

11   For all the host of heaven sings your praise, *
      and your glory is for ever and ever.

      Glory . . .   *Manasseh 1a,2,4,6,7a,b,9a,c,11,12,14b,15b*

      Full of compassion and mercy and love
      is God, the Most High, the Almighty.

New Testament Canticles

39 *A SONG OF THE BLESSÈD*

Refrain: **Rejoice and be glad**
for you are the light of the world,
and great is your reward in heaven.

1   Blessèd are the poor in spirit, *
    for theirs is the kingdom of heaven.

2   Blessèd are those who mourn, *
    for they shall be comforted.

3   Blessèd are the meek, *
    for they shall inherit the earth.

4   Blessèd are those who hunger
        and thirst after righteousness, *
    for they shall be satisfied.

5   Blessèd are the merciful, *
    for they shall obtain mercy.

6   Blessèd are the pure in heart, *
    for they shall see God.

7   Blessèd are the peacemakers, *
    for they shall be called children of God.

8   Blessèd are those who suffer persecution
        for righteousness' sake, *
    for theirs is the kingdom of heaven.

Glory . . .   *Matthew 5.3-10*

Rejoice and be glad
for you are the light of the world,
and great is your reward in heaven.

40a *MAGNIFICAT (THE SONG OF MARY)*

1   My soul proclaims the greatness of the Lord,
        my spirit rejoices in God my Saviour; *
    he has looked with favour on his lowly servant.

2   From this day all generations will call me blessèd; *
    the Almighty has done great things for me
        and holy is his name.

3   He has mercy on those who fear him, *
    from generation to generation.

4   He has shown strength with his arm *
    and has scattered the proud in their conceit,

5   Casting down the mighty from their thrones *
    and lifting up the lowly.

6   He has filled the hungry with good things *
    and sent the rich away empty.

7   He has come to the aid of his servant Israel, *
    to remember his promise of mercy,

8   The promise made to our ancestors, *
    to Abraham and his children for ever.

    Glory . . .   *Luke 1.46-55*

40b *MAGNIFICAT (THE SONG OF MARY)*

1   My soul proclaims the greatness of the Lord, *
    my spirit rejoices in God my Saviour,

2   For you, Lord, have looked with favour
        on your lowly servant. *
    From this day all generations will call me blessèd:

3   You, the Almighty, have done great things for me *
    and holy is your name.

4   You have mercy on those who fear you, *
    from generation to generation.

5   You have shown strength with your arm *
    and scattered the proud in their conceit,

6   Casting down the mighty from their thrones *
    and lifting up the lowly.

7   You have filled the hungry with good things *
    and sent the rich away empty.

8   You have come to the aid of your servant Israel, *
       to remember the promise of mercy,

9   The promise made to our ancestors, *
       to Abraham and his children for ever.

       Glory . . .   *Luke 1.46-55, ELLC Alternative Version*

40c   *AN UNFOLDING OF THE MAGNIFICAT*

1   My soul-body swells with love of my Creator, *
       joy fires my heart for my lover, my God.

2   My belovèd has noticed me and loved me,
         a nobody from among the powerless poor. *
       From this time to the end of days,
         all generations will call me blessèd.

3   For Love has drawn me from the shadows: *
       wonderful indeed is the name of our God.

4   Your loving-kindness embraces those
         who are awestruck with wonder and love, *
       held in eternity's moment in time.

5   Your gentleness has shown great strength: *
       the proud have been scattered
         in the fantasies and deceits of their minds.

6   Those drunk with imperial power
         have fallen from their arrogant thrones. *
       The dispossessed on the scrapheap
         have been empowered one with another.

7   The homeless and the hungry
         have been fed with their share of the harvest. *
       The greedy who hold on to their wealth
         have seen it all crumble and vanish.

8   Just and compassionate God,
         giving a new name to the deprived and invisible,
         you fulfil your covenants of promise. *
       Long ago you gave Abraham your blessing,
         and to Sarah, both faithful and true.

9   Your love reaches every generation, *
     to the earth's little people, for ever.

10   Now is the blessing renewed: *
     I give you my heartfelt thanks
          with eyes that are shining with love,
          with the Presence gestating within me.

     Glory . . .   *Jim Cotter*

41a *BENEDICTUS (THE SONG OF ZECHARIAH)*

1   ✠ Blessèd be the Lord the God of Israel, *
     who has come to his people and set them free.

2   He has raised up for us a mighty Saviour, *
     born of the house of his servant David.

3   Through his holy prophets God promised of old *
     to save us from our enemies,
          from the hands of all that hate us,

4   To show mercy to our ancestors, *
     and to remember his holy covenant.

5   This was the oath God swore to our father Abraham: *
     to set us free from the hands of our enemies,

6   Free to worship him without fear, *
     holy and righteous in his sight
          all the days of our life.

7   And you, child, shall be called the prophet of the Most High, *
     for you will go before the Lord to prepare his way,

8   To give his people knowledge of salvation *
     by the forgiveness of all their sins.

9   In the tender compassion of our God *
     the dawn from on high shall break upon us,

10   To shine on those who dwell in darkness
          and the shadow of death, *
     and to guide our feet into the way of peace.

     Glory . . .   *Luke 1.68-79*

41b *BENEDICTUS (THE SONG OF ZECHARIAH)*

1   Blessèd are you, Lord, the God of Israel, *
      for you have come to your people and set them free.

2   You have raised up for us a mighty Saviour, *
      born of the house of your servant, David.

3   Through your holy prophets, you promised of old *
      to save us from our enemies,
        from the hands of all who hate us,

4   To show mercy to our ancestors, *
      and to remember your holy covenant.

5   This was the oath you swore to our father Abraham, *
      to set us free from the hands of our enemies,

6   Free to worship you without fear, *
      holy and righteous before you,
        all the days of our life.

7   And you, child, shall be called the prophet of the Most High, *
      for you will go before the Lord to prepare the way,

8   To give God's people knowledge of salvation *
      by the forgiveness of their sins.

9   In the tender compassion of our God *
      the dawn from on high shall break upon us,

10 To shine on those who dwell in darkness
        and the shadow of death, *
      and to guide our feet into the way of peace.

      Glory . . .   *Luke 1.68-79, ELLC Alternative Version*

41c *AN UNFOLDING OF THE BENEDICTUS*

1   We praise you, God of freedom, *
      releasing all who are imprisoned,

2   Raising up for us a powerful deliverer, *
      a descendant of God's servant, David.

3   Such was your promise, long, long ago, *
      by the lips of your holy prophets,

4   That you would free us from the grip of evil, *
    from the powers that ensnare us.

5   This was your covenant of old, *
    that you would treat us with justice
        and compassion,

6   That we might serve you without fear, *
    truthful and courageous our whole life long.

7   John, forerunner, from the womb, *
    you were called to be a prophet
        to prepare God's way,

8   Going before the Liberator
        who will lead us to our freedom, *
    disarming the powers of evil
        and opening the prison doors.

9   For in the tender mercies of our God *
    the rising sun has burst upon our lives,

10 Giving light to those who dwell in darkness
        and in the shadow of death, *
    and guiding our feet into ways of peace.

    Glory ...   *Jim Cotter*

42a *NUNC DIMITTIS (THE SONG OF SIMEON)*

1   Now, Lord, you let your servant go in peace: *
    your word has been fulfilled.

2   My own eyes have seen the salvation *
    which you have prepared in the sight of every people:

3   A light to reveal you to the nations *
    and the glory of your people Israel.

    Glory ...   *Luke 2.29-32*

42b AN UNFOLDING OF THE NUNC DIMITTIS

1 Thanks be to God, I have lived to see this day. *
   God's promise is fulfilled, and my duty done.

2 At last you have given me peace,
      for I have seen with my own eyes *
   the revelation you have prepared for all peoples,

3 A light to the world in its darkness, *
   the glory of all who serve your love.

   Glory . . .   *Jim Cotter*

43 A SONG OF THE JUSTIFIED

Refrain: **Our hope is not in vain,
      because God's love has been poured into our hearts.**

1 God reckons as righteous those who believe, *
   who believe in him who raised Jesus from the dead;

2 For Christ was handed over to death for our sins, *
   and raised to life for our justification.

3 Since we are justified by faith, *
   we have peace with God through our Lord Jesus Christ.

4 Through Christ we have gained access
      to the grace in which we stand, *
   and rejoice in our hope of the glory of God.

5 We even exult in our sufferings, *
   for suffering produces endurance,

6 And endurance brings hope, *
   and our hope is not in vain,

7 Because God's love has been poured into our hearts, *
   through the Holy Spirit, given to us.

8 God proves his love for us: *
   while we were yet sinners Christ died for us.

9 Since we have been justified by his death, *
   how much more shall we be saved from God's wrath.

10 Therefore, we exult in God through our Lord Jesus Christ, *
    in whom we have now received our reconciliation.

    Glory . . .   *Romans 4.24,25;5.1-5,8,9,11*

    Our hope is not in vain,
    because God's love has been poured into our hearts.

44 *A SONG OF GOD'S CHILDREN*

Refrain: **The Spirit of the Father,**
       who raised Christ Jesus from the dead,
       gives life to the people of God.

1   The law of the Spirit of life in Christ Jesus *
    has set us free from the law of sin and death.

2   All who are led by the Spirit of God are children of God; *
    for we have received the Spirit that enables us to cry, 'Abba, Father'.

3   The Spirit himself bears witness that we are children of God *
    and if God's children, then heirs of God;

4   If heirs of God, then fellow-heirs with Christ; *
    since we suffer with him now, that we may be glorified with him.

5   These sufferings that we now endure *
    are not worth comparing to the glory that shall be revealed.

6   For the creation waits with eager longing *
    for the revealing of the children of God.

    Glory . . .   *Romans 8.2,14,15b-19*

    The Spirit of the Father,
    who raised Christ Jesus from the dead,
    gives life to the people of God.

45 *A SONG OF DIVINE LOVE*

Refrain: **Love bears all things**
       and will never come to an end.

1   Love is patient and kind, *
    love is not jealous or boastful,
       it is not arrogant or rude.

2   Love does not insist on its own way, *
    it is not angry or resentful.

3   It does not rejoice in wrongdoing *
    but rejoices in the truth.

4   Love bears all things and believes all things; *
    love hopes all things and endures all things.

5   Love will never come to an end, *
    but prophecy will vanish,
        tongues cease and knowledge pass away.

6   Now we know only in part *
    and we prophesy only in part,

7   But when the perfect comes, *
    the partial shall pass away.

8   When I was a child, I spoke like a child, *
    I thought like a child, I reasoned like a child.

9   But when I became mature, *
    I put an end to childish ways.

10 For now we see only puzzling reflections in a mirror, *
    but then we will see face to face.

11 Now I know only in part; *
    then I shall know fully,
        even as I have been fully known.

12 There are three things that last for ever,
        faith, hope and love, *
    but the greatest of these is love.

    Glory . . .   *1 Corinthians 13.4-13*

    **Love bears all things
    and will never come to an end.**

Refrain: **The glorious grace of God**
            is freely bestowed on us in the Beloved.

1   Blessèd are you,
         the God and Father of our Lord Jesus Christ, *
     for you have blest us in Christ Jesus
         with every spiritual blessing in the heavenly places.

2   You chose us to be yours in Christ
         before the foundation of the world, *
     that we should be holy and blameless before you.

3   In love you destined us for adoption as your children,
         through Jesus Christ, *
     according to the purpose of your will,

4   To the praise of your glorious grace, *
     which you freely bestowed on us in the Beloved.

5   In you, we have redemption
         through the blood of Christ, *
     the forgiveness of our sins,

6   According to the riches of your grace, *
     which you have lavished upon us.

7   You have made known to us, in all wisdom and insight, *
     the mystery of your will,

8   According to your purpose
         which you set forth in Christ, *
     as a plan for the fullness of time,

9   To unite all things in Christ, *
     things in heaven and things on earth.

Glory . . .   *Ephesians 1.3-10*

The glorious grace of God
is freely bestowed on us in the Beloved.

47 *THE SONG OF CHRIST'S GLORY*

Refrain: **At the name of Jesus
every knee shall bow.**

1   Christ Jesus was in the form of God, *
    but he did not cling to equality with God.

2   He emptied himself, taking the form of a servant, *
    and was born in our human likeness.

3   Being found in human form he humbled himself, *
    and became obedient unto death, even death on a cross.

4   Therefore God has highly exalted him, *
    and bestowed on him the name above every name,

5   That at the name of Jesus every knee should bow, *
    in heaven and on earth and under the earth;

6   And every tongue confess that Jesus Christ is Lord, *
    to the glory of God the Father.

Glory . . .   *Philippians 2.5-11*

**At the name of Jesus
every knee shall bow.**

48 *A SONG OF REDEMPTION*

Refrain: **Christ is the image of the invisible God,
the firstborn of all creation.**

1   The Father has delivered us from the dominion of darkness, *
    and transferred us to the kingdom of his beloved Son;

2   In whom we have redemption, *
    the forgiveness of our sins.

3   He is the image of the invisible God, *
    the firstborn of all creation.

4   For in him all things were created, *
    in heaven and on earth, visible and invisible.

5   All things were created through him and for him, *
    he is before all things and in him all things hold together.

6   He is the head of the body, the Church, *
       he is the beginning, the firstborn from the dead.

7   In him all the fullness of God was pleased to dwell; *
       and through him God was pleased to reconcile all things.

     Glory . . .   *Colossians 1.13-18a,19,20a*

     Christ is the image of the invisible God,
     the firstborn of all creation.

49 *A SONG OF CHRIST'S APPEARING*

Refrain: **Christ was believed in throughout the world**
          and taken up in glory.

1   Christ Jesus was revealed in the flesh *
       and vindicated in the spirit.

2   He was seen by angels *
       and proclaimed among the nations.

3   Believed in throughout the world, *
       he was taken up in glory.

4   This will be made manifest at the proper time *
       by the blessèd and only Sovereign,

5   Who alone has immortality, *
       and dwells in unapproachable light.

     To the King of kings and Lord of lords *
     be honour and eternal dominion. Amen.

                             1 Timothy 3.16;6.15,16

     Christ was believed in throughout the world
     and taken up in glory.

50 *A SONG OF GOD'S ASSEMBLED*

Refrain: **We have come before the throne of God**
          to share in the inheritance of the saints in light.

1   We have come before God's holy mountain, *
       to the heavenly Jerusalem, the city of the living God.

2   We have come before countless angels making festival, *
    before the assembly of the firstborn citizens of heaven.

3   We have come before God, who is judge of all, *
    before the spirits of the just made perfect.

4   We have come before Jesus, *
    the mediator of the new covenant.

5   We are receiving a kingdom that cannot be shaken: *
    so let us give thanks and offer to God acceptable worship,

6   Full of reverence and awe; *
    for our God is a consuming fire.

Glory . . .   *Hebrews 12.22-24a,28,29*

**We have come before the throne of God
to share in the inheritance of the saints in light.**

51 *A SONG OF FAITH*

Refrain: **God raised Christ from the dead,
          the Lamb without spot or stain.**

1   Blessèd be the God and Father *
    of our Lord Jesus Christ!

2   By his great mercy we have been born anew to a living hope *
    through the resurrection of Jesus Christ from the dead,

3   Into an inheritance that is imperishable, undefiled and unfading, *
    kept in heaven for you,

4   Who are being protected by the power of God through faith, *
    for a salvation ready to be revealed in the last time.

5   You were ransomed from the futile ways of your ancestors *
    not with perishable things like silver or gold

6   But with the precious blood of Christ *
    like that of a lamb without spot or stain.

7   Through him you have confidence in God,
       who raised him from the dead and gave him glory, *
    so that your faith and hope are set on God.

Glory . . .   *1 Peter 1.3-5,18,19,21*

**God raised Christ from the dead,
the Lamb without spot or stain.**

52 *A SONG OF CHRIST THE SERVANT*

Refrain: **Christ committed no sin,
no guile was found on his lips.**

1   Christ suffered for you, leaving you an example, *
    that you should follow in his steps.

2   He committed no sin, no guile was found on his lips, *
    when he was reviled, he did not revile in turn.

3   When he suffered, he did not threaten, *
    but he trusted himself to God who judges justly.

4   Christ himself bore our sins in his body on the tree, *
    that we might die to sin and live to righteousness.

5   By his wounds, you have been healed,
        for you were straying like sheep, *
    but have now returned
        to the shepherd and guardian of your souls.

    Glory . . .   *1 Peter 2.21b-25*

**Christ committed no sin,
no guile was found on his lips.**

53 *A SONG OF REPENTANCE*

Refrain: **Tell the good news of Jesus the Christ
to all who are searching for redemption.**

1   This is the message we have heard from Christ
        and proclaim to you: *
    that God is light,
        in whom there is no darkness at all.

2   If we say that we have fellowship with God
        while we walk in darkness, *
    we lie and do not do what is true.

3   But if we walk in the light
        as God is in the light, *
    we have fellowship with one another.

4   And the blood of Jesus, the Son of God, *
    cleanses us from all our sins.

5   If we say that we have no sin, *
    we deceive ourselves
        and the truth is not in us.

6   If we confess our sins, *
    the One who is faithful and just will forgive us
        and cleanse us from all unrighteousness.

Glory . . .   *1 John 1.5-9*

**Tell the good news of Jesus the Christ
to all who are searching for redemption.**

54 *A SONG OF GOD'S LOVE*

Refrain: **God's love was revealed among us
        so that we might live through Jesus.**

1   Beloved, let us love one another,
        for love is of God; *
    everyone who loves is born of God and knows God.

2   Whoever does not love does not know God, *
    for God is love.

3   In this the love of God was revealed among us, *
    that God sent his only Son into the world,
        so that we might live through him.

4   In this is love,
        not that we loved God but that he loved us, *
    and sent his Son to be the expiation for our sins.

5   Beloved, since God loved us so much, *
    we ought also to love one another.

6   For if we love one another, God abides in us, *
    and God's love will be perfected in us.

Glory . . .   *1 John 4.7-11,12b*

**God's love was revealed among us
so that we might live through Jesus.**

55 *A SONG OF PRAISE*

Refrain: **You created all things, O God,
and are worthy of our praise for ever.**

1   You are worthy, our Lord and God, *
     to receive glory and honour and power.

2   For you have created all things, *
     and by your will they have their being.

3   You are worthy, O Lamb, for you were slain, *
     and by your blood you ransomed for God
         saints from every tribe and language and nation.

4   You have made them to be a kingdom and priests
         serving our God, *
     and they will reign with you on earth.

**To the One who sits on the throne and to the Lamb *
be blessing and honour and glory and might,
for ever and ever. Amen.**

Revelation 4.11;5.9b,10

**You created all things, O God,
and are worthy of our praise for ever.**

56 *A SONG OF THE REDEEMED*

Refrain: **Salvation belongs to our God,
who will guide us to springs of living water.**

1   Behold, a great multitude *
     which no one could number,

2   From every nation,
         from all tribes and peoples and tongues, *
     standing before the throne and the Lamb.

3   They were clothed in white robes
         and had palms in their hands, *
     and they cried with a loud voice, saying,

4   'Salvation belongs to our God
        who sits on the throne, *
    and to the Lamb.'

5   These are they
        who have come out of the great tribulation, *
    they have washed their robes
        and made them white in the blood of the Lamb;

6   Therefore they stand before the throne of God, *
    whom they serve day and night within the temple.

7   And the One who sits upon the throne *
    will shelter them with his presence.

8   They shall never again feel hunger or thirst, *
    the sun shall not strike them,
        nor any scorching heat.

9   For the Lamb at the heart of the throne *
    will be their Shepherd,

10 He will guide them to springs of living water, *
    and God will wipe away every tear from their eyes.

To the One who sits on the throne and to the Lamb *
be blessing and honour and glory and might,
for ever and ever. Amen.

Revelation 7.9,10,14b-17

Salvation belongs to our God,
who will guide us to springs of living water.

57 GREAT AND WONDERFUL

Refrain: **All nations shall come and worship you, O Christ,**
        and share in the feast of your kingdom.

1   Great and wonderful are your deeds, *
    Lord God the Almighty.

2   Just and true are your ways, *
    O ruler of the nations.

3   Who shall not revere and praise your name, O Lord? *
    for you alone are holy.

4   All nations shall come and worship in your presence: *
      for your just dealings have been revealed.

To the One who sits on the throne and to the Lamb *
be blessing and honour and glory and might,
for ever and ever. Amen.

Revelation 15.3,4

All nations shall come and worship you, O Christ,
and share in the feast of your kingdom.

58 *A SONG OF THE LAMB*

Refrain: **Let us rejoice and exult**
       and give glory and homage to our God.

1   Salvation and glory and power belong to our God, *
      whose judgements are true and just.

2   Praise our God, all you his servants, *
      all who fear him, both small and great.

3   The Lord our God, the Almighty, reigns: *
      let us rejoice and exult and give him the glory.

4   For the marriage of the Lamb has come *
      and his bride has made herself ready.

5   Blessèd are those who are invited *
      to the wedding banquet of the Lamb.

To the One who sits on the throne and to the Lamb *
be blessing and honour and glory and might,
for ever and ever. Amen.

Revelation 19.1b,2a,5b,6b,7,9b

Let us rejoice and exult
and give glory and homage to our God.

59 *A SONG OF THE HOLY CITY*

Refrain: **I saw the holy city**
       coming down out of heaven from God.

1   I saw a new heaven and a new earth, *
    for the first heaven and the first earth had passed away
        and the sea was no more.

2   And I saw the holy city, new Jerusalem,
        coming down out of heaven from God, *
    prepared as a bride adorned for her husband.

3   And I heard a great voice from the throne saying, *
    'Behold, the dwelling of God is among mortals.

4   'He will dwell with them and they shall be his peoples, *
    and God himself will be with them.

5   'He will wipe every tear from their eyes, *
    and death shall be no more.

6   'Neither shall there be mourning,
        nor crying, nor pain any more, *
    for the former things have passed away.'

7   And the One who sat upon the throne said, *
    'Behold, I make all things new.'

   To the One who sits on the throne and to the Lamb *
   be blessing and honour and glory and might,
   for ever and ever. Amen.

                                               Revelation 21.1-5a

   I saw the holy city
   coming down out of heaven from God.

60 *A SONG OF THE HEAVENLY CITY*

Refrain: **By the river stood the tree of life,**
       with healing for all the nations.

1   I saw no temple in the city, *
    for its temple is the Lord God the Almighty
        and the Lamb.

2   And the city has no need of sun or moon
        to shine upon it, *
    for the glory of God is its light,
        and its lamp is the Lamb.

3   By its light the nations shall walk, *
    and the rulers of the earth
        shall bring their glory into it.

4   Its gates shall never be shut by day,
        nor shall there be any night; *
    they shall bring into it
        the glory and honour of the nations.

5   I saw the river of the water of life,
        bright as crystal, *
    flowing from the throne of God and of the Lamb.

6   And either side of the river stood the tree of life,
        yielding its fruit each month, *
    and the leaves of the tree
        were for the healing of the nations.

7   The throne of God and of the Lamb shall be there,
        and his servants shall worship him; *
    and they shall see his face
        and his name shall be on their foreheads.

    To the One who sits on the throne and to the Lamb *
    be blessing and honour and glory and might,
    for ever and ever. Amen.

                                    Revelation 21.22-26;22.1,2b,d,3b,4

    By the river stood the tree of life,
    with healing for all the nations.

61 *A SONG OF THE SPIRIT*

Refrain: **Surely I am coming soon.**
            Amen. Come, Lord Jesus!

1   'Behold, I am coming soon', says the Lord,
        'and bringing my reward with me, *
    to give to everyone according to their deeds.

2 'I am the Alpha and the Omega, the first and the last, *
the beginning and the end.'

3 Blessèd are those who do God's commandments,
that they may have the right to the tree of life, *
and may enter into the city through the gates.

4 'I, Jesus, have sent my angel to you, *
with this testimony for all the churches.

5 'I am the root and the offspring of David, *
I am the bright morning star.'

6 'Come!' say the Spirit and the Bride; *
'Come!' let each hearer reply.

7 Come forward, you who are thirsty, *
let those who desire
take the water of life as a gift.

To the One who sits on the throne and to the Lamb *
be blessing and honour and glory and might,
for ever and ever. Amen.

Revelation 22.12-14,16,17

Surely I am coming soon.
Amen. Come, Lord Jesus!

62a *THE EASTER ANTHEMS*

1 Christ our passover has been sacrificed for us: *
so let us celebrate the feast,

2 Not with the old leaven of corruption and wickedness: *
but with the unleavened bread of sincerity and truth.

1 Corinthians 5.7b,8

3 Christ once raised from the dead dies no more: *
death has no more dominion over him.

4 In dying he died to sin once for all: *
in living he lives to God.

5 See yourselves therefore as dead to sin: *
and alive to God in Jesus Christ our Lord.

Romans 6.9-11

6   Christ has been raised from the dead: *
    the first fruits of those who sleep.

7   For since by one man came death: *
    by another has come also the resurrection of the dead;

8   For as in Adam all die: *
    even so in Christ shall all be made alive.

1 Corinthians 15.20-22

Glory . . .

62b *THE EASTER ANTHEMS*

1   We praise you, O Christ, risen from the dead *
    breaking death's dominion, rising from the grave.

2   Absorbing in yourself the force of evil's ways *
    you destroyed death's age-old sting,
        and now you are alive for evermore.

3   Let us find our life in you *
    breaking through our fear of everlasting void.

4   For you are risen from the dead *
    the first fruits of those who sleep.

5   From the days of first awareness
        we betrayed the call of life *
    yet yearned for that communion
        which still we dimly sense.

6   Pain and evil, malice and cruel greed *
    these deepened the sorrow of our hearts.

7   Yet they are done away in light of glorious dawn *
    the victory of resurrection day.

8   At one with all who've lived,
        so all of us have died *
    at one with your humanity,
        all shall be made alive.

Jim Cotter

Glory . . .

Other Canticles

63a *PHOS HILARON – A SONG OF THE LIGHT*

1   O gladdening light, of the holy glory of the immortal Father, *
    heavenly, holy, blessèd, O Jesus Christ.

2   Now that we have come to the setting of the sun
        and see the evening light, *
    we give praise to God, Father, Son and Holy Spirit.

3   Worthy are you at all times to be worshipped
        with holy voices,
        O Son of God and giver of life: *
    therefore all the world glorifies you.

63b *PHOS HILARON – A SONG OF THE LIGHT*

1   O joyful light,
        from the pure glory of God eternal in heaven, *
    O holy, blessèd Jesus Christ.

2   As we come to the setting of the sun *
    and see the evening light,

3   We give thanks and praise to God *
    ever blessèd Trinity.

4   Worthy are you at all times
        to be sung with holy voices,
        O Son of God, O Giver of life, *
    and to be glorified through all creation.

CSF, Province of the Americas

63c *PHOS HILARON – A SONG OF THE LIGHT*

1   Hail, gladdening Light, of his pure glory poured,
        Who is the immortal Father, heavenly, blest,
    Holiest of Holies, Jesus Christ our Lord.

2   Now we are come to the Sun's hour of rest,
        The lights of evening round us shine,
    We hymn the Father, Son and Holy Spirit divine.

3   Worthy are you at all times to be sung
        With undefilèd tongue,
    Son of our God, giver of life, alone:
    Therefore in all the world your glories,
        Lord, they own.

tr. John Keble *

63d   *PHOS HILARON – A SONG OF THE LIGHT*

Light of the world, in grace and beauty,
mirror of God's eternal face,
transparent flame of love's free duty,
you bring salvation to our race.
Now as we see the lights of evening,
we raise our voice in hymns of praise:
worthy are you of endless blessing,
sun of our night, lamp of our days.

Metrical version – tr. Paul Gibson; tune: Rendez à Dieu

63e   *PHOS HILARON – A SONG OF THE LIGHT*

1   O gladsome light, O grace
    Of God the Father's face,
    The eternal splendour wearing;
    Celestial, holy, blest,
    Our Saviour Jesus Christ,
    Joyful in your appearing.

2   As day fades into night,
    We see the evening light,
    Our hymn of praise outpouring:
    Father of might unknown,
    Christ, his incarnate Son,
    And Holy Spirit, adoring.

3   To you of right belongs
    All praise of holy songs,
    O Son of God, Lifegiver;
    You, therefore, O Most High,
    The world will glorify,
    And shall exalt for ever.

tr. Robert Bridges *

64a TE DEUM LAUDAMUS – A SONG OF THE CHURCH

1 We praise you, O God,
we acclaim you as the Lord;

2 all creation worships you,
the Father everlasting.

3 To you all angels, all the powers of heaven,
the cherubim and seraphim, sing in endless praise:

4 **Holy, holy, holy Lord, God of power and might,
heaven and earth are full of your glory.**

5 The glorious company of apostles praise you.
The noble fellowship of prophets praise you.

6 The white-robed army of martyrs praise you.
Throughout the world the holy Church acclaims you:

7 **Father, of majesty unbounded,
your true and only Son, worthy of all praise,
the Holy Spirit, advocate and guide.**

8 You, Christ, are the King of glory,
the eternal Son of the Father.

9 When you took our flesh to set us free
you humbly chose the Virgin's womb.

10 You overcame the sting of death
and opened the kingdom of heaven to all believers.

11 You are seated at God's right hand in glory.
We believe that you will come and be our judge.

12 **Come then, Lord, and help your people,
bought with the price of your own blood,
and bring us with your saints
to glory everlasting.**

64b AN UNFOLDING OF THE TE DEUM

1 Men and women: praise the God of Love.
Earth and sky worship the Creator.

2   Angelic powers of light eternal,
    penetrating the ancient dark:
    lift your voices with the song:

3   Holy, holy, holy, strange mysterious power,
    the whole creation is full of your glory.

4   Saints and holy fools of every generation,
        sing alleluia, alleluia.
    Prophets crying out for justice,
        sing alleluia, alleluia.

5   Martyrs who carried you in their wounds,
    scars embodied in their glory,
        sing alleluia, alleluia.
    Your holy and stumbling people
    in all times and places
        sing alleluia, alleluia.

6   Giver of life, of splendour and wonder,
        tender, of infinite patience!
    Bearer of pain, graceful and true,
        with wounds bringing salve!
    Maker of love, flaming and passionate
        guiding us into the truth!

7   Universal Christ, we greet you in your glory,
        hidden deep in the being of God,
    Word made flesh to deliver us,
        brought to life by human touch,

8   Glad to be born of Mary,
    embodying the divine,
    withdrawing the sting of death,
    terrifying us with love unbounded,
    offering to fulfil all we could desire,
    opening the road to God's presence for ever,

9   Guarding the freedom of the creation,
    yearning for the gathering of the harvest.

10 **Come, then, judge and deliver us,**
    who are freed at the cost of your life,
    give us integrity to refuse what is evil,
    give us your Spirit to discern what is true,
    and lead us with all your saints
    to lands of eternal glory.

Jim Cotter

65 *A SONG OF EPHREM THE SYRIAN*

1   Behold: Fire and Spirit in the womb that bore you: *
    Behold: Fire and Spirit in the river where you were baptized.

2   Fire and Spirit in our baptism: *
    In the Bread and the Cup, Fire and Holy Spirit.

3   In your Bread is hidden a Spirit not to be eaten, *
    In your Wine dwells a Fire not to be drunk.

4   Spirit in your Bread, Fire in your Wine, *
    A wonder set apart, yet received by our lips.

5   How wonderful your footsteps, walking on the waters! *
    You subdued the great sea beneath your feet.

6   Yet to a little stream you subjected your head, *
    Bending down to be baptized in it.

7   The stream was like John who performed the baptism in it, *
    In their smallness each an image of the other.

8   To the stream so little, to the servant so weak, *
    The Lord of them both subjected himself.

66 *SALUS AETERNA – SAVIOUR ETERNAL*

    Saviour eternal,
    life of the world unfailing,
    light everlasting
    and our true redemption.

    Taking our humanity
    in your loving freedom,
    you rescued our lost earth
    and filled the world with joy.

By your first advent, justify us,
by your second, set us free:
that when the great light dawns
and you come as judge of all,
we may be robed in immortality
and ready, Lord, to follow
in your footsteps blest, wherever they may lead.

after the Advent Sequence

67 *A SONG OF ANSELM*

Refrain: **Gather your little ones to you, O God,
as a hen gathers her brood to protect them.**

1   Jesus, like a mother you gather your people to you; *
you are gentle with us as a mother with her children.

2   Often you weep over our sins and our pride, *
tenderly you draw us from hatred and judgement.

3   You comfort us in sorrow and bind up our wounds, *
in sickness you nurse us, and with pure milk you feed us.

4   Jesus, by your dying we are born to new life; *
by your anguish and labour we come forth in joy.

5   Despair turns to hope through your sweet goodness; *
through your gentleness we find comfort in fear.

6   Your warmth gives life to the dead, *
your touch makes sinners righteous.

7   Lord Jesus, in your mercy heal us; *
in your love and tenderness remake us.

8   In your compassion bring grace and forgiveness, *
for the beauty of heaven may your love prepare us.

    Glory . . .   *Anselm of Canterbury, tr. Michael Vasey*

**Gather your little ones to you, O God,
as a hen gathers her brood to protect them.**

68 *VICTIMAE PASCHALI – A SONG OF THE RESURRECTION*

Come, Christians, bring your sacrifice of praise
to Jesus Christ, our conquering victim and our Easter king.
Jesus, the sinless lamb, has saved the sinful flock
and reconciled us to the Father.

Death and life have wrestled
in a wondrous fight,
the leader of the living
fell to the powers of night
dead, yet he reigns in power
his strange victory to share.

Speak, Mary, friend of Christ,
what did you see on sorrow's road?
Tell us your story.

'I saw the tomb of the living Christ.
I saw his resurrection glory.
I saw the witnessing angels.
I saw the head-cloth and the shroud.
Christ my hope has risen,
and goes before his own to Galilee.'

Trust Mary, believers,
for only she has truth to tell,
unlike the falsifying crowd
of rumour-makers and deceivers.

**We know that Christ is truly risen,
defeating death and hell's dark thrall,
so conquering king, have mercy on us all.
Alleluia.**

after the Easter Sequence

69a *THE CANTICLE OF THE CREATURES*

1   Most High, all powerful, good Lord, *
yours are the praises, the glory, the honour
    and all blessing.

2   To you alone, Most High, do they belong *
and no human is worthy to mention your name.

3   Praised be you, my Lord, with all your creatures,
        especially Sir Brother Sun, *
    who is the day and through whom you give us light.

4   And he is beautiful and radiant with great splendour; *
    and bears a likeness of you, Most High One.

5   Praised be you, my Lord, through Sister Moon and the stars: *
    in heaven you formed them clear and precious and beautiful.

6   Praised be you, my Lord, through Brother Wind; *
    and through the air, cloudy and serene, and every kind of weather,
        through which you give sustenance to your creatures.

7   Praised be you, my Lord, through Sister Water, *
    who is very useful and humble and precious and chaste.

8   Praised be you, my Lord, through Brother Fire,
        through whom you light the night: *
    and he is beautiful and playful and robust and strong.

9   Praised be you, my Lord, through our Sister, Mother Earth,
        who sustains and governs us *
    and who produces various fruit
        with coloured flowers and herbs.

10 Praised be you, my Lord,
        through those who give pardon for your love *
    and bear infirmity and tribulation.

11 Blessèd are those who endure in peace: *
    for by you, Most High, shall they be crowned.

12 Praised be you, my Lord, for our Sister,
        Bodily Death, *
    from whom no one living can escape:
        woe to those who die in mortal sin.

13 Blessèd are those whom death will find
        in your most holy will, *
    for the second death shall do them no harm.

14 Praise and bless my Lord and give him thanks *
    and serve him with great humility.

                                            Francis of Assisi

69b *THE CANTICLE OF THE CREATURES (metrical version)*

1   Most High, omnipotent, good Lord,
     To you be ceaseless praise outpoured,
     And blessing without measure;
     From you alone all creatures came;
     No one is worthy you to name.

2   My Lord be praised by Brother Sun,
     Who through the skies his course does run,
     And shines in brilliant splendour;
     With brightness he does fill the day,
     And signifies your boundless sway.

3   My Lord be praised by Sister Moon,
     And all the stars that with her soon
     Will point the glitt'ring heavens.
     Let wind and air and cloud and calm,
     And weathers all, repeat the psalm.

4   By Sister Water, then be blest
     Most humble, useful, precious, chaste.
     Be praised by Brother Fire:
     Cheerful is he, robust and bright,
     And strong to lighten all the night.

5   By Mother Earth my Lord be praised;
     Governed by you, she has upraised
     What for our life is needful.
     Sustained by you through every hour,
     She brings forth fruit and herb and flower.

6   My Lord be praised by those who prove
     In free forgivingness their love,
     Nor shrink from tribulation.
     Happy, who peaceably endure:
     With you, Lord, their reward is sure.

7   By Death, our Sister, praisèd be,
     From whom no one alive can flee.
     Woe to the unpreparèd!
     But blest be those who do your will
     And follow your commandments still.

8   Most High, omnipotent, good Lord,
         To you be ceaseless praise outpoured
         And blessing without measure.
         Let every creature thankful be
         And serve in great humility.

after Francis of Assisi

70a *A SONG OF CLARE OF ASSISI*

Refrain: **Transform your entire being
into the image of the Godhead itself.**

1   Place your mind before the mirror of eternity! *
         Your soul in the brilliance of glory!

2   Your heart in the figure of the divine substance *
         and, through contemplation,

3   Transform your entire being *
         into the image of the Godhead itself,

4   So that you too may feel what God's friends feel *
         in tasting the hidden sweetness,

5   Reserved from the beginning, *
         for all who love God.

6   May you totally love God *
         whose self-giving was totally for your love,

7   At whose beauty the sun and the moon marvel, *
         whose rewards and their uniqueness and grandeur have no limits.

      Glory . . .   *from The Third Letter to Agnes of Prague, Clare of Assisi*

**Transform your entire being
into the image of the Godhead itself.**

70b *A SONG OF CLARE OF ASSISI*

Refrain: *Place your mind in the mirror of eternity!*
            Place your soul in the splendour of glory!
            Place your heart in the icon of the substance divine,
            contemplating, be transformed into the image
                of the Godhead itself.

1   Taste and know the hidden sweetness of God,
     for all time existing to be found by those who love
     the sacred banquet which all may share, if they dare.
     All it costs is everything,
     a heart open, longing, trusting, giving.

     Refrain

2   Taste and know the hidden sweetness of God,
     whose beauty is endless and whose love
        inflames our love;
     Whose contemplation refreshes us, brings us joy –
     All our being overflows with you,
     O Most Holy, fragrant Lover.

Refrain: *Place your mind in the mirror of eternity!*
            Place your soul in the splendour of glory!
            Place your heart in the icon of the substance divine,
            contemplating, be transformed into the image
                of the Godhead itself.

Jean Malcolm, after Clare of Assisi

71 *VENI SANCTE SPIRITUS – COME, HOLY SPIRIT*

Come, Holy Spirit;
send down from heaven's height
your radiant light.

Come, lamp of every heart,
come, parent of the poor;
all gifts are yours.

Comforter beyond all comforting,
sweet unexpected guest,
sweetly refresh.

Rest in hard labour,
coolness in heavy heat,
hurt souls' relief.

Refill the secret hearts
of your faithful,
O most blessèd light.

Without your holy power
nothing can bear your light,
nothing is free from sin.

Wash all that is filthy,
water all that is parched,
heal what is hurt within.

Bend all that is rigid,
warm all that has frozen hard,
lead back the lost.

Give to your faithful ones,
who come in simple trust,
your sevenfold mystery.

Give virtue its reward,
give, in the end, salvation
and joy that has no end.

after the Golden Sequence

72 *A SONG OF MERCY AND GRACE*

Refrain: **God is the light and the grace,
which is all blessèd love.**

1   Jesus is our true mother, *
     the protector of the love which knows no end.

2   We have our being from Jesus, *
     where the foundation of motherhood begins.

3   God revealed that in all things, *
     as truly as God is our father
        so truly God is our mother.

4   God is the power and goodness of fatherhood; *
     God is the wisdom and loving kindness of motherhood.

5 God is the Trinity and God is the Unity; *
   God is all our life:
        nature, mercy and grace.

6 God is the one who makes us to love, *
   and the endless fulfilling of all true desires;

7 For where the soul is highest and noblest, *
   then it is humble and lowly.

8 God desired Christ to be our mother,
        our brother and our Saviour, *
   for God knows us now
        and loved us before time began.

9 In nature, Jesus is our true mother
        by our first creation, *
   and in grace by taking our created nature.

10 All the love of offering and sacrifice
        of belovèd motherhood, *
   are in Christ our Belovèd.

11 For in Jesus we have this godly will, *
   both in nature and in grace.

   Glory . . .   *Julian of Norwich*

   **God is the light and the grace,
   which is all blessèd love.**

73 *A SONG OF TRUE MOTHERHOOD*

Refrain: **Christ came in our poor flesh
        to share a mother's care.**

1 God chose to be our mother in all things *
   and so made the foundation of his work,
        most humble and most pure,
        in the Virgin's womb.

2 God, the perfect wisdom of all, *
   arrayed himself in this humble place.

3 Christ came in our poor flesh *
   to share a mother's care.

4   Our mothers bear us for pain and for death; *
    our true mother, Jesus,
        bears us for joy and endless life.

5   Christ carried us within him in love and travail, *
    until the full time of his passion.

6   And when all was completed
        and he had carried us so for joy, *
    still all this could not satisfy
        the power of his wonderful love.

7   All that we owe is redeemed in truly loving God, *
    for the love of Christ works in us;
        Christ is the one whom we love.

    Glory . . .   *Julian of Norwich*

    **Christ came in our poor flesh
    to share a mother's care.**

74   *A SONG OF OUR TRUE NATURE*

Refrain: **Nature and grace are of one accord,
        for God is one in love, in nature and in grace.**

1   Christ revealed our frailty and our falling, *
    our trespasses and our humiliations.

2   Christ also revealed his blessèd power, *
    his blessèd wisdom and love.

3   He protects us as tenderly and as sweetly
        when we are in greatest need; *
    he raises us in spirit
        and turns everything to glory and joy without ending.

4   God is the ground and the substance,
        the very essence of nature; *
    God is the true father and mother of natures.

5   We are all bound to God by nature, *
    and we are all bound to God by grace.

6   And this grace is for all the world, *
    because it is our precious mother, Christ.

7   For this fair nature was prepared by Christ
        for the honour and nobility of all, *
    and for the joy and bliss of salvation.

   Glory . . .   *Julian of Norwich*

   Nature and grace are of one accord,
   for God is one in love, in nature and in grace.

75 *SAVIOUR OF THE WORLD*

Refrain: **In the greatness of your mercy, O God,**
         forgive the sins of all your people.

1   Jesus, Saviour of the world,
        come to us in your mercy: *
    we look to you to save and help us.

2   By your cross and your life laid down,
        you set your people free: *
    we look to you to save and help us.

3   When they were ready to perish,
        you saved your disciples: *
    we look to you to come to our help.

4   In the greatness of your mercy,
        loose us from our chains, *
    forgive the sins of all your people.

5   Make yourself known
        as our Saviour and mighty deliverer; *
    save and help us that we may praise you.

6   Come now and dwell with us, Lord Christ Jesus: *
    hear our prayer and be with us always.

7   And when you come in your glory: *
    make us to be one with you
        and to share the life of your kingdom.

                                                               Henry Allon

   In the greatness of your mercy, O God,
   forgive the sins of all your people.

The Christian Year
The Seasons (Temporale)
Advent

Form 3 is used for Morning, Evening and Night Prayer.

MIDDAY PRAYER IN ADVENT

Form 1-7 is used with the following propers:

DOXOLOGY TO HYMN

To you, O Christ, all glory be,
Whose advent sets your people free;
Whom with the Father, we adore,
And Holy Spirit, evermore. Amen.

PSALM 119

READING

Sunday	Revelation 22.17,20,21	Thursday	Mark 13.34-end
Monday	Isaiah 11.1-4	Friday	Romans 13.11-end
Tuesday	Mark 1.1-5	Saturday	Luke 1.35,38
Wednesday	Luke 12.35-37		

or, on any day in Advent, one of the following readings is used:

Comfort, O comfort my people, says your God.   *Isaiah 40.1*

Our Lord says, 'Surely I am coming soon.' Amen, come Lord Jesus.
Revelation 22.20

RESPONSE

*Either **A:***

John said, I am the voice of one crying in the wilderness,
    make straight the way of the Lord.
All flesh shall see the salvation of our God.

After me will come one who ranks before me;
he will baptise with the Holy Spirit and with fire.
And the glory of the Lord shall be revealed.

One who is mightier than I is coming;
I bear witness that this is the Chosen One of God.
**All flesh shall see the salvation of our God,
and the glory of the Lord shall be revealed.**

or **B:**

Behold, I send my messenger to prepare my way before me
**and the One whom you seek will suddenly come to God's
temple.**

Who can endure the day of God's coming?
And who can stand when the Most High appears?

For God is like a refiner's fire and like fuller's soap
**and shall sit as a refiner of silver and purify
the offspring of Levi.**

Who can endure the day of God's coming and who can stand
when the Most High appears?
**As for me, I will look to the Most High, I will wait for
the God of my salvation.**

COLLECT – one of the following is used.

Eternal God,
as Mary waited for the birth of your Son,
so we wait for his coming in glory;
bring us through the birth pangs of this present age
to see, with her, our great salvation
in Jesus Christ our Lord. **Amen.**

Keep us, O Lord,
while we tarry on this earth,
in a serious seeking after you,
and in an affectionate walking with you,
every day of our lives;
that when you come,
we may be found not hiding our talent,
nor serving the flesh,
nor yet asleep with our lamp unfurnished,
but waiting and longing for our Lord,
our glorious God for ever. **Amen.**

Richard Baxter (1691)

THE CONCLUSION

May the Lord make us ready for his coming in glory. Amen.

The First Sunday of Advent

COLLECT – one of the following is used.

Almighty God,
give us grace to cast away the works of darkness
and to put on the armour of light,
now in the time of this mortal life,
in which your Son Jesus Christ came to us in great humility;
that on the last day,
when he shall come again in his glorious majesty
    to judge the living and the dead,
we may rise to the life immortal;
through him who is alive and reigns with you,
in the unity of the Holy Spirit,
one God, now and for ever. **Amen.**

Almighty God,
as your kingdom dawns,
turn us from the darkness of sin to the
    light of holiness,
that we may be ready to meet you
in our Lord and Saviour, Jesus Christ. **Amen.**

God our deliverer,
whose approaching birth
still shakes the foundations of our world,
may we so wait for your coming
with eagerness and hope
that we embrace without terror
the labour pangs of the new age,
through Jesus Christ, **Amen.**

Janet Morley

The Second Sunday of Advent

COLLECT – one of the following is used.

O Lord, raise up, we pray, your power
and come among us,
and with great might succour us;
that whereas, through our sins and wickedness
we are grievously hindered
in running the race that is set before us,
your bountiful grace and mercy
may speedily help and deliver us;
through Jesus Christ your Son our Lord,
to whom with you and the Holy Spirit,
be honour and glory, now and for ever. **Amen.**

Almighty God,
purify our hearts and minds,
that when your Son Jesus Christ comes again as
   judge and saviour
we may be ready to receive him,
who is our Lord and our God. **Amen.**

The Third Sunday of Advent

COLLECT – one of the following is used.

O Lord Jesus Christ,
who at your first coming sent your messenger
to prepare your way before you:
grant that the ministers and stewards of your mysteries
may likewise so prepare and make ready your way
by turning the hearts of the disobedient to the wisdom of the just,
that at your second coming to judge the world
we may be found an acceptable people in your sight;
for you are alive and reign with the Father
in the unity of the Holy Spirit,
one God, now and for ever. **Amen.**

God for whom we watch and wait,
you sent John the Baptist to prepare the way of your Son:
give us courage to speak the truth,
to hunger for justice,
and to suffer for the cause of right,
with Jesus Christ our Lord. **Amen.**

The Eight Days before Christmas –
The Advent Refrains on the Magnificat

17 December, O Sapientia

> **O Wisdom, coming forth from the mouth
> of the Most High,
> reaching from one end to the other mightily,
> and sweetly ordering all things:
> Come and teach us the way of prudence.**
>
> *cf Ecclesiasticus 24.3; Wisdom 8.1*

18 December, O Adonai

> **O Adonai, and leader of the House of Israel,
> who appeared to Moses in the fire of the burning bush
> and gave him the law on Sinai:
> Come and redeem us with an outstretched arm.**
>
> *cf Exodus 3.2; 24.12*

O Root of Jesse, standing as a sign among the peoples;
before you kings will shut their mouths,
to you the nations will make their prayer:
Come and deliver us, and delay no longer.

cf Isaiah 11.10; 45.14; 52.15; Romans 15.12

20 December, O Clavis David

O Key of David and sceptre of the House of Israel;
you open and no one can shut;
you shut and no one can open:
Come and lead the prisoners from the prison house,
those who dwell in darkness and the shadow of death.

cf Isaiah 22.22; 42.7

21 December, O Oriens

O Morning Star,
splendour of light eternal and sun of righteousness:
Come and enlighten those who dwell in darkness
and the shadow of death.

cf Malachi 4.2

22 December, O Rex Gentium

O King of the nations, and their desire,
the cornerstone making both one:
Come and save the human race,
which you fashioned from clay.

cf Isaiah 28.16; Ephesians 2.14

23 December, O Emmanuel

O Emmanuel, our king and our lawgiver,
the hope of the nations and their Saviour:
Come and save us, O Lord our God.

cf Isaiah 7.14

The Fourth Sunday of Advent

This provision is not used on weekdays after 23 December.

COLLECT – one of the following is used.

God our redeemer,
who prepared the Blessed Virgin Mary
to be the mother of your Son:
grant that, as she looked for his coming as our saviour,
so we may be ready to greet him
when he comes again as our judge;
who is alive and reigns with you,
in the unity of the Holy Spirit,
one God, now and for ever. **Amen.**

Eternal God,
as Mary waited for the birth of your Son,
so we wait for his coming in glory;
bring us through the birth pangs of this present age
to see, with her, our great salvation
in Jesus Christ our Lord. **Amen.**

24 December – Christmas Eve

Morning

COLLECT

Almighty God,
as we prepare with joy
to celebrate the gift of the Christ-child,
embrace the earth with your glory
and be for us a living hope
in Jesus Christ our Lord. **Amen.**

Evening

Form 4 is used.

COLLECT

Almighty God,
you make us glad with the yearly remembrance
    of the birth of your Son Jesus Christ:
grant that, as we joyfully receive him as our redeemer,
so we may with sure confidence behold him
when he shall come to be our judge;
who is alive and reigns with you,
in the unity of the Holy Spirit,
one God, now and for ever. **Amen.**

Christmas

Form 4 is used for Morning, Evening and Night Prayer.

MIDDAY PRAYER IN CHRISTMAS

Form 1-7 is used with the following propers:

DOXOLOGY TO HYMN

Lord Jesus, King of heaven and earth,
We praise you for your virgin birth;
You are the Father's only Son,
With God the Spirit, ever one. Amen.

PSALMS   Psalms of Ascent *(Pss 121-131, 133)*

READING

Sunday	John 1.14,16-18	Thursday	Galatians 4.4-7
Monday	Isaiah 9.2,6,7	Friday	Titus 2.11-14
Tuesday	Matthew 1.20b-23	Saturday	Hebrews 1.1-3a
Wednesday	Luke 2.16-20		

or, on any day in Christmas, one of the following readings is used:

In him was life, and the life was the light of all people. The light shines in the darkness, and the darkness did not overcome it.   *John 1.4,5*

God's love was revealed among us in this way: God sent his only Son into the world so that we might live through him.   *1 John 4.9*

RESPONSE

Either **A:**

Glory to God in the highest heaven,
and on earth, peace.

The angel said, Do not be afraid Mary,
   for you have found favour with God;
   you will conceive in your womb and bear a son,
   and you will name him Jesus.
Glory to God in the highest heaven.

The Holy Spirit will come upon you,
    and the power of the Most High will overshadow you;
    therefore the child to be born will be holy;
    he will be called Son of God.
Glory to God in the highest heaven.

or B:

That which we heard from the beginning,
**which we saw with our own eyes
    and touched with our hands,**

The Word of life, which was from the beginning,
we now proclaim to you.

The darkness is passing away
and the true light is already shining.

God is our light in whom there is no darkness at all.
If we walk in the light, we have fellowship with Christ.

COLLECT – one of the following is used.

Lord Jesus Christ,
your birth at Bethlehem
draws us to kneel in wonder at heaven touching earth:
accept our heartfelt praise
as we worship you,
our Saviour and our eternal God. **Amen.**

Almighty and everlasting God,
who stooped to raise fallen humanity
through the child-bearing of blessèd Mary:
grant that we, who have seen your glory
    revealed in our human nature
and your love made perfect in our weakness,
may daily be renewed in your image
and conformed to the pattern of your Son,
Jesus Christ our Lord. **Amen.**

Collect of the Blessed Virgin Mary

THE CONCLUSION

May the grace of Christ our Saviour be with us all. Amen.

25 December – Christmas Day

COLLECT – one of the following is used.

Almighty God,
you have given us your only-begotten Son
to take our nature upon him
and as at this time to be born of a pure virgin:
grant that we, who have been born again
and made your children by adoption and grace,
may daily be renewed by your Holy Spirit;
through Jesus Christ our Lord. **Amen.**

Lord Jesus Christ,
your birth at Bethlehem
draws us to kneel in wonder at heaven touching earth:
accept our heartfelt praise
as we worship you,
our Saviour and our eternal God. **Amen.**

God our beloved,
born of a woman's body,
you came that we might look upon you,
and handle you with our own hands.
May we so cherish one another in our bodies
that we may also be touched by you;
through the Word made flesh, Jesus Christ, **Amen.**

Janet Morley

Morning

Opening Canticle: 64

The First Sunday of Christmas

This provision is not used on weekdays after 5 January.

COLLECT – one of the following is used.

Almighty God,
who wonderfully created us in your own image
and yet more wonderfully restored us
through your Son Jesus Christ:
grant that, as he came to share in our humanity,
so we may share the life of his divinity;
who is alive and reigns with you,
in the unity of the Holy Spirit,
one God, now and for ever. **Amen.**

God in Trinity,
eternal unity of perfect love:
gather the nations to be one family,
and draw us into your holy life
through the birth of Emmanuel,
our Lord Jesus Christ. **Amen.**

1 January – The Naming & Circumcision of Jesus   1

COLLECT – one of the following is used.

Almighty God,
whose blessèd Son was circumcised
in obedience to the law for our sake
and given the Name that is above every name:
give us grace faithfully to bear his Name,
to worship him in the freedom of the Spirit,
and to proclaim him as the Saviour of the world;
who is alive and reigns with you,
in the unity of the Holy Spirit,
one God, now and for ever. **Amen.**

Christ our brother,
in you there is neither Jew nor Gentile,
neither male nor female;
yet you received the mark of the covenant
and took upon you
the precious burden of the law.
May we so accept in our bodies
our own particular struggle and promise,
so that we also may break down barriers
in your name, **Amen**.

Janet Morley

	Morning	**Evening**
31 Dec.		*Second Canticle:* 47
1 Jan.	*Opening Canticle:* 64 *Second Canticle:* 13	*Second Canticle:* 57

Magnificat **To us a child is born, to us a Son is given,**
Eve **and he shall be called the Prince of Peace.**

Preparation Alleluia. From the rising of the sun to its setting,
 may the Lord's name be praised.
 O come, let us worship. Alleluia.

Benedictus **You shall call his name Jesus**
 for he will save his people from their sins.

Magnificat **You have done great things, O God,**
 and holy is your name.

Midday, *as for Christmas, with the following propers:*

READING Luke 1.28-31 *or*

From the rising of the sun to its setting, my name is great among the
nations, says the Lord of hosts. *Malachi 1.11*

RESPONSE Christmas A, page 547.

The Second Sunday of Christmas

This provision is not used on weekdays after 5 January.

COLLECT – one of the following is used.

Almighty God,
in the birth of your Son
you have poured on us the new light of your incarnate Word,
and shown us the fullness of your love:
help us to walk in his light and dwell in his love
that we may know the fullness of his joy;
who is alive and reigns with you,
in the unity of the Holy Spirit,
one God, now and for ever. **Amen.**

God our Father,
in love you sent your Son
that the world may have life:
lead us to seek him among the outcast
and to find him in those in need,
for Jesus Christ's sake. **Amen.**

Epiphany

Form 5 is used for Morning, Evening and Night Prayer.

MIDDAY PRAYER IN EPIPHANY

Form 1-7 is used with the following propers:

DOXOLOGY TO HYMN

Your glory, Christ is manifest:
All peoples, Lord, by you are blest;
Whom with the Father, we adore,
And Holy Spirit evermore. Amen.

PSALM 119

READING

Sunday	Malachi 1.11	Thursday	Romans 8.15-17
Monday	John 2.10,11	Friday	Ephesians 1.8b-10
Tuesday	Isaiah 60.1-3	Saturday	Revelation 1.13-16
Wednesday	2 Corinthians 4.5,6		

or, on any day in Epiphany, one of the following readings is used:

Jesus said, 'I am the light of the world. Whoever follows me will never walk in darkness but will have the light of life.'   *John 8.12*

Grace was given to us in Christ Jesus before the ages began, but it has now been revealed through the appearing of our Saviour Christ Jesus, who abolished death and brought life and immortality to light through the gospel.   *2 Timothy 1.9,10*

RESPONSE

Either A:

The Magi hastened with gifts to the royal birth.
When they saw the star, they rejoiced greatly.

This is he who is to baptise in the Holy Spirit;
this is the Chosen One of God.

Now the Church is joined to her heavenly Bridegroom,
for Christ washes away her sins in the Jordan.

The water was made wine at the wedding feast,
the first of the signs by which Christ revealed his glory.

or B:

I have been found by those who did not seek me.
I have shown myself to those who did not ask for me.

They shall see, who have never been told of him,
and they shall understand, who have never heard of him.

The root of Jesse has come,
he who rises to rule the nations.

Rejoice, O nations, with his people,
and let all the peoples praise him.

COLLECT – one of the following is used.

Eternal Lord,
our beginning and our end:
bring us with the whole creation
to your glory, hidden through past ages
and made known
in Jesus Christ our Lord. **Amen.**

O good Jesus,
Word of the Father and
   brightness of his glory,
whom angels desire to behold:
teach me to do your will
that, guided by your Spirit,
I may come to that blessèd city of
   everlasting day,
where all are one in heart and mind,
where there is safety and eternal peace,
happiness and delight,
where you live with the Father and the Holy Spirit,
world without end. **Amen.**   *after Gregory the Great (604)*

THE CONCLUSION

May the light of Christ our Lord shine in all our hearts. Amen.

6 January – The Epiphany

COLLECT – one of the following is used.

O God,
who by the leading of a star
manifested your only Son to the peoples of the earth:
mercifully grant that we,
who know you now by faith,
may at last behold your glory face to face;
through Jesus Christ our Lord. **Amen.**

Creator of the heavens,
who led the Magi by a star
to worship the Christ-child:
guide and sustain us,
that we may find our journey's end
in Jesus Christ our Lord. **Amen.**

O God, the source of all insight,
whose coming was revealed to the nations
not among men of power
but on a woman's lap;
give us grace to seek you
where you may be found,
that the wisdom of this world may be humbled
and discover your unexpected joy,
through Jesus Christ, **Amen.**   *Janet Morley*

Morning

Opening Canticle: 64

The Baptism of Christ
The First Sunday of Epiphany

I

The Second Sunday of Epiphany
when January 6 is a Sunday

COLLECT – one of the following is used.

Eternal Father,
who at the baptism of Jesus
revealed him to be your Son,
anointing him with the Holy Spirit:
grant to us, who are born again by water and the Spirit,
that we may be faithful to our calling as your adopted children;
through Jesus Christ our Lord. **Amen.**

Heavenly Father,
at the Jordan you revealed Jesus as your Son:
may we recognize him as our Lord
and know ourselves to be your beloved children;
through Jesus Christ our Saviour. **Amen.**

Spirit of energy and change,
in whose power Jesus was anointed
to be the hope of the nations;
be poured out also upon us
without reserve or distinction,
that we may have confidence and strength
to plant your justice on the earth,
through Jesus Christ, **Amen.**

Janet Morley

	Morning	*Evening*
Sat.		*Second Canticle:* 56
Sun.	*Opening Canticle:* 64 *Second Canticle:* 22	*Second Canticle:* 65

Magnificat **Behold my Chosen, in whom my soul delights;**
Eve **the one on whom my Spirit rests.**

Preparation Alleluia. Jesus is the belovèd Son of God
in whom the Father is well pleased.
O come, let us worship. Alleluia.

Benedictus **Jesus is baptised and the whole world is made holy; Christ washes away our sins and purifies us with the Holy Spirit.**

Magnificat **Draw water from the wells of salvation, for Christ our Lord has made creation holy.**

Midday, *as for Epiphany with the following propers:*

READING Titus 2.11-13 *or*

The Spirit of the Lord God is upon me, because the Lord has anointed me; he has sent me to bring good news to the oppressed, to bind up the broken-hearted.   *Isaiah 61.1*

RESPONSE

John appeared in the wilderness
**and preached a baptism of repentance
for the forgiveness of sins.**

I baptise you with water,
**but he will baptise you with the Holy Spirit
and with fire.**

As soon as Jesus was baptised, he came up from the water,
and suddenly the heavens were opened.

The voice of God was heard from heaven:
**This is my Son, the Belovèd,
with whom I am well pleased.**

The Second Sunday of Epiphany

When 6 January is a Sunday this provision is used on the Third Sunday of Epiphany

COLLECT – one of the following is used.

Almighty God,
in Christ you make all things new:
transform the poverty of our nature by the riches of your grace,
and in the renewal of our lives
make known your heavenly glory;
through Jesus Christ our Lord. **Amen.**

Eternal Lord,
our beginning and our end:
bring us with the whole creation
to your glory, hidden through past ages
and made known
in Jesus Christ our Lord. **Amen.**

The Third Sunday of Epiphany

*When 6 January is a Sunday this provision is used on the Fourth Sunday
of Epiphany*

COLLECT – one of the following is used.

Almighty God,
whose Son revealed in signs and miracles
the wonder of your saving presence:
renew your people with your heavenly grace,
and in all our weakness
sustain us by your mighty power;
through Jesus Christ our Lord. **Amen.**

God of all mercy,
your Son proclaimed good news to the poor,
release to the captives,
and freedom to the oppressed:
anoint us with your Holy Spirit
and set all your people free
to praise you in Christ our Lord. **Amen.**

The Fourth Sunday of Epiphany

When 6 January is a Sunday this provision is used on Sunday 3 February

COLLECT – one of the following is used.

God our creator,
who in the beginning
commanded the light to shine out of darkness:
we pray that the light of the glorious gospel of Christ
may dispel the darkness of ignorance and unbelief,
shine into the hearts of all your people,
and reveal the knowledge of your glory
   in the face of Jesus Christ your Son our Lord. **Amen.**

God of heaven,
you send the gospel to the ends of the earth
and your messengers to every nation:
send your Holy Spirit to transform us
by the good news of everlasting life
in Jesus Christ our Lord. **Amen.**

2 February – The Presentation of Christ in the Temple, Candlemas 1

COLLECT – one of the following is used.

Almighty and ever-living God,
clothed in majesty,
whose beloved Son was this day presented in the Temple,
in substance of our flesh:
grant that we may be presented to you
with pure and clean hearts,
by your Son Jesus Christ our Lord. **Amen.**

Lord Jesus Christ,
light of the nations and glory of Israel:
make your home among us,
and present us pure and holy
to your heavenly Father,
your God, and our God. **Amen.**

Christ our cornerstone,
you were recognized at your presentation
as a sign of hope for the world,
but also as a stumbling-block for many;
may we so present our bodies to your service,
that, in sharing your scandal,
we may become a people acceptable to you,
in your name, **Amen.**   *Janet Morley*

	Morning	**Evening**
I Feb.		*Second Canticle: 60*
2 Feb.	*Opening Canticle: 64* *Second Canticle: 13*	*Second Canticle: 73*

| *Magnificat*
Eve | **The Lord whom you seek**
will suddenly come to his temple. |

| *Preparation* | Alleluia. The Lord Jesus comes to his chosen people.
O come, let us worship. Alleluia. |

| *Benedictus* | **The parents of Jesus**
marvelled at what was said about him.
And Mary kept all these things
and pondered them in her heart. |

| *Magnificat* | **Simeon held the child in his arms,**
and beheld his salvation;
Anna gave thanks to God
and proclaimed her redeemer. |

Midday, *as for Epiphany, with the following propers:*

READING 1 John 3.1-3 *or*

The Lord whom you seek will suddenly come to his temple. The messenger of the covenant in whom you delight – indeed, he is coming.

Malachi 3.1

RESPONSE

Behold, I send my messenger to prepare my way before me,
and the One whom you seek will suddenly come
to God's temple.

Who can endure the day of God's coming?
And who can stand when the Most High appears?

For God is like a refiner's fire and like fuller's soap
and shall sit as a refiner of silver and purify
the offspring of Levi.

Who can endure the day of God's coming and who can stand
when the Most High appears?
As for me I will look to the Most High, I will wait
for the God of my salvation.

Ordinary Time

The Fifth Sunday before Lent

This provision is always used from the day after the Presentation of Christ in the Temple until the first of the Sundays before Lent.

COLLECT – one of the following is used.

Almighty God,
by whose grace alone we are accepted
    and called to your service:
strengthen us by your Holy Spirit
and make us worthy of our calling;
through Jesus Christ our Lord. **Amen.**

God of our salvation,
help us to turn away from those habits
which harm our bodies and poison our minds
and to choose again your gift of life,
revealed to us in Jesus Christ our Lord. **Amen.**

The Fourth Sunday before Lent

COLLECT – one of the following is used.

O God,
you know us to be set
in the midst of so many and great dangers,
that by reason of the frailty of our nature
we cannot always stand upright:
grant to us such strength and protection
as may support us in all dangers
and carry us through all temptations;
through Jesus Christ our Lord. **Amen.**

Lord of the hosts of heaven,
our salvation and our strength,
without you we are lost:
guard us from all that harms or hurts
and raise us when we fall;
through Jesus Christ our Lord. **Amen.**

The Third Sunday before Lent

COLLECT – one of the following is used.

Almighty God,
who alone can bring order
to the unruly wills and passions of sinful humanity:
give your people grace
so to love what you command
and to desire what you promise,
that, among the many changes of this world,
our hearts may surely there be fixed
where true joys are to be found;
through Jesus Christ our Lord. **Amen.**

Eternal God,
whose Son went among the crowds
    and brought healing with his touch:
help us to show his love,
in your Church as we gather together,
and by our lives as they are transformed
into the image of Christ our Lord. **Amen.**

The Second Sunday before Lent

COLLECT – one of the following is used.

Almighty God,
you have created the heavens and the earth
and made us in your own image:
teach us to discern your hand in all your works
and your likeness in all your children;
through Jesus Christ your Son our Lord,
who with you and the Holy Spirit reigns supreme over all things,
now and for ever. **Amen.**

Almighty God,
give us reverence for all creation
and respect for every person,
that we may mirror your likeness
in Jesus Christ our Lord. **Amen.**

The Sunday next before Lent

This provision is not used on or after Ash Wednesday.

COLLECT – one of the following is used.

Almighty Father,
whose Son was revealed in majesty
before he suffered death upon the cross:
give us grace to perceive his glory,
that we may be strengthened to suffer with him
and be changed into his likeness, from glory to glory;
who is alive and reigns with you,
in the unity of the Holy Spirit,
one God, now and for ever. **Amen.**

Holy God,
you know the disorder of our sinful lives:
set straight our crooked hearts,
and bend our wills to love your goodness
   and your glory
in Jesus Christ our Lord. **Amen.**

On Shrove Tuesday, 'Alleluia, alleluia' may be added to the final versicle and response at Evening Prayer.

After Night Prayer on Shrove Tuesday, 'Alleluia' is not said again until Easter Day.

Lent

Form 6 is used for Morning, Evening and Night Prayer.

MIDDAY PRAYER IN LENT

Form 1-7 is used with the following propers:

DOXOLOGY TO HYMN

Grant, ever blessèd Trinity,
And ever perfect Unity,
That this our fast of forty days,
May work our profit and your praise. Amen.

PSALMS Psalms of Ascent *(Pss 121-131, 133)*

READING

Sunday	Romans 6.3-5	*Thursday*	Isaiah 58.6-9a
Monday	Joel 2.12-14	*Friday*	Matthew 6.1-4
Tuesday	1 Corinthians 9.24-end	*Saturday*	Luke 10.38-end
Wednesday	Romans 7.21-25a		

or, on any day in Lent, one of the following readings is used:

Jesus said, 'There will be more joy in heaven over one sinner who repents than over ninety-nine righteous people who need no repentance.

Luke 15.7

To the Lord our God belong mercy and forgiveness, for we have rebelled against him.   *Daniel 9.9*

RESPONSE

Either A:

Father, we have sinned against heaven and before you;
we are no longer worthy to be called your children.

Heal us and we shall be healed,
save us and we shall be saved; for you are our praise.

Make in us a clean heart, O God,
and renew a right spirit within us.

Jesus Christ, Son of the living God, have mercy upon us;
holy God, holy and strong, holy and immortal,
  have mercy upon us.

or B:

Seek your God who will be found,
search after God with all your heart and soul.

Christ also suffered for you, leaving you an example,
that you should follow in his steps.

For us he faced temptations, suffering and death,
and in him we are brought to life again.

Jesus Christ, Son of the living God, have mercy upon us;
holy God, holy and strong, holy and immortal,
  have mercy upon us.

COLLECT – one of the following is used.

Almighty God,
by the prayer and discipline of Lent
may we enter into the mystery of Christ's sufferings,
and by following in his Way
come to share in his glory;
through Jesus Christ our Lord. **Amen.**

Teach us, good Lord, to serve you as you deserve;
to give and not to count the cost;
to fight and not to heed the wounds;
to toil and not to seek for rest;
to labour and not to seek for any reward,
save that of knowing that we do your will. **Amen.**

Ignatius of Loyola (1556)

THE CONCLUSION

May God bless us and show us compassion and mercy. Amen.

Ash Wednesday

COLLECT – one of the following is used.

Almighty and everlasting God,
you hate nothing that you have made
and forgive the sins of all those who are penitent:
create and make in us new and contrite hearts
that we, worthily lamenting our sins
and acknowledging our wretchedness,
may receive from you, the God of all mercy,
perfect remission and forgiveness;
through Jesus Christ our Lord. **Amen.**

Holy God,
our lives are laid open before you:
rescue us from the chaos of sin
and through the death of your Son
bring us healing and make us whole
in Jesus Christ our Lord. **Amen.**

O God,
you have made us for yourself,
and against your longing there is no defence.
Mark us with your love,
and release in us a passion for your justice
in our disfigured world;
that we may turn from our guilt and face you,
our heart's desire, **Amen.**   *Janet Morley*

The First Sunday of Lent

COLLECT – one of the following is used.

Almighty God,
whose Son Jesus Christ fasted forty days in the wilderness,
and was tempted as we are, yet without sin:
give us grace to discipline ourselves in obedience to your Spirit;
and, as you know our weakness,
so may we know your power to save;
through Jesus Christ our Lord. **Amen.**

Heavenly Father,
your Son battled with the powers of darkness,
and grew closer to you in the desert:
help us to use these days to grow in wisdom and prayer
that we may witness to your saving love
in Jesus Christ our Lord. **Amen.**

The Second Sunday of Lent

COLLECT – one of the following is used.

Almighty God,
you show to those who are in error the light of your truth,
that they may return to the way of righteousness:
grant to all those who are admitted
   into the fellowship of Christ's religion,
that they may reject those things
   that are contrary to their profession,
and follow all such things as are agreeable to the same;
through our Lord Jesus Christ. **Amen.**

Almighty God,
by the prayer and discipline of Lent
may we enter into the mystery of Christ's sufferings,
and by following in his Way
come to share in his glory;
through Jesus Christ our Lord. **Amen.**

The Third Sunday of Lent

COLLECT – one of the following is used.

Almighty God,
whose most dear Son went not up to joy but first he suffered pain,
and entered not into glory before he was crucified:
mercifully grant that we, walking in the way of the cross,
may find it none other than the way of life and peace;
through Jesus Christ our Lord. **Amen.**

Eternal God,
give us insight
to discern your will for us,
to give up what harms us,
and to seek the perfection we are promised
in Jesus Christ our Lord. **Amen.**

The Fourth Sunday of Lent

Mothering Sunday may be celebrated in preference to the provision for the Fourth Sunday of Lent.

COLLECT – one of the following is used.

Merciful Lord,
absolve your people from their offences,
that through your bountiful goodness
we may all be delivered from the chains of those sins
which by our frailty we have committed;
grant this, heavenly Father,
for Jesus Christ's sake, our blessèd Lord and Saviour. **Amen.**

Merciful Lord,
you know our struggle to serve you:
when sin spoils our lives
and overshadows our hearts,
come to our aid
and turn us back to you again;
through Jesus Christ our Lord. **Amen.**

Mothering Sunday

COLLECT — one of the following is used.

God of compassion,
whose Son Jesus Christ, the child of Mary,
shared the life of a home in Nazareth,
and on the cross drew the whole human family to himself:
strengthen us in our daily living
that in joy and in sorrow
we may know the power of your presence
to bind together and to heal;
through Jesus Christ your Son our Lord,
who is alive and reigns with you,
in the unity of the Holy Spirit,
one God, now and for ever. **Amen.**

God of love,
passionate and strong,
tender and careful:
watch over us and hold us
all the days of our life;
through Jesus Christ our Lord. **Amen.**

God our mother,
you hold our life within you;
nourish us at your breast,
and teach us to walk alone.
Help us so to receive your tenderness
and respond to your challenge
that others may draw life from us,
in your name, **Amen.**

Janet Morley

Passiontide

Although Passiontide forms a part of Lent, the propers change to give a greater emphasis on Christ's suffering. Passiontide continues until Easter Eve. The last three days of Holy Week have their own propers.

MIDDAY PRAYER IN PASSIONTIDE

Form 1-7 is used with the following propers:

DOXOLOGY TO HYMN

To you, O saving Three in One,
Let homage due by all be done;
And grant us by the cross restored,
To share the Victor's great reward. Amen.

PSALMS Psalms of Ascent *(Pss 121-131, 133)*

READING

Sunday	Hebrews 2.10-12	Thursday	1 Peter 2.24,25
Monday	Mark 8.31-35	Friday	Romans 5.6-8
Tuesday	Isaiah 53.4-6	Saturday	John 12.23-26
Wednesday	1 Corinthians 1.18,22-25		

or, on any day in Passiontide, one of the following readings is used:

I have been crucified with Christ, and it is no longer I who live, but it is Christ who lives in me. *Galatians 2.19b-20a*

Jesus Christ died for all, so that those who live might live no longer for themselves, but for him who died and was raised for them.
2 Corinthians 5.15

RESPONSE

Either **A:**

If you want to become my follower, you must deny yourself
    and take up your cross and follow me.
May I never boast of anything
    except the cross of our Lord Jesus Christ.

If you want to save your life, you will lose it,
    and if you lose your life for my sake, you will find it.
May I never boast of anything
    except the cross of our Lord Jesus Christ.

For what will it profit you to gain the whole world
    but forfeit your life?
May I never boast of anything
    except the cross of our Lord Jesus Christ.

We adore you, O Christ, and we bless you,
because by your holy cross, you have redeemed the world.

*or **B**:*

Now is the Son of Man glorified,
and God is glorified in him.

Now is the judgement of this world,
now shall the ruler of this world be cast out.

I, when I am lifted up from the earth,
will draw all people to myself.

As Moses lifted up the serpent in the wilderness,
    so must the Son of Man be lifted up;
that whoever believes in him may have eternal life.

We adore you, O Christ, and we bless you:
because by your holy cross, you have redeemed the world.

COLLECT – one of the following is used.

Eternal God,
in the cross of Jesus
we see the cost of our sin
and the depth of your love:
in humble hope and fear
may we place at his feet
all that we have and all that we are,
through Jesus Christ our Lord. **Amen.**

Soul of Christ, sanctify me,
body of Christ, save me,
blood of Christ, inebriate me,
water from the side of Christ, wash me.
Passion of Christ, strengthen me.
O good Jesus, hear me:
hide me within your wounds
and never let me be separated from you.
From the wicked enemy defend me,
in the hour of my death, call me
and bid me come to you,
so that with your saints I may praise you
for ever and ever. **Amen.**

Anima Christi (14th century)

THE CONCLUSION

**May the life-giving cross be the source of all our joy and peace.
Amen.**

The Fifth Sunday of Lent

COLLECT – one of the following is used.

Most merciful God,
who by the death and resurrection of your Son Jesus Christ
delivered and saved the world:
grant that by faith in him who suffered on the cross
we may triumph in the power of his victory;
through Jesus Christ our Lord. **Amen.**

Gracious Father,
you gave up your Son
out of love for the world:
lead us to ponder the mysteries of his passion,
that we may know eternal peace
through the shedding of our Saviour's blood,
Jesus Christ our Lord. **Amen.**

Holy Spirit,
mighty wind of God,
inhabit our darkness
brood over our abyss
and speak to our chaos;
that we may breathe with your life
and share your creation
in the power of Jesus Christ, **Amen.** (Years A & B)

Janet Morley

Christ Jesus,
whose glory was poured out like perfume,
and who chose for our sake
to take the form of a slave:
may we also pour out our love
with holy extravagance,
that our lives may be fragrant with you, **Amen.** (Year C)

Janet Morley

Palm Sunday

COLLECT – one of the following is used.

Almighty and everlasting God,
who in your tender love towards the human race
sent your Son our Saviour Jesus Christ
to take upon him our flesh
and to suffer death upon the cross:
grant that we may follow the example of his patience and humility,
and also be made partakers of his resurrection;
through Jesus Christ our Lord. **Amen.**

True and humble king,
hailed by the crowd as Messiah:
grant us the faith to know you and love you,
that we may be found beside you
on the way of the cross,
which is the path of glory. **Amen.**

God, our hope of victory
whom we constantly betray;
grant us so to recognize your coming
that in our clamour
there may be commitment,
and in our silence
the very stones may cry aloud
in your name, **Amen.**

Janet Morley

Midday, *as for Passiontide, with the following propers:*

READING Matthew 23.37-39 *or*

Hosanna to the Son of David! Blessèd is the one who comes in the name of
the Lord! *Matthew 21.9*

RESPONSE

Let us run with perseverance the race that is set before us,
looking to Jesus, the pioneer and perfecter of our faith.

Who for the joy that was set before him endured the cross,
   disregarding its shame,
and has taken his seat at the right hand of the throne of God.

You who fear God, give praise;
**all you children of Jacob, give glory; stand in awe of God,
      all you children of Israel,**

for you have come to God's holy mountain
and to the city of the living God.

We adore you, O Christ, and we bless you:
because by your holy cross, you have redeemed the world.

Maundy Thursday

COLLECT – one of the following is used.

Almighty Father,
whose Son Jesus Christ has taught us
that what we do for the least
    of our brothers and sisters
we do also for him:
give us the will to be the servant of others
    as he was the servant of all,
who gave up his life and died for us,
yet is alive and reigns with you and the Holy Spirit,
one God, now and for ever. **Amen.**

Christ, whose feet were caressed
With perfume and a woman's hair;
You humbly took a basin and towel
And washed the feet of your friends.
Wash us also in your tenderness
As we touch one another;
That, embracing your service freely,
We may accept no other bondage
In your name, **Amen**.

Janet Morley

Morning	Evening
Second Canticle: 5	*Second Canticle: 54*

Preparation   Christ the Lord was tempted and suffered for us.
O come, let us worship.

Benedictus   **Christ loved those who were his,
and showed them how deep was his love for them.**

Magnificat   **Christ humbled himself for us,
and in obedience accepted death.**

Evening Prayer is said before the Liturgy of the Lord's Supper.

Midday, as for Passiontide, with the following propers:

READING Philippians 2.5-8 *or*

For their sakes I sanctify myself, so that they also may be sanctified in truth.

John 17.19

RESPONSE

This is my commandment,
that you love one another as I have loved you.

No one has greater love than this,
to lay down one's life for one's friends.

You are my friends, if you do what I command you.
This I command you, that you love one another.

As the Father has loved me so I have loved you; abide in my love;
that my joy may be in you, and that your joy may be complete.

We adore you, O Christ, and we bless you:
because by your holy cross, you have redeemed the world.

Night Prayer is said only by those not present at the Watch.

See Note 6 on page 14 regarding the observance of the Triduum.

Good Friday

COLLECT — one of the following is used.

Almighty Father,
look with mercy on this your family
for which our Lord Jesus Christ was content to be betrayed
    and given up into the hands of sinners
    and to suffer death upon the cross;
who is alive and glorified with you and the Holy Spirit,
one God, now and for ever. **Amen.**

Eternal God,
in the cross of Jesus
we see the cost of our sin
and the depth of your love:
in humble hope and fear
may we place at his feet
all that we have and all that we are,
through Jesus Christ our Lord. **Amen.**

Christ, whose bitter agony
was watched from afar by women,
enable us to follow the example
of their persistent love;
that, being steadfast in the face of horror,
we may also know the place of resurrection,
in your name, **Amen.**

Janet Morley

Morning	Evening
Second Canticle: 19	*Second Canticle:* 75

Benedictus **Over his head, they put the charge against him:
this is Jesus of Nazareth, King of the Jews.**

Magnificat **Christ humbled himself for us,
and in obedience accepted death,
even death on a cross.**

Midday, *as for Passiontide, with the following propers:*

READING John 12.23-28 *or*

Jesus Christ died for all, so that those who live might live no longer for
themselves, but for him who died and was raised for them.

2 Corinthians 5.15

RESPONSE

Now is the Son of Man glorified,
and God is glorified in him.

Now is the judgement of this world,
now the ruler of this world will be driven out.

I, when I am lifted up from the earth,
will draw all people to myself.

As Moses lifted up the serpent in the wilderness,
  so must the Son of Man be lifted up;
that whoever believes in him may have eternal life.

We adore you, O Christ, and we bless you:
because by your holy cross, you have redeemed the world.

Easter Eve

COLLECT – one of the following is used.

Grant, Lord,
that we who are baptised into the death
  of your Son our Saviour Jesus Christ
may continually put to death our evil desires
  and be buried with him;
and that through the grave and gate of death
we may pass to our joyful resurrection;
through his merits,
who died and was buried and rose again for us,
your Son Jesus Christ our Lord. **Amen.**

In the depths of our isolation
we cry to you, Lord God:
give light in our darkness
and bring us out of the prison of our despair;
through Jesus Christ our Lord. **Amen.**

O God,
you have searched the depths we cannot know,
and touched what we cannot bear to name;
may we so wait,
enclosed in your darkness,
that we are ready to encounter
the terror of the dawn,
with Jesus Christ, **Amen.**

Janet Morley

Morning	Evening
Second Canticle: 24	*Second Canticle:* 43

Benedictus   **Destroy this temple**
and, in three days,
I will raise it up, says the Lord;
this he said of the temple that was his body.

Magnificat   **Christ humbled himself for us**
and, in obedience,
accepted death,
even death on a cross:
therefore God raised him to the heights
and gave him the name
which is above all other names.

Midday, *as for Passiontide with the following propers:*

READING   Isaiah 38.10-12,17-20 *or*

Shall I ransom them from the power of Sheol? Shall I redeem them from
Death? O Death, where are your plagues? O Sheol, where is your
destruction?   *Hosea 13.14*

RESPONSE

After the Lord had been laid in the tomb,
they set guards to keep watch over it.

You will not leave my soul to Death,
nor suffer your faithful one to see the Pit.

I believe that I shall see the goodness of the Lord
in the land of the living.

We adore you, O Christ, and we bless you:
because by your holy cross, you have redeemed the world.

Easter

Form I is used for Morning, Evening and Night Prayer.

MIDDAY PRAYER IN EASTER

Form 1-7 is used with the following propers:

DOXOLOGY TO HYMN

**All praise be yours, O risen Lord,
From death to endless life restored;
Whom with the Father, we adore
And Holy Spirit evermore. Amen.**

PSALM 119

READING

Sunday	I Peter 1.3-5	*Thursday*	Luke 24.28-32
Monday	Zephaniah 3.14-18	*Friday*	Job 19.23-27a
Tuesday	I Corinthians 15.42-44a, 47-49	*Saturday*	Revelation 1.12,13, 17,18
Wednesday	Colossians 3.1-4		

or, on any day in Easter, one of the following readings is used:

Jesus said, 'This is the will of him who sent me, that I should lose nothing of all that he has given me, but raise it up on the last day.   *John 6.39*

We have been buried with him by baptism into death, so that, just as Christ was raised from the dead by the glory of the Father, so we too might walk in newness of life.   *Romans 6.4*

RESPONSE

Either A:

If you have been raised with Christ, seek the things that are above,
where Christ is, seated at the right hand of God.

Let the peace of Christ rule in your hearts,
to which you were called in the one body.

Let the word of Christ dwell in you richly,
with thankfulness in your hearts to God.

Behold, I tell you a mystery:
Death is swallowed up in victory.

O Death, where is your victory? O Death, where is your sting?
Thanks be to God, who gives us the victory
through our Lord Jesus Christ. Alleluia, alleluia.

or B:

If anyone is in Christ, there is a new creation.
The old has passed away, the new has come.

Jesus said, Father, the hour has come, glorify your Son,
that your Son may glorify you.

I have glorified you on earth,
I have finished the work which you gave me to do.

I have made your name known to those you gave me.
They were yours and they have kept your word.

If anyone is in Christ, there is a new creation.
The old has passed away, the new has come.
Alleluia, alleluia.

COLLECT – one of the following is used.

Risen Christ,
you filled your disciples with boldness and fresh hope:
strengthen us to proclaim your risen life
and fill us with your peace,
to the glory of God the Father. **Amen.**

Christ yesterday and today,
the beginning and the end,
Alpha and Omega,
all time belongs to you,
and all ages;
to you be glory and power
through every age and for ever. **Amen**

from the Easter Vigil

THE CONCLUSION

May the risen Christ give us his peace. Alleluia. Amen.

Easter Day

COLLECT – one of the following is used.

Lord of all life and power,
who through the mighty resurrection of your Son
overcame the old order of sin and death
to make all things new in him:
grant that we, being dead to sin
and alive to you in Jesus Christ,
may reign with him in glory;
to whom with you and the Holy Spirit
be praise and honour, glory and might,
now and in all eternity. **Amen.**

God of glory,
by the raising of your Son
you have broken the chains of death and hell:
fill your Church with faith and hope;
for a new day has dawned
and the way to life stands open
in our Saviour Jesus Christ. **Amen.**

O God, the power of the powerless,
you have chosen as your witnesses
those whose voice is not heard.
Grant that, as women first announced
the resurrection
though they were not believed,
we too may have courage
to persist in proclaiming your word,
in the power of Jesus Christ, **Amen.**

Janet Morley

Morning

Alternative Opening Canticle: 64

The Second Sunday of Easter

COLLECT – one of the following is used.

Almighty Father,
you have given your only Son to die for our sins
and to rise again for our justification:
grant us so to put away the leaven of malice and wickedness
that we may always serve you
in pureness of living and truth;
through the merits of your Son Jesus Christ our Lord. **Amen.**

Risen Christ,
for whom no door is locked, no entrance barred:
open the doors of our hearts,
that we may seek the good of others
and walk the joyful road of sacrifice and peace,
to the praise of God the Father. **Amen.**

The Third Sunday of Easter

COLLECT – one of the following is used.

Almighty Father,
who in your great mercy gladdened the disciples
   with the sight of the risen Lord:
give us such knowledge of his presence with us,
that we may be strengthened and sustained by his risen life
and serve you continually in righteousness and truth;
through Jesus Christ our Lord. **Amen.**

Risen Christ,
you filled your disciples with boldness and fresh hope:
strengthen us to proclaim your risen life
and fill us with your peace,
to the glory of God the Father. **Amen.**

The Fourth Sunday of Easter

COLLECT – one of the following is used.

Almighty God,
whose Son Jesus Christ is the resurrection and the life:
raise us, who trust in him,
from the death of sin to the life of righteousness,
that we may seek those things which are above,
where he reigns with you
in the unity of the Holy Spirit,
one God, now and for ever. **Amen.**

Risen Christ,
faithful shepherd of your Father's sheep:
teach us to hear your voice
and to follow your command,
that all your people may be gathered into one flock,
to the glory of God the Father. **Amen.**

The Fifth Sunday of Easter

COLLECT – one of the following is used.

Almighty God,
who through your only-begotten Son Jesus Christ
have overcome death and opened to us the gate of everlasting life:
grant that, as by your grace going before us
    you put into our minds good desires,
so by your continual help
we may bring them to good effect;
through Jesus Christ our risen Lord. **Amen.**

Risen Christ,
your wounds declare your love for the world
and the wonder of your risen life:
give us compassion and courage
to risk ourselves for those we serve,
to the glory of God the Father. **Amen.**

The Sixth Sunday of Easter

This provision is not used on or after Ascension Day.

COLLECT – one of the following is used.

God our redeemer,
you have delivered us from the power of darkness
and brought us into the kingdom of your Son:
grant, that as by his death he has recalled us to life,
so by his continual presence in us he may raise us
    to eternal joy;
through Jesus Christ our Lord. **Amen.**

Risen Christ,
by the lakeside you renewed your call to your disciples:
help your Church to obey your command
and draw the nations to the fire of your love,
to the glory of God the Father. **Amen.**

Ascension Day

COLLECT – one of the following is used.

Grant, we pray, almighty God,
that as we believe your only-begotten Son our Lord Jesus Christ
to have ascended into the heavens,
so we in heart and mind may also ascend
and with him continually dwell;
who is alive and reigns with you,
in the unity of the Holy Spirit,
one God, now and for ever. **Amen.**

Risen Christ,
you have raised our human nature to the throne of heaven:
help us to seek and serve you,
that we may join you at the Father's side,
where you reign with the Spirit in glory,
now and for ever. **Amen.**

O God,
you withdraw from our sight
that you may be known by our love;
help us to enter the cloud
where you are hidden,
and surrender all our certainty
to the darkness of faith
in Jesus Christ, **Amen.**

Janet Morley

First Evening

THE BLESSING OF THE LIGHT

Blessèd are you, Sovereign God,
creator of light and darkness,
to you be glory and praise for ever.
As evening falls, you renew your promise
to reveal among us the light of your presence.
May your word be a lantern to our feet
and a light upon our path
that we may behold your coming among us.
Strengthen us in our stumbling weakness
and free our tongues to sing your praise,
Father, Son and Holy Spirit.
Blessèd be God for ever.

Second Canticle: 49

Magnificat: **Christ was believed in throughout the world and taken up in glory. Alleluia.**

THE CONCLUSION

May Christ, who has opened the kingdom of heaven, bring us to reign with him in glory. Amen.

Let us bless the Lord. Alleluia, alleluia.
Thanks be to God. Alleluia, alleluia.

Morning

Blessèd are you, Lord of heaven and earth,
to you be glory and praise for ever.
From the darkness of death you have raised your Christ
to the right hand of your majesty on high.
The pioneer of our faith, his passion accomplished,
has opened for us the way to heaven
and sends on us the promised Spirit.
May we be ready to follow the Way
and so be brought into the glory of your presence
where songs of triumph for ever sound:
Father, Son and Holy Spirit.
Blessèd be God for ever.

Alleluia. Christ the Lord ascends into heaven.
O come, let us worship. Alleluia.

Opening Canticle: 64

Second Canticle: 26

Benedictus: **I am ascending to my Father
and to your Father;
to my God and your God. Alleluia.**

THE CONCLUSION

**May Christ, who has opened the kingdom of heaven,
bring us to reign with him in glory. Amen.**

Let us bless the Lord. Alleluia, alleluia.
Thanks be to God. Alleluia, alleluia.

Midday

Form 5 is used with the following propers:

DOXOLOGY TO HYMN

**All praise from every heart and tongue
To you, ascended Lord, be sung;
Whom with the Father we adore,
And Holy Spirit evermore. Amen**

PSALM 119

READING Hebrews 4.14-16 *or*

Jesus led the disciples out as far as Bethany, and lifting up his hands, he blessed them. While he was blessing them, he withdrew from them and was carried up into heaven.   *Luke 24.50-51*

RESPONSE

To the King of the ages, immortal, invisible, the only God,
be honour and glory for ever and ever.

Christ Jesus was revealed in the flesh,
vindicated in the Spirit,

seen by angels,
proclaimed among the nations,

believed in throughout the world
and taken up in glory.

Our Lord Jesus Christ shall appear;
he will be revealed at the proper time by God.
Alleluia, alleluia.

COLLECT

God the Father,
help us to hear the call of Christ the King
and to follow in his service,
whose kingdom has no end;
for he reigns with you and the Holy Spirit,
one God, one glory. **Amen.**

THE CONCLUSION

May the grace of the Holy Spirit enlighten
our hearts and minds. Alleluia. Amen.

Evening

THE BLESSING OF THE LIGHT

Blessèd are you, Sovereign God,
creator of light and darkness,
to you be glory and praise for ever.
As evening falls, you renew your promise
to reveal among us the light of your presence.
May your word be a lantern to our feet
and a light upon our path
that we may behold your coming among us.
Strengthen us in our stumbling weakness
and free our tongues to sing your praise,
Father, Son and Holy Spirit.
Blessèd be God for ever.

Second Canticle: 49

Magnificat: **I have made your name known**
to those you have given me;
and now I pray for them,
for I am coming to you. Alleluia.

THE CONCLUSION

May Christ, who has opened the kingdom of heaven,
bring us to reign with him in glory. Amen.

Let us bless the Lord. Alleluia, alleluia.
Thanks be to God. Alleluia, alleluia.

Pentecost

From the Friday after Ascension Day to the Day of Pentecost., Form 2 is used for Morning, Evening and Night Prayer. On Friday and Saturday after Ascension Day the COLLECT for the Seventh Sunday of Easter is used.

MIDDAY PRAYER IN PENTECOST

Form 1-7 is used with the following propers:

DOXOLOGY TO HYMN

**To God the Father, God the Son,
And God the Spirit praise be done:
May Christ the Lord upon us pour
The Spirit's gift for evermore. Amen.**

PSALM 119

READING

Friday	(1) Hebrews 2.8b-10	(2) 2 Corinthians 1.20-22
Saturday	(1) Romans 8.38,39	(2) 2 Corinthians 3.17,18
Sunday	John 7.37-39a	
Monday	Isaiah 40.28-end	
Tuesday	1 Corinthians 12.4-7	
Wednesday	Joel 2.28,29	
Thursday	Luke 11.9-13	
Day of Pentecost	John 20.21,22	

or, on any day in Pentecost:

You will receive power when the Holy Spirit has come upon you; and you will be my witnesses to the ends of the earth.   *Acts 1.8*

RESPONSE

Either A:

If the Spirit of God who raised Jesus from the dead dwells in you,
**God will give life to your mortal bodies also, through
   the Spirit that dwells in you.**

What no eye has seen, nor ear heard,
  nor the human heart conceived,
God revealed to us through the Spirit;

for the Spirit searches everything,
even the depths of God.

The grace of our Lord Jesus Christ and the love of God
  and the fellowship of the Holy Spirit,
be with us all evermore. Alleluia, alleluia.

or B:

There are diversities of gifts but the same Spirit;
there are differences of service but the same Lord.

To one is given, by the Spirit, the word of wisdom;
to another the word of knowledge, by the same Spirit.

To another, faith, by the same Spirit;
to another, gifts of healing, by the same Spirit.

The grace of our Lord Jesus Christ and the love of God
  and the fellowship of the Holy Spirit,
be with us all evermore. Alleluia, alleluia.

COLLECT – one of the following is used.

Holy Spirit, sent by the Father,
ignite in us your holy fire;
strengthen your children with the gift of faith,
revive your Church with the breath of love,
and renew the face of the earth,
through Jesus Christ our Lord. **Amen.**

O King enthroned on high,
Comforter and Spirit of truth,
you that are in all places and fill all things,
the treasury of blessings and the giver of life,
come and dwell with us,
cleanse us from every stain
and save our souls, O gracious one. **Amen.**

an Orthodox prayer

**May the grace of the Holy Spirit enlighten
our hearts and minds. Alleluia. Amen.**

The Seventh Sunday of Easter
The Sunday after Ascension Day

COLLECT – one of the following is used.

O God the King of glory,
you have exalted your only Son Jesus Christ
with great triumph to your kingdom in heaven:
we beseech you, leave us not comfortless,
but send your Holy Spirit to strengthen us
and exalt us to the place where our Saviour Christ is gone before,
who is alive and reigns with you,
in the unity of the Holy Spirit,
one God, now and for ever. **Amen.**

Risen, ascended Lord,
as we rejoice at your triumph,
fill your Church on earth with power and compassion,
that all who are estranged by sin
may find forgiveness and know your peace,
to the glory of God the Father. **Amen.**

Day of Pentecost
Whit Sunday

This provision is not used on the weekdays after the Day of Pentecost.

COLLECT – one of the following is used.

God, who as at this time
taught the hearts of your faithful people
by sending to them the light of your Holy Spirit:
grant us by the same Spirit
to have a right judgement in all things
and evermore to rejoice in his holy comfort;
through the merits of Christ Jesus our Saviour. **Amen.**

Spirit of truth
whom the world can never grasp,
touch our hearts with the shock of your coming;
fill us with desire for your disturbing peace;
and fire us with longing
to speak your uncomfortable word
through Jesus Christ, **Amen.**

Janet Morley

Morning

Opening Canticle: **64**

Ordinary Time

The Weekdays after the Day of Pentecost

COLLECT

O Lord, from whom all good things come:
grant to us your humble servants,
that by your holy inspiration
we may think those things that are good,
and by your merciful guiding may perform the same;
through our Lord Jesus Christ. **Amen.**

Trinity Sunday

COLLECT – one of the following is used.

Almighty and everlasting God,
you have given us your servants grace,
by the confession of a true faith,
to acknowledge the glory of the eternal Trinity
and in the power of the divine majesty to worship the Unity:
keep us steadfast in this faith,
that we may evermore be defended from all adversities;
through Jesus Christ our Lord. **Amen.**

Holy God,
faithful and unchanging:
enlarge our minds with the knowledge of your truth,
and draw us more deeply into the mystery of your love,
that we may truly worship you,
Father, Son and Holy Spirit,
one God, now and for ever. **Amen.**

	Morning	*Evening*
Sat.		*Second Canticle: 44*
Sun.	*Opening Canticle: 64* *Second Canticle: 27*	*Second Canticle: 72*

Magnificat **Glory and honour be to God**
Eve   **in the unity of the Trinity.**

Alleluia. God in three Persons: blessèd Trinity.
O come, let us worship. Alleluia.

Benedictus **Holy, holy, holy is the God of hosts;**
who was, and who is, and who is to come.

Magnificat **Blessèd be the creator of all things;**
the holy and undivided Trinity.

Midday

PSALM 119

READING Luke 10.21-22 *or*

God's love has been shed abroad in our hearts through the Holy Spirit
that has been given to us.

Romans 5.5

RESPONSE

Holy, holy, holy Lord, God of power and might,
who was, and who is, and who is coming.
We praise and glorify you for ever.

Worthy are you O Lord our God,
to receive glory and honour and power.
We praise and glorify you for ever.

Worthy is the Lamb who was slain
to receive power and divinity and wisdom and strength
and honour and glory and blessing.
We praise and glorify you for ever.

Let us bless the Father, the Son and the Holy Spirit.
We praise and glorify you for ever.

Praise our God all you servants,
and you who fear him, the small and the great.
We praise and glorify you for ever.

Praise God in his glory, heaven and earth,
and every creature that is in heaven and on the earth
and under the earth and such as are on the seas,
and all that are in them.
We praise and glorify you for ever.

Glory to God, Source of all being,
   Eternal Word and Holy Spirit.
We praise and glorify you for ever.

As it was in the beginning, is now and shall be for ever.
We praise and glorify you for ever.

after The Praises to be Said at all the Hours, Francis of Assisi

COLLECT

O God our mystery,
you bring us to life,
call us to freedom,
and move between us with love.
May we so participate
in the dance of your trinity,
that our lives may resonate with you,
now and for ever, **Amen.**

Janet Morley

THE CONCLUSION

May the blessing of the Holy Trinity be with us always. Amen.

The Day of Thanksgiving for the Institution of Holy Communion – Corpus Christi I

Thursday after Trinity Sunday

Form 4 is used for Morning, Evening and Night Prayer.

COLLECT – one of the following is used.

Lord Jesus Christ,
we thank you that in this wonderful sacrament
you have given us the memorial of your passion:
grant us so to reverence the sacred mysteries
   of your body and blood
that we may know within ourselves
and show forth in our lives
the fruits of your redemption;
for you are alive and reign with the Father
in the unity of the Holy Spirit,
one God, now and for ever. **Amen.**

O God who took human flesh
that you might be intimate with us;
may we so taste and touch you
in our bodily life
that we may discern and celebrate
your body in the world,
through Jesus Christ, **Amen.**

Janet Morley

	Morning	**Evening**
Wed.		*Second Canticle: 65*
Thu.	*Opening Canticle: 64* *Second Canticle: 15*	*Second Canticle: 73*

Magnificat **Your people eat the food of angels:**
Eve   **you give them bread from heaven.**

Preparation Alleluia. Christ's flesh is food indeed
            and his blood is drink indeed.
            O come, let us worship. Alleluia.

Benedictus **I am the living bread which came down from heaven;**
            whoever eats of this bread will live for ever.

Magnificat **O sacred feast, in which Christ is received**
            and the memory of his passion renewed:
            our minds are filled with grace
            and a pledge of future glory is given us.

Midday

Form 5 is used with the following propers:

PSALM 119

READING John 6.48-51 *or*

The believers devoted themselves to the apostles' teaching and fellowship,
to the breaking of bread and the prayers.   *Acts 2.42*

The cup of blessing which we bless:
is it not a communion in the blood of Christ?

The bread which we break:
is it not a communion with the body of Christ?

Because there is one bread, we many are one body:
for we all partake of the one bread. Alleluia, alleluia.

The First Sunday after Trinity

COLLECT – one of the following is used.

O God,
the strength of all those who put their trust in you,
mercifully accept our prayers
and, because through the weakness of our mortal nature
we can do no good thing without you,
grant us the help of your grace,
that in the keeping of your commandments
we may please you both in will and deed;
through Jesus Christ our Lord. **Amen.**

God of truth,
help us to keep your law of love
and to walk in ways of wisdom,
that we may find true life
in Jesus Christ your Son. **Amen.**

The Divine Compassion of Christ II

Friday after the First Sunday after Trinity

Form 6 is used for all Offices.

COLLECT

Loving God,
whose Son, our Lord Jesus Christ,
was moved with compassion for all who had gone astray
and with indignation for all who had suffered wrong:
inflame our hearts with the burning fire of your love,
that we may seek out the lost,
have mercy on the fallen
and stand fast for truth and righteousness;
through Jesus Christ our Saviour. **Amen.**

Morning	Evening
Alt. Opening Canticle: 64	
Pss: 108, 146	*Pss:* 97, 98
Second Canticle: 5	*Second Canticle:* 73
Jeremiah 30.18-22	Jeremiah 31.31-34
Ephesians 1.1-14	Romans 8.28-end

Preparation Alleluia. Christ is the King of love.
O come, let us worship. Alleluia.

Benedictus **Christ loves us with an everlasting love
and shows us mercy and compassion.**

Magnificat **The riches of God's grace are ours
in the love revealed to us in Christ Jesus.**

Midday

READING Philippians 2.1-4 *or*

The Lord appeared to him from far away. I have loved you with an
everlasting love; therefore I have continued my faithfulness to you.

Jeremiah 31.3

All nations you have made shall come
and they shall worship the Lord.

They shall glorify your Name,
for you are great and do marvellous things.

The Lord is near to all who call to him;
**the Lord is full of compassion and mercy,
long-suffering and of great goodness.**

Sing to the Lord for he has done excellent things;
this is known in all the earth.

The Second Sunday after Trinity

COLLECT – one of the following is used.

Lord, you have taught us
that all our doings without love are nothing worth:
send your Holy Spirit
and pour into our hearts that most excellent gift of love,
the true bond of peace and of all virtues,
without which whoever lives is counted dead before you.
Grant this for your only Son Jesus Christ's sake. **Amen.**

Faithful Creator,
whose mercy never fails:
deepen our faithfulness to you
and to your living Word,
Jesus Christ our Lord. **Amen.**

The Third Sunday after Trinity

COLLECT – one of the following is used.

Almighty God,
you have broken the tyranny of sin
and have sent the Spirit of your Son into our hearts
    whereby we call you Father:
give us grace to dedicate our freedom to your service,
that we and all creation may be brought
    to the glorious liberty of the children of God;
through Jesus Christ our Lord. **Amen.**

God our saviour,
look on this wounded world
in pity and in power;
hold us fast to your promises of peace
won for us by your Son,
our Saviour Jesus Christ. **Amen.**

The Fourth Sunday after Trinity

COLLECT – one of the following is used.

O God, the protector of all who trust in you,
without whom nothing is strong, nothing is holy:
increase and multiply upon us your mercy;
that with you as our ruler and guide
we may so pass through things temporal
that we lose not our hold on things eternal;
grant this, heavenly Father,
for our Lord Jesus Christ's sake. **Amen.**

Gracious Father,
by the obedience of Jesus
you brought salvation to our wayward world:
draw us into harmony with your will,
that we may find all things restored in him,
our Saviour Jesus Christ. **Amen.**

The Fifth Sunday after Trinity

COLLECT – one of the following is used.

Almighty and everlasting God,
by whose Spirit the whole body of the Church
is governed and sanctified:
hear our prayer which we offer for all your faithful people,
that in their vocation and ministry
they may serve you in holiness and truth
to the glory of your name;
through our Lord and Saviour Jesus Christ. **Amen.**

Almighty God,
send down upon your Church
the riches of your Spirit,
and kindle in all who minister the gospel
your countless gifts of grace;
through Jesus Christ our Lord. **Amen.**

The Sixth Sunday after Trinity

COLLECT – one of the following is used.

Merciful God,
you have prepared for those who love you
such good things as pass our understanding:
pour into our hearts such love toward you
that we, loving you in all things and above all things,
may obtain your promises,
which exceed all that we can desire;
through Jesus Christ our Lord. **Amen.**

Creator God,
you made us all in your image:
may we discern you in all that we see,
and serve you in all that we do;
through Jesus Christ our Lord. **Amen.**

The Seventh Sunday after Trinity

COLLECT — one of the following is used.

Lord of all power and might,
the author and giver of all good things:
graft in our hearts the love of your name,
increase in us true religion,
nourish us with all goodness,
and of your great mercy keep us in the same;
through Jesus Christ our Lord. **Amen.**

Generous God,
you give us gifts and make them grow:
though our faith is small as mustard seed,
make it grow to your glory
and the flourishing of your kingdom;
through Jesus Christ our Lord. **Amen.**

The Eighth Sunday after Trinity

COLLECT — one of the following is used.

Almighty Lord and everlasting God,
we beseech you to direct, sanctify and govern
    both our hearts and bodies
in the ways of your laws
    and the works of your commandments;
that through your most mighty protection, both here and ever,
we may be preserved in body and soul;
through our Lord and Saviour Jesus Christ. **Amen.**

Lord God,
your Son left the riches of heaven
and became poor for our sake:
when we prosper save us from pride,
when we are needy save us from despair,
that we may trust in you alone;
through Jesus Christ our Lord. **Amen.**

The Ninth Sunday after Trinity

COLLECT – one of the following is used.

Almighty God,
who sent your Holy Spirit
to be the life and light of your Church:
open our hearts to the riches of your grace,
that we may bring forth the fruit of the Spirit
in love and joy and peace;
through Jesus Christ our Lord. **Amen.**

Gracious Father,
revive your Church in our day,
and make her holy, strong and faithful,
for your glory's sake
in Jesus Christ our Lord. **Amen.**

The Tenth Sunday after Trinity

COLLECT – one of the following is used.

Let your merciful ears, O Lord,
be open to the prayers of your humble servants;
and that they may obtain their petitions
make them to ask such things as shall please you;
through Jesus Christ our Lord. **Amen.**

Lord of heaven and earth,
as Jesus taught his disciples to be persistent in prayer,
give us patience and courage never to lose hope,
but always to bring our prayers before you;
through Jesus Christ our Lord. **Amen.**

The Eleventh Sunday after Trinity

COLLECT – one of the following is used.

O God, you declare your almighty power
most chiefly in showing mercy and pity:
mercifully grant to us such a measure of your grace,
that we, running the way of your commandments,
may receive your gracious promises,
and be made partakers of your heavenly treasure;
through Jesus Christ our Lord. **Amen.**

God of glory,
the end of our searching,
help us to lay aside
all that prevents us from seeking your kingdom,
and to give all that we have
to gain the pearl beyond all price,
through our Saviour Jesus Christ. **Amen.**

The Twelfth Sunday after Trinity

COLLECT – one of the following is used.

Almighty and everlasting God,
you are always more ready to hear than we to pray
and to give more than either we desire or deserve:
pour down upon us the abundance of your mercy,
forgiving us those things of which our conscience is afraid
and giving us those good things
    which we are not worthy to ask
but through the merits and mediation
of Jesus Christ your Son our Lord. **Amen.**

God of constant mercy,
who sent your Son to save us:
remind us of your goodness,
increase your grace within us,
that our thankfulness may grow,
through Jesus Christ our Lord. **Amen.**

The Thirteenth Sunday after Trinity

COLLECT – one of the following is used.

Almighty God,
who called your Church to bear witness
that you were in Christ reconciling the world to yourself:
help us to proclaim the good news of your love,
that all who hear it may be drawn to you;
through him who was lifted up on the cross,
and reigns with you in the unity of the Holy Spirit,
one God, now and for ever. **Amen.**

Almighty God,
you search us and know us:
may we rely on you in strength
and rest on you in weakness,
now and in all our days;
through Jesus Christ our Lord. **Amen.**

The Fourteenth Sunday after Trinity

COLLECT – one of the following is used.

Almighty God,
whose only Son has opened for us
a new and living way into your presence:
give us pure hearts and steadfast wills
to worship you in spirit and in truth;
through Jesus Christ our Lord. **Amen**

Merciful God,
your Son came to save us
and bore our sins on the cross:
may we trust in your mercy
and know your love,
rejoicing in the righteousness
that is ours through Jesus Christ our Lord. **Amen.**

The Fifteenth Sunday after Trinity

COLLECT – one of the following is used.

God, who in generous mercy sent the Holy Spirit
 upon your Church in the burning fire of your love:
grant that your people may be fervent
 in the fellowship of the gospel
that, always abiding in you,
they may be found steadfast in faith and active in service;
through Jesus Christ our Lord. **Amen**

Lord God,
defend your Church from all false teaching
and give to your people knowledge of your truth,
that we may enjoy eternal life
in Jesus Christ our Lord. **Amen.**

The Sixteenth Sunday after Trinity

COLLECT – one of the following is used.

O Lord, we beseech you mercifully to hear the prayers
 of your people who call upon you;
and grant that they may both perceive and know
 what things they ought to do,
and also may have grace and power faithfully to fulfil them;
through Jesus Christ our Lord. **Amen.**

Lord of creation,
whose glory is around and within us:
open our eyes to your wonders,
that we may serve you with reverence
and know your peace at our lives' end,
through Jesus Christ our Lord. **Amen.**

The Seventeenth Sunday after Trinity

COLLECT – one of the following is used.

Almighty God,
you have made us for yourself,
and our hearts are restless till they find their rest in you:
pour your love into our hearts and draw us to yourself,
and so bring us at last to your heavenly city
where we shall see you face to face;
through Jesus Christ our Lord. **Amen.**

Gracious God,
you call us to fullness of life:
deliver us from unbelief
and banish our anxieties
with the liberating love of Jesus Christ our Lord. **Amen.**

The Eighteenth Sunday after Trinity

COLLECT – one of the following is used.

Almighty and everlasting God,
increase in us your gift of faith
that, forsaking what lies behind
and reaching out to that which is before,
we may run the way of your commandments
and win the crown of everlasting joy;
through Jesus Christ our Lord. **Amen.**

God, our judge and saviour,
teach us to be open to your truth
and to trust in your love,
that we may live each day
with confidence in the salvation which is given
through Jesus Christ our Lord. **Amen.**

The Nineteenth Sunday after Trinity

COLLECT – one of the following is used.

O God, forasmuch as without you
we are not able to please you;
mercifully grant that your Holy Spirit
may in all things direct and rule our hearts;
through Jesus Christ our Lord. **Amen.**

Faithful Lord,
whose steadfast love never ceases
and whose mercies never come to an end:
grant us the grace to trust you
and to receive the gifts of your love,
new every morning,
in Jesus Christ our Lord. **Amen.**

The Twentieth Sunday after Trinity

COLLECT – one of the following is used.

God, the giver of life,
whose Holy Spirit wells up within your Church:
by the Spirit's gifts equip us to live the gospel of Christ
    and make us eager to do your will,
that we may share with the whole creation
    the joys of eternal life;
through Jesus Christ our Lord. **Amen.**

God, our light and our salvation:
illuminate our lives,
that we may see your goodness in the land of the living,
and looking on your beauty
may be changed into the likeness of Jesus Christ our Lord. **Amen.**

The Twenty-first Sunday after Trinity

COLLECT – one of the following is used.

Grant, we beseech you, merciful Lord,
to your faithful people pardon and peace,
that they may be cleansed from all their sins
and serve you with a quiet mind;
through Jesus Christ our Lord. **Amen.**

Almighty God,
in whose service lies perfect freedom:
teach us to obey you
with loving hearts and steadfast wills;
through Jesus Christ our Lord. **Amen.**

*If there are twenty-three Sundays after Trinity, the provision for the Third Sunday
before Lent is used on the Twenty-second Sunday after Trinity.*

The Last Sunday after Trinity

COLLECT – one of the following is used.

Blessèd Lord,
who caused all holy Scriptures to be written for our learning:
help us so to hear them,
to read, mark, learn and inwardly digest them
that, through patience, and the comfort of your holy word,
we may embrace and for ever hold fast
    the hope of everlasting life,
which you have given us in our Saviour Jesus Christ. **Amen.**

Merciful God,
teach us to be faithful in change and uncertainty,
that trusting in your word
and obeying your will
we may enter the unfailing joy of Jesus Christ our Lord. **Amen.**

From All Saints' Day until the day before the First Sunday of Advent

Form 7 is used for Morning, Evening and Night Prayer.

MIDDAY PRAYER IN ALL SAINTS TO ADVENT

Form 1-7 is used with the following propers:

DOXOLOGY TO HYMN

Most loving Father, hear our plea!
You rule the world with equity,
Together with your only Son,
And with your Spirit, three in one. Amen.

PSALMS Psalms of Ascent *(Pss 121-131, 133)*

READING

Sunday	Revelation 4.9-end	*Thursday*	Ephesians 4.11-13
Monday	Philippians 4.4-7	*Friday*	Hebrews 12.1-2
Tuesday	Hebrews 12.22-24	*Saturday*	Daniel 12.2-3
Wednesday	Matthew 24.30-31		

or, on any day in All Saints to Advent, one of the following readings is used:

Our citizenship is in heaven, and it is from there that we are expecting a
Saviour, the Lord Jesus Christ.   *Philippians 3.20*

Blessèd are the poor in spirit, for theirs is the kingdom of heaven.

Matthew 5.3

RESPONSE

Either **A:**

God raised Christ from the dead,
and enthroned him at his right hand in heaven.

He shall be called the Prince of Peace,
and his throne shall be established for ever.

He shall be great to the ends of the earth,
and he shall be their peace.

The Lord has given him the dominion and glory and a kingdom:
that all peoples, nations and languages shall serve him.
Alleluia, alleluia.

or **B:**

To him who loves us and has freed us from our sins by his blood:
to him be glory and dominion for ever.

You are a chosen race, a royal priesthood, a holy nation,
God's own people,
that you may declare the wonderful deeds of him
who has called you out of darkness into his marvellous light.

Once you were no people, but now you are God's people;
once you had not received mercy, but now you
have received mercy.

To him who loves us and has freed us from our sins by his blood:
to him be glory and dominion for ever.

COLLECT – one of the following is used.

God the Father,
help us to hear the call of Christ the King
and to follow in his service,
whose kingdom has no end;
for he reigns with you and the Holy Spirit,
one God, one glory. **Amen.**

Bring us, O Lord God, at our last awakening
into the house and gate of heaven,
to enter that gate and dwell in that house,
where there shall be no darkness nor dazzling,
but one equal light;
no noise nor silence, but one equal music;
no fears nor hopes, but one equal possession;
no ends or beginnings, but one equal eternity;
in the habitations of your glory and dominion,
world without end. **Amen.**

Eric Milner-White (1963)
after John Donne (1631)

May God give us grace to follow his saints in glory. Amen.

1 November – All Saints' Day   1

COLLECT – one of the following is used.

Almighty God,
you have knit together your elect
in one communion and fellowship
   in the mystical body of your Son Christ our Lord:
grant us grace so to follow your blessèd saints
in all virtuous and godly living
that we may come to those inexpressible joys
that you have prepared for those who truly love you;
through Jesus Christ our Lord. **Amen.**

God of holiness,
your glory is proclaimed in every age:
as we rejoice in the faith of your saints,
inspire us to follow their example
with boldness and joy;
through Jesus Christ our Lord. **Amen.**

	Morning	*Evening*
31 Oct.		*Second Canticle:* 50
1 Nov.	*Opening Canticle:* 64 *Second Canticle:* 18	*Second Canticle:* 39

Magnificat **The saints cried out with a loud voice:**
Eve   **Salvation to our God who sits on the throne**
          and to the Lamb.

Preparation Alleluia. Our God is glorious in all the saints.
          O come, let us worship. Alleluia.

Benedictus **The righteous will shine like the sun**
          in the highest heavens.

Magnificat **With one heart and voice, all the saints proclaim:**
          We praise you, blessèd Trinity, one God.

READING   Hebrews 12.22-24 or

I heard the voice of a great multitude crying out, 'Alleluia! For the Lord our God the Almighty reigns.'   *Revelation 19.6*

RESPONSE

A great multitude which no one could number,
  stood before the throne and before the Lamb,
clothed with white robes, and with palms in their hands.

They cried with a loud voice saying:
Salvation to our God who sits on the throne, and to the Lamb.

These are they who have come out of the great tribulation,
**they have washed their robes, and made them white
  in the blood of the Lamb.**

Therefore they are before the throne of God,
  and serve him day and night.
**Salvation to the God who sits on the throne,
  and to the Lamb.**

The Fourth Sunday before Advent

COLLECT – *one of the following is used.*

Almighty and eternal God,
you have kindled the flame of love
  in the hearts of the saints:
grant to us the same faith and power of love,
that, as we rejoice in their triumphs,
we may be sustained by their example and fellowship;
through Jesus Christ our Lord. **Amen.**

God of glory,
touch our lips with the fire of your Spirit,
that we with all creation
may rejoice to sing your praise;
through Jesus Christ our Lord. **Amen.**

The Third Sunday before Advent

COLLECT – one of the following is used.

Almighty Father,
whose will is to restore all things
in your beloved Son, the King of all:
govern the hearts and minds of those in authority,
and bring the families of the nations,
divided and torn apart by the ravages of sin,
to be subject to his just and gentle rule;
who is alive and reigns with you,
in the unity of the Holy Spirit,
one God, now and for ever. **Amen.**

God, our refuge and strength,
bring near the day when wars shall cease
and poverty and pain shall end,
that earth may know the peace of heaven
through Jesus Christ our Lord. **Amen.**

*In years when Remembrance Sunday is observed on the Second Sunday before
Advent, the Collect for the Third Sunday before Advent may be used on
Remembrance Sunday and the Collect for the Second Sunday before Advent may
be used on the Third Sunday before Advent.*

The Second Sunday before Advent

COLLECT – one of the following is used.

Heavenly Father,
whose blessèd Son was revealed
    to destroy the works of the devil
and to make us the children of God and heirs of eternal life:
grant that we, having this hope,
may purify ourselves even as he is pure;
that when he shall appear in power and great glory
we may be made like him in his eternal and glorious kingdom;
where he is alive and reigns with you,
in the unity of the Holy Spirit,
one God, now and for ever. **Amen.**

Heavenly Lord,
you long for the world's salvation:
stir us from apathy,
restrain us from excess
and revive in us new hope
that all creation will one day be healed
in Jesus Christ our Lord. **Amen.**

Christ the King
The Sunday Next before Advent

COLLECT – one of the following is used.

Eternal Father,
whose Son Jesus Christ ascended to the throne of heaven
    that he might rule over all things as Lord and King:
keep the Church in the unity of the Spirit
and in the bond of peace,
and bring the whole created order to worship at his feet;
who is alive and reigns with you,
in the unity of the Holy Spirit,
one God, now and for ever. **Amen.**

Mighty God,
most holy and most humble,
you have chosen to hear our cry
and share our poverty.
Come close to our world,
kindle our hearts
and melt our despair,
that with all your creatures
we may live in hope;
through Jesus Christ our King, **Amen.**

Janet Morley

The following may be used as the Collect at Morning and Evening Prayer during this week.

Stir up, O Lord,
the wills of your faithful people;
that they, plenteously bringing forth the fruit of good works,
may by you be plenteously rewarded;
through Jesus Christ our Lord. **Amen.**

	Morning	**Evening**
Sat.		*Second Canticle: 55*
Sun.	*Opening Canticle: 64* *Second Canticle: 4*	*Second Canticle: 57*

Magnificat **Blessèd is the king**
Eve   **who comes in the name of the Lord.**

Preparation Alleluia. Christ is king: let the earth rejoice.
              O come, let us worship. Alleluia.

Benedictus **God raised Christ from the dead,**
             and enthroned him at his right hand in heaven.

Magnificat **God has given him dominion,**
             glory and all sovereignty;
             that all peoples and nations shall serve him.

Midday, as for All Saints to Advent, with the following propers:

READING I Timothy 6.13-16 *or*

God put his power to work in Christ when he raised him from the dead
and seated him at his right hand in the heavenly places.   *Ephesians 1.20*

RESPONSE

He shall be called the Prince of Peace,
and his throne shall be established for ever.

His kingdom is an everlasting kingdom,
and all nations shall serve and obey him.

He shall be great to the ends of the earth,
and he shall be their peace.

The Lord has given him the dominion and glory and a kingdom:
that all peoples, nations and languages shall serve him.
Alleluia, alleluia.

Festivals and Lesser Festivals (Sanctorale)

| 1 January | **The Naming & Circumcision of Jesus,** see page 550 | I |

| 2 January | **Basil the Great & Gregory of Nazianzus** | III |
| | *Common of Teachers of the Faith, page 706* | |

COLLECT

Lord God,
whose servants Basil and Gregory
proclaimed the mystery of your Word made flesh,
to build up your church in wisdom and strength:
grant that we may rejoice in his presence among us,
and so be brought with them to know the power
of your unending love;
through Jesus Christ our Lord. **Amen.**

| **6 January** | **The Epiphany,** see page 555 | I |

| 12 January | **Aelred of Hexham** | III |
| | *Common of Members of Religious Communities, page 710* | |

COLLECT

Almighty God,
who endowed Aelred the abbot
with the gift of Christian friendship
and the wisdom to lead others in the way of holiness:
grant to your people that same spirit of mutual affection,
so that loving one another,
we may know the love of Christ
and rejoice in the eternal possession
of your supreme goodness;
through Jesus Christ our Lord. **Amen.**

| 13 January | **Hilary** | III |

Common of Teachers of the Faith, page 706

COLLECT

Everlasting God,
whose servant Hilary
steadfastly confessed your Son Jesus Christ
to be both human and divine:
grant us his gentle courtesy
to bring to all the message of redemption
in the incarnate Christ,
who is alive and reigns with you,
in the unity of the Holy Spirit,
one God, now and for ever. **Amen.**

| 16 January | **First Franciscan Martyrs** | III |

Common of Martyrs, page 704

COLLECT

God of our salvation,
we thank you for the first Franciscan martyrs
who shared in the passion of your beloved Son.
May we also persevere until death
  in bearing witness to you
and share with them in the glory of eternity;
through Jesus Christ our Lord. **Amen.**

| 17 January | **Antony of Egypt** | III |

*Common of Members of Religious Communities,
page 710*

COLLECT

Most gracious God,
who called your servant Antony to sell all that he had
and to serve you in the solitude of the desert:
by his example may we learn to deny ourselves
and to love you before all things;
through Jesus Christ our Lord. **Amen.**

SSF

18-25 January   **Week of Prayer for Christian Unity**

Form 5, Common of the Unity of the Church, page 720, is used.

18 January   **Confession of Peter**   II

Form 7, of Apostles, is used for Morning, Evening and Night Prayer.

COLLECT

Almighty God,
you inspired Saint Peter,
first among the apostles,
to confess Jesus as the Messiah
and Son of the living God:
keep your Church steadfast
on the rock of this faith,
through Jesus Christ our Lord. **Amen.**

Church of the Province of Southern Africa

Morning	Evening
Alt. Opening Canticle: 64	
Pss: 71, 117	Pss: 145
Second Canticle: 17	Second Canticle: 51
Ezekiel 12.1-7	Ezekiel 3.4-11
Acts 11.1-18	Matthew 14.22-33

Midday

The appropriate weekday of Form 1-7 is used with the Common of Apostles, page 700.

19 January   **Wulfstan**   III

Common of Bishops and other Pastors, page 708

COLLECT

Lord God,
who raised up Wulfstan to be a bishop among your people
and a leader of your Church:
help us, after his example,
to live simply,
to work diligently
and to make your kingdom known;
through Jesus Christ our Lord. **Amen.**   *Robert Jeffery*

20 January   Founders of Anglican Franciscan
Communities   II

Form 3, of Members of Religious Communities, is used for Morning,
Evening and Night Prayer.

COLLECT

Everlasting God,
we praise you for the founders of Anglican Franciscan
    communities;
grant that as we commemorate them in thanksgiving
    and celebration,
we may know the truth of the gospel in our hearts
and build well on the foundations they have laid,
in Jesus Christ our Lord. **Amen.**   *SSF*

Morning	Evening
Alt. Opening Canticle: 64	
Pss: 1, 15, 148	*Pss:* 65, 84
Second Canticle: 10	*Second Canticle:* 54
Proverbs 16.1-9	2 Kings 2.4-14
2 Corinthians 6.1-10	Romans 8.26-30

Preparation   Alleluia. Christ the poor and lowly in heart.
              O come, let us worship. Alleluia.

Benedictus   **Blessèd are you who are poor,**
              for yours is the kingdom of God.

Magnificat   **Everyone who has left all things**
and followed me
will be repaid a hundred times over
and inherit eternal life.

Midday

The appropriate weekday of Form 1-7 is used with the Common of Members of Religious Communities, page 710.

21 January   **Agnes**   III
               Common of Martyrs, page 704

COLLECT

Eternal God, shepherd of your sheep,
whose child Agnes was strengthened to bear witness
in her living and her dying
to the true love of her redeemer:
grant us the power to understand, with all your saints,
what is the breadth and length and height and depth
and to know the love that surpasses knowledge,
even Jesus Christ your Son our Lord,
who is alive and reigns with you,
in the unity of the Holy Spirit,
one God, now and for ever. **Amen.**

24 January   **Francis de Sales**   III
               Common of Teachers of the Faith, page 706

COLLECT

Holy God,
who called your bishop Francis de Sales
to bring many to Christ through his devout life
and to renew your Church with patience and understanding:
grant that we may, by word and example,
reflect your gentleness and love to all we meet;
through Jesus Christ our Saviour,
who is alive and reigns with you,
in the unity of the Holy Spirit,
one God, now and for ever. **Amen.**

25 January   The Conversion of Paul   II

Form 7, of Apostles, is used for Morning, Evening and Night Prayer.

COLLECT

Almighty God,
who caused the light of the gospel
to shine throughout the world
through the preaching of your servant Saint Paul:
grant that we who celebrate his wonderful conversion
may follow him in bearing witness to your truth;
through Jesus Christ our Lord. **Amen.**

Morning	Evening
Alt. Opening Canticle: 64 *Second Canticle: 17*	*Second Canticle: 43*

Midday

The appropriate weekday of Form 1-7 is used with the Common of Apostles, page 700.

26 January   **Timothy and Titus**   III

Form 2, of Missionaries, is used for Morning and Evening Prayer.
The appropriate weekday of Form 1-7, of Epiphany, is used for Midday.
Form 5 is used for Night Prayer.

COLLECT

Heavenly Father,
who sent your apostle Paul to preach the gospel,
and gave him Timothy and Titus
to be his companions in faith:
grant that our fellowship in the Holy Spirit
may bear witness to the name of Jesus,
who is alive and reigns with you,
in the unity of the Holy Spirit,
one God, now and for ever. **Amen.**

Church of the Province of Southern Africa

Morning	Evening
Pss: 97, 147 part 1	*Pss:* 34
Second Canticle: 13	*Second Canticle:* 47
Numbers 11.16-17,24-25	Numbers 27.15-end
1 Timothy 6.11-16	Galatians 2.1-10

28 January   **Thomas Aquinas**   III

Common of Teachers of the Faith, page 706

COLLECT

Eternal God,
who enriched your Church with the learning and holiness
of your servant Thomas Aquinas:
give to all who seek you
a humble mind and a pure heart
that they may know your Son Jesus Christ
as the way, the truth and the life;
who is alive and reigns with you,
in the unity of the Holy Spirit,
one God, now and for ever. **Amen.**

30 January   **Charles**   III

Common of Martyrs, page 704

COLLECT

King of kings and Lord of lords,
whose faithful servant Charles
prayed for those who persecuted him
and died in the living hope of your eternal kingdom:
grant us by your grace so to follow his example
that we may love and bless our enemies,
through the intercession of your Son, our Lord Jesus Christ. **Amen.**

2 February   **The Presentation of Christ in the Temple,** *see page 559*   I

| 3 February | **Anskar** | III |

Common of Missionaries, page 712

COLLECT

God of grace and might,
who sent your servant Anskar
to spread the gospel to the Nordic peoples:
raise up, we pray, in our generation
messengers of your good news
and heralds of your kingdom
that the world may come to know
the immeasurable riches of our Saviour Jesus Christ. **Amen.**

| 7 February | **Colette** | III |

Common of Members of Religious Communities,
page 710

COLLECT

God our sustainer,
who inspired Colette to be an example
and leader of evangelical perfection for many:
grant that the spirit of Francis and Clare
which she wisely taught
and wondrously confirmed by her example
may ever abide in us;
through Jesus Christ our Lord. **Amen.**

| 14 February | **Cyril and Methodius** | III |

Common of Missionaries, page 712

COLLECT

Lord of all,
who gave to your servants Cyril and Methodius
the gift of tongues to proclaim the gospel to the Slavs:
make your whole Church one as you are one
that all Christians may honour one another,
and east and west acknowledge
one Lord, one faith, one baptism,
and you, the God and Father of all;
through Jesus Christ our Lord. **Amen.**

17 February   **Janani Luwum**   III

Common of Martyrs, page 704

COLLECT

God of truth,
whose servant Janani Luwum walked in the light,
and in his death defied the powers of darkness:
free us from fear of those who kill the body,
that we too may walk as children of light,
through him who overcame darkness by the power of the cross,
Jesus Christ our Lord. **Amen.**

23 February   **Polycarp**   III

Common of Martyrs, page 704

COLLECT

Almighty God,
who gave to your servant Polycarp
boldness to confess the name of our Saviour Jesus Christ
before the rulers of this world
and courage to die for his faith:
grant that we also may be ready
to give an answer for the faith that is in us
and to suffer gladly for the sake of our Lord Jesus Christ. **Amen.**

TEC

24 February   **The Vocation of Francis**   III

Common of Ministry, page 723

COLLECT

Most High and glorious God,
enlighten the darkness of our hearts
and give us a true faith, a certain hope
and a perfect love.
Give us a sense of the divine
and knowledge of yourself,
so that we may do everything
in fulfilment of your holy will;
through Jesus Christ our Lord. **Amen.**

The Prayer before the Crucifix, Francis of Assisi

27 February   **George Herbert**   III
Common of Bishops and other Pastors, page 708

COLLECT

King of glory, king of peace,
who called your servant George Herbert
from the pursuit of worldly honours
to be a priest in the temple of his God and king:
grant us also the grace to offer ourselves
with singleness of heart in humble obedience to your service;
through Jesus Christ our Lord. **Amen.**

SSF

I March   David   II

*Form 5, of Bishops and other Pastors, is used for Morning,
Evening and Night Prayer.*

COLLECT

Almighty God,
who called your servant David
to be a faithful and wise steward of your mysteries
    for the people of Wales:
in your mercy, grant that,
following his purity of life and zeal for the gospel of Christ,
we may with him receive the crown of everlasting life;
through Jesus Christ our Lord. **Amen**

The Church in Wales

Morning	Evening
Alt. Opening Canticle: 64	
Pss: 112, 147 part 1	*Pss:* 92, 99
Second Canticle: 31	*Second Canticle:* 53
Wisdom 5.1-16	Ezekiel 2.1-7
Hebrews 11.8-16	2 Timothy 4.1-8

Midday

*The appropriate weekday of Form 1-7 is used with the Common of Bishops and
other Pastors, page 708.*

| 2 March | **Chad** | III |

Common of Missionaries, page 712

COLLECT

Almighty God,
from the first fruits of the English nation who turned to Christ,
you called your servant Chad
to be an evangelist and bishop of his own people:
give us grace so to follow his peaceable nature,
humble spirit and prayerful life,
that we may truly commend to others
the faith which we ourselves profess;
through Jesus Christ our Lord. **Amen.**

SSF

| 7 March | **Perpetua, Felicity & their Companions** | III |

Common of Martyrs, page 704

COLLECT

Holy God,
who gave great courage
to Perpetua, Felicity and their companions:
grant that we may be worthy
to climb the ladder of sacrifice
and be received into the garden of peace;
through Jesus Christ our Lord. **Amen.**   *SSF *

| 8 March | **Edward King** | III |

Common of Bishops and other Pastors, page 708

COLLECT

God of peace,
who gave such grace to your servant Edward King
that whomever he met he drew to Christ:
fill us, we pray, with tender sympathy and joyful faith,
that we also may win others
to know the love that passes knowledge;
through him who is the shepherd and guardian of our souls,
Jesus Christ your Son our Lord. **Amen.**

17 March　　Patrick

Form 2, of Missionaries, is used for Morning, Evening and Night Prayer.

COLLECT

Almighty God,
who in your providence chose your servant Patrick
to be the apostle of the Irish people:
keep alive in us the fire of the faith he kindled
and strengthen us in our pilgrimage
towards the light of everlasting life;
through Jesus Christ your Son our Lord. **Amen.**

Morning	Evening
Alt. Opening Canticle: 64 *Pss:* 106.1-9, 147 part 1 *Second Canticle:* 9 Isaiah 51.1-8 Acts 16.6-15	*Pss:* 46, 96 *Second Canticle:* 53 Isaiah 8.19 – 9.2 Luke 6.20-31

Midday

The appropriate weekday of Form 1-7 is used with the Common of Missionaries, page 712.

19 March　　Joseph of Nazareth

Form 4 is used for Morning, Evening and Night Prayer.

COLLECT

God our Father,
who from the family of your servant David
raised up Joseph the carpenter
to be the guardian of your incarnate Son
and husband of the Blessed Virgin Mary:
give us grace to follow him
in faithful obedience to your commands;
through Jesus Christ our Lord. **Amen.**

Morning	Evening
Alt. Opening Canticle: 64 *Second Canticle:* 7	*Second Canticle:* 45

Preparation (Alleluia.) The Lord became the carpenter's Son.
O come, let us worship. (Alleluia.)

Benedictus **Behold the faithful and wise servant**
whom the Master placed over his household.
(Alleluia.)

Magnificat **Joseph of Nazareth went up to Bethlehem**
to be enrolled with Mary his betrothed,
who was with child. (Alleluia.)

Midday

Form 1-7 is used with the following propers:

READING Luke 2.41-51 *or*

You know that from the Lord you will receive the inheritance as your
reward; you serve the Lord Christ.   *Colossians 3.24*

RESPONSE

Joseph was the husband of Mary,
who gave birth to Jesus, called Messiah.

A faithful man who abounds with blessings,
he who guards his master will be honoured.

Behold the faithful and wise servant:
whom the master placed over his household.

Joseph was the husband of Mary,
who gave birth to Jesus, called Messiah.

| 20 March | **Cuthbert** | III |
| | *Common of Missionaries, page 712* | |

COLLECT

Almighty God,
who called your servant Cuthbert from following the flock
to follow your Son and to be a shepherd of your people:
in your mercy, grant that we, following his example,
may bring those who are lost home to your fold;
through Jesus Christ our Lord. **Amen.**

| 21 March | **Thomas Cranmer** | III |
| | *Common of Martyrs, page 704* | |

COLLECT

Father of all mercies,
who through the work of your servant Thomas Cranmer
    renewed the worship of your Church
and through his death revealed your strength
    in human weakness:
by your grace strengthen us to worship you
in spirit and in truth
and so to come to the joys of your everlasting kingdom;
through Jesus Christ our Mediator and Advocate. **Amen.**

25 March   The Annunciation of Our Lord   I

Form 4 is used for Morning, Evening and Night Prayer.

COLLECT – one of the following is used.

We beseech you, O Lord,
pour your grace into our hearts,
that as we have known the incarnation of your Son Jesus Christ
    by the message of an angel,
so by his cross and passion
we may be brought to the glory of his resurrection;
through Jesus Christ our Lord. **Amen.**

O God,
you fulfil our desire
beyond what we can bear;
as Mary gave her appalled assent
to your intimate promise,
so may we open ourselves also
to contain your life within us,
through Jesus Christ. **Amen.**   *Janet Morley*

	Morning	*Evening*
24 Mar.		*Second Canticle: 47*
25 Mar.	*Opening Canticle: 64* *Second Canticle: 7*	*Second Canticle: 73*

Magnificat   **The Holy Spirit will come upon you, Mary,**
Eve   **and the power of the Most High**
                will overshadow you. (Alleluia.)

Preparation   (Alleluia.) The Word was made flesh.
                O come, let us worship. (Alleluia.)

Benedictus   **The Word of God,**
                begotten of the Father
                before time began, humbled himself for us
                and was incarnate from the Holy Spirit and
                the Virgin Mary. (Alleluia.)

Magnificat   **Mary received the word of the Lord**
                and conceived the Word of life. (Alleluia.)

Midday

The appropriate weekday of Form 1-7 is used with the following propers:

DOXOLOGY TO HYMN

Lord Jesus, King of heaven and earth,
We praise you for your virgin birth;
You are the Father's only Son,
With God the Spirit, ever one. Amen.

Christ Jesus, though he was in the form of God, did not regard equality with God as something to be exploited, but emptied himself, taking the form of a slave, being born in human likeness.   *Philippians 2.6,7*

RESPONSE

It was there from the beginning:
we have heard it and we have seen it with our own eyes.

We looked upon it:
and touched it with our own hands.

We speak of the Word of life,
and this life was made visible.

We here declare to you the eternal life which dwelt with the Father,
and was made visible to us.

We share a common life with the Father and his Son Jesus Christ:
that the joy of us all may be complete. (Alleluia, alleluia.)

10 April	**William Law**	III
	Common of Teachers of the Faith, page 706	

COLLECT

Almighty God,
who called your servant William Law
to a devout and holy life:
grant that by your spirit of love
and through faithfulness in prayer
we may find the way to divine knowledge
and so come to see the hidden things of God;
through Jesus Christ our Lord. **Amen.**

SSF

16 April	**Taking of Vows by Francis**
	& Renewal of Commitment (p. 748) III
	Common of Members of Religious Communities,
	page 710

COLLECT

Creator God
rekindle in us your gifts of grace;
renew our Franciscan life,
and bring to completion
all that your calling has begun in *us*
through following the teaching and footprints
of your Son, our Saviour, Jesus Christ. **Amen.**

SSF

| 19 April | **Alphege** | III |
| | *Common of Martyrs, page 704* |

COLLECT

Merciful God,
who raised up your servant Alphege
to be a pastor of your people
and gave him grace to suffer for justice and true religion:
grant that we who celebrate his martyrdom
may know the power of the risen Christ in our hearts
and share his peace in lives offered to your service;
through Jesus Christ our Lord. **Amen.**

| 21 April | **Anselm** | III |
| | *Common of Teachers of the Faith, page 706* |

COLLECT

Eternal God,
who gave great gifts to your servant Anselm
as a pastor and teacher:
grant that we, like him, may desire you with our whole heart
and, so desiring, may seek you
and, seeking, may find you;
through Jesus Christ our Lord. **Amen.**

SSF *

23 April   George   II

Form 6, of Martyrs, is used for Morning, Evening and Night Prayer.

COLLECT

God of hosts,
who so kindled the flame of love
in the heart of your servant George
that he bore witness to the risen Lord
by his life and by his death:
give us the same faith and power of love
that we who rejoice in his triumphs
may come to share with him the fullness of the resurrection;
through Jesus Christ our Lord. **Amen.**

Michael Perham

Morning	Evening
Alt. Opening Canticle: 64 Second Canticle: 28	Second Canticle: 43

Midday

The appropriate weekday of Form 1-7 is used with the Common of Martyrs, page 704.

25 April   Mark   II

Form 2, of Evangelists, is used for Morning, Evening and Night Prayer.

COLLECT

Almighty God,
who enlightened your holy Church
through the inspired witness of your evangelist Saint Mark:
grant that we, being firmly grounded
   in the truth of the gospel,
may be faithful to its teaching both in word and deed;
through Jesus Christ our Lord. **Amen.**

Morning	Evening
Alt. Opening Canticle: 64 Second Canticle: 34	Second Canticle: 55

Midday

The appropriate weekday of Form 1-7 is used with the Common of Evangelists, page 702.

| 29 April | **Catherine of Siena** | III |

Common of Teachers of the Faith, page 706

COLLECT

God of compassion,
who gave your servant Catherine of Siena
a wondrous love of the passion of Christ:
grant that your people may be united to him in his majesty
and rejoice for ever in the revelation of his glory;
who is alive and reigns with you,
in the unity of the Holy Spirit,
one God, now and for ever. **Amen.**

SSF

| 1 May | **Philip and James** | II |

Form 7, of Apostles, is used for Morning, Evening and Night Prayer.

COLLECT

Almighty Father,
whom truly to know is eternal life:
teach us to know your Son Jesus Christ
as the way, the truth, and the life;
that we may follow the steps
    of your holy apostles Philip and James,
and walk steadfastly in the way that leads to your glory;
through Jesus Christ our Lord. **Amen.**

Morning	Evening
Alt. Opening Canticle: 64 Second Canticle: 22	Second Canticle: 50

Midday

The appropriate weekday of Form 1-7 is used with the Common of Apostles, page 700.

2 May	**Athanasius**	III

Common of Teachers of the Faith, page 706

COLLECT

Ever-living God,
whose servant Athanasius testified
   to the mystery of the Word made flesh for our salvation:
help us, with all your saints,
to contend for the truth
and to grow into the likeness of your Son,
Jesus Christ our Lord. **Amen.**

4 May	**English Saints and Martyrs** **of the Reformation Era**	III

Common of Any Saint, page 714

COLLECT

Merciful God,
who, when your Church on earth was torn apart
   by the ravages of sin,
raised up men and women in this land
who witnessed to their faith with courage and constancy:
give to your Church that peace which is your will,
and grant that those who have been divided on earth
   may be reconciled in heaven
and share together in the vision of your glory;
through Jesus Christ our Lord. **Amen.**

8 May   **Julian of Norwich**   III

Common of Members of Religious Communities,
page 710

COLLECT – one of the following is used.

Most holy God, the ground of our beseeching,
who through your servant Julian
revealed the wonders of your love:
grant that as we are created in your nature
    and restored by your grace,
our wills may be so made one with yours
that we may come to see you face to face
and gaze on you for ever;
through Jesus Christ our Lord. **Amen.**

Christ our true mother,
you have carried us within you,
laboured with us,
and brought us forth to bliss.
Enclose us in your care,
that in stumbling we may not fall,
nor be overcome by evil,
but know that all shall be well, **Amen.**

Janet Morley

14 May   Matthias   II

Form 7, of Apostles, is used for Morning, Evening and Night Prayer.

COLLECT

Almighty God,
who in the place of the traitor Judas
chose your faithful servant Matthias
to be of the number of the Twelve:
preserve your Church from false apostles
and, by the ministry of faithful pastors and teachers,
keep us steadfast in your truth;
through Jesus Christ our Lord. **Amen.**

Morning	Evening
Alt. Opening Canticle: 64 Second Canticle: 32	Second Canticle: 53

Midday

The appropriate weekday of Form 1-7 is used with the Common of Apostles, page 700.

15 May	**Pachomius**	III

Common of Members of Religious Communities, page 710

COLLECT

Everliving God,
who called your servant Pachomius
to live the evangelical counsels
dedicated to the common life:
grant to all Christians living in community
the spirit of forgiveness, acceptance and love;
through Jesus Christ our Lord. **Amen.**

16 May	**Margaret of Cortona**	III

Common of Members of Religious Communities, page 710

COLLECT

God of mercy,
give us grace that we may truly repent of our sins
following the example of your servant, Margaret of Cortona;
and that, by a living faith,
we may obtain full forgiveness;
through the merits of Jesus Christ our Lord. **Amen.**

19 May	**Dunstan**	III

Common of Bishops and other Pastors, page 708

COLLECT

Almighty God,
who raised up Dunstan to be a true shepherd of the flock,
a restorer of monastic life
and a faithful counsellor to those in authority:
give to all pastors the same gifts of your Holy Spirit
that they may be true servants of Christ and of all his people;
through Jesus Christ our Lord. **Amen.**

SSF

20 May	**Bernardine of Siena**	III

*Common of Members of Religious Communities,
page 710*

COLLECT

God of glory,
who gave your servant Bernardine
a most tender love of the Holy Name of Jesus:
grant that we may always be alive
with the spirit of your love;
through Jesus Christ our Lord. **Amen.**

24 May	**John and Charles Wesley**	III

Common of Bishops and other Pastors, page 708

COLLECT

God of mercy,
who inspired John and Charles Wesley
with zeal for your gospel:
grant to all people boldness to proclaim your word
and a heart ever to rejoice in singing your praises;
through Jesus Christ our Lord. **Amen.**

SSF *

| 25 May | **The Venerable Bede** | III |

Common of Members of Religious Communities,
page 710

COLLECT

God our maker,
whose Son Jesus Christ gave to your servant Bede
grace to drink in with joy the word
   that leads us to know you and to love you:
in your goodness
grant that we also may come at length to you,
the source of all wisdom,
and stand before your face;
through Jesus Christ our Lord. **Amen.**

| **26 May** | **Augustine of Canterbury** | II |

Form 5, of Bishops and other Pastors, is used for Morning,
Evening and Night Prayer.

COLLECT

Almighty God,
whose servant Augustine was sent as the apostle
   of the English people:
grant that as he laboured in the Spirit
   to preach Christ's gospel in this land,
so all who hear the good news
may strive to make your truth known in all the world;
through Jesus Christ our Lord. **Amen.**   *SSF* *

Morning	Evening
Alt. Opening Canticle: 64	
Pss: 47, 147 part 1	*Pss:* 67, 98, 99
Second Canticle: 35	*Second Canticle:* 53
Isaiah 61.1-9	Deuteronomy 30.11-end
Acts 17.16-31	2 Corinthians 5.11 – 6.2

Midday

The appropriate weekday of Form 1-7 is used with the Common of Bishops and
other Pastors, page 708.

30 May   **Josephine Butler**   III

Common of Any Saint, page 714

Common of Any Saint, page 714

COLLECT

God of compassion and love,
by whose grace your servant Josephine Butler
followed in the way of your Son
in caring for those in need:
help us like her to work with strength
for the restoration of all to the dignity
    and freedom of those created in your image;
through Jesus Christ our Saviour. **Amen.**   *SSF *

31 May   **The Visit of the BVM to Elizabeth II**

Form 4, of the BVM, is used for Morning, Evening and Night Prayer.

COLLECT – one of the following is used.

Mighty God,
by whose grace Elizabeth rejoiced with Mary
and greeted her as the mother of the Lord:
look with favour on your lowly servants
that, with Mary, we may magnify your holy name
and rejoice to acclaim her Son our Saviour,
who is alive and reigns with you,
in the unity of the Holy Spirit,
one God, now and for ever. **Amen.**

O God our deliverer,
you cast down the mighty,
and lift up those of no account;
as Elizabeth and Mary embraced
with songs of liberation,
so may we also be pregnant with your Spirit,
and affirm one another in hope for the world,
through Jesus Christ, **Amen.**

Janet Morley

Morning	Evening
Alt. Opening Canticle: 64 Second Canticle: 30	Second Canticle: 67

Midday

The appropriate weekday of Form 1-7 is used with the Common of the BVM, page 698.

I June   **Justin**   III
                Common of Martyrs, page 704

COLLECT

God our redeemer,
who through the folly of the cross taught your martyr Justin
the surpassing knowledge of Jesus Christ:
remove from us every kind of error
that we, like him, may be firmly grounded in the faith,
and make your name known to all peoples;
through Jesus Christ our Lord. **Amen.**

SSF

5 June   **Boniface (Wynfrith) of Crediton**   III
                Common of Martyrs, page 704

COLLECT

God our redeemer,
who called your servant Boniface
to preach the gospel among the German people
and to build up your Church in holiness:
grant that we may preserve in our hearts
that faith which he taught with his words
    and sealed with his blood,
and profess it in lives dedicated to your Son
Jesus Christ our Lord. **Amen.**

| 8 June | **Thomas Ken** | III |

Common of Bishops and other Pastors, page 708

COLLECT

O God, from whom all blessings flow,
by whose providence we are kept
and by whose grace we are directed:
help us, through the example of your servant Thomas Ken,
faithfully to keep your word,
humbly to accept adversity
and steadfastly to worship you;
through Jesus Christ our Lord. **Amen.**

SSF

| 9 June | **Columba** | III |

Common of Missionaries, page 712

COLLECT

Almighty God,
who filled the heart of Columba
with the joy of the Holy Spirit
and with deep love for those in his care:
may your pilgrim people follow him,
strong in faith, sustained by hope,
and one in the love that binds us to you;
through Jesus Christ our Lord. **Amen.**

| **11 June** | **Barnabas** | **II** |

Form 7, of Apostles, is used for Morning, Evening and Night Prayer.

COLLECT

Bountiful God, giver of all gifts,
who poured your Spirit upon your servant Barnabas
and gave him grace to encourage others:
help us, by his example,
to be generous in our judgements
and unselfish in our service;
through Jesus Christ our Lord. **Amen.**

Morning	Evening
Alt. Opening Canticle: 64 Second Canticle: 17	Second Canticle: 51

Midday

The appropriate weekday of Form 1-7 is used with the Common of Apostles, page 700.

13 June   **Antony of Padua**   III
Common of Members of Religious Communities, page 710

COLLECT

Grant, O God,
that as you servant Antony of Padua
proclaimed your gospel both in word and deed,
so may we bear witness
to the eternal kingdom of your Son;
through Jesus Christ our Lord. **Amen.**

16 June   **Richard**   III
Common of Bishops and other Pastors, page 708

COLLECT

Most merciful redeemer,
who gave to your bishop Richard a love of learning,
a zeal for souls and a devotion to the poor:
grant that, encouraged by his example,
we may know you more clearly,
   love you more dearly,
   and follow you more nearly, day by day,
who with the Father and the Holy Spirit are alive and reign,
one God, now and for ever. **Amen.**

22 June   Alban   II

Form 6, of Martyrs, is used for Morning, Evening and Night Prayer.

COLLECT

Eternal Father,
when the gospel of Christ first came to our land
you gloriously confirmed the faith of Alban
by making him the first to win a martyr's crown:
grant that, following his example,
in the fellowship of the saints
we may worship you, the living God,
and give true witness to Jesus Christ your Son our Lord. **Amen.**

Morning	*Evening*
Alt. Opening Canticle: 64	
Pss: 40, 117	*Pss:* 11, 116
Second Canticle: 28	*Second Canticle:* 43
Daniel 12.1-3	Wisdom 4.7-15
Hebrews 11.32 – 12.2	Luke 12.4-12

Midday

*The appropriate weekday of Form 1-7 is used with the Common of Martyrs,
page 704.*

23 June   **Etheldreda**   III

*Common of Members of Religious Communities,
page 710*

COLLECT

Eternal God,
who bestowed such grace upon your servant Etheldreda
that she gave herself wholly to the life of prayer
   and to the service of your true religion:
grant that we, like her,
may so live our lives on earth seeking your kingdom
that by your guiding
we may be joined to the glorious fellowship of your saints;
through Jesus Christ our Lord. **Amen.**

24 June   The Birth of John the Baptist   1

Form 3 is used for Morning, Evening and Night Prayer.

COLLECT

Almighty God,
by whose providence your servant John the Baptist
    was wonderfully born,
and sent to prepare the way of your Son our Saviour
by the preaching of repentance:
lead us to repent according to his preaching
and, after his example,
constantly to speak the truth, boldly to rebuke vice,
and patiently to suffer for the truth's sake;
through Jesus Christ our Lord. **Amen.**

Day	Morning	Evening
23 Jun.		*Second Canticle:* 51
24 Jun.	*Opening Canticle:* 64 *Second Canticle:* 11	*Second Canticle:* 61

Magnificat **The angel Gabriel**
Eve **appeared to Zechariah in the temple,**
  standing by the altar of incense.

Preparation Alleluia. John rejoiced and pointed to the Lamb of God.
  O come, let us worship. Alleluia.

Benedictus **Elizabeth, the wife of Zechariah, brought forth a son;**
  he grew and became strong in spirit.

Magnificat **The child born of Elizabeth is more than a prophet,**
  for he will proclaim the way of the Lord.

Midday

The appropriate weekday of Form 1-7 is used with the following propers:

DOXOLOGY TO HYMN

**To you, O Christ, all glory be,
Whose advent sets your people free;
Whom with the Father, we adore,
And Holy Spirit, evermore. Amen.**

READING John 3.25-30 *or*

The Lord called me before I was born, while I was in my mother's womb he named me. *Isaiah 49.1*

RESPONSE

There was a man sent from God,
whose name was John.

He came as a witness to bear witness to the light,
that all might believe through him.

He was not the light,
but came to bear witness to the light,

for the true light that enlightens everyone
was coming into the world.

28 June	**Irenaeus**	III
	Common of Teachers of the Faith, page 706	

COLLECT

God of peace,
who through the ministry of your servant Irenaeus
strengthened the true faith
and brought harmony to your Church:
keep us steadfast in your true religion,
and renew us in faith and love,
that we may always walk in the way that leads to eternal life;
through Jesus Christ our Lord. **Amen.**

SSF *

29 June   Peter and Paul   II

Form 7, of Apostles, is used for Morning, Evening and Night Prayer.

COLLECT

Almighty God,
whose blessèd apostles Peter and Paul
glorified you in their death as in their life:
grant that your Church,
inspired by their teaching and example,
and made one by your Spirit,
may ever stand firm upon the one foundation,
Jesus Christ your Son our Lord. **Amen.**

Morning	Evening
Alt. Opening Canticle: 64 *Second Canticle:* 17	*Second Canticle:* 56

Midday

The appropriate weekday of Form 1-7 is used with the Common of Apostles, page 700.

3 July   Thomas   II

Form 7, of Apostles, is used for Morning, Evening and Night Prayer.

COLLECT

Almighty and eternal God,
who, for the firmer foundation of our faith,
allowed your holy apostle Thomas
  to doubt the resurrection of your Son
till word and sight convinced him:
grant to us, who have not seen, that we also may believe
and so confess Christ as our Lord and our God;
who is alive and reigns with you,
in the unity of the Holy Spirit,
one God, now and for ever. **Amen.**

Morning	Evening
Alt. Opening Canticle: 64 Second Canticle: 22	Second Canticle: 50

Midday

The appropriate weekday of Form 1-7 is used with the Common of Apostles, page 700.

11 July   **Benedict of Nursia**   11

Form 3, of Members of Religious Communities, is used for Morning, Evening and Night Prayer.

COLLECT

Eternal God,
who made Benedict a wise master
   in the school of your service
and a guide to many called into community
   to follow the rule of Christ:
grant that we may put your love before all else
and seek with joy the way of your commandments;
through Jesus Christ our Lord. **Amen.**

SSF

Morning	Evening
Alt. Opening Canticle: 64 Pss: 16, 148 Second Canticle: 34 Wisdom 1.1-7 Romans 12.1-13	Pss: 1, 15, 112 Second Canticle: 54 Proverbs 11.27 – 12.3 Romans 8.26-30

Midday

The appropriate weekday of Form 1-7 is used with the Common of Members of Religious Communities, page 710.

| 14 July | **John Keble** | III |

Common of Bishops and other Pastors, page 708

COLLECT

Father of the eternal Word,
in whose encompassing love
all things in peace and order move:
grant that, as your servant John Keble
adored you in all creation,
so we may have a humble heart of love
for the mysteries of your Church
and know your love to be new every morning,
in Jesus Christ your Son our Lord. **Amen.**

Keble College, Oxford

| 15 July | **Bonaventure** | III |

Common of Members of Religious Communities, page 710

COLLECT

God our Father
we thank you for the blessings given to your Church
through the holiness and wisdom
of your servant Bonaventure:
grant that we may follow him
in the way that leads to eternal life;
through Jesus Christ our Lord. **Amen.**

| 19 July | **Gregory and Macrina** | III |

Common of Teachers of the Faith, page 706

COLLECT

Lord of eternity, creator of all things,
in your Son Jesus Christ you open for us the way to resurrection
that we may enjoy your bountiful goodness:
may we who celebrate your servants Gregory and Macrina
press onwards in faith to your boundless love
and ever wonder at the miracle of your presence among us;
through Jesus Christ our Lord. **Amen.**

Festivals and Lesser Festivals

22 July   Mary Magdalene   II

Form 1 is used for Morning, Evening and Night Prayer.

COLLECT – one of the following is used.

Almighty God,
whose Son restored Mary Magdalene
    to health of mind and body
and called her to be a witness to his resurrection:
forgive our sins and heal us by your grace,
that we may serve you in the power of his risen life;
who is alive and reigns with you,
in the unity of the Holy Spirit,
one God, now and for ever. **Amen.**

Christ our healer,
beloved and remembered by women,
speak to the grief which makes us forget,
and the terror that makes us cling,
and give us back our name;
that we may greet you clearly,
and proclaim your risen life, **Amen.**

Janet Morley

Morning	**Evening**
Alt. Opening Canticle: 64	
Second Canticle: 5	*Second Canticle:* 51

Preparation Alleluia. The Lord appeared first to Mary of Magdala.
            O come, let us worship. Alleluia.

Benedictus **After the Sabbath,**
            towards the dawn of the first day of the week,
            Mary Magdalene went to the tomb.

Magnificat **Mary came and told the disciples**
            that she had seen the Lord.

Midday

The appropriate weekday of Form 1-7 is used with the following propers:

DOXOLOGY TO HYMN

**All praise be yours, O risen Lord,
From death to endless life restored;
Whom with the Father, we adore
And Holy Spirit evermore. Amen.**

READING 2 Corinthians 1.3-7 *or*

Now after Jesus rose early on the first day of the week, he appeared first to Mary Magdalene, from whom he had cast out seven demons.

Mark 16.9

RESPONSE

Very early on the Sunday morning, as the sun was rising,
Mary Magdalene came to the tomb.

Mary was weeping and she looked into the tomb.
There she saw two angels in brilliant clothes.

Jesus said to Mary, Woman, why are you weeping, whom do you seek?
**They have taken away my Lord, she said,
and I do not know where they have put him**

Jesus said, Mary.
**She turned to him and said, Rabboni, which means Master.
Alleluia, alleluia.**

25 July   James   II

Form 7, of Apostles, is used for Morning, Evening and Night Prayer.

COLLECT

Merciful God,
whose holy apostle Saint James,
leaving his father and all that he had,
was obedient to the calling of your Son Jesus Christ
and followed him even to death:
help us, forsaking the false attractions of the world,
to be ready at all times to answer your call without delay;
through Jesus Christ our Lord. **Amen.**

Morning	Evening
Alt. Opening Canticle: 64 *Second Canticle:* 11	*Second Canticle:* 46

Midday

The appropriate weekday of Form 1-7 is used with the Common of Apostles, page 700.

26 July   **Anne and Joachim**   III
Common of Any Saint, page 714

COLLECT

Lord God of Israel,
who bestowed such grace on Anne and Joachim
that their daughter Mary grew up obedient to your word
and made ready to be the mother of your Son:
help us to commit ourselves in all things to your keeping
and grant us the salvation you promised to your people;
through Jesus Christ our Lord. **Amen.**

29 July   **Mary, Martha and Lazarus**   III

Common of Any Saint, page 714

COLLECT

God our Father,
whose Son enjoyed the love of his friends,
   Mary, Martha and Lazarus,
in learning, argument and hospitality:
may we so rejoice in your love
that the world may come to know
   the depths of your wisdom, the wonder of your compassion,
   and your power to bring life out of death;
through the merits of Jesus Christ,
our friend and brother,
who is alive and reigns with you,
in the unity of the Holy Spirit,
one God, now and for ever. **Amen.**

30 July   **Thomas Clarkson,
Olaudah Equiano
and William Wilberforce**   III

Common of Any Saint, page 714

COLLECT

God our deliverer,
who sent your Son Jesus Christ
to set your people free from the slavery of sin:
grant that, as your servants Thomas Clarkson,
   Olaudah Equiano and William Wilberforce
toiled against the sin of slavery,
so we may bring compassion to all
and work for the freedom of all the children of God;
through Jesus Christ our Lord. **Amen.**

| 2 August | **Mary of the Angels** | III |

Common of the BVM, page 698

COLLECT

Loving God,
by the message of an angel
Mary received your word
and by her willing obedience
brought forth him who is the world's redemption:
may we, like her, share the good news of his coming
and with the angels and archangels
give praise and glory to you for ever:
through Jesus Christ our Lord. **Amen.**

| 4 August | **John Vianney** | III |

Common of Bishops and other Pastors, page 708

COLLECT

God of love
who filled your servant John Vianney
with zeal as a priest, pastor and confessor:
help us, by your grace,
to win all our brothers and sisters for Christ
and to share with them in eternal glory;
through Jesus Christ our Lord. **Amen.**

| 5 August | **Oswald** | III |

Common of Martyrs, page 704

COLLECT

Lord God almighty,
who so kindled the faith of King Oswald with your Spirit
that he set up the sign of the cross in his kingdom
and turned his people to the light of Christ:
grant that we, being fired by the same Spirit,
may always bear our cross before the world
and be found faithful servants of the gospel;
through Jesus Christ our Lord. **Amen.**

*St Oswald's Church, Durham ** *

6 August   The Transfiguration of Our Lord   I

Form 5, is used for Morning, Evening and Night Prayer.

COLLECT – one of the following is used.

Father in heaven,
whose Son Jesus Christ was wonderfully transfigured
before chosen witnesses upon the holy mountain,
and spoke of the exodus he would accomplish at Jerusalem:
give us strength so to hear his voice and bear our cross
that in the world to come we may see him as he is;
who is alive and reigns with you,
in the unity of the Holy Spirit,
one God, now and for ever. **Amen.**

Christ our only true light,
before whose bright cloud
your friends fell to the ground;
we bow before your cross
that we may remember in our bodies
the dead who fell like shadows;
and that we may refuse to be prostrated
before the brightness
of any other light,
looking to your power alone
for hope of the resurrection from the dead, **Amen.**   *Janet Morley*

Day	Morning	Evening
5 Aug.		*Second Canticle:* 50
6 Aug.	*Opening Canticle:* 64 *Second Canticle:* 4	*Second Canticle:* 66

Magnificat   **This is my Son, my Belovèd;**
Eve   **listen to my Chosen One.**

Preparation   Alleluia. Christ is the Lord of glory.
             O come, let us worship. Alleluia.

Benedictus   **Christ, who is the very image of the Father,**
             was revealed in glory upon the holy mountain.

Magnificat **It is good that we are here
and to behold the glory that is Christ.**

Midday

The appropriate weekday of Form 1-7 is used with the following propers:

READING 2 Corinthians 4.2-6 *or*

The Lord Jesus will transform the body of our humiliation so that it may be
conformed to the body of his glory. *Philippians 3.21*

RESPONSE

Arise, shine, for your light has come
and the glory of the Lord has risen upon you.

For darkness shall cover the earth
and thick darkness the peoples.

But the Lord will arise upon you
and his glory will appear over you.

Glory to God, Source of all being, Eternal Word and Holy Spirit.
The glory of the Lord has risen upon you.

8 August	**Dominic**	III
	Common of Members of Religious Communities,	
	page 710	

COLLECT

Almighty God,
whose servant Dominic grew in the knowledge of your truth
and formed an order of preachers to proclaim the faith of Christ:
by your grace give to all your people a love for your word
and a longing to share the gospel,
so that the whole world may come to know you
and your Son Jesus Christ our Lord. **Amen.**

| 9 August | **Mary Sumner** | III |

Common of Any Saint, page 714

COLLECT

Faithful and loving God,
who called Mary Sumner to strive for the renewal of family life:
give us the gift of your Holy Spirit,
that through word, prayer and deed
   your family may be strengthened and your people served;
through Jesus Christ our Lord. **Amen.**

| 10 August | **Laurence** | III |

Common of Martyrs, page 704

COLLECT

Almighty God,
who made Laurence a loving servant of your people
and a wise steward of the treasures of your Church:
fire us with his example to love as he loved
and to walk in the way that leads to eternal life;
through Jesus Christ our Lord. **Amen.**

SSF *

| **11 August** | **Clare of Assisi** | **I** |

Form 3 is used for Morning, Evening and Night Prayer.

COLLECT

God of peace,
who in the poverty of the blessèd Clare
gave us a clear light to shine in the darkness of this world:
give us grace so to follow in her footsteps
that we may, at the last, rejoice with her
   in your eternal glory;
through Jesus Christ our Lord. **Amen.**

SSF

Day	Morning	Evening
10 Aug.		Pss: 27, 113 *Second Canticle:* 39 Song of Songs 8.3-7a Revelation 19.1-9
11 Aug.	*Opening Canticle:* 64 Pss: 63, 148 *Second Canticle:* 29 Ecclesiasticus 2.1-9 Matthew 13.44-51	Pss: 61, 66 *Second Canticle:* 70 Isaiah 54.1-8 Matthew 11.25-end

Magnificat **Come, O child of God,**
Eve **and look to your Redeemer,**
and you will shine with glory.

Preparation Alleluia. Clare loved the Lord with her whole heart.
O come, let us worship. Alleluia.

Benedictus **It is your Father's good pleasure**
to give you the kingdom of heaven.

Magnificat **You have left all things and followed me;**
you will be repaid a hundred times over
and gain eternal life.

Midday

The appropriate weekday of Form 1-7 is used with the following propers:

READING Luke 12.32-34 *or*

I regard everything as loss because of the surpassing value of knowing
Christ Jesus my Lord.   *Philippians 3.8*

RESPONSE

O holy poverty! To those who possess and desire her
God promises the kingdom of heaven.

Clare said to her soul, 'Go now, it is quite safe to leave,
for you have a good guide for the journey;

Go now, for the one who created you
   has always kept you safe
and loved you with a tender love,
   as a mother loves her child.'

| 13 August | **Jeremy Taylor** | III |

Common of Teachers of the Faith, page 706

COLLECT

Holy and loving God,
you dwell in the human heart
and make us partakers of the divine nature
in Christ our great high priest:
help us who remember your servant Jeremy Taylor
to put our trust in your heavenly promises
and follow a holy life in virtue and true godliness;
through Jesus Christ our Lord. **Amen.**

| 14 August | **Maximilian Kolbe** | III |

Common of Martyrs, page 704

COLLECT

God of life and hope,
we praise you that you can turn our weakness into your strength.
As you called Maximilian Kolbe to give his life for a brother,
and always to have faith in the final victory of the good,
grant us the grace to bear witness to your love
and to serve our brothers and sisters even to death,
through Jesus Christ our Redeemer. **Amen.**

SSF

15 August   The Blessed Virgin Mary   I

Form 4, of the BVM, is used for Morning, Evening and Night Prayer.

COLLECT

Almighty God,
who looked upon the lowliness of the Blessed Virgin Mary
and chose her to be the mother of your only Son:
grant that we who are redeemed by his blood
may share with her in the glory of your eternal kingdom;
through Jesus Christ our Lord. **Amen.**

	Morning	Evening
14 Aug.		*Second Canticle: 50*
15 Aug.	*Opening Canticle: 64* *Second Canticle: 30*	*Second Canticle: 73*

Midday

*The appropriate weekday of Form 1-7 is used with the Common of the BVM,
page 698.*

20 August   **Bernard**   III
Common of Teachers of the Faith, page 706

COLLECT

Merciful redeemer,
who, by the life and preaching of your servant Bernard,
rekindled the radiant light of your Church:
grant us, in our generation,
to be inflamed with the same spirit of discipline and love
and ever to walk before you as children of light;
through Jesus Christ our Lord. **Amen.**

SSF

24 August   Bartholomew   II

Form 7, of Apostles, is used for Morning, Evening and Night Prayer.

COLLECT

Almighty and everlasting God,
who gave to your apostle Bartholomew grace
    truly to believe and to preach your word:
grant that your Church
may love that word which he believed
and may faithfully preach and receive the same;
through Jesus Christ our Lord. **Amen.**

Morning	Evening
Alt. Opening Canticle: 64 *Second Canticle:* 34	*Second Canticle:* 55

Midday

The appropriate weekday of Form 1-7 is used with the Common of Apostles, page 700.

25 August   Louis Capet   II

Form 7, of Any Saint, is used for Morning, Evening and Night Prayer.

COLLECT

Sovereign God,
who raised your servant Louis
from the cares of earthly rule
to the glory of your heavenly Kingdom:
grant, we pray, that with him
we may have fellowship with the King of kings,
your Son, Jesus Christ our Lord. **Amen.**

Morning	Evening
Alt. Opening Canticle: 64	
Pss: 21, 92	Pss: 15, 112
Second Canticle: 10	Second Canticle: 60
Isaiah 58.6-11	Leviticus 19.1-2, 17-18
Romans 8.26-30	Luke 19.12-19

Midday

The appropriate weekday of Form 1-7 is used with the Common of Any Saint., page 714.

27 August	**Monica**	III

Common of Any Saint, page 714

COLLECT

Faithful God,
who strengthened Monica, the mother of Augustine, with wisdom,
and through her patient endurance encouraged him
   to seek after you:
give us the will to persist in prayer
that those who stray from you may be brought to faith
   in your Son Jesus Christ our Lord. **Amen.**

28 August	**Augustine of Hippo**	III

Common of Teachers of the Faith, page 706

COLLECT

Merciful Lord,
who turned Augustine from his sins
   to be a faithful bishop and teacher:
grant that we may follow him in penitence and discipline
till our restless hearts find their rest in you;
through Jesus Christ our Lord. **Amen.**

29 August   **The Beheading of John the Baptist**   III

Form 3 is used with Refrains for 24 June, page 648, for Morning and Evening Prayer.
The appropriate weekday of Form 1-7 is used for Midday and Night Prayer.

COLLECT

Almighty God,
who called your servant John the Baptist
to be the forerunner of your Son in birth and death:
strengthen us by your grace
that, as he suffered for the truth,
so we may boldly resist corruption and vice
and receive with him the unfading crown of glory;
through Jesus Christ our Lord. **Amen.**

Morning	Evening
Pss: 3, 11, 146	*Pss:* 13, 116
Second Canticle: 12	*Second Canticle:* 44
Jeremiah 1.14-19	Ecclesiasticus 51.1-12
Luke 3.1-20	Revelation 6.9-11

30 August   **John Bunyan**   III
Common of Teachers of the Faith, page 706

COLLECT

God of peace,
who called your servant John Bunyan
to be valiant for truth:
grant that as strangers and pilgrims
we may at the last rejoice with all Christian people
    in your heavenly city;
through Jesus Christ our Lord. **Amen.**

SSF

31 August   **Aidan**   III
               Common of Missionaries, page 712

COLLECT

Everlasting God,
you sent the gentle bishop Aidan
to proclaim the gospel in this land:
grant us to live as he taught
in simplicity, humility and love for the poor;
through Jesus Christ our Lord. **Amen.**

3 September   **Gregory the Great**   III
               Common of Teachers of the Faith, page 706

COLLECT

Merciful Father,
who chose your bishop Gregory
to be a servant of the servants of God:
grant that, like him, we may ever long to serve you
by proclaiming your gospel to the nations,
and may ever rejoice to sing your praises;
through Jesus Christ our Lord. **Amen.**

                                                            SSF

8 September   The Birth of the
                Blessed Virgin Mary   II

Form 4, of the BVM, is used for Morning, Evening and Night Prayer.

COLLECT

Almighty and everlasting God,
who stooped to raise fallen humanity
through the child-bearing of blessèd Mary:
grant that we, who have seen your glory
   revealed in our human nature
and your love made perfect in our weakness,
may daily be renewed in your image
and conformed to the pattern of your Son,
Jesus Christ our Lord. **Amen.**

Morning	Evening
Alt. Opening Canticle: 64	
Pss: 72, 147 part 2	Pss: 87, 113, 138
Second Canticle: 3	Second Canticle: 59
Isaiah 66.10-14	Ecclesiasticus 24.17-22
Galatians 4.1-7	John 2.1-12

Midday
The appropriate weekday of Form 1-7 is used with the Common of the BVM,
page 698.

10 September   **Agnellus of Pisa & the Coming**
                   of the Friars Minor to England   III
                   Common of Members of Religious Communities,
                   page 710

COLLECT

Maker of all,
you helped blessèd Agnellus
and the first Franciscans who came to this land
to reflect the image of Christ,
through a life of poverty and humility.
By walking in their footsteps
and imitating their joyful love,
may we follow faithfully the pattern of your Son
Jesus Christ our Saviour. **Amen.**   *SSF*

13 September   **John Chrysostom**   III
                   Common of Teachers of the Faith, page 706

COLLECT

God of truth and love,
who gave to your servant John Chrysostom
eloquence to declare your righteousness
    in the great congregation
and courage to bear reproach
for the honour of your name:
mercifully grant to those who minister your word

such excellence in preaching,
that all people may share with them
in the glory that shall be revealed;
through Jesus Christ our Lord. **Amen.** *TEC*

14 September   Holy Cross Day   II

Form 6 is used for Morning, Evening and Night Prayer.

COLLECT

Almighty God,
who in the passion of your blessèd Son
made an instrument of painful death
to be for us the means of life and peace:
grant us so to glory in the cross of Christ
that we may gladly suffer for his sake;
who is alive and reigns with you,
in the unity of the Holy Spirit,
one God, now and for ever. **Amen.**

Morning	*Evening*
Opening Canticle: 21 *Second Canticle:* 5	*Second Canticle:* 52

Preparation   Alleluia. Christ Jesus was raised high on the cross
for our sake.
O come, let us worship. Alleluia.

Benedictus   **Far be it from me to glory,
save in the cross of our Lord Jesus Christ.**

Magnificat   **If you would come after me, you must deny yourself,
and take up your cross and follow me.**

Midday

The appropriate weekday of Form 1-7 is used with the following propers:

DOXOLOGY TO HYMN

**To you, O saving Three in One,
Let homage due by all be done;
And grant us by the cross restored,
To share the Victor's great reward. Amen.**

READING Hebrews 2.9-10 *or*

We proclaim Christ crucified, a stumbling block to Jews and foolishness to Gentiles, but to those who are the called, both Jews and Greeks, Christ the power of God and the wisdom of God. *1 Corinthians 1.23-24*

RESPONSE

If any want to become my followers, let them deny themselves
and take up their cross and follow me.
May I never boast of anything except the cross
of our Lord Jesus Christ.

For those who want to save their life will lose it,
and those who lose their life for my sake will find it.
May I never boast of anything except the cross
of our Lord Jesus Christ.

For what will it profit them if they gain the whole world
but forfeit their life?
May I never boast of anything except the cross
of our Lord Jesus Christ, by which the world
has been crucified to me, and I to the world.

15 September   **Mary at the Cross**   III
Common of the BVM, page 698.

COLLECT

Lord Jesus Christ,
when you were raised upon the cross,
your mother Mary stood beside you in your passion:
may your Church, as it shares in your suffering and death,
come to share more deeply in your risen life:
for, with the Father and the Holy Spirit,
you are alive and reign, one God,
now and for ever. **Amen.**

SSF

Morning	Evening
Pss: 25, 146	*Pss:* 13, 88
Second Canticle: 5	*Second Canticle:* 75
Lamentations 1.1-12; 2.13	Ruth 1.18-21
Luke 2.22-40	Galatians 6.11-end

16 September **Ninian** III
Common of Missionaries, page 712

COLLECT

Almighty and everlasting God,
who called your servant Ninian to preach the gospel
    to the people of northern Britain:
raise up in this and every land
heralds and evangelists of your kingdom,
that your Church may make known the immeasurable riches
    of your Son our Saviour Jesus Christ. **Amen.**

17 September   Stigmata of Francis II

Form 6 is used for Morning, Evening and Night Prayer.

COLLECT

Lord Jesus Christ,
who when the world was growing cold,
to the inflaming of our hearts by the fire of your love
raised up blessèd Francis
bearing in his body the marks of your passion:
mercifully grant to us, your people,
true penitence and grace to bear the Cross for love of you;
who live and reign with the Father and the Holy Spirit,
one God, now and for ever. **Amen.**

Morning	Evening
Opening Canticle: 21 *Pss:* 27, 148 *Second Canticle:* 5 Isaiah 6.1-8 John 12.20-41	*Pss:* 34, 121 *Second Canticle:* 52 Ecclesiasticus 39.5-11 *or* 1 Kings 19.4-13a 2 Corinthians 4.5-18

Preparation   Alleluia. Christ crucified is the power and wisdom of God.
          O come, let us worship. Alleluia.

Benedictus   **There will appear in heaven
the sign that heralds the Redeemer,
whom they will see coming in power and glory.**

Magnificat   **Christ carried our sins in his body to the cross;
through his wounds, we have been healed.**

Midday

The appropriate weekday of Form 1-7 is used with the following propers:

DOXOLOGY TO HYMN

To you, O saving Three in One,
Let homage due by all be done;
And grant us by the cross restored,
To share the Victor's great reward. Amen.

READING   Romans 6.5-8 *or*

Those whom God foreknew he also predestined to be conformed to the
image of his Son, in order that he might be the firstborn within a large
family.   *Romans 8.29*

RESPONSE

God has shone in our hearts
**to give the light of the knowledge of the glory of God
in the face of Jesus Christ.**

We carry in our bodies the death of Jesus,
**so that the life of Jesus may also be made visible
in our bodies.**

While we live, we are always being given up to death
for Jesus' sake,
**so that the life of Jesus may be made visible
in our mortal flesh.**

20 September **John Coleridge Patteson III**
and his Companions
Common of Martyrs, page 704

COLLECT

God of all tribes and peoples and tongues,
who called your servant John Coleridge Patteson
to witness in life and death to the gospel of Christ
amongst the peoples of Melanesia:
grant us to hear your call to service
and to respond trustfully and joyfully
to Jesus Christ our redeemer,
who is alive and reigns with you,
in the unity of the Holy Spirit,
one God, now and for ever. **Amen.**

21 September Matthew   II

Form 7, of Apostles, is used for Morning, Evening and Night Prayer.

COLLECT

O Almighty God,
whose blessèd Son called Matthew the tax collector
to be an apostle and evangelist:
give us grace to forsake the selfish pursuit of gain
    and the possessive love of riches
that we may follow in the way of your Son Jesus Christ,
who is alive and reigns with you,
in the unity of the Holy Spirit,
one God, now and for ever. **Amen.**

Morning	Evening
Alt. Opening Canticle: 64 Second Canticle: 32	Second Canticle: 50

Midday

The appropriate weekday of Form 1-7 is used with Common of Apostles, page 700.

Lancelot Andrewes III

Common of Bishops and other Pastors, page 708

COLLECT

Lord God,
who gave to Lancelot Andrewes many gifts of your Holy Spirit,
making him a man of prayer and a pastor of your people:
perfect in us that which is lacking in your gifts,
  of faith, to increase it,
  of hope, to establish it,
  of love, to kindle it,
that we may live in the light of your grace and glory;
through Jesus Christ our Lord. **Amen.**

27 September **Vincent de Paul** III

*Common of Members of Religious Communities,
page 710*

COLLECT

Merciful God,
whose servant Vincent de Paul,
by his ministry of preaching and pastoral care,
brought your love to the sick and the poor:
give to all your people a heart of compassion
that by word and action they may serve you
  in serving others in their need;
through Jesus Christ our Lord. **Amen.**

29 September   Michael and All Angels   II

Form 7 is used for Morning, Evening and Night Prayer.

COLLECT

Everlasting God,
you have ordained and constituted
  the ministries of angels and mortals in a wonderful order:
grant that as your holy angels always serve you in heaven,
so, at your command,
they may help and defend us on earth;
through Jesus Christ our Lord. **Amen.**

Morning	Evening
Alt. Opening Canticle: 64 Second Canticle: 36	Second Canticle: 50

Preparation Alleluia. God is worshipped and adored by all the angels.
O come, let us worship. Alleluia.

Benedictus **There was silence in heaven
while the dragon waged war;
and Michael and his angels fought against him,
and won the victory.**

Magnificat **Then I saw an angel soaring in the heavens,
with an eternal gospel to proclaim to all
who live on the earth.**

Midday

The appropriate weekday of Form 1-7 is used with the following propers:

READING Hebrews 1.5-9 *or*

I heard the voice of many angels surrounding the throne and the living creatures and the elders, singing with full voice: 'Worthy is the Lamb that was slaughtered.' *Revelation 5.11a,12a*

RESPONSE

God shall give the angels charge over you,
to keep you in all your ways.

Bless God, all you angels,
you mighty ones who do God's bidding,
and hearken to the voice of God's word.

Bless God, all you heavenly hosts,
you ministers who do God's will.

Bless God, all creation,
in all places of God's dominion;
bless the Holy One, O my soul.

4 October   Francis of Assisi   I

Form 3 is used for Morning, Evening and Night Prayer.
The Transitus, *page 751, is celebrated on the evening of 3 October.*

COLLECT

O God, you ever delight to reveal yourself
to the childlike and lowly of heart:
grant that, following the example of the blessèd Francis,
we may count the wisdom of this world as foolishness
and know only Jesus Christ and him crucified,
who is alive and reigns with you,
in the unity of the Holy Spirit,
one God, now and for ever. **Amen.**

SSF

Day	Morning	Evening
3 Oct.		*Pss:* 104 *Second Canticle:* 39 Genesis 1.24-end 1 Corinthians 1.17-end
4 Oct.	*Opening Canticle:* 64 *Pss:* 19, 148 *Second Canticle:* 33 Isaiah 52.7-end Luke 14.25-33	*Pss:* 8, 145 *Second Canticle:* 69 Isaiah 55 Matthew 10.5-22

Magnificat   **The life that I now live,**
Eve   **I live by faith in the Son of God.**

Preparation   Alleluia. Christ exalts the humble and meek.
             O come, let us worship. Alleluia.

Benedictus   **He was as the morning star,**
             and as the sun shining upon the temple
             of the Most High.

Magnificat   **Christ will be honoured in my body,**
             whether by life or by death;
             for me to live is Christ and to die is gain.

The appropriate weekday of Form 1-7 is used with the following propers:

READING   Matthew 6.19-23, 33 *or*

For Christ's sake, I have suffered the loss of all things, in order that I may
gain Christ and be found in him.   *Philippians 3.8*

RESPONSE

I have been crucified with Christ;
and it is no longer I who live,
but it is Christ who lives in me.

The life I now live in the flesh,
I live by faith in the Son of God,
who loved me and gave himself for me.

I have done what is mine;
may Christ teach you what is yours.

Praise and bless my Lord, and give him thanks;
and serve him with great humility.

6 October   **William Tyndale**   III
                    Common of Martyrs, page 704

COLLECT

Lord, give to your people grace to hear and keep your word
that, after the example of your servant William Tyndale,
we may not only profess your gospel
but also be ready to suffer and die for it,
to the honour of your name;
through Jesus Christ our Lord. **Amen.**   *TEC*

10 October	**Paulinus**	III

Common of Missionaries, page 712

COLLECT

God our Saviour,
who sent Paulinus to preach and to baptise,
and so to build up your Church in this land:
grant that, inspired by his example,
we may tell all the world of your truth,
that with him we may receive the reward
   you prepare for all your faithful servants;
through Jesus Christ our Lord. **Amen.**

12 October	**Wilfrid of Ripon**	III

Common of Missionaries, page 712

COLLECT

Almighty God,
who called our forebears to the light of the gospel
   by the preaching of your servant Wilfrid:
help us, who keep his life and labour in remembrance,
to glorify your name by following the example
   of his zeal and perseverance;
through Jesus Christ our Lord. **Amen.**

13 October	**Edward the Confessor**	III

Common of Any Saint, page 714

COLLECT

Sovereign God,
who set your servant Edward
   upon the throne of an earthly kingdom
and inspired him with zeal for the kingdom of heaven:
grant that we may so confess the faith of Christ
   by word and deed,
that we may, with all your saints, inherit your eternal glory;
through Jesus Christ our Lord. **Amen.**

| 15 October | **Teresa of Avila** | III |

Common of Teachers of the Faith, page 706

COLLECT

Merciful God,
who by your Spirit raised up your servant Teresa of Avila
to reveal to your Church the way of perfection:
grant that her teaching
may awaken in us a longing for holiness,
until we attain to the perfect union of love
in Jesus Christ your Son our Lord. **Amen.**

| 17 October | **Ignatius of Antioch** | III |

Common of Martyrs, page 704

COLLECT

Feed us, O Lord, with the living bread
and make us drink deep of the cup of salvation
that, following the teaching of your bishop Ignatius
and rejoicing in the faith
    with which he embraced a martyr's death,
we may be nourished for that eternal life
    for which he longed;
through Jesus Christ our Lord. **Amen.**

18 October   Luke   II

Form 2, of Evangelists, is used for Morning, Evening and Night Prayer.

COLLECT

Almighty God,
you called Luke the physician,
whose praise is in the gospel,
to be an evangelist and physician of the soul:
by the grace of the Spirit
and through the wholesome medicine of the gospel,
give your Church the same love and power to heal;
through Jesus Christ our Lord. **Amen.**

Morning	Evening
Alt. Opening Canticle: 64 *Second Canticle:* 29	*Second Canticle:* 53

Midday

The appropriate weekday of Form 1-7 is used with the Common of Evangelists, page 702.

19 October   **Henry Martyn**   III
                              Common of Missionaries, page 712

COLLECT

Almighty God,
who by your Holy Spirit gave Henry Martyn
a longing to tell the good news of Christ
and skill to translate the Scriptures:
by the same Spirit give us grace to offer you our gifts,
wherever you may lead, at whatever the cost;
through Jesus Christ our Lord. **Amen.**

22 October   **Peter of Alcantara**   III
                              Common of Members of Religious Communities,
                              page 710

COLLECT

God of peace,
who gave blessèd Peter of Alcantara
great gifts of penitence and prayer:
may we follow his example
and casting aside all that is the enemy of the Spirit
lay hold upon your heavenly treasure,
which you give us
through Jesus Christ our Lord. **Amen.**

26 October   **Alfred the Great**   III

Common of Any Saint, page 714

COLLECT

God, our maker and redeemer,
we pray you of your great mercy
and by the power of your holy cross
to guide us by your will and to shield us from our foes:
that, after the example of your servant Alfred,
we may inwardly love you above all things;
through Jesus Christ our Lord. **Amen.**

28 October   Simon and Jude   II

Form 7, of Apostles, is used for Morning, Evening and Night Prayer.

COLLECT

Almighty God,
who built your Church upon the foundation
   of the apostles and prophets,
with Jesus Christ himself as the chief cornerstone:
so join us together in unity of spirit by their doctrine,
that we may be made a holy temple acceptable to you;
through Jesus Christ our Lord. **Amen.**

Morning	*Evening*
Alt. Opening Canticle: 64 Second Canticle: 32	Second Canticle: 56

Midday

The appropriate weekday of Form 1-7 is used with the Common of Apostles, page 700.

29 October　　**James Hannington**　　　　　III
　　　　　　　　　Common of Martyrs, page 704

COLLECT

Most merciful God,
who strengthened your Church by the steadfast courage
　of your martyr James Hannington:
grant that we also,
thankfully remembering his victory of faith,
may overcome what is evil
and glorify your holy name;
through Jesus Christ our Lord. **Amen.**

SSF

30 October　　**Dedication of All Franciscan
　　　　　　　　Churches or Chapels**　　　I

Form 1 is used for Morning, Evening and Night Prayer.

COLLECT

Almighty God,
to whose glory we celebrate
the dedication of this house of prayer:
we praise you for the many blessings
you have given to those who worship here;
and we pray that all who seek you in this place may find you,
and, being filled with the Holy Spirit,
may become a living temple acceptable to you;
through Jesus Christ our Lord. **Amen.**

Day	*Morning*	*Evening*
29 Oct.		*Pss:* 29, 93, 99 *Second Canticle:* 59 1 Chronicles 28.20-29.5 1 Corinthians 3.9-17
30 Oct.	*Opening Canticle:* 64 *Pss:* 48, 150 *Second Canticle:* 16 Haggai 2.6-9 Hebrews 10.19-25	*Pss:* 132 *Second Canticle:* 50 Jeremiah 7.1-11 Luke 19.1-10

| *Magnificat* | **How awesome is this place!** |
| *Eve* | **It is none other than the house of God.** |

| *Preparation* | Alleluia. God is dwelling in our hearts. |
| | **O come, let us worship. Alleluia.** |

| *Benedictus* | **My house shall be called a house of prayer;** |
| | **a refuge for all peoples.** |

Magnificat	**This is the place where we call**
	on the holy name of God;
	of which it is written, My name shall be there.

Midday

The appropriate weekday of Form 1-7 is used with the following propers:

READING   Hebrews 8.1-7 *or*

We are the temple of the living God; as God said, I will live in them and move among them, and I will be their God and they shall be my people.

2 Corinthians 6.16

RESPONSE

The Lord will bring us to his holy mountain
and make us joyful in his house of prayer.

Enter the gates of the Lord with thanksgiving.
Walk into his courts with praise.

All our offerings and sacrifices
will be accepted on your altar.

For your house shall be called
a house of prayer for all peoples.

1 November   All Saints' Day, *page 613*   1

2 November   Commemoration of the Faithful Departed, All Souls Day   II

Form 7 is used for Morning, Evening and Night Prayer.

COLLECT

Eternal God, our maker and redeemer,
grant us, with all the faithful departed,
the sure benefits of your Son's saving passion
   and glorious resurrection
that, in the last day,
when you gather up all things in Christ,
we may with them enjoy the fullness of your promises;
through Jesus Christ our Lord. **Amen.**

Church of the Province of Southern Africa

Morning	Evening
Opening Canticle: 62	
Pss: 90, 130	Pss: 116
Second Canticle: 28	Second Canticle: 44
Job 14.1-14	Job 19.21-27
1 Thessalonians 4.13-end	1 Corinthians 15.20-28, 51-57

Preparation   God is our Redeemer, for whom all are alive.
                 O come, let us worship.

Benedictus   **I am the resurrection and the life;**
                 whoever believes in me, even though they die,
                 will live.

Magnificat   **All that the Father gives to me will come to me;**
                 and the one who comes to me I will not cast out.

The doxology at the end of canticles and psalms may be replaced with:

Rest eternal grant unto them, O Lord,
and let light perpetual shine upon them.

Midday

The appropriate weekday of Form 1-7 is used with the following propers:

READING   John 11.25-27 *or*

God will swallow up death for ever and will wipe away the tears
from all faces.   *Isaiah 25.8*

RESPONSE

I heard a voice from heaven saying:
blessèd are the dead who die in the Lord.

For since death came through a human being,
**the resurrection of the dead has also come
through a human being.**

For as all die in Adam,
so all will be made alive in Christ.

For he must reign until he has put all his enemies under his feet.
The last enemy to be destroyed is death.

3 November   **Richard Hooker**   III
                       Common of Teachers of the Faith, page 706

COLLECT

God of peace, the bond of all love,
who in your Son Jesus Christ have made the human race
   your inseparable dwelling place:
after the example of your servant Richard Hooker,
give grace to us your servants ever to rejoice
   in the true inheritance of your adopted children
and to show forth your praises now and ever;
through Jesus Christ our Lord. **Amen.**

                                                        Kenneth Stevenson

7 November **Willibrord of York** III
Common of Missionaries, page 712

COLLECT

God, the Saviour of all,
you sent your bishop Willibrord from this land
to proclaim the good news to many peoples
and confirm them in their faith:
help us also to witness to your steadfast love
   by word and deed
so that your Church may increase
   and grow strong in holiness;
through Jesus Christ our Lord. **Amen.**

8 November **The Saints and Martyrs of England** III
Common of Any Saint, page 714

COLLECT

God, whom the glorious company of the redeemed adore,
assembled from all times and places of your dominion:
we praise you for the saints of our own land
and for the many lamps their holiness has lit;
and we pray that we also may be numbered at last
with those who have done your will
   and declared your righteousness;
through Jesus Christ our Lord. **Amen.**

10 November **Leo the Great** III
Common of Teachers of the Faith, page 706

COLLECT

God our Father,
who made your servant Leo
strong in the defence of the faith:
fill your Church with the spirit of truth
that, guided by humility and governed by love,
she may prevail against the powers of evil;
through Jesus Christ our Lord. **Amen.**

SSF *

11 November   **Martin of Tours**   III
Common of Bishops and other Pastors, page 708

COLLECT

God all powerful,
who called Martin from the armies of this world
to be a faithful soldier of Christ:
give us grace to follow him
in his love and compassion for the needy,
and enable your Church to claim for all people
their inheritance as children of God;
through Jesus Christ our Lord. **Amen.**

SSF

13 November   **Charles Simeon**   III
Common of Teachers of the Faith, page 706

COLLECT

Eternal God,
who raised up Charles Simeon
   to preach the good news of Jesus Christ
and inspire your people in service and mission:
grant that we with all your Church may worship the Saviour,
turn in sorrow from our sins and walk in the way of holiness;
through Jesus Christ our Lord. **Amen.**

16 November   **Margaret of Scotland**   III
Common of Any Saint, page 714

COLLECT

God, the ruler of all,
who called your servant Margaret to an earthly throne
and gave her zeal for your Church and love for your people
that she might advance your heavenly kingdom:
mercifully grant that we who commemorate her example
   may be fruitful in good works
and attain to the glorious crown of your saints;
through Jesus Christ our Lord. **Amen.**

17 November   **Hugh**   III
Common of Bishops and other Pastors, page 708

COLLECT

O God,
who endowed your servant Hugh
with a wise and cheerful boldness
and taught him to commend to earthly rulers
   the discipline of a holy life:
give us grace like him to be bold in the service of the gospel,
putting our confidence in Christ alone,
who is alive and reigns with you,
in the unity of the Holy Spirit,
one God, now and for ever. **Amen.**   *Lincoln Cathedral* *

18 November   Elizabeth of Hungary   II

Form 7, of Any Saint, is used for Morning, Evening and Night Prayer.

COLLECT

Merciful God,
who taught Elizabeth of Hungary
   to recognize and reverence Christ in the poor of this world:
by her example
strengthen us to love and serve the afflicted and the needy
and so to honour your Son, the servant king,
who is alive and reigns with you,
in the unity of the Holy Spirit,
one God, now and for ever. **Amen.**

Morning	Evening
Alt. Opening Canticle: 64	
Pss: 45	*Pss:* 122, 127
Second Canticle: 34	*Second Canticle:* 67
Proverbs 31.10-31	Isaiah 58.7-8
Romans 12.1-13	Revelation 19.7-9

Midday

*The appropriate weekday of Form 1-7 is used with the Common of Any Saint,
page 714.*

19 November	**Hilda**	III

Common of Members of Religious Communities, page 710

COLLECT

Eternal God,
who made the abbess Hilda to shine like a jewel in our land
and through her holiness and leadership
   blessed your Church with new life and unity:
help us, like her, to yearn for the gospel of Christ
and to reconcile those who are divided;
through him who is alive and reigns with you,
in the unity of the Holy Spirit,
one God, now and for ever. **Amen.**

20 November	**Edmund**	III

Common of Martyrs, page 704

COLLECT

Eternal God,
whose servant Edmund kept faith to the end,
both with you and with his people,
and glorified you by his death:
grant us such steadfastness of faith
that, with the noble army of martyrs,
we may come to enjoy the fullness of the resurrection life;
through Jesus Christ our Lord. **Amen.**

23 November	**Clement**	III

Common of Martyrs, page 704

COLLECT

Creator and Father of eternity,
whose martyr Clement bore witness with his blood
to the love he proclaimed and the gospel that he preached:
give us thankful hearts as we celebrate your faithfulness,
   revealed to us in the lives of your saints,
and strengthen us in our pilgrimage as we follow your Son,
Jesus Christ our Lord. **Amen.**

24 November **All Departed Franciscans** III
Common of the Departed, page 716

COLLECT

Lord God, creator of all,
you have made us creatures of this earth,
but have also promised us a share in life eternal.
According to your promises,
may our Franciscan brothers and sisters,
with all who have died in the peace of Christ,
come with your saints to the joys of your kingdom,
where there will be neither sorrow nor pain,
but life everlasting. **Amen.**   *SSF*

29 November **All Franciscan Saints** III
Common of Members of Religious Communities, page 710

COLLECT

Everlasting God,
you have adorned your Church
with the splendours of the saintly followers
of our holy brother Francis:
grant that as we commemorate their holiness
we may come at last with all the pure of heart
to share the vision of your eternal glory;
through Jesus Christ our Lord. **Amen.**

30 November   Andrew II

Form 7, of Apostles, is used for Morning, Evening and Night Prayer.

COLLECT – one of the following is used.

Almighty God,
who gave such grace to your apostle Saint Andrew
that he readily obeyed the call of your Son Jesus Christ
   and brought his brother with him:
call us by your holy word,
and give us grace to follow you without delay
   and to tell the good news of your kingdom;
through Jesus Christ our Lord. **Amen.**

Christ, whose insistent call
disturbs our settled lives,
give us discernment to hear your word,
grace to relinquish our tasks,
and courage to follow empty-handed
wherever you may lead;
that the voice of your gospel
may reach the ends of the earth, **Amen.**

Janet Morley

Morning	**Evening**
Alt. Opening Canticle: 64 *Second Canticle: 34*	*Second Canticle: 60*

Midday

The appropriate weekday of Form 1-7 is used with the Common of Apostles, page 700.

6 December   **Nicholas**   III

Common of Bishops and other Pastors, page 708

COLLECT

Almighty Father, lover of souls,
who chose your servant Nicholas
    to be a bishop in the Church,
that he might give freely out of the treasures of your grace:
make us mindful of the needs of others
and, as we have received, so teach us also to give;
through Jesus Christ our Lord. **Amen.**

7 December   **Ambrose**   III

Common of Teachers of the Faith, page 706

COLLECT

God of hosts,
who called Ambrose from the governor's throne
to be a bishop in your Church
and an intrepid champion of your faithful people:
mercifully grant that, as he did not fear to rebuke rulers,
so we, with like courage,
    may contend for the faith we have received;
through Jesus Christ our Lord. **Amen.**

8 December   The Conception of
the Blessed Virgin Mary   II

Form 4, of the BVM, is used for Morning, Evening and Night Prayer.

COLLECT

Eternal God,
who prepared the Blessed Virgin Mary
to be the mother of your Son:
grant that, as we rejoice in his coming as our Saviour,
so we may be ready to greet him
when he comes as our Judge;
for he is alive and reigns with you and the Holy Spirit,
one God, now and for ever. **Amen.**

SSF

Morning	Evening
Alt. Opening Canticle: 64	
Pss: 85, 147 part 2	Pss: 46, 87
Second Canticle: 20	Second Canticle: 67
Genesis 12.1-7	Isaiah 10.33 – 11.10
Romans 8.28-30	Revelation 21.1-7

Midday

The appropriate weekday of Form 1-7 is used with the Common of the BVM, page 698.

13 December **Lucy** III
Common of Martyrs, page 704

COLLECT

God our redeemer,
who gave light to the world that was in darkness
by the healing power of the Saviour's cross:
shed that light on us, we pray,
that with your martyr Lucy
we may, by the purity of our lives,
   reflect the light of Christ
and, by the merits of his passion,
   come to the light of everlasting life;
through Jesus Christ our Lord. **Amen.**

14 December **John of the Cross** III
Common of Teachers of the Faith, page 706

COLLECT

O God, the judge of all,
who gave your servant John of the Cross
a warmth of nature, a strength of purpose
   and a mystical faith
that sustained him even in the darkness:
shed your light on all who love you
and grant them union of body and soul
in your Son Jesus Christ our Lord. **Amen.**

24 December **Christmas Eve,** *page 545*

25 December Christmas Day, *page 549* I

26 December   Stephen   II

*Form 4 is used for Morning, Evening and Night Prayer with Canticles
and Refrains for Christmas.*
*The appropriate weekday of Form 1-7, of Christmas, is used
for Midday Prayer.*

COLLECT

Gracious Father,
who gave the first martyr Stephen
grace to pray for those who took up stones against him:
grant that in all our sufferings for the truth
we may learn to love even our enemies
and to seek forgiveness for those who desire our hurt,
looking up to heaven to him who was crucified for us,
Jesus Christ, our mediator and advocate. **Amen.**

27 December   John   II

*Form 4 is used for Morning, Evening and Night Prayer with Canticles
and Refrains for Christmas.*
*The appropriate weekday of Form 1-7, of Christmas, is used
for Midday Prayer.*

COLLECT

Merciful Lord,
cast your bright beams of light upon the Church:
that, being enlightened by the teaching
    of your blessèd apostle and evangelist Saint John,
we may so walk in the light of your truth
that we may at last attain to the light of everlasting life;
through Jesus Christ your incarnate Son our Lord. **Amen.**

28 December   The Holy Innocents   II

*Form 4 for Morning, Evening and Night Prayer with Canticles
and Refrains for Christmas.
The appropriate weekday of Form 1-7, of Christmas, is used
for Midday Prayer.*

COLLECT – *one of the following is used.*

Heavenly Father,
whose children suffered at the hands of Herod,
though they had done no wrong:
by the suffering of your Son
and by the innocence of our lives
frustrate all evil designs
and establish your reign of justice and peace;
through Jesus Christ our Lord. **Amen.**

God of the dispossessed,
defender of the helpless,
you grieve with all the women who weep
because their children are no more;
may we also refuse to be comforted
until the violence of the strong
has been confounded,
and the broken victims have been set free
in the name of Jesus Christ, **Amen.**

Janet Morley

29 December   **Thomas Becket**   III
Refrains for Christmas

COLLECT

Lord God,
who gave grace to your servant Thomas Becket
to put aside all earthly fear
   and be faithful even to death:
grant that we, disregarding worldly esteem,
may fight all wrong,
uphold your rule,
and serve you to our life's end;
through Jesus Christ our Lord. **Amen.**   *SSF **

Dedication Festival   I

Form I is used for Morning, Evening and Night Prayer.

COLLECT

Almighty God,
to whose glory we celebrate
the dedication of this house of prayer:
we praise you for the many blessings
you have given to those who worship here;
and we pray that all who seek you in this place may find you,
and, being filled with the Holy Spirit,
may become a living temple acceptable to you;
through Jesus Christ our Lord. **Amen.**

Morning	Evening
	Pss: 29, 93, 99 *Second Canticle:* 59 I Chronicles 28.20 – 29.5 I Corinthians 3.9-17
Opening Canticle: 64 *Pss:* 48, 150 *Second Canticle:* 16 Haggai 2.6-9 Hebrews 10.19-25	*Pss:* 132 *Second Canticle:* 50 Jeremiah 7.1-11 Luke 19.1-10

Magnificat **How awesome is this place!**
Eve **It is none other than the house of God.**

Preparation Alleluia. God is dwelling in our hearts.
O come, let us worship. Alleluia.

Benedictus **My house shall be called a house of prayer;
a refuge for all peoples.**

Magnificat **This is the place where we call
on the holy name of God;
of which it is written, My name shall be there.**

Midday

The appropriate weekday of Form 1-7 is used with the following propers:

READING Hebrews 8.1-7 *or*

We are the temple of the living God; as God said, 'I will live in them and walk among them, and I will be their God and they shall be my people.'

2 Corinthians 6.16

RESPONSE

The Lord will bring us to his holy mountain
and make us joyful in his house of prayer.

Enter the gates of the Lord with thanksgiving.
Walk into his courts with praise.

All our offerings and sacrifices
will be accepted on your altar.

For your house shall be called
a house of prayer for all peoples.

Common of the Saints and the Departed

Of the Blessed Virgin Mary

Also found in Form 4

COLLECT – one of the following is used.

Living God,
with grace you made the Blessed Virgin Mary
   to be the mother of your only Son,
fill us now with that same grace
that, through faith and obedience,
we may all rejoice in your mercy and walk in your light;
for the sake of Jesus Christ our Lord. **Amen.**

Almighty and everlasting God,
who stooped to raise fallen humanity
through the child-bearing of blessèd Mary:
grant that we, who have seen your glory
   revealed in our human nature
and your love made perfect in our weakness,
may daily be renewed in your image
and conformed to the pattern of your Son,
Jesus Christ our Lord. **Amen.**

Doxology	**Lord Jesus, King of heaven and earth,** **We praise you for your virgin birth;** **You are the Father's only Son,** **With God the Spirit, ever one. Amen.**

Eve

Second Canticle	58 *or* 73
Magnificat	**Blessèd are you, Mary,** **for you believed that what was said to you** **by the Lord would be fulfilled. (Alleluia.)**

Morning

Preparation	(Alleluia.) Christ is the Son of Mary. **O come, let us worship. (Alleluia.)**

Opening Canticle	64
Second Canticle	3 *or* 30
Benedictus	**In the womb of Mary, you found a dwelling place on earth, O Christ; remain for ever in our hearts. (Alleluia.)**

Midday

The appropriate weekday of Form 1-7 is used on Class I & II Holy Days.

Reading

    31 May   Song of Songs 2.8-13
    15 Aug. Ephesians 2.4-7
     8 Sep.   Galatians 4.3-5
     8 Dec.   Romans 8.29-30
or
A virgin shall conceive and bear a son, and his name shall be called Emmanuel, God with us.   *Matthew 1.23*

Response

Hail Mary, full of grace, the Lord is with you,
because God has blest you for ever.

Fear not, Mary, for you have found favour with God,
because God has blest you for ever.

You shall conceive and bring forth a Son,
because God has blest you for ever.

Blessèd are you among women
  and blessèd is the fruit of your womb,
**for out of you arose the Sun of Righteousness,
    Christ our God. (Alleluia, alleluia.)**

Evening

Second Canticle	54 *or* 59
Magnificat	**Mary gave birth to the Word of God; truly she is the ever-blessèd mother of Christ our Lord. (Alleluia.)**

Night

Nunc Dimittis	**Blessèd are you, Mary, the Lord is with you: through you we received our Redeemer, the Lord Jesus Christ.**

Of Apostles

Also found in Form 7

COLLECT

O God,
we thank you for the glorious company of the apostles,
and especially on this day for your servant N.
We pray that as the apostles
   were faithful and zealous in their mission,
so we may, with ardent devotion,
make known the love and mercy
of our Lord and Saviour Jesus Christ. **Amen.**   *TEC*

Eve
Second Canticle   46 *or* 49
Magnificat   **When all is made new,**
                    and the Christ is on his throne of glory,
                    you will sit on the twelve thrones
                    to judge the tribes of Israel. (Alleluia.)

Morning
Preparation   (Alleluia.) Christ the cornerstone has built his
                    Church upon the apostles and prophets.
                    O come, let us worship. (Alleluia.)

Alt Opening Canticle 64
Second Canticle   17 *or* 32
Benedictus   **You did not choose me but I chose you**
                    and I appointed you to go out and bear fruit,
                    fruit that shall last. (Alleluia.)

Midday
The appropriate weekday of Form 1-7 is used with the following propers:

Reading   Ephesians 2.19-21 *or*

                    Go into all the world and proclaim the good news to
                    the whole creation.   *Mark 16.15*

Response   Their voice has gone out to all the earth,
                    and their words to the ends of the world.

How are people to call on God
in whom they have not believed?
**How are they to believe in God,
of whom they have not heard?**

How shall they hear without a preacher?
How shall they preach except they be sent?

For faith comes by hearing,
and hearing through the word of Christ.

Their voice has gone out to all the earth,
**and their words to the ends of the earth.
(Alleluia, alleluia.)**

Evening
Second Canticle   55 *or* 56
Magnificat   **On the foundation stones of the heavenly city
                      are written the names of the apostles of the
                      Lamb. (Alleluia.)**

Of Evangelists

Also found in Form 2

COLLECT

Ever-living God,
by the hand of *N* your evangelist
you have given to your Church
the gospel of Jesus Christ:
giving thanks for this witness
we pray that we may be firmly grounded
    in its truth;
through Jesus Christ our Lord. **Amen.**   *SSF*

Eve

Second Canticle	53 *or* 57
Magnificat	**Your word is a lantern to my feet**
	and a light upon my path. (Alleluia.)

Morning

Preparation	(Alleluia.) Christ has proclaimed his gospel in all lands.
	O come, let us worship. (Alleluia.)
Alt Opening Canticle	64
Second Canticle	9 *or* 17
Benedictus	**We bring you the good news**
	that what God promised to our ancestors,
	he has fulfilled for us their children
	by raising Jesus. (Alleluia.)

Midday

The appropriate weekday of Form 1-7 is used with the following propers:

Reading	Ephesians 3.5-7 *or*
	I have become a servant of this gospel according to the gift of God's grace that was given me by the working of his power. *Ephesians 3.7*
Response	Give praise you servants of the Lord,
	O praise the name of the Lord.
	We will tell of all his wonderful deeds
	and be glad and exalt in him.

Blessèd be the name of the Lord,
from this time forth and for evermore.

From the rising of the sun to its setting
let the name of the Lord be praised.
(Alleluia, alleluia.)

Evening
Second Canticle   49 *or* 56
Magnificat   **The one who saw what Jesus did**
has borne witness,
that you also may believe. (Alleluia.)

Of Martyrs

Also found in Form 6

COLLECT

Almighty God,
by whose grace and power your holy martyr N
triumphed over suffering and was faithful unto death:
strengthen us with your grace,
that we may endure reproach and persecution
and faithfully bear witness to the name
    of Jesus Christ your Son our Lord. **Amen.**

Morning	Evening
	Pss: 11, 13, 21 *Second Canticle:* 43 *or* 73 Isaiah 43.1-7 *or* Wisdom 4.7-15 1 Peter 4.12-end *or* Revelation 7.9-end
Alt. Opening Canticle: 64 *Pss:* 57, 148 *Second Canticle:* 5 *or* 28 Jeremiah 15.15-21 *or* Wisdom 2.12-22 Matthew 10.16-22, 28-33 *or* Hebrews 10.32-end	*Pss:* 3, 116 *Second Canticle:* 56 *or* 67 Jeremiah 11.18-20 *or* Ecclesiasticus 51.1-12 John 12.24-26 *or* Romans 8.31-end

Magnificat
Eve
**Whoever follows me will not walk in darkness
but will have the light of life. (Alleluia.)**

Preparation
(Alleluia.) Christ is the strength of the martyrs.
O come, let us worship. (Alleluia.)

Benedictus
**Blessèd are those who are persecuted
for the cause of right,
for theirs is the kingdom of heaven. (Alleluia.)**

Magnificat
**Those who gave up their life for Christ
and followed in the Way
rejoice with God now and for ever. (Alleluia.)**

Midday

The appropriate weekday of Form 1-7 is used on Class I & II Holy Days with the following propers:

Reading   Revelation 6.9-11   *or*

I saw under the altar the souls of those who had been
slaughtered for the word of God and for the testimony they
had given.   *Revelation 6.9*

Response   Unless a grain of wheat falls into the earth and dies,
it remains just a single grain;

but if it dies,
it bears much fruit.

Whoever serves me must follow me,
and where I am, there will my servant be also.

Whoever serves me,
God will honour. (Alleluia, alleluia.)

Of Teachers of the Faith

Also found in Form 5

COLLECT

Almighty God,
who enlightened your Church
   by the teaching of your servant N:
enrich it evermore with your heavenly grace,
and raise up faithful witnesses,
who by their life and teaching
may proclaim the truth of your salvation;
through Jesus Christ our Lord. Amen.

Morning	Evening
	Ps: 37 *Second Canticle:* 53 *or* 61 Proverbs 4.1-9 *or* Wisdom 7.7-16 Matthew 5.13-20 *or* 2 Timothy 4.1-8
Alt. Opening Canticle: 64 *Pss:* 19, 147 part 2 *Second Canticle:* 15 *or* 30 Nehemiah 8.1-10 *or* Malachi 2.5-7 Mark 4.1-10, 13-20 *or* John 8.25-32	*Ps:* 34 *Second Canticle:* 46 *or* 49 Proverbs 8.1-21 *or* Ecclesiasticus 39.1-10 Matthew 7.15-27 *or* 1 Corinthians 2.1-13

Magnificat
Eve
Wisdom is treasure without end,
those who attain it are God's friends.
(Alleluia.)

Preparation
(Alleluia.) Christ speaks the truth in every age.
O come, let us worship. (Alleluia.)

Benedictus
Those who are wise will shine as brightly
as the heavens,
and those who have instructed many in virtue
will shine like stars for all eternity. (Alleluia.)

Magnificat
Those who keep and teach the commandments
will be considered great in heaven. (Alleluia.)

                                           Common of the Saints

Midday

The appropriate weekday of Form 1-7 is used on Class I & II Holy Days with the following propers:

Reading   James 3.17-18 *or*

Wisdom guided them along a marvellous way and
became a shelter to them by day and a starry flame
through the night.   *Wisdom 10.17*

Response   There is one God over all and in all,
to whom Christ ascended on high.

Grace is given to each of us
according to the measure of Christ's gift.

Some are apostles, some prophets,
some evangelists, some pastors and teachers,

for building up the body of Christ, to minister together,
**to be mature in the fullness of Christ.
(Alleluia, alleluia.)**

Of Bishops and other Pastors

Also found in Form 5

COLLECT – one of the following is used.

Eternal God,
you called N to proclaim your glory
   in a life of prayer and pastoral zeal:
keep the leaders of your Church faithful
and bless your people through their ministry,
that the Church may grow into the full stature
   of your Son Jesus Christ our Lord. **Amen.**

(for a bishop)

Almighty God,
the light of the faithful and shepherd of souls,
who set your servant N to be a bishop in the Church,
to feed your sheep by the word of Christ
and to guide them by good example:
give us grace to keep the faith of the Church
and to follow in the footsteps
   of Jesus Christ our Lord. **Amen.**

Morning	Evening
	Pss: 4, 5 *Second Canticle:* 47 *or* 53 Ezekiel 34.1-16 *or* Malachi 2.4-7 John 10.11-16 *or* 1 Peter 5.1-4
Alt. Opening Canticle: 64 *Pss:* 84, 99, 149 *Second Canticle:* 8 *or* 31 Numbers 27.15-end *or* Jeremiah 1.4-10 John 21.15-17 *or* Ephesians 4.7-16	*Ps:* 25 *Second Canticle:* 47 *or* 54 Isaiah 6.1-8 *or* Ezekiel 3.16-21 Luke 12.35-48 *or* Acts 20.24-35

Magnificat	**The word of God is alive and active,**
Eve	**and speaks to us of salvation. (Alleluia.)**
Preparation	(Alleluia.) Christ feeds his flock in every age.
	O come, let us worship. (Alleluia.)
Benedictus	**I will give you shepherds after my own heart**
	who will feed you with knowledge and
	understanding. (Alleluia.)
Magnificat	**Well done, good and faithful servant:**
	you have been faithful over a little, I will make you
	ruler over much. (Alleluia.)

Midday

The appropriate weekday of Form 1-7 is used on Class I & II Holy Days with the following propers:

Reading	Luke 4.18-19 *or*
	Remember your leaders who preached the word of God
	to you; consider the outcome of their way of life,
	and imitate their faith. *Hebrews 13.7*
Response	Jesus says: I am the good shepherd.
	The good shepherd lays down his life for the sheep.
	I will search for my sheep and seek them out;
	I will rescue them from where they have been
	scattered.
	I will bring them into their own land,
	and watch over them in righteousness.
	I will save my flock
	for they shall no longer be a prey. (Alleluia, alleluia.)

Of Members of Religious Communities

Also found in Form 3

COLLECT

Almighty God,
by whose grace *N* kindled with the fire of your love,
became a burning and a shining light in the Church:
inflame us with the same spirit of discipline and love,
that we may ever walk before you as children of light;
through Jesus Christ your Son our Lord. **Amen.**

Morning	Evening
	Ps: 77
	Second Canticle: 39 or 61
	Kings 19.1-16 or
	Isaiah 61.10 – 62.5
	Matthew 19.16-end or
	Romans 8.18-27
Alt. Opening Canticle: 64	
Pss: 16, 148	Pss: 61, 63, 131
Second Canticle: 27 or 34	Second Canticle: 45 or 54
Song of Songs 8.6-7,13 or	Proverbs 2.1-11 or
Proverbs 10.27-end	Wisdom 6.10-20
Matthew 25.1-13 or	Matthew 19.16-end or
Philippians 3.7-end	Luke 12.32-40

Magnificat	**Like everlasting foundations on a rock**
Eve	**are the commandments of God in the hearts**
	of the blessèd. (Alleluia.)
Preparation	(Alleluia.) Christ the pure and lowly in heart.
	O come, let us worship. (Alleluia.)
Benedictus	**They who wait upon the Lord**
	shall renew their strength;
	they shall mount up with wings as an eagle.
	(Alleluia.)

Magnificat   **You have left all things and followed me:**
            you will be rewarded a hundred times over
            and gain eternal life. (Alleluia.)

Midday

The appropriate weekday of Form 1-7 is used on Class I & II Holy Days with the following propers:

Reading   1 John 2.15-17 *or*

            I will meditate on your commandments
            and contemplate your ways, O Lord.   *Psalm 119.15*

Response   My soul thirsts for God,
            for the living God.

            As for me, I am poor and needy,
            but the Lord cares for me.

            My flesh and my heart fail.
            God is the strength of my heart
            and my possession for ever.

            My soul thirsts for God,
            for the living God.   (Alleluia, alleluia.)

Of Missionaries

Also found in Form 2

COLLECT

Everlasting God,
whose servant *N* carried the good news of your Son
   to the people of ... :
grant that we who commemorate *his/her* service
may know the hope of the gospel in our hearts
and manifest its light in all our ways;
through Jesus Christ our Lord. **Amen.**

Morning	Evening
	Pss: 67, 97, 126 *Second Canticle:* 45 *or* 49 Jonah 3 *or* Ezekiel 3.16-21 Luke 5.1-11 *or* 2 Corinthians 5.11-6.2
Alt. Opening Canticle: 64 *Pss:* 98, 147 part 1 *Second Canticle:* 11 *or* 22 Isaiah 49.1-6 *or* Ezekiel 34.11-16 Romans 15.18-21 *or* 1 Corinthians 9.15-23	*Pss:* 89.1-18, 100 *Second Canticle:* 45 *or* 49 Isaiah 52.7-10 *or* Isaiah 61.1-3a Mark 4.26-32 *or* Acts 17.16-31

Magnificat *Eve*	**May our whole nature be transformed** **that we may come to discern the will of God.** **(Alleluia.)**
Preparation	(Alleluia.) Christ has proclaimed his gospel in all lands. **O come, let us worship. (Alleluia.)**
Benedictus	**Christ gave them as a light to the nations** **that his salvation might reach to the ends** **of the earth. (Alleluia.)**
Magnificat	**How beautiful on the mountains** **are the feet of those who bring good news** **and proclaim the gospel of peace. (Alleluia.)**

Midday

The appropriate weekday of Form 1-7 is used on Class I & II Holy Days with the following propers:

Reading　　Acts 13.47-49　*or*

O give thanks to the Lord and call upon his name;
make known his deeds among the peoples.　　*Psalm 105.1*

Response　　Give praise you servants of the Lord,
O praise the name of the Lord.

We will tell of his wonderful deeds
and be glad and exalt in him.

Blessèd be the name of the Lord,
from this time forth and for evermore.

From the rising of the sun to its setting
let the name of the Lord be praised.
(Alleluia, alleluia.)

Of Any Saint

Also found in Form 7

COLLECT

Almighty God,
you have built up your Church
through the love and devotion of your saints:
inspire us to follow the example of *N*,
whom we commemorate today,
that we in our generation may rejoice with *him/her*
in the vision of your glory;
through Jesus Christ our Lord. **Amen.**

Morning	Evening
	Ps: 18.21-36, 47-51 *Second Canticle:* 58 *or* 59 Deuteronomy 6.1-9 *or* Ecclesiasticus 2.1-11 Ephesians 2.1-10 *or* Matthew 25.31-end
Alt. Opening Canticle: 64 *Pss:* 92, 150 *Second Canticle:* 10 *or* 35 Proverbs 8.1-17 *or* Isaiah 61.1-9 John 17.10-19 *or* 1 John 3.14-end	*Pss:* 1, 15, 112 *Second Canticle:* 50 *or* 56 Isaiah 51.1-8 *or* Micah 6.1-8 2 Corinthians 4.1-12 *or* Luke 10.38-end

Magnificat *Eve*	**The Lord guides the humble in the right path** **and teaches his way to the poor. (Alleluia.)**
Preparation	(Alleluia.) Our God is the God of peace, whom to serve is perfect freedom. **O come, let us worship. (Alleluia.)**
Benedictus	**They were faithful until death** **and God has given them the crown of life. (Alleluia.)**
Magnificat	**In the heavenly kingdom,** **the blessèd have their dwelling place** **and their rest for ever and ever. (Alleluia.)**

Midday

The appropriate weekday of Form 1-7 is used on Class I & II Holy Days with the following propers:

Reading   1 Peter 2.4-10 *or*

Jesus said, The Son of Man did not come to be served but to serve and to give up his life as a ransom for many.

Mark 10.45

Response   My mouth shall speak the praise of the Lord:
let all flesh bless his holy name for ever and ever.

One generation shall praise your works to another:
and shall declare your power.

All your works praise you, Lord:
and your faithful servants bless you.

They make known the glory of your kingdom:
and speak of your power. (Alleluia, alleluia.)

Of the Departed

Also found in Form 7

COLLECT

Lord God, creator of all,
you have made us creatures of this earth,
but have also promised us a share in life eternal.
According to your promises,
may our *brother/sister N,*
with all who have died in the peace of Christ,
come with your saints to the joys of your kingdom,
where there will be neither sorrow nor pain,
but life everlasting. Amen.

Morning	Evening
Opening Canticle: 62	
Pss: 42, 43, 147 part 1	Pss: 121, 139
Second Canticle: 5 or 28	Second Canticle: 43 or 67
Lamentations 3.17-26	Wisdom 4.8-15
Romans 14.7-12	2 Corinthians 4.16-5.10

Preparation   God is our Redeemer, for whom all are alive.
O come, let us worship.

Benedictus   **I am the resurrection and the life;
whoever believes in me, even though they die,
will live.**

Magnificat   **All that the Father gives to me will come to me;
and the one who comes to me I will not cast out.**

The doxology at the end of the psalms and canticles may be replaced with:

**Rest eternal grant unto them, O Lord,
and let light perpetual shine upon them.**

The 'Kontakion', following, may be used as the Office hymn.

Give rest, O Christ, to your servants, with your saints:
where sorrow and pain are no more,
neither sighing, but life everlasting.
You only are immortal, the creator and maker of all:
and we are mortal, formed of the earth,
and unto earth shall we return.
For so you did ordain when you created me, saying:
'Dust thou art and unto dust shalt thou return.'
All we go down to the dust;
and weeping o'er the grave, we make our song:
Alleluia, alleluia, alleluia.
Give rest . . .

Midday

The appropriate weekday of Form 1-7 is used on Class I & II Holy Days with the propers of 2 November, All Souls Day, page 684.

Special Occasions

The Guidance of the Holy Spirit

Form 2 is used.

COLLECT – one of the following is used.

God, who from of old
taught the hearts of your faithful people
by sending to them the light of your Holy Spirit:
grant us by the same Spirit
to have a right judgement in all things
and evermore to rejoice in his holy comfort;
through the merits of Christ Jesus our Saviour. **Amen.**

Almighty God,
you have given your Holy Spirit to the Church
to lead us into all truth:
bless with the Spirit's grace and presence
   the members of this *Community/Chapter etc.*;
keep *us/them* steadfast in faith and united in love,
that *we/they* may manifest your glory
and prepare the way of your kingdom;
through Jesus Christ our Lord. **Amen.**

Morning	Evening
Pss: 68.1-18, 147 part 2	Ps: 139.1-18, 23,24
Second Canticle: 22 or 30	*Second Canticle:* 44 or 71
Joel 2.23-29	Isaiah 61.1-4
1 John 4.9-15	John 15.26 – 16.14

Benedictus **I will pour out my Spirit on the earth
and everyone who calls on the name of the Lord
shall be saved. (Alleluia.)**

Magnificat **The Lord is the Spirit,
and where the Spirit of the Lord is,
there is freedom. (Alleluia.)**

Midday

The appropriate weekday of Form 1-7 is used with the following propers:

Reading   Romans 5.1-5 *or*

                   God's love has been poured into our hearts through the
                   Holy Spirit that has been given to us.   *Romans 5.5*

Response   *as for Pentecost, page 590*

The Unity of the Church

Form 5 is used.

COLLECT – one of the following is used.

Heavenly Father,
you have called us in the Body of your Son Jesus Christ
to continue his work of reconciliation
and reveal you to the world:
forgive us the sins which tear us apart;
give us the courage to overcome our fears
and to seek that unity which is your gift and your will;
through Jesus Christ our Lord. **Amen.**

Lord Jesus Christ,
who said to your apostles,
'Peace I leave with you, my peace I give to you':
look not on our sins but on the faith of your Church
and grant it the peace and unity of your kingdom;
where you are alive and reign with the Father
in the unity of the Holy Spirit,
one God, now and for ever. **Amen.**

Morning	Evening
Pss: 118, 147 part 1	*Pss:* 122, 125, 133
Second Canticle: 14 or 20	*Second Canticle:* 65 or 67
Ezekiel 37.15-end	Ecclesiastes 4.9-12
1 John 4.7-21	John 11.45-52

Benedictus   **This is the message that we have heard
from the beginning,
that we should love one another. (Alleluia.)**

Magnificat   **Christ is our peace, who has made us one
and has broken down the barriers
which divided us. (Alleluia.)**

Midday

The appropriate weekday of Form 1-7 is used with the following propers:

Reading   John 17.20-23 *or*

'May all be one. As you Father, are in me and I am in you, may they also be in us, so that the world may believe that you have sent me.'   *John 17.21*

Response   *Form 5, Response A, page 166*

Mission and Evangelism

Form 5 is used.

COLLECT

Almighty God,
who called your Church to witness
that you were in Christ reconciling the world to yourself:
help us to proclaim the good news of your love,
that all who hear it may be drawn to you;
through him who was lifted up on the cross,
and reigns with you
in the unity of the Holy Spirit,
one God, now and for ever. **Amen.**

Morning	Evening
Pss: 96, 146	*Ps:* 145
Second Canticle: 11 *or* 13	*Second Canticle:* 49 *or* 57
Isaiah 12.1-6	Isaiah 61.1-11
Acts 2.29-42	Matthew 9.27-38

Benedictus **You are the light of the world.**
A city built on a hill cannot be hid. (Alleluia.)

Magnificat **Go and make disciples of all nations,**
baptizing them in the name of the Father
and of the Son and of the Holy Spirit. (Alleluia.)

Midday

The appropriate weekday of Form 1-7 is used with the following propers:

Reading 2 Corinthians 4.1-6 *or*

We do not proclaim ourselves; we proclaim Jesus Christ as
Lord and ourselves as your slaves for Jesus' sake.

2 Corinthians 4.5

Response *Form 2, Response A, page 80*

Ministry (including Prayer for Vocations & for Ember Days)

Form 5 is used.

COLLECT – *one of the following is used.*

(for the ministry of all Christian people)

Almighty and everlasting God,
by whose Spirit the whole body of the Church
   is governed and sanctified:
hear our prayer which we offer for all your faithful people,
that in their vocation and ministry
they may serve you in holiness and truth
to the glory of your name;
through our Lord and Saviour Jesus Christ. **Amen.**

(for vocations to the Religious Life)

Almighty God,
you have entrusted to your Church
a share in the ministry of your Son our great high priest:
inspire by your Holy Spirit the hearts of many
to offer themselves for the Religious Life,
that strengthened by his power,
they may work for the increase of your kingdom
and set forward the eternal praise of your name;
through Jesus Christ your Son our Lord. **Amen.**

(for vocations to the Franciscan life)

God of life,
guide with your Spirit
all those you are calling to offer themselves
to live the gospel in the way of blessèd Francis and Clare,
that we all may serve you in humility, love and joy,
to the glory of your name,
Jesus Christ our Saviour. **Amen.**

Morning	Evening
Pss: 23, 84, 146	*Pss:* 42, 43
Second Canticle: 13 or 17	*Second Canticle:* 53 or 67
I Samuel 3.1-11	Ezekiel 34.11-16
John 4.31-38	Luke 10.1-9

Benedictus   **Whoever wishes to become great among you must be your servant, and whoever wishes to be first among you must be the servant of all. (Alleluia.)**

Magnificat   **Jesus said, Do you love me? Then feed my sheep. (Alleluia.)**

Midday

The appropriate weekday of Form 1-7 is used with the following propers:

Reading   John 15.12-17 *or*

I appointed you to go and bear fruit, fruit that will last, so that the Father will give you whatever you ask him in my name.   *John 15.16b*

Response   *Form 5, Response A, page 166*

Creation (including Rogation Days & Harvest Thanksgiving)

Form 1 is used.

COLLECT – one of the following is used.

Maker of all,
you have created the heavens and the earth
and made us in your own image:
may we discern your hand in all your works
and serve you with reverence and thanksgiving;
through Jesus Christ our Lord,
who with you and the Holy Spirit
reigns supreme over all things
now and for ever. **Amen.**

Eternal God,
you crown the year with your goodness
and you give us the fruits of the earth in their season:
grant that we may use them to your glory,
for the relief of those in need and for our own well-being;
through Jesus Christ our Lord. **Amen.**

God our Father,
you never cease the work you have begun
and prosper with your blessing all human labour:
make us wise and faithful stewards of your gifts
that we may serve the common good,
maintain the fabric of our world
and seek that justice where all may share
   the good things you pour upon us;
through Jesus Christ our Lord. **Amen.**

Morning	Evening
Pss: 107.1-3,23-43, 148 *Second Canticle:* 4 *or* 37 Genesis 9.8-17 *or* Ecclesiasticus 43.1-26 Revelation 10.1-7	Ps: 104 *Second Canticle:* 55 *or* 69 Job 38.1-18 Matthew 6.25-33

| *Benedictus* | **The Lord will indeed give all that is good,**
and our land will yield its increase. |
| *Magnificat* | **Consider the lilies of the field,**
yet even Solomon in all his glory
was not clothed like one of these. |

Midday

The appropriate weekday of Form 1-7 is used with the following propers:

Reading	Romans 8.18-25 *or*
	God saw everything that he had made, and indeed, it was very good. *Genesis 1.31*
Response	*Form 1, Response A, page 51*

The Peace of the World

Form 5 is used.

COLLECT

Almighty God,
from whom all thoughts of truth and peace proceed:
kindle, we pray, in the hearts of all, the true love of peace
and guide with your pure and peaceable wisdom
those who take counsel for the nations of the earth
that in tranquillity your kingdom may go forward,
till the earth is filled with the knowledge of your love;
through Jesus Christ our Lord. **Amen.**

Morning	Evening
Pss: 85, 147 part 2	*Pss:* 46, 47
Second Canticle: 6 or 10	*Second Canticle:* 39 or 45
Isaiah 11.1-9	Isaiah 2.1-5
Ephesians 2.13-22	John 16.22-33

Benedictus **Peace I leave with you, my own peace I give you;
do not let your hearts be troubled or afraid.
(Alleluia.)**

Magnificat **Live with one another in peace,
and the God of peace will be with you. (Alleluia.)**

Midday

The appropriate weekday of Form 1-7 is used with the following propers:

Reading Micah 6.6-8 *or*

What does the Lord require of you but to do justice, and to
love kindness, and to walk humbly with your God.

Micah 6.8

Response *Form 6, Response A, page 198*

Social Justice & Responsibility

Form 4 is used.

COLLECT

Eternal God,
in whose perfect realm
no sword is drawn but the sword of righteousness,
and no strength known but the strength of love:
so guide and inspire the work of those who seek your kingdom
that all your people may find their security
in that love which casts out fear
and in the fellowship revealed to us
in Jesus Christ our Saviour. **Amen.**

Morning	Evening
Pss: 85, 146	*Ps:* 33
Second Canticle: 3 *or* 11	*Second Canticle:* 39 *or* 60
Isaiah 58.6-9	Amos 5.21-24
Colossians 3.12-15	Luke 3.7-14

Benedictus   **Blessèd are the merciful,
for they will receive mercy. (Alleluia.)**

Magnificat   **Blessèd are the meek,
for they will inherit the earth. (Alleluia.)**

Midday

The appropriate weekday of Form 1-7 is used with the following propers:

Reading   Matthew 25.34-36 *or*

'Truly I tell you, just as you did it to one of the least of these who are members of my family, you did it to me.'

Matthew 25.40

Response   *Form 4, Response A, page 137*

Additional Liturgies

These liturgies may be used in conjunction with an Office, replacing the Prayers section, unless otherwise stated. They may stand as a form of worship on their own.

1. THANKSGIVING FOR HOLY BAPTISM

If possible, this should be celebrated at the font; or a simple bowl of water may be used.

I saw water flowing from the threshold of the temple.
Wherever the river flows
everything will spring to life. Alleluia.

On the banks of the river grow trees bearing every kind of fruit.
Their leaves will not wither nor their fruit fail.

Their fruit will serve for food,
their leaves for the healing of the nations.
For the river of the water of life
flows from the throne of God and of the Lamb.

Water may be poured into the font or bowl as the following prayer is said.

God in Christ gives us water welling up for eternal life.
With joy you will draw water from the wells of salvation.
Lord, give us this water and we shall thirst no more.

Let us give thanks to the Lord our God.
It is right to give thanks and praise.

Blessèd are you, sovereign God of all,
to you be glory and praise for ever.
You are our light and our salvation.
From the deep waters of death
you have raised your Son to life in triumph.
Grant that all who have been born anew by water and the Spirit
may daily be renewed in your image,
walk by the light of faith,
and serve you in newness of life;
through your anointed Son, Jesus Christ,
to whom with you and the Holy Spirit

we lift our voices of praise,
Father, Son and Holy Spirit.
Blessèd be God for ever.

THE APOSTLES' CREED or another affirmation of faith may be said.

Let us affirm the faith into which we have been baptised.

**I believe in God, the Father almighty,
creator of heaven and earth.**

**I believe in Jesus Christ, his only Son, our Lord,
who was conceived by the Holy Spirit,
born of the Virgin Mary,
suffered under Pontius Pilate,
was crucified, died, and was buried;
he descended to the dead.
On the third day he rose again;
he ascended into heaven,
he is seated at the right hand of the Father,
and he will come to judge the living and the dead.**

**I believe in the Holy Spirit,
the holy catholic Church,
the communion of saints,
the forgiveness of sins,
the resurrection of the body,
and the life everlasting. Amen.**

INTERCESSIONS and THANKSGIVINGS may be offered.

COLLECT

Almighty God,
in our baptism you have consecrated us
to be temples of your Holy Spirit.
May we, whom you have counted worthy,
nurture this gift of your indwelling Spirit with a lively faith,
and worship you with upright lives;
through Jesus Christ our Lord. **Amen.**

*The water may be sprinkled over the people or they may be invited to
use it to sign themselves with the cross.*

Rejoicing in God's new creation
as our Saviour taught us, so we pray
Our Father in heaven, . . .

THE CONCLUSION

Either:

God has made us one in Christ.
He has set his seal upon us and, as a pledge of what is to come,
has given the Spirit to dwell in our hearts.

The peace of the Lord be always with you
and also with you.

or:

May God, who in Christ gives us a spring of water
    welling up to eternal life,
perfect in *you* the image of his glory:
and may the blessing of God almighty,
the Father, the Son and the Holy Spirit
be among *you* and remain with *you* always. **Amen.**

Let us bless the Lord. (Alleluia, alleluia.)
Thanks be to God. (Alleluia, alleluia.)

2. PRAYERS FOR THE UNITY OF THE CHURCH

These prayers are particularly appropriate for use on Thursdays and during the Week of Prayer for Christian Unity, 18-25 January, and other suitable occasions. They may take place around a unity candle, the font or some other symbol of the Church.

Jesus prayed that his followers may all be one.
In the power of the Spirit, we join our prayers with his.

The following may be used.

O God, the Father of our Lord Jesus Christ,
our only Saviour, the Prince of Peace:
give us grace seriously to lay to heart
    the great dangers we are in by our unhappy divisions.

Take away all hatred and prejudice,
and whatever else may hinder us
    from godly union and concord;
that, as there is but one body and one Spirit,
one hope of our calling,
one Lord, one faith, one baptism,
one God and Father of us all,
so we may henceforth be all of one heart and of one soul,
united in one holy bond of peace, of faith and charity,
and may with one mind and one mouth glorify you;
through Jesus Christ our Lord. **Amen.**

I am the vine and you are the branches.
Abide in me as I abide in you.

As the Father has loved me, so have I loved you.
Abide in me as I abide in you.

No one has greater love than this,
to lay down one's life for one's friends.
Abide in me as I abide in you.

You are my friends if you do what I command you;
love one another as I have loved you.
Abide in me as I abide in you.

INTERCESSIONS are offered for the unity of the Church.

This response may be used.

Lord of the Church
hear your people's prayer.

Silence may be kept.

COLLECT

Lord Jesus Christ,
who said to your apostles,
'Peace I leave with you, my peace I give to you':
look not on our sins but on the faith of your Church
and grant it the peace and unity of your kingdom;
where you are alive and reign with the Father
in the unity of the Holy Spirit,
one God, now and for ever. **Amen.**

THE LORD'S PRAYER may be said.

Looking for the unity of all peoples on earth,
as our Saviour taught us, so we pray
Our Father in heaven, . . .

THE CONCLUSION

The peace of the Lord be always with you
and also with you.

Let us offer one another a sign of peace,
God's seal on our prayers.

3. EUCHARISTIC DEVOTIONS

For use on Thursdays and other appropriate occasions.

The following or some other suitable hymn may be sung.

O salutaris hostia
O Priest and Victim, Word of Life,
Throw wide the gates of Paradise.
We face our foes in mortal strife;
You are our strength! O heed our cries.

To Father, Son and Spirit blest,
One only God, be ceaseless praise.
May you in goodness grant us rest
In heaven, our home, for endless days. Amen.

tr. James Quinn SJ

*Here may follow suitable prayers, songs and readings, in honour of our Lord Jesus
Christ and the Eucharist. There may be a homily or meditation and a period of
silence may be kept, which may conclude with the following:*

THE LORD'S PRAYER may be said.

Rejoicing in the presence of Christ, our daily bread,
as our Saviour taught us, so we pray
Our Father in heaven, . . .

Tantum ergo
Come, adore this wondrous presence;
Bow to Christ, the source of grace.
Here is kept the ancient promise
Of God's earthly dwelling place.
Sight is blind before God's glory,
Faith alone may see his face.

Glory be to God the Father,
Praise to his co-equal Son,
Adoration to the Spirit,
Bond of love, in Godhead one.
Blest be God by all creation
Joyously while ages run. Amen.

tr. James Quinn SJ

Your people eat the food of angels. (Alleluia.)
You give them bread from heaven. (Alleluia.)

The following or some other suitable prayer may be used.

Lord Jesus Christ,
we thank you that in this wonderful sacrament
you have given us the memorial of your passion:
grant us so to reverence the sacred mysteries
    of your body and blood
that we may know within ourselves
and show forth in our lives
the fruits of your redemption;
for you are alive and reign with the Father
in the unity of the Holy Spirit,
one God, now and for ever. **Amen.**

A period of silent prayer may be kept.

THE DIVINE PRAISES

Blessèd be God.
Blessèd be the holy and undivided Trinity.
Blessèd be God the Father, maker of heaven and earth.
Blessèd be Jesus Christ, truly divine and truly human.
Blessèd be the holy Name of Jesus.
Blessèd be Jesus Christ in his death and resurrection.

Blessèd be Jesus Christ on his throne of glory.
Blessèd be Jesus Christ in the Sacrament of his body and blood.
Blessèd be God the Holy Spirit, the giver and sustainer of life.
Blessèd be God in the Virgin Mary,
   Mother of our Lord and God.
Blessèd be God in the angels and saints.
Blessèd be God.

The following or some other suitable acclamation may be used.

Let us adore Christ the Lord in the most holy Sacrament.

1   O praise the Lord, all you nations; *
     praise him, all you peoples.

2   For great is his steadfast love towards us, *
     and the faithfulness of the Lord endures for ever.
     (Alleluia.)   *Psalm 117*

Glory . . .

Let us adore Christ the Lord in the most holy Sacrament.

4. PRAYERS AT THE FOOT OF THE CROSS

*These prayers are for use on Fridays and other appropriate occasions
but not during the Christmas, Epiphany or Easter season.*

*A procession may be made towards a suitable cross, before which lights
may be burning, or a cross may be carried in. It may be mounted upright
or laid on the ground, with lights burning around it.*

On the cross, Jesus offered himself to the Father for the whole
world. At the foot of his cross, we join our prayers with his.

Either:

We adore you, O Christ, and we bless you:
because by your holy cross you have redeemed the world.

Holy God,
Holy and strong,
Holy and immortal,
have mercy upon us.

or:

We glory in your cross, O Lord,
and praise and glorify your holy resurrection:
for by virtue of the cross,
joy has come to the whole world.

God be gracious to us and bless us
and make his face to shine upon us,
that your way may be known upon earth,
your saving power among all nations.

We glory in your cross, O Lord,
and praise and glorify your holy resurrection:
for by virtue of the cross,
joy has come to the whole world.

While silence is kept, or appropriate hymns or chants are sung,
any of those present may come forward to touch the cross.
They may, for example, place their forehead on it as a sign
of entrusting to God, in union with Christ and his suffering, their
own burdens as well as those of others.

Other forms of intercessions may be offered.

Lord, we come to the cross;
in your mercy, hear us.

Almighty Father,
look with mercy on this your family
for which our Lord Jesus Christ was content to be betrayed
    and given up into the hands of sinners
    and to suffer death upon the cross;
who is alive and glorified with you and the Holy Spirit,
one God, now and for ever. **Amen.**

THE LORD'S PRAYER may be said.

Kneeling (*or* standing) at the foot of the cross,
as our Saviour taught us, so we pray
Our Father in heaven, . . .

May the life-giving cross be the source of all our joy and peace.
Amen.

Let us bless the Lord.
Thanks be to God.

5. CROSS PRAYERS

This devotion is normally observed at either Midday Prayer or Evening Prayer on
Fridays except in Christmas and Easter. It may be used on other suitable
occasions.

Having in mind Saint Francis' devotion to the passion of Christ
and looking upon the figure of the Crucified,
with arms outstretched, let us pray to the Lord.

A silence is observed for reflection on Christ's Passion.

You have sealed, O Lord, your servant Francis
with the signs of our redemption.

Either:

Lord Jesus Christ,
who when the world was growing cold,
to the inflaming of our hearts by the fire of your love
raised up blessèd Francis
bearing in his body the marks of your passion:
mercifully grant to us, your people,
true penitence
and grace to bear the cross for love of you;
who live and reign with the Father and the Holy Spirit,
one God, now and for ever. **Amen.**

or:

Most High and glorious God,
enlighten the darkness of our hearts
and give us a true faith, a certain hope
and a perfect love.
Give us a sense of the divine
and knowledge of yourself,
so that we may do everything
in fulfilment of your holy will;
through Jesus Christ our Lord. **Amen.**

The Prayer before the crucifix, Francis of Assisi

THE LORD'S PRAYER may be said.

Kneeling (*or* standing) at the foot of the cross,
as our Saviour taught us, so we pray
Our Father in heaven, . . .

THE CONCLUSION

**May Christ who bore our sins on the cross,
set us free to serve him with joy. Amen.**

Let us bless the Lord.
Thanks be to God.

6. THE GOSPEL PROCLAMATION

At the end of Evening Prayer or Night prayer, the gospel reading for the following day may be introduced by this acclamation:

We proclaim not ourselves, but Christ Jesus as Lord
and ourselves as your servants for Jesus' sake.

For the God who said, Let light shine out of darkness,
has caused the light to shine within us.

To give the light of the knowledge of the glory of God
in the face of Jesus Christ.

THE GOSPEL

Hear the gospel of our Lord Jesus Christ according to . . .
Glory to you, O Lord.

After the gospel reading:

This is the gospel of the Lord.
Praise to you, O Christ.

THE SONG OF TIMOTHY

Here are words you can trust:
Remember Jesus Christ, risen from the dead.
He is our salvation, our eternal glory.

If we have died with him, we shall also live with him;
if we endure, we shall also reign with him.

If we are faithless, he keeps faith;
for he has broken the power of death
and brought life and immortality to light
   through the gospel.

THE COLLECT

This may be either the Collect of the following day or a concluding Collect, as appropriate.

THE LORD'S PRAYER may be said.

Awaiting the fulfilment of all God's promises,
as our Saviour taught us, so we pray
Our Father in heaven, . . .

THE CONCLUSION

Let us bless the living God:
he was born of the Virgin Mary,
revealed in his glory,

worshipped by angels,
proclaimed among the nations,

believed in throughout the world,
exalted to the highest heavens.

Blessèd be God, our strength and our salvation,
now and for ever. Amen.

Let us bless the Lord. (Alleluia, alleluia.)
Thanks be to God. (Alleluia, alleluia.)

7. A CELEBRATION OF THE WORD

A Bible may be carried in and placed on the altar table or lectern.

Your word is a lantern to our feet
and a light upon our path.

Almighty God,
we thank you for the gift of your holy word.
May it be a lantern to our feet, a light upon our paths,
and a strength to our lives.
Take us and use us to love and serve all people
in the power of the Holy Spirit
and in the name of your Son, Jesus Christ our Lord. **Amen.**

A Bible Study or Lectio Divina (see page 741) may be shared.
After a suitable period, the service continues.

The Word of life which was from the beginning
we proclaim to you.

The darkness is passing away
and the true light is already shining.
The Word of life which was from the beginning.

That which we heard, which we saw with our eyes,
and touched with our hands,
we proclaim to you.

For our fellowship is with the Father,
and with his Son, Jesus Christ our Lord.
The Word of life which was from the beginning
we proclaim to you.

O God,
by whose command the order of time runs its course:
forgive our restlessness, perfect our faith
and, while we await the fulfilment of your promise,
grant us to have a good hope through the Word made flesh,
even Jesus Christ our Lord. **Amen.**

Gregory Nazianzus

THE LORD'S PRAYER may be said.

Rejoicing in the presence of the Word of God here among us,
as our Saviour taught us, so we pray
Our Father in heaven, . . .

THE CONCLUSION

**May the grace of Christ the incarnate Word be with us all.
Amen.**

Let us bless the Lord. (Alleluia, alleluia.)
Thanks be to God. (Alleluia, alleluia.)

A GROUP 'LECTIO DIVINA' METHOD

*Before starting decide on a leader to be responsible for an opening prayer and for
keeping time. Also decide who shall read the passage of scripture each time.
Anyone may 'pass' at any time instead of sharing aloud with the group, by stating
this. At the end, praying silently may be preferred, concluding with an 'Amen'
aloud.*

Listening for Christ the Word
- **Reading**: one person reads aloud the passage of scripture, as all
  listen for the word or phrase that attracts them.
- **Silence**: for two minutes as each person reflects on the word or
  phrase that attracted them.
- **Sharing aloud**: each may make a single sentence statement of
  the word or phrase, with no elaboration.

How Christ the Word speaks to me
- **Second Reading**: of the same passage by another.
- **Silence**: for two minutes reflecting on 'How does the content of
  this reading touch my life today?'
- **Sharing aloud**: briefly, beginning 'I hear ...' or 'I see ...'.

What Christ the Word is inviting me to do
- **Third Reading**: of the same passage by another.
- **Silence**: for two minutes reflecting on 'I believe that God wants
  me to ... today'.
- **Sharing aloud**: the result of each person's reflection, being
  especially aware of what is shared by the person on your right.

Pray, in turn, for the person on your right.

8. THE MINISTRY OF HEALING

Bless the Lord, O my soul;
and forget not all his benefits.

God forgives all our iniquities;
and heals all our diseases.

God redeems our life from the pit;
and crowns us with love and mercy.

READING

This or another suitable reading such as Mark 1.29-34 or Acts 3.1-10 follows.

Are any among you suffering? They should pray. Are any cheerful? They should sing songs of praise. Are any among you sick? They should call for the elders of the church and have them pray over them, anointing them with oil in the name of the Lord. The prayer of faith will save the sick, and the Lord will raise them up; and anyone who has committed sins will be forgiven. Therefore confess your sins to one another, and pray for one another, so that you may be healed. *James 5.13-16a*

This prayer of thanksgiving may be said.

Blessèd are you, sovereign God, gentle and merciful,
creator of heaven and earth.
Your word brought light out of darkness.
In Jesus Christ you proclaim good news to the poor,
liberty to captives, sight to the blind,
and freedom for the oppressed.
Daily your Spirit renews the face of the earth,
bringing life and health, wholeness and peace.
In the renewal of our lives
you make known your heavenly glory.
Father, Son and Holy Spirit.
Blessèd be God for ever.

THE APOSTLES' CREED, page 785, or an affirmation of faith may be said.

INTERCESSIONS for those in need and those who care for them may be offered in this or another form.

Holy God, in whom we live and move and have our being,
we make our prayer to you, saying,
Lord, hear us.
Lord, graciously hear us.

Grant to [*N and*] all who seek you
the assurance of your presence, your power and your peace.
Lord, hear us.
Lord, graciously hear us.

Grant your healing grace to [*N and*] all who are sick
that they may be made whole in body, mind and spirit.
Lord, hear us.
Lord, graciously hear us.

Grant to all who minister to the suffering
wisdom and skill, sympathy and patience.
Lord, hear us.
Lord, graciously hear us.

Sustain and support the anxious and fearful
and lift up all who are brought low.
Lord, hear us.
Lord, graciously hear us.

Hear us, Lord of life.
Heal us, and make us whole.

Almighty God,
whose Son revealed in signs and miracles
the wonder of your saving presence:
renew [*N, N, ... and*] all your people
with your heavenly grace,
and in all our weakness
sustain us by your mighty power,
through Jesus Christ our Lord. **Amen.**

THE LORD'S PRAYER

Rejoicing in the healing power of God's love,
as our Saviour taught us, so we pray
Our Father in heaven, . . .

The MINISTRY OF HEALING may take place here using these or other suitable prayers.

Be with us, Spirit of God;
nothing can separate us from your love.

Breathe on us, breath of God;
fill us with your saving power.

Speak in us, wisdom of God;
bring strength, healing and peace.

The Lord is here.
His Spirit is with us.

Silence is kept.

If anointing is to be administered, a priest may use this prayer over the oil, if it has not previously been blessed.

Lord, holy Father, giver of health and salvation,
as your apostles anointed those who were sick and healed them,
so continue the ministry of healing in your Church.
Sanctify this oil, that those who are anointed with it
may be freed from suffering and distress,
find inward peace, and know the joy of your salvation,
through your Son, our Saviour Jesus Christ. **Amen.**

THE LAYING ON OF HANDS may be administered using these or other suitable words.

In the name of God and trusting in his might alone,
receive Christ's healing touch to make you whole.

May Christ bring you wholeness
of body, mind and spirit,
deliver you from every evil,
and give you his peace. **Amen.**

If ANOINTING is administered by an authorised minister, these or other suitable words may be used.

N, I anoint you in the name of God who gives you life.
Receive Christ's forgiveness, his healing and his love.

May the Father of our Lord Jesus Christ
grant you the riches of his grace,
his wholeness and his peace. **Amen.**

This prayer concludes the Ministry of Healing.

The almighty Lord,
who is a strong tower for all who put their trust in him,
whom all things in heaven, on earth, and under the earth obey,
be now and evermore your defence.
May you believe and trust that the only name under heaven
given for health and salvation
is the name of our Lord Jesus Christ. **Amen.**

O magnify the Lord with me;
let us exalt his name together.
O magnify the Lord with me;
let us exalt his name together.

I sought the Lord and he answered me;
he delivered me from all my fears.
O magnify the Lord with me.

In my weakness I cried to the Lord;
he heard me and saved me from my troubles.
Let us exalt his name together.

Glory to the Father and to the Son
and to the Holy Spirit.
O magnify the Lord with me;
let us exalt his name together.

cf Psalm 34

THE CONCLUSION

Peace to you from God our Father who hears our cry.
Peace from his Son Jesus Christ whose death brings healing.
Peace from the Holy Spirit who gives us life and strength.
The peace of the Lord be always with you
and also with you.

9. THANKSGIVING FOR MISSION

This Thanksgiving should be celebrated near or facing the main door of the building.

A suitable Gospel reading may be introduced by this acclamation:

We proclaim not ourselves, but Christ Jesus as Lord
and ourselves as your servants for Jesus' sake.

For the God who said, Let light shine out of darkness,
has caused the light to shine within us.

To give the light of the knowledge of the glory of God
in the face of Jesus Christ.

THE GOSPEL READING

Hear the gospel of our Lord Jesus Christ according to . . .
Glory to you, O Lord.

After the gospel reading:

This is the gospel of the Lord.
Praise to you, O Christ.

This prayer of thanksgiving may be said.

Blessèd are you,
the God and Father of our Lord Jesus Christ,
for you have blessed us in Christ with every spiritual blessing.
You chose us in Christ before the foundation of the world
and destined us for adoption as your children.
In Christ we have the forgiveness of sins,
an inheritance in your kingdom, the seal of your Spirit,
and in him we live for the praise of your glory,
Father, Son and Holy Spirit.
Blessèd be God for ever.

The commissioning of those called to mission and ministry may take place here.

Will you continue in the apostles' teaching and fellowship,
in the breaking of the bread, and in the prayers?
With the help of God, I will.

Will you persevere in resisting evil,
and, whenever you fall into sin, repent and return to the Lord?
With the help of God, I will.

Will you proclaim by word and example
the good news of God in Christ?
With the help of God, I will.

Will you seek and serve Christ in all people,
loving your neighbour as yourself?
With the help of God, I will.

Will you acknowledge Christ's authority over human society,
by prayer for the world and its leaders,
by defending the weak, and by seeking peace and justice?
With the help of God, I will.

May Christ dwell in your hearts through faith,
that you may be rooted and grounded in love
and bring forth the fruit of the Spirit.
Amen.

*INTERCESSIONS for those engaged in ministry and other prayers for the mission
of the Church may be offered.*

COLLECT

Almighty God,
who called your Church to witness
that in Christ you were reconciling the world to yourself:
help us so to proclaim the good news of your love,
that all who hear it may be reconciled to you
through him who died for us and rose again
and reigns with you in the unity of the Holy Spirit,
one God, now and for ever. **Amen.**

THE LORD'S PRAYER may be said.

Looking for the coming of the Kingdom,
as our Saviour taught us, so we pray
Our Father in heaven, . . .

THE CONCLUSION

Let us bless the living God:
he was born of the Virgin Mary,
revealed in his glory,

worshipped by angels,
proclaimed among the nations,

believed in throughout the world.
exalted to the highest heavens.

Blessèd be God, our strength and our salvation,
now and for ever. Amen.

Let us bless the Lord. (Alleluia, alleluia.)
Thanks be to God. (Alleluia, alleluia.)

10. RENEWAL OF COMMITMENT

*The Renewal of Commitment shall be used on 16 April each year, the traditional
date of the taking of vows by Saint Francis. It may be used on other suitable
occasions, such as during a Community retreat or on Saint Francis' Day.*

*It may take place either at the Eucharist, after the gospel, or at an Office, as
the Prayers section. It may form a rite of its own.*

*Some of the following symbols may be used: Paschal Candle; Habit and Rope; The
Manual SSF; San Damiano Crucifix; a Book of the Gospels.*

The Lord give you peace!

Let us recall the words of Saint Francis:
'Most beloved brothers and sisters,
blessèd children, hear me, hear the voice of your father.
We have promised great things,
still greater things are promised to us.
Let us keep our promises
and strive to attain what has been promised to us.'

*READING from a Franciscan source, for example, that under 16 April
in 'A Sense of the Divine'.*

A HOMILY may be preached.

INTERCESSIONS may be offered and may include:
thanksgiving for the religious life in the Church;
thanksgiving for those who have encouraged and supported us in our vocation;
the Second and Third Orders SSF;
other Franciscans;
those who minister to us in our vocation.

THE LORD'S PRAYER may be said.

Being made one by the power of the Spirit,
as our Saviour taught us, so we pray
Our Father in heaven, . . .

**United with our Franciscan brothers and sisters
throughout the world,
we now renew our commitment.**

All the brothers and sisters in profession say together:

**Most High and everlasting God,
accept us now as we come to renew our love and service.
Gathered in your name and by your grace
we affirm once again our promise and vow to you,
in the sight of the holy angels,
    and of all the company of heaven,
and dedicate ourselves to the service
of our Lord Jesus Christ in the way of the blessèd Francis
by living in obedience, without property,
    and in chastity,
according to the Rule of our Community
and the life of the gospel,
God being our helper.**

All the novices then say together:

**Most High and everlasting God,
accept us now as we come to renew our love and service.
Gathered in your name and by your grace
we affirm once again our promise to you,
in the sight of the holy angels
and of all the company of heaven,
and dedicate ourselves to the service**

of our Lord Jesus Christ in the way of the blessèd Francis
by living in obedience,
according to the Rule of our Community
and the life of the gospel,
God being our helper.

All say together:

**Most High and glorious God,
enlighten the darkness of our hearts
and give us a true faith, a certain hope
and a perfect love.
Give us a sense of the divine
and knowledge of yourself,
so that we may do everything
in fulfilment of your holy will;
through Jesus Christ our Lord. Amen.**

THE CONCLUSION

In the words of the blessèd Francis, I bless you.
'May whoever observes all these things
be filled in heaven with the blessings of the Most High
and on earth with the blessing of Jesus Christ
in union with the blessing of the Holy Spirit,
    the Comforter,
and all the powers of heaven and all the saints.
And I, your poor servant,
as much as I am able,
confirm for you ✠ this most holy blessing.' **Amen.**

The peace of the Lord be always with you.
And also with you.

Let us offer one another a sign of peace,
God's seal on our prayers.

11. A CELEBRATION OF THE TRANSITUS OF OUR BROTHER FRANCIS

The Transitus is celebrated in the evening of 3 October and may follow the Lord's Prayer in the Prayers section in an Office or the Dismissal at a Eucharist or as a separate act of worship. Hymns may be sung at appropriate points and the congregation may gather around appropriate symbols: for example, a habit and a cord; an icon of Francis; a San Damiano crucifix; a book of the Gospels; a loaf of bread.

The Officiant begins:

Francis died at sunset on 3 October 1226 in a small hut near the Chapel of St Mary of the Angels in the woods below Assisi. On this evening each year it is our custom to gather together to celebrate all that God did in the life and person of Francis and to rededicate ourselves to living the gospel life, to which his life, words and deeds bore such powerful witness.

Let us hear what was written about Francis as he approached death in the early Sources of his life.

Reader 1   When Francis saw his final day drawing near,
as shown to him two years earlier by divine revelation,
he called to him the brothers he chose.
He blessed each one as it was given to him from above.

1 Celano

Reader 2   Although racked with sickness, blessèd Francis praised God
with great fervour of spirit and joy of body and soul, and told
his brother, 'If I am to die soon, call Brother Angelo and
Brother Leo that they may sing to me about Sister Death.'

Those brothers came to him and, with many tears, sang the
Canticle of Brother Sun and the other creatures of the Lord,
which the saint himself had composed in his illness for the
praise of the Lord and the consolation of his own soul and
that of others. Before the last stanza he added one about Sister
Death.

The Assisi Compilation [7]

CANTICLE   THE CANTICLE OF THE CREATURES (69b), page 532

Reader 3   As the brothers shed bitter tears and wept inconsolably, the
               holy father had bread brought to him. Francis blessed and
               broke it, and gave each of them a piece to eat.

Bread may be blessed and then shared by all present.

               He also ordered a book of the Gospels to be brought and
               asked that the Gospel according to Saint John be read to
               him starting from that place which begins, *Before the feast of the
               Passover.* He was remembering that most sacred supper, the
               last one the Lord celebrated with his disciples. In reverent
               memory of this, to show his brothers how much he loved
               them, he did all of this.

John 13.1-5,12-17 may be read.

Reader 4   The few days that remained to him before his passing he spent
               in praise of God, teaching his belovèd companions how to
               praise Christ with him. As best he could, he broke out into
               this psalm:

                        Thomas of Celano, 'The Remembrance of the Desire of a Soul'

Psalm 142 is recited together.

1   **I cry aloud to the Lord; ***
     to the Lord I make my supplication.

2   **I pour out my complaint before him ***
     and tell him of my trouble.

3   **When my spirit faints within me, you know my path; ***
     in the way wherein I walk have they laid a snare for me.

4   **I look to my right hand, and find no one who knows me; ***
     I have no place to flee to, and no one cares for my soul.

5   **I cry out to you, O Lord, and say: ***
     'You are my refuge, my portion in the land of the living.

6   **'Listen to my cry, for I am brought very low; ***
     save me from my persecutors,
        for they are too strong for me.

7   **'Bring my soul out of prison,**
        that I may give thanks to your name; *
     when you have dealt bountifully with me,
        then shall the righteous gather around me.'

Reader 5   That evening before nightfall, after vespers, when blessèd
Francis passed to the Lord, many birds called larks flew low
above the roof of the house where blessèd Francis lay,
wheeling in a circle and singing.

The Assisi Compilation [14]

The hour came.
All the mysteries of Christ
were fulfilled in him,
and he happily took flight to God.
One of his disciples, a brother of no small fame, saw the soul
of the most holy father like a star ascending to heaven, having
the immensity of the moon and the brightness of the sun,
extending over many waters carried by a little white cloud.

Thomas of Celano, 'The Remembrance of the Desire of a Soul'

The Officiant continues:

I have done what is mine;
may Christ teach you what is yours.

Francis raised his hands to heaven and glorified Christ.
Free from all things, he went to God free.

Welcome, my Sister Death.
She will be the gate of life.

Francis, poor and lowly, enters heaven rich,
while saints and angels sing their songs of praise.

With arms outstretched, let us pray to the Lord.

Silence

Let us pray.

O God,
who made your Church rich
through the poverty of the blessèd Francis:
help us, who remember his death,
not to trust in earthly things
but to seek your heavenly gifts;
through Jesus Christ our Saviour. **Amen.**

*Then the Officiant gives the solemn blessing and the bell is tolled forty-four times
(to mark the years of Francis' life).*

To the prayers of the saints I commend you.
May the most pure Virgin, Mother of God,
Patroness of all Franciscans, pray for you.
May Saint Francis, our brother,
who bore the marks of the Lord Jesus, pray for you.
May Saint Antony, illustrious preacher, pray for you.
May Saint Bonaventure, seraphic doctor, pray for you.
May Saint Bernardine, lover of the Holy Name of Jesus,
     pray for you.
May Saint Clare, first-born of the Second Order, pray for you.
May Saint Louis, Saint Elizabeth and the illustrious saints
     of the Third Order, pray for you.
May all the saints of God, pray for you.
May the holy angels befriend you and watch around you
     to protect you.
And I will pronounce upon you the blessing
     which our holy brother, Francis,
Gave to Brother Leo, his companion:

✠ The Lord bless you and keep you;
the Lord make his face shine upon you
     and be gracious to you;
the Lord lift up the light of his countenance upon you
     and give you peace.
May the Lord give you his holy benediction.   **Amen.**

12. THANKSGIVING FOR THE HOLY ONES OF GOD

This Litany of Thanksgiving is appropriate for various occasions. It is particularly suitable for use at Morning or Evening Prayer at All Saints' tide.

The following responses may be said or sung.

Let us bless the Lord.
Thanks be to God.

or:

Alleluia, alleluia, alleluia.

For Abraham and Sarah, our ancestors in faith,
and all who journey into the unknown trusting God's promises:
For Jacob, deceitful younger brother, yet chosen by God,
the father of all who are called by virtue not of their own:
For Moses the lawgiver and Aaron the priest,
and all who lead God's people to freedom and newness of life: **R**

For Esther and Deborah, saviours of their nation,
and for all who dare to act courageously at God's call:
For Hannah and Ruth, and all who through love and devotion
witness to the faithfulness of God:
For Isaiah, John the Baptist and all the prophets,
and all who speak the truth without counting the cost: **R**

For Mary the Virgin, the mother of our Lord and God,
and all who obey God's call without question:
For Andrew and John and the first disciples,
and for all who forsake everything to follow Jesus:
For Mary Magdalene, Salome and Mary,
first witnesses of the resurrection,
and for all who bear witness to Christ: **R**

For Peter and Paul, [N] and the apostles,
who preached the gospel to Jew and Gentile,
and for all who take the good news to the ends of the earth:
For Barnabas, Silas and Timothy,
and for all who bring encouragement and steadfastness:

*In the following sections names may be added or omitted
to reflect local traditions.*

For the writers of the Gospels
and for all who bring the faith of Christ alive for each generation: **R**

For Ambrose, Augustine, Gregory and Jerome,
and for all who contend for the truth of the gospel:
For Basil, Gregory of Nazianzus, Athanasius and John Chrysostom,
and all who enable us to reflect on the mystery of Christ:
For Cyprian, Antony and Ephrem,
and for all who lead the Church into new paths of discipleship: **R**

For Stephen, Alban, Agnes, Lucy and the whole army of martyrs,
and all who have faced death for love of Christ:
For Augustine of Canterbury and Aidan, for Boniface and Patrick,
and for all who have carried the gospel to this and other lands:
For Aelred, Bernard and Cuthbert,
and for all who live and teach the love of God: **R**

For Anselm and Richard Hooker,
and for all who reveal to us the depths of God's wisdom:
For Benedict and Scholastica, Francis and Clare, Hilda and Bede,
and for all who deepen our common life in Christ:
For Julian of Norwich, Bridget of Sweden and Teresa of Avila,
and for all who renew our vision of the mystery of God: **R**

For Thomas Cranmer
and all who reform the Church of God:
For Thomas More
and all who hold firm to its continuing faith:
For Gregory and Dunstan, George Herbert and John Keble,
and for all who praise God in poetry and song: **R**

For Lancelot Andrewes, John Wesley and Charles Simeon,
and for all who preach the word of God:
For William Wilberforce and Josephine Butler,
and for all who work to transform the world:
For Monica, and for Mary Sumner,
and for all who nurture faith in home and family: **R**

For the martyrs and peacemakers of our own time,
who shine as lights in the darkness:
For all the unsung heroes and heroines of our faith,
whose names are known to God alone:
For all those in our own lives
who have revealed to us the love of God
and shown to us the way of holiness: **R**

For *NN* ... **R**

Let us rejoice and praise them with thankful hearts
and glorify our God in whom they put their trust.

THE COLLECT

God of holiness,
your glory is proclaimed in every age:
as we rejoice in the faith of your saints,
inspire us to follow their example
with boldness and joy;
through Jesus Christ our Lord. **Amen.**

THE LORD'S PRAYER may be said.

Uniting our prayers with the whole company of heaven
as our Saviour taught us, so we pray
Our Father in heaven, . . .

THE CONCLUSION

May the infinite and glorious Trinity,
the Father, the Son, and the Holy Spirit,
direct our life in good works,
and after our journey through this world,
grant us eternal rest with the saints. **Amen.**

13. PRAYERS FOR TRAVELLERS, PILGRIMS AND THOSE GOING ON MISSION

The following may take the place of the Conclusion at an Office, or the Dismissal at the Eucharist.

O Lord save your servants,
who put their trust in you.

Send them help from your holy sanctuary,
and ever more mightily defend them.

Be unto them, O Lord, a strong tower
from the face of the enemy.

Show them your ways, O Lord,
and teach them your paths.

O God, give your angels charge over them,
to keep them in all their ways.

For Travellers:

PSALM 16

> **You will show me the path of life.**

1   Preserve me, O God, for in you have I taken refuge; *
    I have said to the Lord, 'You are my lord,
        all my good depends on you.'

2   All my delight is upon the godly that are in the land, *
    upon those who are noble in heart.

3   Though the idols are legion that many run after, *
    their drink offerings of blood I will not offer,
        neither make mention of their names upon my lips.

4   The Lord himself is my portion and my cup; *
    in your hands alone is my fortune.

5   My share has fallen in a fair land; *
    indeed, I have a goodly heritage.

6   I will bless the Lord who has given me counsel, *
    and in the night watches he instructs my heart.

7   I have set the Lord always before me; *
    he is at my right hand; I shall not fall.

8   Wherefore my heart is glad and my spirit rejoices; *
    my flesh also shall rest secure.

9   For you will not abandon my soul to Death, *
    nor suffer your faithful one to see the Pit.

10 You will show me the path of life;
        in your presence is the fullness of joy *
    and in your right hand are pleasures for evermore.

You will show me the path of life.

READING Luke 10.25-37

PRAYER

Merciful God, giver of life and health,
guide, we pray, with your wisdom
all who are striving to protect travellers
from injury and harm;
grant to those who travel consideration for others,
and to those who walk and play
a thoughtful caution and care;
so that without fear or misfortune
we all may come safely to our journey's end,
by your mercy, who care for each one of us;
through Jesus Christ our Saviour. **Amen.**

Douglas Crick (1885-1973)

For Pilgrims:

PSALM 121

The Lord himself watches over you.

1   I lift up my eyes to the hills; *
    from where is my help to come?

2   My help comes from the Lord, *
    the maker of heaven and earth.

3   He will not suffer your foot to stumble; *
    he who watches over you will not sleep.

4   Behold, he who keeps watch over Israel *
     shall neither slumber nor sleep.

5   The Lord himself watches over you; *
     the Lord is your shade at your right hand,

6   So that the sun shall not strike you by day, *
     neither the moon by night.

7   The Lord shall keep you from all evil; *
     it is he who shall keep your soul.

8   The Lord shall keep watch over your going out
     and your coming in, *
     from this time forth for evermore.

The Lord himself watches over you.

READING 3 John 2-8

PRAYER

God of the journey
and protector of all who trust in you;
you led your people in safety through the desert
and brought them to a land of plenty.
Be with your servants
and fill them with your Spirit of love.
Preserve them from all harm
and bring them in safety to their destination.
We ask this through Christ our Redeemer. **Amen.**

For those going on Mission:

PSALM 96

Tell out his salvation from day to day.

1   Sing to the Lord a new song; *
     sing to the Lord, all the earth.

2   Sing to the Lord and bless his name; *
     tell out his salvation from day to day.

3   Declare his glory among the nations *
     and his wonders among all peoples.

4   For great is the Lord and greatly to be praised; *
         he is more to be feared than all gods.

5   For all the gods of the nations are but idols; *
         it is the Lord who made the heavens.

6   Honour and majesty are before him; *
         power and splendour are in his sanctuary.

7   Ascribe to the Lord, you families of the peoples; *
         ascribe to the Lord honour and strength.

8   Ascribe to the Lord the honour due to his name; *
         bring offerings and come into his courts.

9   O worship the Lord in the beauty of holiness; *
         let the whole earth tremble before him.

10   Tell it out among the nations that the Lord is king. *
         He has made the world so firm that it cannot be moved;
          he will judge the peoples with equity.

11   Let the heavens rejoice and let the earth be glad; *
         let the sea thunder and all that is in it;

12   Let the fields be joyful and all that is in them; *
         let all the trees of the wood shout for joy before the Lord.

13   For he comes, he comes to judge the earth; *
         with righteousness he will judge the world
          and the peoples with his truth.

Tell out his salvation from day to day.

READING Matthew 28.16-20

PRAYER

Heavenly Father,
draw your servant nearer to yourself
that *s/he* may know your will;
Loving Lord Jesus,
fill *her/him* with all joy and peace;
Holy Spirit, inspire *her/him*
that *s/he* may celebrate and proclaim *her/his* faith
and give glory to God,
ever blessèd Trinity,
now and for ever. **Amen.**

THE CONCLUSION

May our blessèd Lady pray for you.
May Saint Francis and Saint Clare pray for you.
May all the saints of God pray for you.
May the holy angels befriend you
   and watch around you to protect you.

Brother/Sister N, ✠ may the Lord bless you. **Amen.**

Go in peace to love and serve the Lord.
In the name of Christ. Amen.

14. WELCOMING A NEW MEMBER TO A HOUSE

This prayer may be used in the context of the Eucharist, an Office, an informal meal together or a social gathering.

The Guardian shall normally be the Officiant.

Trinity of love,
We joyfully celebrate the arrival of *N*
to this Franciscan household.
We thank you for the gifts *N* will bring
to our community life.
May we grow together in love and service,
and strengthen and support each other
in our common vocation,
that your Kingdom may be seen among us. **Amen.**

***N*, we welcome you.**

15. BLESSING OF MINISTRY

After the 'Ministry of the Word' in the Eucharist, or after the Lord's Prayer in the Prayers section of an Office, the candidate for blessing comes and stands before the Officiant. The Community stands around the candidate, but not obscuring the view of the people.

Officiant   We are gathered here to welcome and bless N, who has been chosen to serve as *Minister/Guardian* of N.

The Officiant then addresses the candidate:

N, in the presence of the Community, do you commit yourself to this trust and responsibility?

Candidate   I do.

Officiant   Will you guard those put in your care, nurture them in the faith and, by your life and example, proclaim the living Word among them, after the spirit of the blessèd Francis?

Candidate   I will, God being my helper.

Officiant   Will you see that the observance of the Rule is maintained, with love, patience and understanding?

Candidate   I will, God being my helper.

The candidate steps aside and the Officiant addresses the Community:

Brothers and Sisters, will you love and support N in this ministry?

Community   We will.

Officiant   Let us then silently offer our prayers to God and ask a blessing on N in this ministry.

The candidate kneels before the Officiant and a period of silence is observed.

The Officiant and the Community stretch out their right hands over the candidate and the Officiant says:

> May our blessèd Lady pray for you.
> May Saint Francis, who bore the marks
>   of the Lord Jesus, pray for you.
> May Saint Clare pray for you.
> May all the saints of the three Orders
>   pray for you.
> May the holy angels befriend you
> and watch around you to protect you.
>
> And I will pronounce upon you
> the blessing which our holy father, Francis,
> gave to Brother Leo, his companion:
>
> ✠ The Lord bless you and watch over you,
> the Lord make his face shine upon you
>   and be gracious to you,
> the Lord look kindly on you
>   and give you peace.
> N, the Lord bless you.

And all present proclaim:
Amen.

The Officiant then gives the Peace to the newly blessed.
The Community expresses its approval in a suitable manner.

If the blessing is in the context of a Eucharist, the President then continues, offering the Peace to all present, and the Eucharist proceeds with the Preparation of the Table.

16. THE CELEBRATION OF A PROFESSION ANNIVERSARY

The celebration of a significant Profession anniversary shall normally take place in the context of the Eucharist. The Minister Provincial or their representative shall officiate. Propers and texts from 'The Receiving of Profession in Life Vows' may be used. A homily may be given.

After the Ministry of the Word, following the gospel (and homily), the Minister shall be seated in front of the altar facing the congregation.

Brother/Sister N shall stand in front of him/her, facing the congregation.

N   My brothers and sisters,
         xx years ago, in response to God's call,
         I made my profession of poverty, chastity and obedience.
         As I continue my Christian pilgrimage,
         today, through Christ and his body the Church,
         with gladness, I repeat my vow:

N kneels in front of the Minister.

         I, *Brother/Sister N*
         do hereby dedicate myself
         for my whole life,
         in company with the *brothers/sisters*
         of the First Order of the
         Society of Saint Francis,
         to the service of our Lord Jesus Christ,
         to follow him under the conditions of
         poverty, chastity and obedience
         in the way of the blessèd Francis;
         and I promise and vow
         in the presence of almighty God
         that I will live according to the
         Rule of this Community,
         God being my helper.

The Community say together:

Creator Spirit,
rekindle in *N* your gifts of grace,
renew *her/his* life in Christ
and bring to completion
all that your calling has begun in *her/him*. Amen.

The Minister stands to bless Brother/Sister N.

May our blessèd Lady pray for you.
May Saint Francis, who bore the marks
    of the Lord Jesus, pray for you.
May Saint Clare pray for you.
May all the saints of the three Orders pray for you.
May the holy angels befriend you
    and watch around you to protect you.
And I will pronounce upon you
the blessing which our holy father, Francis,
gave to Brother Leo, his companion:

✠ The Lord bless you and watch over you,
the Lord make his face to shine upon you
and be gracious to you,
the Lord look kindly on you and give you peace.
Brother/Sister N, the Lord bless you.

And all present shall say:
Amen.

The Eucharist continues with either the Intercessions or the Peace.

17. PRAYING FAREWELL

This rite may be used when anyone is departing from the local Community. It may be adapted according to circumstances, including the absence of the person leaving. If used at the Eucharist it replaces the Blessing and Dismissal. At an Office it follows the Lord's Prayer in the Prayers section. To symbolise continuing love and concern, the group may gather in a circle.

God of our beginnings and endings,
we celebrate all we have shared with *N and N*
and ask your blessing as *they* continues on *their* journey.
May the love that is in our hearts
be a bond that unites us forever,
wherever we may be.
May the power of your presence
bless this moment of our leave-taking;
this we ask for the sake of Jesus Christ, our Redeemer. **Amen.**

THE PSALMS The following may be said or some other.

1   **You, O God, will guard us from all evil:**
    you will protect our lives.

2   **You will protect our going out and our coming in:**
    both now and for ever.

3   **Where can I flee from your Spirit:**
    or where can I flee from your presence?

4   **If I climb to heaven, you are there:**
    if I lie in the grave, you are there also.

5   **If I take the wings of the morning:**
    and dwell in the depths of the sea,

6   **Even there, your hand shall lead me:**
    your hand shall hold me fast.

from Psalms 121 & 139

Come to our help, comfort us and give us life,
in your merciful goodness, O God,
for we are yours;
keep our feet from the evil path
and save us through Jesus Christ,
your Word and Wisdom. **Amen.**

I thank my God, every time I remember you, constantly praying with joy for all of you, because of your sharing in the gospel. And this is my prayer, that love may overflow more and more with knowledge and full insight to help to determine what is best, so that in the day of Christ we may be pure and blameless, having produced the harvest of righteousness that comes through Jesus Christ for the glory and praise of God.

Philippians 1.3,4,9

or Exodus 13.21-22; John 3.5-8; John 16.21-24; 2 Corinthians 4.7-9

THE RESPONSE

The Community may say their words together or different individuals take a particular part.

Community (1)	**As you journey onward,** **we ask forgiveness where we have failed you;** **we give thanks for all you have given us;** **we assure you of our love and prayers.**
Leaver(s)	As I leave, I ask forgiveness where I have failed you; I give thanks for all that you have given to me; I assure you of my love and prayers.
Community (2)	**As you experience the pain of change,** **and the insecurity of moving on,** **we pray that you may also experience** **the blessing of inner growth.**
Leaver(s)	I know that God goes with me.
Community (3)	**As you meet the poor, the pained,** **and the stranger on the Way,** **we pray that you may see in each one** **the face of Christ.**
Leaver(s)	I know that God goes with me.
Community (4)	**As you walk through the good times and the bad,** **we pray that you may never lose sight** **of the shelter of God's loving arms.**
Leaver(s)	I know that God goes with me.

Community (5)	**As you ponder your decisions**
	and wonder over the fruits of your choice,
	we pray that the peace of Christ
	may reign in your heart.

Leaver(s)	I know that God goes with me.

THE CONCLUSION

We praise and thank you, God of the journey,
for our *brothers and sisters* who *are* soon to leave us.
We entrust *them* into your loving care,
knowing that you are always the faithful traveller
   and companion on the Way.
Shelter and protect *them* from all harm and anxiety.
Grant *them* the courage to meet the future,
and grace to let go into new life;
through Jesus Christ our Saviour. **Amen.**

N and N, ✠ may God bless you. **Amen.**

Then each person present may make the sign of the cross on the forehead of those leaving, saying:

Go in peace, for our God goes with you.

The Peace may be exchanged.

18. ON HEARING OF THE DEATH OF A BROTHER OR SISTER

This service may be used on the hearing of the death or on the day of the funeral by those not able to be present or on any other suitable occasion.

We shall not all die
but we shall be changed.
The trumpet shall sound and the dead will rise immortal
and we shall be changed.
The perishable must be clothed with the imperishable
and the mortal must be clothed with immortality.
We shall not all die
but we shall be changed.

HYMN
One of the following may be sung, or some other:
'Dies Irae', or the 'Kontakion', or 'Jesus, remember me when you come into your kingdom'.

PSALMS
Any of the following may be said:
Pss. 23, 42, 43, 121, 130, 139

SCRIPTURE READINGS
One of the following may be used, or some other:
Isaiah 25.6-9; Hosea 6.1-3; John 11.21-27; John 14.1-3;
Romans 6.3-9; Philippians 1.20-26; 1 Thessalonians 4.13-18

MEMORIES OF THE DEPARTED may be shared, ending with one of the following prayers:

Either:

God in heaven,
we thank you that you have made each one of us
in your own image,
and given us gifts and talents
with which to serve you.
We thank you for N,
the years we shared with *her/him*,
the good we saw in *her/him*,
the love we received from *her/him*.
Now give us strength and courage,
to leave *her/him* in your care,
confident in your promise of eternal life,
through Jesus Christ our Lord. **Amen.**

or:

O God,
who brought us to birth
and in whose arms we die:
in our grief and shock
contain and comfort us,
embrace us with your love,
give us hope in our confusion
and grace to let go into new life;
through Jesus Christ. **Amen**

Janet Morley

CANTICLE
One of the following is said or sung: 27, 28, 43, 51 *or* 59.

THE PRAYERS

INTERCESSION may be offered.

Lord, have mercy.
Lord, have mercy.

Christ, have mercy.
Christ, have mercy.

Lord, have mercy.
Lord, have mercy.

We commend *N* to you, O God,
as *s/he* journeys beyond our sight.

Either:

God of all consolation,
in your unending love and mercy
you turn the darkness of death
into the dawn of new life.
Your Son, by dying for us, conquered death
and, by rising again,
restored to us eternal life:
may we then go forward eagerly to meet our Redeemer
and, after our life on earth,
be reunited with all our brothers and sisters
in that place where every tear is wiped away
and all things are made new;
through Jesus Christ our Saviour. **Amen.**

or:

Heavenly Father,
into whose hands Jesus Christ
commended his spirit at the last hour:
into those same hands we now commend your servant *N*,
that death may be for *her/him*
the gate to life and to eternal fellowship with you;
through Jesus Christ our Lord. **Amen.**

THE LORD'S PRAYER may be said.

Lord Jesus, remember us in your kingdom and teach us to pray
Our Father in heaven, . . .

Either:

N, our companion in faith and *brother/sister* in Christ,
we entrust you to God who created you.
May you return to the Most High who formed you
    from the dust of the earth.
May the angels and the saints come to meet you
    as you go forth from this life.
May Christ, who was crucified for you,
    take you into his Kingdom.
May Christ the Good Shepherd
    give you a place within his flock.
May Christ forgive you your sins
    and keep you among his people.
May you see your Redeemer face to face
    and delight in the vision of God for ever. **Amen.**

or:

N, may Christ give you rest in the land of the living
and open for you the gates of paradise;
may he receive you as a citizen of the Kingdom,
and grant you forgiveness of your sins:
for you were his friend. **Amen.**

Orthodox Funeral Rite

THE CONCLUSION

We remember the living and the departed.

Either:

Now to the One who is able to keep us from falling
and set us in the presence of the divine glory,
to the only God our Saviour
be glory and majesty, dominion and praise,
now and for ever. **Amen.**

or the Kaddish, page 776, may be said.

A time of silence may be kept.

Prayers for Various Occasions

1. LITANIES

a) MORNING

That this day may be holy, good and joyful:
we pray to you, O Lord.

That we may offer to you our worship and our work:
we pray to you, O Lord.

That we may strive for the well-being of all creation:
we pray to you, O Lord.

That in the pleasures and pains of life,
we may know the love of Christ and be thankful:
we pray to you, O Lord.

That we may be bound together by your Holy Spirit,
in communion with [N and with] all your saints,
entrusting one another and all our life to Christ:
we pray to you, O Lord.

Let us commend ourselves, and all for whom we pray,
to the mercy and protection of God.

Open prayer may be offered and silence is kept.

The Collect and Lord's Prayer follow.

b) EVENING

That this evening may be holy, good and peaceful:
we pray to you, O Lord.

That your holy angels may lead us in the paths of peace
  and goodwill:
we pray to you, O Lord.

That we may be pardoned and forgiven for our sins and offences:
we pray to you, O Lord.

That there may be peace in your Church and for the whole world:
we pray to you, O Lord.

That we may be bound together by your Holy Spirit,
in communion with [N and with] all your saints,
entrusting one another and all our life to Christ:
we pray to you, O Lord.

Let us commend ourselves, and all for whom we pray,
to the mercy and protection of God.

Open prayer may be offered and silence is kept.

The Collect and Lord's Prayer follow.

c) SAINTS' DAYS

Rejoicing in our fellowship with N and all the saints,
we make our prayer to our gracious God.

For your grace revealed in N,
and for all that inspires us from *her/his* life:

God of love,
hear our prayer.

For *her/his* insight into the mystery of Christ
and for every way in which *her/his* faith continues to speak today: **R**

That following *her/his* good example,
we may hear afresh your call to holiness of life: **R**

That we may receive grace to grow into the likeness of Christ: **R**

That we may persevere in prayer
and seek new light and truth from your word: **R**

That we may draw other people to the fire of your love: **R**

That we may be faithful to Christ even to death: **R**

In communion with N and all the saints,
let us commend the world to the mercy and protection of God.

Open prayer may be offered and silence is kept.

The Collect and Lord's Prayer follow.

2. TRADITIONAL PRAYERS AND ANTHEMS

a) MARIAN ANTHEMS

Traditionally, these anthems are sung at the end of Night Prayer.

SALVE REGINA, from after Pentecost to Advent

The Latin text may be found at the end of Night Prayer, Forms 1-7.

Hail, O Queen, mother of mercy;
our life, our sweetness and our hope, hail.
To you do we cry, the banished children of Eve;
to you do we sigh,
lamenting and weeping in this vale of tears;
therefore, our advocate,
your eyes of mercy turn towards us,
and Jesus, the blessèd fruit of your womb,
to us, after this exile, reveal.
O clement, O devoted, O sweet Virgin Mary.

ALMA REDEMPTORIS MATER, from Advent until Candlemas

O Loving Mother of the Redeemer,
you remain an ever open gateway to heaven,
and star of the sea;
come to the aid of the fallen people who strive to rise again:
you brought forth to the wonder of all nature
your own holy creator;
pure of heart, now and always,
from the lips of Gabriel you received the Ave:
on us sinners have mercy.

AVE REGINA CAELORUM, from February 3 until Maundy Thursday

Queen of the heavens, we greet you:
Hail to you, Our Lady of Angels;
You the dawn, the door of morning,
from whom rose the world's salvation;
Joy to you, O Virgin glorious,
radiant beyond all other;
Mary, most precious and gracious,
pray for us to your Son, Jesus our Saviour.

REGINA COELI, from Easter Day until Pentecost Sunday

Queen of Heaven, rejoice this day, Alleluia.
He whom you were called to bear, Alleluia.
As he promised has arisen, Alleluia.
Pour for us, to God, your prayer, Alleluia.

ANTHEM TO THE THEOTOKOS

Into his joy, the Lord has received you,
Virgin God-bearer, Mother of Christ.

You have beheld the King in his beauty,
Mary, daughter of Israel.

You have made answer for the creation
to the redeeming will of God.

Light, fire and life, divine and immortal,
joined to our nature you have brought forth,

that to the glory of God the Father,
heaven and earth might be restored.

OSB West Malling

b) **WORLD PRAYER FOR PEACE**

O God,
lead us from death to life,
from falsehood to truth.
Lead us from despair to hope,
from fear to trust.
Lead us from hate to love,
from war to peace.
Let peace fill our hearts, our world, our universe. **Amen.**

Satish Kumar

c) **KADDISH**

The Kaddish is an affirmation of faith in the face of death, said by the chief mourner, surrounded by the congregation.

Magnified and sanctified be the great name of God
in the world which he created according to his will.
May he establish his kingdom in your life and in your days,

and in the lifetime of all his people:
quickly and speedily may it come; and let us say Amen.

Blessèd be God for ever.

Blessed, praised and glorified,
exalted, extolled and honoured,
magnified and lauded be the name of the Holy One;
blessèd be God.
Though he be high above all the blessings and hymns,
praises and consolations,
which are uttered in the world; and let us say Amen.

Blessèd be God for ever.

May there be abundant peace from heaven
and life for us and for all people; let us say Amen.

Blessèd be God for ever.

d) **CHRIST ARAKSHA**

For individuals to say before sleep.

May the cross of the Son of God,
which is mightier than all the hosts of Satan,
and more glorious than all the hosts of heaven,
abide with me in my going out and my coming in.
By day and by night, at morning and at evening,
at all times and in all places may it protect and defend me.
From the wrath of evildoers, from the assaults of evil spirits,
from foes visible and invisible, from the snares of the devil,
from all passions that beguile the soul and body:
may it guard, protect and deliver me. **Amen.**

an Indian prayer

e) **AN ARMENIAN ORTHODOX DISMISSAL**

Keep us in peace, O Christ our God,
under the protection of your holy and venerable cross;
save us from our enemies, visible and invisible,
and count us worthy to glorify you with thanksgiving,
with the Father and the Holy Spirit,
now and for ever, world without end. **Amen.**

3. FRANCISCAN PRAYERS

Other Franciscan prayers will be found in Midday Prayer, Forms 1-7:
Absorbeat, page 199
19th-century French Prayer, page 229
The prayer in 'A Letter to the Entire Order', page 53
Admonitions XXVII, page 81
The Praises to be Said at all the Hours, pages 109, 595
The Praises of God, page 138
The Prayer before the Crucifix, page 168
A Salutation of the BVM, page 230 and with 'The Principles of the First
Order', page 786
Prayer from The Praises to be Said at all the Hours, page 796

a) A SALUTATION OF THE VIRTUES

Hail, Queen Wisdom! may the Lord protect you,
with your Sister, holy pure Simplicity!
Lady holy Poverty, may the Lord protect you,
with your Sister, holy Humility!
Lady holy Charity, may the Lord protect you,
with your Sister holy Obedience.
Most holy Virtues, may the Lord protect all of you
from whom you come and proceed.

There is surely no one in the whole world
who can possess any one of you without dying first.
Whoever possesses one and does not offend
the others possesses all.
Whoever offends one does not possess
any and offends all.
And each one confounds vice and sin.
Holy Wisdom confounds Satan and all his cunning.
Pure holy Simplicity confounds all the wisdom
of this world and the wisdom of the body.
Holy Poverty confounds the desire for riches,
greed, and the cares of this world.
Holy Humility confounds pride, all people
who are in the world and all this is in the world.
Holy Charity confounds every diabolical
and carnal temptation and every carnal fear.
Holy Obedience confounds every corporal
and carnal wish, binds its mortified body

to obedience of the Spirit and obedience
to one's brother, so that it is subject
and submissive to everyone in the world,
not only to people but to every beast
and wild animal as well that they may do
whatever they want with it, insofar
as it has been given to them from above by the Lord.

Francis of Assisi

b) A PRAYER INSPIRED BY THE OUR FATHER

O Our Father most holy: our Creator,
Redeemer, Consoler, and Saviour:

Who are in heaven: in the angels and the saints,
enlightening them to know, for you, Lord, are light;
inflaming them to love, for you, Lord, are love;
dwelling in them and filling them with happiness,
for you Lord, are Supreme Good,
the Eternal Good, from whom all good
comes without whom there is no good.

Holy be your name: may knowledge of you
become clearer in us that we may know the breadth
of your blessings, the length of your promises,
the height of your majesty, the depth of your judgements.

Your kingdom come: that you may rule in us through
your grace and enable us to come to your kingdom,
where there is clear vision of you, perfect love of you,
eternal enjoyment of you.

Your will be done on earth as in heaven: that we may
love you with our whole heart by always thinking of you,
with our whole soul by always desiring you,
with our whole mind by always directing all our intentions to you,
and by seeking your glory in everything,
with all our whole strength by exerting all our energies
and affections of body and soul in the service of your love
and of nothing else: and we may love our neighbour as ourselves
by drawing them all to your love with our whole strength,
by rejoicing in the good of others as in our own,
by suffering with others at their misfortunes,
and by giving offence to no one.

Give us this day: in remembrance, understanding and reverence of that love which [our Lord Jesus Christ] had for us and of those things that he said and did and suffered for us.

Our daily Bread: your own beloved Son, our Lord Jesus Christ.

Forgive us our trespasses: through your ineffable mercy, through the power of the passion of your beloved Son and through the merits and intercession of the ever blessèd Virgin and all your elect.

As we forgive those who trespass against us: and what we do not completely forgive, make us, Lord, forgive completely, that we may truly love our enemies because of you and we may fervently intercede for them before you, returning no one evil for evil and we may strive to help everyone in you.

Lead us not into temptation: hidden or obvious, sudden or persistent.

But deliver us from evil: past, present, and to come.

Francis of Assisi

c) ANTIPHON OF THE BLESSED VIRGIN MARY

Holy Virgin Mary,
among women born into the world,
there is no one like you.
Daughter and servant of the most high
and supreme King and of the Father in heaven,
Mother of our most holy Lord Jesus Christ,
Spouse of the Holy Spirit, pray for us
with Saint Michael the Archangel,
and all the powers of heaven and all the saints,
at the side of your most holy beloved Son,
our Lord and Teacher.

The Office of the Passion, Francis of Assisi

d) FOR THE SECOND ORDER

Generous God,
pour your abundant blessing
on those who after the pattern of blessèd Clare
have left all to follow you
in a life of poverty, prayer and penance;
assist them with your grace
that they may persevere
in their vocation to the end
and that all their needs may be supplied;
through Jesus Christ our Lord. **Amen.**

e) FOR THE THIRD ORDER

Lord God,
who opened the eyes of the blessèd Francis
to the vocation of those you call to serve you
    in the world:
grant such grace to the members of the Third Order
that being crucified with Christ
they may show forth among all
the radiance of his risen life;
who with you and the Holy Spirit
is alive and reigns, one God, now and for ever. **Amen.**

f) FOR A MEETING OF A CHAPTER

Almighty God,
you have given your Holy Spirit to the Church
to lead us into all truth.
Bless with your grace and presence
the members of *this* Chapter;
keep *us* steadfast in faith and united in love,
that *we* may reveal your glory
and prepare the way of your kingdom;
through Jesus Christ our Lord. **Amen.**

4. FOR MISSION AND EVANGELISM

a) Give to your Church, O God,
a bold vision and a daring charity,
a refreshed wisdom and a courteous understanding,
that the eternal message of your Son
may be acclaimed as the good news of the age;
through him who makes all things new,
even Jesus Christ our Lord. **Amen.**   *Percy Dearmer (1867-1936)*

b) Heavenly Father, draw us nearer to yourself
that we may know your will;
loving Lord Jesus, fill us with all joy and peace
that we may respond to your call;
Holy Spirit, inspire us
that we may celebrate our faith
and give glory to you, God,
ever blessèd Trinity,
now and for ever. **Amen.**

c) O God,
take our minds and think through them,
take our lips and speak through them,
take our hearts and set them on fire
    with love for you;
may your kingdom come,
on earth as it is in heaven. **Amen.**

d) Spirit of God,
make us open to others in listening,
generous to others in giving
and sensitive to others in praying;
through Jesus Christ our Lord. **Amen.**

e) O God,
may we live in faith,
walk in hope
and be renewed in love,
until the world reflects your glory
and you are all in all. **Amen.**

5. FOR RETREATS & QUIET DAYS

a) Loving God,
   look with mercy on your servants
   who seek in solitude and silence
   refreshment of soul and strengthening for service;
   grant them your abundant blessing
   in the peace of Christ our Lord. **Amen.**

b) Grant us, O merciful God,
   the will to seek you, whom we desire above all,
   that we may find you and be found in you;
   may your love and wisdom guide words spoken in your name;
   may we find faith and hope
   in the still small voice which tells us of your presence;
   may we be one with you in Jesus our Redeemer. **Amen.**

c) Lord Jesus Christ,
   speak to our hearts in the stillness,
   keep us steadfast in the foundation that cannot be shaken,
   lift up our eyes to behold the vision of your glory;
   and perfect our faith, now and always. **Amen.**

d) Loving Father,
   all our wants are tempered through the needs of others
   and all our needs are met through your grace:
   lift us above our doubts and uncertainties
   into the calmness of your presence,
   that safeguarded by your peace
   we may serve you and all your creation
   through the love which is eternal,
   even your Son, Jesus Christ our Lord. **Amen.**

e) Eternal Spirit of God, breathe on us
   that we may know quiet and contented minds
   and lay all our burdens on Christ;
   take from us all anxiety and disquiet
   and draw our hearts to the Father
   by the power of your love;
   lead us to the peace that passes all understanding,
   to the silence which reveals you among us. **Amen.**

6. CREATION

a) God of unchangeable power,
when you fashioned the world
the morning stars sang together
and the host of heaven shouted for joy;
open our eyes to the wonder of creation
and teach us to use all things for good,
to the honour of your glorious name;
through Jesus Christ our Lord. **Amen.**

A New Zealand Prayer Book

b) God of mercy,
you have blessed us beyond our dreams;
you have set before us promises and perils
beyond our understanding;
help us to struggle and pray
that the perils may be averted
and your promises fulfilled;
through Jesus Christ our Redeemer. **Amen.**

A New Zealand Prayer Book

c) God our creator,
your servant Francis
proclaimed your praise and glory
by, with and through all created beings;
give us your grace
to treasure all your gifts,
treating them with reverence and love,
that we may be willing to share your bounty
with all your children
in the name of Jesus Christ, our Saviour. **Amen.**

d) God of creation,
at this time of gradual awakening
to the ways in which we imperil our planet earth;
open our hearts and minds
that we may learn to nurture in love
rather than destroy in ignorance;
this we pray in the name of Jesus Christ our Saviour. **Amen.**

7. A GENERAL THANKSGIVING

Almighty God, Father of all mercies,
we your unworthy servants give you most humble and hearty thanks
for all your goodness and loving kindness.
We bless you for our creation, preservation,
    and all the blessings of this life;
but above all for your immeasurable love
in the redemption of the world by our Lord Jesus Christ,
for the means of grace, and for the hope of glory.
And give us, we pray, such a sense of all your mercies
that our hearts may be unfeignedly thankful,
and that we show forth your praise, not only with our lips,
    but in our lives,
by giving up ourselves to your service,
and by walking before you in holiness and righteousness all our days;
through Jesus Christ our Lord,
to whom, with you and the Holy Spirit,
be all honour and glory, for ever and ever. **Amen.**

8. THE APOSTLES' CREED

**I believe in God, the Father almighty,
creator of heaven and earth.**

**I believe in Jesus Christ, his only Son, our Lord,
who was conceived by the Holy Spirit,
born of the Virgin Mary,
suffered under Pontius Pilate,
was crucified, died, and was buried;
he descended to the dead.
On the third day he rose again;
he ascended into heaven,
he is seated at the right hand of the Father,
and he will come to judge the living and the dead.**

**I believe in the Holy Spirit,
the holy catholic Church,
the communion of saints,
the forgiveness of sins,
the resurrection of the body,
and the life everlasting. Amen.**

The Principles
of the First Order SSF

The Collects, at the end of each day's reading, are optional.

THE OBJECT OF THE ORDER

DAY 1   Jesus the Master speaks, *Very truly, I tell you, unless a grain of wheat falls into the earth and dies, it remains just a single grain; but if it dies, it bears much fruit. Those who love their life lose it, and those who hate their life in this world will keep it for eternal life. Whoever serves me must follow me, and where I am, there will my servant be also. Whoever serves me, the Father will honour.*[1]

The Master sets before us in the example of his own sacrifice the secret of fruit-bearing. He surrenders himself to death, and lo! he becomes the source of new life to myriads. Lifted up from the earth in sacrifice, he draws unto him all those multitudes of which the Greeks, whose coming kindled his vision,[2] are the foretaste and prophecy. The life that is cherished perishes: the life that is renounced is eternal.

[O God,
you gave us blessèd Francis
to be a teacher and a leader
in following the ways of your only-begotten Son.
Grant, we pray,
that we who honour his memory here on earth
may share his glory in heaven;
through Jesus Christ our Lord. Amen.]

DAY 2   This law of renunciation and sacrifice, which is the law of the Master's own life and fruit-bearing, he lays also upon his servants, bidding them follow him in the same path. To those who thus follow he promises the ineffable reward of union with himself and acceptance by the Father. The object, therefore, of the First Order, is to build up a body of men and women who, accepting Christ as their Lord and Master, will seek to follow

---

1   John 12.24-26.
2   cf John 12.20-21.

him in the way of renunciation and sacrifice as an act of witness and for the loving service of his brothers and sisters in the world.

[O Friend of the forsaken
and Lover of the unloved,
make us bearers of your presence to all.
Teach us to walk in the poverty of your Son
and to be among your people as those who serve;
in the name of him who for our sakes
became poor, Jesus Christ our Lord. Amen.]

THE THREE CONDITIONS OF LIFE

DAY 3   The community, recognising that God has at all times called certain of his children to embrace a state of celibacy for the kingdom of heaven's sake, that they may be free to give themselves without distraction to his service, sets before itself the aim of building up a body of men and women who shall be completely dedicated to him alone both in body and spirit.

These, after a sufficient period of probation, voluntarily in response to God's call, dedicate themselves to a life of devotion to our Lord under the conditions of poverty, chastity and obedience.

[Eternal God,
source of all mercies and consolation,
may we live to praise you.
Make the homage we pay you reasonable;
season our sacrifices with the salt of wisdom,
that our entire being may be transformed into your image,
through Jesus Christ our Saviour. Amen.]

after Clare of Assisi

DAY 4   It is not without reason that these three conditions have ever been embraced by those desiring to live the life of religious detachment; for they stand for the ideal of perfect renunciation of the world, the flesh and the devil, which are the three great enemies of the spiritual life.

[O Lord Jesus Christ,
you raised up Francis
to renew in your Church
the life of simplicity and evangelical poverty
and imprinted on his flesh the marks of your wounds.
Pour out your Spirit on us,
that, following you in the nakedness of the cross
and bearing your wounds in our hearts,
we may at length attain to your perfect likeness;
who with the Father and the Holy Spirit,
live and reign, one God, now and for ever. Amen.]

THE FIRST CONDITION OF LIFE: POVERTY

DAY 5   The Master willingly embraced a life of poverty in this world. *He was rich, yet for your sakes he became poor.*[3] He chose a stable for his birthplace and for his upbringing the house of a village carpenter. Even that home he left in early manhood and became a wayfarer, with *nowhere to lay his head.*[4]

Us also he calls to poverty. *Whoever serves me must follow me. None of you can become my disciple if you do not give up all your possessions.*[5] The brothers and sisters, therefore, seek to be poor in spirit. They desire to escape from the love of the world and the things that are in the world and rather, like their patron Saint Francis, to be in love with poverty. They covet only the unsearchable riches of Christ. They recognise, indeed, that while some of their members may be called to a literal following of Saint Francis in a life of actual penury and extreme simplicity, for most so high an ideal will not be possible.

[Merciful God,
you made your Church rich
through the poverty of blessèd Francis.
Help us, like him,
not to trust in earthly things
but to seek your heavenly gifts;
through Jesus Christ our Saviour. Amen.]

---

3   *2 Corinthians 8.9.*

4   *Matthew 8.20.*

5   *John 12.26; Luke 14.33.*

DAY 6   The brothers and sisters desire to possess nothing which cannot be shared by those around them and such things as will help to satisfy their needs.

They receive no pay and own no personal possessions. They live as a family having all things in common. They receive for their use the simple necessities of life. Yet what they receive they regard not as their own but rather as lent to them for a season.

Nor must they, while excluding the snare of the world from their individual lives, allow it to return in the corporate community, where it may work a wider and more fatal destruction. It would be small gain were they to surrender their personal possessions only to live in luxury through the abundance of the common stock. Therefore the community must turn away from excess. The buildings it erects and the style and manner of life which it permits must be the simplest that are consistent with good health and efficient work. If there is money beyond what such simple needs require, let it be spent in works of mercy and service, or else be used for the house of God, which it is right and seemly with proper moderation to adorn, or for the purchase of books which are necessary to the work of study.

[God of peace,
who in the poverty of the blessèd Clare
gave us a clear light to shine in the darkness of this world:
give us grace so to follow in her footsteps
that we may, at the last, rejoice with her
   in your eternal glory;
through Jesus Christ our Lord. Amen.]
Collect for Saint Clare's Day, Common Worship

DAY 7   In all things let the brothers and sisters exhibit the simplicity of true Franciscans who, caring little for the world where they are but strangers and pilgrims, have their hearts set on that spiritual home *where their treasure is.*[6]

---

6   *Matthew 6.21.*

[O God, by the life of blessèd Francis,
you moved your people to a love of simple things.
May we, after his example,
hold lightly to the things of this world
and store up for ourselves treasure in heaven;
through Jesus Christ our Lord. Amen.]

THE SECOND CONDITION OF LIFE: CHASTITY

DAY 8 The brothers and sisters are bound, like all Christians, to resist and by God's grace to conquer the temptations of the flesh and to live lives of purity and self-control. They must ever strive through faithful self-discipline and prayer to be chaste both in mind and body. Furthermore, that they may *promote unhindered devotion to the Lord,*[7] and give themselves wholly to his work, being wedded only to Christ, their true spouse, they embrace of their own will the vocation of celibacy.

They do this not because they believe that the unmarried state is in itself higher than the married, but because they believe that for them the unmarried state is that in which God wishes them to serve him. Therefore they look to him with confidence to give them the grace needed for this life which, if they should undertake it contrary to his will, would be to them a state of greater rather than less distraction than that of marriage.

[May the power of your love, Lord Christ,
fiery and sweet as honey,
so absorb our hearts
as to withdraw them from all that is under heaven.
Grant that we may be ready
*   to die for love of your love,*
as you died for love of our love. Amen.]

Absorbeat, after Francis of Assisi

DAY 9 In thus accepting the state of chastity, the brothers and sisters must ever be on their guard against the temptation to self-centredness, coldness or a lack of sympathy with the interests of others. Their espousal to Christ must not weaken or mar their human affections. Rather must their union with him enable them to love more richly with his love all with whom they are brought in contact.

---

7   *I Corinthians* 7.35.

[O God,
your love led Francis and Clare
to establish our three Orders.
Draw us into your love, that,
in its perfection,
we may grow in love towards all
with whom we have to do;
for the sake of your Son, Jesus Christ,
who gives himself in love to all. Amen.]

THE THIRD CONDITION OF LIFE: OBEDIENCE

DAY 10   The Master, who, coming into the world not to do his own will but the will of him that sent him, *became obedient to the point of death – even death on a cross,*[8] says to those who follow him, *Take my yoke upon you, and learn from me; for I am gentle and humble in heart, and you will find rest for your souls.*[9]

The brothers and sisters desire, therefore, to surrender their wills to the will of God, in the spirit of perfect obedience, that being delivered from self-will and pride they may find true freedom and peace and be ready instruments which he can use for his purposes.

[Most High and glorious God,
enlighten the darkness of our hearts
and give us a true faith, a certain hope
and a perfect love.
Give us a sense of the divine
and knowledge of yourself,
so that we may do everything
in fulfilment of your holy will;
through Jesus Christ our Lord. Amen.]
                                         The Prayer before the crucifix, Francis of Assisi

DAY 11   Further, by voluntarily accepting the Rule as binding upon them, the brothers and sisters pledge themselves to abide by this Rule and to obey the decisions of the Chapter, by which the common mind of the community is expressed and interpreted.

---

8   *Philippians 2.8.*
9   *Matthew 11.29.*

It is the work of the Ministers to administer the Rule and to see that the decisions of the Chapter are observed. Their directions, therefore, unless they order something contrary to the Rule or in itself sinful, must be promptly and cheerfully carried out. In their absence obedience is due to their Assistants. Brothers or sisters put in charge of a department of work are also to be obeyed in that department. But none may on any authority act contrary to the guiding of their own consciences. The Ministers are, like the other members, under obedience to the Rule and Chapter and are bound to exercise their authority, not in a spirit of partiality or pride or selfishness, but with equal consideration and love and with humble prayer for the divine wisdom.

[O God, you ever delight to reveal yourself
to the childlike and lowly of heart:
grant that, following the example of the blessèd Francis,
we may count the wisdom of this world as foolishness
and know only Jesus Christ and him crucified,
who is alive and reigns with you,
in the unity of the Holy Spirit,
one God, now and for ever. Amen.]

Collect for Saint Francis' Day, Common Worship

DAY 12   The obligation of particular obedience within the community is gladly accepted by the members, not as something different from the obedience which they owe to God, but rather as part of that obedience. They are confident that, if God has called them to a life under Rule, they will, in fulfilling the obligations of that life, be most truly obeying him and that whatever limitations or humiliations their obedience may involve will, if cheerfully accepted, be a means by which pride is vanquished and a more perfect consecration achieved.

When working away from the community, the brothers and sisters should put themselves under the discipline of the parish or society in which they are staying.

[Almighty, eternal, just and merciful God,
give to us poor creatures the grace to do for you alone
    that which we know to be your will,
and always desire that which pleases you,
so that, inwardly purified, enlightened
and inflamed by the fire of your Holy Spirit,
we may be enabled to follow in the footprints
    of your belovèd Son, our Lord Jesus Christ,
and, by your grace alone, make our way to you,
    the Most High;
who in perfect Trinity and simple Unity,
live and reign, God all-powerful,
for ever and ever. Amen.]

A Letter to the Entire Order, Francis of Assisi

THE THREE WAYS OF SERVICE

DAY 13   The brothers and sisters seek to serve their Master by the
life of devotion, by sacred study and by works. In the life of the community
as a whole all these three ways must find full and balanced expression. It is
not, indeed, to be expected that all will devote themselves equally to each
of these three tasks. It is right that their several employments should vary
according to the particular ability which God has given them, as that some
should, with the approval of their Minister, give themselves in large measure
to prayer and contemplation, others to the pursuit of learning and the
writing of books and others mainly to the ministry of active service. Yet
must room be found in the lives of all for at least some measure of each of
these three employments.

[Grant us, O God, day by day,
the joy of true living:
that all who seek your service
may find your peace,
and grow into the loving likeness
of your Son, our Lord Jesus Christ. Amen.]

THE FIRST WAY OF SERVICE: PRAYER

DAY 14   Praise and prayer constitute the atmosphere in which the brothers and sisters must strive to live. They must endeavour to maintain a constant recollection of the presence of God and of the unseen world. An ever-deepening devotion to Christ is the hidden source of all their strength and joy. He is for them the One all-lovely and adorable, God incarnate, crucified and risen, whose love is the inspiration of service and the reward of sacrifice.

[O God, by your servant, Francis,
you taught us renewed reverence
for the Incarnation of your Son Jesus Christ.
As we learn to serve him on earth,
so may we know more truly
his presence in our hearts with great joy;
through Jesus Christ our Redeemer. Amen.]

DAY 15   That their union with this Lord and Master may be ever renewed and strengthened, the brothers and sisters unite in offering daily before God the memorial of his death and passion and feeding often upon his sacrificial life. The Holy Eucharist is the centre round which their life revolves. It is above all the heart of their prayer life.

The time of morning prayer is the preparation of mind and spirit for entrance within the sanctuary. The meditation which follows later is the opportunity for quiet tryst with him who through the sacrament is present inwardly, and for feeding on him in the heart by faith with thanksgiving. The services of intercession and thanksgiving are times when those who have been thus joined with him in communion and meditation may plead with God in sure reliance on his promise: *if you abide in me, and my words abide in you, ask for whatever you wish, and it will be done for you,*[10] and also thank him for continuous experience of its fulfilment.

The evening office is the renewed offering of praise and prayer to the same Lord at the end of the day's work, and in its closing silence the hearts of all are together steeped afresh in the peace of that inward uncreated light which, as the shadows of life deepen, abides unchanged. Compline is the Master's blessing of protection and peace.

---

10 John 15.7.

[Christ our Lord,
we ask you humbly
to gather us under the wings of your love.
Keep us alive
with the water of remorse,
the air of contemplation,
the fire of love
and the earth of humility,
so that we may join you, who are life itself
and blessed through all ages. Amen.]   *Sermons II.394, Anthony of Padua*

DAY 16   The brothers and sisters must strive ever to remember how essential is the work of prayer to every department of their lives. Without the constant renewal of divine grace the spirit flags, the will is weakened, the conscience grows dull, the mind loses its freshness and even the bodily vigour is impaired. They must, therefore, always be on their guard against the constant temptation to let other work encroach upon the hours of prayer, remembering that if they seek in this way to increase the bulk of their activity it can only be at the cost of its true quality and value. They must be regular and punctual in their attendance at corporate prayer. They must also bear in mind that it is of little value to be present at the common devotions in a formal or careless spirit. They must seek to make of each office an offering of true devotion from the heart. The reverent, ordered and earnest offering of the corporate worship is the very heart of the community's life.

[Lord Jesus Christ,
may we sing the song of your praise,
rejoice only in you,
live modestly, abandon our worries
and tell you all our needs,
so that in the refuge of your peace
we can live in the heavenly Jerusalem,
with your help,
who are blessèd and glorious,
for eternal ages. Amen.]   *Sermons II.50, Anthony of Padua*

DAY 17   So, too, the brothers and sisters must guard with jealous watchfulness the times of private prayer. They must remember that corporate worship is not a substitute for the quiet communion of the individual soul with God, and they must strive to go forward to ever fuller

enjoyment of such communion, till they are living in so constant a
remembrance of God's presence that they do indeed *pray without ceasing.*[11]

[God, all-powerful, most holy,
sublime ruler of all,
you alone are good, fully, completely good;
may we render to you all praise,
all glory, all thanksgiving,
all honour and all blessing;
may we always ascribe to you alone
everything that is good. Amen.]

Prayer from The Praises to be Said at all the Hours, Francis of Assisi

DAY 18   It is to assist such an attitude and practice of recollection
that the rules of silence have been laid down and the brothers and sisters
will welcome and use such silence, regarding it not as the imposition of an
artificial restraint, nor merely as an external rule to be observed by
refraining from speech, but as the opportunity for growing in the sense of
the divine presence. They will welcome in a like spirit the retreats and days
of quiet which the community's Rule provides as times when, in the
withdrawal from all external distractions, the life of the spirit may be
renewed and deepened.

In these and suchlike ways, the brothers and sisters will seek to keep ever
fresh and living their devotion to Christ their Lord; and when through
human frailty they fail in their high endeavour, they will yet return again to
Christ with humble contrition and earnest purpose of amendment; and they
will hold in special esteem that sacrament of penance and absolution
whereby they are cleansed from sin and renewed in the life of grace.

[Lord Jesus,
in your servant Francis
you displayed the wonderful power of the cross.
Help us always to follow you
in the way of the holy cross,
and give us strength to resist all temptation;
to whom with the Father and the Holy Spirit,
be all glory for ever. Amen.]

---

11 *1 Thessalonians 5.17.*

THE SECOND WAY OF SERVICE: STUDY

DAY 19   The true knowledge is the knowledge of God. The highest
wisdom is that holy wisdom whereby the soul is made one with God. The
first place, therefore, in the brothers' and sisters' work of study will always
be given to the study and practice of the way of the soul's ascent to God
and the devotional study of the scriptures as one of the chief aids to that
end. They will study also the teaching of the Christian saints concerning the
spiritual life.

It is the hope of the community that some of its houses may be not only
homes of prayer but also homes of learning. It is out of this recognition of
the value and importance of study that some of the hours each day are set
apart for this purpose under the Rule; and it is mainly for the uninterrupted
securing of these hours that the rule of the lesser silence is laid down
whenever possible.

[Believing, hoping, loving,
with our whole heart,
with our whole mind,
and with our whole strength,
may we be carried to you, belovèd Jesus,
as to the goal of all things,
because you alone are sufficient,
you alone are good and pleasing. Amen.]   *The Tree of Life, Bonaventure* *

THE THIRD WAY OF SERVICE: WORKS

DAY 20   Jesus the Master took on himself the form of a servant. *He*
came not to be served but to serve.[12] *He went about doing good; curing all who*
were sick;[13] *bringing good news to the poor; binding up the broken-hearted.*[14]
Those who would claim to be his servants and follow him must be diligent
in ministry to others.

The active works by which the brothers and sisters seek to serve their
Master begin within the house and garden. The sweeping, dusting and other
menial offices, as well as certain forms of manual work, are apportioned
among them so that all may contribute their share to the work of the
household and the cost of their own living. All must be capable of engaging

---

12 *Mark 10.45.*
13 *Acts 10.38; Matthew 8.16.*
14 *Luke 4.18; Isaiah 61.1.*

in some form of manual work. All must consider the interests of the community in its work for God and study strict economy. Brothers and sisters will do their own work as far as possible. Saint Francis said that *the idle (member) has no place in the community.*

[Keep us faithful, O God,
to the inspiration of blessèd Francis,
that seeking nothing for ourselves
we may bring true riches to the world;
through him who gave us himself,
Jesus Christ our Lord. Amen.]

DAY 21   Outside the special works of service to the community itself there are many opportunities of ministry, particularly to the uncared-for, the sick, the suffering and needy. The community sets before it, as the special programme of service which it would like to be able to carry out, those acts of mercy the doing of which even to the humblest the Master declares that he will accept as done unto himself. By helping in the relief of poverty we may give him food and drink. By hospitality to strangers we may take him in. By relieving those homeless and naked we may clothe him. By caring for the sick we may relieve him. By visiting the prisoners we may cheer him.[15]

The community does not, indeed, expect ever to have at its disposal many funds for the administration of charitable relief, but it will gladly lend its members in the work of such relief and co-operate with others who are doing it. In all such work, the community will seek to serve all irrespective of creed, offering its services not as a bribe but as a reflection of the love of Christ himself.

[O God,
you came among us as a servant.
Fill us with your humility
that we may, like Francis our brother,
forget ourselves in love for you
and in compassion for others;
and in the lonely, the rejected,
the deprived and the imprisoned,
find Christ our Lord. Amen.]

---

15   *cf Matthew 25.35-45.*

DAY 22   But chiefest of all forms of service that the brothers and sisters can offer must ever be the effort to show others in his beauty and power the Christ who is the inspiration and joy of their own lives. They will seek to do this, not in a spirit of aggression, nor with contempt for the beliefs of others, but rather because, knowing in their own experience the power of Christ to save from sin and to give newness of life, they must needs seek to share their own supreme treasure. Out of the fullness, therefore, of devoted love they would seek to give their belovèd Master to all.

They must remember that, in this task of showing Christ to others the witness of life is more eloquent than that of words. Franciscans must, therefore, seek rather to be living lives through which Christ can manifest himself than to preach much in public. Nevertheless, there will be some amongst them called more particularly to the ministry of the Word, and all must be ready at all times to give an answer for the faith that is in them,[16] and particularly to guide all who are sincerely seeking after truth. They must also be ready by instruction and prayer and spiritual direction to strengthen the faith of Christians and lead them forward in the spiritual life.

[O God,
by whose inspiration
Francis became a little brother to all
and did not fear to take the message of peace
and love even into the heart of the enemy:
give us, who follow him,
a like spirit of reconciliation and generosity
in our own day;
through Jesus Christ our Lord. Amen.]

DAY 23   The brothers and sisters must be glad at all times to relieve those who come to them for help or counsel. They must never give the impression that they have no time for such ministry. Rather must they be ready to lay aside all other work, including even the work of prayer, where such service is immediately required, confident that such a negligence will surely be well-pleasing to the Servant of all.

---

16 *cf I Peter 3.15.*

[O God,
you called Francis
to be an instrument of peace
in a divided world and a weakling church:
make us, too, agents of reconciliation
in a church moving towards unity
and in a world still torn by faction and fear;
through Jesus Christ our Saviour. Amen.]

THE THREE NOTES OF THE ORDER

DAY 24   The three notes which must ever in special degree mark the lives of the brothers and sisters are humility, love and joy. If these prevail within its members, the object of the community will be fulfilled and its work fruitful. If they are lacking, it will be unprofitable and barren.

[Maker of all,
you helped the blessèd Francis
to reflect the image of Christ
by following his teaching and footprints.
Grant that, through a life of poverty, humility
*   and joyful love,*
we may follow faithfully the pattern of your Son,
Jesus Christ our Lord. Amen.]

THE FIRST NOTE: HUMILITY

DAY 25   The brothers and sisters will strive to keep ever before them the example of him who *emptied himself, taking the form of a slave*[17] and who, on the last night of his life, humbly in the guise of a slave washed his disciples' feet.[18] They will ever seek after his pattern to *clothe themselves with humility in their dealings with one another.*[19]

Humility is the recognition of the truth about God and ourselves, the recognition of our own insufficiency and dependence, seeing that we have nothing which we have not received. It is the mother of all Christian virtues. As Saint Bernard of Clairvaux has said, *No spiritual house can stand for a moment save on the foundation of humility.* It is the first condition of a

---

17 *Philippians 2.7.*
18 *cf John 13.4-5.*
19 *I Peter 5.5.*

happy life within the family. Thus those in the house must remember that brothers and sisters who are always confident that they are right and eager to impose their opinion on others, will themselves be unhappy as chafing under the discipline of subordination and correction and will also make the life of the family unhappy by marring that distinctive atmosphere of harmony and order which depends on everyone doing their allotted task with cheerfulness. The glad acceptance of the rule of obedience, and the loyal fulfilment of orders that are distasteful or difficult, will be one sure means of growing in this grace.

[O God,
you resist the proud and give grace to the humble.
Help us not to think proudly
but to serve you with the humility
    which pleases you;
grant that, like your servant Francis,
we may walk in the footsteps of your Son, Jesus Christ,
and through him receive the gift of your grace. Amen.]

DAY 26   The brothers and sisters must also refrain from all contemptuous thoughts one of another, and not seeking for pre-eminence must *regard others as better than themselves.*[20] The faults that they see in others must be subjects for prayer rather than criticism and they must be more diligent to *take the log out of their own eye* than *the speck out of their neighbour's eye.*[21] They must be ready not only gladly, *when invited, to go and sit down at the lowest place,*[22] but rather of their own accord take it. Nevertheless, if entrusted with a work of which they feel incapable or unworthy, they must not shrink from accepting it on the plea of humility, but attempt it confidently through *the power (of Christ) made perfect in weakness.*[23]

In their relations also with those outside, the brothers and sisters must strive to show their Master's humility. They must welcome gladly all opportunities of humble service that come to them and never desire pre-eminence or praise. In particular they must resist the temptation to consider themselves superior to others because dedicated to a life of religion, realising how much greater often are the sacrifices and difficulties

---

20 *Philippians 2.3.*
21 *Matthew 7.5.*
22 *Luke 14.10.*
23 *2 Corinthians 12.9.*

of those engaged in the ordinary professions of life and how much more nobly they face them.

[God our creator,
by your gift Francis followed Christ
in poverty and humility;
may we, after his example,
serve you without faltering,
and come with joy
to the riches of eternal life,
through Jesus Christ our Saviour. Amen.]

THE SECOND NOTE: LOVE

DAY 27   The Master says, *By this everyone will know that you are my disciples, if you have love for one another.*[24] Love is thus the distinguishing feature of all true disciples of Christ. It must be specially an outstanding note in the lives of those who are seeking to be specially consecrated to Christ as his servants. *God is love*[25] and, for those whose lives are *hidden with Christ in God,*[26] love will be the very atmosphere which surrounds all that they do.

This love the brothers and sisters must show towards all to whom they are united by natural ties of relationship or friendship. They will love them not less but more as their love for Christ grows deeper.

They will love also with a special affection those to whom they are united within the family of the community, praying for each individually and seeking to grow in love for each. They must be on their guard against all that injures this love: the bitter thought, the hasty retort, the angry gesture; and never fail to ask forgiveness of any against whom they have sinned. They must seek to love equally with others those with whom they have least natural affinity. For this love of one another is not simply the welling up of natural affection but a supernatural love which God gives them through their common union with Christ. As such it bears testimony to its divine origin. Our Lord intended the unity of those who believe in him to be a special witness to the world of his divine mission. The community must show the spectacle of a Christian family whose members, even though they

---

24 John 13.35.
25 1 John 4.8.
26 Colossians 3.3.

be of varied race and education and character, are bound into a living fellowship by this supernatural love.

Lastly, in all their relationships with those, whether Christians or not, with whom their work brings them in contact they will seek to show forth this same supernatural Christ-like love; and, remembering that love is measured by sacrifice, they will seek gladly to spend whatever gifts they may possess of body, mind and spirit in the service of those to whom God calls them to minister.

[Grant, O God,
that as your servant Francis carried
the love and peace of Christ
into the hearts of all who knew him;
so may we who seek to follow his example
shed abroad that same love and peace
in the minds of all and in the dark places
   of the earth;
through Jesus Christ our Lord. Amen.]

THE THIRD NOTE: JOY

DAY 28   Finally, the brothers and sisters, *rejoicing in the Lord always,*[27] must show forth in their lives the grace and beauty of divine joy. They must remember that they follow the Son of Man, *who came eating and drinking,*[28] who loved the birds and the flowers, who blessed little children, who was *a friend of tax collectors and sinners,*[29] who sat at the tables alike of the rich and the poor. They will, therefore, put aside all gloom and moroseness, all undue aloofness from the common interests of people and delight in laughter and good fellowship. They will rejoice in God's world and all its beauty and its living creatures, *calling (nothing) profane or unclean.*[30] They will mingle freely with all kinds of people, seeking to banish sorrow and to bring good cheer into other lives. They will carry with them an inner secret of happiness and peace which all will feel, if they may not know its source.

---

27 *Philippians 4.4.*
28 *Luke 7.34.*
29 *cf Mark 10.16.*
30 *Acts 10.28.*

[Blessèd Lord,
as Francis found joy in creation,
in beauty and simplicity,
but perfect joy in sharing the sufferings of the world:
so may we, abiding in your love,
receive your gift of perfect joy,
and by the power of your Spirit
radiate your peace,
and find, even in suffering,
the glory of God. Amen.]

DAY 29   This joy, likewise, is a divine gift and comes only from union with God in Christ. As such it can abide even in days of darkness and difficulty, giving cheerful courage in the face of disappointment and an inward serenity and confidence in sickness and suffering. Those who possess it can be *content with weaknesses, insults, hardships, persecutions, and calamities for the sake of Christ; for whenever they are weak, then they are strong.*[31]

[God in heaven,
your servant Francis
found perfect joy in being rejected.
Help us also to draw near
to our crucified Lord,
that the joy of his triumph may shine in us
to your glory and the healing of your world;
through Jesus Christ our Lord. Amen.]

THE THREE NOTES

DAY 30   These three notes of humility, love and joy, which should mark the lives of the brothers and sisters, are all supernatural graces which can be won only from the divine bounty. They can never be attained through our own unaided exertions. They are miraculous gifts of the Holy Spirit. But it is the purpose of Christ our Master to work miracles through his servants; and, if they will but be emptied of self and utterly surrendered to him, they will become chosen vessels of his Spirit and effective

---

31 *2 Corinthians 12.10.*

instruments of his mighty working, *who is able to accomplish abundantly far more than all we can ask or imagine.*[32]

[O Most High, almighty, good Lord, God,
grant your people grace
to renounce the vanities of this world;
that, after the example of blessèd Francis,
we may delight in all your creatures, for love of you,
with perfectness of joy;
through Jesus Christ our Lord. Amen.]

Revised 1996

---

32 *Ephesians 3.20.*

Principles, First Order

Community Obedience
of the Third Order SSF

In all Provinces of the Third Order this offering of prayer should be made daily, either on its own or in the context of Morning or Evening Prayer.

Either A:

**We adore you, most holy Lord Jesus Christ,
here, and in all your churches
    throughout all the world;
and we bless you
because, by your holy cross,
you have redeemed the world.**

*from The Testament, Francis of Assisi
after the European Province SSF*

or B:

**Both here, and in all your churches
    throughout the whole world,
we adore you, O Christ, and we bless you,
because by your holy cross,
you have redeemed the world.**

*from The Testament, Francis of Assisi
after the Province of the Americas SSF*

DAILY READING from The Principles of the Third Order, pages 810-16.

INTERCESSIONS may be offered from the Third Order Intercession List or the Address List.

**O God,
we give you thanks
for the Third Order of the Society of Saint Francis.
Grant, we pray, that being knit together
    in community and prayer,
we your servants may glorify your holy name
    after the example of Saint Francis,
and win others to your love;
through Jesus Christ our Lord. Amen.**

The offering of prayer may continue with either Morning or Evening Prayer, or one of the following optional Collects,

[*SUNDAY*

O God,
your love led Francis and Clare
to establish our three Orders.
Draw us into your love, that,
in its perfection,
we may grow in love towards all
with whom we have to do;
for the sake of your Son, Jesus Christ,
who gives himself in love to all. **Amen**.

MONDAY

O God, you ever delight to reveal yourself
to the childlike and lowly of heart:
grant that, following the example of the blessèd Francis,
we may count the wisdom of this world as foolishness
and know only Jesus Christ and him crucified,
who is alive and reigns with you,
in the unity of the Holy Spirit,
one God, now and for ever. **Amen**.

Collect for Saint Francis' Day, Common Worship

TUESDAY

O God,
you resist the proud and give grace to the humble.
Help us not to think proudly
but to serve you with the humility
  which pleases you;
grant that, like your servant Francis,
we may walk in the footsteps of your Son, Jesus Christ,
and through him receive the gift of your grace. **Amen**.

WEDNESDAY

Merciful God,
you made your church rich
through the poverty of blessèd Francis.
Help us, like him,
not to trust in earthly things,
but to seek your heavenly gifts
through Jesus Christ our Lord. **Amen**.

THURSDAY

Lord,
without you our labour is wasted,
but with you all who are weak can find strength.
Pour your Spirit on the Society of Saint Francis;
give your labourers a pure intention,
patient faith, sufficient success on earth,
and the joy of serving you in heaven,
through Jesus Christ our Lord. **Amen**.

FRIDAY

Lord Jesus,
in your servant Francis
you displayed the wonderful power of the cross.
Help us always to follow you in the way of the holy cross,
and give us strength to resist all temptation,
to whom with the Father and the Holy Spirit
be all glory for ever. **Amen**.

SATURDAY

O God,
by the life of blessèd Francis
you moved your people to a love of simple things.
May we, after his example,
hold lightly to the things of this world
and store up for ourselves treasure in heaven;
through Jesus Christ our Lord. **Amen**.]

and conclude with:

Either A:

May our blessèd Lady pray for us;
May Saint Francis pray for us;
May Saint Clare pray for us;
May all the Saints of the Third Order pray for us;
May the holy angels watch over us and befriend us;
May our Lord Jesus give us his blessing and his peace. Amen.

or B:

The grace of our Lord Jesus Christ,
and the love of God,
and the fellowship of the Holy Spirit
be with us all evermore. Amen.

The Principles
of the Third Order SSF

THE OBJECT

DAY 1   Jesus said, *Very truly, I tell you, unless a grain of wheat falls into the earth and dies, it remains just a single grain; but if it dies, it bears much fruit. Those who love their life lose it, and those who hate their life in this world will keep it for eternal life. Whoever serves me must follow me, and where I am, there will my servant be also. Whoever serves me, the Father will honour.* [33]

DAY 2   In the example of his own sacrifice, Jesus reveals the secret of bearing fruit. In surrendering himself to death, he becomes the source of new life. Lifted from the earth on the cross, he draws all people to himself. Clinging to life causes life to decay; the life that is freely given is eternal.

DAY 3   Jesus calls those who would serve him to follow his example and choose for themselves the same path of renunciation and sacrifice. To those who hear and obey, he promises union with God. The object of the Society of Saint Francis is to build a community of those who accept Christ as their Lord and Master, and are dedicated to him in body and spirit. They surrender their lives to him and to the service of his people. The Third Order of the Society consists of those who, while following the ordinary professions of life, feel called to dedicate their lives under a definite discipline and vows. They may be female or male, married or single, ordained or lay.

DAY 4   When Saint Francis encouraged the formation of the Third Order he recognised that many are called to serve God in the spirit of Poverty, Chastity and Obedience in everyday life (rather than in a literal acceptance of these principles as in the vows of the Brothers and Sisters of the First and Second Orders). The Rule of the Third Order is intended to enable the duties and conditions of daily living to be carried out in this spirit.

---

33 John 12.24-26.

THE THREE AIMS OF THE ORDER

THE FIRST AIM: TO MAKE OUR LORD KNOWN AND LOVED EVERYWHERE

DAY 5   The Order is founded on the conviction that Jesus Christ is the perfect revelation of God; that true life has been made available to us through his Incarnation and ministry; by his cross and resurrection; and by the sending of his Holy Spirit. Our Order believes that it is the commission of the church to make the gospel known to all, and therefore accepts the duty of bringing others to know Christ, and of praying and working for the coming of the Kingdom of God.

DAY 6   The primary aim for us as Tertiaries is therefore to make Christ known. This shapes our lives and attitudes to reflect the obedience of those whom our Lord chose to be with him and sent out as his witnesses. Like them, by word and example, we bear witness to Christ in our own immediate environment and pray and work for the fulfilment of his command to make disciples of all nations.

THE SECOND AIM: TO SPREAD THE SPIRIT OF LOVE AND HARMONY

DAY 7   The Order sets out, in the name of Christ, to break down barriers between people and to seek equality for all. We accept as our second aim the spreading of a spirit of love and harmony among all people. We are pledged to fight against the ignorance, pride and prejudice that breed injustice or partiality of any kind.

DAY 8   Members of The Third Order fight against all injustice in the name of Christ, in whom there can be neither Jew nor Greek, slave nor free, male nor female; for in him all are one. Our chief object is to reflect that openness to all which was characteristic of Jesus. This can only be achieved in a spirit of chastity, which sees others as belonging to God and not as a means of self-fulfilment.

DAY 9   As Tertiaries, we are prepared not only to speak out for social justice and international peace, but to put these principles into practice in our own lives, cheerfully facing any scorn or persecution to which this may lead.

DAY 10   The first Christians surrendered completely to our Lord and recklessly gave all that they had, offering the world a new vision of a society in which a fresh attitude was taken towards material possessions. This vision was renewed by Saint Francis when he chose Lady Poverty as his bride, desiring that all barriers set up by privilege based on wealth should be overcome by love. This is the inspiration for the third aim of the Society, to live simply.

DAY 11   Although we possess property and earn money to support ourselves and our families, we show ourselves true followers of Christ and of Saint Francis by our readiness to live simply and to share with others. We recognise that some of our members may be called to a literal following of Saint Francis in a life of extreme simplicity. All of us, however, accept that we avoid luxury and waste, and regard our possessions as being held in trust for God.

DAY 12   Personal spending is limited to what is necessary for our health and well-being and that of our dependants. We aim to stay free from all attachment to wealth, keeping ourselves constantly aware of the poverty in the world and its claim on us. We are concerned more for the generosity that gives all, rather than for the value of poverty in itself. In this way we reflect in spirit the acceptance of Jesus' challenge to sell all, give to the poor, and follow him.

THE THREE WAYS OF SERVICE

DAY 13   Tertiaries desire to be conformed to the image of Jesus Christ, whom we serve in the three ways of prayer, study and work. In the life of the Order as a whole these three ways must each find full and balanced expression, but it is not to be expected that all members devote themselves equally to each of them. Each individual's service will vary according to his or her abilities and circumstances, yet each individual member's personal Rule of Life must include each of the three ways.

THE FIRST WAY OF SERVICE: PRAYER

DAY 14   Tertiaries seek to live in an atmosphere of praise and prayer. We aim to be constantly aware of God's presence, so that we may indeed pray without ceasing. Our ever-deepening devotion to the indwelling Christ is a source of strength and joy. It is Christ's love that inspires us to service, and strengthens us for sacrifice.

DAY 15   The heart of our prayer is the Eucharist, in which we share with other Christians the renewal of our union with our Lord and Saviour in his sacrifice, remembering his death and receiving his spiritual food.

DAY 16   Tertiaries recognise the power of intercessory prayer for furthering the purposes of God's Kingdom, and therefore seek a deepening fellowship with God in personal devotion, and constantly intercede for the needs of his church and his world. Those of us who have much time at our disposal give prayer a large part in our daily lives. Those of us with less time must not fail to see the importance of prayer and to guard the time we have allotted to it from interruption. Lastly, we are encouraged to avail ourselves of the sacrament of Reconciliation, through which the burden of past sin and failure is lifted and peace and hope restored.

THE SECOND WAY OF SERVICE: STUDY

DAY 17   *This is eternal life: to know you, the only true God, and Jesus Christ, whom you have sent.*[34]   True knowledge is knowledge of God. Tertiaries therefore give priority to devotional study of Scripture as one of the chief means of attaining that knowledge of God that leads to eternal life.

DAY 18   As well as the devotional study of Scripture, we all recognise our Christian responsibility to pursue other branches of study, both sacred and secular. In particular some of us accept the duty of contributing, through research and writing, to a better understanding of the church's mission in the world: the application of Christian principles to the use and distribution of wealth; questions concerning justice and peace; and of all other questions concerning the life of faith.

---

34 *John 17.3.*

THE THIRD WAY OF SERVICE: WORK

DAY 19 Jesus took on himself the form of a servant. He came not to be served, but to serve. He went about doing good: healing the sick, preaching good news to the poor, and binding up the broken-hearted.

DAY 20 Tertiaries endeavour to serve others in active work. We try to find expression for each of the three aims of the Order in our lives, and whenever possible actively help others who are engaged in similar work. The chief form of service that we have to offer is to reflect the love of Christ, who, in his beauty and power, is the inspiration and joy of our lives.

THE THREE NOTES OF THE ORDER

DAY 21 Humility, love and joy are the three notes that mark the lives of Tertiaries. When these characteristics are evident throughout the Order, its work will be fruitful. Without them all that it attempts will be in vain.

THE FIRST NOTE: HUMILITY

DAY 22 We always keep before us the example of Christ, who emptied himself, taking the form of a servant, and who, on the last night of his life, humbly washed his disciples' feet. We likewise seek to serve one another with humility.

DAY 23 Humility confesses that we have nothing that we have not received and admits the fact of our insufficiency and our dependence upon God. It is the basis of all Christian virtues. Saint Bernard of Clairvaux said, 'No spiritual house can stand for a moment except on the foundation of humility.' It is the first condition of a joyful life within any community.

DAY 24 The faults that we see in others are the subject of prayer rather than of criticism. We take care to cast out the beam from our own eye before offering to remove the speck from another's. We are ready to accept the lowest place when asked, and to volunteer to take it. Nevertheless, when asked to undertake work of which we feel unworthy or incapable, we do not shrink from it on the grounds of humility, but confidently attempt it through the power that is made perfect in weakness.

THE SECOND NOTE: LOVE

DAY 25   Jesus said, *I give you a new commandment, that you love one another. Just as I have loved you, you also should love one another. By this everyone will know that you are my disciples, if you have love for one another.*[35] Love is the distinguishing feature of all true disciples of Christ who wish to dedicate themselves to him as his servants.

DAY 26   Therefore, we seek to love all those to whom we are bound by ties of family or friendship. Our love for them increases, as our love for Christ grows deeper. We have a special love and affection for members of the Third Order, praying for each other individually and seeking to grow in that love. We are on our guard against anything that might injure this love, and we seek reconciliation with those from whom we are estranged. We seek the same love for those with whom we have little natural affinity, for this kind of love is not a welling-up of emotion, but is a bond founded in our common union with Christ.

DAY 27   The Third Order is a Christian community whose members, though varied in race, education and character, are bound into a living whole through the love we share in Christ. This unity of all who believe in him will become, as our Lord intended, a witness to the world of his divine mission. In our relationships with those outside the Order, we show the same Christ-like love, and gladly give of ourselves, remembering that love is measured by sacrifice.

THE THIRD NOTE: JOY

DAY 28   Tertiaries, rejoicing in the Lord always, show in our lives the grace and beauty of divine joy. We remember that we follow the Son of Man, who came eating and drinking, who loved the birds and the flowers, who blessed little children, who was a friend to tax collectors and sinners and who sat at the tables of both the rich and the poor. We delight in fun and laughter, rejoicing in God's world, its beauty and its living creatures, calling nothing common or unclean. We mix freely with all people, ready to bind up the broken-hearted and to bring joy into the lives of others. We carry within us an inner peace and happiness, which others may perceive, even if they do not know its source.

---

35 John 13.34-35.

DAY 29   This joy is a divine gift, coming from union with God in Christ. It is still there even in times of darkness and difficulty, giving cheerful courage in the face of disappointment, and an inward serenity and confidence through sickness and suffering. Those who possess it can rejoice in weakness, insults, hardships and persecutions for Christ's sake; for when we are weak, then we are strong.

THE THREE NOTES

DAY 30   The humility, love and joy, which mark the lives of Tertiaries, are all God-given graces. They can never be obtained by human effort. They are gifts of the Holy Spirit. The purpose of Christ is to work miracles through people who are willing to be emptied of self and to surrender to him. We then become channels of grace through whom his mighty work is done.

Revised 2005

Alternative Table of Psalms

At Morning Prayer a Praise Psalm may be added as follows: Sunday 117; Monday 146; Tuesday 147 part 1; Wednesday 147 part 2; Thursday 148; Friday 149; Saturday 150.

Temporale

		Sun	Mon	Tue	Wed	Thu	Fri	Sat
Advent	M	25	70, 75	50	28, 76	62, 82	40	9
	E	80	94	144	44	11, 12	42, 43	123, 130
Christmas	M	89.5-18	85	112	19	113	20	96
	E	89.1-4,19-29	2, 110	84	45	127, 128	132	98
Epiphany	M	93	99	97	66	24	57	21
	E	72	47, 48	145	81	98	36, 46	8, 20
Lent	M	26	32	56	3, 6	25	39	13, 124
	E	86	102	38	90	27	69	31
Passion	M	20	73	35	55	40	69	23, 88
	E	61, 62	26, 27	64, 86	41, 56	42, 43	31	13, 130
Easter	M	118	81	135	139	33	30	66
	E	113, 114	115	105.1-22 or 23-45	103	136	107.1-32 or 33-43	116
Asc to Pent	M	15, 24	2	110	8	47	46	29
	E	96, 98	18 pt 1	21, 36.5-10	122, 126	84	93, 97	139
All Ss to Adv	M	33	139	116	65	145	23, 125	92, 97
	E	74	15, 16	73	77	34	142, 143	84

Ordinary Time

Week 1 begins from the day following the Presentation and on the Monday following the Day of Pentecost and the other weeks follow in sequence.

		Sun	Mon	Tue	Wed	Thu	Fri	Sat
Week 1	M	118	145	25	89.5-18	93	26	33
	E	113, 114	33	80	89.1-4,19-29	72	86	74
Week 2	M	81	65	70, 75	85	99	32	139
	E	115	68.1-19, 32-35	94	2, 110	47, 48	102	15, 16
Week 3	M	135	121	50	112	97	56	116
	E	105.1-22 or 23-45	122, 126	144	84	145	38	73
Week 4	M	139	99	28, 76	19	66	3, 6	65
	E	103	18.1-20 or 21-50	44	45	81	90	77
Week 5	M	33	47	62, 82	113	24	25	145
	E	136	8, 29	11, 12	127, 128	98	27	34
Week 6	M	30	111	40	20	57	39	23, 125
	E	107.1-32 or 33-43	133, 138	42, 43	132	36, 46	69	142, 143
Week 7	M	66	93	9	96	21	13, 124	92, 97
	E	116	139	123, 130	98	8, 20	31	84

Historical Note & Acknowledgements

HISTORICAL NOTE

The Daily Office SSF, a prayer book for the use of the Society of Saint Francis, an Anglican religious community, was first published in 1970. Revisions of this book were made in 1972 and in 1976: inevitably these were only interim measures in view of the rapid liturgical changes that were taking place in the Church at large and in the Church of England in particular.

With the advent of *The Alternative Service Book 1980 (ASB),* it was felt that the time was right for the daily cycle of prayer used by the Society to reflect that authorised for use in the Church of England. This had been the custom of the Society until 1970. A completely new edition of *The Daily Office SSF* was published in 1981, to supplement and enrich that provided for the Daily Office in *ASB.* Accordingly, *The Daily Office SSF* contained four daily Offices, of which Morning and Evening Prayer followed the order and text used in *ASB,* together with the collects and canticles plus a large number of other collects, canticles and prayers. This book was reprinted in 1986.

The Daily Office SSF came to be used in far more places and by far more people than had even been envisaged. In 1989 a revision was authorised by the Provincial Chapters of the First Order SSF in the European Province, in the light of increased liturgical knowledge, advances made in other parts of the Church and not least in the use of inclusive language. A joint Advisory Panel was formed with the SSF Committee on Liturgy and some members of the Liturgical Commission of the Church of England. There was the expressed desire to meet the needs of a wider public, longing for a form of daily office to enrich their common worship at the Sunday Eucharist. The result was the publication of two slightly differing versions: *Celebrating Common Prayer,* the non-Franciscan edition with its supplement including a simple form of celebrating the Office; and *The Daily Office SSF,* with its supplement having an emphasis on the Religious Life and Franciscan spirituality. Both books were published in 1992 and reprinted in 1996 and 2003. *Celebrating Common Prayer* was a huge success in that it was used extensively by individuals, religious communities, parish churches and cathedrals of the Church of England as well as in other Provinces of the

Anglican Communion. It made a significant contribution towards the work of preparation for *Common Worship: Daily Prayer.*

Again, with the publication of *Common Worship* in 2000, and *Common Worship: Daily Prayer* in 2005, SSF in the European Province wanted an Office that was aligned with *Common Worship* because there were significant liturgical changes from *ASB*. At the Joint Meeting of the Provincial Chapters in 2005, a revised edition of *The Daily Office SSF* was authorised 'to retain the familiar pattern but make adjustments for the use of the *Common Worship Lectionary*, together with some user-friendly changes in the light of community experience'. It is worth noting that *The Daily Office SSF* is used in all Provinces of the First Order, adjustments being made in accordance with the appropriate Anglican Provincial Lectionary, also by the Second Order SSF and by many members of the Third Order SSF.

ACKNOWLEDGEMENTS

The Society of Saint Francis owes an immeasurable debt of gratitude to the late Br Tristam SSF who served many years on the SSF Committees on Liturgy and the Liturgical Commission of the Church of England before his untimely death in December 2002.

Br Colin Wilfred SSF, Guardian of the Canterbury Friary, and Sr Joyce CSF, Minister General CSF, were the revision editors. They are grateful to the Rt Revd David Stancliffe, the Rt Revd Stephen Platten TSSF, Dr Philip Tovey TSSF, Thomas Allain-Chapman of Church House Publishing and Robin Baird-Smith of Continuum International Publishing Group for their encouragement and assistance in the production of this revision.

The Society is grateful to the following for permission to reproduce material, some of which is copyright. A text accompanied by the symbol * indicates that minor alterations have been made.

The Archbishops' Council of the Church of England: material from *Common Worship: Daily Prayer* and *Common Worship: Times and Seasons* © The Archbishops' Council, 2005, 2006 is reproduced by permission.

The Division of Christian Education of the National Council of the Churches of Christ in the United States of America: Scripture quotations from The New Revised Standard Version of the Bible, Anglicized Edition, copyright © 1989, 1995 by the Division of Christian Education of the National Council of the Churches of Christ in the United States of America. Used by permission. All rights reserved.

The English Language Liturgical Consultation: English translation of The Lord's Prayer (adapted),The Apostles' Creed (adapted), Gloria Patri (adapted), Te Deum Laudamus (adapted),Benedictus (adapted), Magnificat (adapted), Nunc Dimittis, © English Language Liturgical Consultation (ELLC), 1988, and used by permission. See www.englishtexts.org

The International Committee on English in the Liturgy: the English translation of the collects for Saint Elizabeth of Hungary (p. 688), Saint Clement (p. 689), and the Unity of the Church (p. 720), based on (or excerpted from) The Roman Missal © 1973, International Committee on English in the Liturgy, Inc. All rights reserved.

The Continuum International Publishing Group Ltd: collects for Epiphany 4 (p. 558), Trinity 15 (p. 607), 4 before Advent (p. 614), The Birth of the Blessed Virgin Mary (p. 667), Lucy (p. 693), Of the Blessed Virgin Mary (2) (p. 698) and Creation (1) (p. 725), based on (or excerpted from) David Silk (ed.), Prayers for Use at the Alternative Services, 1980 © Mowbray, an imprint of the Continuum International Publishing Group Ltd. The hymns Tantum ergo and O salutaris hostia (p. 733) from New Hymns for All Seasons © 1969 James Quinn SJ and Geoffrey Chapman, an imprint of The Continuum International Publishing Group Ltd. Used by permission.

Church of the Province of Southern Africa: collects for Epiphany 2 (p. 557), Epiphany 3 (p. 558), Lent 5 (p. 572), Confession of Peter (p. 621), Timothy and Titus (p. 624), Thomas (p. 650), Augustine of Hippo (p. 665), Bishops and other Pastors (p. 708), Any Saint (p. 714), and Harvest (p. 725), based on (or excerpted from) An Anglican Prayer Book, 1989 © Provincial Trustees of the Anglican Church of Southern Africa. Produced with permission from the Publishing Committee.

The Revd Jim Cotter: Benedictus, Magnificat, Te Deum, Nunc Dimittis and Easter Anthems, excerpted from Out of the Silence . . . Into the Silence, Cairns Publications, 2006, © Jim Cotter. Used by permission.

Saint Oswald's Church, Durham: collect for Oswald (p. 657). Used by permission.

The Dean and Chapter of Durham Cathedral: collects for Bede (p. 642) and Cuthbert (p. 632). Used by permission.

The Warden, Fellows and Scholars of Keble College, Oxford: collect for John Keble (p. 652). Used by permission.

Church in Wales Publications: collect for David (p. 628). Used by permission.

The Alcuin Club: collects for Ignatius (p. 679), Nicholas (p. 691) and Ambrose (p. 692), based on (or excerpted from) Martin Draper (ed.), *The Cloud of Witnesses,* 1982 © G.B. Timms. Used by permission.

The Episcopal Church USA: collects for Polycarp (p. 627), John Chrysostom (p. 668), William Tyndale (p. 677) and of Apostles (p. 700) adapted (or excerpted from) *The Book of Common Prayer* (1979).

New City Press: texts of Canticle of the Creatures (p. 530) and from pp. 751-3, excerpted from Regis J. Armstrong OFM Cap., J. A. Wayne Hellmann OFM Conv. and William Short OFM (eds.) *Francis of Assisi: Early Documents, Volumes I & II,* © 1999, 2000 Franciscan Institute of St Bonaventure University, St Bonaventure, N.Y. Used by permission.

New City Press: texts (pp. 533, 534) adapted from Regis J. Armstrong OFM Cap., editor and translator of the revised edition, *Clare of Assisi: Early Documents, The Lady,* © 2006 The Province of St Mary of the Capuchin Order as represented by Regis J. Armstrong OFM Cap. Used by permission.

The Church of Ireland: collects for Christmas 2 (p. 552) and the Transfiguration of Our Lord (p. 658), adapted (or excerpted from) *The Book of Common Prayer 2004.*© Representative Body of the Church of Ireland. Used by permission.

Oxford University Press: collects for Evening Prayer Form 7 (p. 238), The Baptism of Christ (p. 556), 2 before Lent (p. 562), Corpus Christi (p. 596), based on (or excerpted from) *The Book of Common Worship of the Church of South India.* Used by permission.

Methodist Publishing: collect for Morning Prayer Form 2 (1) (p. 74) from *The Methodist Worship Book* © 1999 Trustees for Methodist Church Purposes. Used by permission of Methodist Publishing.

The Cathedral and Abbey Church of Saint Alban: collect for Alban (p. 647).

OSB, West Malling: Anthem to Theotokos (p. 776) and Confession (pp. 62, 90, 119, 177).

The Rt Revd Michael Perham: collects for Joseph of Nazareth (p. 630) and George (p. 636), adapted (or excerpted) from *Celebrating Common Prayer* © SSF European Province 1992, 1996.

The Community of Saint Francis, Province of the Americas: Phos Hilaron, (63b, p.524). Used by permission.

The Revd Jean Malcolm: *A Song of Clare of Assisi* adapted for singing (p. 534).

Stanbrook Abbey: the office hymns (pp. 194, 225) adapted (or excerpted) from John Harper (ed.), *Hymns for Prayer and Praise,* Canterbury Press © 1974, 1995 Stanbrook Abbey.

Order of the Holy Cross, New York: translation of the office hymn *Rerum Deus tenax vigor* (p. 162) excerpted from *OHC Breviary* © OHC, New York.

Order of Preachers, Blackfriars, Oxford: translation of the office hymn *Die parente temporum* (p. 47) adapted (or excerpted) from John Harper (ed.), *Hymns for Prayer and Praise,* Canterbury Press © 1995 Order of Preachers, Blackfriars, Oxford.

The Catholic Bishops' Conference of England and Wales: collects for Aelred of Hexham (p. 619), Columba (p. 645), Aidan (p. 667), Paulinus (p. 678), Willibrord of York (p. 686), and Hilda (p. 689). Used by permission.

Hodder and Stoughton Publishers: collect for Social Justice and Responsibility (p. 728), based on (or excerpted from) *Parish Prayers* © Frank Colquhoun 1967.

SPCK: collect for Mothering Sunday (p. 569), adapted (or excerpted from) *Enriching the Christian Year,* © Michael Perham 1993; collects excerpted from *All Desires Known* © Janet Morley 2005. Used by permission of the publishers.

Kevin Mayhew Ltd: prayers by Saint Anthony of Padua (p. 795) and Saint Bonaventure (p. 797), adapted (or excerpted) from *Praying in the Franciscan Spirit,* Frances Teresa OSC © 1999 Sister Frances Teresa.

The Anglican Church in Aotearoa, NZ and Polynesia: prayers (p. 784) from *A New Zealand Prayer Book.*

The Dean and Chapter of Lincoln Cathedral: collect for Edward King (p. 629).

The Very Revd Robert Jeffery: collect for Wulfstan (p. 622).

The Revd Paul Gibson: metrical version of Phos Hilaron (63d, p. 525).

Panel of Monastic Musicians: the office hymn (p.133) adapted (or excerpted) from John Harper (ed.), *Hymns for Prayer and Praise,* Canterbury Press © Panel of Monastic Musicians 1995.

If any copyright has been unwittingly transgressed, or a necessary gratitude gone unexpressed, the Society offers its apologies and will rectify any such oversight in future editions.

The Lord's Prayer

Our Father in heaven,
hallowed be your name,
your kingdom come,
your will be done,
on earth as in heaven.
Give us today our daily bread.
Forgive us our sins
as we forgive those who sin against us.
Lead us not into temptation
but deliver us from evil.
For the kingdom, the power,
and the glory are yours
now and for ever. Amen.

Common Worship

Our Father in heaven,
hallowed be your name,
your kingdom come,
your will be done,
on earth as in heaven.
Give us today our daily bread.
Forgive us our sins
as we forgive those who sin against us.
Save us from the time of trial
and deliver us from evil.
For the kingdom, the power,
and the glory are yours
now and for ever. Amen.

ELLC

Our Father in heaven,
hallowed be your name,
your kingdom come,
your will be done,
on earth as in heaven.
Give us today our daily bread.
Forgive us our sins
as we forgive those who sin against us.
Do not bring us to the time of trial
but deliver us from evil.
For the kingdom, the power,
and the glory are yours
now and for ever. Amen.

The Scottish Episcopal Church

41b *BENEDICTUS (THE SONG OF ZECHARIAH)*

1   ✠ Blessèd are you, Lord, the God of Israel, *
    for you have come to your people and set them free.

2   You have raised up for us a mighty Saviour, *
    born of the house of your servant, David.

3   Through your holy prophets, you promised of old *
    to save us from our enemies,
      from the hands of all who hate us,

4   To show mercy to our ancestors, *
    and to remember your holy covenant.

5   This was the oath you swore to our father Abraham: *
    to set us free from the hands of our enemies,

6   Free to worship you without fear, *
    holy and righteous before you,
      all the days of our life.

7   And you, child, shall be called the prophet of the Most High, *
    for you will go before the Lord to prepare the way,

8   To give God's people knowledge of salvation *
    by the forgiveness of their sins.

9   In the tender compassion of our God *
    the dawn from on high shall break upon us,

10 To shine on those who dwell in darkness
      and the shadow of death, *
    and to guide our feet into the way of peace.

Luke 1.68-79, ELLC Alternative Version *

Either:

**Glory to the Father and to the Son
  and to the Holy Spirit; ***
**as it was in the beginning, is now,
  and shall be for ever. Amen.**

or:

**Glory to God, Source of all being,
  Eternal Word and Holy Spirit; ***
**as it was in the beginning, is now,
  and shall be for ever. Amen.**

40b *MAGNIFICAT (THE SONG OF MARY)*

1   ✠ My soul proclaims the greatness of the Lord, *
    my spirit rejoices in God my Saviour,

2   For you, Lord, have looked with favour
        on your lowly servant. *
    From this day all generations will call me blessèd:

3   You, the Almighty, have done great things for me *
    and holy is your name.

4   You have mercy on those who fear you, *
    from generation to generation.

5   You have shown strength with your arm *
    and scattered the proud in their conceit,

6   Casting down the mighty from their thrones *
    and lifting up the lowly.

7   You have filled the hungry with good things *
    and sent the rich away empty.

8   You have come to the aid of your servant Israel, *
    to remember the promise of mercy,

9   The promise made to our ancestors, *
    to Abraham and his children for ever.

Luke 1.46-55, ELLC Alternative Version *

Either:

**Glory to the Father and to the Son
   and to the Holy Spirit; ***
**as it was in the beginning, is now,
   and shall be for ever. Amen.**

or:

**Glory to God, Source of all being,
   Eternal Word and Holy Spirit; ***
**as it was in the beginning, is now,
   and shall be for ever. Amen.**